DATE DUE

D1015004

Directory of Blacks
in the Performing Arts

by

EDWARD MAPP

The Scarecrow Press, Inc.

Metuchen, N.J. & London

1978

PN
1590
B53
M3

EERL Withdrawn
Surplus Duplicate

ELMER E. RASMUSON LIBRARY
UNIVERSITY OF ALASKA

Library of Congress Cataloging in Publication Data

Mapp, Edward.
    Directory of Blacks in the performing arts.

    Bibliography: p.
    Includes index.
    1.   Blacks in the performing arts--Directories.   I.   Title.
PN1590. B53M3   792'. 0295'73   78-2436
ISBN 0-8108-1126-X

Copyright © 1978 by Edward Mapp

Manufactured in the United States of America

Dedicated with love and affection
to
Estelle Viola and Andrew Wayne
and to the memory of
Edward Cameron and Clements Hamden
Each one a branch on the Mapp family tree

CONTENTS

FOREWORD

To the unknowing, "show business" can be an illusive invalid as well as a glamorous occupation. There was a time, however, when for the black performer, it was not too illusive nor was it an invalid. For many years, being in show business was fabulous and most times glamorous. It was fabulous in 1821 when the African Company, with John Hewlett as its star, presented the classics at Brown's Theatre on Bleecker and Mercer Sts., in what was later to become Greenwich Village. The company was so successful that they graciously made a partition in the back of the house to accommodate the whites. It was fabulous when Ira Aldridge was world famous for his portrayals of Othello and the Moor in "Titus Andronicus"; when the black performer decided to make some of the big money being made by the minstrel shows that imitated him by imitating the imitators; and when the Lafayette Players sent out two acting companies a season with such stars as Laura Bowman, Abbie Mitchell, Clarence Brooks, Frank Wilson, Rose McClendon and many others.

When Harlem had little theatre groups like the Allied Re Players, the Rose McClendon Players, The American Negro Theatre, The Suitcase Theatre and various church groups--these groups were the proving grounds for Ossie Davis, Ruby Dee, Frederick O'Neal, Earle Hyman, Sidney Poitier, Harry Belafonte, Alice Childress and on and on--these were more of the fabulous days! It was fabulous when Williams and Walker captured the crowned heads of Europe with their production of "In Dahomey," and when Broadway would present at least two major black productions a year, such as "Shuffle Along," "Liza," "Africana," "Running Wild," "Chocolate Dandies," "Blackbirds," "7 Come 11," plus large touring musicals like "The

Models," and "Desires." The glamor was evident when we had not two but many film stars like Clarence Muse, Stepin Fetchit, Louise Beavers, Nina Mae McKinney, Daniel Haynes and matinee idol, Lorenzo Tucker.

It was fabulous when Oscar Micheaux, Toddy and Million Dollar Films produced rather good films without using the trite racial conflicts so overworked by Hollywood. I might add that Oscar Micheaux produced, wrote, directed and edited his films and we haven't had one black person or company attempt to take his place in this lucrative field that has a ready market hungry for such a product. No, the films were not all fabulous, nor were the stage productions, but the artists were great and they were able to learn and practice their trade in the only way possible ... by working at it.

It was fabulous when every social gathering hired a black band and the choices were Duke Ellington, Cab Calloway, Noble Sissle, Eddie South, Chick Webb, or one of many small singing and playing combos all over the country; when Harlem was peppered with night spots like the Cotton Club, Dickie Wells', Connie's 101 Ranch, and the Plantation, with full stage shows and not just weekend combos; when Harlem had not just one theatre with stage presentations, but the Lafayette, the Odeon, the Lincoln and the Alhambra with full stage shows every night in the week; when variety theatres over the country didn't feel that they had a good "bill" unless there was a black act starred; when the performer could be certain of at least fifty weeks a year on tour, with shows managed, written and staged by blacks; and when there were scores of chorus girls and show girls plus many singing and dancing novelty acts.

From these opportunities came the stars like Florence Mills, George Walker, Josephine Baker, Bessie Smith, Ada Ward, Ethel Waters, Bob Cole and Bert Williams. It was fabulous when we had serious singers like Caterina Jarboro, Marian Anderson, Etta Moten, Roland Hayes, Hall Johnson Choir, Paul Robeson and Black Patti and when we had the Hemsley Winfield Dancers, the Van Grona Negro Ballet and the always working and touring Katherine Dunham group. It was fabulous when we had comics like Tim Moore, and

viii

a host of fine straight men like Slick Chester. These performers would be tops today without the aid of the black face make-up that was their stock in trade.

I don't want to convey the notion that we don't have great artists today, for we well know that we have. I am saying, however, that we have too few in some fields and none at all in others. Sadder still is the fact that we have few places for our talented young people to get their feet wet and few producers to give them the opportunity to prove their talent. If you look into the backgrounds of the stars of today, such as Lena Horne, Ella Fitzgerald, Sidney Poitier, Harry Belafonte, and Sammy Davis Jr., you will find that they all started in small bistros, churches, and experimental theatres in Harlem or in their hometowns where their own people had faith in their ability and gave them the initial help and chance of exposure to eventually make the grade. Believe me when I tell you the big Broadway agents didn't snap them up for the big money jobs until they were well on their way to stardom. I have said all this to express that, if the old invalid of black show business would throw away the crutch of the white producer, director, writer, and agent, and would crawl backward, black performers just might once again become fabulous and success not so illusive.

The names in this Directory are those show biz folk who have achieved recognition in some way and who serve as building blocks to inspire those who are still unknown in the performing arts.

Kenn Freeman, Historian
Negro Actors Guild

PREFACE

Directory of Blacks in the Performing Arts is an unprece-
dented reference source to black performing artists in film, television, night-clubs, stage, opera, ballet, jazz and classical concert.
The Directory responds to the need for a single source of information on the subject. It is a compendium of biographical and career
facts on over 850 black individuals, living and deceased, who have
earned a degree of recognition for their work in the performing
arts. The term "blacks" is not used in a delimiting way and there-
fore includes Americans, Africans, West Indians, Canadians and
others. The term "performing arts" is used comprehensively to
cover the broad spectrum of dance, film, music, radio, television
and theatre. Individuals listed are either engaged in performance
or performance-related activities. Persons engaged in the performing arts but who are equally noted for their work in other fields
are listed; for example, athletes Jim Brown, Archie Moore, and
O. J. Simpson. Although every effort was made to include all
black performing artists of some prominence, some exclusion is in-
evitable in a work of this magnitude. It was decided to exclude
groups such as The Supremes and The Ink Spots because their composition changes. An artist who earns personal recognition apart
from a group, such as Diana Ross, will be included. A performing artist who makes even a single contribution of significance is included while one with a lengthy list of credits comprised solely of
college and local repertory work, "bit parts," "walk-ons," understudy assignments and summer stock activity is excluded. To do
otherwise would be to ignore past achievement and to speculate
about future careers.

A questionnaire was prepared and distributed to as many

x

black performing artists as could be contacted through direct mailings and announcements in the media. Many general and specialized reference resources, television programs, films and audio tapes were consulted. See the "Bibliography" for a partial listing.

Entries are listed in alphabetical order. Appropriate cross-references are provided (example: JONES, LEROI see BARAKA, IMAMU AMIRI). Each entry includes name, brief relevant personal information, e.g., birth and education. A listing of professional credits follows, arranged alphabetically by medium since many artists have worked in more than one entertainment field. "Honors" is another useful feature, listing "Emmy," "Oscar," "Grammy," "Tony," etc. Access to individuals for whom current addresses were not available can be obtained from member affiliations or other career data provided. The location of individuals, although certainly a subsidiary function, is not the primary purpose of this work. The profession is far too mobile and international for such a goal to be feasible. Several persons have changed addresses and jobs even while the manuscript was in preparation.

It has been a source of amazement to the author to discover that a fair number of performing arts people are related to other black people in the performing arts by birth or marriage. Thus the origin of the category "Relationships." The category "Career Data" serves in most instances as a catchall for relevant personal information inappropriate for listing under any other category, i.e., tours, non-performing arts activities, participation in festivals and appointments with repertory companies (exclusive of specific performances). Work with an orchestra, band, opera or ballet company, teaching appointments and roles associated with an artist's repertoire are listed here. Under "Theater" is cited performances in plays and appearances in specific theatres, concert halls and opera houses. The notation "Series" is used under the "Television" and "Radio" categories to indicate that an artist is a permanent member of a show or assumes a recurrent role in a program.

The compiler makes no claim that listings under any individual are all-inclusive. The aim was to provide sufficient information to be representative of a particular artist's work.

For ease of use, the "Classified Index" of all entries permits an approach to the work by type of activity performed, e.g., actor, composer, director, musician, playwright, or singer. A "List of Abbreviations" preceding the body of the work should clarify items which have been abbreviated to save space and avoid repetition within entries.

The Directory of Blacks in the Performing Arts was conceived and executed as a permanent record of the significant contributions by blacks to the world of performing arts and as a tribute to the unheralded accomplishments of many who were and are trailblazing in this field. The work attempts to present in one volume brief and accurate facts needed by the general reader or performing arts buff who might want to know the real name of Redd Foxx, the birthplace of Sidney Poitier or the first film made by Eartha Kitt. The book also attempts to satisfy the more specialized research requirements of members of the industry who might want to know if comedian Nipsey Russell has any background as a television show host or if singer Leslie Uggams has any experience as a dramatic actress or where to locate silent screen star Lorenzo Tucker.

The Directory will be useful to individuals interested in or involved in any way with the performing arts as well as to all libraries (public, college, university, school) serving these people. Artist representatives, media managers, theatre groups, studios, performing arts associations, casting directors, publicists, booking agencies and concert bureaus are all potential users. Newspapers and magazines (even those peripherally related to the performing arts) will find the Directory an important resource for writing articles and releases on performers. Individuals and institutions engaged in black studies will find it a useful tool. All constructive suggestions are welcome for future editions of Directory of Blacks in the Performing Arts.

I wish to thank first my dear friend Helen T. Wittner for her secretarial assistance, infinite patience and loyal support in the preparation of this work. Appreciation is extended to staff members of the Theatre Collection at New York Public Library, the Library/Learning Resource Center at New York City Community

College, the Film Collection at the Museum of Modern Art, Actors Equity Association, British Actors Equity Association, Negro Actors Guild, Screen Actors Guild and the Schomburg Center for Research in Black Culture, and to Helen Chedekel and Thomas Galvin among many individuals who helped.

E. M.

ACRONYMS AND ABBREVIATIONS

AAAA	Associated Actors and Artistes of America
AAAS	American Academy of Arts and Sciences
ACA	American Composers Alliance
AEA	Actors Equity Association
AFI	American Film Institute
AFM	American Federation of Musicians
AFTRA	American Federation of Television and Radio Artists
AGMA	American Guild of Musical Artists
AGVA	American Guild of Variety Artists
a.k.a.	also known as
AMPAS	Academy of Motion Picture Arts and Sciences
ANT	American Negro Theatre
ANTA	American National Theatre Academy
ASCAP	American Society of Composers Authors and Publishers
ASF	American Shakespeare Festival
ASMA	American Society of Music Arrangers
Assn.	Association
asst.	assistant
ATPAM	Association of Theatrical Press Agents and Managers
AUDELCO	Audience Development Co.
b.	born
BBC	British Broadcasting Corporation
bd.	board
Bklyn.	Brooklyn
Brit.	British
BTA	Black Theatre Alliance
Bway	Broadway
c.	circa, approximately
CC	City Center
C.C.C.	Civilian Conservation Corps
C.C.L.A.	City College of Los Angeles
CCNY	City College of New York
choreog.	choreographed
CLGA	Composers and Lyricists Guild of America
Co.	Company
CORE	Congress of Racial Equality
Corp.	Corporation
d.	died
Dept.	Department
DGA	Directors Guild of America
dir.	directed, director

doc.	documentary
ELT	Equity Library Theatre
Exec.	Executive
Fr.	French
gov.	government
H. S.	High School
Ital.	Italian
L. A.	Los Angeles
LCR	Lincoln Center Repertory
L. I.	Long Island
Mgr.	Manager
NAACP	National Association for the Advancement of Colored People
NAG	Negro Actors Guild
NARAS	National Academy of Recording Arts and Sciences
NATAS	National Academy of Television Arts and Sciences
NBT	National Black Theater
NEC	Negro Ensemble Company
NET	National Educational Television
N. J.	New Jersey
NRT	National Repertory Theatre
N. Y.	New York
N. Y. C.	New York City
NYSF	New York Shakespeare Festival
O. B.	Off Broadway
PASLA	Performing Arts Society of Los Angeles
PBS	Public Broadcasting Service
PEN	Poets, Essayists and Novelists
Philad.	Philadelphia
Pitts.	Pittsburgh
Pr.	Press
pre-Bway	pre-Broadway
Pres.	President
SAG.	Screen Actors Guild
SSDC	Society of Stage Directors and Choreographers
TOBA	Theatre Owners Booking Association
U. or Univ.	University
UC	University of California
UCLA	University of California at Los Angeles
U. S.	United States
USN	United States Navy
USO	United Service Organizations
U. S. S. R.	Union of Soviet Socialist Republics
v. or vol., or vols.	volume, volumes
Wash. (D. C.)	Washington, District of Columbia
WGA	Writers Guild of America
W. P. A.	Work Projects Administration
WSF	Washington Shakespeare Festival
YMHA	Young Men's Hebrew Association
YWCA	Young Women's Christian Association

ABDUL, RAOUL
(Critic/Singer)
b. November 7, 1929, Cleveland, Ohio.
Education: Vienna Academy of Music and Dramatic Arts; New
    School for Social Research; Cleveland Institute of Music; New
    York College of Music; Mannes College of Music; studied voice
    with Alexander Kipnis; Harvard University 1966.
Address: 360 West 22 St., New York, N.Y. 10011.
Career Data: Editorial asst. to Langston Hughes; operatic notes in
    first U.S. staged production of Orff's Die Kluge and title role
    in Milhaud's Les Malheures d'Orphée; concerts in U.S., Can-
    ada, Austria, Netherlands, Hungary and Germany; sang in
    Marlboro Music Festival 1956; organized and directed Coffee
    Concerts (Harlem's first subscription series of chamber
    music concerts) 1958-63; sang in Vienna Music Festival
    1962; music critic, Associated Negro Press and Amster-
    dam News N.Y.; lecturer on music, Atlanta University
    1976.
Memberships: Advisory Board; Symphony of the New World.
Publications: Famous Black Entertainers of Today, Dodd, Mead,
    1974.
Theater: Carnegie Hall (debut) 1967; Cosi Fan Tutte; Amahl and the
    Night Visitors (Karamu Theatre, Cleveland).

ADAMS, CAROLYN
(Dancer)
b. August 16, 1943.
Special Interests: Writing.
Address: 144 West 121 St., New York, N.Y. 10027.
Career Data: Member, Paul Taylor Dance Co., 1965-; founder,
    Harlem Dance Foundation and Studio; repertoire includes Tablet
    1960, Aureole 1962.
Television: Midday Live 1976.
Theater: Billy Rose Theatre 1976.
Relationships: Niece of Anna Arnold Hedgman, public official.

ADAMS, JOE (Joseph Edward Adams)
(Actor)

b. April 11, 1922, Los Angeles, Calif.
Education: Campton City College.
Films: Husky Miller in Carmen Jones 1954; psychiatrist in Man-
    churian Candidate 1962; Blues for Lovers (Brit.) 1966.
Radio: Disc jockey, KOWL (L.A.).

ADAMS, ROBERT
    (Actor)
b. 1910, Georgetown, Guiana.
Education: London University, Middle Temple; National Institute of
    Engineering.
Special Interests: Teaching (acting), singing, writing.
Career Data: Founder, London Negro Repertory Theatre; heavy-
    weight wrestling champion of British Empire; star of British
    films and London stage.
Films: Sanders of the River 1935; King Solomon's Mines 1937; Song
    of Freedom 1938; Midshipman Easy; An African in London; It
    Happened One Sunday; Dreaming; Caesar and Cleopatra 1946;
    Kisenga, Man of Africa (a.k.a. Man of Two Worlds) 1952;
    Sapphire 1959.
Theater: London stage appearances: Stevedore (West End debut) 1937;
    Toussaint L'Ouverture 1938; All God's Chillun Got Wings 1946;
    The House of Jeffreys; The Judgment of Dr. Johnson; Chastity
    My Brother; You Can't Take It with You; The Little Foxes;
    Cellar Caviar; Colony (alternating with Orlando Martins); title
    role in Emperor Jones.

ADDERLEY, JULIAN EDWIN "Cannonball"
    (Jazz Musician)
b. September 15, 1928, Tampa, Fla. d. August 8, 1975, Gary, Ind.
Education: U.S. Naval School of Music; Florida A. & M. College.
Special Interests: Alto saxophone.
Honors: Down Beat magazine New Alto Star of the Year 1959; Play-
    boy magazine Readers Poll for First Alto Sax 1962-71; Ebony
    Music Award 1975.
Career Data: Played with Miles Davis group 1957; toured with
    George Shearing 1959; played with Lionel Hampton, Woody Her-
    man, J. J. Johnson; Montreux Jazz Festival (Switzerland)
    1973; Newport Jazz Festival 1975.
Clubs: Café Bohemia 1955.
Films: A Man Called Adam (music) 1966; Save the Children 1973.
Musical Compositions: Co-composer: Work Song; Big Man: The
    Legend of John Henry.
Records: Love, Sex and the Zodiac (Fantasy); Mercy, Mercy,
    Mercy!; Cannonball Adderley and the Poll Winners (Riverside)
    1960; Cannonball Adderley and Friends (Capitol) 1973; Phenix
    (Fantasy); Black Messiah; Country Preacher (Capitol); Walk
    Tall; Quiet Nights; Fiddler on the Roof; Big Man (Fantasy)
    1975; The Legend of John Henry; Music; You All (Capitol);
    The Japanese Concerts (Milestones); Spontaneous Combustion
    (Savoy).

Television: Battle Hymn episode, Kung Fu 1974.
Theater: Carnegie Hall 1962; Apollo Theatre 1974; Nassau Coliseum.
Relationships: Husband of Olga James, actress/singer; brother of
    Nathaniel Adderley, jazz musician.

ADDERLEY, NAT (Nathaniel Adderley)
    (Jazz Musician)
b. November 25, 1931, Tampa, Fla.
Special Interests: Cornet, mellophone, trumpet.
Career Data: Played with Lionel Hampton 1954-55; toured with
    Cannonball Adderley's combo 1956-57; J. J. Johnson combo
    1957-58; Woody Herman 1959.
Clubs: Top of the Gate 1976.
Musical Compositions: Co-composer, Big Man: The Legend of
    John Henry.
Relationships: Brother of Julian "Cannonball" Adderley, jazz mu-
    sician.

ADDISON, ADELE
    (Concert Singer)
b. July 24, 1925, New York, N.Y.
Education: Mus. B., Westminster Choir College 1946.
Special Interests: German lieder.
Career Data: Aspen Music Festival 1956; performed with Boston,
    Cleveland, New York Philharmonic, National, Chicago, Pitts-
    burgh, Los Angeles, San Francisco, Indianapolis orchestras;
    Soviet Union tour (Cultural Exchange Program) 1963; premier
    performances include Montaigne's Fragments from Song of
    Songs (New Haven Symphony) 1959; Foss' Time Cycle (New York
    Philharmonic) 1960; Poulenc's Gloria (Boston Symphony) 1961.
Films: Porgy and Bess (voice) 1958.
Theater: Town Hall (recital debut) 1952; Mimi in New York City
    Opera Co. production of La Bohème (City Center debut) 1953;
    Philharmonic Hall 1962.

AILEY, ALVIN
    (Dancer/Choreographer)
b. January 5, 1931, Rogers, Texas.
Education: University of California Los Angeles 1949-50; Los
    Angeles City College 1950-51; San Francisco State College
    1952-53; studied dance with Lester Horton Dance Theatre
    (L.A.) 1949-51, 53; Hanya Holm 1949-55; Martha Graham
    1956; Anna Sokolow 1956; studied acting with Stella Adler
    1960-62.
Special Interests: Acting, writing.
Honors: Spingarn award 1977.
Career Data: Lester Horton Dance Theatre Co. (debut) 1950,
    (choreographer) 1953; performed at Jacobs Pillow Dance
    Festival 1954, 1959-60; formed Alvin Ailey American Dance

Theatre Co. 1958; performed at Boston Arts Festival 1961;
U. S. State Dept. tour (Australia, South East Asia) 1962; per-
formed at International Music Festival (Brazil) 1963; tour of
Soviet Union 1970; founder, American Dance Center 1975;
choreographed dances for Harkness Ballet
Films: Lydia Bailey 1952; Carmen Jones 1954.
Memberships: AEA; AFTRA; AGMA; AGVA.
Television: Choreographer and dancer on Party at Ciro's 1954; Red
        Skelton Show 1954; Jack Benny Show 1954; Dave Garroway To-
        day Show 1959; Camera Three 1962-63; Look Up and Live 1962;
        choreographed Parade 1964; Soul; Alvin Ailey: Memories and
        Vision 1971; Ailey Celebrates Ellington (Festival of the Arts
        for Young People) 1974; Straight Talk 1976.
Theater: Choreographed Macumba, Love Songs, Reflections in D,
        Child of Earth, Dance for Six, Hidden Rites, Streams, Fan-
        ga, Choral Dances, Gymnopedias, Flowers, Revelations, Knox-
        ville, Summer 1915; danced in House of Flowers (debut) 1954;
        the Purple Bandit in The Carefree Tree (O. B,) 1955; toured
        with Harry Belafonte's Sing, Man, Sing 1956; danced in Show
        Boat (Jones Beach, N. Y.) 1957; danced in Jamaica 1957; ap-
        peared with Ailey Dance Co. at Kaufmann Concert Hall YMHA
        (N. Y. C.) 1958; choreographed Carmen Jones (Theatre in the
        Park) 1959; performed with his dance company at World Dance
        Festival (Central Park, N. Y. C.) 1959; Dark of the Moon (ELT)
        1960; directed tour of African Holiday 1960; choreographed
        Creation of the World 1960; Lewisohn Stadium 1961; choreo-
        graphed Roots of the Blues 1961; Paul in Call Me by My
        Rightful Name (O. B.) 1961; Ding Dong Bell (stock) 1961; Talk-
        ing to You (Two by Saroyan) (O. B.) 1961; choreographed Her-
        mit Songs, Been Here and Gone, Feast of Ashes 1962; Tiger,
        Tiger Burning Bright 1962; My People (Chicago) 1963; staged
        Jerico-Jim Crow (O. B.) 1964; choreographed Ariadne 1964;
        appeared at Théâtre des Champs Elysées (Paris) 1964; choreo-
        graphed After Eden 1966; choreographed Cry, Mary Lou's
        Mass 1971; choreographed The River Carmen 1972; Palais de
        Sports 1975; choreographed The Mooche, Night Creature 1975.

AJAYE, FRANKLIN
        (Comedian/Actor)
b. Brooklyn, N. Y.
Education: Columbia University Law School.
Clubs: Comedy Store (L. A.); Roxy (L. A.); Improvisation; The Other
        End 1977.
Films: Car Wash 1976; Sweet Revenge 1977.
Memberships: SAG.
Records: Don't Smoke Dope; Fry Your Hair; I Am a Comedian (A&M).
Television: Keep on Truckin'; Barney Miller; Midnight Special 1976;
        Sammy and Company 1976; Celebrity Sweepstakes 1976; Dinah
        1976; Don Kirshner's Rock Concert 1976; Merv Griffin Show
        1977.

ALDRIDGE, IRA (Frederick Ira Aldrich)
  (Actor)
b. July 24, 1807, New York, N. Y. d. August 7, 1867, Lodz, Po-
  land.
Education: African Free School, New York (1820-24); University of
  Glasgow; Schenectady College.
Honors: Prussian Gold Medal Award for Arts & Science from King
  Frederick; Medal of Ferdinand from Franz Joseph of Austria
  for Othello; honored by Haiti for service to his race 1827;
  Golden Cross of Leopold by Czar of Russia; Golden Order of
  Service from Royal House of Saxony; Maltese Cross (Berne,
  Switzerland); chair named in his honor at Shakespeare Mem-
  orial Theatre, Stratford-on-Avon, England.
Career Data: Began acting career at African Grove Theater, New
  York, 1821 and amateur corps at Brown's Theater.
Publications: The Black Doctor (adaptor), 1847
Theater: The Death of Christophe; Titus Andronicus; King Lear;
  Macbeth; Richard III; Shylock in Merchant of Venice; Mungo
  in The Paddock; Ginger Blue in The Virginia Mummy; Rollo
  in Sheridan's Pizarro; Hamlet; Surinam (a. k. a. A Slave's Revenge) (London) 1825; Aboan in Oroonoko (Belfast) 1829; Iago
  in Othello (London) 1833; Fabian in The Black Doctor (London) 1846; Gambia in The Slave (England) 1855; title role in
  Othello (London) 1865.

ALI, RASHIED
  (Jazz Musician)
b. July 1, 1933, Philadelphia, Pa.
Education: Granoff School.
Address: 77 Greene St. , New York, N. Y. 10012
Special Interests: Drums.
Career Data: Worked with Sonny Rollins, Archie Shepp, Sun Ra and
  others; joined John Coltrane combo 1965; formed his own
  quintet; owner of Ali's Alley, a jazz club.

ALICE, MARY
  (Actress)
b. December 3, 1941, Indianola, Miss.
Career Data: Member, NEC.
Films: The Education of Sonny Carson 1974; Sparkle 1976.
Memberships: AEA.
Television: Sty of the Blind Pig, Police Woman 1974; Sanford and
  Son 1975; Good Times 1975; Family Holvak 1975; Nancy in
  Requiem for a Nun 1975; Just an Old Sweet Song (General
  Electric Theatre) 1976; Serpico 1976; Monkey in the Middle
  1976.
Theater: In the Deepest Part of Sleep (O. B.); Trials of Brother
  Jero (NEC) 1968; Happy Ending (O. B.) 1965; Thoughts (O. B.);
  Tell Pharaoh (O. B.); The Strong Breed (NEC) 1968; A Rat's
  Mass (O. B.); No Place to Be Somebody (Bway debut) 1971;
  Duplex (LCR) 1972; House Party (American Place Theatre)

Allen 6

1973; Black Sunlight (NEC) 1974; Heaven and Hell's Agreement (NEC) 1974; Terraces (NEC) 1974; Truckin' (BTA production at Harlem Cultural Council) 1974; You're Too Tall
but Come Back in Two Weeks (New Haven) 1975.

ALLEN, BETTY (Lou)
         (Concert Singer)
b. Campbell, Ohio.
Education: Wilberforce University 1944-46; Hartford School of Mus-
        ic 1952; studied voice with Zinka Milanov.
Address: 159 West 87 St., New York, N.Y. 10024.
Honors: Marian Anderson Award 1953-54; National Music League
        Management Award 1953; John Hay Whitney Fellowship 1953-
        54; Martha Baird Rockefeller Aid to Musicians Grant 1953,
        1958; Ford Foundation Grant 1963-64.
Career Data: Soloist, Leonard Bernstein's Jeremiah Symphony 1951;
        New York City Opera Co. 1953; toured Europe, North Africa,
        Caribbean, Far East, South America; taught at Manhattan
        School of Music; sang Liszt's The Legend of Saint Elizabeth;
        Katisha in the Mikado; Ericlea in Monteverdi's Il Ritorno
        d' Ulisse; Copeland's In the Beginning; Il Tabarro; alto solo-
        ist in Mahler's Third Symphony; performed with Philadelphia,
        New York, San Antoniò, Cleveland and Kansas City orchestras,
        honorary chairman, Symphony of the New World; participated
        in festivals at Carmel, Tanglewood, Ravinia, Saratoga.
Memberships: AFTRA; Metropolitan Opera Guild; National Negro
        Musicians Assn.; NAACP; Urban League.
Records: Treemonisha; St. Matthew Passion.
Theater: Four Saints in Three Acts 1952; Town Hall (Debut) 1958;
        Teatro Coleen, Buenos Aires (opera debut) 1964; Treemonisha
        1975; Sing Out America, Town Hall 1976; Avery Fisher Hall.

ALLEN, DEBORAH
         (Actress/Dancer)
b. January 16, 1950, Houston, Texas.
Education: B.F.A. Howard University; Studied with Ballet Nacional
        and Ballet Folklorico (Mexico); Houston Ballet Foundation
        (Texas); N.Y. School of Ballet.
Special Interests: Choreography, teaching.
Address: 1270 Fifth Ave., New York, N.Y. 10029.
Honors: Ford Foundation grant.
Career Data: Worked with George Faison Universal Dance Exper-
        ience; NYSF; AMAS Repertory Theatre; taught dance at Duke
        Ellington School of Performing Arts.
Memberships: AEA.
Television: Pampers commercial; Black Journal 1975; Jim Stafford
        (variety) 1975; Good Times 1976; Three Girls Three (special)
        1977; Merv Griffin Show 1977.
Theater: Purlie 1971; danced at Delacorte Theatre (Central Park,
        N.Y.C.) 1972; Ti-Jean and His Brothers (O.B.) 1972; asst.
        to choreographer, Via Galactica (O.B.) 1973; Beneatha Young-

er in Raisin 1973; Truckload 1975; Music Magic (Billie Holiday Theatre, Brooklyn); Guys and Dolls (Westbury Music Fair)
1977.

ALLEN, JONELLE
        (Singer/Actress)
b.   July 18, 1944, New York, N. Y.
Education: Professional Children's School (N. Y. C.).
Address: 377 Edgecombe Ave., New York, N. Y. 10031.
Honors: Theatre World Award 1972; Tony nomination 1972.
Films: That Kind of Woman 1959; A Man Called Adam 1966; How
        to Succeed in Business Without Really Trying 1967; Cotton
        Comes to Harlem 1970; The Cross and the Switchblade; Come
        Back Charleston Blue 1972; The River Niger 1976.
Memberships: Urban Arts Corps.
Radio: Eternal Light; Clark Chewing Gum and Post Cereal Com-
        mercials.
Television: Cliff Dwellers; Monty Hall at Sea World; Profiles in
        Courage; Trials of O'Brien; Another World; As the World
        Turns; Look Up and Live; Edge of Night; Walter Winchell
        Variety Show 1952; The Green Pastures (Hallmark Hall of
        Fame) 1957; Cotton Club '75 (special) 1974; Police Woman
        1974, 1975; Jacqueline Foster in Foster and Laurie 1975;
        Smoganza (special) 1975; Police Story 1975; Cage Without a
        Key 1975; Legacy of Blood (Wide World Mystery) 1975; Opry-
        land U. S. A. 1975; Musical Chairs 1975; Halfway to Danger
        (Wide World Mystery) 1975; Barney Miller 1975; Tonight Show
        1976; Joe Forrester 1976; Merv Griffin Show 1976; American
        Woman: Portraits of Courage 1976; Dinah! 1976; Sammy and
        Company 1976.
Theater: Someone's Comin' Hungry (O. B.); The Last Sweet Days of
        Isaac (San Francisco); Small War on Murray Hill; Silvia in
        Wisteria Trees (Bway debut) 1950; Finian's Rainbow (City Cen-
        ter) 1955; Moon on a Rainbow Shawl (O. B.) 1962; Fever for
        Life (stock) 1967; Hair 1967-68; George M 1968; House of
        Leather (La Mama Theater) 1970; Five on the Black Hand
        Side (O. B.) 1970; Bury the Dead (Urban Arts Corp. Produc-
        tion) 1971; Two Gentlemen of Verona 1972.

ALONZO, CECIL
        (Playwright/Director)
b.   Virginia.
Education: Norfolk State College; American Academy of Dramatic
        Arts 1966.
Special Interests: Acting.
Address: 395 Clinton Ave. , Brooklyn, N. Y. 11238.
Career Data: Founder, The Alonzo Players 1967; toured local the-
        aters, community centers, and colleges.
Films: Wrote One of Us (screen play).
Theater: Wrote Strike One Blow; Somewhere Between Us Two;
        Black Voices; Breakfast Is Served; Four Hundred Years Over-

due; O. T. B.; wrote and directed 1999 (based on concept of
John A. Williams) 1975; produced Day of Absence (Alonzo
Players); Seafood Playhouse 1975.

AMOS, JOHN
(Actor)
b. December 27, 1939, Newark, N. J.
Education: Long Beach City College (Calif.); Colorado State Univer-
sity; Bronx Community College.
Career Data: Played football for several colleges and for the United
Football League; Chairman, United Negro College Fund for
Southern California.
Clubs: Cafe Wha.
Films: Sweet Sweetback's Baadasssss Song 1971; The World's Great-
est Athlete 1973; Let's Do It Again 1975.
Television: Wrote for The Leslie Uggams Show; Bill Cosby Show;
Two's Company; acted in The Funny Side 1971; Gordy the
Weatherman on The Mary Tyler Moore Show; Maude; James
Evans in Good Times (series) 1974-76; Mike Douglas Show
1975; Tony Orlando and Dawn 1975; Dinah 1975; Hollywood
Squares 1975; Police Story 1976; Kunta Kinte (the adult) in
Roots 1977; Future Cop (series) 1977; National Disaster Sur-
vival Test (special) 1977.
Theater: Norman, Is That You? (L. A.)

ANDERSON, CARL
(Singer/Actor)
Clubs: Hotel Drake.
Films: Judas in Jesus Christ Superstar 1973.
Television: Mike Douglas Show.

ANDERSON, EDDIE "Rochester" (Edmund Lincoln Anderson)
(Actor/Comedian)
b. September 18, 1905, Oakland, Calif. d. February 28, 1977
Los Angeles, Calif.
Honors: Black Film-Makers Hall of Fame, 1975.
Career Data: Formed song and dance vaudeville team with his bro-
ther Cornelius 1923-33; formerly with The Three Black Aces
(vocal trio); Strut Mitchell Troupe; toured with California
Collegians.
Clubs: Sebastian's Cotton Club (L. A.), Apex (L. A.).
Films: What Price Hollywood 1932; Transient Lady, Rainbow on
the River, Three Men on a Horse, Noah in Green Pastures
1936; Melody for Two, Bill Cracks Down, On Such a Night,
White Bondage, One Mile from Heaven, Over the Goal 1937;
Jezebel, You Can't Take It with You, Kentucky, Thanks for
the Memory, Reckless Living, Gold Diggers in Paris, Ex-
posed 1938; Going Places, Honolulu, Gone with the Wind,
You Can't Cheat an Honest Man, Man About Town 1939; Buck
Benny Rides Again, Love Thy Neighbor 1940; Topper Returns,

Kiss the Boys Goodbye, Birth of the Blues 1941; Tales of
Manhattan, Star Spangled Rhythm 1942; The Meanest Man in
the World, Cabin in the Sky, What's Buzzin', Cousin? 1943;
Broadway Rhythm 1944; Brewster's Millions, I Love a Band-
leader 1945; The Sailor Takes a Wife, Memory for Two 1946;
The Show-Off 1947; It's A Mad Mad Mad Mad World 1963.
Memberships: SAG.
Radio: Rochester (Jack Benny's butler) on the Jack Benny Show 1937-
49.
Television: Rochester on The Jack Benny Show 1953-65; The Green
Pastures (Hallmark Hall of Fame) 1957; Bachelor Father 1962;
Last of the Private Eyes (Dick Powell Theater) 1963; Love,
American Style 1969; What's My Line?; Harlem Globetrotters
(cartoon voice).
Theater: Struttin' Along.

ANDERSON, ERNEST
(Actor)
Education: Northwestern University.
Films: In This Our Life 1942; Till The End of Time 1946; The Well
1951; 3 for Bedroom C 1952; North by Northwest 1959; What-
ever Happened to Baby Jane 1962; Tick... Tick... Tick... 1970.
Television: Sanford and Son 1975.

ANDERSON, ESTHER
(Actress)
b.   Jamaica, West Indies.
Special Interests: Directing, writing.
Films: Theatre of Death 1967; The Touchables 1968; Two Gentle-
men Sharing 1969; One More Time 1970; A Warm December
1973.
Television: The Rookies (guest).

ANDERSON, GARLAND
(Playwright)
b.   c. 1887, Kansas.
Theater: Wrote Appearances 1925 (first play on Broadway written
by a black); Extortion 1929.

ANDERSON, MARIAN
(Concert Singer/Opera Singer)
b.   February 27, 1902, Philadelphia, Pa.
Education: The Philadelphia Choral Society.
Address: 46 Joe's Hill Road, Danbury, Conn. 06810.
Honors: First black to sing as featured member at the Metropolitan
Opera; more than 40 honorary degrees, American and foreign
institutions; New York Philharmonic Competitions (First Place)
1925; Rosenwald Fellowship 1930; Spingarn Medal for highest
achievement by a Negro 1939; Finnish Probenignitate Humana

1940; Bok Award 1940; U. S. delegate to UN 1958; Presidential Medal of Freedom 1963.

Career Data: Narrated Aaron Copland's Lincoln Portrait with Boston Pops; numerous tours throughout the world beginning 1924; Lewisohn Stadium (debut) 1926; Town Hall 1935; Carnegie Hall 1936; Lincoln Memorial Concert 1939; performed Ulrica in Un Ballo in Maschera at Metropolitan Opera (debut) 1955; farewell concert with Philadelphia Orchestra 1965.

Films: Carnegie Hall 1947.

Publications: My Lord, What a Morning (autobiography), Viking, 1956.

Records: Spirituals; Songs at Eventide; Christmas Carols.

Television: What's My Line?; Ed Sullivan Show 1952; Criss Awards 1976.

Relationships: Aunt of James De Priest, musician/conductor.

ANDERSON, MYRTLE
    (Actress)
Films: Green Pastures 1936; The Lady Is Willing, Tales of Manhattan 1942; I Walked with a Zombie, Cabin in the Sky 1943; Oh, You Beautiful Doll 1949; Whirlpool 1950; White Witch Doctor 1953.
Theater: Green Pastures 1935.

ANDERSON, THOMAS
    (Actor)
b. November 28, 1906, Pasadena, Calif.
Education: Pasadena Junior College; American Theatre Wing.
Films: Don't Play Us Cheap; The Learning Tree 1969; The Legend of Nigger Charley 1972; Gordon's War, Trick Baby 1973.
Theater: Four Saints in Three Acts (debut) 1934; Roll Sweet Chariot 1934; asst. director to Orson Welles on Harlem Federal Theatre production of Macbeth 1936; Cabin in the Sky 1940; Native Son 1941; Set My People Free 1948; How Long Till Summer 1949; A Hole in the Head 1957; The Great White Hope 1968; Hello Dolly! 1969; 70 Girls 70 1971; Don't Play Us Cheap 1972; Conquering Thursday (O. B.); The Peddler (O. B.); The Dodo Bird (O. B.).

ANDREWS, INEZ
    (Gospel Singer)
Records: Golden Gems of Gospel, Vol. 2 (Peacock); Gospel at Its Best (Peacock); I'm Free (ABC); Live at Munich; Lord Don't Move This Mountain; This Is Not the First Time, I've Been Last; A Letter to Jesus; Mary Don't You Weep.

ANGELOU, MAYA (Marguerite Annie Johnson)
    (Actress/Playwright)
b. April 4, 1928, St. Louis, Mo.

Education: Mission High School (San Francisco); studied dance with
       Pearl Primus; studied acting with Frank Silvera.
Special Interests: Dance, teaching, songwriting, languages, poetry.
Address: Sonoma, Calif. 95476.
Career Data: Writer, Ghanaian Broadcasting Corp., Accra, 1963-
       65; professor, University of Ghana; Chubb Professor, Yale
       Univ.
Clubs: Hungry Eye, (San Francisco); Purple Onion (San Francisco);
       Mr. Kelly's (Chicago); Village Vanguard; The Blue Angel.
Films: Porgy and Bess 1959; wrote screenplay and score for Georgia
       Georgia 1972.
Memberships: AFI (board member).
Publications: The Least of These (play); The Clawing Within (play);
       The True Believers (poems in collaboration with Abbey Lin-
       coln); Adjoa Amissah (play) 1967; I Know Why the Caged Bird
       Sings (autobiography), Random House, 1970; Gather Together
       in My Name (autobiography), Random House, 1975; Singin' and
       Swingin' and Gettin' Merry Like Christmas (autobiography),
       Random House, 1976.
Radio: Arlene Francis Show.
Television: Wrote, produced, directed and hosted Black! Blues!
       Black! (NET series); narrated Black African Heritage (series)
       1972; Bill Moyers Journal 1973; Merv Griffin Show 1974, 1975;
       Assignment America 1975; Bicentennial Minutes 1975; Phil
       Donahue Show 1975; Positively Black 1975; Black Pride 1975;
       Black News 1975; Sunday 1975; Sammy and Company 1975;
       Knowledge 1976, Dinah 1976; Today 1976; Roots 1977; Friends
       of ... 1977; The Richard Pryor Special? 1977.
Theater: Porgy and Bess (premier danseuse in European tour) 1954-
       55; Calypso Heat Wave 1957; wrote, produced, and acted in
       Cabaret for Freedom; the Queen in The Blacks (O.B.) 1961-
       64; Jean Anouilh's Medea (Hollywood) 1966; Look Away 1973;
       adapted Sophocles' Ajax (L.A.) 1974.

ARANHA, RAY
       (Playwright)
b. May 1, 1939, Miami, Fl.
Education: Florida A & M University 1961.
Special Interests: Acting.
Honors: Drama Desk Award 1973-74.
Theater: My Sister, My Sister 1973; The Prodigal Sister 1974; The
       Estate 1975.

ARCHER, OSCEOLA
       (Actress/Director)
b. Albany, Ga.
Education: Howard University B.A. 1913; New York University M.A.
       (drama) 1936.
Address: 66 West 88 St. New York, N.Y. 10024.
Career Data: Studied acting at Repertory Playhouse Associates;
       Equity Library Theatre; dir., Putnam County Playhouse Ma-

hopac, N. Y. (productions of The Glass Menagerie, The Oc-
toroon, The Lady's Not for Burning); instructor, dramatic
Arts and dir. Little Theatre, Bennett College (Greensboro,
N. C.) 1937-39; dir. and teacher, American Negro Theatre
1944-48; Prospect Park Summer Theatre (Bklyn) 1965; Hun-
ter College Chelsea Theatre Playwrights Project 1967.
Films: An Affair of the Skin 1963.
Memberships: AEA; AFTRA; SAG; SSDC.
Radio: Joyce Jordan, M. D. 1940s; Angelina in The Right to Hap-
piness (series) 1950s.
Television: The Power and the Glory (Play of the Week); Rashomon
(Play of the Week); Pygmalion (Hallmark Hall of Fame); Tea-
house of the August Moon (Hallmark Hall of Fame); Panama
Hattie (Best of Broadway); The Edge of Night.
Theater: The Cat Screams; Riders to the Sea (American Negro The-
atre); Hippolytus (ANTA); Skin of Our Teeth (Olney Theatre);
Strange House (Putney, Vt.); Between Two Worlds 1934; Panic
1934; Emperor Jones (tour) 1939; Romeo and Juliet (NYSF)
1961; Ring Round the Moon (NRT) 1963-64; Tituba in The Crucible (NRT) 1963-64; The Sea Gull (NRT) 1963-64; Blood Wedding (Pennsylvania State University Theatre) 1966; The Phy-
sicists (Pennsylvania State University Theatre) 1966; The
Three Sisters (Hartford) 1966-67; The Guide 1968; The Screens
(O. B.) 1971; directed The Silver Box.

ARMSTRONG, LIL (Lillian Hardin)
     (Jazz Musician)
b. February 3, 1898, Memphis, Tenn. d. August 27, 1971, Chi-
     cago, Ill.
Education: Fisk University; Chicago School of Music (diploma) 1928;
     New York College of Music 1929.
Special Interests: Arranging, composing, conducting, piano.
Career Data: Played with King Oliver 1921-24; Louis Armstrong
     (Hot Five and Hot Seven) 1925-27.
Clubs: Nob Hill (Chicago); Tin Pan Alley (Chicago); Garrick Stage
     Bar (Chicago); Mark Twain Lounge (Chicago); East Town Bar
     (Milwaukee).
Memberships: ASCAP 1957.
Musical Compositions: Brown Gal; Just for a Thrill; Perdido Street
     Blues; Some Barbecue.
Theater: Shuffle Along 1921; Hot Chocolates 1929; conducted all-
     girl orchestra at Regal Theatre (Chicago) 1934.
Relationships: Former wife of Louis Armstrong, jazz musician.

ARMSTRONG, LOUIS "Satchmo" (Daniel Louis Armstrong)
     (Jazz Musician)
b. July 4, 1900, New Orleans, La. d. July 6, 1971, Queens, N. Y.
Special Interests: Conducting, trumpet, scat singing.
Honors: Esquire Award 1944-47; Record Changer All Time All Star
     1951; Down Beat Hall of Fame 1952; Down Beat International
     Critics' Poll 1953-54; Grammy award 1964; Ebony Music A-
     ward (posthumously) 1975.

Career Data: Performed with Tuxedo Brass Band and Kid Ory 1917;
King Oliver 1922; Fletcher Henderson 1924; his own band 1935;
toured Europe, U.S., Africa, Australia, Canada, South America, New Zealand, Mexico, Asia; formed all-stars 1947; Nice,
France, Jazz Festival 1948.

Clubs: Sunset Cafe (Chicago); Savoy Ballroom; Connie's Inn; Sebastian's Cotton Club (Culver City, Ca.); Royal Gardens (Chicago); Roseland; Billy Berg's Club 1947.

Films: Ex-Flame 1930; Rhapsody in Black and Blue, Paramount
shorts 1932; I'll Be Glad When You're Dead You Rascal You;
Pennies from Heaven 1936; Artists and Models, Every Day's
a Holiday 1937;   Doctor Rhythm 1938; Going Places 1939; Cabin in the Sky 1943; Jam Session, Atlantic City 1944; Pillow
to Post 1945; New Orleans 1947; A Song Is Born 1948; The
Strip, Here Comes the Groom 1951; Glory Alley 1952; The
Glenn Miller Story 1954; High Society 1956; Satchmo the Great
(doc.) 1958; The Five Pennies 1959; The Beat Generation,
Jazz on a Summer's Day (doc) 1960; Paris Blues 1961; When
the Boys Meet the Girls 1965; A Man Called Adam 1966; Hello
Dolly! 1969; Newport Jazz Festival (doc.) 1970; Auf Wieder-
sehen (German).

Memberships: ASCAP 1939.

Musical Compositions: Satchel Mouth Swing; Wild Man Blues; Sugar
Foot Stomp; Ol' Man Mose; Struttin' with Some Barbecue; Jo-
seph'n' His Brudders; No Variety Blues; Hear Me Talkin' to
Ya; Where Did You Stay Last Night; I've Got a Heart Full of
Rhythm; Back O' Town Blues.

Publications: Swing That Music (autobiography), Longmans, Green,
1936; Satchmo: My Life in New Orleans (autobiography), Prentice-Hall, 1954.

Records: Louis Armstrong and Earl Hines 1928 (Smithsonian); The
Louis Armstrong Story; Blues Heritage; The Genius of Louis
Armstrong vol. 1 1923-33 (Columbia); When We Were Young;
Louis Armstrong and Al Hirt Play Dixieland Trumpet; Am-
bassador Satch; I Get Ideas and A Kiss to Build a Dream
(Decca) 1951; Takes Two to Tango (Decca) 1952; Blueberry
Hill 1953; Hello Dolly! (Knapp) 1964; At the Crescendo (MCA);
Best (Audio Fidelity); Definitive Album (Audio Fidelity); Dis-
ney Songs the Satchmo Way (Buena Vista); Essential (Van-
guard); I Will Wait for You (Brunswick); Mame (Pickwick);
What a Wonderful World (ABC); Louis Armstrong with Dukes
of Dixieland (Audio Fidelity); Louis Armstrong with His
Friends (Amsterdam); Early Portrait (Milestone); Ambassador
Satch (Columbia Special Products); Greatest Hits (Columbia);
Great Soloists (Biograph); July 4, 1900-July 6, 1971 (RCA);
Louis Armstrong (Trip); One and Only (Vocation); ... Plays
Fats (Columbia Special Products); ... Plays the Blues (Bi-
ograph); ... Plays W.C. Handy (Columbia Special Products);
Satchmo-Autobiography (MCA); Satchmo at Symphony Hall
(MCA); Satchmo the Great (Columbia Special Products); Story
(Columbia); V.S.O.P. (Columbia Special Products).

Television: What's My Line?; Ed Sullivan Show; The Lord Don't Play
Favorites (Producers Showcase) 1956; Academy Awards Show
1968.

Theater: Appeared at Lafayette Theatre; Regal Theatre (Chicago);
          Olympia Theatre (Paris); Hot Chocolates 1929; Palladium (Lon-
          don) 1932; Bottom in Swingin' the Dream 1939; New York Met-
          ropolitan Opera House (first jazz concert) 1944; Apollo Thea-
          tre 1953.
Relationships: Former husband of Lil Hardin Armstrong, jazz mu-
          sician.

ASHLEY, FRANK
          (Dancer/Choreographer)
b.   April 10, 1941, Kingston, Jamaica.
Education: Studied with Ivy Baxter, Martha Graham.
Special Interests: Teaching.
Address: 424 East 13 St., New York, N. Y. 10009.
Career Data: Danced with National Dance Theatre of Jamaica, Pearl
          Lang, Martha Graham, Eleo Pomare, and others; founder and
          artistic director, Frank Ashley Dance Co. 1975.
Theater: Choreographed Games; West Indian Hello; The In-Crowd
          (O. B.) 1977; Macbeth (O. B.) 1977.

ATKINS, PERVIS
          (Director)
Education: New Mexico State University B. A. 1961.
Special Interests: Football, theatrical agent, producing.
Address: 9255 Sunset Blvd., Los Angeles, Calif. 90046.
Honors: U. S. O. Commendation for Meritorious Service 1971.
Career Data: Played professional football with Los Angeles Rams,
          Washington Redskins, Oakland Raiders 1961-68; theatrical a-
          gent, Jack Fields and Associates.
Films: The Longest Yard 1954; Melinda 1972.
Television: Sports commentator KIIZ 1962; Police Woman 1974; asst.
          dir. of motion pictures for ABC; acted in Ellery Queen 1976,
          Delvecchio 1976.

ATTAWAY, RUTH
          (Actress)
b.   Greenville, Miss.
Education: University of Illinois B. A. 1933; University of Chicago
          1933-34.
Address: Box 635, Radio City Station, New York, N. Y. 10019.
Honors: Coordinating Council for Negro Performers Citation for her
          contribution to the theatrical profession 1953.
Films: The President's Lady 1953; The Young Don't Cry, Raintree
          Country 1957; Serena in Porgy and Bess 1959; Terror in the
          City 1966; The Taking of Pelham 1-2-3, Conrack 1974.
Memberships: AEA; AFTRA; SAG.
Television: Hidden Faces; The Defenders; Studio One; High Tension;
          Kraft Television Theatre; Harlem Detective 1953, 1955; Three's
          Company (pilot) 1954.
Theater: The Little Foxes (Stock); Decision (O. B.); The Country
          Wife (LCR); Danton's Death (LCR); The Caucasion Chalk Circle

(LCR); You Can't Take It with You 1937; The Grass Harp
(O. B.) 1953; mother in Mrs. Patterson 1954; Mister Johnson
1956; The Egghead 1957; Nat Turner (O. B.) 1960s; A Raisin
in the Sun (stand-by for Claudia McNeil) 1961; Tiger, Tiger
Burning Bright (stand-by for Claudia McNeil) 1962; After the
Fall (LCR) 1964; Yerma (LCR) 1966.

ATTLES, JOSEPH E.
        (Actor /Singer)
b.   April 7, 1903, Charleston, S. C.
Education: Harlem Musical Conservatory.
Films: The Swimmer, For the Love of Ivy 1968; The Liberation of
        L. B. Jones 1970; Across 110th Street 1972; The Gambler 1974.
Membership: AEA; NAG.
Television: Positively Black 1976.
Theater: Blackbirds of 1928 1928; John Henry 1940; Sportin' Life
        in Porgy and Bess (tour) 1953; Prodigal Son (O. B.) 1957;
        Kwamina 1961; Tambourines to Glory 1963; Jerico-Jim Crow
        (O. B.) 1964; Cabin in the Sky (O. B.) 1964; The Reckoning
        (NEC) 1969; A Cry of Players (LCR) 1969; King Lear (LCR)
        1969; Day of Absence (NEC) 1970; Duplex (O. B.) 1973; The
        Last of Mrs. Lincoln 1973; Bubbling Brown Sugar 1975-76.

AVERY, MARGARET
        (Actress)
Films: The Folks at Red Wolf Inn; Cool Breeze 1972; Magnum
        Force, Hell Up in Harlem 1973; Which Way Is Up? 1977.
Memberships: SAG.
Television: Kojak 1974; Harry O 1974; Sanford and Son 1975; Night
        Stalker 1975; The Rookies 1975; Louis Armstrong Chicago
        Style 1976.

AYLER, ETHEL
        (Actress)
b.   c. 1934, Whistler, Ala.
Education: Fisk University; De Paul University (Chicago).
Special Interests: Singing.
Address: 252 West 77 St., New York, N. Y. 10024.
Clubs: Blue Angel.
Memberships: NEC.
Television: Black Pride 1976.
Theater: Porgy and Bess (Rome) 1955; (tour) 1957; Simply Heaven-
        ly 1957; Jamaica (understudy for Lena Horne) 1959; title role
        in Carmen Jones (Theatre in the Park) 1959; The Cool World
        1960; The Blacks (O. B.) 1961; Ododo (NEC) 1969; The First
        Breeze of Summer (NEC) 1975; Eden (NEC) 1976; The Browns-
        ville Raid (NEC) 1976; Macbeth (O. B.) 1977.

BAILEY, PEARL (Mae)
        (Singer /Actress)

b. March 29, 1918, Newport News, Va.
Education: William Penn High School, Philadelphia, Pa.
Special Interests: Song writing.
Address: Box 52, Northridge, Calif. 91324.
Honors: USO Man of the Year; March of Dimes Woman of the Year;
     First Order in Arts & Sciences from President Sadat of Egypt;
     Donaldson Award 1946; Entertainer of the Year (Cue) 1967;
     Special Tony Award (Hello, Dolly!) 1967-68; Ambassador of
     Love (by Pres. Nixon) 1968; U. S. delegate to UN 1975.
Career Data: Performed with Noble Sissle, Cootie Williams, Count
     Basie.
Clubs: Village Vanguard 1944; Venetian Room; Fairmont Hotel (San
     Francisco); Blue Angel; Ciro's (L. A.); Mocambo (L. A.); Zan-
     zibar.
Films: Variety Girl (debut) 1947; Isn't It Romantic? 1948; Carmen
     Jones 1954; That Certain Feeling 1956; St. Louis Blues 1958;
     Porgy and Bess 1959; All the Fine Young Cannibals 1960; The
     Landlord 1970; Norman, Is That You? 1976.
Memberships: ASCAP 1958.
Musical Compositions: A Five Pound Box of Money; I'm Gonna Keep
     On Doin'; Don't Be Afraid to Love; Jingle Bells Cha Cha Cha.
Publications: The Raw Pearl (autobiography), Harcourt Brace &
     World, 1968; Talking to Myself (autobiography), Harcourt
     Brace & World, 1971.
Records: The Bad Old Days; For Adult Listening; Tired; Takes Two
     to Tango; Legalize My Name.
Television: Yoohoo commercial; Paramount Chicken commercial; Ed
     Sullivan Show; Milton Berle Show; Flip Wilson Show; Johnny
     Carson Show; Oral Roberts; Hollywood Squares; Pearl Bailey
     Show (variety series) 1970; An Evening with Pearl (special)
     1974; Bing Crosby and His Friends 1974; Captain Kangaroo
     1974; Feeling Good 1975; Dinah! 1975; Mike Douglas Show
     1975; Merv Griffin Show 1975; Kup's Show 1975; A. M. Amer-
     ica 1975; Grammy awards show 1976; Evening at Pops 1976;
     Pat Collins Show 1976; Gong Show 1977; Bing (special) 1977.
Theater: Appeared at Strand Theatre; Apollo Theatre; Earl Theatre
     (Philadelphia); St. Louis Woman (Bway debut) 1946; Arms and
     the Girl 1950; Bless You All 1950; House of Flowers 1954;
     Hello, Dolly! 1969, 1975; Constitution Hall (Philadelphia) 1977.
Relationships: Former wife of Slappy White, comedian.

BAKER, JOSEPHINE
     (Entertainer)
b. June 3, 1906, St. Louis, Mo. d. April 12, 1975, Paris, France
Special Interests: Singing, dancing, race relations, orphan children.
Honors: Chevalier of the Légion d'Honneur; Croix de Guerre 1939-45;
     Rosette de la Résistance; NAACP Woman of the Year Award
     1951; Black Filmmakers Hall of Fame (posthumously) 1976.
Career Data: Toured Europe, South America, South Africa and U. S.
Clubs: Plantation Club (Plantation Revue) 1924; Casino de Paris
     (Paris Qui Remue Revue) 1931; Chez Josephine (her own club);
     Copa City (Miami Beach) 1951; Last Frontier (Las Vegas) 1952;
     Sporting Club (Monte Carlo) 1961.

Films: La Revue des Revues 1927; La Sirène des Tropiques 1927;
        La Folie du Jour 1927; Zou Zou 1934; Princess Tam-Tam
        1935; Fausse Alerte 1939; Moulin Rouge 1944; The French
        Way 1959.
Publications: Les Memoires de Josephine Baker 1927; Voyages et
        Aventures de Josephine Baker 1931.
Records: J'ai Deux Amours (theme song); Josephine Baker.
Television: Kate Smith Show 1951; Merv Griffin Show 1973; Tonight
        Show 1973; Black News 1973.
Theater: Shuffle Along (chorus) 1922; The Chocolate Dandies 1924;
        La Revue Nègre (Paris) 1925; Teatro Lirico (Milan) 1932;
        Prince Edward Theatre (London) 1933; La Créole (Paris) 1935;
        Ziegfeld Follies 1936; Théâtre aux Armées 1945; Paris Sings
        Again (pre-Bway run) 1947; Strand Theatre 1951; Hill Street
        Theatre (L. A.) 1951; Apollo Theatre 1952; Roxy Theatre
        1952; Mes Amours (Paris) 1958; Olympia Theatre (Paris)
        1958; Carnegie Hall 1963; Josephine Baker and Her Company
        1964; Ahmanson Theatre (L. A.) 1973; Carnegie Hall 1973;
        Palladium (London) 1974; The Twelve Dresses of Josephine
        Baker (Monaco) 1974; Bobino Music Hall (Paris) 1975.

BALTHROP, CARMEN
        (Singer)
b. c. 1954, Washington, D. C.
Education: Catholic University of America.
Honors: Metropolitan Opera Awards Singer 1975.
Career Data: Sang for Oratorio Society of New York.
Records: Treemonisha.
Television: Sunday 1975; Merv Griffin Show 1977.
Theater: Title role in Treemonisha 1975; Handel's Messiah at Car-
        negie Hall 1975.

BARAKA, IMAMU AMIRI (Everett Leroi Jones)
        (Playwright)
b. October 7, 1934, Newark, N. J.
Education: Rutgers University 1951-52; Howard University B. A.
        1954; Columbia University; New School Social Research.
Address: 502 High Street, Newark, N. J. 07102.
Honors: Whitney Fellowship 1963; Obie (for Dutchman) 1964; Gug-
        genheim Fellowship 1965; Yoruba Academy Fellow 1965.
Career Data: Founder Black Arts Repertory Theater School (Har-
        lem) 1964; Spirit House (Newark) 1966; member, Black
        Scholar's Speaker's Bureau; co-convenor, National Black Po-
        litical Convention; taught at New School for Social Research,
        Columbia University, University of Buffalo, San Francisco
        State College; visiting lecturer, Yale University 1977-78.
Films: Dutchman 1964.
Memberships: Black Academy of Arts & Letters.
Radio: Black New Ark--Unity of Struggle 1969-75.
Records: Black and Beautiful 1966; Black Mass 1967; Nation Time
        (Motown) 1972.

Television: Soul; Black New Ark 1971; A. M. New York 1974.
Theater: Dante 1962; Dutchman 1964; The Slave 1964; The Dead Lec-
     turer, A Recent Killing 1964; Baptism 1965; Toilet 1965;
     J-E-L-L-O 1965, 1970; Experimental Death Unit 1965; The
     Death of Malcolm X 1965; Black Mass 1966; Mad Heart 1967;
     Slave Ship 1967; Arm Yourself or Harm Yourself 1967; Home
     on the Range 1967; Great Goodness of Life: A Coon Show
     1968; Insurrection 1968; Board of Education 1968; Chant 1968;
     Police 1968; The Coronation of the Black Queen 1969; Sidnee
     Poet Heroical 1969; The Kid Poeta Tragical 1969; Junkies
     Are Full of (SHHH ...) 1970; Bloodrite, a Ritual 1970; Co-
     lumbia, the Gem of the Ocean 1972; New Ark's a Moverin
     (Newark) 1973; Incredible Rocky 1974; Stop Killer Cop (New-
     wark) 1975.

BARNES, MAE (Edith Mae Stith)
     (Singer/Actress)
b. January 23, 1907, New York, N. Y.
Special Interests: Dancing, drums, piano.
Address: 185-24 Jordan Ave. St. Albans, N. Y. 11412.
Clubs: Pod's and Jerry's; Bon Soir; Blue Angel.
Films: Odds against Tomorrow 1959.
Memberships: AEA; AFTRA; AGVA; SAG.
Television: Steve Allen Show; Garry Moore Show; The Today Show;
     Merv Griffin Show; Dupont Show of the Month; Kitty Foyle
     (Series); Ed Sullivan Show 1964.
Theater: Running Wild (debut) 1923; Lucky Sambo 1925; Shuffle A-
     long (tour) 1926; Rang Tang 1927; The Rainbow 1928; Hot Rhy-
     thm 1930; Ebony Scandals (vaudeville tour) 1932-33; By the
     Beautiful Sea 1954; Ziegfeld Follies (pre-Bway tour) 1956.

BASIE, COUNT (William James Basie)
     (Composer/Musician)
b. August 21, 1904, Red Bank, N. J.
Special Interests: Conducting, piano, organ.
Honors: Musicians of America most popular band award 1933; Top
     Band, Pittsburg Courier annual popularity poll 1941; Metro-
     nome Poll 1942-43; All-American Band award, Esquire 1945;
     Jazz Merit Award, The Lamplighter 1945; Down Beat Inter-
     national Critics' Poll winner 1952-56; command performance,
     Buckingham Palace 1957; Down Beat Hall of Fame 1958; Gram-
     my Awards 1958, 1960, 1963; performed at President Ken-
     nedy's Inaugural Ball 1961; Ebony Black Music Hall of Fame
     1975; Playboy Hall of Fame; Newport Jazz Hall of Fame 1976.
Career Data: Played with Benny Moten (Kansas City) 1929-36; form-
     ed own band 1936.
Clubs: Capitol Lounge (Chicago); Grand Terrace (Chicago); White
     Horse Tavern (Kansas City); Tropicana (Las Vegas). Caesar's
     Palace (Las Vegas); Copacabana 1936; Roseland 1938; Savoy
     Ballroom 1938; The Famous Door Club 1938-39; Hotel Lincoln
     1944; The Riverboat 1974; The Bottom Line 1976.

Films: Mister Big; The Hit Parade of 1943; Reveille with Beverly;
         I Dood It (score); Crazy House; Stage Door Canteen; Top Man
         1943; Ebony Parade 1947; Sex and the Single Girl 1964; Made
         in Paris 1966; One More Time 1970.
Memberships: ASCAP 1943; Dance Orchestra Leaders Assn.; NAACP.
Musical Compositions: Two O'Clock Jump; Good Morning Blues; Pan-
         assie Stomp; Basie Boogie; Blue and Sentimental; One O'Clock
         Jump (theme); The Comeback; Everyday; All Right O. K. You
         Win; Every Tub; Jumping at the Woodside; 920 Special; John's
         Idea; Gone with the Wind; Good Bait, Miss Thing; Riff Inter-
         lude; Futile Frustration; Hollywood Jump.
Records: The Best of Count Basie (MCA); A Night at the Apollo;
         April in Paris; Jam Session (Clef); Basie Jazz (Clef); Dance
         Session (Clef); The Bosses (Pablo); The Old Count and The
         New Count (Epic); Blues by Basie; Basie Jam (Pablo); Afrique
         (Flying Dutchman); Basic Basie (BASF); Basie's in the Bag
         (Brunswick); Best (Roulette); Big Band (Pablo); Board of Di-
         rectors (Dot); Broadway Basie's Way (Command); Echoes of
         an Era (Roulette); Everything's Coming Up Roses (Pickwick);
         Fantail (Roulette); Jam Montreux '75 (Pablo); Kid from Red
         Bank (Roulette); Basie Meets Bond (Solid State); Straight A-
         head (Dot); Standing Ovation (Dot); Songs of Bessie Smith
         (Flying Dutchman); 16 Great Performances (ABC); Kansas
         City 7 (Impulse); Kansas City Suite/Easin' It (Roulette); Basie
         with Eckstine (Roulette); Basie with Joe Williams (Verve); Ba-
         sie with Vaughan (Roulette); Satch and Josh (Pablo); I Told
         You So (Pablo); One O'Clock Jump (Columbia Special Pro-
         ducts); Super Chief (Columbia); The First Time (with Duke
         Ellington) 1962.
Television: Ed Sullivan Show; Joey Bishop Show; Tonight Show;
         Showtime at the Apollo 1954; Sammy and Company 1975; Pos-
         itively Black 1975; Mike Douglas Show 1976; John Denver and
         Friend (special) 1976; Merv Griffin Show 1976.
Theater: Appeared at Carnegie Hall 1939; Apollo Theatre 1940;
         Strand Theatre; Salle Pleyel (Paris) 1964; Avery Fisher Hall
         1975; Palladium (London) 1975; Westbury Music Fair 1975;
         The Concert (with Ella Fitzgerald and Frank Sinatra) at the
         Uris Theatre 1975.

BASKETT, JAMES
         (Actor)
b. February 16, 1904, Indianapolis, Ind. d. July 9, 1948, Los
         Angeles Calif.
Honors: Special Academy Award (for Song of the South) 1947.
Career Data: performed with Lafayette Players.
Films: Harlem Is Heaven 1932; The Policy Man 1938; Gone Harlem,
         Straight to Heaven 1939; Comes Midnight 1940; Uncle Remus
         in Song of the South 1946.

BASSEY, SHIRLEY (Veronica)
         (Singer)
b. January 8, 1937, Cardiff, Wales.

Address: Via Forengo, 6 Lugano, Switzerland.
Honors: AGVA Entertainer of the Year award 1975.
Career Data: London stage debut 1956.
Clubs: Tropicoro; Talk of the Town (London); Persian Room-Hotel
Plaza 1961; Empire Room-Waldorf Astoria 1971; El San Juan
Hotel (Puerto Rico) 1975.
Films: Goldfinger (sang theme) 1964; The Liquidators (sang theme)
1966; Diamonds Are Forever (sang theme) 1971.
Records: Belts the Best (United Artists); And We Were Lovers (Uni-
ted Artists); How About You (Pickwick); I Capricorn (United
Artists); I Love You So (United Artists); In Person (United
Artists); Shirley Bassey (United Artists); Shirley Means Bas-
sey (United Artists); ... Sings the Hits from Oliver (United
Artists); I Who Have Nothing; This Is My Life (United Art
ists); Something Else; Shirley Bassey at Her Best; The Best
of Bassey; And I Love You So; Nobody Does It Like Me (U-
nited Artists); Shirley Bassey Live at Carnegie Hall (United
Artists); Never, Never, Never, (United Artists); Shirley Bassey Is Really Something (United Artists); Does Anybody Miss
Me? (United Artists); Good, Bad But Beautiful (United Artists).
Television: Mike Douglas Show 1973; Saturday Night Live with Howard Cosell 1975; AGVA Entertainer of the Year Awards Show
1976; Shirley Bassey Show 1976.
Theater: Dorothy Chandler Pavillion (L. A.); Carnegie Hall 1973,
1975; Westchester Premier Theatre 1975, 1976; Westbury Music Fair 1976.

BATES, PEG LEG (Clayton Bates)
      (Dancer)
b.   October 11, 1907, Greenville, S. C.
Address: Kerhonkson, N. Y. 12486.
Career Data: Owner, Peg Leg Bates Country Club 1952-.
Clubs: Cotton Club.
Television: Ed Sullivan Show; Mike Douglas Show 1973.
Theater: Appeared at Apollo Theatre.

BATSON, SUSAN
      (Actress)
b.   c. 1944, Roxbury, Mass.
Education: Emerson College (drama) 1964; studied with Uta Hagen,
Herbert Berghof Studio, Actors Studio.
Honors: Obie; John Hay Whitney Fellowship.
Films: WUSA 1970.
Television: Merv Griffin Show; Gidget Grows Up; The New People;
Delvecchio 1976; Good Times 1976.
Theater: Threepenny Opera; Who's Got His Own (Center Stage, Bal-
timore); The Adventures of the Black Girl in Search for Her
God (L. A.); Hair 1967; In White America (tour) 1967; George
M! 1968; The Creation of the World and Other Business (pre-
Bway) 1972; The Leaf People (O. B.) 1975.

BEARD, MATTHEW "Stymie"
>   (Actor)
b. January 1, 1925, Los Angeles, Calif.
Films: Our Gang (series) 1930-35; Kid Millions 1934; Captain Blood
>   1935; Rainbow on the River 1936; Jezebel, Beloved Brat 1938;
>   Way Down South 1939; The Return of Frank James, Broken
>   Strings 1940; Stormy Weather 1943; Moss in the Pond 1974.
>   Truck Turner 1974.
Television: Hawkins; The First Woman President; Good Times; Fire-
>   house 1972; Sanford and Son 1973; Tomorrow Show 1974; It's
>   Good to Be Alive 1974; Good Times 1976.
Theater: Appeared at Capitol Theatre (Passaic, N. J.) 1974.

BEATTY, TALLEY
>   (Dancer/Choreographer)
Education: Studied dance with Katherine Dunham.
Special Interests: Teaching.
Career Data: Member, Katherine Dunham Dance Group 1940-42;
>   Ballet Society (later New York City Ballet) 1947; founder,
>   Talley Beatty Dance Co.; artist-in-residence, Elma Lewis
>   School of Fine Arts (Roxbury, Mass.); dance roles include
>   the priest in Yanvalou, the fugitive in Tropic Death (Swamp
>   Suite).
Films: Study in Choreography for Camera (doc.) 1945; Carnival in
>   Rhythm 1940.
Memberships: AEA.
Theater: Choreographed Sing Me Sunshine; Migration; Negro Dance
>   Evening YMHA 1937; Tropics and Le Jazz Hot 1940; Tropical
>   Revue 1942; Blue Holiday 1945; Spring in Brazil 1946; Show-
>   boat 1946; Bal Negre 1946; Blackface 1947; Tropicana (Bos-
>   ton) 1952; choreographed The Road of the Phoebe Snow 1959;
>   Come and Get the Beauty of It Hot 1960; The Blacks (O.B.)
>   1961; Concerts for Harpsichord 1961; Fly Blackbird 1962;
>   Ballad for Bimshire 1963; Montgomery Variations 1967; House
>   of Flowers (O.B.) 1968; But Never Jam Today 1969; The
>   Black Belt 1969; Ari; Alice in Wonderland (Afro-American
>   adaptation).

BEAVERS, LOUISE
>   (Actress)
b. 1902, Cincinnati, Ohio. d. October 26, 1962, Hollywood, Calif.
Education: Pasadena High School.
Honors: Black Filmmakers Hall of Fame 1976.
Films: Uncle Tom's Cabin 1927; Wall Street, Gold Diggers of Broad-
>   way, Glad Rag Doll, Barnum Was Right, Coquette, Nix on
>   Dames 1929; Our Blushing Brides, Back Pay, She Couldn't
>   Say No, Wide Open, Safety in Numbers 1930; Up for Murder,
>   Party Husbands, Reckless Living, Sundown Trail, Annabelle's
>   Affairs, Six-Cylinder Love, Good Sport, Girls About Town
>   1931; Freaks, Ladies of the Big House, Old Man Minick, Un-
>   ashamed, It's Tough to Be Famous, Night World, What Price

Hollywood?, Street of Women, We Humans, The Expert, Wild
Girl, Jubilo, Young America, Divorce in the Family, Too
Busy to Work 1932; Girl Missing, What Price Innocence?,
Her Bodyguard, Bombshell, Her Splendid Folly, Notorious
but Nice, She Done Him Wrong, Pick Up, A Shriek in the
Night, I'm No Angel 1933; In the Money, Delilah in Imita-
tion of Life, I've Got Your Number, Bedside, The Merry
Frinks, Cheaters, Glamour, I Believed in You, I Give My
Love, Merry Wives of Reno, A Modern Hero, Registered
Nurse, Hat, Coat and Glove, Dr. Monica, West of the Pecos
1934; Annapolis Farewell 1935; Bullets or Ballots, General
Spanky, Wives Never Know, Rainbow on the River 1936; The
Last Gangster, Make Way for Tomorrow, Wings over Hono-
lulu, Love in a Bungalow 1937; Scandal Street, The Headleys
at Home, Life Goes On, Brother Rat, Reckless Living 1938;
Peck's Bad Boy with the Circus, Made for Each Other, The
Lady's from Kentucky, Reform School 1939; Parole Fixer,
Women Without Names, I Want a Divorce, No Time for Com-
edy 1940; Virginia, Sign of the Wolf, Belle Starr, Shadow of
the Thin Man 1941; The Vanishing Virginian, Reap the Wild
Wind, Holiday Inn, The Big Street, Seven Sweethearts (a. k. a.
Tulip Time), Tennessee Johnson 1942; There's Something A-
bout a Soldier, Good Morning Judge, DuBarry Was a Lady,
All by Myself, Top Man 1943; Jack London, Dixie Jamboree,
South of Dixie, Follow the Boys, Barbary Coast Gent 1944;
Delightfully Dangerous 1945; Lover Come Back, Young Widow
1946; Banjo 1947; Mr. Blandings Builds His Dream House,
For the Love of Mary, Good Sam 1948; Tell It to the Judge,
My Blue Heaven 1949; Girls School, Jackie Robinson's mother
in The Jackie Robinson Story 1950; Colorado Sundown, I Dream
of Jeannie 1952; Never Wave at a Wac 1953; Goodbye My La-
dy, You Can't Run Away from It, Teenage Rebel 1956; Tam-
my and the Bachelor 1957; The Goddess 1958; All the Fine
Young Cannibals 1960; The Facts of Life 1961.
Memberships: SAG (board member).
Television: Title role in Beulah (series) 1952-53; Cleopatra Collins
(Star Stage) 1956; The Hostess with the Mostess (Playhouse 90)
1957; The Swamp Fox (World of Disney Series) 1959; Groucho
Marx--You Bet Your Life 1959.
Theater: Vaudeville act at Loews State Theatre.

BECHET, SIDNEY
(Jazz Musician)
b. May 14, 1897, New Orleans, La. **d.** May 14, 1959, Paris,
France.
Special Interests: Saxophone, composing, conducting, cornet, clar-
inet.
Honors: Winner Record Changer All Star Poll 1951.
Career Data: Performed with numerous bands and groups, including
King Oliver, Benny Peyton, Noble Sissle, Louis Armstrong,
Clarence Williams, Duke Ellington; joined Will Marion Cook's
Southern Syncopated Orchestra (Chicago); toured Europe, South

America; vice-president, Jazz Inc. 1945-49; led all-star band
at Brussels World Fair 1958.
Clubs: Big 25, Pete Lala's (New Orleans); Dreamland, DeLuxe Café,
Pekin Cabaret (Chicago); Rector's Club, Hammersmith Palais
(London); Rhythm Club; Club Basha; Nest Club; Les Ambassa-
deurs Club (Paris) 1928; Enduro Restaurant (Brooklyn) 1940;
Savoy (Boston) 1945; Jimmie Ryan's 1947, 1949; Jazz LTD.
(Chicago) 1948.
Films: Blues (Fr.) 1955; La Souffle au Coeur (music) 1971.
Musical Compositions: Nouvelles Orleans; The Night Is a Witch.
Publications: Treat It Gentle (autobiography), 1960.
Records: Master Musician (Bluebird).
Theater: Appeared at Monogram Theatre (Chicago) 1917; acted and
played with Bruce and Bruce Touring Co. 1917; How Come?
1922; Jimmy Cooper's Black and White Revue (tour) 1924;
Seven Eleven Show (tour) 1925; Revue Negre (tour) 1925-26;
Eddie Condon's Town Hall concerts; Hear That Trumpet 1946.

BELAFONTE, HARRY (Harold George Belafonte)
        (Singer/Actor)
b.   March 1, 1927, New York, N.Y.
Education: Studied with Erwin Piscator's Dramatic Workshop at New
School for Social Research.
Special Interests: Calypso, guitar, producing, black history and cul-
ture, civil rights.
Address: c/o Belafonte Enterprises, Inc., 157 West 57 St., New
York, N.Y. 10019, and 300 West End Ave., New York, N.Y.
10023.
Honors: Donaldson, Tony, and Theatre World awards (for John
Murray Anderson's Almanac) 1954; Diners' Club Award 1955-
56; U.S. Dept. of State Award 1958; Emmy Award (for Tonight with Belafonte) 1959; Grammy Award 1960; Black Filmmakers Hall of Fame 1976.
Career Data: Member, American Negro Theatre and Community for
the Negro in the Arts; toured as concert performer throughout Europe, U.S., Australia, Israel, Japan and Philippines;
appeared at Brussels World's Fair (Belgium) 1958; bd. member, Southern Christian Leadership Conference; furthered career of Miriam Makeba, singer; formed Har Bel production
company 1959; president, Belafonte Enterprises Inc.
Clubs: Royal Roost (debut); Village Vanguard 1951; Blue Angel; Riviera (Las Vegas) 1955; Palmer House (Chicago) 1955; Fairmont Hotel (San Francisco) 1955; Mocambo (Hollywood); Coconut Grove (L.A.) 1955; Caesar's Palace (Las Vegas); Thunderbird Hotel (Las Vegas); Latin Casino (Philadelphia).
Films: Bright Road (debut) 1953; Carmen Jones 1954; David Boyer
in Island in the Sun 1957; Odds Against Tomorrow; produced
and acted in The World, the Flesh and the Devil 1959; produced and acted in The Angel Levine 1970; co-produced and
acted in Buck and the Preacher 1972; Uptown Saturday Night
1974.
Memberships: AEA; AFTRA; AGVA; SAG.

Musical Compositions: Turn Around; Glory Manger; Shake That Little Foot; Mark Twain.

Records: Shenandoah; Belafonte; Calypso (RCA); Scarlet Ribbons; An
Evening with Belafonte (RCA); Harry Belafonte Sings of the
Caribbean; To Wish You a Merry Christmas; Pure Gold (RCA);
In My Quiet Room; Matilda; Come Back Liza; Brown Skin
Girl; Jamaica Farewell, Mary's Boy Child 1956; Banana Boat
Song, or Day-O; Hold'Em Joe; Mama Look at Bubu; Island
in the Sun; Coconut Woman 1957; Belafonte at Carnegie Hall
(RCA); Porgy and Bess; Love Is a Gentle Thing 1959; Swing
Dat Hammer; Belafonte Sings the Blues; My Lord, What a
Morning; Belafonte Returns to Carnegie Hall 1960; Jump Up
at Calypso 1961; Many Moods of Belafonte; Midnight Special
1962; Streets I Have Walked 1963; Belafonte at the Greek
Theatre 1964.

Television: What's My Line?; Ed Sullivan Show; Flip Wilson Show;
Colgate Variety Hour (special) 1955; Three for Tonight (special) 1955; Winner by Decision (G. E. Theatre) 1955; Tonight
with Belafonte (special) 1959; New York 19 (special) 1960;
The Strollin' Twenties (special) 1966; A Time for Laughter
(special) 1967; guest host on Tonight Show 1968; Petula Clark
(special) 1968; Harry and Lena (special) 1969; Today Is Ours
(special); Dick Cavett Show 1972; Sunday 1974; Mike Douglas
Show 1974; Free to Be ... You and Me (Marlo Thomas Special) 1975; Paul Robeson (The People) 1976; Like It Is 1976;
Kup's Show 1976; Jubilee 1976; Golden Globe Awards show
(emcee) 1977.

Theater: John Murray Anderson's Almanac (debut) 1953; Three for
Tonight 1955; appeared at Lewisohn Stadium 1956; Sing, Man
Sing (tour) 1956; The Greek Theatre (L. A.) 1957, 1963; pro-
duced Moonbirds 1959; appeared at Palace Theatre 1959; A
Night with Belafonte; appeared at Avery Fisher Hall; Salle
Wilfrid-Pelletier (Montreal) 1976.

BELGRAVE, CYNTHIA
    (Actress/Director)
b. August 6, 1926, Boston, Mass.
Education: Massachusetts School of Fine Arts B. F. A.; studied at
    Paul Mann Acting Studio 1958-60.
Special Interests: Singing, commercial art.
Address: 357 Bergen Street, Brooklyn, N. Y. 11217.
Honors: N. Y. Times season's outstanding performance 1964.
Career Data: Dir., plays, Greenwich Mews Theatre; associate prof.,
    Performing Arts, Staten Island Community College; teacher,
    Y. W. C. A. Brooklyn; dir., Farris/Belgrave Theatre Work-
    shop.
Films: I the People; Odds Against Tomorrow 1959; Requiem for a
    Heavyweight 1962; Black Like Me 1964; The Hospital 1972;
    The Taking of Pelham 1-2-3 1974.
Memberships: AEA; AFTRA; SAG.
Television: Brother Jess; The Reporter; Commercial: She Sure
    Loves You; The Defenders 1962-63; The Naked City 1962-63;
    East Side West Side 1965; Kojak 1977.

Theater: Lovey; directed Malcolm X: The Black Messiah; The Amen
    Corner; Cities in Bezique (O. B.); And the Wind Blows; A
    Raisin in the Sun (O. B.); The Blacks (O. B.) 1961; Funny
    House of a Negro (O. B.) 1964; Mr. Grossman (O. B.) 1964;
    Junebug Graduates Tonight (O. B.) 1967; directed and acted
    in Trials of Brother Jero (O. B.) 1968; directed The Strong
    Breed (O. B.) 1968; Twelfth Night (LCR) 1972; The Sunshine
    Boys 1973; directed Jasper (O. B.) 1975; Twin Bit Garden
    (O. B.) 1975.

BELL, JEANNE (Annie Lee Morgan)
    (Actress)
b. c. 1944.
Career Data: Former model, Playboy's first black centerfold 1969.
Films: Melinda 1972; Mean Streets 1973; The Klansman, Three the
    Hard Way 1974; title role in TNT Jackson 1975; Jackpot (un-
    finished film); Disco 9000 1977.
Memberships: SAG.
Television: Dial soap and Dodge automobile commercials; Police
    Woman 1974.

BENJAMIN, BENNIE
    (Musician/Composer)
b. November 4, 1907, Christiansted, St. Croix, Virgin Islands.
Special Interests: Banjo, guitar.
Career Data: Song writing team with George Weiss.
Memberships: ASCAP 1942.
Musical Compositions: I Don't Want to Set the World on Fire; When
    the Lights Go On Again All Over the World; Oh, What It
    Seemed to Be (with G. Weiss); Wheel of Fortune (with G.
    Weiss); Cancel the Flowers; Strictly Instrumental; I'll Keep
    the Love Light Burning; Rumors Are Flying; I Don't See Me
    in Your Eyes Anymore; Can Anyone Explain; Surrender; I'll
    Never Be Free; Confess; Just for Tonight; These Things I
    Offer You; Cross Over the Bridge; A Girl a Girl!; How Im-
    portant Can It Be?; I Ran All the Way Home; Of This I'm
    Sure; Lonely Man; Lonesome and Blue; I Want to Thank Your
    Folks.

BENNETT, FRAN
    (Actress)
b. August 14, 1935, Malvern, Ark.
Education: University of Wisconsin.
Address: c/o Jeff Hunter, 119 West 57 St., New York, N. Y. 10019.
Career Data: Minnesota Repertory Theatre Co. 1967-69 (acted in
    House of Atreus among other plays).
Films: Giant 1956; That Night 1957.
Memberships: AEA; AFTRA; AGVA; SAG.
Television: The Guiding Light (series); The Nurses (series).
Theater: The Cat and the Canary (O. B.); By Jupiter (O. B.); Brecht

on Brecht (O. B.); Land Beyond the River (O. B.) 1957; Man-
dingo 1961; Octoroon (O. B.) 1961; The Cantilevered Terrace
(O. B.) 1962; Ballad for Bimshire 1963; In White America
(O. B.).

BENSON, GEORGE
      (Jazz Musician)
b. c. 1942, Pittsburgh, Pa.
Special Interests: Composing, singing, guitar.
Honors: Grammy awards 1977.
Career Data: Performed at Metropolitan Museum of Art 1977.
Films: The Greatest (score) 1977.
Records: White Rabbit (CTI); The Other Side of Abby Road (A&M);
      Masquerade 1976; Breezin' (Warner Bro.) 1976; In Flight
      (Warner Bro.) 1977; Good King Bad (CTI).
Television: Tonight Show 1977; Saturday Night Live 1977.
Theater: Palladium 1977; Avery Fisher Hall 1977.

BENTON, BROOK (Benjamin Franklin Peay)
      (Singer)
b. September 19, 1931, Camden, S. C.
Clubs: Barney Google's 1975; Copa (Bklyn) 1975; Rainbow Grill 1975;
      Waldorf's Starlight Roof 1975.
Records: For Mercury: It's Just a Matter of Time 1959; Thank
      You Pretty Baby 1959; So Many Ways 1959; Baby You've Got
      What It Takes (with Dinah Washington) 1960; A Rockin' Good
      Way (with Dinah Washington) 1960; Fools Rush In 1960; Kiddio
      1960; The Boll Weevil Song 1961; Think Twice 1961; Hotel
      Happiness 1962; Walk on the Wild Side 1962; I Got What I
      Wanted 1963; A House Is Not a Home 1964; Do It Right 1964;
      Love Me Now 1965, for RCA: Mother Nature, Father Time
      1965. For Cotillion: Do Your Own Thing 1968; Nothing Takes
      the Place of You 1969, Rainy Night in Georgia 1970; My Way
      1970.

BERNARD, ED
      (Actor)
b. July 4, 1939, Philadelphia, Pa.
Education: Temple University; studied at Herbert Berghof Studio.
Career Data: Performed at Hedgerow Theatre.
Films: Shaft 1971; The Hot Rock, Across 110th Street 1972; Trader
      Horn 1973; Together Brothers 1974.
Memberships: SAG.
Television: Styles on Police Woman (series); Cool Million; That's
      My Mama (series) 1974; Reflections on Murder 1974; Unwed
      Father 1974.
Theater: To Be Young, Gifted and Black (O. B.) 1969; Five on the
      Black Hand Side (O. B.) 1970; Goat Without Horns (L. A.);
      Boesman and Lena (L. A.) 1977; Short Eyes 1977.

BERRY, CHUCK (Charles Edward Anderson Berry)
       (Singer)
b.   January 15, 1926, San Jose, Calif.
Special Interests: Composing, guitar.
Address: Universal Attractions, 888 Seventh Ave., New York, N.Y.
       10010 and Berry Park, Wentzville, Mo. 63385.
Honors: Rock 'n' Roll Hall of Fame.
Career Data: Formed his own combo 1952.
Clubs: Cosmopolitan (St. Louis, Mo.); My Mother's Place (Wash-
       ington D.C.) 1970.
Films: Rock Rock Rock 1956; Go, Johnny Go 1959; Jazz on a Sum-
       mer's Day (doc.) 1960; Let the Good Times Roll 1973.
Musical Compositions: Roll Over Beethoven; Maybelline; Nadine;
       Johnny B. Goode; Sweet Little Sixteen; Reelin' & Rockin';
       Rock 'n' Roll Music; Surfin' U.S.A.; Wee Wee Hours.
Records: On Stage (Chess); Chuck Berry Bio; Chuck and His Friends;
       Chuck Berry; After School Session (Chess); Berry's On Top
       (Chess); Flashback (Pickwick); Golden Hits (Mercury); Johnny
       B. Goode (Pickwick); London Sessions (Chess); More Chuck
       Berry (Chess); No Particular Place to Go; (Chess); One Doz-
       en Berrys (Chess); St. Louis to Liverpool (Chess); Sweet Lit-
       tle Rock & Roller (Pickwick); Wild Berrys (Pickwick); Great
       Guitars (Checker); You Never Can Tell; On Chess: Maybel-
       line 1955; Too Much Monkey Business/Brown-Eyed Handsome
       Man 1956; Oh Baby Doll 1957; Rock'n Roll Music 1957; Sweet
       Little Sixteen 1958; Johnny B. Goode 1958; Beautiful Delilah
       1958; Almost Grown 1959; Too Pooped to Pop 1960; Little
       Marie 1964; Greatest Hits 1964; Dear Dad 1965; Chuck Ber-
       ry's Golden Decade 1967; At the Fillmore Auditorium 1967;
       Concerto in B. Goode 1969; Back Home Again 1970; San Fran-
       cisco Dues 1971; Rollin' and Rockin' 1972; My Ding-A-Ling
       1972.
Television: Mike Douglas Show; Merv Griffin Show; Don Kirshner
       Playboy 20th Anniversary Party (Wide World Special); Salute
       to the Beatles (Wide World Special) 1975; Midnight Special
       1975; Rock Music Awards 1975; Don Kirshner's Rock Concert
       1975; Sammy and Company 1975; Dinah! 1975; Saturday Night
       1977.
Theater: Rock & Roll Revival (Madison Square Garden) 1975; West-
       bury Music Fair 1975; Casino (Asbury Park, N.J.) 1976; Pa-
       lace Lido (Douglas, Isle of Man) 1976.

BEST, WILLIE "Sleep'n Eat"
       (Actor)
b.   1915, Mississippi. d. February 27, 1962, Hollywood, Calif.
Films: Up Pops the Devil, The Monster Walks 1931; Little Miss
       Marker, West of the Pecos, Kentucky Kernels 1934; Murder
       on the Bridal Path, The Bride Walks Out, Mummy's Boys,
       Racing Lady, Make Way for a Lady, Thank You, Jeeves,
       General Spanky, Two in Revolt (first time billed as Willie
       Best), Down the Stretch 1936; Breezing Home, The Lady
       Fights Back, Super Sleuth, Saturday's Heroes, Meet the Missus

1937; Gold Is Where You Find It, Blondie, Merrily We Live,
Goodbye Broadway, Youth Takes a Fling, Vivacious Lady
1938; Nancy Drew, Trouble Shooter, The Covered Trailer,
At the Circus 1939; I Take This Woman, The Ghost Breakers,
Money and the Woman, Who Killed Aunt Maggie? 1940; Road
Show, The Lady from Cheyenne, High Sierra, Flight from
Destiny, Scattergood Baines, Nothing but the Truth, Highway
West, The Smiling Ghost 1941; Juke Girl, Whispering Ghosts,
A Haunting-We Will Go, Busses Roar, The Hidden Hand, Scat-
tergood Survives a Murder, The Body Disappears 1942; Cabin
in the Sky, Thank Your Lucky Stars, Cinderella Swings It,
The Kansan 1943; Adventures of Mark Twain, Home in Indi-
ana, The Girl Who Dared 1944; Hold that Blonde, Pillow to
Post 1945; The Bride Wore Boots, Dangerous Money, The
Face of Marble, Red Dragon 1946; Suddenly It's Spring, The
Red Stallion 1947; Smart Woman, Half Past Midnight, The
Shanghai Chest 1948; Jiggs and Maggie in Jackpot Jitters, The
Hidden Hand 1949; South of Caliente 1951.
Television: Trouble with Father (series) 1950-52; My Little Margie
(series) 1952-55.

BEY, LA ROCQUE "Harlem's Godfather of Dance"
       (Dancer/Choreographer)
b.   Detroit, Mich.
Education: Northwestern School of Music, Dance and Drama; De-
       troit Conservatory of Music; Detroit Institute of Musical Arts.
Special Interests: Piano, drums, teaching.
Address: 169 West 133 St., New York, N.Y. 10030.
Career Data: Founded La Rocque Bey School of Dance 1960; appear-
       ances with Josephine Baker, Aretha Franklin, Miriam Makeba,
       Duke Ellington, Sammy Davis Jr.
Clubs: Smalls Paradise 1976.
Theater: Performed at Town Hall 1975; Savoy Manor 1976; Harlem
       Performance Center 1976.

BEY, MARKI
       (Actress)
b.   c. 1946, Philadelphia, Pa.
Clubs: The Improvisation.
Films: The Landlord 1970; Sugar Hill 1974; Super Dude 1975.
Memberships: AEA; SAG.
Television: Merv Griffin Show 1970; Rookies 1975.
Theater: Hello, Dolly! 1969; Every Night When the Sun Goes Down
       1976.

BIBB, LEON (Charles Leon Bibb)
       (Actor/Singer)
b.   c. 1926, Louisville, Ky.
Special Interests: Folk singing, guitar.
Address: 199-17 111 Ave., Hollis, N.Y. 11412.

Honors: Tony nomination (for A Hand Is on the Gate) 1966.
Career Data: Participated in Newport Folk Festival 1959; toured
       Russia in 1964.
Clubs: Village Gate; The Bitter End; Hungry Eye (San Francisco);
       Cellar Door (Wash. D. C.).
Films: For Love of Ivy, Uptight 1968; The Lost Man 1969.
Records: Leon Bibb Sings Folk Songs (Vanguard) 1959; Leon Bibb
       Sings Love Songs (Vanguard) 1960; Tol' My Captain (Vanguard)
       1960; Oh Freedom and Other Spirituals (Washington) 1960;
       Leon Bibb in Concert (Liberty); Cherries and Plums (Liberty);
       Leon Bibb Sings (Columbia) 1961.
Television: Tonight Show; Ed Sullivan Show; Merv Griffin Show; Mike
       Douglas Show; The Electric Company; Someone New 1969.
Theater: Ailey's Blues Suite; Livin' the Life (O. B.) 1957; Lost in
       the Stars (O. B.) 1958; Annie Get Your Gun (O. B.) 1958;
       Finian's Rainbow (O. B.) 1960; A Hand Is on the Gate 1966;
       Carnival (City Center) 1969; Duet: An Evening of Theatre in
       Song (Vancouver) 1975.

BLACK PATTI see JONES, SISSERETTA

BLAKE, EUBIE "Mouse" (James Hubert Blake)
       (Pianist/Composer)
b. February 7, 1883, Baltimore, Md.
Education: New York University 1946.
Special Interests: Conducting, producing, lecturing.
Address: 284-A Stuyvesant Avenue, Brooklyn, N. Y. 11221.
Honors: Songwriters' Hall of Fame; Bronze Bust in Museum of City
       of New York 1967; Oscar Micheaux Award (Black Filmmakers
       Hall of Fame) 1976.
Career Data: Toured with medicine show 1901; teamed with Noble
       Sissle since 1915 as vocal-piano duo (The Dixie Duo), joint
       orchestra leaders and co-composers; appeared with James
       Reese Europe's society orchestra 1916-19; appearances at New
       Orleans Jazz Festival 1969; Newport Jazz Festival 1971, 73,
       76; Monterey Jazz Festival 1974.
Clubs: Goldfield Hotel (Baltimore) 1907-15.
Films: Snappy Tunes 1923; Eubie Blake Plays 1927; Pie Pie Black-
       bird (short) 1931; Harlem Is Heaven 1932; score for From
       These Roots (doc.) 1974.
Memberships: ASCAP 1922.
Musical Compositions: 315 songs including As Long As You Live;
       You're Lucky to Me; Memories of You; Love Will Find a Way;
       Lovin' You the Way I Do; Eubie's Boogie; Gypsy Blues; Ban-
       danna Days; Troublesome Ivories; Brittwood Rag; Blue Rags
       in Twelve Keys; Fizz Water 1914; Chevy Chase 1914; It's All
       Your Fault 1915; Charleston Rag (a. k. a. Sounds of Africa)
       1919; I'm Just Wild About Harry 1921; You Were Meant for
       Me 1924; Bugle Call Rag 1926.
Records: Blues and Spirituals (Biograph); Song Hits (Eubie Blake
       Music); The Eighty-Six Years of Eubie Blake (Columbia) 1969;

Eubie Blake Live Rags To Classics; Charleston Rag (Eubie
Blake Music); Concert; Blues and Ragtime (Biograph); Eubie
Blake & His Proteges (Eubie Blake Music); Early Rare Re-
cordings (Eubie Blake Music); Wild About Eubie.

Television: Jack Paar Show; Today Show; Ragtime; Johnny Carson
Show; Black Omnibus; Black Arts 1972; Mike Douglas Show
1974; What's My Line? 1975; Interface 1975; A. M. America
1975; Evening at Pops 1975; The People 1975; Like It Is
1976; Midday Live 1976; Merv Griffin Show 1976; Black News
1976.

Theater: Wrote, co-produced and starred in Shuffle Along 1921;
wrote songs for Elsie 1923; wrote songs for Charlot's Revue
of 1924; The Chocolate Dandies (a. k. a. In Bamville) 1924;
wrote songs for Folies Bergere 1930; Hot Rhythm 1930;
Blackbirds of 1930; conducted Singin' the Blues 1931; Olsen
and Johnson's Atrocities of 1932; Shuffle Along of 1933; Swing
It 1937; Shuffle Along of 1952; The Rhythms of America
(Bklyn.) 1967; appearances at Alice Tully Hall 1972; Town
Hall (5:45 Interlude Series) 1972; Philharmonic Hall 1973;
Carnegie Hall 1975; Bubbling Brown Sugar (score) 1976; Mu-
sic for Dance (Brooklyn Academy of Music) 1976.

BLAKELY, DON(ALD)
          (Actor)
Films: Cross and the Switchblade, Shaft's Big Score 1972; The
          Spook Who Sat by the Door 1973; Strike Force 1975; Short
          Eyes 1977.
Television: Grant Piper in Beacon Hill (series) 1975; The Adams
          Chronicle 1976; Sanford and Son 1976.
Theater: Lost in the Stars (ELT) 1968; American Night Cry (O. B.)
          1973; Big Man: The Legend of John Henry (Carnegie Hall)
          1976; The Basic Training of Pavlo Hummel 1977.

BLAKEY, ART (Abdullah Ibn Buhaina)
          (Jazz Musician)
b.   October 11, 1919, Pittsburgh, Pa.
Special Interests: Drums.
Address: Shaw Artists Corp. , 656 Fifth Ave. , New York, N. Y.
          10017.
Honors: Down Beat Critics New Star Award 1953.
Career Data: Worked with Fletcher Henderson band 1939, pianist
          Mary Lou Williams 1940, Billy Eckstine band 1944-47, Lucky
          Millinder 1949, Buddy De Franco's Quartet 1951-53, The
          Jazz Messengers (his own quintet) 1955; toured U. S. , Europe
          and Japan.
Clubs: Five Spot; The Village Gate; Mikell's; Tic Toc (Boston)
          1941; Birdland 1954; Top of the Gate 1975-76.
Records: Three Blind Mice.
Television: Jazz Adventures.
Theater: appeared at Apollo Theatre 1950; Avery Fisher Hall (New-
          port Jazz Festival) 1975; Carnegie Hall (Newport Jazz Festi-
          val) 1976; Radio City Music Hall 1976.

BLAND, BOBBY "Blue"
>   (Singer)
b.   January 27, 1930, Rosemark, Tenn.
Records: On Duke: Two Steps from the Blues; Best; Here's the
>   Man; Spotlighting the Man; Touch of the Blues; Introspective
>   Early Years; Like 'Er Red Hot; Soul of the Man; Farther Up
>   the Road 1957; Cry, Cry Cry 1960; I Pity the Fool 1961;
>   Turn on Your Love Light 1961; Who Will the Next Fool Be
>   1962; Stormy Monday Blues 1962; Call on Me 1963; Some-
>   times You Gotta Cry a Little 1963; Share Your Love with
>   Me 1964; Aint Nothing You Can Do 1964; Blind Man 1965;
>   These Hands (Small But Mighty) 1965; I'm Too Far Gone (To
>   Turn Around) 1966; Good Time Charlie 1966; You're All I
>   Need 1967; Driftin Blues 1968; Rockin' in the Same Old Boat
>   1968; Gotta Get to Know You 1969; Chains of Love 1969; If
>   You've Got a Heart 1970; Keep on Loving Me (You'll
>   See the Change) 1970; I'm Sorry 1971. On Dunhill: This
>   Time I'm Gone for Good 1973; Together for the First
>   Time with B. B. King; Get On Down with Bobby Bland;
>   Together Live (Impulse); California (Dunhill); Dreamer (Dun-
>   hill).
Television: Soul Train 1975; Midnight Special 1977.
Theater: Appeared at Beacon Theatre 1976; Radio City Music Hall
>   (Newport Jazz Festival) 1976.

BLAND, JAMES A.
>   (Composer)
b.   October 22, 1854, Flushing, N. Y.
d.   May 5, 1911, Philadelphia, Pa.
Education: Howard University.
Special Interests: Banjo.
Career Data: Known as "The World's Greatest Minstrel Man"; in-
>   novated "Bland Banjo" (instrument includes 5th string).
Musical Compositions: Carry Me Back to Old Virginny 1878; In the
>   Evening by the Moonlight; Oh, Dem Golden Slippers; Pretty
>   Little Caroline Rose; Dandy Black Brigade; In Morning by the
>   Bright Light; The Missouri Hound Dog.
Theater: The Sporting Girl; appeared at Her Majesty's Theatre
>   (London) 1881.

BLEDSOE, JULES (Julius C. Bledsoe)
>   (Actor/Singer)
b.   December 29, 1898, Waco, Texas.
d.   July 14, 1943, Hollywood, Calif.
Education: Bishop College (Marshall, Texas).
Films: Show Boat 1929; Drums of the Congo 1942.
Radio: Show Boat.
Theater: Sang in Gruenberg's The Emperor Jones (opera) and The
>   Creation (orchestration of James Weldon Johnson poem);
>   Amonasro in Verdi's Aida; concert debut at Aeolian Hall
>   1924; Deep River 1926; In Abraham's Bosom 1926; Joe in
>   Show Boat 1927.

BLIND, TOM (Thomas Wiggins, a. k. a. Thomas Green Bethune)
       (Musician)
b.   May 25, 1849, Muscogee County, Ga.
d.   June 13, 1908, Hoboken, N. J.
Education: Studied with Prof. Joseph Poznanski.
Special Interests: Classical music, singing, composing, piano.
Career Data: Performed throughout U. S. , Canada and Europe; per-
       formed for President Abraham Lincoln and for Queen Vic-
       toria of England; played Bach, Beethoven, Mozart, Verdi, etc.
Musical Compositions: The Rain Storm; Timpani Galop; Mary Samp-
       lian; Wellin Klange; Grand March de Concert; Delta Kappa
       Epsilon; General Ripley's March; Amazon March; The Ma-
       sonic Grand March; Battle of Manassas; The Music Boy;
       Banjo Scotch Bagpipe; Scotch Fiddler; Church Organ; Guitar;
       The Cascade.
Theater: Appeared at Great St. James and Egyptian Halls (London);
       Irving Hall 1868.

BLIND LEMON see JEFFERSON, BLIND LEMON

BOATNER, EDWARD (Hammond)
       (Composer/Musician)
b.   November 13, 1898, New Orleans, La.
Education: Chicago College of Music.
Special Interests: Singing, conducting, arranging.
Address: 76 West 69 St. , New York, N. Y. 10023.
Career Data: Concert singer 1926-30; music director, National
       Baptist Convention, 1925-33.
Musical Compositions: Arrangements include O What a Beautiful
       City, Trampin', I Want Jesus to Walk with Me, On My Jour-
       ney; wrote Trouble in Mind (an opera).

BOATWRIGHT, McHENRY (Rutherford)
       (Singer)
b.   February 29, 1928, Tennille, Ga.
Education: New England Conservatory of Music B. Mus. 1950.
Address: National Artists Corp. , 711 Fifth Ave. , New York, N. Y.
       10022.
Honors: National Competition for Soloist award, Boston Pops Or-
       chestra 1949; Marian Anderson award 1953, 54; National
       Federation of Music Clubs award 1957.
Career Data: Boston Post Music Festival; Chicagoland Music Festi-
       val 1953; concert tour of U. S. , Canada, Japan, Hong Kong,
       Philippines; repertoire includes Gunther Schiller's The Visita-
       tion, Boito's Mefistofele, Boris Godunov and Porgy and Bess;
       associate professor (voice) Ohio State University; sang with
       orchestras: Boston Symphony, Chicago Philharmonic, L. A.
       Philharmonic, Philadelphia Orchestra, N. Y. Philharmonic.
Records: Crown in Porgy and Bess (London) 1976.
Television: Ed Sullivan Show; The Today Show; Mike Douglas Show;
       Like It Is 1975.

Theater: Appeared at Blossom Music Center (Ohio); New England
Opera Theatre; Hollywood Bowl (L. A.); Jordan Hall (Boston)
1956; N. Y. Metropolitan Opera House 1967; Heritage Society
Chorus' An Evening of Negro Spirituals--Alice Tully Hall
1975; Carnegie Hall 1976.

BOJANGLES see ROBINSON, BILL

BONDS, MARGARET (Allison)
(Pianist/Composer)
b.   March 3, 1913, Chicago, Ill.
d.   April 26, 1972, Los Angeles, Calif.
Education: Julliard School of Music; Northwestern University B. M. ,
M. M. ; studied composition with Roy Harris, Emerson Har-
per and Robert Starer.
Special Interests: Producing, teaching.
Honors: Rosenwald Fellowship; Roy Harris Scholarship; National
Association of Negro Musicians Award; Rodman Wanamaker
Award 1932.
Career Data: Taught at American Theatre Wing; performed with
the Chicago Symphony Orchestra, the Woman's Symphony
Orchestra, the New York City Symphony; guest soloist Chi-
cago World's Fair 1933; performed with the Scranton, Pa.
Philharmonic Orchestra 1950; worked with Inner City Cul-
tural Center (Los Angeles) 1968-72.
Clubs: Cafe Society; Spivy's Roof; Cerutti's, Ritz Tower Hotel;
Hurricane Restaurant.
Memberships: National Association of Negro Musicians; ASCAP
1952.
Musical Compositions: The Negro Speaks of Rivers; Three Dream
Portraits; Peter and the Bells; Mass in D Minor; Troubled
Waters; Spiritual Suite for Piano; Ballad of the Brown King
Cantata; Migration (ballet); Empty Interlude; Peachtree Street;
Spring Will Be So Sad; Fields of Wonder; King, He's Got the
Whole World in His Hands; Georgia; Sit Down Servant; Dry
Bones; I'll Reach to Heaven; Lord I Just Can't Keep from
Crying.
Radio: Mary Astor's Hollywood Showcase.
Theater: Federal Theatre (Chicago); Orchestra Hall (Chicago); ANTA
Theatre; Paper Mill Playhouse (N. J.); Goodman Theatre (Chi-
cago); Migration (Talley Beatty Dance Co.); Town Hall (debut)
1952; Happy Hunting (score) 1956; Shakespeare in Harlem
(score) 1960; Clandestine on the Morning Line (score) 1961.

BORDE, PERCIVAL (Sebastian)
(Dancer/Choreographer)
b.   December 31, 1922, Trinidad.
Education: Queen's Royal College Annex (Trinidad); New York Uni-
versity.
Special Interests: Teaching.

Address: c/o SUNY Binghamton, New York 13901.

Career Data: Participated in African Carnival '61 at 69th Regiment
      Armory 1961; lectured and danced at Jacobs Pillow 1965;
      associate professor, SUNY Binghamton; executive board mem-
      ber & adjudicator, Southern Tier Civic Ballet Co.; artistic
      director, Afro-American Dance Theatre Workshop, SUNY
      Binghamton; executive director, Pearl Primus-Borde School
      of Dance.

Theater: Dancer with Pearl Primus Company at Brooklyn Academy
      of Music 1956; performed at St. Mark Playhouse 1958, 59;
      presented Black Rhythm Program at Circle in the Square
      Theatre 1965; appeared in Mister Johnson 1965; choreographed
      Man Better Man (O. B.) 1969; choreographed The Harangues
      (O. B.) 1970; choreographed Akokawe (O. B.) 1970.

Relationships: husband of Pearl Primus, choreographer/dancer.

BOSAN, ALONZO
      (Actor)

b. October 7, 1886, Shelbyville, Ohio.

d. June 24, 1959, New York, N. Y.

Special Interests: Singing.

Career Data: Appeared in vaudeville in U. S., England and Australia;
      played Palace Theatre 1928.

Films: Virgin Island 1960 (posthumously).

Theater: Hummin' Sam 1933; Turpentine 1936; Walk Together Chil-
      lun 1936; Androcles and the Lion 1938; Dark Hammock 1944;
      Strange Fruit 1945; A Long Way from Home 1948; Set My
      People Free 1948; 2 Blind Mice 1949; The Wisteria Trees
      1950; The Green Pastures 1951; Seventeen 1951; My Darlin'
      Aida 1952; Mrs. Patterson (pre-Bway tour) 1954; The Wis-
      teria Trees (City Center) 1955.

BOSTIC, EARL (O.)
      (Jazz Musician)

b. April 25, 1913, Tulsa, Okla.

d. October 28, 1965, Rochester, N. Y.

Education: Xavier University (New Orleans).

Special Interests: Alto saxophone, composing, arranging, conducting.

Honors: Playboy Magazine Jazz Poll winner 1959.

Career Data: Worked with bands of Bennie Moten 1933, Don Redman
      1938, Hot Lips Page 1941, Lionel Hampton 1943, Cab Callo-
      way; led his own band 1945; associated with rhythm and blues
      hits including Temptation; Flamingo; 845 Stomp; Moonglow
      and Cherokee.

Clubs: Mimo 1941; Smalls 1944; Bengasi (Washington, D. C.) 1947.

Musical Compositions: Let Me Off Uptown; The Major and the Minor;
      Brooklyn Boogie.

Records: Jam Session at the Savoy (Savoy); Flamingo (King) 1951;
      Sleep (King) 1951; Temptation.

BOURNE, ST. CLAIR (Cecil)
    (Director/Producer)
b. February 16, 1943, New York, N. Y.
Education: Georgetown University; Syracuse University B. A. 1967;
    Columbia University.
Special Interests: Film, travel, international affairs, journalism.
Address: 230 W. 105 St., New York, N. Y. 10025.
Honors: John Russworm Award (New York Urban League) 1969;
    Bronze Award (N. Y. International Film-TV Festival) 1974.
Career Data: Peace Corps 1964-66; taught film courses at Queens
    College 1968, California State College 1970, Cornell Univer-
    sity 1972 and U. C. L. A. 1975; film critic for Black Scholar
    and Amsterdam News (N. Y.); film coordinator for World
    Black and African Festival of the Arts (Lagos, Nigeria) 1976;
    founder and president, The Chamba Organization (film pro-
    ductions).
Films: Produced, directed and wrote Something to Build On (doc.)
    1971; produced Statues Hardly Ever Smile (doc.) 1971; di-
    rected Ourselves (doc.) 1971; produced, directed and wrote
    Nothing But Common Sense (doc.) 1972; directed Pusher Man
    (doc.) 1972; produced and directed A Piece of the Block (doc.)
    1972; directed and produced Let the Church Say Amen! (doc.)
    1973; Zaire 1974 (production consultant) 1974; produced, di-
    rected and wrote A Nation of Common Sense 1975; co-produced
    The Long Night 1976.
Publications: Chamba Notes (a periodical) 1970-72.
Radio: WBAI-FM (engineer) 1967-68.
Television: Produced and directed Telephone (Sesame Street) 1971;
    producer, writer, director for Black Journal (NET series)
    1968-70.
Relationships: Son of St. Clair Bourne Sr., communicator.

BOWEN, RUTH "Mother Goose" (Ruth Jean Baskerville)
    (Theatrical Agent)
b. September 13, 1930, Danville, Va.
Education: New York University; U. C. L. A.
Address: Queen Booking Corp., 1650 Broadway, New York, N. Y.
    10019.
Honors: Testimonial from Black Ivory, 1973.
Career Data: Student/Gal Friday to Hume Cronyn, actor; founder
    and pres., Queen Booking Corp. (largest black owned clear-
    inghouse for entertainment) 1962; clients include(d) Dinah
    Washington, Aretha Franklin, Ray Charles, Gladys Knight
    and the Pips, Sammy Davis Jr., Josephine Baker, Earl Bos-
    tic, Isley Brothers, Esther Phillips, Richard Pryor, James
    Cleveland, Lola Falana.
Television: Co-produced Ebony Music Awards 1975; Positively
    Black 1976.
Relationships: Former wife of Billy Bowen, one of original Ink
    Spots, singing group.

BOWMAN, LAURA
(Actress)
b.   October 3, 1881, Quincy, Ill.
d.   March 29, 1957, Hollywood, Calif.
Career Data: Lafayette Players (14 years); toured Europe (10 years).
Films: Drums O'Voodoo 1933; Lem Hawkins' Confession 1935; God's
        Stepchildren 1938; Birthright 1939; The Son of Ingagi, The
        Notorious Elinor Lee 1940.
Memberships: AEA; AFTRA; NAG; SAG.
Radio: Fred Allen Show; Rudy Vallee Show; The O'Neils; Southern-
        aires; Stella Dallas; John's Other Wife; Pepper Young's
        Family; Pretty Kitty Kelly.
Theater: In Dahomey 1902; The Southerners 1904; In Abraham's
        Bosom 1926; Wade in the Water (Negro Art Theatre) 1929;
        Harlem 1929; Sentinels 1931; Jezebel 1933; Louisiana 1933;
        Plumes in the Dust 1936; Conjur (Brooklyn) 1938; Please
        Mrs. Garibaldi 1939; Jeb 1946.

BRADFORD, ALEX "Professor"
(Singer)
b.   1927, Bessemer, Ala.
Special Interests: Gospel, composing.
Address: 103 Lyons Avenue, Newark, N. J. 07112.
Honors: Obie and Drama Desk Awards (for Don't Bother Me, I
        Can't Cope) 1972.
Career Data: Sang with the Protective Harmoneers, The Willie
        Webb Singers and with Mahalia Jackson; formed his own
        singing group The Bradfordettes, then the Bradford Specials
        (1st all male gospel group) 1954, then Professor Alex Brad-
        ford singers; ordained a minister; director of music dept.,
        Greater Abyssinian Baptist Choir, Newark, N. J.; toured
        throughout world; appeared at Newport Jazz Festival.
Musical Compositions: Too Close to Heaven.
Records: The Black Man's Lament (Atlantic); The Best of Alex
        Bradford; Walking with the King (Gospel); I Found the Answer
        (Gospel); Don't Bother Me I Can't Cope.
Theater: Dark of the Moon (O. B.); Sounds of Gospel at Apollo
        Theatre 1960; Black Nativity 1961; But Never Jam Today
        1969; Bury the Dead (O. B.) 1971; Don't Bother Me, I Can't
        Cope 1972; New York Gospel Music Festival (Robert F. Ken-
        nedy Theatre) 1975; Your Arms Too Short to Box with God
        (Washington, D. C.) 1975.
Relationships: Husband of Alberta Bradford, singer and pianist.

BRANCH, WILLIAM (Blackwell)
(Playwright)
b.   September 11, 1927, New Haven, Conn.
Education: Northwestern University B. S. 1949; Columbia University
        M. F. A. 1958; Yale University School of Drama (American
        Broadcasting Company Fellowship) 1965-66.
Special Interests: Acting, teaching.

Address: 53 Cortlandt Avenue, New Rochelle, N. Y. 10801.
Honors: Hannah Del Vecchio Award (Columbia University) 1958;
        Robert E. Sherwood Television Award and National Council
        of Christians and Jews Citation (both for television drama
        Light in the Southern Sky) 1958; John Simon Guggenheim Fel-
        lowship (for creative writing in drama) 1959-60; American
        Film Festival Blue Ribbon Award and Emmy nomination (both
        for Still a Brother: Inside the Negro Middle Class) 1969.
Career Data: Actor 1946-55; field representative for Ebony 1946-
        55; taught or lectured at Harvard, Columbia, UCLA, UC
        Santa Barbara, San Jose State, Spelman, Univ. of Utah,
        Univ. of Ghana; Visiting Playwright at Smith College, North
        Carolina Central Univ. and St. Laurence Univ; wrote for
        The Jackie Robinson column in N. Y. Post 1959-61; delegate
        to International Conference on the Arts (Lagos, Nigeria)
        1961; wrote articles for N. Y. Times and Amsterdam News
        (N. Y.); staff producer-writer Educational Broadcasting Corp.,
        Channel 13, 1962-64; Producer, Special Unit, NBC News
        1972-73; President, William Branch Associates (firm to create,
        write, produce and provide consultant service for films and
        television programs).
Films: Together for Days (script) 1971.
Memberships: Dramatists Guild; National Assn. of Broadcast Em-
        ployees & Technicians; Writers Guild of America, East.
Radio: Directed the Jackie Robinson Show 1959; wrote and directed
        The Alma John Show 1963-65.
Television: The Way 1955; What Is Conscience? 1955; Let's Find
        Out 1956; Light in the Southern Sky 1958; The Explorers
        Club 1963; Gypsy in My Soul 1964; Legacy of a Prophet 1964;
        Fair Game 1964; Still a Brother: Inside the Negro Middle
        Class 1968; The Case of the Non-Working Workers 1972;
        Build Baby Build 1972; The 20 Billion Dollar Rip-off 1972;
        No Room to Run, No Place to Hide 1972; The Black Church
        in New York 1973; Afro-American Perspectives 1973-75.
Theater: Acted in Anna Lucasta (tour); plays include A Medal for
        Willie 1951; In Splendid Error 1954; To Follow the Phoenix
        1960; A Wreath for Udomo 1961; Baccalaureate 1970; Experi-
        ment in Black.

BRICE, CAROL (Carol Lovette Hawkins Brice)
        (Concert Singer)
b.   April 16, 1918, Sedalia, N. C.
Education: Palmer Memorial Institute (Sedalia, N. C.) 1935; Talla-
        dega College B. Mus. 1939; Juilliard School of Music 1939-
        44.
Honors: Walter Naumberg award 1944; selected Woman of the Year
        (National Council of Negro Women).
Career Data: Soloist at St. George's Episcopal Church 1939-43;
        guest, program commemorating 3rd inauguration of F. D. R.
        1941; sang with symphonies including: Kansas City 1944;
        Pittsburgh 1945-46, Boston (at Berkshire Music Festival,
        Tanglewood) 1946, 1948, San Francisco 1948; Prof. (music),

University of Oklahoma (Norman); toured Europe and South
America.

Memberships: AEA; AFTRA; AGMA.

Records: The Ordering of Moses (Silver Crest); Leider Eines Fah-
renden Gesellen and El Amor Brujo (Columbia) 1946; Bach
Aria Album 1949; a Carol Brice Album 1950.

Theater: The Hot Mikado (N. Y. World's Fair) 1939; Town Hall
(debut) 1945; Voodoo Princess in Ouanga (Metropolitan Opera
House) 1956; Kakou in Saratoga 1959; Finian's Rainbow (City
Center) 1960; Queenie in Show Boat (City Center) 1961; Maria
in Porgy and Bess (City Center) 1961; Harriet Tubman in
Gentlemen Be Seated 1963; Carnegie Hall 1975.

Relationships: Sister of Jonathan Brice, pianist.

BRICKTOP (Ada Beatrice Smith Du Conge)
(Entertainer)

b.   July, 1894, Alderson, Va.

Special Interests: Singing.

Honors: Cole Porter's song "Miss Otis Regrets" written for her.

Career Data: Member, Panama Trio (with Florence Mills, Cora
Greene); opened her own clubs in Paris 1926-39 and Rome
1951-64.

Clubs: Barron Wilkin's Club; Connie's Inn 1924; Café de Champ
(Chicago); The Cotton Club; Le Gran Duc (Paris); Cherute's;
Panama Club; Bricktop's (Paris and Rome); Soerabaja 1974;
Tango (Chicago) 1975; Cleo 1976.

Films: Honeybaby, Honeybaby 1974.

Television: David Susskind Show; Kup's Show 1975.

Theater: Appeared Carnegie Hall (with Josephine Baker) 1973;
Avery Fisher Hall (with Eartha Kitt) 1974.

BRIDGEWATER, DEE DEE (Denise Garret)
(Singer/Actress)

b.   May 27, 1950, Memphis, Tenn.

Education: Michigan State University 1968-69, University of Illinois
1969.

Address: 463 West St., New York, N. Y. 10014.

Honors: Down Beat Critics Poll Vocalist of the Year 1972, 74;
Swing Magazine (Japan) best vocalist 1973; Tony award (for
The Wiz) 1975.

Career Data: Toured Soviet Union and Japan with Thad Jones/Mel
Lewis group 1972; vocalist with Andy Goodrich quartet and
Norman Connors group 1973-74; performed at Monterey Jazz
Festival and Illinois Jazz Festival.

Clubs: Hopper's; Village Vanguard.

Films: Sang title song in Coffey 1973.

Records: The Wiz; Dee Bridgewater; Love in the Middle of the Air.

Television: Woman Alive 1975; At the Top 1976; Tonight Show 1977.

Theater: Glinda, the good witch in The Wiz 1975-76; Satchmo '76
Show at Beacon Theatre 1976.

BRISTOL, JOHNNY
        (Singer)
b.   Morgantown, N. C.
Career Data: Teamed with Jackie Beavers as Johnny and Jackie;
        writer and producer for Diana Ross, Smokey Robinson, Jerry
        Butler, Gladys Knight, Johnny Mathis, The Tavares and others.
Records: Hang On in There, Baby (MGM); Feeling the Magic (MGM).
Television: Soul Train 1974; Dinah! 1975; American Bandstand 1975.

BROOKS, CLARENCE
        (Actor)
b.   c. 1895 San Antonio, Texas.
Films: Realization of a Negro's Ambition 1915; Law of Nature
        1918; A Man's Duty 1919; By Right of Birth 1921; Welcome
        Strangers 1924; Absent 1928; Georgia Rose 1930; Dr. Mar-
        chand in Arrowsmith 1931; Okay America 1932; Nagana 1933;
        Harlem After Midnight 1934; Lem Hawkins' Confession 1935;
        Two-Gun Man from Harlem 1936; Dark Manhattan 1937; The
        Spirit of Youth 1938; Bargain with Bullets, Bronze Buckaroo,
        Harlem on the Prairie, Harlem Rides the Range 1939; Am I
        Guilty? 1940; Son of Ingagi 1940; Up Jumped the Devil 1941;
        The Negro Soldier 1944.
Theater: Porgy 1929; Cabin Echoes (L. A.) 1933.

BROWN, ANNE (Wiggins)
        (Singer)
b.   1915, Baltimore, Md.
Education: Morgan College; Columbia University; Julliard School
        of Music 1932; studied voice with Lotte Lehmann.
Special Interests: Acting.
Career Data: Has performed with The Philadelphia Orchestra, the
        N. Y. Philharmonic, the Toronto Symphony 1942 and Beetho-
        ven's 9th Symphony with Arturo Toscanini and the NBC Sym-
        phony.
Films: Rhapsody in Blue 1945.
Radio: Coca Cola Hour; RCA Magic Key Program; Lincoln Highway
        (NBC) 1942.
Records: Bess in Porgy and Bess (Decca).
Theater: Hollywood Bowl; Lewisohn Stadium; Lew Leslie's Black-
        birds (London); Bess in Porgy and Bess 1935; Labor Stage
        1938; Mamba's Daughters 1939; Pins and Needles (revue)
        1939; Ravel's L'Heure Espagnole 1939; Offenbach's Helen
        (Negro version) 1941; Bess in Porgy and Bess (revival) 1942;
        concert at Brooklyn Academy of Music 1942; Robin Hood Dell
        1942; Miranda in Virginia (St. Louis Opera Co.); concert at
        Town Hall 1945; Menotti's The Medium and the Telephone
        (Norway) 1950.

BROWN, CHELSEA
        (Actress)
b.   Chicago, Ill.

Education: Studied modeling.
Special Interests: Dancing.
Address: c/o Goldin-Dennis & Associates, 470 South Sanvicente
          Blvd. , Los Angeles, Calif. 90048.
Career Data: Danced in Portrait in Bronze (a revue); appeared
          with The Bill Williams troupe (Puerto Rico) and Larry Steel
          Company (Las Vegas); performed with Ray Charles show;
          toured Orient (Saigon, Hong Kong, Taiwan) with a musical
          trio.
Films: The Thing with Two Heads 1972.
Television: Laugh-In (series); The Flying Nun; Love, American
          Style; The Name of the Game 1970; Dial Hot Line 1970;
          Matt Lincoln 1971; Marcus Welby, M. D. 1972; Police Story
          1973; That's My Mama 1975; Human Dimension 1975; Bronk
          1976.

BROWN, EVERETT
          (Actor)
Films: I Am a Fugitive from a Chain Gang, Nagana 1933; Gone
          with the Wind 1939; Congo Maisie 1940; White Witch Doctor
          1953.

BROWN, GEORG STANFORD
          (Actor)
b.   June 24, 1943, Havana, Cuba.
Education: William H. Taft H. S. ; Los Angeles City College, Insti-
          tute of Vocal Arts; American Musical and Dramatic Academy
          1964.
Honors: Emmy nomination for Roots 1977.
Career Data: New York Shakespeare Festival 1966.
Films: The Comedians 1967; Bullitt, Dayton's Devils 1968; Forbin
          Project 1970; The Man, Wild in the Sky 1972.
Television: It Takes a Thief; Mannix; Julia; The Bold Ones; Medi-
          cal Center; Room 222; Terry Webster in The Rookies (series);
          The Time Is Now (The Name of the Game) 1970; Here Come
          the Brides 1970; Ritual of Evil 1970; Dinah! 1975; S. W. A. T.
          1975; Dawn: Portrait of a Teenage Runaway 1976; Roots
          1977; directed episode of Starsky and Hutch 1977; directed
          episodes of Charlie's Angels 1977.
Theater: Richard III (NYSF); Macbeth (NYSF); Measure for Measure
          (NYSF) 1966; All's Well that Ends Well (NYSF) 1966.

BROWN, GRAHAM (Robert E. Brown)
          (Actor)
b.   October 24, 1924, New York, N. Y.
Education: Howard University B. A. 1949; Columbia University 1951;
          American Theatre Wing 1950.
Address: 240 West 10 Street, New York, N. Y. 10014.
Memberships: AEA; AFTRA; SAG.
Television: Matt Lincoln; The Storefront Lawyers; The Interns;

N. Y. P. D.; The Guiding Light; The Edge of Night; The Doctors; The Days of Our Lives (series); Ironside; Medical Center; Owen Marshall; Sanford and Son.

Theater: Widower's Houses (O. B.); Time of Storm (O. B.); The
Emperor's Clothes (O. B.); Major Barbara (O. B.); A Land
Beyond the River (O. B.) 1957; The Blacks (O. B.); The Fire-
bugs (O. B.) 1963; performed with Tyrone Guthrie Repertory
Theatre, Minneapolis (Hamlet, The Three Sisters, Henry V.,
Volpone, St. Joan, Richard III, The Way of the World, The
Caucasian Chalk Circle, The Miser) 1963-65; performed with
Center Stage Repertory, Baltimore (Babu in Benito Cereno,
The Balcony, Noah, Titus Andronicus, A Penny for a Song)
1966-67; performed with Inner City Repertory Theatre, Los
Angeles (chorus in Antigone) 1971; The Man in the Glass
Booth; Ride a Black Horse (NEC); Man Better Man (NEC)
1969; Malcochon (NEC) 1969; God Is a (Guess What?) (NEC)
1968; Daddy Goodness (NEC) 1968; Song of the Lusitanian
Bogey (NEC) 1968; Dr. Hampton in Weekend 1968; World
Theatre Festival with NEC (London) 1970; Behold Cometh the
Vanderkellans (O. B.) 1972; Dr. Stanton in the River Niger
(NEC) 1973; Black Picture Show (NYSF) 1974; Pericles (NYSF)
1974; The Great Mac Daddy (NEC) 1974; Waiting for Mongo
(NEC) 1975; title role in Gilbeau (New Federal Theatre) 1976;
Eden (NEC) 1976, The Brownsville Raid (NEC) 1976.

BROWN, JAMES "Godfather of Soul"; "Soul Brother Number 1"
        (Singer)
b.   May 3, 1933, Augusta, Ga.
Special Interests: Composing.
Address: 1122 Greene Street, Augusta, Ga. 30902.
Honors: Thirty-eight gold records in over 20 years; Grammy 1965;
        Humanitarian award, B'nai B'rith Performing Arts Lodge
        1969; Black Record, National Youth Movement.
Career Data: Member of Famous Flames, singing group; chairman
        of the board, James Brown Productions, James Brown Enter-
        prises & Man's World (includes 2 record companies, 3 radio
        stations); performed at Zaire Festival 1974.
Films: Ski Party 1965; The Phynx 1970; Black Caesar (voice) 1973.
Musical Compositions: Please, Please, Please.
Radio: Host, WRDW (Augusta) 1975.
Records: On Polydor: The Payback; Hell; Reality; Sex Machine
        Today; Love Machine; My Thang; Hot; Goodfoot; Everybody's
        Doing the Hustle; Poppa Don' Take No Mess.
Television: Tonight Show; Mike Douglas Show; Flip Wilson Show;
        Midnight Special; In Concert 1974; The American Music Awards
        1975; Merv Griffin Show 1975; Tattletales 1975; Soul Train
        1975; Dinah! 1975, 76; Future Shock (WTCG, Georgia) 1976.
Theater: Appeared at Astrodome (Houston); Apollo Theatre (on and
        off 1959-74); Madison Square Garden; Wide World in Concert
        1974.

BROWN, JIM (James Nathaniel Brown)
(Actor)
b.   February 17, 1935, St. Simons Island, Ga.
Education: Manhasset High School 1953; Syracuse University.
Honors: Hickok Belt-Athlete of the Year 1964; Player of the Year
         1958; 1963; 1965.
Career Data: Pro-Football (formerly All-American Halfback 1956;
         Cleveland Browns Fullback 1957-66); founder, Black Economic
         Union.
Films: Rio Conchos 1964; Dirty Dozen 1967; The Split, Ice Station
         Zebra, Dark of the Sun 1968; 100 Rifles, Riot, Kenner 1969;
         Tick... Tick... Tick..., El Condor, The Grasshopper 1970;
         Slaughter, Black Gunn 1972; Slaughter's Big Ripoff, I Escaped
         from Devils Island, The Slams 1973; Three the Hard Way
         1974; Take a Hard Ride 1975.
Publications: Off My Chest (autobiography), Doubleday, 1964.
Television: Midday Live; I Spy (Cops and Robbers) 1967; Wide
         World Special 1974; Playboy Bunny of the Year 1975; Don
         Adams Screen Test 1976.

BROWN, JOHNNY
(Comedian)
b.   Florida.
Career Data: Toured with Sam Taylor's band; member of team
         Hines, Hines and Brown; protégé of Sammy Davis Jr.; or-
         ganized The Johnny Brown All-Stars, a basketball team.
Clubs: Latin Casino (Camden); Thunderbird (Las Vegas); Plaza;
         Statler-Hilton; Harrah's (Lake Tahoe).
Films: A Man Called Adam 1966; The Lost Man 1969; The Out of
         Towners 1970.
Memberships: AEA; SAG.
Television: Ed Sullivan Show; Merv Griffin Show; Beat the Clock;
         Julia; Leslie Uggams Show 1969; Rookies; Rowan and Mar-
         tin's Laugh-In (series); Tonight Show; Love, American Style
         1971; commercials: Cool Whip and Gillette Blades; The Mouse
         Factory 1972; Good Times (series) 1975; Get Christie Love
         1975; Mike Douglas Show 1975; Where's the Fire? (pilot)
         1975; Match Game 1975; Dinah! 1975; Sammy and Company
         (series) 1975; Rhyme and Reason 1975; Chico and the Man
         1976; Cross-Wits 1977.
Theater: Appearance at Mill Run Theatre (Chicago); Golden Boy
         (debut) 1964; Carry Me Back to Morningside Heights 1968.

BROWN, MAXINE
(Singer)
b.   Kingstree, S. C.
Education: Fashion Institute of Technology.
Special Interests: Composing.
Honors: Gold record (for Funny).
Career Data: Worked with Manhattans vocal group.
Clubs: Seafood Playhouse 1975; Le Club Magnet 1976.

Musical Compositions: All in My Mind 1961; Funny 1961.
Records: Hold On, I'm Coming; Something You've Got; All in My
Mind (NOMAR) 1961; Funny (NOMAR) 1961; Oh No, Not My
Baby (WAND) 1964; If You Gotta Make a Fool of Somebody
(WAND) 1965.
Television: Soul.
Theater: Don't Bother Me, I Can't Cope (Bway debut) 1974.

BROWN, OSCAR JR.
        (Entertainer/Composer)
b.   October 10, 1926, Chicago, Ill.
Special Interests: Directing, producing.
Clubs: The Fisherman's Cove; Village Vanguard 1961; Blue Angel
1962; Hungry I (San Francisco) 1962; Crescendo 1962; Berns
(Stockholm) 1963; Waldorf Astoria 1963; Cool Elephant (Lon-
don) 1965.
Memberships: Authors League of America.
Musical Compositions: Dat Der 1960; Brown Baby 1960; Work Song
1960; The Sanke 1963; Muffled Drums 1975.
Records: Fresh (Atlantic); Brother Where Are You? (Atlantic); Be-
tween Heaven and Hell (Columbia); Movin' On (Atlantic).
Television: Today Show 1961; One of a Kind (special) 1974; Posi-
tively Black; Kup's Show 1976.
Theater: Wrote Slave Song; wrote Crecie; wrote and performed in
Sunshine and Shadows; wrote and performed in Kicks and
Company 1961; Summer in the City 1965; wrote songs for
Big Time Buck White 1968; Joy 1970; appearances at Apollo
Theatre 1961; Carnegie Hall 1962; Gaugin (Chicago) 1976;
wrote In Da Beginning 1977.
Relationships: Husband of Jean Pace, singer; brother-in-law of
Judy Pace, actress.

BROWN, RAY (Raymond Matthews Brown)
        (Jazz Musician)
b.   October 13, 1926, Pittsburgh, Pa.
Special Interests: Bass.
Honors: Esquire New Star Award 1947; Down Beat Poll winner
1953-59, Down Beat Critics' Poll 1954; Metronome Poll win-
ner 1955-60; Playboy Poll winner 1958-60; Playboy All Stars
Poll winner 1959-60; Grammy 1963; Ebony Music award 1975.
Career Data: Performed with Dizzy Gillespie, Oscar Peterson trio
from 1951; Jazz at the Philaharmonic tours 1957, 58; faculty,
School of Jazz, Lenox, Mass. 1957.
Television: Merv Griffin Show (series); Ebony Music Awards Show
1975.
Relationships: Former husband of Ella Fitzgerald, singer.

BROWN, RUTH "Miss Rhythm"
        (Singer)
b.   January 30, 1928, Portsmouth, Va.

Career Data: Vocalist with bands of Count Basie, Billy Eckstine,
         Lucky Millinder 1948.
Clubs: Baby Grand; The Crystal Caverns (Washington, D. C.).
Records: On Atlantic: So Long 1949; Teardrops from My Eyes
         1950; I'll Wait for You 1951; 5-10-15 Hours 1952; Daddy
         Daddy 1952; (Mama) He Treats Your Daughter Mean 1953;
         Oh What a Dream 1954; It's Love Baby 1955; Luck Lips 1957;
         This Little Girl's Gone Rockin' 1958; I Don't Know 1959;
         Don't Deceive Me 1960; Shake a Hand (Philips) 1962.
Theater: Guys and Dolls (Aladdin Hotel, Las Vegas) 1977.

BROWN, TIMOTHY (WAYNE) (Thomas Allen Brown)
         (Actor)
b. 1937, Chicago, Ill.
Education: Ball State University (Muncie, Indiana); studied with
         Herbert Berghof.
Special Interests: Singing.
Career Data: Vocalist with local band in Indiana; male model for
         Jantzen Sportswear; played professional football with Phila-
         delphia Eagles, Green Bay Packers and Baltimore Colts.
Films: M*A*S*H 1970; Black Gunn 1972; Sweet Sugar, Bonnie's
         Kids, Girls Are for Loving, Superchick 1973; The Dynamite
         Brothers 1974; Nashville 1975; Black Heat 1976.
Television: Appearances on Merv Griffin Show; Joey Bishop Show;
         Steve Allen Show; Mike Douglas Show; Spearchucker in
         M*A*S*H 1972; Mobile One 1975; S. W. A. T. 1975; Adam-12
         1975; Cannon 1975.

BROWN, TONY (William Anthony Brown)
         (Broadcaster/Producer)
b. April 11, 1933, Charleston, W. Va.
Education: Wayne State University B. A. 1959; M. S. W. 1961.
Special Interests: Directing, writing.
Address: c/o WNET-TV, 356 West 58 Street, New York, N. Y.
         10019.
Honors: Emmy 1972; Communicator for Freedom Award from
         Operation PUSH 1973; Frederick Douglass Liberation Award
         from Howard University 1974.
Career Data: City Editor, Detroit Courier; Howard University,
         Professor 1961-71; Dean, School of Communications, 1971-
         74.
Memberships: National Center of Afro American Artists (Board
         Member); National Communications Council (Board of Gov-
         ernors); The National Institute of Mental Health (Communi-
         cations Committee).
Television: Executive producer, host and moderator of Black Jour-
         nal (series) 1970-.

BROWNE, ROSCOE LEE
         (Actor)
b. May 2, 1925, Woodbury, N. J.

Education: Lincoln University (Pa.); University of Florence (Italy);
       Middlebury College (Vermont); Columbia University.
Special Interests: Sports, writing poetry, teaching, directing.
Honors: Obie (for Benito Cereno); Black Filmmakers Hall of Fame
       award 1977.
Career Data: Twice All-American (indoor 1,000 yard run) and
       world champion (800 meter run) Paris 1951; member of ten
       A.A.U. teams; instructor (French and English literature)
       Lincoln University 1946-47, 1949-50.
Films: The Connection 1962; Black Like Me, The Cool World 1964;
       Terror in the City 1966; The Comedians 1967; Uptight 1968;
       Topaz, Me and My Brother 1969; The Liberation of L.B.
       Jones 1970; Cisco Pike, The Cowboys 1972; Super Fly T.N.T.,
       World's Greatest Athlete 1973; Uptown Saturday Night 1974;
       Logan's Run 1976; Twilights Last Gleaming 1977.
Memberships: AEA; AFTRA; SAG.
Publications: Pool Beyond the Blues (poetry).
Records: Roses and Revolution.
Television: The Green Pastures (Hallmark Hall of Fame) 1957;
       The Defenders; East Side/West Side; The Whistling Shrimp
       (Espionage) 1963; Benito Cereno (Festival of the Arts) 1965;
       Mannix 1968; Invaders 1968; Outcasts 1969; The Third Choice
       (Name of the Game) 1969; Bonanza 1972; All in the Family;
       Flip Wilson Show; Good Times; Planet of the Apes 1974; The
       Big Rip Off 1975; Barney Miller 1975; Today 1975; Gideon
       on McCoy (series); The Streets of San Francisco; This Far
       by Faith 1977; Maude 1977.
Theater: Julius Caesar (NYSF) 1956; Taming of the Shrew (East
       River Park) 1956; Aaron the Moor in Titus Andronicus 1957;
       Aria de Capo (O.B.) 1958; The Cool World 1960; Dark of the
       Moon (ELT) 1960; The Pretender (O.B.) 1960; Archibald Wel-
       lington in The Blacks (O.B.) 1961; Brecht on Brecht (O.B.)
       1962; General Seeger 1962; Tiger, Tiger Burning Bright
       1962; Fool in King Lear (NYSF) 1962; The Threepenny Opera
       (Arena Theatre, Wash. D.C.) 1963; The Winter's Tale
       (Delacorte Theatre) 1963; Narrator in The Ballad of the Sad
       Cafe 1963; The Old Glory (O.B.) 1964; directed and acted
       in A Hand Is on the Gate 1966; Volpone (NYSF) 1967; The
       Dream on Monkey Mountain (O.B.) 1971; Babu in Benito
       Cereno (O.B.); Broken Words (Evening of Poetry, Wash.
       D.C.) 1974; Desire Under the Elms (Lake Forest, Illinois)
       1974; An Evening of Edna St. Vincent Millay (Alice Tully
       Hall) 1975.

BRYANT, HAZEL (Joan)
       (Producer/Playwright)
b. September 8, 1939, Zanesville, Ohio.
Education: B.A. Oberlin Conservatory 1962; studied at Mozarteum
       School of Music, Salzburg, Austria; Columbia University.
Special Interests: Acting, singing, directing.
Address: c/o Empire Hotel, 44 West 63rd Street, New York, N.Y.
Career Data: Sang soprano roles in operas in Italy, France, Ger-

many, Austria and the U. S. 1968; co-coordinated, Lincoln
Center Community Street Theatre 1972; president, Black
Theater Alliance; member, Theater Panel, N. Y. State Coun-
cil on the Arts; founder and Executive Artistic Director,
Afro-American Total Theater, 1963-date; director, Richard
Allen Center for Cultural Art 1976; executive editor, Muses;
N. Y. City Board of Cultural Affairs.

Films: Hazel Hazel Hazel Hazel Hazel (short doc.) 1971.
Television: Black News 1976.
Theater: Acted in Lost in the Stars (ELT) 1968; acted in That's
the Game, Jack (Milwaukee Repertory Theatre) 1969; wrote
Keys to the Kingdom; wrote Mae's Amis (with Hope Clarke
and Hank Johnson) 1969; wrote Origins (with Beverly Todd
and Hank Johnson) 1969; wrote Black Circles 'Round Angela
(with Jimmy Justice) 1971; wrote Sheba (with Jimmy Justice)
1972; wrote Makin' It (with Jimmy Justice) 1972; directed
Wildflowers, Laundry and Indiana Avenue (3 one-act plays
for NEC) 1973; directed Ma Louis Daughters; directed Carnival Song 1973.

BRYANT, JOYCE
     (Singer)
b. c. 1927, San Francisco?, Calif.
Education: Oakwood College (Huntsville, Ala.).
Career Data: Retired from show business to pursue religious study
and evangelical work 1956-76.
Clubs: Cafe Society; Ciro's (Hollywood); Riviera (New Jersey);
Fontainebleu Hotel (Miami Beach); La Martinique 1951; Ben
Maksik's Town and Country Club (Brooklyn) 1952; Algiers
Hotel (Miami Beach) 1953; Thunderbird (Las Vegas) 1953;
Copacabana 1953; Cleo's 1977.
Records: Drunk with Love; Running Wild; Love for Sale.
Television: Sammy and Company 1977.
Theater: Porgy and Bess; Apollo Theatre 1955.

BRYANT, WILLIE (William Steven Brown)
     (Singer)
b. August 30, 1908, New Orleans, La.
d. February 9, 1964, Los Angeles, Calif.
Special Interests: Acting, composing.
Honors: Unofficial Mayor of Harlem 1952.
Career Data: Harlem's Alhambra Theatre Stock Company; partner
with Bessie Smith in Big Fat Ma and Skinny Pa act; led own
dance band 1934-38, 1946-48; U. S. O. tours 1940-45; per-
formed with Buck and Bubbles.
Memberships: ASCAP 1960.
Musical Compositions: It's Over Because We're Through.
Radio: Disc jockey on WXYZ (Detroit) and WHOM (N. Y. C.) 1950s.
Records: Made over twenty during 1935-36.
Television: NBC Series (with his band) 1949; hosted Showtime at
the Apollo (series) 1954.

Theater: Chocolate Revue 1934; Mamba's Daughters 1939; master
     of ceremonies, Apollo Theatre amateur nights; Blue Holiday
     1945.

BUBBLES, JOHN (John William Sublett)
     (Dancer)
b. February 19, 1902, Louisville, Ky.
Special Interests: Singing, comedy.
Career Data: Teamed with Ford Lee Washington as Buck and Bub-
     bles, vaudeville team 1909-53; toured Vietnam with Bob Hope;
     teamed with Anna Maria Alberghetti in nightclub act 1964.
Films: Varsity Show 1937; Cabin in the Sky 1943; Atlantic City
     1944; Buck and Bubbles Laugh Jubilee 1945; A Song Is Born
     1948.
Television: Tonight Show; Lucy Show.
Theater: George White's Varieties; appearances at Apollo Theatre;
     At Home at the Palace; Show Time; Curtain Time; Ziegfeld
     Follies of 1921; Palladium (London) 1931; Sportin' Life in
     Porgy and Bess 1935; Frolics of 1938; Laugh Time 1943;
     Capitol Theatre 1943; Carmen Jones 1944.

BUCK see WASHINGTON, FORD LEE

BULLINS, ED
     (Playwright)
b. July 2, 1935, Philadelphia, Pa.
Education: Los Angeles City College; San Francisco State College.
Special Interests: Directing, teaching.
Address: 932 East 212 Street, Bronx, N.Y. 10469 and 425 Lafayette
     Street, New York, N.Y. 10003.
Honors: American Place Theatre Grant; Guggenheim Fellowship;
     Rockefeller Foundation Playwriting Grant; Creative Artists
     Program Service Grant for Playwriting; National Endowment
     for the Arts Grant for Playwriting; Obie awards 1968, 75;
     Drama Desk-Vernon Rice Award 1968; N.Y. Drama Critics
     Circle award 1975.
Career Data: Writer/producing director, The Surviving Theatre;
     editor, Black Theatre Magazine 1968; member, playwright-
     in-residence, American Place Theatre 1973; co-founder,
     Community Experimental Theatre, Black Arts/West (San
     Francisco); lectured Fordham University, Columbia Univer-
     sity, University of Massachusetts, Dartmouth College, Clark
     College, Talladega College, University of California, Ber-
     keley; playwright-in-residence/associate director, New La-
     fayette Theatre.
Memberships: Black Arts Alliance (organization of Black Theatre
     groups); Dramatists Guild; Writers Guild of America, East.
Television: Positively Black 1975.
Theater: Storyville; Sepia Star; wrote: Next Time; The Devil
     Catchers; Night of the Beast; House Party; I Am Lucy Terry;

It Bees That Way 1960; Clara's Ole Man 1965; How Do You
Do: A Nonsense Drama 1965; Dialect Determinism or The
Rally 1965; The Game of Adam and Eve 1966; The Theme
Is Blackness 1966; A Minor Scene 1966; The Gentleman Caller
1966; It Has No Choice 1966; In the Wine Time 1966; Goin a
Buffalo 1966; The Helper 1966; The Black Revolutionary Com-
mercial 1967; The Man Who Dug Fish 1967; The Corner 1967;
In New England Winter 1967; Electronic Nigger 1968; A Son
Come Home 1968; We Righteous Bombers (under pseudonym
Kingsley B. Bass) 1969; American Flag Ritual 1969; The Du-
plex: 1969; A Black Love Fable in Four Movements; State
Office Building Curse 1970; One Minute Commercial 1970;
The Pig Pen 1970; Street Sounds 1970; Death List 1970; The
Fabulous Miss Marie 1971; Malcolm:71 1971; You Gonna Let
Me Take You Out Tonight Baby? 1972; Soulful Happening
1973; Homeboy 1973; The Sirens 1974; The Taking of Miss
Janie 1975; Jo Anne!!! 1975; The Mystery of Phillis Wheat-
ley 1976; Do Wah 1976; Daddy 1977.

BUMBRY, GRACE (Ann)
(Opera Singer)
b. January 4, 1937, St. Louis, Mo.
Education: Boston University 1954-55; Music Academy of the West
1956-59; Northwestern University; studied with Lotte Leh-
mann.
Address: c/o Metropolitan Opera Assn., Lincoln Center Plaza,
New York, N.Y. 10023.
Honors: John Hay Whitney award 1959; White House command per-
formance 1962.
Career Data: Honorary chairman, Symphony of the New World;
sang (1st black) at Bayreuth Festival 1961; protégé of Sol
Hurok (impressario); repertoire includes Eboli in Don Carlos,
Santuzza in Cavalleria Rusticana, Amneris in Aida, Venus in
Tannhauser, Chimene in Le Cid, title roles in Salome and
Carmen.
Records: Carmen.
Television: Arthur Godfrey's Talent Scouts 1954; Mike Douglas Show
1975; Not For Women Only 1976.
Theater: Appearances at Paris Opera House 1960; Carnegie Hall
1962; Covent Garden (London) 1963; La Scala (Milan) 1965;
Teatro Colon (Buenos Aires); Vienna State Opera; Chicago
Opera House; Metropolitan Opera House; Rome Opera House;
Avery Fisher Hall 1974; Bolshoi Opera 1976.

BURBRIDGE, EDWARD (De Joie)
(Designer)
b. May 23, 1933, New Orleans, La.
Education: Pratt Institute (Brooklyn) 1956-59; studied at Sevilla
Forte Studio 1959; Polakov Studio and Forum 1959.
Special Interests: Acting, singing.
Address: 34 Hicks Street, Brooklyn, N.Y. 11201.

Honors: John Hay Whitney Fellowship 1955-56.
Career Data: Toured with Wings Over Jordan Choir; designed nu-
    merous theatrical productions including The First Breeze of
    Summer, Song of the Lusitanian Bogey, Absurd Person Singu-
    lar, Jimmy Shine, Marat/Sade, The Visit, Chemin de Fer;
    Designed for Robert Joffrey Ballet Co.; Alvin Ailey Dance
    Theatre (City Center); Metropolitan Opera Studio; Los Angeles
    Forum Theatre.
Films: Acted in An Affair of the Skin 1963; designed for Hello,
    Dolly! 1969; designed for Book of Numbers 1973.
Memberships: United Scenic Artists Local 829; NEC.
Television: Black New World (NET); designed Ceremonies in Dark
    Old Men 1969.

BURGHARDT, ARTHUR N. (Arthur Burghardt-Banks)
    (Actor)
b. c. 1947, Georgia.
Honors: Emmy award 1976.
Career Data: Noted for characterization of Frederick Douglass on
    stage, film and television.
Films: Network 1976.
Memberships: AEA.
Television: Like It Is; Black Journal 1976; The Life and Times of
    Frederick Douglass (Close Up) 1976.
Theater: Appeared in one man show on Frederick Douglass at Town
    Hall and Triangle Theatre 1971; co-wrote Frederick Doug-
    lass ... Through His Own Words; appeared in Sherlock
    Holmes 1974.

BURGIE, IRVING "Lord Burgess" (Irving Burgie Page)
    (Composer/Singer)
b. July 28, 1924, Brooklyn, N.Y.
Education: Juilliard School of Music; University of Arizona, Uni-
    versity of Southern California.
Special Interests: Calypso, guitar, playwriting.
Address: Variety Sound Corp., 130 West 42 Street, New York,
    N.Y. 10036.
Films: Wrote songs for Island in the Sun 1957; wrote Calalou (un-
    produced screenplay).
Musical Compositions: Jamaica Farewell; Island in the Sun; I Do
    Adore Her; Come Back Lisa; Day of Angelina; Land of the
    Sea and Sun; Dolly Dawn.
Theater: Wrote score for Ballad for Bimshire (O.B.) 1963.

BURKE, GEORGIA (Gracie Maldell Burke)
    (Actress)
b. February 27, 1906, LaGrange, Ga.
Education: Claflin University (Orangeburg, S.C.) 1930; New York
    University 1932-34.
Special Interests: Teaching.

Address: 465 West 152 Street, New York, N. Y. 10031.
Honors: Donaldson Award (for Decision) 1944.
Career Data: Toured Europe, U. S. S. R. and South America 1952-56.
Films: Anna Lucasta 1959; Grandma Custis in The Cool World 1964.
Memberships: AEA; AFTRA; NAG; SAG.
Radio: Big Story (series) 1932; Lily the maid in When a Girl Mar-
         ries (series).
Television: Goodyear Theatre 1950; The Little Foxes 1957; The
         Grass Harp (Play of the Week) 1960.
Theater: Lew Leslie's Blackbirds; Old Man Satan; Five Star Final;
         Savage Rhythm; Sun Fields; In Abraham's Bosom 1926; They
         Shall Not Die 1934; Coquette (New Hope, Pa.) 1934; Mamba's
         Daughters 1939; No Time for Comedy 1939; Cabin in the Sky
         1940; Virgie in Decision 1944; Anna Lucasta 1944; The Wis-
         teria Trees 1952; The Grass Harp 1952; Maria in Porgy and
         Bess 1953; Tambourines to Glory (stock) 1958; Interlock
         (ANTA) 1958; The Killer (O. B.) 1960; Two Queens of Love
         and Beauty (New Hope, Pa.) 1961.

BURLEIGH, HARRY T(HACKER) (Henry Thacher Burleigh)
         (Musician/Composer)
b.   December 2, 1866, Erie, Pa.
d.   September 12, 1949, Stamford, Conn.
Education: National Conservatory of Music.
Special Interests: Arranging.
Honors: National Conservatory of Music Scholarship; NAACP Spin-
         garn medal 1917; Harmon award 1930.
Career Data: Soloist, St. George's Episcopal Church 1894-1946,
         Temple Emmanuel 1900-1925.
Memberships: ASCAP 1914.
Musical Compositions: I Want to Die While You Love Me; Every-
         time I Feel de Spirit; Just You; Six Plantation Melodies for
         Violin and Piano 1901; I Love My Jean 1914; Saracen Songs
         1914; From the Southland for Piano 1914; The Prayer 1915;
         Deep River 1916; Ethiopia Saluting the Colors 1916; The
         Young Warrior 1916; Southland Sketches for Violin and Piano
         1916; Jubilee Songs of the United States of America 1916;
         Little Mother of Mine 1917; Dear Old Pal of Mine 1918; Un-
         der a Blazing Star 1918; Five Songs 1919; In the Great Some-
         where 1919; Old Songs Hymnal 1929; One Year 1914-1915;
         The Soldier; In the Wood of Finvara; Down by the Sea.

BURRELL, KENNY (Kenneth Earl Burrell)
         (Jazz Musician)
b.   July 31, 1931, Detroit, Mich.
Education: Wayne State University Mus. B. 1955.
Special Interests: Guitar, composing.
Honors: International Jazz Critics awards 1957, 1960, 1965, 1969-
         73.
Career Data: Worked with Oscar Peterson trio 1955-57, Benny
         Goodman orchestra 1957-59, Kenny Burrell trio 1960, Kenny

Burrell quartet 1963; founder and president, Jingle Bells & Jazz (a corp. to promote jazz) 1975.

Clubs: Across 110th Street; Half Note; Village Vanguard; El Matador (San Francisco); Bottom Line 1976; Hopper's 1977.

Memberships: ASCAP 1959.

Musical Compositions: Sugar Hill; Kenny's Blues.

Records: God Bless the Child.

Theater: Bye Bye Birdie 1960; appeared at Alice Tully Hall; Town Hall 1975; Radio City Music Hall 1976.

BURRELL, WALTER (PRICE) JR.
    (Publicist/Critic)

b. November 4, 1944, Portsmouth, Va.

Education: Hampton Institute B. A.; University of California at Los Angeles M. A.

Special Interests: Acting, writing.

Address: P. O. Box 900, Beverly Hills, Calif. 90213.

Career Data: Critic/columnist, Black Stars magazine; member, Coalition Against Blaxploitation Committee; unit publicist, 20th Century-Fox Studios and Universal Studios.

Memberships: Publicists Guild 1969.

Radio: Producer/moderator, The Record.

Theater: Wrote and acted in All for a Place and Free Black & 21.

BURROWS, VINIE
    (Actress)

b. November 15, 1928, New York, N. Y.

Education: New York University B. A.

Special Interests: Directing, producing, teaching.

Address: 63 Avenue A, New York, N. Y. 10009.

Honors: AUDELCO Black Theatre Recognition award.

Career Data: Adjunct professor, St. Peters College; lecturer, New School of Social Research; drama director, Franklin Marshall College; performed at 1st African Cultural Festival, Algiers 1969.

Films: Walk Together Children 1972.

Memberships: AEA; AFTRA; BTA; The Committee for the Negro in the Arts, SAG.

Television: Straight Talk; Like It Is; Christopher Closeup; Camera Three; Merv Griffin Show; Tonight Show.

Theater: The Wisteria Trees 1950; The Green Pastures 1951; Mrs. Patterson 1954; The Skin of Our Teeth 1955; The Ponder Heart 1956; Nat Turner (O. B.) 1960; Mandingo 1961; Bolo in The Blacks (O. B.) 1961; The Worlds of Shakespeare (O. B.) 1963; Spring Beginning; African Family Festival (Billie Holiday Theatre, Brooklyn); Walk Together Children (one woman show) 1968-72; appeared at Apollo Theatre (Harlem Childrens Theatre) 1974; Dark Fire (one woman show) 1974; Song of Lawino (reading at Paterson New Jersey Free Public Library) 1974.

BUSH, ANITA
    (Actress)
b.   c. 1883, Washington, D. C.
d.   February 16, 1974, New York, N. Y.
Special Interests: Producing.
Career Data: Toured with Williams and Walker in London; toured
    with black vaudeville troupe 1903; appeared before King Ed-
    ward VII of England; founded Anita Bush Stock Company
    which appeared at Lincoln Theatre and Lafayette Theatre
    1915.
Films: The Crimson Skull 1921; The Bulldogger 1922.
Memberships: NAG (executive secretary 1971).
Television: Free Time 1971.
Theater: In Dahomey 1902-03; The Girl at the Fort 1915; Swing It
    (W. P. A. Federal Theatre) 1938; Androcles and the Lion (W.
    P. A. Federal Theatre) 1939.

BUSH, NORMAN
    (Actor)
b.   April 11, 1933, Louisville, Ky.
Education: American Academy of Dramatic Arts, American Mime
    Theatre.
Special Interests: Photography.
Address: 311 East 23rd Street, New York, N. Y. 10010.
Career Data: Appeared at World Theatre Festival (London) 1969
    and Premio Roma Rassegna Internationale Arte dello Spet-
    tacolo (Rome) 1969.
Films: The Pawnbroker 1965; Serpico 1973; The Supercops, Death
    Wish, Harry and Tonto 1974; Three Days of the Condor 1975.
Memberships: AEA; AFTRA; NEC (1967-70); SAG.
Radio: Funnyhouse of a Negro (BBC) 1964.
Television: The Catholic Hour 1963; The Nurses; The Defenders;
    Day of Absence 1967; N. Y. P. D. 1968; You Are There 1970;
    The Connection 1973; The Silent Countdown: Hypertension
    (doc.) 1976.
Theater: The Connection (O. B.) 1959; The Goose (O. B.) 1960; The
    Toilet (O. B.) 1964; Funnyhouse of a Negro (O. B.) 1964; The
    Servant for Two Masters (O. B.) 1966; The Weary Blues
    (O. B.) 1967; Song of the Lusitanian Bogey (NEC) 1968; Sum-
    mer of the Seventeenth Doll (NEC) 1968; Kongi's Harvest
    (NEC) 1968; Daddy Goodness (NEC) 1968; God Is a (Guess
    What?) (NEC) 1968; Man Better Man (NEC) 1969; Malcochon
    (O. B.) 1969; Day of Absence (NEC) 1970; Akokawe (NEC)
    1970; Brotherhood (NEC) 1970; In New England Winter (NEC)
    1971; directed The One (O. B.) 1971; Sleep 1972.

BUTLER, JERRY "Iceman"
    (Singer)
b.   December 8, 1939, Sunflower, Miss.
Special Interests: Composing.
Career Data: Former member, The Roosters, later, The Impres-
    sions.

Clubs: Latin Casino (Philadelphia) 1975.
Films: Save the Children 1973.
Records: Power of Love; On Vee Jay: For Your Precious Love
        1958; He Will Break Your Heart 1960; Find Another Girl
        1961; Make It Easy On Yourself 1963; Whatever You Want
        1963; Giving Up on Love 1964; Good Times 1965. On Mer-
        cury: Sweet Sixteen; I Dig You Baby 1967; Mr. Dream Mer-
        chant 1967; Only the Strong Survive 1968; Hey Western Union
        Man 1968; Moody Woman 1969; Got to See If I Can't Get
        Mommy to Come Back Home 1970; How Did We Lose It Baby
        1971; Close to You 1972; Love's On (Motown); Very Best
        (United Artists); All Time Hits (Trip); Best (Mercury); Star-
        ring (Tradition); Suite for the Single Girl (Motown) 1977;
        Thelma and Jerry (Motown) 1977.
Television: David Frost Show; Upbeat; Tonight Show; Soul.
Theater: Appeared at Apollo Theatre; Amphitheatre (Washington,
        D. C.); Forum (Inglewood, Calif.); Felt Forum 1976.

BYRD, DONALD(SON) T.
        (Jazz Musician)
b. December 9, 1932, Detroit, Mich.
Education: Manhattan School of Music B. MM. 1963; Columbia
        Teachers College Ed. D. ; studied with Nadia Boulanger in
        France.
Special Interests: Arranging, composing, producing.
Address: 1625 Woods Drive, Los Angeles, Calif. 90069.
Honors: Down Beat award; Record World award; Billboard award;
        gold records; Playboy Magazine Poll winner.
Career Data: Chairman, Music Dept. , Howard University 1968-75;
        taught at New York University, Rutgers University; chair-
        man, Jazz Studies, North Carolina Central University (Dur-
        ham) 1977; founder, Black Byrd Productions.
Records: For Blue Note: Blackjack; Black Byrd; Byrd in Flight;
        Electric; Ethiopian Knights; Fancy Free; Free Form; Fuego;
        I'm Tryin to Get Home; New Perspectives; Royal Flush;
        Slow Drag; Steppin' Into Tomorrow; Street Lady, Places and
        Spaces; Trumpets All Out (Prestige); Two Sides of ... (Trip);
        Early Byrd (Columbia); Caricatures (Blue Note).
Television: Presenter on Ebony Music Awards 1975; Mark of Jazz
        1976; This Far by Faith 1977; American Bandstand 1977.
Theater: Appearances at Avery Fisher Hall (Newport Jazz Festi-
        val) 1975; Beacon Theatre 1975; Carnegie Hall 1976; Wollman
        Rink Central Park (Schaefer Music Festival) 1976; West-
        chester Premier Theatre 1976.

CAESAR, SHIRLEY
        (Singer)
b. 1939, Durham, N. C.
Special Interests: Composing, gospel music.
Honors: Grammy award, Ebony Awards Peoples Choice 1975.
Career Data: Leader, Shirley Caesar singers; member The Cara-
        vans 1958-66.

Musical Compositions: To Be Like Jesus.
Records: On Hob: Be Careful; The King and Queen of Gospel (with
           James Cleveland); Go Take a Bath; No Change; Grace; First
           Lady (Roadshow) 1977.
Television: Musical Chairs; The Today Show; Merv Griffin Show;
           Positively Black 1975; Ebony Music Awards 1975.
Theater: Appearances at Astrodome (Houston); Alice Tully Hall
           (Black Arts Festival) 1972; Robert F. Kennedy Theatre 1975.

CALDWELL, BEN
           (Playwright)
Address: 400 East 167 Street, Bronx, N. Y. 10456.
Career Data: Plays performed at Brooklyn Academy of Music,
           Boston Center for the Arts, Boston's Loeb Experimental
           Theatre and Newark's Spirit House.
Theater: Wrote The Obscene Play for Adults Only; Right Attitude
           or Is You Is or Is You Ain't a Revolutionary; Uptight or ... ;
           What Is Going On; The Job 1966; Hypnotism 1966; The Wall
           1967; Prayer Meeting or The First Militant Minister 1967;
           The Fanatic 1968; Riot Sale or Dollar Psyche Fake Out 1968;
           Mission Accomplished 1968; Recognition 1968; Top Secret or
           a Few Million After B. C. 1968; Unpresidented 1968; Family
           Portrait 1969; The King of Soul or The Devil and Otis Red-
           ding 1969; All White Caste 1971.

CALLOWAY, CAB (Cabell)
           (Singer/Musician)
b.   December 25, 1907, Rochester N. Y.
Education: Crane College (Chicago).
Special Interests: Composing, conducting, dancing, acting.
Address: 1040 Knollwood Rd. , White Plains, N. Y. 10603.
Career Data: Leader, Alabamians (Chicago) 1928, (N. Y. C.) 1929;
           leader Missourians, 1930; Cab Calloway band 1931-48.
Clubs: Crazy Cat; Sunset Cafe (Chicago); Savoy Ballroom; Cotton
           Club; Connie's Inn; Palladium (L. A.); Stevensville Country
           Club; Riverboat 1975; Reno Sweeney 1976.
Films: The Big Broadcast 1932; International House: The Old Man
           of the Mountain 1933; The Singing Kid 1936; Manhattan Merry
           Go Round, Hi De Ho 1937; Stormy Weather 1943; Sensations
           of 1945; Ebony Parade 1947; St. Louis Blues 1958; The Cin-
           cinnati Kid 1965; A Man Called Adam 1966; Brother Can
           You Spare a Dime 1975.
Memberships: ASCAP 1942.
Musical Compositions: Minnie the Moocher; Hi De Ho Man; Geechy
           Joe; Are You All Reet?; The Jumpin' Jive; Lady with the
           Fan; Zaz Zuh Zaz; Peck-a Doodle Doo; Rustle of Swing;
           Boog It; Are You in Love with Me Again; Three Swings and
           Out; Are You Hep to That Jive?; Hot Air, Let's Go Joe,
           Chinese Rhythm.
Publications: Of Minnie the Moocher and Me (autobiography), Cro-
           well, 1976.

Radio: Cab Calloway's Quizicale (NBC).
Television: Kup's Show; Showtime at the Apollo 1954; Ed Sullivan
    Show 1967; The Littlest Angel (Hallmark Hall of Fame) 1969;
    A. M. New York 1974; Harry O 1975; Vaudeville 1975; What's
    My Line? 1975; Midday Live 1976; Apollo Theatre (special)
    1976; Sunday 1976; Not for Women Only 1976.
Theater: Plantation Days (revue); Connie's Hot Chocolates 1929;
    appeared at Paramount, State-Lake (Chicago) and Strand
    Theatres; Sportin' Life in Porgy and Bess (U. S. and Europe)
    1952-54; Cotton Club Revue (Central Park's Theatre Under
    the Stars) 1957; Hello, Dolly! 1969; Pajama Game 1973; ap-
    pearance at Carnegie Hall 1975, 1976.
Relationships: Father of Chris Calloway, actress and Cecelia (Lael)
    Calloway, singer.

CALLOWAY, KIRK (E.)
    (Actor)
b.   September 22, 1960, Los Angeles, Calif.
Honors: Unity award; Golden Globe nomination as best newcomer.
Films: Summertree 1971; Doug in Cinderella Liberty, The Soul of
    Nigger Charley 1973.
Memberships: AFTRA, SAG.
Television: The Bold Ones.

CALLOWAY, NORTHERN J. (Jesse James)
    (Actor)
b.   New York, N. Y.
Education: High School for the Performing Arts.
Special Interests: Songwriting, storytelling.
Address: 115 West 87th Street, New York, N. Y. 10024.
Career Data: Appeared in repertory at Stratford (Ontario) Shake-
    speare Festival.
Films: Panic in Needle Park 1971; Together for Days 1973.
Television: David Frost Show; Secret Storm; Love of Life; On
    Being Black (series); David on Sesame Street 1971-75; Go-
    U. S. A. 1975.
Theater: Salvation (O. B.); Pied Piper (NYSF tour); Saint Joan
    (LCR) 1968; Tiger at the Gates (LCR) 1968; Cyrano de Ber-
    gerac (LCR) 1968; The Me Nobody Knows 1970; replaced Ben
    Vereen in Pippin 1975; The Poison Tree 1976.

CAMBRIDGE, ED (Edmund)
    (Director/Actor)
b.   New York, N. Y.
Special Interests: Teaching (acting).
Films: Hit Man, Melinda, Trouble Man 1972.
Memberships: AEA; NEC.
Television: Bracken's World; Harry O 1974; Kojak 1974; Sanford
    and Son 1975; Mannix 1975; Starsky and Hutch 1975; This
    Far by Faith 1977.

Theater: Acted in: Reveille Is Always (O. B.);   Macbeth (O. B.);
          No Count Boy (O. B.);   Taming of the Shrew (City Center);
          Our Lan' (O. B.) 1947;   Clandestine on the Morning Line (O. -
          B.) 1961;   Stage Manager: A Hand Is on the Gate;   Amen
          Corner 1965;   Associate producer: Trials of Brother Jero
          and The Strong Breed (O. B.) 1968;   Directed: Ballad for
          Bimshire 1963;   The Milk Train Doesn't Stop Here Anymore
          (Barter Theater, Abingdon Va.) 1963;   Summer of the 17th
          Doll (NEC) 1968;   String (NEC) and Malcochon (NEC) 1969;
          Ceremonies in Dark Old Men (NEC) 1969;   The Toilet and
          Dutchman (Brooklyn College) 1970;   Eden (NEC) 1976;   The
          Trap Play (NEC) 1976;   Macbeth (O. B.) 1977.

CAMBRIDGE, GODFREY (MacArthur)
          (Comedian)
b.   February 26, 1933, New York, N. Y.
d.   November 29, 1976, Los Angeles, Calif.
Education: Hofstra University;   City College of New York 1954.
Special Interests: Acting, photography.
Honors: Obie (for The Blacks) 1961;   Tony nomination (for Purlie
          Victorious) 1962.
Clubs: Blue Angel;   Village Vanguard;   Village Gate;   Act IV (De-
          troit);   St. Regis Maisonette 1971;   Jimmy's 1974;   Playboy
          Club (Geneva, N. Y.);   The Cellar Door (Wash. D. C.);   Cres-
          cendo (Hollywood);   Aladdin Hotel (Las Vegas);   Basin Street
          West (San Francisco);   Cal-Neva Lodge (Tahoe);   Playboy Club
          (Chicago) 1976.
Films: The Last Angry Man 1959;   Gone Are the Days 1963;   The
          Troublemaker 1964;   The Busy Body, The President's Analyst
          1967;   Bye Bye Braverman, The Biggest Bundle of Them All
          1968;   Cotton Comes to Harlem, Watermelon Man 1970;   Come
          Back Charleston Blue, The Biscuit Eater, Beware! The Blob,
          produced and wrote Pusher Man (doc.) 1972;   Five on the
          Black Hand Side (cameo) 1973;   Dead Is Dead (doc.) 1974;
          Friday Foster 1975;   Whiffs 1976.
Memberships: Friars.
Publications: Put-Downs and Put-Ons, Parallax, 1967.
Records: On Epic: Ready or Not Here's Godfrey Cambridge 1964;
          Those Cotton-Pickin Days Are Over;   Godfrey Cambridge Toys
          with the World;   The Godfrey Cambridge Show.
Television: Jerry Visits;   You'll Never Get Rich;   Search for Tomor-
          row;   Naked City;   Ellery Queen;   Sergeant Bilko Show;   I've
          Got a Secret 1956;   Male Call (U. S. Steel Hour) 1962;   Jack
          Paar Show 1964;   Dick Van Dyke Show 1966;   Daktari 1966;
          A Time for Laughter (special) 1967;   The Late Great 1968;
          Sesame Street 1971;   Night Gallery 1971;   David Frost Show
          1971;   U. S. Treasury 1972;   The Furst Family (pilot for
          That's My Mama series) 1973;   Ceremonies in Dark Old Men
          1975;   Police Story 1975;   Metropolitan Transit Authority com-
          mercial 1975;   Today at Night: America the Humorous 1975;
          Merv Griffin Show 1975;   Tattletales 1975;   Kup's Show 1975;
          The Late Great 1975;   Captain Kangaroo 1976;   Ice Palace 1976.

Theater: Take a Giant Step (O. B.) 1956; Mister Johnson 1956;
Nature's Way 1957; Detective Story (ELT) 1960; Gitloe in
Purlie Victorious 1961; Diouf in The Blacks (O. B.) 1961;
The Living Premise 1963; Pseudolus the slave in A Funny
Thing Happened on the Way to the Forum (tour) 1967; How
to Be a Jewish Mother 1968; Lost in the Stars (City Center)
1968; The River Niger (tour) 1974; God's Favorite (stock)
1975.
Relationships: Former husband of Barbara Ann Teer, actress/
director.

CAMERON, EARL
      (Actor)
b.   August 8, 1917, Hamilton, Bermuda.
Address: c/o Eric L'Epine-Smith Ltd. , 10 Wyndham Place, London
      W. 1 England.
Career Data: Chairman, United Kingdom, African Festival Commit-
      tee, 1977.
Films: Pool of London, Emergency Call 1951; Hundred Hour Hunt
      1953; The Heart of the Matter 1954; Simba 1955; A Woman
      for Joe, Safari, Odongo 1956; Mark of the Hawk 1958; Sap-
      phire 1959; The Killers of Kilimanjaro 1960; Flame in the
      Streets 1962; Term of Trial 1963; Guns at Batasi 1964;
      Thunderball 1965; Battle Beneath the Earth 1968; Two Gentle-
      men Sharing 1969; The Revolutionary 1970; A Warm December
      1973.
Memberships: BAEA.
Television: Fear of Strangers (Brit.); Wind Versus Polygamy,
      Theatre 625 series (Brit.) 1968.
Theater: Deep Are the Roots (London); Anna Lucasta (London); 13
      Death Street, Harlem (Brit. tour); The Petrified Forest (Lon-
      don) 1943; Janie Jackson (London) 1968.

CAMPBELL, DICK (Cornelius C. Campbell)
      (Director/Producer)
b.   June 27, 1903, Beaumont, Texas.
Education: Paul Quinn College (Waco) B. S. ; Long Island Univer-
      sity; Columbia University Teachers College; Prairieville
      College.
Special Interests: Singing, acting, writing, publicity.
Address: 321 West 24 Street, New York, N. Y. 10011.
Honors: Harold Jackman Memorial Award 1970; Seagram's Man of
      the Year Award 1975.
Career Data: ANTA's Representative to Africa; The American Ne-
      gro Theatre; executive director, Symphony of the New World;
      U. S. State Dept. tour, Africa, South East Asia; co-founder
      and director, Rose McClendon Players 1937-41; director,
      Camp Shows Inc. 1942-45; director, Federal Theatre 1949.
Clubs: Cotton Club; Smalls Paradise.
Films: Come Back Charleston Blue 1972.
Memberships: AEA; AGMA; ATPAM; NAG; Harlem Cultural Council;
      Coordinating Council for Negro Performers.

Publications: Toll the Liberty Bell, 1952; Jim Crow Must Go, 1953.
Radio: Bell Telephone Hour; Community Dialogue; 51st State; Rudy
    Vallee's Fleischman Yeast Hour (with Eddie Green) 1930-31.
Television: Like It Is.
Theater: Produced Tambourines to Glory; acted in Singing the
    Blues; performed in Black Birds 1928; performed in Hot
    Chocolates 1929; acted in Brain Sweat 1934; Town Hall 1940-
    41; acted in Cabin in the Sky 1941-42; acted in Man with the
    Golden Arm 1957; produced and acted in Ballad for Bimshire
    1963.
Relationships: Husband of Muriel Rahn (deceased), singer/actress.

CANTY, MARIETTA
      (Actress)
b.   c. 1906.
Career Data: Noted for portraying servant roles in films of the
    1940s and 1950s; Member, Charles Gilpin Players (Hartford,
    Conn.).
Films: Emperor Jones 1933, The Lady Is Willing, The Spoilers,
    The Magnificent Dope 1942; Three Hearts for Julia 1943;
    Lady in the Dark 1944; Sunday Dinner for a Soldier 1945;
    The Searching Wind 1946; Mother is a Freshman 1949; Dear
    Wife, My Foolish Heart, Father of the Bride, Bright Leaf
    1950; Valentino, Father's Little Dividend, Belle Le Grand
    1951; A Man Called Peter, Rebel Without a Cause 1955.
Theater: Run Little Chillun (debut) 1933; Co-Respondent Unknown
    1936; Kiss the Boys Goodbye 1939; No Time for Comedy
    1939; Horse Fever 1940; On Striver's Row 1940.

CAPERS, VIRGINIA (Eliza Virginia Capers)
      (Actress)
b.   September 22, 1925, Sumter, S. C.
Education: Howard University 1943-45; Juilliard School of Music
    1946-50.
Special Interests: Singing, Yiddish.
Honors: Emmy nomination as best supporting actress (for Mannix
    episode); Tony award for best actress in a musical (Raisin)
    1974; First Lady of Broadway (by Eastern Center Poetry
    Society of England) 1974; Lorraine Hansberry Arts award
    1975.
Clubs: Grossingers 1975.
Films: House of Women 1962; The Ride to Hangman's Tree 1967;
    The Lost Man, Trouble Man 1969; Norwood, The Great
    White Hope 1970; Big Jake, Support Your Local Sheriff 1971;
    Billie Holiday's mother in Lady Sings the Blues 1972; The
    World's Greatest Athlete, Five on the Black Hand Side 1973.
Memberships: AEA; NATAS.
Television: The Rookies; Julia (series); Mannix; The Untouchables;
    Joe Franklin Show 1974; One to One Telethon 1974; Pat Col-
    lins Show 1974; Straight Talk 1974; Midday Live 1975; Sunday
    1975; Today Show 1975; United Jewish Appeal Telethon 1975;

Dinah! 1976; Kup's Show 1976; Jigsaw John 1976; Patterns for
Living 1976; Jerry Lewis Telethon 1976; Waltons 1976.
Theater: Queenie in Show Boat; Porgy and Bess (tour) 1954; Ja-
    maica 1957; Saratoga 1959; Sadie in Sister Sadie and the Sons
    of Sam (Mark Tabor Forum, L. A.) 1969; (New Dramatists
    Workshop) 1975; Lena Younger in Raisin 1973.

CARA, IRENE
    (Actress/Singer)
b.   March 18, 1959.
Honors: Obie (for The Me Nobody Knows).
Films: Angela in Aaron Loves Angela 1975; title role in Sparkle
    1976.
Memberships: AEA.
Musical Compositions: Funky Train.
Records: Esta es Irene; Maggie Flynn.
Television: The Electric Company; Search for Tomorrow; Love of
    Life; The Everything Show; Positively Black 1969, 1976; Kojak
    1976; Timex commercial 1976.
Theater: Maggie Flynn 1968; The Me Nobody Knows 1971.

CARPENTER, THELMA
    (Singer)
b.   January 15, 1922, Brooklyn, N. Y.
Education: Girls H. S. (Brooklyn) 1935-38; Studied voice with Bernie
    Thall 1942-52.
Special Interests: Acting.
Honors: Esquire award as vocalist on radio 1945-46.
Career Data: Sang with the orchestras of Teddy Wilson 1939-40,
    Coleman Hawkins 1940-41, Count Basie 1942-44 and Duke El-
    lington; hit songs include Hurry Home, Sitting and Rocking,
    and These Foolish Things; appeared at Newport Jazz Festival
    1974.
Clubs: Copacabana; Shelbourne Hotel; Ruban Bleu; Cafe Society;
    Zanzibar; Rio Cabana (Chicago); Fenimina Renard Bleu (Athens);
    Le Papillon (Hollywood); Copacabana (London 1953, Rome 1953,
    1957, 1959); Dinar Zard (Paris, 1953, 1957, 1959); The River-
    boat 1974; Downbeat 1975; Soerabaja 1975; Vincent's Place
    1976; Hopper's 1976.
Memberships: AEA; AFTRA; AGVA.
Radio: Jack Darrell Kiddie Hour (WNYC) 1932; Major Bowes Pro-
    gram 1934; J. C. Flippen Program (WHN); Eddie Cantor Show
    (NBC) 1945-46.
Television: The Ed Sullivan Show; The Steve Allen Show; The Jackie
    Gleason Show; the first television show in Rome (ITA) 1953;
    on BBC (London) 1957; Eddie Condon Show; Sugar Hill Times;
    Mother-in-law in Barefoot in the Park (series) 1970.
Theater: Memphis Bound (debut) 1945; Inside U. S. A. 1948; Shuffle
    Along 1952; Ankles Away 1955; Hello, Dolly! 1969; Bubbling
    Brown Sugar (tour) 1975.

CARROLL, DIAHANN (Carol Diahann Johnson)
      (Singer/Actress)
b.   July 17, 1935, New York, N. Y.
Education: H. S. of Music and Art; New York University.
Honors: Metropolitan Opera Scholarship 1945; Cue Entertainer of
      the Year award 1961; Tony (for No Strings) 1962; Emmy nomi-
      nations (for Naked City episode) 1962 and (for Julia) 1969; Os-
      car nomination (for Claudine) 1975; NAACP's 8th annual image
      award (for best actress); Black Filmmakers Hall of Fame 1976.
Clubs: Persian Room-Plaza Hotel; Royal Box (Americana Hotel);
      Sands Hotel (Las Vegas); M. G. M. Grand Hotel (Las Vegas);
      Cafe Society Downtown; Latin Quarter; Palmer House (Chicago);
      Kutsher's (Monticello); Concord (Kiamesha Lake); Grossingers;
      Ciro's (Hollywood).
Films: Myrt in Carmen Jones (debut) 1954; Clara in Porgy and
      Bess 1959; Goodbye Again, Paris Blues 1961; Hurry Sundown
      1967; The Split 1968; title role in Claudine 1974.
Memberships: AEA; AFTRA; SAG.
Records: Diahann Carroll (Motown).
Television: Dennis James' Chance of a Lifetime; Arthur Godfrey's
      Talent Scout Show; Danny Kaye Show; Jack Paar Show; David
      Frost Show; Red Skelton Show; Ed Sullivan Show; Pepsodent
      commercial; Democrat National Telethon; Garry Moore Show;
      Judy Garland Show; Peter Gunn 1960; A Horse Has a Big Head
      (Naked City) 1962; And Man Created Vanity (Eleventh Hour)
      1963; Strollin' Twenties (special) 1966; title role in Julia (series)
      1968-71; Cole Porter in Paris (special) 1972; Jack Lemmon's
      Get Happy (special) 1973; Flip Wilson (special) 1974; Christmas
      in New York (Wide World Special) 1974; Merv Griffin Show
      1975, 1976; Mike Douglas Show 1975; Kup's Show 1975; Tonight
      Show 1975; Fashion Awards Show 1975; Dinah! 1975; Women of
      the Year 1975; Sammy and Company 1975; Death Scream 1975;
      guest host on Black Journal 1975; Who Loves Ya Baby (Telly
      Savalas special) 1976; Sonny and Cher 1976; Symphonic Soul
      1976; Entertainment Hall of Fame Awards '76 1976; Celebrity
      Concert 1976; Diahann Carroll Show 1976; America Salutes
      Richard Rodgers: The Sound of His Music 1976.
Theater: Ottilie in House of Flowers (debut) 1954; Barbara in No
      Strings 1962; Philharmonic Hall 1962; Same Time Next Year
      (L. A.) 1977.

CARROLL, VINNETTE (Justine)
      (Actress/Director)
b.   March 11, 1922, New York, N. Y.
Education: Long Island University B. A. 1944; New York University
      M. A. 1946; New School for Social Research 1948-50 and Colum-
      bia University (Ph. D. Candidate); studied with Erwin Piscator
      at Dramatic Workshop; with Lee Strasberg 1948-50; with Stella
      Adler 1954-55.
Special Interests: Teaching.
Address: 26 West 20 Street, New York, N. Y. 10011.
Honors: Ford Foundation grant for directors 1960-61; Obie (for

performance in Moon on a Rainbow Shawl) 1961; Emmy (for
directing Beyond the Blues) 1964; Outer Critics Circle Award
for directing 1971-72; NAACP Image Award 1972; L. A. Drama
Critics Circle Award, distinguished directing 1972; Harold
Jackman Memorial award 1973; Tony nomination (directing)
1973; Tony nomination (directing) 1977.

Career Data: Teacher of Drama, High School of Performing Arts,
1955-66; formerly director Ghetto Arts Program, N. Y. State
Council on the Arts; artistic director, Urban Arts Corps.

Films: A Morning for Jimmy 1960; One Potato Two Potato 1964;
Up the Down Staircase 1967; The Reivers, Alice's Restaurant
1969.

Memberships: AEA; AFTRA; SAG; Actors' Studio (directors unit).

Radio: CBS Mystery Theatre 1974.

Television: Prodigal Son; Member of the Wedding (Granada TV London) 1960; narrated and directed Black Nativity 1962; adapted
and directed Beyond the Blues 1964; Jubilation 1964; We the
Women (American Parade series) 1974; title role in Sojourner
(American Parade series) 1975; All in the Family 1976; Positively Black 1977.

Theater: Acted in: The Crucible (O. B.); Ftatateeta in Caesar and
Cleopatra 1955; Small War on Murray Hill 1956; Jolly's Progress 1959; Moon on a Rainbow Shawl (London) 1959; (O. B.)
1962; Prodigal Son (London); The Octoroon (O. B.) 1961; Black
Nativity (London); Directed: Dark of the Moon (ELT) 1960;
Ondine 1961; Kicks and Company 1961; The Disenchanted (ELT)
1962; Black Nativity (O. B.) 1962; Spoleto Festival of Two
Worlds 1963; The Prodigal Son (O. B.) 1965; The Flies (O. B.)
1966; Slow Dance on a Killing Ground (O. B.) 1967; Old Judge
Mose Is Dead (O. B.) 1967; The Lottery (O. B.) 1967; Trumpets
of the Lord (O. B.) 1968; But Never Jam Today (O. B.) 1969;
Don't Bother Me, I Can't Cope 1971; Bury the Dead (O. B.)
1971; Come Back to Harlem (a. k. a. Harlem Homecoming) 1972;
Step Lively Boy (O. B.) 1973; Croesus and the Witch (O. B.)
1973; The Flies (O. B.) 1974; All the King's Men (O. B.) 1974;
The Ups and Downs of Theophilus Maitland (O. B.) 1974; De-
sire Under the Elms (Lake Forest, Illinois) 1974; Your Arms
Too Short to Box with God, Spoleto Festival 1975; Play Mas
(O. B.) 1976; The Music Magic of Neal Tate (O. B.) 1976.

CARTER, BEN
    (Actor)
b. 1912, Fairfield, Iowa.
d. 1946.
Honors: International Film and Radio Guild award (for Crash Dive).
Career Data: Former theatrical agent for black performers; part-
ner in comedy vaudeville act with Mantan Moreland.
Films: Gone with the Wind 1939; Tin Pan Alley, Shadrack in Mary-
land, Sporting Blood, Little Old New York, South to Karanga,
Chad Hanna, Safari 1940; Sleepers West, Ride on Vaquero,
Dressed to Kill 1941; Her Cardboard Lover, Reap the Wild
Wind 1942; Crash Dive, Happy Go Lucky 1943; Bowery to

Broadway, Dixie Jamboree 1944; Lady on a Train 1945; John
Henry in The Harvey Girls, The Scarlet Clue 1946.
Radio: Happy-Go-Lucky series; Bob Burns Show 1944-45.

CARTER, BENNY "The King" (Bennett Lester Carter)
(Jazz Musician)
b. August 8, 1907, New York, N. Y.
Education: Wilberforce University.
Special Interests: Arranging, conducting, alto and tenor saxophone,
trombone, trumpet, clarinet, piano.
Address: 2752 Hollyridge Drive, Hollywood, Calif. 90028.
Honors: Metronome poll winner 1942-46; Esquire (silver) award
1945, (gold) award 1946, 1947.
Career Data: Played with McKinny's Cotton Pickers and bands of
Duke Ellington, Earl Hines 1924, Fletcher Henderson 1928,
1930, Chick Webb 1931, Willie Bryant 1934 and his own band
on and off until 1955; performed in Europe and Japan; taught
at Princeton University 1975; State Dept. tour of Middle East
1975.
Clubs: Plantation Club; Casa Manana; Trocadero (L. A.); Billy Berg's
(L. A.); Boeuf Sur le Toit (Paris); Savoy Ballroom; Michael's
Pub.
Films: Thousands Cheer, Stormy Weather 1943; Snows of Kiliman-
jaro, Clash by Night 1952; View from Pompey's Head 1955.
Musical Compositions: Some Day Sweetheart.
Radio: BBC (London) 1936.
Records: The King (Pablo); Jazz Giant (Contemporary); Additions
(Impulse); Further Definitions (Impulse); 1933 (Prestige); Swing-
in' the Twenties (Contemporary); Bounce (Capitol).
Television: Arranged and scored Alfred Hitchcock Presents; Chrys-
ler Theatre; Soundstage.
Theater: Appeared at Apollo Theatre; Capitol Theatre; Lafayette
Theatre.

CARTER, BETTY
(Singer)
b. c. 1930.
Special Interests: Jazz.
Career Data: Vocalist with Lionel Hampton 1947-50; founder and
recorded on own label--Bet-Car.
Clubs: The Bottom Line 1975; Seafood Playhouse 1975.
Records: The Invisible Betty Carter 1964; Baby It's Cold Outside
(with Ray Charles) 1966; Betty Carter (Bet-Car); Betty Carter
Album (Bet-Car).
Television: Interface 1975; Saturday Night Live 1976.
Theater: Appeared at Apollo Theatre 1953; Don't Call Me Man
(Billie Holiday Theatre, Brooklyn).

CARTER, RALPH
(Actor/Singer)
b. June 30, 1961, New York, N. Y.

Honors: Tony nomination as best supporting actor in a musical;
    Drama Desk award as most promising young actor; Theatre
    World award (for Raisin) 1974.
Memberships: AEA; AFTRA.
Records: Young and in Love (Mercury).
Television: Michael Evans in Good Times (series) 1974-; Dinah!
    1974, 1975; Arnold Bread Rolls commercial; Not for Women
    Only 1974; American Bandstand 1975; Soul Train 1975; Musi-
    cal Chairs 1975; The Dyn-O-Mite Saturday Preview Special
    1975; Wonderama 1975.
Theater: Tough to Get Help (O. B.); Dude (O. B.); The Karl Marx
    Play (O. B.); The Me Nobody Knows (Bway debut) 1971; Travis
    Younger in Raisin 1973; Via Galactica (O. B.) 1973.

CARTER, TERRY
    (Actor)
b. Brooklyn, N. Y.
Education: Northeastern University, St. John's University School of
    Law.
Special Interests: Piano.
Career Data: Member, Greenwich Mews Theatre Co. ; founder, Pied
    Piper Productions (film commercials).
Films: Parrish 1961; Black on White (a. k. a. The Artful Penetra-
    tion) 1969; Company of Killers 1970; Boots Turner 1972; Brother
    on the Run 1973; Abby, Foxy Brown 1974; Benji 1975.
Memberships: AFTRA; SAG.
Radio: The Story of Ruby Valentine; 21st Precinct.
Television: Newscaster/anchorman (WBZ Boston) 1965; The Time of
    Your Life (Playhouse 90); Big Story; Philco TV Playhouse; Play
    of the Week; Search for Tomorrow; Danger; Naked City; Ga-
    briel in the Green Pastures (Hallmark Hall of Fame); Pvt.
    Sugarman "Shugie" on Sergeant Bilko (series); Standard Oil
    commercial; Sgt. Joe Broadhurst in McCloud (series) 1970-;
    Six Million Dollar Man 1975; Cross-Wits 1976; Rhyme and
    Reason 1976; Tattletales 1976.
Theater: Decision (O. B.); Mondays Heroes (O. B.); Of Mice and
    Men (O. B.); The Other Foot (O. B.); Mrs. Patterson 1954;
    Finian's Rainbow (City Center) 1955; A Raisin in the Sun 1960;
    The Hostage (tour) 1961; Kwamina 1961.

CASEY, BERNIE
    (Actor)
b. June 8, 1939, Wyco, W. Va.
Education: M. F. A. Bowling Green University.
Honors: Best actor award (for Maurie) at Jamaica Black Film Fes-
    tival 1974.
Career Data: Played football six seasons for San Francisco Forty-
    Niners.
Films: The Guns of the Magnificent Seven 1969; Tick... Tick...
    Tick... 1970; Black Chariot 1971; title role in Hit Man, Black
    Gunn, Boxcar Bertha 1972; title role in Maurie, Cleopatra

Jones 1973; Cornbread, Earl and Me 1975; Dr. Black Mr.
Hyde, Brothers 1977.
Memberships: SAG.
Television: Snoop Sisters; Slay Ride 1972; Panic on the 5:22 1974;
New England Journal 1975; Tony Orlando and Dawn 1975; Police
Story 1975; Joe Forrester 1976; Black News 1977; Kup's Show
1977.

CASH, ROSALIND
        (Actress)
b. December 31, 1938, Atlantic City, N. J.
Education: City College of New York.
Career Data: Worked with Negro Ensemble Company, YMCA Little
        Theatre.
Films: Klute, Omega Man 1971; Melinda, The New Centurions
        Hickey and Boggs 1972; The All-American Boy 1973; Uptown
        Saturday Night, Amazing Grace 1974; Cornbread, Earl and
        Me 1975; Dr. Black Mr. Hyde, The Monkey Hustle 1976.
Television: What's Happening 1976; Good Times 1976; Police Woman
        1976; A Killing Affair 1977.
Theater: Charlie Was Here and Now He's Gone; Dark of the Moon
        (ELT) 1960; understudy for Barbara McNair in No Strings 1962;
        Fiorello! (City Center) 1962; The Wayward Stork 1966; To Bury
        a Cousin (O. B.) 1967; Junebug Graduates Tonight (O. B.) 1967;
        Kongi's Harvest (NEC) 1968; God Is a (Guess What?) (NEC)
        1968; Song of the Lusitanian Bogey (NEC) 1968; Daddy Good-
        ness (NEC) 1968; Man Better Man (NEC) 1969; Ceremonies in
        Dark Old Men (NEC) 1969; An Evening of One Acts (NEC)
        1969; Day of Absence (NEC) 1970; Brotherhood (NEC) 1970;
        The Harangues (NEC) 1970; Goneril in King Lear (NYSF) 1973;
        Boesman and Lena (L. A.) 1977.

CHALLENGER, RUDY
        (Actor)
b. October 2, 1928, New York, N. Y.
Films: Change of Mind 1969; Cool Breeze, Hit Man 1972; Detroit
        9000 1973; Sheba, Baby 1975.
Memberships: SAG.
Television: Sanford and Son; Lieut. Trask on Banacek (series);
        Rockford Files 1974--; Caribe 1975; McCloud 1975; Night
        Stalker 1975; Six Million Dollar Man 1976; Delvecchio 1976;
        Kojak 1976.

CHANTICLEER, RAVEN
        (Entertainer/Designer)
b. September 13, 1933, New York, N. Y.
Education: Fashion Institute of Technology.
Special Interests: Fashion, acting, singing, dancing, painting.
Address: 167 West 23 Street, New York, N. Y. 10011.
Career Data: Opened his House of Fashion 1969; designed clothes

for Sarah Vaughan, Della Reese, Josephine Baker, Eartha
Kitt, Mahalia Jackson and other celebrities.

Clubs: Baby Grand; Tamiment (Pa.); Downington Inn (Pa.); Caesar's
Palace (Las Vegas).

Films: Carmen Jones 1954; Porgy and Bess 1959; Cotton Comes to
Harlem 1970.

Radio: Leon Lewis 1972; Barry Gray Show 1973; Bobby Murray
Show 1974; Joe Franklin Show 1975; Bob Grant Show 1975.

Records: Strawberries (Zell) 1965.

Television: Joe Pine Show 1967; Joe Franklin Show 1968-75; Alan
Burke Show 1969; David Frost Show 1969; Mike Douglas Show
1969, 73, 75; Dick Cavett Show 1970; Merv Griffin Show 1970-
75; The Tonight Show 1973-75; Geraldo Rivera's One to One
Telethon 1973-75; The Arthritis Telethon 1975; Black News
1975.

Theater: Chorus boy in numerous shows including House of Flowers
1955; Jamaica 1957; Golden Boy 1964; Hello, Dolly! 1969;
appeared at Apollo Theatre, Howard Theatre (Washington, D. C.).

CHARLES, RAY (Ray Charles Robinson)
(Singer)
b. September 23, 1930, Albany, Ga.

Education: St. Augustine School for the Blind (Florida).

Special Interests: Composing, piano, saxophone.

Address: c/o Queens Booking Corp. , 1650 Broadway, New York,
N. Y. 10019.

Honors: French Republic bronze medallion; Grammy award 1960-
63, 1976; Playboy Magazine Music Hall of Fame 1968; Ebony
Black Music Poll Hall of Fame 1975.

Career Data: Formed Swing Time Trio in 1950s; founder of Ray
Charles Enterprises, Crossover Records, Tangerine Label
(all his own production units); concert tours of Europe, Mexico,
Australia, New Zealand, Japan, Indonesia and Malaysia.

Films: Blues for Lovers (Brit.) 1966; In the Heat of the Night
(sang theme) 1967.

Records: Ray Charles at Newport; The Best of Ray Charles (At-
lantic); Through The Eyes of Love; Living for the City; On
Atlantic: Genius; Great; Greatest; Live; In Person; I Got a
Woman 1955; What'd I Say 1959. On ABC: Georgia On My
Mind 1960; Ruby 1960; I Can't Stop Loving You 1962; Born To
Lose 1962; You Are My Sunshine 1962; Your Cheating Heart
1962; That Lucky Old Sun 1963; My Heart Cries For You 1964;
Cry 1965; In The Heat of The Night 1967. On Crossover:
Come Live With Me; Renaissance; Ray Charles (Archive of
Folk & Jazz Music); Porgy and Bess (RCA) 1976.

Television: Ed Sullivan Show; Bob Hope Show (special); host of
Cotton Club '75 (special) 1974; Tonight Show 1974, 75; The
Mac Davis Show 1975; Midnight Special 1975; Sammy and Com-
pany 1975; Dinah! 1975; co-host, Ebony Music Awards 1975;
A Salute to the Best Years of "Your Hit Parade" (Wide World
Special) 1975; Cher Show 1975; Comedy in America Report
1976; Touch of Gold '75 1976; Mike Douglas Show 1976.

Theater: Appeared at Nanuet Theatre-Go-Round, Apollo Theatre
        1957; America the Beautiful (tour) 1976; Carnegie Hall 1976;
        Soul at Shea Stadium 1976; Aitken Centre (University of New
        Brunswick) Canada 1976.

CHASE, ANNAZETTE
        (Actress)
Films: The Mack, Blume in Love 1973; Truck Turner 1974; Bogard
        1975; Part II Sounder 1976; The Greatest 1977.
Memberships: SAG.
Television: The Law 1975; Saturday Night 1975; Rockford Files 1976;
        Harry O 1976.

CHECKER, CHUBBY (Ernest Evans)
        (Singer)
b.   October 3, 1941, Philadelphia, Pa.
Special Interests: Composing, dancing.
Address: c/o Cameo Records 1405 Locust Street, Philadelphia, Pa.
        19102.
Honors: Grammy award 1961.
Career Data: Popularized "the Twist" dance.
Clubs: Camelot Inn; Le Jardin; Peppermint Lounge; Speak Easy
        (Long Island) 1976; Bali Hai (Northport, L. I.) 1976.
Films: Teenage Millionaire (music) 1961; Twist Around the Clock,
        Don't Knock the Twist 1962; Let the Good Times Roll 1973.
Memberships: ASCAP 1964.
Musical Compositions: Spread Joy, She Said.
Records: On Parkway: The Class 1959; The Twist 1960; The
        Hucklebuck 1960; Whole Lotta Shakin Goin' On 1960; Pony Time
        1961; Let's Twist Again 1961; Limbo Rock 1962; Hey You Little
        Boo-Ga-Loo 1966. On Buddah: Back in the U. S. S. R. 1969.
Television: American Bandstand; Midnight Special 1973; Mike Douglas
        Show 1974, 1975; Rock'n'Roll Revival (Wide World Special)
        1975; Rock'n'Roll at the Hop 1975; Discomania 1976.
Theater: Appearances at Madison Square Garden 1974; Nanuet
        Theatre-Go-Round 1974.

CHENAULT, LAWRENCE E.
        (Actor)
b.   1877, Mount Sterling, Ky.
Career Data: Performed with A. G. Fields Co. ; Black Patti's
        Troubadours; M. B. Curtis Minstrels; Williams & Walker Co. ;
        Pekin Stock Co. (Chicago); Lafayette Players Stock Co. ; ap-
        peared in vaudeville as member of teams of Allen and Chenault
        and Martin and Chenault.
Films: The Brute, The Symbol of the Unconquered 1920; The Bur-
        den of Race, The Crimson Skull, The Gunsaulus Mystery 1921;
        The Call of His People, A Prince of His Race, The Schemers,
        Secret Sorrow, Spitfire 1922; The Sport of Gods 1923; Birth-
        right, The House Behind the Cedars, Son of Satan 1924; The

Devil's Disciple, Ten Nights in a Barroom 1926; The Scar of
Shame 1927; Children of Fate 1929; Crimson Fog, Ten Minutes
to Live 1932; The Ghost of Tolston's Manor, Harlem After
Midnight 1934.
Theater: Smart Set 1905; In Abyssinia 1908.

CHERRY, DON (Donald E.)
    (Musician)
b. November 18, 1936, Oklahoma City, Okla.
Special Interests: Trumpet, conducting.
Address: Blue Note Records, 43 West 61 Street, New York, N. Y.
        10023.
Career Data: Played with Ornette Coleman Quintet 1959, Sonny
    Rollins 1963; led Donald Cherry Quintet.

CHESTER, SLICK "The Colored Cagney" (Alfred George Chester)
    (Actor)
b. February 26, 1900, New York, N. Y.
Address: 596 Edgecombe Avenue, New York, N. Y. 10032.
Honors: Black Filmmakers Hall of Fame 1976.
Career Data: Appeared with Five Cubanolas; one of the earliest
    black actors in silent films.
Films: The Girl from Chicago 1932; Dixie Love 1934; Harlem After
    Midnight 1934; Temptation 1936; The Underworld 1937; Miracle
    in Harlem 1948.
Memberships: NAG.
Theater: Seven Eleven; Watermelons; Chocolate Dandies 1924.

CHEVALIER DE SAINT GEORGES, JOSEPH BOULOGNE
    (Composer)
b. 1739, Guadeloupe.
d. 1799.
Education: Studied with Francois Gossec.
Special Interests: Violin, viola.
Honors: Colonel of all-black regiment known as Les Hussards Amér-
    icains et du Midi.
Career Data: Concertmaster of Concert des Amateurs 1769.
Musical Compositions: Symphonie Concertante in G Major for Two
    Violins and Orchestra Opus 13; Ernestine (an opera); String
    Quartet no. 1 in C Major Opus no. 1; Symphony no. 1 in G
    Major Opus 11 no. 1.

CHILDRESS, ALICE
    (Playwright)
b. 1920, Charleston, S. C.
Special Interests: Acting, directing.
Address: c/o Flora Roberts Inc., 116 East 59 Street, New York,
        N. Y. 10022.
Honors: Obie award (for Trouble in Mind) 1956; John Golden Fund

for Playwrights 1957; National Negro Business and Professional
Women's Clubs Sojourner Truth Achievement Award 1975; Black
Filmmakers 1st Paul Robeson Medal of Distinction 1977.
Career Data: Actress/director, American Negro Theatre; scholar-
writer, Radcliffe Institute (Harvard University) 1966-68.
Memberships: AEA; AFTRA; Dramatists Guild; Harlem Writers
Guild; New Dramatists, Screen and TV Writers, East; SCSD.
Publications: Black Scenes: Collection of Scenes from Plays Writ-
ten by Black People About Black Experience, Doubleday, 1971.
Television: A Roundtable Discussion on Black Theatre (BBC); wrote
Wine in the Wilderness 1969; wrote Wedding Band 1974; Straight
Talk 1975; Paul Robeson (The People) 1976.
Theater: Acted in Anna Lucasta 1944, The World of Sholom Alei-
chem (O. B.) 1953, The Cool World 1960. Wrote: The Free-
dom Drum, The World on a Hill, A Man Bearing a Pitcher,
Vashti's Magic Mirror, Just a Little Simple (adaptation) 1950,
Florence 1951, Gold Through the Trees 1952, Trouble in
Mind 1955, Wedding Band 1962, String 1969, Young Martin
Luther King 1969, Mojo: A Black Love Story 1971.

CHILDRESS, ALVIN
(Actor)
b. Meridian, Miss.
Education: Rust College (Mississippi) B. A. , 1931.
Honors: Black Filmmakers Hall of Fame 1974.
Career Data: Member, American Negro Theatre, Federal Theatre.
Films: Crimson Fog, Harlem Is Heaven 1932; Dixie Love 1934;
Hell's Alley 1938; Keep Punching 1939; Anna Lucasta, The
Man in the Net 1959; Thunderbolt and Lightfoot 1974; The Day
of the Locust 1975; Bingo Long Traveling All-Stars and Motor
Kings 1976.
Memberships: SAG.
Television: Banyon; Cowboy in Africa; Amos on Amos 'n' Andy
(series) 1951-54; Playhouse 90; Juvenile Court; Night Court;
Sanford and Son; Good Times 1974; The Jeffersons 1975;
Eleanor and Franklin 1976.
Theater: Wrote Hell's Alley (with Alice Herndon); acted in Sweet
Land; Savage Rhythm 1931; Brown Sugar 1937; The Case of
Philip Lawrence 1937; Haiti 1938; Two on an Island 1940;
Natural Man (ANT) 1941; Anna Lucasta 1944; On Striver's
Row (ANT) 1946; The Amen Corner (L. A.).

CHRISTIAN, ROBERT
(Actor)
b. December 27, 1939, Los Angeles, Calif.
Education: University of California, Los Angeles.
Address: 5 Minetta Street, New York, N. Y. 10012.
Television: I Love Lucy; Joey Bishop Show; Andy Griffith Show;
Malibu Run; Gomer Pyle Show.
Theater: The Happening (O. B.); Hornblend (O. B.); Does a Tiger
Wear a Necktie?; Fortune and Men's Eyes (O. B.); Mary

Stuart (O. B.); Narrow Road to the Deep North (O. B.); Twelfth
Night (O. B.); An Evening with Richard Nixon; Boys in the
Band (O. B.) 1967-68; We Bombed in New Haven 1968; Behold
Cometh the Vanderkellans (O. B.) 1971; The Past Is the Past
(O. B.) 1973; Going Through Changes (O. B.) 1973; Black Sun-
light (NEC) 1974; Terraces (NEC) 1974; All God's Chillun Got
Wings (revival) 1975; In the Wine Time (O. B.) 1976; Boesman
and Lena (O. B.) 1977.

CHURCHILL, SAVANNAH
    (Singer/Actress)
b.   August 21, 1919, New Orleans, La.
Career Data: Vocalist with Benny Carter band 1940s.
Clubs: Bamville; Ubangi 1942.
Films: Miracle in Harlem 1948; Souls of Sin 1949.
Records: Sin; My Affair, Hurry Hurry (Capitol) 1943; I'm So Lone-
    some I Could Cry 1952.
Theater: Appeared at Apollo Theatre.

CLANTON, RONY (Hampton Clanton)
    (Actor)
b.   Terrace, N. C.
Education: Studied acting with Dick Anthony Williams and Ed Cam-
    bridge.
Special Interests: Karate.
Career Data: Worked with Negro Ensemble Company; Ju Ju Play-
    ers; New Federal Theatre.
Films: Willie in De Rochemont's Option on Tomorrow (doc.); Get-
    ting It Together (industrial); Duke in The Cool World 1964;
    title role in The Education of Sonny Carson 1974.
Memberships: SAG.
Radio: What's Goin' On?.
Television: Another World; Secret Storm; Search for Tomorrow,
    For the People 1965; Judge Horton and the Scottsboro Boys
    1976.
Theater: The Time Now (HARYOU-Actors Studio); Late Real Cool,
    The Corner (O. B.); His First Step (O. B.); Don't Let It Go to
    Your Head (O. B.); Toilet (O. B.) 1965.

CLARK, MARLENE
    (Actress)
Films: For Love of Ivy 1968; The Landlord 1970; Slaughter, Be-
    ware the Blob, Clay Pigeon 1972; Ganja and Hess (a. k. a.
    Blood Couple) 1973; Newman's Law 1974; Lord Shango, This
    Beast Must Die 1975; Baron Wolfgang Von Tripps 1976.
Memberships: SAG.
Television: Bill Cosby Show; Sanford and Son, Rookies 1976.

CLAYTON, BUCK (Wilbur Clayton)
  (Jazz Musician)
b. November 12, 1911, Parsons, Kan.
Special Interests: Trumpet, arranging.
Honors: Esquire gold award 1945.
Career Data: Played with Count Basie band 1936-43; toured with
    Jazz at Philharmonic 1946; toured France 1949-50; played with
    Joe Bushkin's Quartet 1951-53; Brussels World's Fair 1958;
    played with Eddie Condon band 1959-60; toured Japan and Aus-
    tralia 1964; New Orleans Jazz Festival 1969.
Clubs: Sebastian's Cotton Club (Culver City, Calif.); Cafe' Society
    Downtown 1947; Basin Street 1954; Michael's Pub 1976.
Films: The Benny Goodman Story 1955.
Records: Jammin' with Buck (Epic); Buck Meets Ruby (Van); Ameri-
    cans Abroad (Pax), Jam Session (Chiaroscuro).

CLEVELAND, JAMES
  (Singer)
b. December 5, 1931, Chicago, Ill.
Education: Roosevelt University.
Special Interests: Gospel music, piano, composing.
Address: 3701 Northland Drive, Los Angeles, Calif. 90008.
Honors: Grammy (best soul gospel performance) 1974; Ebony Music
    award 1975; NAACP Image award (gospel artist) 1976; numerous
    gold records.
Career Data: Worked with Angelic Choir of Nutley, N.J.; piano ac-
    companist for Caravans and Roberta Martin Singers; formed
    own group, The James Cleveland Singers; national president
    and founder, Gospel Music Workshop of America; pastor, Cor-
    nerstone Instl Baptist Church (L.A.).
Films: Save the Children 1973.
Records: On Savoy: Merry Christmas; Jesus Is the Best Thing
    That Ever Happened to Me; I'll Do His Will; God Has Smiled
    on Me; To the Glory of God; Gospel Workshop Live in Cleve-
    land; James Cleveland and the Angelic Choir; James Cleveland
    Sings Solos; Touch Me. On Hob: The Best of Cleveland; Hal-
    lelujah I Love Her So 1959; The Love of God 1960; Peace Be
    Still; In the Ghetto; Give It to Me; The King and Queen of Gos-
    pel (with Shirley Caesar); I Stood on the Bank.
Television: Like It Is 1975; Ebony Music Awards show 1975.
Theater: Appeared at Apollo Theatre.

CLIFF, JIMMY
  (Singer)
b. St. James, Jamaica, West Indies.
Special Interests: Reggae; calypso.
Films: The Harder They Come 1973.
Memberships: BAEA.
Records: Unlimited (Reprise); Music Maker (Reprise); Follow My
    Mind (Reprise); Wonderful World, Beautiful People (A&M);
    The Harder They Come; Struggling Man (Island); In Concert;
    The Best of. . . .

Television: Reggae; Jamaican Soul (Camera Three) 1975; Don Kirsh-
ner's Rock Concert 1975.
Theater: Carnegie Hall 1974; Beacon Theatre 1975; Madison Square
Garden 1976; Wollman Theatre (Schaefer Music Festival) 1976.

COBB, ARNETT CLEOPHUS
(Jazz Musician)
b.   August 10, 1918, Houston, Texas.
Education: Phillis Wheatley High School (Houston).
Special Interests: Tenor saxophone.
Address: 292 Washington Place, Englewood, N. J. 07631.
Career Data: Played with Chester Boone 1934-36, Milton Larkin
1936-42, Lionel Hampton 1942-47; organized his own band Cobb
and The Mobb 1947-48, reorganized 1951-56; toured Europe
1973; guest soloist, Texas Jazz Festival (Corpus Christi, Texas)
1974.
Clubs: El Dorado (Houston) 1960; Magnavox 1970.
Records: Jazz at Town Hall v. 1; Very Saxy; Saxomania (Apollo).

COBHAM, BILLY
(Musician)
b.   c. 1947, Panama.
Special Interests: Drums, composing.
Career Data: played with Miles Davis; toured Europe (summer)
1974; formed band with George Duke 1976.
Clubs: Renaissance (Cincinnati) 1975; The Bottom Line 1976.
Films: Salsa (doc.) 1976.
Records: On Atlantic: Shabazz; Life & Times; Total Eclipse; A
Funky Thide of Sings; Crosswinds; Spectrum.
Theater: Appeared at Carnegie Hall 1974, 1976; Avery Fisher Hall
1974, 1975, The Palladium 1976.

COLE, CAROL
(Actress)
b.   October 17, 1944, West Medford, Mass.
Education: Cazenovia College A. A.
Address: 463 West Street, New York, N. Y. 10014.
Films: The Silencers 1967; The Mad Room, Model Shop 1969; Pro-
mise at Dawn 1970; The Taking of Pelham 1-2-3 1974.
Memberships: AEA; AFTRA; SAG.
Television: Daughter in Grady (series) 1975; The Cat (L. A.) 1966;
Positively Black 1975; Sanford and Son 1975.
Theater: The Three Marias; The Owl and the Pussy Cat (L. A.);
Weekend 1968; What If It Had Turned Up Heads (O. B.) 1972;
Pericles (N. Y. S. F.) 1974; Black Picture Show 1974; Parto
(O. B.) 1975.
Relationships: Daughter of Nat "King" Cole, singer; sister of
Natalie Cole, singer.

COLE, COZY (William Randolph Cole)
(Jazz Musician)
b.   October 17, 1909, East Orange, N. J.
Education: Juilliard School of Music 1942-45.
Special Interests: Drums.
Honors: Esquire Silver award 1944.
Career Data: Played with bands of Benny Carter 1933-34, Willie
     Bryant 1935-36, Cab Calloway 1939-42, Benny Goodman 1945-
     46, Louis Armstrong 1949-53; started drum school with Gene
     Krupa 1954; led his own group; played with Jonah Jones 1969-
     75.
Clubs: Onyx 1944; Metropole 1955-58; Rainbow Room 1975.
Films: Make Mine Music 1944; The Strip 1951; The Glenn Miller
     Story 1954.
Radio: Worked with Raymond Scott (CBS) 1942-45.
Records: Crescendo in Drums; Paradiddle; Ratamacue; Topsy I
     1958; Cozy's Caravan; Concerto for Cozy (Savoy); After Hours;
     Topsy II 1958; Turvy II 1958.
Theater: Played in Carmen Jones 1944; Seven Lively Arts 1946.

COLE, NAT "King" (Nathaniel Adams Coles)
(Singer)
b.   March 17, 1919, Montgomery, Ala.
d.   February 15, 1965, Santa Monica, Calif.
Special Interests: Piano, composing.
Honors: Gold Records, Down Beat Poll winner 1944-47, Esquire
     award 1946-47, Metronome poll 1947-49, Grammy 1959, Ebony
     Music award (posthumously) 1975.
Career Data: Formed and worked with musical groups including The
     Royal Dukes 1934, Rogues of Rhythm, Nat Cole Swingsters and
     The King Cole Trio 1937; victim of on-stage (racially motivated)
     attack, Birmingham, Alabama 1956.
Clubs: Swanee Inn (Hollywood); Radio Room (Hollywood); Sands (Las
     Vegas); Coconut Grove (Hollywood).
Films: Pistol Packin' Mama 1943; See My Lawyer (music) 1945;
     Breakfast in Hollywood 1946; Make Believe Ballroom 1949;
     The Blue Gardenia, Small Town Girl 1953; The Adventures of
     Hajji Baba 1954; Kiss Me Deadly 1955; Autumn Leaves (sang
     theme) 1956; Raintree County (sang theme), Istanbul, China
     Gate 1957; W. C. Handy in St. Louis Blues 1958; The Night of
     the Quarter Moon 1959; Cat Ballou 1965.
Memberships: ASCAP; SAG.
Musical Compositions: Straighten Up and Fly Right; I'm a Shy Guy;
     That Ain't Right; It's Better to Be by Yourself; Calypso Blues;
     With You on My Mind; To Whom It May Concern; Just for Old
     Times Sake.
Radio: King Cole Trio 1948-49; Chesterfield Supper Club.
Records: Sweet Lorraine; Route 66; Love Is a Many Splendored
     Thing; Paper Moon; King Cole for Kids; After Midnight; Nat
     King Cole Treasury; On Capitol: Live at the Sands; Cole
     Sings/Shearing Plays; A Mis Amigos; Best; Cole Espanol; More
     Cole Espanol; Story; Straighten Up and Fly Right 1944; I Love

You for Sentimental Reasons 1946; The Christmas Song 1946;
Nature Boy 1948; Mona Lisa 1950; Orange Colored Sky 1950;
Too Young 1951, Red Sails in the Sunset 1951, Unforgettable
1951; Somewhere Along the Way 1952; Walkin' My Baby Back
Home 1952; Because You're Mine 1952; Faith Can Move Moun-
tains 1952; Pretend 1953; Answer Me, My Love 1954; Smile
1954; Darling Je Vous Aime Beaucoup 1955; That's All There
Is to That 1956; Ballerina 1957; Non Dimenticar 1958; Midnight Flyer 1959; Ramblin' Rose 1962; L-O-V-E 1964; Love Is
the Thing; The Greatest of Nat King Cole; Trio Days; Love Is
Here to Stay; Blossom Fell (Pickwick); Love Is a Many Splendored Thing (Pickwick); Stay As Sweet As You Are (Pickwick);
Anatomy of a Jam Session (Black Lion); From the Very Beginning (MCA).

Television: Juke Box Jury; What's My Line?; Showtime at the Apollo
1954; Ed Sullivan Show 1955; Nat King Cole Show (series)
1956-57; This Is Your Life 1960.

Theater: Shuffle Along (tour) 1936; appeared at Paramount Theatre;
Apollo Theatre 1952; I'm With You (tour) 1960; Sight and
Sounds (tour) 1964.

Relationships: Father of Natalie Cole, singer and Carol Cole, actress.

COLE, NATALIE (Stephanie Natalie Maria Cole)
(Singer)
b. February 5, 1950.
Education: University of Massachusetts. B.A. 1972.
Special Interests: Piano.
Honors: NAACP award as best female recording artist 1976; Gram-
my awards as best new artist and best rhythm and blues vo-
calist 1976, 1977; Grand Prize, 5th Tokyo Music Festival
1976.
Career Data: Toured Japan and participated in Tokyo Song Festival
1976.
Clubs: Buddy's Place; Copacabana; Mr. Kelly's (Chicago); Shep-
heard's in the Drake Hotel; Hilton (Las Vegas); Latin Casino;
High Schaparral (Chicago).
Records: Inseparable (Capitol); This Will Be (Capitol); Sophisticated
Lady (Columbia); Natalie (Capitol); Unpredictable (Capitol).
Television: American Bandstand 1975, 1976; Merv Griffin Show
1975; Don Kirshner's Rock Concert 1975; Dinah! 1975; Mid-
night Special 1975, 1976; Tonight Show 1975, 1976; Party
1975; Mike Douglas Show 1976; Positively Black 1976; Grammy
Awards Show 1976; Glen Campbell 1976.
Theater: I'm with You (Calif.) 1960; Apollo 1975; Westchester
Premier Theatre 1975; Beacon Theatre 1975; Kennedy Center
for the Performing Arts (Wash. D.C.) 1976; Winter Garden
1976.
Relationships: Daughter of Nat "King" Cole, singer; sister of Carol
Cole, actress.

COLE, OLIVIA
    (Actress)
b. November 26, Memphis, Tenn.
Education: Bard College; University of Minnesota M. A.; Royal
    Academy of Dramatic Arts (London) 1964.
Address: 611 West 148 Street, New York, N. Y. 10031 and Writers
    and Artists, 9720 Wilshire Blvd., Beverly Hills, Calif. 90212.
Honors: Amanda Steel Scholar; Emmy award (for Roots) 1977.
Career Data: Performed for Seattle Repertory Co.; Arena Stage
    (Washington, D. C.); Minnesota Theatre Co.; Long Wharf
    Theatre (New Haven); Playhouse in the Park (Philadelphia);
    A. P. A. Phoenix Repertory Co. 1966-67.
Films: Heroes 1977.
Memberships: AEA; AFTRA; SAG.
Television: Deborah in The Guiding Light (series); Police Woman;
    Family; Matilda in Roots 1977; Rafferty; Szysznyk (series)
    1977.
Theater: Lady Capulet in Romeo and Juliet (ASF); Merchant of
    Venice (LRC); The Duchess of Malfi (L. A.); Adelaide in Guys
    and Dolls (Williamstown, Mass.); title role in Electra (NYSF)
    1969.

COLE, ROBERT "Bob"
    (Playwright/Lyricist)
b. 1869, Athens, Ga.
d. August 2, 1911.
Education: Atlanta University.
Special Interests: Music, producing, directing.
Memberships: The Frogs (a theatrical association).
Musical Compositions: The Maiden with the Dreamy Eyes; Oh,
    Didn't He Ramble; Under the Bamboo Tree; My Castle on the
    Nile.
Theater: Produced Black Patti's Troubadours 1897; wrote, produced
    and directed A Trip to Coontown (with Billy Johnson) 1898;
    produced (with Glen MacDonough) Belle of Bridgeport 1900;
    headed All Negro Star Stock Co. N. Y. 1901-09; Evolution of
    Ragtime 1903; produced (with John McNally) Humpty Dumpty
    1904; produced (with James Weldon Johnson and John McNally)
    In Newport 1904; The Shoofly Regiment (operetta with Rosa-
    mund Johnson) 1909.

COLEMAN, ORNETTE
    (Composer/Musician)
b. March 9, 1930, Fort Worth, Texas.
Education: School of Jazz, Lenox, Massachusetts 1959.
Special Interests: Alto and tenor saxophone.
Address: c/o Columbia Records, 51 West 52nd Street, New York,
    N. Y. 10019.
Honors: Guggenheim Foundation Fellowship 1967; Recipient, Number
    1 Jazz Man of the Year, Jazz & Pop 3rd Annual Poll 1968.
Career Data: Toured with Pee Wee Clayton 1950; formed quartet

with Don Cherry and others 1959; toured Europe with his own
trio 1965; participated in Newport and Monterey Jazz Festivals;
developed a new atonal style and pioneered the use of double
quartets.
Clubs: 5 Spot 1959; Village Vanguard 1965.
Musical Compositions: Lonely Woman; Antiques; Broadway Blues;
    Round Trip Sadness; Complete Communion; Mapa; Ramblin';
    Cross Breeding; Snowflakes and Sunshine; Dawn; Turn-Around;
    Congeniality, Focus on Sanity; Peace, Sphinx; Chippie; Some-
    thing Else; Circle with a Hole in the Middle.
Records: John Lewis Presents Jazz Abstractions; At 12 (Impulse);
    Best of Ornette Coleman (Atlantic); Free Jazz (Atlantic); Friends
    and Neighbors (Flying Dutchman); Tomorrow Is the Question
    (Contemporary); Shape of Jazz to Come (Atlantic) 1959; Some-
    thing Else (Contemporary) 1959; Change of the Century (Atlan-
    tic) 1960; This Is Our Music (Atlantic) 1961; Town Hall Con-
    cert (Mainstream) 1962; Ornette! (Atlantic) 1962; Ornette on
    Tenor (Atlantic) 1963; At the Golden Circle vols. 1 & 2 (Blue)
    1966; Empty Fox Hole (Blue) 1967; Science Fiction (Columbia)
    1972; Skies of America (Columbia) 1972.
Theater: Directed Death-Life-Patience; appeared at Town Hall 1962.

COLERIDGE-TAYLOR, SAMUEL
    (Composer)
b.   August 15, 1875, London, England.
d.   September 1, 1912, London, England.
Education: Royal College of Music 1890.
Special Interests: Piano, violin.
Honors: Lesley Alexander Prize (composition) 1895; The Coleridge-
    Taylor Society, Washington, D.C. (a group of musicians) named
    in his honor.
Career Data: Organized Croydon String Orchestra; conductor, Royal
    Rochester Choral Society 1902; conductor, Handel Society Lon-
    don 1904; founder, String Players' Club 1906; taught music,
    Trinity College of Music 1906.
Musical Compositions: African Suite; Violin Concerto; Symphonic
    Variations on an African Air; A Trilogy: Hiawatha's Wedding
    Feast, The Death of Minnehaha, Hiawatha's Departure; Bam-
    boula; Twenty Four Negro Melodies Transcribed for the Piano;
    A Tale of Old Japan; Violin Concerto; African Romances;
    Danse Nègre; In Thee O Lord 1891; The Blind Girl of Castel-
    cuille 1901; Meg Blane 1902; Kubla Khan 1906.
Theater: Performed at Shire Hall (Gloucester) 1898; Pekin Theatre
    (Chicago) 1906; wrote accompaniments to Herod, Ulysees, Nero,
    Faust (all dramas performed in London).

COLES, HONI (Charles Coles)
    (Entertainer)
Special Interests: Dancing, producing.
Address: c/o Negro Actors Guild, 1674 Broadway, New York, N.Y.
    10019.

Career Data: Member, Copacetico; part of Miller Brothers 1932;
      teamed with Bert Howell as Howell and Coles 1938; Lucky
      Seven Trio; half of dance team, Coles and Atkins 1947-49.
Memberships: NAG (president 1976-).
Theater: Appearances at Apollo Theatre 1938-40; Strand Theatre
      1947; Gentlemen Prefer Blondes 1949; production manager at
      Apollo Theatre 1967-date; Bubbling Brown Sugar (tour) 1976.

COLES, ZAIDA
      (Actress)
b. September 10, 1933, Lynchburg, Va.
Education: Howard University.
Special Interests: Speech therapy.
Address: 90 Vaughn Avenue, New Rochelle, N. Y. 10801.
Honors: AUDELCO Black Theatre Recognition Award 1975.
Career Data: Howard University Players.
Films: Such Good Friends 1971.
Memberships: AEA; AFTRA; NEC; SAG.
Radio: Sounds of the City (series).
Television: The Doctors (series).
Theater: The Father (O. B.); Cherry Orchard (O. B.); Striver's
      Row (New Heritage Theatre); Beast Story (La Mama); Bayou
      Legend (AMAS Repertory); Pins and Needles (O. B.) 1967;
      Weekend 1968; Zelda 1969; The Life and Times of J. Walter
      Smintheus (O. B.) 1970; One Woman Show (New Rochelle);
      Scenes and Songs of Love and Freedom (one woman show; Ur-
      ban Arts Corps) 1975; Cotillion (New Federal Theatre) 1975;
      Sisyphus and the Blue-Eyed Cyclops (O. B.) 1975; Showdown
      (New Federal Theatre) 1976; Divine Comedy (O. B.) 1977.

COLLEY, DON PEDRO
      (Actor)
Films: Beneath the Planet of the Apes 1970; THX 1138 1971; The
      Legend of Nigger Charley 1972; Black Caesar, The World's
      Greatest Athlete, This Is a Hijack 1973; Sugar Hill 1974.
Memberships: AEA.
Television: Bill Cosby Show; Toma; Streets of San Francisco 1974;
      Celebrity Tennis 1976.

COLLINS, JANET
      (Dancer/Choreographer)
b. March 2, 1917, New Orleans, La.
Education: Los Angeles City College; studied dance with Carmelita
      Maracci, Lester Horton, Mia Slavenska.
Special Interests: Teaching.
Honors: Toscanini Scholarship in Ballet; Hanya Holm Scholarship in
      Modern Dance; Dance magazine award 1949; Mademoiselle mag-
      azine award Woman of the Year 1950; Donaldson award 1950-
      51.
Career Data: Toured with Katharine Dunham Dance Co. ; made N. Y.

debut at YM-YWHA 1949; first black prima ballerina, Metropolitan Opera 1951-54; Solo dance tours of U. S. and Canada
1952-55; teacher of modern dance, School of American Ballet
1949-52, 1966-69, St. Joseph School for Deaf 1959-61, Marymount Manhattan College 1959-69, Manhattanville College of
Sacred Heart 1961-65, Harkness House for Ballet Arts 1966-
67.
Musical Compositions: Spirituals; Canticle of the Elements.
Theater: Principal dancer, Musical Productions (Los Angeles) 1940;
concert at Las Palmas Theatre (Los Angeles) 1948; principal
dancer in Out of This World 1950-51.
Relationships: Cousin of Carmen DeLavallade, dancer/choreographer.

COLTRANE, JOHN "Trane" (William)
(Jazz Musician/Composer)
b. September 23, 1926, Hamlet, N. C.
d. July 17, 1967, Huntington, L. I.
Special Interests: Soprano and tenor saxophone, Eastern music.
Honors: Down Beat Poll winner (top tenor saxophonist and jazzman
of the year) 1965.
Career Data: Developed musical style "sheets of sound" (a. k. a.
honking, bleating); worked with Eddie Vinson's band 1947-48,
Dizzy Gillespie band 1950, Miles Davis 1955-60, Johnny Hodges,
Earl Bostic, Thelonius Monk; Advisory Council, Jazz Magazine
1962-67.
Clubs: Birdland; Village Vanguard.
Musical Compositions: Trane's Blues; A Love Supreme.
Records: The Best of John Coltrane (a. k. a. Chasin' the Trane)
(Impulse); A Love Supreme (Impulse); Alternate Takes (Atlan-
tic); Cannonball & Coltrane; Coltrane Jazz (Atlantic); Coltrane
Live at Birdland (Impulse); My Favorite Things (Atlantic); John
Coltrane/Wilbur Harden Countdown (Savoy); Expression (Im-
pulse) 1967; Ascension (Impulse); Giant Steps (Atlantic); Impres-
sions (Impulse); Africa/Brass (Impulse); Art (Atlantic); Avant-
Garde (Atlantic); Bahia (Prestige); Ballads (Impulse); Believer
(Prestige); Best of ... (Atlantic); Best/Greatest Years (Im-
pulse); Black Pearls (Prestige); Blue Train (Blue Note); Col-
trane (Impulse); Concert in Japan (Impulse); Cosmic Music
(Impulse); Crescent (Impulse); First Trane (Prestige); Gentle
Side (Impulse); Infinity (Impulse); Interstellar Space (Impulse);
John Coltrane (Prestige); Kulu Se' Mama (Impulse); Last Trane
(Prestige); Legacy (Atlantic); Live at Village Vanguard (Impulse);
Live at the Vanguard Again (Impulse); Live in Seattle (Impulse);
Lust Life (Prestige); Master (Prestige); Meditations (Impulse);
More Lasting Than Bronze (Prestige); Ole' Coltrane (Atlantic);
Plays for Lovers (Prestige); Plays the Blues (Atlantic); Quartet
Plays (Impulse); Selflessness (Impulse); Soultrane (Prestige);
Sound (Atlantic); Stardust (Prestige); Stardust Session (Prestige);
Sun Ship (Impulse); Trane Tracks (Trip); Traneing (Prestige);
Trane's Reign (Prestige); Transition (Impulse); 2 Tenors (Pres-
tige).

COOK, LAWRENCE
    (Actor)
Education: New York University, Actors Studio.
Address: c/o Leaverton Associates Ltd. , 1650 Broadway, New York,
    N. Y. 10019.
Honors: Third World Film Festival best actor award (for The Spook
    Who Sat by the Door) 1975.
Films: Title role in The Spook Who Sat by the Door 1973; Lord
    Shango 1975.
Television: Get Smart; Dan August 1960; The Rookies 1975; Ad-
    venturizing with the Chopper (pilot) 1976.
Theater: Macbird (O. B.); The Degenerate (New Dramatists Society);
    Dark Light in May (Yale Drama Society); The Toilet (Actors
    Studio); Macbeth (NYSF) 1966; Volpone (NYSF) 1967; The Great
    White Hope 1968; The Wrong Way Light Bulb 1969; The Dream
    on Monkey Mountain (O. B.) 1971.

COOK, WILL MARION
    (Composer)
b.   January 27, 1869, Washington, D. C.
d.   July 19, 1944, New York, N. Y.
Education: Oberlin College, New York Conservatory of Music;
    Studied with Anton Dvorak.
Special Interests: Violin, conducting.
Honors: Command performance for King George V of England, Buck-
    ingham Palace 1919.
Career Data: Formed all Negro Group called N. Y. Syncopated Or-
    chestra 1918 (became American Syncopated orchestra 1919);
    trained and directed Memphis students band.
Musical Compositions: Bon Bon Buddy; Rain Song; I May Be Crazy
    But I Ain't No Fool; My Lady; Springtime; Exhortation-A Negro
    Sermon; I'm Comin' Virginia; On Emancipation Day; That's
    How the Cakewalk's Done; Swing Along Children; Happy Jim;
    Mandy Lou; Down the Lover's Lane; Red Red Rose; Mammy;
    Lovey Joe; A Little Bit of Heaven Called Home; Darktown Is
    Out Tonight; Who Dat Say Chicken in dis Crowd?; Wid de Moon,
    Moon, Moon.
Theater: Co-wrote Clorindy-The Origin of the Cakewalk 1898; Jes
    Lak White Folk: A Musical Playlet 1899; The Policy Players
    1900; In Dahomey 1902; Abyssinia 1906; Bandanna Land 1907;
    Darkydom 1914; wrote for Black Patti's Troubadours; vocal
    coach for Great Day 1929; wrote the Cannibal King (unproduced).
Relationships: Husband of Abbie Mitchell, actress/singer.

COOKE, SAM
    (Composer/Singer)
b.   January 22, 1935, Chicago, Ill.
d.   December 11, 1964, Los Angeles, Calif.
Career Data: Member of The Soul Stirrers, a gospel group.
Records: The Legendary Sam Cooke; For Keen: You Send Me 1957;
    I Love You for Sentimental Reasons 1957; There I've Said It

Again 1959; Only Sixteen 1959; Wonderful World 1960. For
RCA: Teenage Sonata 1960; Chain Gang 1960; That's It-I Quit-
I'm Movin' On 1961; Twistin' the Night Away 1962; Having a
Party 1962; Send Me Some Lovin' 1963; Tennessee Waltz 1964;
A Change Is Gonna Come 1965; The Best of Sam Cooke (2
vols.); The Man Who Invented Soul.

COOLEY, ISABELLE
    (Actress)
Education: Cleveland College.
Address: 8730 Sunset Blvd., Los Angeles, Calif. 90069.
Career Data: Worked with Karamu House Theatre, Cleveland.
Clubs: La Nouvelle Eve (Paris).
Films: Raintree County 1957; I Want To Live 1958; Anna Lucasta
    1959; I Passed for White, Never So Few 1960; Charmian in
    Cleopatra 1963.
Television: Bill Cosby Show; Medical Story 1975.
Theater: Anna Lucasta 1947; The Long Dream 1960.

COOPER, RALPH "The Bronze Bogart"
    (Actor/Musician)
b. New York, N.Y.
Special Interests: Producing, dancing, comedy, public relations.
Career Data: Formed his own orchestra 1931; formed Million Dol-
    lar Productions (films) 1938; dance act with Eddie Rector as
    partner; community coordinator, New York State Governor's
    Office of Urban Affairs 1976.
Films: Wrote Life Goes On, Gang Smashers, Mr. Smith Goes
    Ghost; Harlem Cabaret 1930; White Hunter 1936; Dark Man-
    hattan, Bargain with Bullets 1937; The Duke Is Tops 1938;
    Bronze Venus, Am I Guilty? (a.k.a. Racket Doctor), Gang
    War 1940.
Radio: Jump 'n' Jive (WMCA); disc jockey on WHOM 1962.
Television: Produced Harlem Spotlight (series).
Theater: Chocolate Blondes; Tan Town Topics; Runnin' Wild 1923;
    Harlem Opera House 1931; Palace Theater 1932; Apollo Theatre
    1938, 1962 (master of ceremonies for amateur night).

COPAGE, MARC
    (Actor)
b. 1962.
Education: American Academy of Dramatic Arts.
Special Interests: Football.
Memberships: SAG.
Television: Corey Baker in Julia (series) 1968-71; Flip Wilson
    Special; Diahann Carroll Special; The Happening Show; Merv
    Griffin Show; Virginia Graham Show; Soul Train; Tony Awards
    Show; Sanford and Son 1975; The Cop and the Kid 1976.

CORBIN, CLAYTON (Clayton Booker Washington Smeltz)
    (Actor)
b.   May 4, 1928, Tacoma, Wash.
Education: Studied drama with Benno Frank 1948-54; studied voice
      with Frank Eels 1948-56.
Address: 13 West 106 Street, New York, N. Y. 10025.
Honors: Joseph Jefferson award (Chicago Drama Critics) 1970.
Career Data: Appeared in more than 30 productions at Karamu
      Theatre, Cleveland 1951-54, 1957-58, 1972-73; appeared in
      various plays with repertory companies throughout the U. S.
      1967-71.
Memberships: AEA; AFTRA; SAG.
Television: Kraft Theatre; Omnibus; Big Story; Frontiers of Faith;
      Justice; Ohio Story; Studio One; Odyssey; For the People;
      Breakthrough; Naked City; Carol for Another Christmas; Trials
      of O'Brien; Our Street (series).
Theater: Lenny in Of Mice and Men (O. B.) 1954; Queequeg in Moby
      Dick (O. B.) 1955; understudied title role in Mr. Johnson 1956;
      Henry Simpson in Toys in the Attic 1960-62; The Blacks (O. B.)
      1962; Henri Christophe in Defiant Island (Howard University
      Players, Wash. D. C.) 1962; Telemachus Clay (O. B.) 1963;
      Atufal in The Old Glory (O. B.) 1964; Royal Hunt in The Sun
      1965-66; title role in The Emperor Jones 1967; Prometheus
      Bound (Yale University) 1967; Marcus in Titus Andronicus
      (NYSF) 1967; Black River (NEC) 1975.

CORDERO, ROQUE
    (Composer)
b.   1917, Panama.
Honors: Koussevitsky International Recording Award 1974.
Career Data: Instructor, Illinois State University.
Musical Compositions: Quintet for Flute, Clarinet, Violin, Cello,
      Piano; Concerto for Violin and Orchestra; Eight Miniatures.

CORNELIUS, DON
    (Producer)
b.   c. 1937, Chicago, Ill.
Radio: Disc jockey, WVON (Chicago).
Records: The Soul Train Gang (RCA).
Television: Host of Soul Train (series).

COSBY, BILL (William Henry Cosby)
    (Comedian)
b.   July 12, 1937, Germantown, Pa.
Education: Temple University; University of Massachusetts M. A.
      and Ph. D.
Special Interests: Acting.
Address: c/o Marietta Mandell, 4000 Warner Blvd. , Burbank, Calif.
      91505.
Honors: Emmy awards 1966, 1967, 1968, 1969; Grammy award

1964, 1965, 1966, 1967, 1969; NAACP Image award (for Let's Do It Again) 1976.

Career Data: President, Jemmin, Inc. (own production company).

Clubs: Playboy Club; Gaslight; Harrah's (Lake Tahoe) 1975; Hilton (Las Vegas).

Films: Hickey and Boggs, Man and Boy 1972; Uptown Saturday Night 1974; Let's Do It Again 1975; Mother, Jugs & Speed 1976; A Piece of the Action 1977.

Radio: Bill Cosby Radio Program.

Records: Bill Cosby Is a Very Funny Fellow ... Right (Warner Bros.); I Started Out as a Child (Warner Bros.); Revenge (Warner Bros.); To Russell (Warner Bros.); My Brother Whom I Slept With (Warner Bros.); 200 MPH (Warner Bros.); It's True, It's True (Warner Bros.); 8:15, 12:15; Silverthroat; Hooray for the Salvation Army Band; When I Was a Kid (Warner Bros.); Why Is There Air? (Warner Bros.); Wonderfulness (Warner Bros.); Bill Cosby Is Not Himself These Days (Capitol); Rat Own, Rat Own, Rat Own (Capitol); Best (Warner Bros.); Bill Cosby (MCA); Fat Albert (MCA); For Adults Only (MCA); Inside The Mind (MCA); More of the Best (Warner Bros.); Congressional Black Caucas (Black Forum); My Father Confused Me (Capitol).

Television: Jack Paar Show; Andy Williams Show; Family Theatre; Kup's Show; Del Monte commercial; Jello Pudding commercial; Jonathan Winters Show; A New Ballgame for Willie Mays (Cameo); The Electric Company; I Spy (series) 1965-68; The First Bill Cosby Special 1968; Bill Cosby Show (series) 1969; Black History; Lost Stolen or Strayed 1969; The Dick Cavett Show 1971; To All My Friends on Shore 1972; Fat Albert (cartoon) 1972; Aesop's Fables 1974; Mike Douglas Show 1974; The Playboy 20th Anniversary Party (Wide World Special) 1974; Circus Highlights 1975; Saturday Night Live with Howard Cosell 1975; The First Comedy Awards 1975; host on The World of Magic 1975; Victor Awards 1975; Merv Griffin Show 1975; Tonight Show 1975; Cher Show 1975; Sammy and Company 1975; Bill Cosby Comedy Hour (special) 1975; Second Bill Cosby Special; Friends 1976; Rich Little Show 1976; Rock'n'Fun Magic Show 1976; Ford commercial 1976; Journey Back to Oz 1976; Cos 1976.

Theater: Appearance at Uris Theatre.

CRAIN, WILLIAM
        (Director)
b.   Columbus, Ohio.
Education: University of California Los Angeles (Cinema).
Films: Apprentice director, Brother John 1971; Blacula 1972.
Memberships: Directors Guild of America.
Television: Mod Squad 1970.

CROCKER, FRANKIE
        (Disc Jockey)
b.   c. 1944, Buffalo, N. Y.

Education: University of Buffalo.
Clubs: Cheetah 1967.
Films: Cleopatra Jones, Five on the Black Hand Side, Jimi Hendrix
       1973; That's the Way of the World, Darktown Strutters 1975.
Radio: Disc jockey WWRL 1965-67, WMCA 1967-71; manager and
       disc jockey WBLS (formerly WLIB) 1972.
Theater: Emcee, Barry White Show (Felt Forum) 1974; emcee/
       guest host, Apollo Theatre 1974, 1975; Felt Forum 1975.

CROSSE, RUPERT
    (Actor)
b. c. 1927, New York, N. Y.
d. March 5, 1973, Nevis, West Indies.
Education: Bloomfield College and Seminary (New Jersey).
Honors: Oscar nomination for best actor in a supporting role (The
       Reivers) 1970.
Films: Shadows 1961; Too Late Blues 1962; To Trap a Spy 1966;
       Waterhole #3 1967; The Reivers 1969.
Television: Bracken's World; The Monkees; Bill Cosby Show; Part-
       ners (series) 1971.

CROTHERS, SCATMAN (Benjamin Sherman Crothers)
    (Actor/Singer)
b. May 23, 1910, Terre Haute, Ind.
Special Interests: Guitar.
Address: 1877 West 38th Street, Los Angeles, Calif. 90062.
Career Data: Started performing at 15 as a drummer; formed his
       own band in 1930 and toured Midwest.
Clubs: Bingo, later known as Sahara (Las Vegas) 1949; Ice House
       (Pasadena) 1975.
Films: Walking My Baby Back Home, Meet Me at the Fair, East
       of Sumatra 1953; The Sins of Rachel Cade 1961; Lady in a
       Cage 1964; Bloody Mama 1960; The King of Marvin Gardens,
       Lady Sings the Blues, Chandler 1972; Detroit 9000 1973;
       Black Belt Jones, Truck Turner 1974; Coon Skin, One Flew
       Over the Cuckoo's Nest, Friday Foster, The Fortune 1975;
       Stay Hungry, The Shootist, Silver Streak 1976.
Memberships: ASCAP 1959.
Musical Compositions: Dearest One; The Gal Looks Good; Nobody
       Knows Why; I Was There; A Man's Gotta Eat; When, Oh When.
Television: Harlem Globetrotters (cartoon voice); Hong Kong Phooey
       (cartoon voice); Dixie Showboat (L. A.); Beany and Cecil (voices);
       Colgate Comedy Hour; Night Stalker; Ironside; Louis the Gar-
       bage Man in Chico and the Man (series) 1974; The Odd Couple
       1974; Man on the Outside 1975; Mike Douglas Show 1975; To-
       night Show 1975; Dinah! 1975; Say Brother 1975; Sanford and
       Son (The Stand-ins episode) 1975; Merv Griffin Show 1975;
       Jonathan Winters Presents 200 Years of American Humor
       (special) 1976; Joys (Bob Hope Special) 1976; Sammy and Com-
       pany 1976; Starsky and Hutch 1976; Celebrity Sweepstakes 1976;
       Rich Little Show 1976; Roots 1977; Dean Martin Roasts Angie
       Dickinson 1977.

CROWDER, JACK see RASULALA, THALMUS

CRUDUP, CARL W.
  (Actor)
Address: 130 Lexington Avenue, New York, N. Y. 10016.
Films: The Gambler 1974; J. D. 's Revenge 1976.
Television: The Blue Knight 1975; Six Million Dollar Man 1976;
    The First Breeze of Summer 1976.
Theater: The First Breeze of Summer 1975.

CULLEN, COUNTEE (Porter)
  (Playwright)
b. May 30, 1903, New York, N. Y.
d. January 9, 1946, New York, N. Y.
Education: New York University B. A. 1926, Harvard University
    M. A. 1926.
Honors: Phi Beta Kappa; Guggenheim Fellowship 1928.
Theater: Wrote Byword for Evil (a. k. a. Medea) 1935; One Way to
    Heaven 1936; The Third Fourth of July (with Owen Dodson)
    1946; St. Louis Woman (a musical co-authored with Arna Bon-
    temps) 1946.

CULLY, ZARA
  (Actress)
b. January 26, Worcester, Mass.
Education: Normal School (Worcester).
Career Data: Taught drama in her own studio in Florida and at Ed-
    ward Waters College.
Films: The Learning Tree 1969; The Great White Hope, The Liber-
    ation of L. B. Jones 1970; Brother John 1971; Sugar Hill 1974.
Memberships: AEA.
Television: Run for Your Life; Playhouse 90; All in the Family;
    The Name of the Game; Mod Squad; Mother Jefferson in The
    Jeffersons (series) 1975-.
Theater: Appeared at Town Hall; Detective Story (L. A.); Take a
    Giant Step (L. A.).

CUMBUKA, JI-TU
  (Actor)
Address: c/o Paul Kohner Inc. 9169 Sunset Boulevard, Los Angeles,
    Calif. 90069.
Films: Uptight 1968; Change of Habit 1969; Maurie 1973; Lost in
    the Stars 1974; Mandingo 1975; Bound for Glory 1976; Fun with
    Dick and Jane 1977.
Television: Lucas Tanner; Kojak 1974; Kung Fu 1974; Chase 1974;
    Get Christie Love 1975; Caribe 1975; The Blue Knight 1975;
    S. W. A. T. 1976; Rockford Files 1976; Roots 1977; Sanford and
    Son 1977.

CUNNINGHAM, ARTHUR H.
(Musician/Composer)
b. November 11, 1928, Piermont, N.Y.
Education: Metropolitan Music School 1941-45; Juilliard School of
Music 1945-46, 1951-52; Fisk University B.A. (music educa-
tion) 1951; Columbia Teachers' College M.A. (theory and con-
ducting) 1957; studied with John W. Work, Teddy Wilson.
Special Interests: Piano, conducting.
Address: P.O. Box 614, 4 North Pine, Nyack, N.Y. 10960.
Honors: Recipient of 5th ASCAP award for composition 1972; Na-
tional Endowment for the Arts grant 1974.
Career Data: Music director summer stock Rockland County Play-
house 1963; lectured at Morehouse, Spelman and Morris Brown
colleges 1968; lecturer at Albany State College and Cheney
State College 1972; composer-in-residence, A & T State Col-
lege, Greensboro, N.C. 1973; guest lecturer at University of
Conn., Storrs; owner, Cunningham Music Corp.
Memberships: ACA; ASCAP.
Musical Compositions: Adagio for String Orchestra and Oboe 1954;
He Met Her at the Dolphin (choral work) 1963; Patsy Patch
and Susan's Dream (children's musicals) 1963; Violetta (a
musical) 1964; Ostrich Feathers (children's musical) 1964;
Perimeters 1965; House by the Sea (libretto) 1966; Dialogue
for Piano and Chamber Orchestra 1967; String and Jazz Quartet Ballet 1968; Louey Louey (mini-rock opera) 1968; Concen-
trics 1968; Midsummer Night's Dream 1968; The Garden of
Phobos (choral piece) 1969; Shango 1969; Minakesh (work for
oboe/piano) 1969; His Natural Grace (one-act rock opera) 1969;
Dim Du Mim (for orchestra/oboe) 1969; Engrams (for piano)
1969; Trinities (for cello and 2 double basses) 1969; Lullabye
for a Jazz Baby 1970; Eclatette for Cello 1970; The Prince
1971; Call His Name (gospel) 1972; Litany for the Flower
Children 1972; Covenant 1972; Born a Slave 1972; World Goin
Down 1972; Hinkty Woman (Harlem Suite) 1974; Night Song
1974; Sunday Stone 1974.
Theater: Orchestrated sections of Ballad for Bimshire 1963; arranged choral concert at Town Hall 1965.

DA COSTA, NOEL
(Composer)
b. 1930, Lagos, Nigeria.
Education: Queens College, Columbia University.
Special Interests: Violin, teaching.
Honors: Fulbright Scholarship 1958-60.
Career Data: Taught at Rutgers University, Hampton Institute,
Hunter College, Queens College.
Memberships: Black Society of Composers.
Musical Compositions: Five Verses with Vamps; The Confessional
Stone 1969; Extempore Blue; The Singing Tortoise; Cikan Ci-
malo; Silver Blue; Three Short Pieces; In the Circle 1969;
The Last Judgement 1970.
Theater: Violinist in Promises Promises 1969.

DAFORA, ASADATA (John Warner Dafora Horton)
    (Dancer/Choreographer)
b. August 4, 1890, Freetown, Sierra Leone, West Africa.
d. March 4, 1965, New York, N. Y.
Education: Studied voice at La Scala, Milan 1910-12.
Special Interests: Acting, composing, directing, singing.
Career Data: First African dancer to present African dance in con-
    cert form in U. S.; made debut 1912; formed Asadata Dafora
    dance group; toured Europe, U. S. and Canada.
Theater: Choreographed Kykunkor (a. k. a. Witch Woman) (Carnegie
    Hall) 1934; choreographed voodoo dance scene in Orson Welles
    production of Macbeth 1936; performed in Negro Dance Evening
    (YMHA) 1937 and Campbell Fairbank's Sportsmen's Show (Bos-
    ton) 1937; played witch doctor in Emperor Jones (White Plains,
    N. Y.) 1939; choreographed and danced in Zunguru (O. B.) 1940;
    Africana Dance Festival (Carnegie Hall) 1943; directed and
    danced Africa: A Tribal Operetta (YMHA) 1944; choreographed
    and danced in A Tale of Old Africa (Carnegie Hall) 1946; pro-
    duced and danced in Batanga (O. B.) 1952.

DANCY, MEL (Melville Frank Dancy)
    (Actor/Singer)
b. April 23, 1937, Flushing, N. Y.
Education: Studied acting at The Theatre of Arts, Los Angeles;
    studied music with Edward Boatner.
Special Interests: Piano, composing.
Address: 220 West 98 Street, New York, N. Y. 10025.
Honors: United States Air Force championship in musical and vocal
    execution.
Career Data: Worked as vocalist with Riverliers; made State Dept.
    tour of Russia with Thad Jones and Mel Lewis.
Clubs: The Half Note; The Embers; Muggs; Village Vanguard; French-
    man's Reef (St. Thomas, V. I.); Gulliver's (N. J.); Sugarbush
    Inn (Vt.); Steak & Brew; Nathans.
Films: Played piano on soundtrack and acted in Galliano (industrial
    film) 1974.
Memberships: Local 802, Musicians Union.
Musical Compositions: Day Star (lyrics); See Saw (music); Let Me
    Do What I Want to Do (lyrics); Let Your Love Come Out (lyrics);
    You Touched Me (lyrics); Brother Martin (lyrics).
Radio: Joe Franklin Show 1973; Gene Shepherd interview; Barry Far-
    ber Show 1973; Live Broadcast from Boomers (WRVR).
Records: Letta (Chisa) 1961; A Little Lovin' (Mainstream) 1973.
Television: The New Yorkers 1969; The Edge of Night 1974; The
    Dating Game.
Theater: Performed at Sacred Concert, Carnegie Hall 1973; Newport
    Jazz Festival 1974.

DANDRIDGE, DOROTHY
    (Actress)
b. November, c. 1923, Cleveland, Ohio.

d.   September 8, 1965, West Hollywood, Calif.
Honors: Foreign Press Award for Porgy and Bess; Academy Award
    Nominee Best Actress for Carmen Jones 1954; Black Film-
    makers Hall of Fame (posthumously) 1977.
Career Data: Appeared as The Wonder Kids with sister Vivian;
    Performed as member of Dandridge Sisters (with sister Vivian
    and another girl) with Jimmie Lunceford Band.
Clubs: Cotton Club 1938; El Rancho (Las Vegas); Riviera (Las
    Vegas); Key Club-Shamrock Hotel (Texas); Ciro's (L. A.); Cafe
    de Paris (London); Empire Room-Waldorf; Mocambo 1951; La
    Vie en Rose 1952; Copacabana (Rio de Janeiro) 1953; Chi Chi
    (Palm Springs) 1963.
Films: A Day at the Races 1937; Four Shall Die 1940; Sundown,
    Lady from Louisiana, Sun Valley Serenade 1941; Bahama Pas-
    sage, Drums of the Congo 1942; Hit Parade of 1943, Moo Cow
    Boogie (all black) 1943; Atlantic City, Since You Went Away
    1944; Pillow to Post 1946; Flamingo, Ebony Parade (all black)
    1947; Harlem Globetrotters 1951; Remains to Be Seen, Bright
    Road 1953; Title role in Carmen Jones 1954; Island in the Sun,
    The Happy Road 1957; The Decks Ran Red 1958; Porgy and
    Bess, Tamango 1959; Moment of Danger 1960; Malaga 1962.
Publications: Everything and Nothing (autobiography), Abelard, 1970.
Radio: Beulah (series).
Television: Gleason's Cavalcade of Stars; Steve Allen's Songs for
    Sale; Ed Sullivan Show; Cain's Hundred 1962; Light's Diamond
    Jubilee 1964.
Theater: Jump for Joy (L. A.) 1941; Julie in Show Boat (Burlingame,
    Calif.) 1964.
Relationships: Daughter of Ruby Dandridge, actress; former wife of
    Harold Nicholas, dancer.

DANDRIDGE, RUBY (Jean)
    (Actress)
b.   March 3, 1904, Memphis, Tenn.
Education: Topeka Institute, Kansas 1917-19; College of Emporia
    (Kansas) 1920-22; Cleveland School of Dramatics.
Career Data: WPA Project with Hall Johnson choir.
Films: Midnight Shadow 1939; Tish, A Night for Crime 1942; Cabin
    in the Sky, Corregidor, Gallant Lady, Melody Parade 1943;
    Ladies in Washington 1944; Junior Miss 1945; Home in Okla-
    homa, Three Little Girls in Blue 1946; The Arnelo Affair, Dead
    Reckoning, My Wild Irish Rose 1947; Tap Roots 1948; Carmen
    Jones 1954; A Hole in the Head 1959.
Memberships: AEA; AFTRA; SAG.
Radio: Oriole on Beulah (series); Geranium on Judy Canova Show
    1943; Raindrop on Gene Autry Show; Ella Rose in Tonight at
    Hoagy's (series) 1944.
Television: Beulah (series); Delilah on Father of the Bride (series)
    1961-62.
Theater: Show Boat; Hit the Deck; The Rosary; Not a Man in the
    House.
Relationships: Mother of Dorothy Dandridge, actress.

DANIELS, BILLY (William Boone)
    (Singer)
b.   c. 1915, Jacksonville, Fla.
Education: Florida Normal College.
Honors: Command performances for Royal Family of England, Mayor
    of Dublin and King Leopold of Belgium.
Career Data: Vocalist with Erskine Hawkins band; toured Europe,
    Australia, Viet Nam, Philippines, Thailand, Singapore; popu-
    larized song "Black Magic".
Clubs: St. Regis; Ebony Club; Cafe Society; Riviera (Palisades,
    N. J.); 400 Club (Atlantic City); Copacabana; Famous Door;
    The Black Cat; Onyx; Kelly's Stable; Jack's Club Baron; Sa-
    hara (Las Vegas); El Rancho (Las Vegas); Caesar's Place
    (Las Vegas); Rainbow Grill 1975; Pocono Gardens 1976; Stevens-
    ville Country Club 1976; Hopper's 1977.
Films: Sepia Cinderella 1947; When You're Smiling 1950; On the
    Sunny Side of the Street 1951; Rainbow Round My Shoulder
    1952; Cruising Down the River 1953; Mr. Black Magic 1956;
    The Big Operator, Night of the Quarter Moon, The Beat Gen-
    eration 1959.
Memberships: AEA.
Records: Too Marvelous for Words; I Get a Kick Out of You; Ol'
    Black Magic; At the Crescendo (GNP Crescendo).
Television: Ed Sullivan Show; Mod Squad; Run for Your Life; Andy
    Williams Show; Mike Douglas Show; Anything Goes (Canadian
    series); The Billy Daniels Show (series) 1956; Cotton Club '75
    (special) 1974; The Tonight Show 1974; Dinah! 1974; Joe Frank-
    lin Show 1975.
Theater: Appearance at Roxy Theatre 1951; Palladium (London)
    1952; Memphis Bound 1945; Golden Boy 1964; Norman, Is That
    You? (Washington, D. C.) 1975; Hello, Dolly! 1975; Bubbling
    Brown Sugar (London) 1977.

DAVIS, ALTOVISE see GORE, ALTOVISE

DAVIS, CLIFTON
    (Singer/Actor)
b.   October 4, 1945, Chicago, Ill.
Education: Oakwood College (Huntsville, Ala.).
Special Interests: Composing.
Address: c/o International Famous Agency, 1301 Avenue of the
    Americas, New York, N. Y. 10019.
Honors: Theatre World award (for Do It Again) 1971; Tony nomina-
    tion (for Two Gentlemen of Verona); Gold record (for Never
    Can Say Goodbye); Torch award (American Heart Assn.) 1975.
Clubs: Improvisation 1967-68; Reno Sweeneys 1975.
Films: Together for Days 1973; Lost in the Stars 1974.
Memberships: AEA; AFTRA; SAG.
Musical Compositions: Never Can Say Goodbye; Looking Through
    the Window.
Television: A Glow of Dying Embers (Love Story); Police Story;

Love, American Style; David Frost Show; The Tonight Show;
On Being Black; Melba Moore/Clifton Davis Show (summer
series) 1972; That's My Mama (series) 1974-75; Cotton Club
'75 1974; Sonny Comedy Revue 1974; Celebrity Sweepstakes
1974-75; Mike Douglas Show 1974-75; Dinah! 1974; $10,000
Pyramid 1974; Legacy of Blood (Wide World Mystery) 1974;
Captain Kangaroo 1975; Gladys Knight and the Pips 1975; Show-
offs 1975; Positively Black 1975; Merv Griffin Show 1975,
1976; Midnight Special 1975; Match Game 1975; guest co-host
Black Journal 1975; Tony Awards 1975; Fashion Awards 1975;
Bobby Vinton Show 1975; Black News 1975; The American Mu-
sic Awards 1975; Mitzi and 100 Guys (special) 1975; Blankety
Blanks 1975; United Jewish Appeal Telethon 1975; Tattletales
1976; Celebration: The American Spirit 1976; The Clifton
Davis Special 1976; Tony Awards Show 1976; Little Ladies of
the Night 1977; The Gong Show 1977.
Theater: Dutchman (tour) 1966; Slaves (tour) 1966; Hunger and
Thirst (tour); Slow Dance on a Killing Ground (tour); How to
Steal an Election (O. B. debut) 1968; Jimmy Shine 1968; To Be
Young, Gifted and Black (O. B.) 1969; Horseman Pass By (O.
B.); Hello, Dolly! 1969; Look to the Lilies 1970; The Engage-
ment Baby 1970; Do It Again (O. B.) 1971; No Place to Be
Somebody 1971; Valentine in Two Gentlemen of Verona 1972;
Guys and Dolls (Aladdin Hotel, Las Vegas) 1977.

DAVIS, ELLABELLE
    (Concert Singer)
b.   March 17, 1907, New Rochelle, N. Y.
d.   November 15, 1960, New Rochelle, N. Y.
Special Interests: Opera.
Career Data: Soloist with Philadelphia Orchestra (under Ormandy);
    Indianapolis Symphony (under Savitsky); performed: The Chap-
    let (opera); Aida (at Opera Nacional of Mexico City and at
    Santiago, Chile) 1946; The Song of Songs (a cantata commis-
    sioned by League of Composers from Lukas Foss) with Boston
    Symphony 1947; toured Europe 1948; Berkshire Music Festival
    1950; performed Richard Strauss' Four Last Songs with The
    National Symphony 1959; toured South America 1960.
Theater: Town Hall (debut) 1942; Teatro Gran Rex (Buenos Aires)
    1946; Carnegie Hall (debut) 1948.

DAVIS, MILES (Dewey)
    (Jazz Musician)
b.   May 25, 1926, Alton, Ill.
Education: Juilliard School of Music 1945.
Special Interests: Composing, trumpet.
Address: c/o Neil Reshen, 53 East 54 Street, New York, N. Y.
    10022.
Honors: Esquire new star award 1947; Metronome poll winner 1951-
    53; Grammy award 1960.
Career Data: Played with Coleman Hawkins, Billy Eckstine bands;

leader of his own band; Paris Jazz Festival 1949; toured with
Jazz Inc. 1952; Newport Jazz Festival 1975.

Clubs: Royal Roost, Cafe Bohemia 1957; The Bottom Line 1974,
1975.

Films: Elevator to the Gallows (French) 1958; Jack Johnson 1971.

Records: At Carnegie Hall (Columbia); Live at Fillmore (Columbia);
Basic Miles (Columbia); Blue Moods (Fantasy); Four & More
(Columbia); Get Up with It (Columbia); Greatest Hits (Colum-
bia); In a Silent Way (Columbia); In Concert (Columbia); In
Europe (Columbia); In Person at the Blackhawk (Columbia);
Jazz at the Plaza (Columbia); Live-Evil (Columbia); Miles
Ahead (Prestige); Miles in the Sky (Columbia); Miles Smiles
(Columbia); My Funny Valentine (Columbia); Nefertiti (Colum-
bia); Porgy and Bess (Columbia); Quiet Nights (Columbia);
'Round About Midnight (Columbia); 7 Steps to Heaven (Colum-
bia); Sketches of Spain (Columbia); Some Day My Prince Will
Come (Columbia); Sorcerer (Columbia) Tribute to Jack Johnson
(Columbia); Collectors Items (Prestige); Conception (Prestige);
Dig (Prestige); Early Miles (Prestige); For Lovers (Prestige);
Greatest Hits (Prestige); Jazz Classics (Prestige); Miles of
Jazz (Trip); Modern Jazz Giants (Prestige); Odyssey (Prestige);
Oleo (Prestige); Tallest Trees (Prestige); Steamin' (Prestige);
Filles de Kilimanjaro (Columbia); The Complete Birth of The
Cool (Capitol); Milestone (Columbia); Miles and Monk at New-
port; Miles Davis in Person; Modern Idiom; Miles Davis Plus
19; Relaxin; Cookin'; Bags; Groove; Big Fun (Columbia); On
the Corner (Columbia); Agharta (Columbia); Walkin (Prestige)
1954; King of Blue (Columbia) 1959; Bitch's Brew (Columbia)
1968; Water Babies (CBS) 1977.

Theater: Appeared at Fillmore; Avery Fisher Hall 1974, 1975; Carnegie Hall 1975; Wollman Theatre, Central Park (Schaefer Music Festival) 1975.

DAVIS, OSSIE
    (Actor/Playwright/Director)
b. December 18, 1917, Cogdell, Ga.
Education: Howard University 1938-41.
Special Interests: Film production, civil rights, black culture and
    history.
Address: 44 Cortlandt Avenue, New Rochelle, N.Y. 10801.
Honors: Frederick Douglass award 1970, Actors Equity Paul Robe-
    son citation 1975, Black Filmmakers Hall of Fame 1974.
Career Data: Member, Rose McClendon Players 1941; Member of
    Black Scholar Speaker's Bureau; Founder and President, Third
    World Cinema Productions Inc.
Films: No Way Out 1950; Fourteen Hours 1951; The Joe Louis Story
    1953; The Cardinal, Gone Are the Days 1963; Shock Treatment
    1964; The Hill (Brit.) 1965; A Man Called Adam 1966; The
    Scalphunters 1968; Sam Whiskey, The Slaves 1969; co-scripted
    and co-directed Cotton Comes to Harlem 1970; directed Kongi's
    Harvest 1971; directed Black Girl 1972; directed Gordon's War
    1973; directed Countdown at Kusini 1974; Let's Do It Again 1975.

Memberships: AEA; AFTRA; NAG; SAG; NAACP; NATAS; CORE.

Radio: Spoken words.

Records: Simple (Caedmon); Silhouettes in Courage; Simple's Uncle Sam; Congressional Black Caucas (Black Forum).

Television: N. Y. P. D. ; Showtime U. S. A. 1951; The Emperor Jones (Kraft Theatre) 1955; John Brown's Raid 1960; Seven Times Monday (Play of the Week) 1960; Defenders 1961, 1963, 1965; wrote episode of The Eleventh Hour 1963; wrote episode of East Side West Side 1963; Go Down Moses (Great Adventure) 1963; Car 54 Where Are You? (series) 1963; Doctors/Nurses 1964; Slattery's People 1965; Look Up and Live 1966; Name of the Game; To Tell the Truth; Night Gallery 1969; Free Time; The Sheriff; A Holiday Celebration (special) 1971; Black Journal 1974; Pat Collins Show; Hawaii Five O 1974; Soul; narrated Black Shadows on a Silver Screen (American Documents); The Tenth Level (CBS Playhouse 90) 1976; Good Morning, America 1976; Phil Donahue Show 1976; narrated The Greatest Story Never Told (Bicentennial special) 1976; Black Conversations 1976; co-host, N. Y. Area Emmy Awards 1977.

Theater: Wrote The Big Deal; wrote Alice in Wonder; Joy Exceeding Glory (Harlem) 1941; Jeb 1946; Anna Lucasta (Bway and tour) 1946-47; The Leading Lady 1948; Stevedore (ELT) 1949; The Smile of the World 1949; The Wisteria Trees 1950; The Royal Family (City Center) 1951; The Green Pastures 1951; Remains to Be Seen 1951; Touchstone 1953; stage manager of The World of Sholom Aleichem 1954-55; No Time for Sergeants 1955; The Wisteria Trees (City Center) 1955; Jamaica 1957; replaced Sidney Poitier in A Raisin in the Sun 1959; wrote and starred in Purlie Victorious 1961; co-produced and starred in Ballad for Bimshire 1963; wrote Curtain Call, Mr. Aldridge, Sir (O. B.) 1963; The Zulu and the Zayda 1965.

Relationships: Husband of Ruby Dee, actress.

DAVIS, SAMMY, JR.

(Entertainer)

b. December 8, 1925, New York, N. Y.

Special Interests: Acting, dancing, singing, impressions, producing.

Awards: NAACP Spingarn Medal 1968; The Achievement Freedom Award; Photoplay Gold Medal Award; Knight of Malta; Grand Prix for TV commercial (Cannes Film Festival) 1974; Black Filmmakers Hall of Fame 1974.

Career Data: Vaudeville appearances (with Will Mastin Trio) 1930-48; formed his own production companies (Sammy Davis Enterprises, Altovise Productions).

Clubs: Big Charlie's; Bill Miller's Riviera (N. J.), Coconut Grove (L. A.), Harrah's (Tahoe and Reno), Front Row (Cleveland), Tropicana, Slapsie Maxie's (Hollywood) 1946, Last Frontier (Las Vegas) 1954, Ciro's (Hollywood) 1955, Copa City (Miami) 1955, Caesar's Palace (Las Vegas) 1974, Deauville (Miami) 1975, Latin Casino (Cherry Hill, N. J.).

Films: Rufus Jones for President (debut) 1931; Season's Greetings 1931; The Benny Goodman Story 1956; Anna Lucasta, Sportin'

Life in Porgy and Bess 1959; Pepe, Ocean's Eleven 1960; Sergeants Three, Convicts Four 1962; Of Love and Desire (sang
title song), Johnny Cool, The Threepenny Opera 1963; Robin
and the Seven Hoods 1964; A Man Called Adam 1966; Salt and
Pepper 1968; Sweet Charity, If It's Tuesday, This Must Be
Belgium (cameo) 1969; produced and acted in One More Time
1970; Save the Children 1973.

Memberships: Friars Club; American Society of Magazine Photo-
graphers; Operation PUSH; United Negro College Fund.

Publications: Yes I Can (autobiography), Farrar Straus & Giroux,
1965.

Records: For Decca: Hey There 1954; Something's Gotta Give 1955;
That Old Black Magic 1955; For Reprise: What Kind of Fool
Am I 1962; As Long As She Needs Me 1963; I've Gotta Be Me
1968. For M. G. M. : Candy Man 1972; That's Entertainment;
Mr. Bojangles; Mr. Wonderful.

Television: Hollywood Palace; Ed Sullivan's Toast of the Town;
Three's Company (pilot with Will Mastin Trio) 1954; Colgate
Comedy Hour 1957; G. E. Theater 1958; Zane Grey Theater
1959; G. E. Theater; Lawman 1961; Frontier Circus; Hennesey;
Dick Powell Theater; Rifleman 1962; Ben Casey 1963; Will the
Real Sammy Davis Stand Up (Patty Duke Show) 1965; Sammy
Davis Jr. Show (series); Alice in Wonderland (voice); Wild,
Wild West 1966; I Dream of Jeannie; Danny Thomas Show 1967;
Mod Squad; The Pigeon; Beverly Hillbillies 1969; Mod Squad;
Name of the Game 1970; The Trackers 1971; What's My Line?;
The Movie Game; Hollywood Squares; NBC Follies (special);
Kup's Show; Black Journal; All in the Family; Make Room for
Daddy; Lucy Show; Courtship of Eddie's Father; Laugh-In; Merv
Griffin Show; 1974 Las Vegas Awards from Caesar's Palace;
James Dean (Wide World Special) 1974; Love of Life 1975;
Oscar Awards Show (co-emcee) 1975; Gladys Knight and the
Pips (variety) 1975; Tattletales 1975; Carol Burnett Show 1975;
People's Choice Awards 1975; Sammy and Company (series)
1975; Phil Donahue Show 1975; Chico and the Man 1975; Baretta
(theme song) 1975; Dinah! 1975; Entertainer of the Year Awards
1975; Tonight Show 1975; Bob Hope Show; Manischewitz Wine
commercial 1975; Second Annual Comedy Awards 1976; Bob
Hope Bicentennial Special 1976; America Salutes Richard Rodgers: The Sound of His Music 1976.

Theater: Minsky's (Burlesque) 1930; Desperate Hours (stock); Mr.
Wonderful 1956-57; Golden Boy 1964; Sammy on Broadway
(Uris Theater) 1975; Personal appearances at Garden State
Arts Center; Nanuet Theater; Felt Forum; Mill Run Theater
(Chicago); Palace (Columbus Ohio); Capital Theatre; Carnegie
Hall 1976.

Relationships: Son of Sammy Davis Sr. and Elvira "Baby" Sanchez,
entertainers; nephew of Will Mastin, entertainer; husband of
Altovise Gore, singer/actress.

DAVY, GLORIA
(Opera Singer)
b. March 29, 1931, Brooklyn, N. Y.

Education: Juilliard School of Music BS.
Address: c/o S. A. Gorlinsky, 35 Dover Street, London W1, Eng-
land.
Honors: Marian Anderson award 1951; Marian Anderson Special
award 1952; Music Education League, N. Y. C. award 1953.
Career Data: Operatic roles include: Bess in Porgy and Bess,
Leonora in Il Trovatore, Aida, Cio Cio San in Madame Butter-
fly, Nedda in Il Pagliacci, Pamina in The Magic Flute among
others; toured Europe 1955-56.
Television: Camera Three.
Theater: Sang at Town Hall (debut) 1954; Metropolitan Opera House;
Carnegie Hall; La Scala (Milan); Vienna State Opera; Nice
Opera 1957; Stuttgart Opera House; Covent Garden (London)
1958; Vienna State Opera 1959; San Carlo Opera (Naples);
Teatro Communale (Bologna); Teatro Massimo (Palermo);
Teatre Reggio (Parma); Deutsche Oper (Berlin) 1962-64.

DAWN, MARPESSA
(Actress)
b. 1935, Pittsburgh, Pa.
Films: Black Orpheus, The Woman Eater 1959.
Theater: Cherie Noire (Paris); Hotel de La Nuit Qui Tombe (a. k. a.
Nightfall Hotel), The Boss Woman (pre-London tour) 1962; Le
Jardin Des Delices 1969; Beckett's Waiting for Godot (O. B.)
1974.

DAWSON, WILLIAM LEVI
(Composer/Conductor)
b. September 23, 1898, Anniston, Ala.
Education: Tuskegee Institute 1914-21; Washburn College (Topeka
Kansas) 1921-22; Chicago Musical College; Horner Institute of
Fine Arts B. Mus. 1925; American Conservatory (Chicago)
M. A. Mus. 1927.
Special Interests: Trombone, arranging.
Honors: Alabama Arts Hall of Fame 1975.
Career Data: First trombonist, Chicago Symphony orchestra 1926-
30; Director, School of Music and Choir, Tuskegee Institute
1931-55; trained choral groups in Spain for U. S. State Dept.;
conducted Birmingham (Alabama) Symphony Orchestra 1976.
Musical Compositions: I Couldn't Hear Nobody Pray 1921; Jump
Back Henry Jump Back 1922; Talk About a Child That Do Love
Jesus 1925; Negro Folk Symphony No. 1, 1934.

DEAN, PHILLIP HAYES
(Playwright)
b. Chicago, Ill.
Address: 403 West 57 Street, New York, N. Y. 10019.
Honors: Drama Desk Award 1971.
Career Data: Organized Tucon Public Theatre.
Television: Wrote Johnny Ghost 1969.

Theater: Wrote: The Collapse of the Great I Am; The Bird of
Dawning Singeth All Night Long (one act) 1968; Every Night
When the Sun Goes Down 1969; An American Night Cry (trilogy
including The Minstrel Boy, The Thunder in the Index, An
American Night Cry) 1971; Freeman 1971; Sty of the Blind Pig
1971; The Owl Killer 1971; Rip Off 1974; Relationship.

DE ANDA, PETER
(Actor)
b. March 10, 1940, Pittsburgh, Pa.
Education: Actors Workshop.
Special Interests: Playwriting.
Career Data: Worked at Pittsburgh Playhouse.
Films: Lady Liberty 1971, The New Centurions, Come Back Charles-
ton Blue 1972.
Memberships: AEA.
Television: One Life to Live 1971; title role in Cutter 1972; Cannon
1975; Joe Forrester 1976; Police Woman 1976.
Theater: The Blacks (O. B.) 1963; Ulysses in Night Town (O. B.)
1964; The Dutchman (O. B.) 1964; The Zulu and the Zayda
(Bway debut) 1965; The Kitchen (O. B.) 1966; wrote Ladies in
Waiting 1968 (performed in 1974 by Alonzo Players at Billie
Holiday Theatre, Brooklyn); The Guide (O. B.) 1968; Passing
Through from Exotic Places (O. B.) 1969; The House of Leather
(O. B.) 1970; A Sound of Silence (O. B.).

DEE, RUBY (Ruby Ann Wallace)
(Actress)
b. October 27, 1923, Cleveland, Ohio.
Education: Hunter College B. A. 1945; studied acting with Morris
Carnovsky 1958-60; Paul Mann; Lloyd Richards; at actors work-
shop.
Special Interests: Writing, music, black history and culture, civil
rights.
Address: 44 Cortlandt Avenue, New Rochelle, N. Y. 10801.
Honors: Frederick Douglass N. Y. Urban League Award 1970; Obie
(for Boesman and Lena) 1971; Actors Equity Assn. Paul Robe-
son Citation 1975; Black Filmmakers Hall of Fame 1975.
Career Data: Worked at American Negro Theatre 1941-44; member
Black Scholar Speaker's Bureau; active with Southern Christian
Leadership Conference and Student Non-Violent Coordinating
Committee; appeared in all black cast productions (Arsenic and
Old Lace, John Loves Mary) in 1940s.
Films: Love in Syncopation 1946; The Fight Never Ends, That Man
of Mine, What a Guy 1947; No Way Out, The Jackie Robinson
Story 1950; The Tall Target 1951; Go Man Go! 1954; Edge of
the City 1957; St. Louis Blues 1958; Virgin Island 1960; Take
a Giant Step, A Raisin in the Sun 1961; The Balcony, Gone
Are the Days 1963; The Incident 1967; scripted and acted in
Uptight 1968; cameo role in Black Girl, Buck and the Preacher
1972; Countdown at Kusini 1975.

Memberships: AEA; AFTRA; CORE; NAACP; SAG.
Radio: The Story of Ruby Valentine (series) 1955; title role in This
    Is Norah Drake 1955; The Ossie Davis and Ruby Dee Story
    Hour (series) 1974-76.
Television: The Guiding Light; Actor's Choice (Camera Three) 1960;
    Seven Times (Play of the Week) 1960; Black Monday (Play of
    the Week) 1961; Alcoa Premiere 1962; Express Stop from Lenox
    Avenue (The Nurses) 1963; The Fugitive 1963; Go Down Moses
    (Great Adventure); No Hiding Place (East Side, West Side) 1963;
    Defenders 1965; Look Up and Live 1966; Peyton Place (series)
    1968; Deadlock 1969; The Sheriff 1971; A Holiday Celebration
    1971; To Be Young, Gifted and Black (N. E. T. Playhouse) 1972;
    Tenafly 1973; On Being Black (series); Wedding Band 1974;
    Ruth Campanella in It's Good to Be Alive 1974; Police Woman
    1974; Positively Black 1975; The People 1975; narrated Foster
    Care (New York Illustrated) 1976; Anyone for Tennyson? 1976;
    Good Morning America 1976; Phil Donahue Show 1976; Black
    Conversations 1976; Union Carbide commercial; co-host N. Y.
    Area Emmy Awards 1977; The Fight Against Slavery 1977.
Theater: South Pacific (debut) 1943; Three's a Family (ANT) 1943;
    Walk Hard (ANT) 1944; Jeb 1946; On Striver's Row (ANT)
    1946; title role in Anna Lucasta (tour) 1946-1947; Long Way
    from Home 1948; Smile of the World 1949; Alice in Wonder
    (O. B.) 1952; The World of Sholom Aleichem (O. B.) 1953; Ruth
    Younger in A Raisin in the Sun 1959; Lutiebelle in Purlie Vic-
    torious 1961; Taming of the Shrew (ASF) 1965; Boesman and
    Lena (O. B.) 1970; Tell Pharaoh (O. B.) 1972; Wedding Band
    (O. B.) 1973; Queen Gertrude in Hamlet 1975.
Relationships: Wife of Ossie Davis, actor/playwright/director.

DE LAVALLADE, CARMEN (Carmen Paula de Lavallade)
    (Dancer/Actress)
b.   March 6, 1931, Los Angeles, Calif.
Education: Los Angeles City College 1950-52; studied acting with
    Stella Adler, singing with Carlo Menotti.
Special Interests: Singing.
Address: 215 West 92 Street, New York, N. Y. 10025.
Career Data: Lester Horton Dance Co. 1950-54; Metropolitan Opera
    Co. (Premier danseuse) 1955-56; John Butler Dance Co. at
    The Festival of Two Worlds (Spoleto) 1958; asst. dir., U. S.
    State Dept. tour of South East Asia with de Lavallade-Ailey
    Dance Co. 1962; soloist Donald McKayle Co. 1963; numerous
    appearances at Jacob's Pillow Dance Festival, Mass. ; prof.
    and member, Repertory Theatre, Yale University.
Clubs: Ciro's (Hollywood) 1953; Coconut Grove (L. A.) 1958; Fla-
    mingo Hotel (Las Vegas) 1961.
Films: The Golden Hawk 1950; Lydia Bailey 1952; The Egyptian,
    Demetrius and the Gladiators 1954, Carmen Jones 1954; Kitty
    in Odds Against Tomorrow 1959.
Memberships: AEA; AFTRA; AGMA; SAG.
Television: Bob Herridge Theatre 1956; A Drum is a Woman 1956;
    Amahl and the Night Visitors; Look Up and Live 1959; The

Gershwin Years 1961; Lamp Unto My Feet 1965; Evening at
Pops; Dance for Camera 1976.
Theater: Danced as Salome (L. A.) 1950; Yerma and Salome (YMHA)
1952; Carmen in House of Flowers 1954; danced in Aida and
Samson et Dalila (Metropolitan Opera) 1956; Impulse (pre-
Bway) 1961; danced Cocaine Lil and the Comet in Ballet Bal-
lads (O. B.) 1961; Iram and Rami in Hot Spot 1963; Naomi in
The Chanukkah Festival (Madison Square Garden) 1963; Girl
in Reflections in the Park 1964; appeared with Josephine Baker
and Her Company 1964; The Four Marys (American Ballet
Theatre) 1965; Tally-Ho (a. k. a. The Frail Quarry) (American
Ballet Theatre) 1965; Titania in Midsummer Night's Dream;
and Molière's Don Juan (Yale University) 1975; Countee Cullen
Great Storytelling Services (Afro-American Total Theatre)
1975; General Gorgeous (Yale University) 1976; Les Chansons
de Bilitis (N. Y. Dance Festival, NYSF) 1976.
Relationships: Wife of Geoffrey Holder, dancer/choreographer;
cousin of Janet Collins, dancer/choreographer.

DE PAUR, LEONARD
        (Conductor)
b.   1919, Summit, N. J.
Education: Juilliard School of Music.
Special Interests: Arranging, composing, directing, producing.
Address: 746 St. Nicholas Avenue, New York, N. Y. 10031.
Honors: Harold Jackman Memorial award.
Career Data: Community Relations Director, Lincoln Center 1971-
        date; produced First (1971) and Second (1972) annual Lincoln
        Center Community Street Theater Festival; organized Lincoln
        Center's International Choral Festival; directed De Paur In-
        fantry Chorus 1946-57; organized Infantry Glee Club in Army
        during 1943-45; musical director for Federal Theatre Project
        1936-39; directed Hall Johnson Choir 1932-36.
Films: Led chorus in Winged Victory 1944.
Records: Songs of New Nations (Mercury); Swing Low Sweet Chariot
        (RCA); On Columbia: Latin American Songs; Choral Caravan;
        A Choral Concert (Songs of Faith); Work Songs and Spirituals.
Television: Positively Black 1975.
Theater: Composed or arranged and directed music for Orson
        Welles' Macbeth, Haiti and Eugene O'Neill's 4 plays of the
        Sea 1936; directed choral work for John Henry 1940; com-
        posed music for Speak of the Devil (O. B.); directed chorus
        for Winged Victory 1943; choral director for Four Saints in
        Three Acts 1952; choral director for Carmen Jones (City Cen-
        ter) 1956; organized De Paur's Opera Gala at Carnegie Hall
        1957; conducted Orchestra of America at Philharmonic Hall
        1964.

DE PRIEST, JAMES
        (Musician/Conductor)
b.   November 21, 1936, Philadelphia, Pa.

Education: University of Pennsylvania B. A., M. A. 1961; Phila-
delphia Conservatory of Music 1959-61.
Special Interests: Composing.
Honors: First prize gold medal, Dimitri Mitropoulos International
Music competition for conductors 1964.
Career Data: Appearances with orchestras: Stockholm Symphony,
Boston Symphony, Chicago Symphony, Philadelphia Orchestra,
Cleveland Orchestra; music director, Contemporary Music
Guild, Philadelphia 1959-62; American specialist in music, U.
S. State Dept. 1962-63; conductor-in-residence, Bangkok,
Thailand 1963-64; music director, summer music program of
Westchester County 1965, 1966; asst. conductor to Leonard
Bernstein, N. Y. Philharmonic Orchestra 1965-66; guest con-
ductor Rotterdam Symphony 1969; assoc. conductor, National
Symphony Orchestra (Wash. D. C.) 1972-75; director, Quebec
Symphony Orchestra 1976.
Musical Compositions: Vision of America (ballet score) 1960; Ten-
drils 1961; A Sprig of Lilac 1964; Requiem (concert) 1965.
Records: On Delos: De Priest Conducts Mozart.
Television: Music director, WCAU (Philadelphia) 1965-66; Sunday
1975.
Theater: Appearance at Avery Fisher Hall 1975.
Relationships: Nephew of Marian Anderson, concert singer/opera
singer.

DESTINE, JEAN-LEON (Leon Destiné)
(Dancer/Choreographer)
b. March 26, 1928, St. Marc, Haiti.
Education: Ethnological Institute (Haiti) 1941-42; Lycee Petion (Haiti)
1940-43.
Special Interests: Teaching, directing.
Address: 676 Riverside Drive, New York, N. Y. 10031.
Honors: Rockefeller Foundation Scholarship 1944-46; Chevalier
Honneur et Mérite 1951; Venice and Edinburgh Film Festivals
1952; Officier de L'ordre National Honneur et Mérite 1958;
Cultural attache-for Haiti in U. S. 1960; Award of Merit (Haitian-
American Citizens Society, Inc.) 1970; Award of Merit (Haitian-
American Artists Society, Inc.) 1975.
Career Data: Teaches at New Dance Group Studio; formed his own
Afro-Haitian Dance Company; performed at Belasco, Roxy,
Madison Square Garden and City Center Theatres; performed
in Bal Nègre (with Dunham troupe) 1946; soloist and choreo-
grapher for Troubled Island (City Center) 1949; performed at
Jacob's Pillow Dance Festival 1949-61.
Clubs: Café Society Uptown; Martinique; Basin Street.
Films: Witch Doctor; Cantiones Unidas (Mexico) 1957.
Memberships: Association of American Dance Companies.
Records: Festival in Haiti (Elektra) 1954.
Television: Ed Sullivan Show; Merv Griffin Show; Eddie Albert Show;
Frank Sinatra (special).

DETT, ROBERT NATHANIEL
    (Composer)
b.   October 11, 1882, Drummondville, Quebec, Canada.
d.   October 2, 1943, Battle Creek, Mich.
Education: Oberlin College B. Mus. 1908; Harvard University 1920-
    21; Eastman School of Music M. M. ; Columbia University; Uni-
    versity of Pennsylvania; American Conservatory of Music (Chi-
    cago); Oliver Willis Halstead Conservatory (Lockport, N. Y.).
Special Interests: Arranging, conducting.
Honors: Harmon Foundation award, Palm and Ribbon award, Royal
    Belgian Band; Harvard Bowdoin Prize 1920; Frances Batt Prize
    for Composition.
Career Data: Director of Music, Lane College (Jackson, Tenn.)
    1908-11 and Lincoln Institute (Jefferson, Mo.) 1911-13; direc-
    tor of music and conductor of choir, Hampton Institute 1913-
    35; director of music, Bennett College 1937; director USO
    chorus 1943; founder, Musical Art Society.
Memberships: ASCAP 1925
Musical Compositions: Drink to Me Only with Thine Eyes; Folk
    Songs of the South; Don't Be Weary; Traveler; Listen to the
    Lambs; Juba Dance; I'll Never Turn Back No More; Magic
    Moon of Molten Gold; A Thousand Years or More; After the
    Cakewalk March Cakewalk; Barcarolle; Magnolia Suite 1912;
    Music in the Mine 1916; The Chariot Jubilee 1921; Enchant-
    ment Suite 1922; In the Bottoms Suite 1926; Cinnamon Grove
    Suite 1928; The Ordering of Moses 1937; Tropic Suite 1938;
    Noon Siesta; A Bayou Garden; To a Closed Casement; Legend
    of the Atoll; Negro Folk Songs.
Publications: Religious Folksongs of the Negro, 1926; The Dett
    Collection of Negro Spirituals, 4v. , 1937.

DIDDLEY, BO (Elias McDaniels)
    (Musician)
b.   December 30, 1928, McComb, Miss.
Special Interests: Guitar, composing.
Address: Los Lunas, N. Mex. 87031.
Clubs: 708 Club (Chicago) 1951; Max's Kansas City 1977.
Films: The Big T. N. T. Show 1966; Let the Good Times Roll 1973.
Musical Compositions: Uncle John.
Records: For Checker: Bo Diddley/I'm a Man 1955; Diddley Daddy
    1955; I'm Sorry 1959; Crackin Up 1959; Say Man 1959; Say
    Man; Say Man; Back Again 1959; Road Runner 1960; You Can't
    Judge a Book by the Cover 1962; Ooh Babe 1967; Boss Man;
    Black Gladiator; ... and Company; Bo Diddley; 500% More Man;
    Go; Gunslinger; Have Guitar; In the Spotlight; Lover; Originator;
    16 Hits; Great Guitars; 20th Anniversary (RCA); Another Dimen-
    sion (Chess); Bag of Tricks (Chess); London Sessions (Chess);
    Where It All Began (Chess); Big Bad Bo (Chess).
Television: Midnight Special 1975.
Theater: Appeared at Apollo Theatre; Nanuet Theatre-Go-Round
    1974; Rock & Roll Revival Spectacular 1974; Madison Square
    Garden 1975; Radio City Music Hall 1975.

DILLARD, WILLIAM
(Actor/Musician)
b. Philadelphia, Pa.
Career Data: Played trumpet with bands of Chick Webb, Benny Car-
ter, Lucky Millinder, Coleman Hawkins, Teddy Wilson and
Louis Armstrong.
Memberships: AEA.
Television: Joe the bartender in Love of Life (series); Arthur God-
frey's Talent Scouts; Easy Does It; King of Babylon in The
Green Pastures.
Theater: A Temporary Island (O. B.); Carmen Jones 1943; Memphis
Bound 1945; Beggars Holiday 1946; Anna Lucasta 1947; The
Power of Darkness (O. B.) 1948; Regina 1949; The Green Pas-
tures 1951; My Darlin' Aida 1952; Shuffle Along 1952; Crown
in Porgy and Bess 1964.

DITON, CARL (Rossini)
(Composer/Pianist)
b. October 30, 1886, Philadelphia, Pa.
d. January 25, 1962, New York, N. Y.
Education: University of Pennsylvania 1909; Julliard School of
Music; Columbia University Ph. D. (music).
Special Interests: Singing, teaching.
Honors: Harmon Award 1929.
Career Data: Organized National Association of Musicians; director
of music, Paine College (Georgia), Wiley College (Texas), Tal-
ladega College (Alabama) 1911-18; instructor of concert piano,
Juilliard School of Music.
Musical Compositions: Four Spirituals 1914; The Hymn of Nebraska
(Oratorio) 1921.

DIXON, DEAN (Charles)
(Musician/Conductor)
b. January 10, 1915, New York, N. Y.
d. November 3, 1976, Zurich, Switzerland.
Education: Juilliard School of Music B. S. 1936; Columbia University
Teachers College M. A. 1939.
Special Interests: Violin.
Honors: ASCAP award of merit 1945; Newspaper Guild Page One
award 1945; Lincoln Steffens Lodge award for outstanding mu-
sicianship 1945; Alice M. Ditson award as outstanding conductor of the year 1948.
Career Data: Founder, Dean Dixon Symphony Society and Dean Dixon
Choral Society 1932; teacher of conducting, Juilliard 1948-49;
conducted chamber orchestra of League of Music Lovers 1937;
guest conductor, NBC Summer Symphony Orchestra 1941; conducted Shoestring Opera Co. 1943; organized American Youth
Orchestra 1944; conductor, N. Y. Philharmonic Orchestra 1948;
conducted Radiodiffusion Française, Paris 1949; conductor, Göte-
borg Symphony Orchestra 1953-60; head conductor, Hessicher
Rundfunk (Radio & TV) Symphony orchestra, Frankfurt, Germany

1961-64; head conductor Mozarteum Salzburg 1962; conductor,
Dutch Radio Society (Hilversuim) 1963; music director, Sydney
Symphony orchestra, Australia 1964-67; guest conductor in
Israel, Japan, South America, Mexico and throughout Europe
and U. S.; originator, Music for Millions Concerts; conducted
for American Negro Ballet Co.
Memberships: N. Y. Violin Teachers Guild.
Records: Gershwin (Everest).
Theater: Conducted for John Henry (musical) 1940; appeared as
conductor at Carnegie Hall, Lewisohn Stadium, Town Hall.

DIXON, IVAN N. III
(Actor/Director)
b. April 6, 1931, New York, N. Y.
Education: North Carolina College B. A. (Political Science), Western
Reserve University.
Address: 2345 Hanning Avenue, Altadena, Calif. 91002.
Films: Something of Value 1957; Porgy and Bess 1959; A Raisin
in the Sun 1961; Nothing But a Man 1964; A Patch of Blue
1965; To Trap a Spy 1966; Suppose They Gave a War and No-
body Came 1970; Clay Pigeon, directed Trouble Man 1972;
produced and directed Spook Who Sat by the Door 1973; Car
Wash 1976.
Television: Chain Reaction; Big Story; Armstrong Circle Theater;
Studio One; Arrowsmith (Dupont Show of the Month) 1960; Twi-
light Zone 1960, 1964; Have Gun, Will Travel 1961; Cain's
Hundred 1962; Target Corruptors 1962; Alcoa Presents; The
Eleventh Hour; Dr. Kildare 1962; Laramie 1962; Defenders
1963, 1965; Stoney Burke 1963; Perry Mason 1963; Outer
Limits 1963, 1964; Great Adventures 1964; The New Breed;
The Man from U. N. C. L. E. 1964; Fugitive 1964, 1967; I Spy
1965; Kinchloe in Hogan's Heroes (series) 1965-1968; Felony
Squad 1967; Ironside 1967; directed episode The Bill Cosby
Show; directed episode Julia; It Takes a Thief 1969; Name of
the Game 1968; Mod Squad 1970; F. B. I. 1970; Love, American
Style 1971; Fer-de-Lance 1974; directed episode Get Christie
Love; directed episode Apples Way; directed episode The Wal-
tons; The Sty of the Blind Pig; directed episode Khan! 1975;
directed "The Bait" episode Starsky and Hutch 1976; directed
episode McCloud 1976.
Theater: Karamu House (Cleveland); Wedding in Japan 1957; The
Cave Dwellers 1957; Asagai in A Raisin in the Sun 1959.

DOBBS, MATTIWILDA
(Opera Singer)
b. July 11, 1925, Atlanta, Ga.
Education: Spelman College (Atlanta) B. A. 1946; Teachers College;
Columbia University M. A. 1948; Mannes College of Music
1948-49; studied voice with Lotte Lehmann 1946-50; French
music with Pierre Bernac (Paris) 1950-52.
Address: c/o Joanne Rile Management 119 N. 18th Street, Philadelphia, Pa. 19103.

ELMER E. RASMUSON LIBRARY
UNIVERSITY OF ALASKA

Honors: Marian Anderson award 2nd prize 1947; John Hay Whitney
        Fellowship 1950; International Music Performers Competition
        1st prize Geneva Conservatory of Music 1951; Order of the
        North Star (Sweden) 1954.
Career Data: Dutch Opera, Holland Festival 1952; recitals and con-
        certs in Europe, Scandinavia 1953-54; U. S. 1954; Australia
        1955, 1959, 1972; Israel 1957, 1959; U. S. S. R. 1959; professor
        of voice, University of Texas (Austin) 1973-74, professor of
        music, University of Illinois at Urbana-Champaign 1975; reper-
        toire includes Role of Zerbinetta in Ariadne auf Naxos; El-
        vira in L'Italiana in Algeri; Olympia in Tales of Hoffman;
        Gilda in Rigoletto; Queen of the Night in The Magic Flute;
        the Queen in Le Coq d'Or.
Memberships: Metropolitan Opera Assn. 1957.
Records: The Pearl Fishers; Zaide.
Theater: Bolshoi Theatre (U. S. S. R.); Covent Garden (London) 1953;
        Municipal Hall (Atlanta) 1952; La Scala (Milan) 1953; Town Hall
        (debut) 1954; San Francisco Opera House (debut) 1955; Metro-
        politan Opera House (debut) 1956; Hamburg State Opera 1961-
        62.

DOBSON, TAMARA
        (Actress)
b.   1947, Baltimore, Md.
Education: Maryland Institute of Art B. F. A.
Special Interests: Modeling, karate.
Address: 100 West 57 Street, New York, N. Y. 10019.
Films: Fuzz, Come Back Charleston Blue 1972; title role in Cleo-
        patra Jones 1973; Cleopatra Jones and the Casino of Gold 1975;
        Norman, Is That You? 1976.
Television: Black Journal 1974; Dinah! 1975; Mike Douglas Show
        1977.

DODSON, OWEN (Vincent)
        (Playwright)
b.   November 28, 1914, Brooklyn, N. Y.
Education: Bates College B. A. 1936; Yale University M. F. A. 1939.
Special Interests: Directing, poetry.
Honors: General Education Board Fellowship 1938, 1939; Maxwell
        Anderson Verse Play Contest Winner, Stanford University
        1940; Rosenwald Fellowship 1944; Guggenheim Fellowship 1953;
        2nd Prize, Paris Review short story contest 1955; AUDELCO
        Black Theatre Outstanding Pioneer Award 1975.
Career Data: Directed drama: Atlanta University 1938-42, Spel-
        man College 1938-42; Howard University, director of Howard
        Players since 1947, chairman and professor of Drama Dept.
        since 1960; co-founder and member, Negro Ensemble Co.
Memberships: AETA; ANTA.
Theater: Authored: Americus; Black Mother Saying; Climbing to
        the Soul; Don't Give Up the Ship; Lord Nelson, Naval Hero;
        Jonathan's Song; Old Ironsides; Including Laughter 1936;

Gargoyles in Florida 1936; Divine Comedy 1938; The Garden
of Time 1939; Amistad 1939; The Southern Star 1940; Dooms-
day Tale 1941; Everybody Join Hands 1942; Someday We're
Gonna Tear the Pillars Down 1942; Freedom the Banner 1942;
The Ballad of Dorie Miller 1942; New World A-Coming 1944;
Bayou Legend 1946; The Third Fourth of July (with Countee
Cullen) 1946; The Christmas Miracle 1955; Till Victory Is Won
(Opera with Mark Fax) 1967; Owen's Song 1974.   Directed:
Mamba's Daughters (Howard Players European Tour) 1949;
The Amen Corner (Howard University) 1954; Countee Cullen's
Medea in Africa 1963.

DOMINO, FATS (Antoine Domino)
     (Singer)
b.   February 26, 1928, New Orleans, La.
Special Interests: Composing.
Honors: 21 gold records.
Career Data: Newport Jazz Festival 1976.
Clubs: Flamingo (Las Vegas); The Hideaway (New Orleans); Copa
     (Brooklyn).
Films: Shake, Rattle and Roll 1956; Jamboree 1957; Let the Good
     Times Roll 1973.
Musical Compositions: I'm Walkin'; Blueberry Hill.
Records: Very Best (United Artists); My Blue Heaven (Pickwick);
     Fats Domino (Pickwick); Million Settlers by Fats.   On Imperial:
     The Fat Man 1950; Ain't It a Shame 1955; Poor Me 1955; Blue
     Monday 1956; Bo-Weevil 1956; I'm in Love Again 1956; Blue-
     berry Hill 1956; I'm Walkin' 1957; Whole Lotta Loving 1958;
     Natural Born Lover 1960; I Hear You Knocking 1961; Jam-
     balaya 1961.   On ABC: Red Sails in the Sunset 1963; Heart-
     break Hill 1964.
Television: American Bandstand; Midnight Special 1974; Merv Grif-
     fin Show 1975.
Theater: Appeared at Apollo Theatre; Westbury Music Theatre 1975;
     Academy of Music 1975; Sam Houston Coliseum (Texas) 1975;
     Radio City Music Hall 1976; Madison Square Garden 1976.

DONALDSON, NORMA
     (Singer/Actress)
b.   New York, N.Y.
Education: Studied acting with Gabriel Dell.
Special Interests: Dancing.
Career Data: Singing tour with John Davidson Company and E.Y.
     Harburg Concerts.
Films: Across 110th Street 1972; Willie Dynamite 1974.
Memberships: AEA; NAG.
Television: Good Times; The Jeffersons; Joe Franklin Show; Midday
     Live 1976.
Theater: A Quarter for the Ladies Room (O.B.); Until the Monkey
     Comes (O.B.); Clara in The Great White Hope; Missy in Pur-
     lie; Bianca in Kiss Me, Kate; Eve in No Place to be Somebody;

Clytemnestra in The Flies; Miss Adelaide in Guys and Dolls 1976.

DONEGAN, DOROTHY
(Pianist)
b.   April 6, 1924, Chicago, Ill.
Education: Chicago Conservatory; Chicago Music College 1942-44; University of Southern California 1953-54.
Special Interests: Composing.
Address: 745 Fifth Avenue, New York, N. Y. 10022.
Career Data: Appeared at Newport Jazz Festival 1974.
Clubs: Zanzibar 1944; Embers 1954; Jimmy Weston's 1974-76.
Films: Sensations of 1945.
Musical Compositions: Piano Boogie 1939; Kilroy Was Here 1947; DDT Blues 1953.
Records: The Feminine Touch (Decca).
Television: Sunday 1975.
Theater: Appearances at Orchestral Hall (Chicago) 1942; Chicago Stadium 1943; Star Time 1945; Town Hall 1975; Carnegie Hall 1975.

DOQUI, ROBERT
(Actor)
Career Data: Chairman, Ethnic Minorities Committee, Screen Actors Guild 1971.
Films: The Cincinnati Kid 1965; The Fortune Cookie 1966; Uptight 1968; The Devil's Eight 1969; Deadly Silence 1970; Soul Soldier 1971; The Man 1972; Coffy 1973; Walking Tall-Pt. 2, Nashville 1975; Buffalo Bill and the Indians or Sitting Bull's History Lesson, Treasure of Matecumbe 1976.
Memberships: SAG.
Television: Harlem Globetrotters (Cartoon voice); Ironside; Name of the Game; I Dream of Jeannie; Insight; Happy Days; Kolchak; A Dream for Christmas 1973; Adam-12 1975; Sanford and Son 1975; Six Million Dollar Man 1975; Blue Knight 1976.

DORSEY, THOMAS ANDREW "Father of Gospel Music"
(Musician/Composer)
b.   July 1, 1899, Villa Rica, Ga.
Special Interests: Blues, gospel, singing, arranging.
Career Data: Co-organized National Convention of Gospel Choirs and Choruses 1932; founder, Dorsey House of Music, Chicago 1932; performed with Ma Rainey; toured with Mahalia Jackson 1939-44; led group The Whispering Syncopaters; a. k. a. "Barrelhouse Tom" and "Georgia Tom. "
Musical Compositions: Composed and/or arranged approximately 800 songs including: Precious Lord; If You See My Savior 1926; How About You?; There'll Be Peace in the Valley; Hold Me; Life Can Be Beautiful; If You Ever Needed the Lord Before; I'll Tell It Wherever I Go; Broken Hearted Blues; Broken Soul Blues; My Desire; When I've Done My Best; Let Us Work

Together-Let Us Sing Together; In the Scheme of Things;
Watching and Waiting; Search Me, Lord; Say a Little Prayer
for Me; Rain on the Ocean; Rain on the Deep Blue Sea.
Theater: Appeared in Temple Theatre (Cleveland); Carnegie Hall
(Newport Jazz Festival) 1975.

DOWDY, HELEN
(Singer/Actress)
b. New York, N. Y.
Education: Teachers College, Columbia University; studied with Eva
Jessye.
Memberships: AEA; NAG.
Theater: Scarlet Sister Mary (debut) 1930; Rhapsody in Black 1931;
Mamba's Daughters 1939; Cabin in the Sky 1940; Strawberry
woman in Porgy and Bess 1942, 1953; Run Little Chillun 1943;
Tropical Revue 1943-44; Memphis Bound 1945; Tobacco Road
(black cast); Queenie in Show Boat 1946, Four Saints in Three
Acts 1952; By the Beautiful Sea 1954; Mrs. Patterson 1954;
Kiss Me, Kate.

DOWNING, DAVID (Leon)
(Actor)
b. July 21, 1943, New York, N. Y.
Education: H. S. of Performing Arts; studied acting at American
Community Theatre with Maxwell Glanville.
Special Interests: Comedy.
Address: 1111 Hacienda Place, West Hollywood, Calif. 90069.
Honors: Best actor, American Community Theatre, 1966.
Career Data: Charter member of Negro Ensemble Co., 1967-69.
Films: Been Down So Long It Looks Like Up to Me 1971; Sounder,
Up the Sandbox 1972; Gordon's War 1973.
Memberships: AEA; AFTRA; SAG.
Television: Day of Absence; Shake and Bake commercial; Sylvania
commercial; Movin' On 1975; Baretta 1975; That's My Mama
1975; All in the Family 1976; Little House on the Prairie 1977.
Theater: The Cool World 1960; God Is a (Guess What?) (NEC) 1968;
Ceremonies in Dark Old Men (NEC) 1969; Mack the Knife in
Threepenny Opera (O. B.) 1972; My Sister, My Sister (O. B.)
1973-1974; Duke of Norfolk in Richard III 1974; Desire Under
the Elms 1974.

DU BOIS, JA'NET (Jeanette Du Bois)
(Actress)
b. August 5, 1938, Philadelphia, Pa.
Education: Hunter College (drama) 1958; studied dance with Alvin
Ailey and Syvilla Fort, acting with Lloyd Richards, Paul Mann,
Gene Frankel, voice with Gian-Carlo Menotti.
Special Interests: Music (guitar, piano), composing, playwriting,
singing.
Films: Love with the Proper Stranger 1963; The World of Henry

Orient 1964; The Pawnbroker 1965; A Man Called Adam 1966; Stormy Monday in Five on the Black Hand Side 1973; A Piece of the Action 1977.

Memberships: AEA; AGVA; SAG.

Musical Compositions: Co-authored Movin' on Up theme for The Jeffersons (television series) 1975.

Television: Naked City; The Defenders; As The World Turns; East Side West Side; Nurse Allen in Love of Life (series); Shaft; The Blue Knight; Resolution of Mossie 1974; Kojak 1974; Wilona on Good Times (series) 197?-date; A Beautiful Killing (Wide World Mystery) 1975; Caribe 1975; Dinah! 1975; Ebony Music Awards 1975; Sammy and Company 1975; Celebrity Sweepstakes 1976; Break the Bank 1976; Tattletales 1976.

Theater: Cab Calloway Revues (tour) 1959; The Long Dream (understudy) 1960; A Raisin in the Sun (understudy) 1960; Nobody Loves an Albatross (understudy) 1963; Jump for Joy (Florida); Golden Boy 1964; wrote unproduced one-act plays: The Peepers, The Sisters.

DUMAS, ALEXANDRE (fils)
    (Playwright)
b. July 27, 1824, Paris, France.
d. November 27, 1895, Marly-Le-Roi.
Honors: Elected to French Academy 1874.
Theater: Wrote La Dame aux Camélias (The Lady of The Camellias, a. k. a. Camille) 1852; Le Demi-Monde 1855; La Question d'Argent (A Question of Money) 1857; Le Fils Naturel 1858; The Ideas of Madame Aubray 1867; The Wife of Claude 1873; Denise 1885; Francillon 1887.

DUNCAN, TODD (Robert Todd Duncan)
    (Concert Singer)
b. February 12, 1903, Danville, Ky.
Education: Butler University B. A. 1925; Columbia University M. A. 1930; Howard University Ph. D. (music) 1938.
Special Interests: Acting, teaching.
Address: 1600 Upshur Street, N. W. Washington, D. C. 20011.
Honors: White House concert for Pres. Franklin D. Roosevelt 1935; Medal of Honor and Merit, Haiti 1945; Donaldson award and N. Y. Drama Critics award (for Lost in the Stars) 1950.
Career Data: Professor, Howard University 1931-45; more than 1500 concert appearances in U. S. , Europe, Australia and South America since 1944; Soloist with Symphonies: Philadelphia, St. Louis, Los Angeles, N. B. C. , B. B. C. and National; N. Y. City Center Opera Co. 1945; soloist, Beethoven's Ninth Symphony with N. Y. Philharmonic Orchestra 1946.
Films: Syncopation 1942; Unchained 1955.
Memberships: NAG.
Records: Porgy in Porgy and Bess (Decca).
Theater: Lewisohn Stadium (annual Gershwin concert); Alfio in Cavalleria Rusticana (debut) 1934; Porgy and Bess 1935, (Calif.

tour) 1937, 1942, 1943; The Sun Never Sets (London) 1939;
Cabin in the Sky 1940; Tonio in Pagliacci and Escamillo in
Carmen 1945; Stephan Kumalo in Lost in the Stars 1949; The
Barrier 1951.

DUNHAM, KATHERINE
       (Dancer/Choreographer)
b.   June 22, 1910, Joliet, Ill.
Education: University of Chicago, Ph. B. , M. A. ; Northwestern Uni-
       versity Ph. D.
Special Interests: Anthropology, painting.
Address: c/o Residence Le Clerc, Port Au Prince, Haiti.
Honors: Rosenwald Travel Fellowship (West Indies) 1936-37; Che-
       valier (1950) and Commander (1962) Legion of Honor and
       Merit, Haiti; Honorary Citizen of Haiti 1957; Dance Magazine
       award 1969; Eight Lively Arts award 1969; Black Academy of
       Arts and Letters award 1972; National Center of Afro-American
       artists (Elma Lewis School of Fine Arts) 1972; Black Film-
       makers Hall of Fame award 1973; American Dance Guild an-
       nual award 1975.
Career Data: Performed at Chicago Beaux Arts Ball 1931; 1st
       appearance as a dancer with Chicago, Illinois Opera Co. 1933;
       danced at Chicago World's Fair 1934 and in ballet L'Ag'Ya for
       W. P. A. Federal Theatre Project 1938; supervised City Theatre
       (Chicago) Writer's Project 1939; Dance director of Labor Stage
       (N. Y. C.) 1939-40; formed Dunham School of Cultural Arts
       1943; guest artist, San Francisco Symphony 1943, Los Angeles
       Symphony 1955; producer-director Katherine Dunham Dance
       Company 1945; Artist in Residence and Director of Perform-
       ing Arts Training Center, Southern Illinois University 1966.
Films: Carnival of Rhythm 1942; Star Spangled Rhythm 1942; choreo-
       graphed dances for Pardon My Sarong 1942; Stormy Weather
       1943; Casbah 1948; choreographed Native Son 1951; Botte e
       Risposta 1952; Mambo (Italian) 1955; Musica en la Noche (Mexi-
       can) 1957.
Memberships: AEA; AFTRA; AGMA (Bd. of Gov.); AGVA; ASCAP
       1964; Authors Guild Inc. ; NAG; SAG; Royal Society of Anthro-
       pology.
Musical Compositions: New Love, New Wine; Coco da Mata; dances
       include: Shango Bhahiana, Rites du Passage, Flaming Youth,
       Blues and Ragtime, Burrell House.
Publications: Katherine Dunham's Journey to Accompong, 1946
       (Greenwood Press reprint 1972); A Touch of Innocence, Har-
       court, Brace, World, 1959; Dances of Haiti 1949, 1959; Ode
       to Taylor Jones (a play written with Eugene Redmond), 1967-
       68.
Television: Lee Graham Show 1975; wrote scripts for productions
       in Mexico, France, England, Italy and Australia.
Theater: Pins and Needles 1939; Georgia Brown in Cabin in the
       Sky 1940; Tropics and Le Jazz Hot 1940; Tropical Revue 1943-
       44; appeared at Hollywood Bowl 1943-44; Carib Song 1945;
       choreographed Windy City 1946; Bal Negre 1946; New Tropical

Revue (London, Paris) 1948; Bamboche 1962; choreographed
Aida (Metropolitan Opera House) 1963.

DYSON, RONNIE (Ronald Dyson)
    (Singer)
b.   June 5, 1950, Washington, D. C.
Films: Putney Swope 1969.
Memberships: AEA.
Records: If You Let Me Make Love to You; We Can Make It Last
    Forever; One Man Band (Columbia); The More You Do It
    (Columbia); Why Can't I Touch You (Columbia).
Television: Merv Griffin Show; Soul! 1974; Black Journal 1975.
Theater: Hair 1968; appearance at Billie Holiday Theatre, Brooklyn;
    appearance at Avery Fisher Hall (tribute to Duke Ellington);
    Mill Run Theatre (Chicago) 1976.

ECKSTINE, BILLY "Mr. B" (William Clarence Eckstein)
    (Singer)
b.   July 18, 1914, Pittsburgh, Pa.
Education: Howard University; Shaw University B. A. (music) 1974;
    University of Southern California.
Special Interests: Trombone, acting, composing, conducting.
Address: c/o William Morris Agency, 151 El Camino Drive, Bever-
    ly Hills, Calif. 90212.
Honors: Amateur show winner (Wash. D. C.) 1935; Esquire new
    star award 1946; Down Beat poll winner 1948-52; Metronome
    poll winner 1949-54; voted number 1 crooner 1950.
Career Data: Organized his own band 1943-47; vocalist with Earl
    Hines band 1939-43.
Clubs: Club de Lisa (Chicago); Desert Inn (Las Vegas); Birdland;
    Copacabana; Persian Room-Hotel Plaza 1972, 1975; Caesar's
    Palace (Las Vegas) 1975; Maisonette-Regis Sheraton 1975.
Films: Skirts Ahoy 1952; Let's Do It Again 1975.
Musical Compositions: Jelly Jelly; Stormy Monday Blues; That's
    the Way I Feel.
Radio: The Blue Ribbon Salute 1943; Robbins Nest 1949.
Records: Every Thing I Have Is Yours; Prisoner of Love; I Apolo-
    gize; My Way; Jelly Jelly (Bluebird) 1940; I'm Falling for You
    (Bluebird) 1940; Prime of My Life 1963; For the Love of Ivy
    1968; The Best Thing (A & M) 1976.
Television: Saturday Night at the Apollo; The Jazz Show with Billy
    Eckstine 1972; Sanford and Son 1975; Mike Douglas Show 1975;
    Sammy and Company 1975; Dinah! 1975; Positively Black 1975;
    Saturday Night Live with Howard Cosell 1976; Like It Is 1976;
    Performance at Wolf Trap 1976.
Theater: Appeared at Paramount Theatre; Carnegie Hall; Apollo
    Theatre; Earl Theatre (Philadelphia); Circle Star Theatre (San
    Francisco) 1972; Howard Theatre (Washington, D. C.) 1973;
    Mill Run Theatre (Chicago, Ill.) 1973; Nanuet Star Theatre
    1975; Westbury Music Fair 1975.

EDMONDS, RANDOLPH SHEPPARD "Dean of Black Academic Theatre"
    (Playwright)
b.   1900, Lawrenceville, Va.
Education: Oberlin College; Columbia University; Yale University;
    Dublin University; London School of Speech Training and Dra-
    matic Art.
Career Data: Faculty member, Morgan State College, Dillard Uni-
    versity, Florida A & M University (chairman, Theatre Arts
    Dept. 23 years); organized Negro Inter-Collegiate Drama Assn.
    1930 and Southern Assn. of Drama and Speech Arts 1936 (fore-
    runner of National Assn. of Dramatic and Speech Arts) 1970.
Theater: Wrote more than 40 plays including Badman; Bleeding
    Hearts; The Breeders; The Call of Jubah; Everyman's Land;
    Gangsters Over Harlem; Hewers of the Wood; Meek Mose (one
    act); Nat Turner; The New Window; Old Man Pete; The Phan-
    tom Treasure; Shades and Shadows; Silas Brown; The Tribal
    Chief; Yellow Death; This Is Your Life; FAMU's Objective IV;
    Job Hunting (one act) 1922; Christmas Gift (one act) 1923; A
    Merchant of Dixie (one act) 1923; Peter Stith (one act) 1923;
    Doom (one act) 1924; Rocky Roads 1926; Illicit Love 1927; The
    Virginia Politician (one act) 1927; Stock Exchange (musical)
    1927; One Side of Harlem 1928; Sirlock Bones (one act) 1928;
    Takazee: A Pageant of Ethiopia 1928; Denmark Vesey (one
    act) 1929; The Devil's Price 1930; Drama Enters the Curricu-
    lum: A Purpose Play (one act) 1930; The Man of God 1931;
    For Fatherland (one act) 1934; The Highwayman (one act) 1934;
    The Outer Room (one act) 1935; Wives and Blues 1938; The
    High Court of Historia (one act) 1939; Simon in Cyrene 1939;
    The Land of Cotton 1942; G. I. Rhapsody 1943; The Shadow
    Across the Path (one act) 1943; The Shape of Wars to Come
    (one act) 1943; The Trial and Banishment of Uncle Tom (one
    act) 1945; Earth and Stars 1946 (revised 1961); Whatever the
    Battle Be: A Symphonic Drama 1950; Prometheus and the
    Atom 1955; Career or College (one act) 1956.

EDWARDS, GLORIA
    (Actress)
Address: 100 Riverside Drive #11E, New York, N. Y. 10024.
Career Data: Worked with American Theatre of Being.
Films: Black Girl 1972.
Television: Ironside; Starsky and Hutch 1975.
Theater: The Amen Corner 1965; Medea (O. B.); Clara in The Great
    White Hope (tour) 1969; Liz in In New England Winter (O. B.)
    1971; Norma Faye in Black Girl (O. B.) 1971; Ain't Supposed
    to Die a Natural Death 1971; What the Winesellers Buy 1973;
    Showdown (New Federal Theatre) 1976.
Relationships: Wife of Dick Anthony Williams, actor.

EDWARDS, JAMES
    (Actor)
b.   1916, Muncie, Ind.

d.   January 4, 1970, San Diego, Calif.
Education: Northwestern University B. S. 1938; Indiana University;
         Knoxville College.
Honors: Oscar nomination best supporting performance (Home of
         The Brave) 1950.
Career Data: Skylight Players (Chicago).
Films: Man Handled, The Set-Up, Home of the Brave 1949; Bright
         Victory, The Steel Helmet 1951; The Member of the Wedding
         1952; The Joe Louis Story 1953; The Caine Mutiny 1954; Seven
         Angry Men, The Phoenix City Story 1955; Battle Hymn 1956;
         African Manhunt, Men in War 1957; Anna Lucasta, Fraulein,
         Tarzan's Fight for Life 1958; Pork Chop Hill, Night of the
         Quarter Moon, Blood and Steel 1959; The Manchurian Candidate
         1962; The Sandpiper 1965; Coogan's Bluff, The Young Runaways
         1968, Patton 1970.
Television: Toward Tomorrow (Cavalcade Theatre) 1955); The Last
         Patriarch (20th Century-Fox Hour) 1956; Meet McGraw (series)
         1957; Climax 1958; Silent Thunder (Desilu Playhouse) 1958;
         Peter Gunn 1960; Lloyd Bridges Show 1962; Fugitive 1963;
         East Side West Side 1963; Eleventh Hour 1964; Nurses 1964;
         Outcasts 1968; Outsider 1968; Virginian 1968; Mannix 1969.
Theater: Almost Faithful; Deep Are the Roots 1945; Lady Passing
         Fair (pre-Bway) 1947.

EDWARDS, TOMMY
         (Singer)
b.   February 17, 1922, Richmond, Va.
d.   October 22, 1969, Henrico County, Va.
Musical Compositions: That Chick's Too Young to Fry 1946.
Records: On MGM: It's All in the Game 1958; Please Mr. Sun
         1959; The Morning Side of the Mountain 1959; I Really Don't
         Want to Know 1960.

ELDER, LONNE III
         (Playwright)
b.   c. 1932, Americus, Ga.
Education: Rutgers University; Yale University School of Drama;
         Mary Welch's Studio; Brett Warren's Actor's Mobile Theatre.
Special Interests: Producing.
Address: c/o 20th Century-Fox Films, 10201 W. Pico, Los Angeles,
         Calif. 90024.
Honors: John Golden Fellowship in Playwriting (Yale U.); Joseph E.
         Levine Fellowship in film writing (Yale U.); John Hay Whitney
         Fellowship; Pulitzer Prize; Outer Critics Circle award; Ver-
         non Rice Drama Desk award; Stella Holt Memorial Playwrights
         award; American National Theatre Academy Hamilton K. Bishop
         award in playwriting; L. A. Drama Critics award.
Films: Acted in and wrote Melinda; wrote Sounder 1972.
Memberships: Harlem Writer's Guild; Black Academy of Arts and
         Letters; Black Artists Alliance.
Records: Reading Poetry to Jazz (R. C. A.).

Television: Wrote for N. Y. P. D. (series); wrote Deadly Circle of
Violence; wrote for McCloud (series); Ceremonies in Dark Old
Men 1975.
Theater: Appeared in Raisin in the Sun 1959; wrote: A Hysterical
Turtle in a Rabbit Race 1961; The Terrible Veil 1963; Cere-
monies in Dark Old Men 1965; Kissin' Rattlesnakes Can Be
Fun 1966; Seven Comes Up, Seven Comes Down 1966; Charades
on East Fourth Street 1967.

ELDRIDGE, ROY "Little Jazz" (David Roy Eldridge)
(Jazz Musician/Conductor)
b. January 30, 1911, Pittsburgh, Pa.
Special Interests: Trumpet, Flugelhorn, drums, singing.
Address: 270 Convent Avenue, New York, N. Y. 10027.
Honors: Down Beat Poll winner 1942, 1946; Metronome Poll winner
1944-46; Esquire (silver) 1945; Westinghouse Trophy award.
Career Data: Played with McKinney's Cotton Pickers 1934, Fletcher
Henderson 1936-37, Gene Krupa 1941-43, 1949, Artie Shaw
1944-45, Benny Goodman sextet (Europe) 1950; Jazz at the
Philharmonic 1945-51; worked with Ella Fitzgerald 1963-65;
New Orleans Jazz Festival 1969; Monterey Jazz Festival 1971.
Clubs: Three Deuces (Chicago); The Embers; The Village Vanguard;
Smalls; Arcadia Ballroom (Chicago); Famous Door 1938; Savoy
Ballroom 1938; Half Note 1969; London House (Chicago) 1971;
Jimmy Ryan's 1976.
Radio: With Paul Baron orchestra 1943-44; Mildred Bailey (series).
Records: Let Me Off Uptown 1941; Roy's Got Rhythm. On Verve:
Little Jazz; Rockin' Chair; Dale's Wail; Swing Goes Dixie.
Theater: Chocolate Dandies 1924; Hot Chocolates 1929; appeared at
Apollo Theatre; Avery Fisher Hall (with Ella Fitzgerald) 1976.

ELLINGTON, DUKE (Edward Kennedy Ellington)
(Musician/Band Leader)
b. April 29, 1899, Washington, D. C.
d. May 24, 1974, New York, N. Y.
Education: Pratt Institute (Brooklyn); Studied with Henry Grant.
Special Interests: Composing, piano.
Honors: N. Y. School of Music award 1933; ASCAP Prize 1934;
Down Beat polls 1945-72; Esquire awards 1945-47; Metronome
polls 1945-46; Pittsburgh Courier award 1947; NAACP Spingarn
Medal 1959; Grammy 1959, 1965; Playboy award 1962-70; Jazz
World award 1963; N. Y. C. Mayor's Musician of Every Year
award 1965; Record World award 1968; Presidential Medal of
Freedom 1969; Songwriters Hall of Fame 1971; Ebony Media
award 1974; Posthumously: Entertainment Hall of Fame;
Black Filmmakers Hall of Fame 1975.
Career Data: Toured Europe 1933, 1939; performed at Newport
Jazz Festival 1956, 1958, 1963; wrote composition for Mon-
terey Jazz Festival 1960; performed at Jazz Festival Washing-
ton, D. C. 1962; toured Middle and Far East 1963; White House
Festival of the Arts 1965; toured South America and Mexico
1968.

Clubs: Barons 1923; Hollywood Club 1925; Kentucky Club 1926;
   Cotton Club 1927-32; Rainbow Grill; Zanzibar; Basin Street
   East 1961.

Films: Black and Tan Fantasy 1929; Check and Double Check 1930;
   Belle of the Nineties 1934; Murder at the Vanities 1934; The
   Hit Parade 1937; New Faces of 1937; Cabin in the Sky 1943;
   Reveille with Beverly 1943; Rock and Roll Revue 1955; Anatomy
   of a Murder (score) 1959; Paris Blues (score) 1961; Assault on
   a Queen (score) 1966; Change of Mind (score) 1969.

Memberships: AFM; ASCAP 1953; Dramatists Guild.

Musical Compositions: Soda Fountain Rag; Sonnet for the Moor; Cop
   Out; Sonnet for Sister Kate; Lady Mac; Sonnet for Caesar; New
   York City Blues; The Clotted Woman; Reflections in D; Do
   Nothing Till You Hear from Me; Creole Love Song; Traffic
   Jam; Black Beauty; Don't Get Around Much Any More; Satin
   Doll; Day Dream; Sophisticated Lady; I Got It Bad and That
   Aint Good; I Let a Song Go out of My Heart; New World A'
   Comin; The Deep South Suite; The Perfume Suite; The Liberian
   Suite; Togo Brava; The Telecasters; Drop Me Off in Harlem;
   Harlem Flat Blues; The Mooche; The Road of the Phoebe Snow;
   Clarinet Lament; Jack the Bear; Blutopia; Flaming Youth;
   Conga Brava; Chelsea Bridge; Koko; Tatooed Bride; Warm
   Valley; I'm Beginning to See the Light; Bojangles; Harlem Air-
   shaft; Riding a Blue Note; In a Sentimental Mood; It Don't
   Mean a Thing If It Aint Got That Swing; Breakfast Dance; Har-
   mony in Harlem; Manhattan Murals; Mood Indigo 1931; Soli-
   tude; Reminiscing in Tempo 1934; Echos of Harlem 1935; Blue
   Bells of Harlem 1938; Jump for Joy; Take the "A" Train 1941;
   Black Brown and Beige 1943; Night Creature 1955; Sweet Thunder 1957; Suite Thursday 1960; My People 1963; The Golden
   Brown and Green Apple Suite 1965; Traffic Jam; The River
   1970.

Publications: Music Is My Mistress (autobiography), Doubleday
   1974.

Records: Duke Ellington & John Coltrane (Impulse); Best (Capitol);
   Black, Brown & Beige (Columbia Special Products); Collages
   (BASF); Duke's Big 4 (Pablo); Echoes of an Era (Roulette);
   Eastbourne (RCA); Ellington at Newport (Columbia); Ellington
   Indigos (Columbia); Ellingtonia-Reevaluations (Impulse); Elling-
   tonia (Impulse); For Always (Stanyan); Great Paris Concert
   (Atlantic); Greatest Hits (Reprise); It Don't Mean a Thing (Fly-
   ing Dutchman); Jazz at The Plaza (Columbia); Jazz Party
   (Columbia Special Products); Latin American Suite (Fantasy);
   My People (Flying Dutchman); New Orleans Suite (Atlantic);
   The Pianist (Fantasy); Recollections Band Era (Atlantic); Se-
   cond Sacred Concert (Prestige); 70th Birthday (Solid State);
   Highlights (United Artists); Suites '59'71'72 (Pablo); Third
   Sacred Concert (RCA); Violin Session (Atlantic); Yale Concert
   (Fantasy); Beginning (MCA); Bethlehem Years (Bethlehem);
   Duke Ellington (Super Majestic); Drum Is a Woman (Columbia
   Special Products); Early Duke Ellington (Archive of Folk &
   Jazz Music); Hi-Fi Ellington Uptown (Columbia Special Pro-
   ducts); Hot in Harlem (MCA); Masterpieces (Columbia Special

Products); Mood Indigo (Camden); Most Important 2nd War Con-
cert (CMS); Music of Ellington (Columbia Special Products);
Piano Reflections (Capitol); ... Presents Ivy Anderson (Colum-
bia); Rockin' in Rhythm (MCA); Such Sweet Thunder (Columbia
Special Products); We Love You Madly (Pickwick); The World
of 1947 (Columbia); The Ellington Era vol. 1 (Columbia); The
Duke at Tanglewood; This Is Duke Ellington (RCA); Jumpin'
Punkins; At His Very Best (RCA); The Afro-Eurasian Eclipse
(Fantasy); The Golden Duke (Prestige); The First Time (Co-
lumbia) 1962.

Television: A Drum Is a Woman (U. S. Steel Hour) 1957; Strollin'
Twenties (special) 1966; What's My Line?; Love You Madly
(special) 1973; Ella Fitzgerald Special.

Theater: Soda Fountain Rag 1915; Apollo Theatre 1932; composed
music for Jump for Joy (Hollywood) 1941; Capitol Theatre
1943; annual concerts at Carnegie Hall 1943-50; Beggar's Holiday 1946; musical director for concert at Lewisohn Stadium
1958; concert at Town Hall 1961; composed music for Timon
of Athens (Stratford, Ontario) 1963; appeared at Singer Bowl;
First Sacred Concert (San Francisco) 1965; Pousse Café 1966;
Third Sacred Concert (London) 1973; Bubbling Brown Sugar
(score) 1976.

Relationships: Father of Mercer Ellington, conductor/composer.

ELLINGTON, MERCER (Kennedy)
    (Conductor/Composer)
b. March 11, 1919, Washington, D. C.
Education: Columbia University 1939; New York University; Juilliard
    School of Music.
Special Interests: Trumpet.
Career Data: Played with Sy Oliver; formed his own band 1939;
    played with Cootie Williams 1954; assistant to Duke Ellington
    1955-59; led Duke Ellington band 1974-.
Clubs: London House (Chicago); Birdland.
Memberships: ASCAP 1957.
Musical Compositions: Things Ain't What They Used to Be; Blue
    Serge; Moon Mist; The Girl in My Dreams; Jumpin' Punkins.
Radio: WLIB (commentator).
Records: On Coral: Stepping into Swing Society; Colors in Rhythm;
    Continuum (Fantasy) 1975.
Television: Mike Douglas Show 1975.
Theater: Appeared at Steel Pier (Atlantic City) 1974; Town Hall
    (N. Y. Nights Presentation) 1975.
Relationships: Son of Duke Ellington, musician.

ELLIOTT, BILL (William David Elliott)
    (Actor)
b. June 4, 1934, Baltimore, Md.
Special Interests: Directing, producing, music.
Address: 5901 W. Sunset Blvd., Hollywood, Calif. 90069.
Career Data: President, Elliott Studio Productions; musician (drums,
    vocals, bandleader) for 12 years.

Films: Change of Habit 1969; Where Does It Hurt? 1972; Coffy
_____1973; Superdude 1975.
Television: Bridget Loves Bernie (series) 1972-73; The Old Man
_____Who Cried Wolf 1970; They Call It Murder 1971; That's My
        Mama 1974; Adam-12 1974; Ironside 1974; Police Story 1975;
        Tattletales 1975; Celebrity Sweepstakes 1975; Rookies 1976.
Relationships: Former husband of Dionne Warwick, singer.

ELLIS, EVELYN
        (Actress)
b.   February 2, 1894, Boston, Mass.
d.   June 5, 1958, Saranac Lake, N. Y.
Career Data: Member, Lafayette Players Company.
Films: The Lady from Shanghai 1948; The Joe Louis Story 1953;
_____Interrupted Melody 1955.
Theater: Othello (Lafayette Theatre) 1919; Roseanne 1923; Goat
_____Alley 1927; Bess in Porgy 1927; Native Son 1941; Blue Holiday
        1945; Deep Are the Roots 1945; Tobacco Road (black cast)
        1950; The Royal Family (City Center) 1951; Touchstone 1953;
        Supper for the Dead (O. B.) 1954.

ESTES, SIMON   (Lamont)
        (Opera Singer)
b.   February 2, 1938, Centerville, Iowa.
Education: University of Iowa; Juilliard School of Music.
Address: 165 West 57 Street, New York, N. Y. 10028.
Honors: Martha Bard Rockefeller Foundation grant; Tchaikovsky
_____vocal competition medal 1966; Munich International music
        competition.
Career Data: Began career with Old Gold singers, University of
_____Iowa; sang with Lubeck (Germany), Hamburg, (Germany) and
        San Francisco Opera companies; repertoire includes roles in
        Offenbach's Tales of Hoffman, The Magic Flute, The Marriage
        of Figaro and Banquo in Macbeth; performed at San Sebastian
        Festival (Spain); sang with New York Philharmonic.
Memberships: American Opera Society.

EUROPE, JAMES REESE
        (Conductor/Musician)
b.   February 22, 1881, Mobile, Ala.
d.   May 9, 1919, Boston, Mass.
Career Data: Formed New Amsterdam Musical Assn. in New York
_____1906; organized Clef Club (black musicians union) 1910; worked
        with Irene and Vernon Castle, dance team; contract with Victor
        Record Co. 1914; director, 15th Regiment Band, 369th Infantry
        during World War I (performed at Aix Les Bains 1918).
Memberships: "The Frogs" (a theatrical association).
Theater: Musical director, The Shoo-Fly Regiment 1907; Mr. Lode
_____of Koal 1909; Watch Your Step 1914; appeared at Manhattan
        Casino (later named Rockland Palace) 1910; Carnegie Hall

(jazz concert) 1912; Symphony Hall (Boston); Theatre des
Champs Elysees (Paris) 1918; Manhattan Opera House 1919.

EVANS, DAMON
(Actor)
b. November 24, 1950, Baltimore, Md.
Education: Children's Theater Assn.; Peabody Conservatory; Inter-
    lochen Arts Academy (Michigan); Boston Conservatory of Music;
    Manhattan School of Music 1974.
Special Interests: Dancing, singing, teaching.
Memberships: AEA.
Television: Love of Life 1973; Lionel (replacing Mike Evans) in
    The Jeffersons (series) 1975; The Silence 1975; The Tenth
    Level (New CBS Playhouse 90) 1975; Merv Griffin Show 1976;
    Captain Kangaroo 1976; Black News 1976; Roots 1977; Tony
    Awards Show 1977.
Theater: Two If by Sea; Hair (tour); A Day in the Life of Just about
    Everyone (O. B.); Lost in the Stars; Love Me, Love My Chil-
    dren (O. B.); Godspell; Jesus Christ Superstar (tour); Hello,
    Dolly! (tour); The Me Nobody Knows 1971; Don't Bother Me I
    Can't Cope 1973; Via Galactica (O. B.) 1973.

EVANS, ESTELLE
(Actress)
b. Bahamas.
Education: Hunter College (Speech and dramatics).
Career Data: Joined American Negro Theatre; director, Our Theatre
    Workshop; director, The Pilot Players (church performers).
Films: The Quiet One (doc.) 1949; To Kill a Mockingbird 1963; The
    Learning Tree 1969.
Radio: American Negro Theatre on the Air (WNEW) 1946-47.
Television: Naked City; CBS Chronicle; Du Pont Show of the Week;
    The Jeffersons 1975; Good Times 1975.
Theater: Our Lan' 1947; Mary Scott in Take a Giant Step 1953;
    Who's Got His Own (O. B.) 1966; Clara's Ole Man (O. B.) 1968;
    A Son Come Home (O. B.) 1968; The Electronic Nigger and
    Others (O. B.) 1968; Halloween Bride (O. B.); Freeman 1973.
Relationships: Mother of Marti Evans-Charles, playwright; sister
    of Esther Rolle, actress.

EVANS, MICHAEL
(Actor)
Education: Los Angeles City College; studied at Watts Workshop
    1970.
Special Interests: Writing, guitar, piano, composing lyrics.
Films: The Love Ins 1967; Now You See Him, Now You Don't 1972.
Television: Lionel Jefferson in All in the Family (series) 1971-75;
    The Voyage of Yes 1973; For Good or Evil episode on Streets
    of San Francisco 1974; co-creator of Good Times (series) 1974;
    Match Game 1974; Password All Stars 1974; Dinah! 1974, 1975;

Celebrity Sweepstakes 1975; Far Out Space Nuts 1975; Lionel
Jefferson in The Jeffersons (series) 1975; Rich Man, Poor
Man 1976; The Practice (series) 1976; The Richard Pryor
Special? 1977.

EVANS-CHARLES, MARTI
(Playwright)
Education: Fisk University; Hunter College, B. A. M. A.
Career Data: Asst. professor, Speech and Drama, Medgar Evers
College, Brooklyn.
Theater: Wrote: Every Inch a Lady; Jamimma 1972; African Inter-
lude 1976.
Relationships: Daughter of Estelle Evans, actress; niece of Esther
Rolle, actress.

FAISON, GEORGE (William)
(Dancer/Choreographer)
b. December 21, 1945, Washington, D. C.
Education: Howard University; studied dance at Harkness House for
the Ballet Arts and with Thelma Hill at Clarke Center and
with Louis Johnson; studied acting with Clarice Taylor.
Special Interests: Acting, costume designing, directing.
Address: c/o Universal Dance Experience, 109 West 96 Street, New
York, N. Y. 10025.
Honors: Tony and Drama Desk awards (for The Wiz) 1975.
Career Data: Dance concerts performed throughout the U. S., Europe
and Africa; formerly with Alvin Ailey American Dance Theater;
choreographed for Negro Ensemble Company, the Afro-Ameri-
can Total Theatre and the Lincoln Center Repertory Company;
founded the George Faison Universal Dance Experience 1971;
lecture tours of colleges.
Clubs: Choreographed night club acts for Dionne Warwick, Roberta
Flack and Eartha Kitt (concert act).
Films: Baron Wolfgang von Tripps (choreog.) 1976.
Memberships: AEA; AFTRA; AGMA; ASCAP; SAG; Society of Stage
Directors and Choreographers (SSDC);
Records: Purlie (RCA) 1971; co-composed The Tornado in The Wiz
(Atlantic) 1975.
Television: Soul (choreog.) 1971-73; Talking with a Giant, Roberta
Flack (choreog.) 1973; Black News 1975; Nor for Women Only
1975; Saturday Night Live with Howard Cosell 1975; Positively
Black 1976; Festival of Lively Arts for Young People (choreog.)
1976.
Theater: Choreographed Poppy; choreographed Slaves; choreographed
Suite Otis 1971; choreographed The Dolls 1971; choreographed
Nigger Nightmare 1971; Purlie 1971; choreographed Don't Bother
Me, I Can't Cope 1972; choreographed Ti-Jean and His Brothers
1972; assistant director for Via Galactica 1973; choreographed
Sheeba 1973; Inner City (Washington, D. C.) 1974; appeared at
Harkness Theatre 1974; choreographed The Wiz 1975; appeared
at Town Hall (Interlude series) 1975; co-directed 1600 Pennsyl-

vania Avenue 1976; Big Man: The Legend of John Henry 1976; choreographed Hobo Sapiens 1976; choreographed Gazelle 1976.

FALANA, LOLA (Loletha Elaine Falana)
    (Actress/Singer)
b.   September 11, c. 1944, Camden, N. J.
Education: Germantown High School (Philadelphia).
Special Interests: Dancing.
Address: 151 El Camino Drive, Beverly Hills, Calif. 90212.
Honors: Performer of the Year (Italy); Tony nomination (Best act-
    ress-musical, Dr. Jazz) 1975; Theatre World award (most
    outstanding new performer) 1975; CLIO award (for Tigress
    commercial) 1976.
Career Data: Discovered at different times by Dinah Washington
    and Sammy Davis Jr. , U. S. O. South East Asia Tour (with
    Bob Hope) 1972.
Clubs: Sands (Las Vegas); The Blue Angel; Riviera (Las Vegas);
    M. G. M. Grand (Las Vegas); Blue Max Room-O'Hare Regency
    Hyatt Hotel (Chicago); Basin Street East 1966; Westside Room
    (Los Angeles) 1971; Kutscher's (Monticello) 1975.
Films: Pop Goes the Weasel; Lola Colt (Ital.); A Man Called Adam
    1966; The Liberation of L. B. Jones 1970; The Klansman 1974;
    Lady Coco 1976.
Television: Mod Squad; Tonight Show; Streets of San Francisco;
    Merv Griffin Show; The F. B. I. 1969; The New Bill Cosby Show
    1973; Bob Hope Special 1973; Hollywood Squares 1974; Celebrity
    Sweepstakes 1975; Mike Douglas Show 1975; Dinah! 1975; Sammy
    and Company 1975; Gladys Knight and the Pips 1975; Comin' at
    Ya (summer series) 1975; Fabergé Tigress commercials 1975;
    Midday Live 1975; Black News 1975; Lola (special) 1975; Kup's
    Show 1975; Emmy Awards Show 1976; Switch 1976.
Theater: Golden Boy 1965, and tour 1968; Dr. Jazz 1975; Westchester
    Premier Theatre 1976.
Relationships: Former wife of Butch Tavares, singer.

FANN, AL (Albert Louis Fann)
    (Actor/Director)
b.   February 21, 1925, Cleveland, Ohio.
Education: Cleveland Institute of Music 1956.
Special Interests: Writing, producing.
Address: 207 West 133 Street, New York, N. Y. 10030.
Honors: Andy award (The Advertising Club of N. Y.) 1969; 1st Black
    Theatre Recognition Award 1973.
Career Data: Asst. Dir. , Karamu Theatre, Cleveland 15 years;
    founder, Al Fann Theatrical Ensemble 1967.
Films: Queen Boxer (trailer); The Tong Father (trailer); asst. dir.
    and acted in Cotton Comes to Harlem 1970; The French Con-
    nection 1971; assoc. prod. and acted in Come Back Charleston
    Blue 1972; Buck and the Preacher (trailer) 1972; Supercops
    1974; E Lillipop 1975; The Circuit Rider.
Memberships: AEA; AFTRA; SAG.

Radio: Commercials for Ex Lax, Nyquil, National Shoes, Easy-Off,
        Yuban Coffee, New York Telephone, Prudential Insurance.
Television: Voice over for Chase Manhattan Bank; Bob Hope Show
        1952; Al in Search for Tomorrow (series) 1971; Lieut. Bolling
        in How to Survive a Marriage (series) 1974; Love of Life
        (series); Edge of Night (series).
Theater: Porgy and Bess (City Center) 1964; Tambourines to Glory;
        wrote and acted in King Heroin (O. B. and tour) 1971; Masks
        in Black (O. B.) 1974, 1975; From This Time Forward (O. B.
        musical) 1975; The Wiz 1975-76; wrote, directed and choreo-
        graphed Strivin' (for Beaux Arts Ball) 1975.

FARGAS, ANTONIO
       (Actor)
b. c. 1947, Bronx, N. Y.
Education: Haryou Drama Workshop.
Address: Phil Gersh Agency, 222 N. Canon Drive, Beverly Hills,
       Calif.
Films: The Cool World 1964; Putney Swope 1969; Pound, Where's
       Poppa, W. U. S. A. 1970; Believe in Me, Shaft 1971; Cisco Pike,
       Across 110th Street 1972; Cleopatra Jones 1973; Foxy Brown,
       The Gambler, Busting, Conrack 1974; Cornbread Earl and Me
       1975; Next Stop, Greenwich Village, Car Wash 1976.
Memberships: AEA; SAG.
Television: The Bill Cosby Show (debut); Ironside; Toma; Night
       Stalker; Sanford and Son; Hereafter; Police Story; Police Woman
       1974; Kojak 1974; Jim in Huckleberry Finn 1975; Huggy Bear in
       Starsky and Hutch (series) 1975; Advertising with the Chopper
       (pilot) 1976.
Theater: The Slave (O. B.) 1964; The Toilet (O. B.) 1965; The Amen
       Corner (European tour) 1965; Day of Absence (NEC) 1966;
       Dream on Monkey Mountain (L. A.); Scipio in The Great White
       Hope 1968; Ceremonies in Dark Old Men (NEC) 1969; Glass
       Menagerie; The Pelican.

FARINA see HOSKINS, ALLEN

FETCHIT, STEPIN (Lincoln Theodore Monroe Andrew Skeeter Perry)
       (Actor)
b. May 30, 1892, Key West, Fla.
Honors: Black Filmmakers Hall of Fame 1974.
Films: In Old Kentucky 1927; The Devil's Skipper, Nameless Man,
       The Tragedy of Youth 1928; Show Boat, Big Time, Fox Movie-
       tone Follies, Gummy in Hearts in Dixie, Salute, The Kid's
       Clever, Thru Different Eyes, The Galloping Ghost, Ghost Talks
       1929; Cameo Kirby, Swing High, Big Fight 1930; The Prodigal;
       Neck and Neck 1931; Slow Poke 1932; Wild Horse Mesa 1933;
       Stand Up and Cheer, Carolina, David Harum, Judge Priest,
       The World Moves On, Marie Galante, Bachelor of Arts 1934;
       County Chairman, Helldorado, One More Spring, Charlie Chan

in Egypt, Steamboat 'Round the Bend, The Virginia Judge 1935;
36 Hours to Kill, Dimples 1936; On the Avenue, Love Is News,
50 Roads to Town 1937; Elephants Never Forget, Zenobia, His
Exciting Night, It's Spring Again 1939; Big Timers 1945; Mir-
acle in Harlem 1948; Bend of the River 1952; The Sun Shines
Bright, Sudden Fear 1954; Malcolm X 1972; Amazing Grace
1974; Won Ton-Ton 1976.
Memberships: SAG.
Television: Black History: Lost, Stolen or Strayed (special) 1968;
    Cutter 1972.
Theater: Flamingo Follies (revue on tour) 1943.

FISHER, GAIL
    (Actress)
b.   August 18, c. 1935, Orange, N. J.
Education: American Academy of Dramatic Arts; American Modeling
    Agency; Lincoln Center Repertory Theatre.
Special Interests: Writing lyrics.
Address: c/o International Creative Management 9255 West Sunset
    Blvd. , Los Angeles, Calif. 90065.
Honors: NAACP Image award 1969; Emmy award (first black actress
    to be recipient) 1969; Golden Globe award 1970, 1972.
Musical Compositions: Wrote lyrics for Do-Do-Do; What Could Be
    More Right?; Hang On In; Below ... Above; Mercy, Mercy,
    Mercy.
Television: My Three Sons; Peggy Fair in Mannix (series) 1968-75;
    Love, American Style 1969, 1971; Room 222 1972; Every Man
    Needs One 1972; Masquerade Party 1974; Bicentennial Minutes
    1974; Emmy Awards Show 1974; Merv Griffin Show 1975; Medi-
    cal Center 1975; Cross-Wits 1976.
Theater: A Raisin in the Sun; The Rock Cried Out; Susan Slept Here.

FITZGERALD, ELLA "First Lady of Song"
    (Singer)
b.   April 25, 1918, Newport News, Va.
Address: c/o Virginia Wicks, 236 East 68th Street, New York,
    N. Y. 10023.
Honors: Down Beat Magazine awards 1937-39-1953-54; Grammy
    winner 1958-60, 1962, 1977; Metronome Poll winner 1954; Es-
    quire Magazine awards (gold) 1946, (silver) 1947; Ella Fitz-
    gerald Center for Performing Arts dedicated to her at Univer-
    sity of Maryland.
Career Data: Discovered at Apollo Theatre amateur night; vocalist
    with Chick Webb band 1934-39, led his band 1939-42; per-
    formed with Duke Ellington band; performed at Newport Jazz
    Festival 1973; hit numbers include Hard Hearted Hannah, Lady
    Be Good and How High the Moon.
Clubs: Caesar's Palace; Mocambo (Hollywood); Venetian Room-Fair-
    mont Hotel (San Francisco).
Films: Ride 'Em Cowboy 1942; Pete Kelly's Blues 1955; St. Louis
    Blues 1958; Let No Man Write My Epitaph 1958.

Flack 118

Memberships: ASCAP 1940.

Musical Compositions: A Tisket a Tasket 1938; You Showed Me the Way; I Found My Yellow Basket; Just One of Those Nights; Oh! But I Do; Please Tell Me the Truth; Chew, Chew, Chew; Spinnin' the Web.

Records: At Duke's Place (Verve); At Montreux '75 (Pablo); Best (Verve); Best of ... (MCA); Carnegie Hall; Newport Jazz Festival 1975 (Columbia); Cote d'Azur (Verve); Ella Fitzgerald (Pickwick); Ella Loves Cole (Atlantic); History (Verve); Mack the Knife; Ella in Berlin (Verve); Watch What Happens (BASF); Porgy & Bess (Verve); Ella Fitzgerald (Archive of Folk & Jazz Music); Take Love Easy (Pablo); Best (MCA); ... Sings Gershwin (MCA); Stairway to the Stars; Ella Fitzgerald Sings Sweet Songs for Swingers; Ella in London (Pablo); Newport Jazz Festival Live at Carnegie Hall July 5, 1973.

Television: Mike Douglas Show; Dean Martin Show; Flip Wilson Show; Memorex commercial; Evening at Pops 1974; Ella Fitzgerald Show (special) 1975; Positively Black 1975; Dinah! 1976; The Tonight Show 1976; Grammy awards show 1976.

Theater: Appeared at Apollo Theatre, Paramount Theatre, Avery Fisher Hall, Hollywood Bowl, Town Hall, Carnegie Hall 1973, Nanuet Theatre-Go-Round 1975, Westbury Music Fair 1975, The Concert at Uris Theatre (with Sinatra and Basie) 1975.

Relationships: Former wife of Ray Brown, jazz musician.

FLACK, ROBERTA
(Singer)
b. February 10, 1940, Asheville, N. C.
Education: Howard University B. A. (Music).
Special Interests: Teaching.
Address: 600 New Hampshire Avenue, N. W. Washington, D. C. 22307.
Honors: Down Beat Female Vocalist of the Year 1971; Grammy award 1974; Ebony Music award 1975; gold record; Roberta Flack Human Kindness Day, Washington, D. C.
Career Data: Owns two music publishing firms; elected trustee, Atlanta University; accompanist for operatic school; piano teacher; performed at festivals: Montreux Pop (Switzerland), Schaefer, Newport Jazz, Hampton Jazz, Cincinnati Jazz.
Clubs: Shelley's Manne-Hole (Hollywood).
Films: Play Misty for Me (voice), Soul to Soul 1971; Save the Children 1973.
Records: On Atlantic: The First Time Ever I Saw Your Face; First Take 1968; Chapter Two 1970; Quiet Fire 1971; Roberta Flack and Donny Hathaway 1972; Killing Me Softly with His Song 1973; Feel Like Makin' Love.
Television: Boboquivari; Bill Cosby Show 1970; The First Time Ever (special) 1973; Celebrity Concert Tonight 1975; Saturday Night Live with Howard Cosell 1975; Marlo Thomas and Friends Free to Be You and Me (special) 1975; The Grammy Awards Show 1975, 1976.
Theater: Appearances at N. Y. Philharmonic Hall 1970; Felt Forum

(with Quincy Jones 1973 and with Richard Pryor 1975); Black
Music at Apollo Theatre 1975; Amphitheatre (L. A.) 1976.

FLUELLEN, JOEL (M.)
   (Actor)
b. December 1, Monroe, La.
Education: Studied with Morris Carnovsky, Maria Ouspenskaya,
   Hume Cronyn, Charles Laughton.
Address: Paul Kohner, 9169 Sunset Blvd. , Los Angeles, Calif.
   90069.
Honors: Black Filmmakers Hall of Fame award 1975.
Career Data: Organized Negro Art Theatre, Los Angeles 1950;
   worked for N. A. A. C. P. 's Performers Charity Club.
Films: The Negro Sailor (doc.) 1945; The Burning Cross 1947;
   Good Sam 1948; The Jackie Robinson Story 1950; Riot in Cell
   Block 11, Sitting Bull, Duffy of San Quentin 1954; Lucy Gallant
   1955; Friendly Persuasion 1956; Run Silent, Run Deep, The
   Decks Ran Red 1958; Porgy and Bess, Imitation of Life 1959;
   The Young Savages, A Raisin in the Sun 1961; Roustabout, He
   Rides Tall 1964; The Chase 1966; The Learning Tree 1969;
   The Great White Hope 1970; Skin Game 1971; Thomasine and
   Bushrod 1974; Man Friday 1975; The Bingo Long Traveling
   All-Stars and Motor Kings 1976.
Memberships: AEA; SAG.
Television: The F. B. I. ; I Spy; Gidget; Tarzan; Laramie; The In-
   vaders; Ben Casey; The Iron Horse; The Road West; Wild
   Wild West; The Breaking Point; Death Valley Days; Slattery's
   People; Dick Van Dyke Show; Ramar of the Jungle; The Great
   Adventure; Alfred Hitchcock Presents; Marcus Welby, M. D. ;
   Columbo; Insight; Adam-12; The Sheriff 1971; A Dream for
   Christmas 1973; The Autobiography of Miss Jane Pittman 1974;
   Apple's Way 1974; Barnaby Jones 1976.
Theater: Paper on the Wind; Three Men on a Horse 1942; The Respect-
   ful Prostitute 1948; Freight 1950; Billy Budd 1951; Noah 1954;
   The Iceman Cometh (O. B.) 1956; All Aboard; Golden Boy 1964.

FORD, CLEBERT
   (Actor)
Films: Trick Baby 1973.
Memberships: AEA.
Publications: A Guide to the Big Apple, Louis J. Martin Associates,
   1977.
Television: Co-produced and wrote We Shall Overcome and After-
   wards (Finland); Tom M'Aboko (Finland); Directions '61; John
   Brown's Body; East Side/West Side.
Theater: Threepenny Opera (Sweden); The Slave (Sweden); Sarah
   and the Sax (Sweden); The Kitchen (Sweden); Pantagleize (Swe-
   den); Trumpets of the Lord (Italy); Jerico-Jim Crow (Italy);
   title role in Othello (Buffalo Arena Theatre); Guildenstern in
   Rosencrantz and Guildenstern Are Dead (tour); The Cool
   World 1960; Dark of the Moon (ELT) 1960; The Blacks (O. B.)

1961; Romeo and Juliet (NYSF) 1961; Ballad for Bimshire
1963; Antony and Cleopatra (NYSF) 1963; Folk Studio (Rome)
1965, Les Blancs 1970, Aint Supposed to Die a Natural Death
1972; Gilbeau (New Federal Theatre) 1976; Showdown (New
Federal Theatre) 1976; Sounds in Motion (tribute to Paul Robeson, Marymount Manhattan Theatre) 1976; Daddy (O. B.) 1977.

FORT, SYVILLA
    (Dancer/Choreographer)
b.   1917, Seattle, Wash.
d.   November 8, 1975, New York, N. Y.
Education: Cornish School of The Arts (Seattle).
Special Interests: Teaching.
Career Data: Dance director, Katherine Dunham School 1948-54;
    instructor, Teachers College, Columbia University; teacher,
    Syvilla Fort Studio 1955-75 (students included Butterfly Mc-
    Queen, Alvin Ailey, Eartha Kitt, James Earl Jones and others);
    consultant to Government of Guinea.
Films: Stormy Weather 1943; Jammin' the Blues 1945.
Television: Positively Black 1975.
Theater: Palace Theatre (Seattle).
Relationships: Wife of Buddy Phillips, dancer.

FOSTER, FRANCES (Frances Helen Brown)
    (Actress)
b.   June 11, 1924, Yonkers, N. Y.
Education: American Theatre Wing 1949-51.
Address: 146 East 49 Street, New York, N. Y. 10017.
Special Interests: Directing.
Honors: Sara Siddons Award 1960; Bergen Record Poll (Best actress)
    1971-72; Encore Salute to Excellence 1973.
Career Data: Associate Professor and Artist in Residence, Theatre
    Dept. , City College of New York.
Films: Edge of the City 1957; Take a Giant Step 1961; Tammy and
    the Doctor 1962; Cops and Robbers 1973; A Piece of the Action
    1977.
Memberships: AEA; AFTRA; NEC (1967-date); SAG (1967-date).
Television: Our Street (series); Grace Trainor in One Life to Live
    (series); The Nurses; Dr. Kildare; The Guiding Light; Omnibus;
    Day in Court; Armstrong Circle Theatre; Dupont Show of the
    Month; U. S. Steel Hour; Legacy of Blood (Wide World Mystery)
    1974; Good Times 1975; Positively Black 1975, 1976; The First
    Breeze of Summer (PBS) 1976; Kojak 1976.
Theater: Raisin in the Sun; The Crucible (O. B.); Ballet Behind the
    Bridge (O. B.); Good Woman of Setzuan (London); Orrin; Ride
    the Right Bus (People's Showcase Theatre) 1951; The Wisteria
    Trees (Bway debut) 1955; Take a Giant Step (O. B.) 1956; No-
    body Loves an Albatross 1963; The Last Minstrel (O. B.) 1963;
    Happy Ending 1966; Song of the Lusitanian Bogey (NEC) 1968;
    God Is a (Guess What?) (NEC) 1968; Summer of the Seventeenth
    Doll (NEC) 1968; Kongi's Harvest 1968; Man Better Man (NEC)

1969; An Evening of One Acts (NEC) 1969; Day of Absence
(NEC) 1970; Brotherhood 1970; Akokawe (NEC) 1970; Behold!
Cometh the Vanderkellans (O. B.) 1971; Sty of the Blind Pig
(NEC) 1972; Rosalee Prichett (NEC) 1972; The River Niger
(NEC) 1973-1974; directed Terraces (NEC) 1974; directed A
Love Play (NEC) 1976; Livin' Fat (NEC) 1976; Boesman and
Lena (O. B.) 1977.

FOSTER, GLORIA
        (Actress)
b.   November 15, 1936, Chicago, Ill.
Education: Illinois State University, Chicago Teachers College.
Address: c/o Smith Stevens Ltd. , 1650 Broadway, New York, N. Y.
        10019.
Honors: Theatre World Award for Medea 1966; Obie and Vernon
        Rice Desk Award (In White America) 1963-64.
Films: Nothing But a Man, The Cool World 1964; The Comedians
        1967; The Angel Levine 1970; Man and Boy 1972.
Memberships: AEA; AFTRA; SAG.
Television: Bill Cosby Show; The Outcasts 1968; Mod Squad 1970;
        To All My Friends on Shore 1972.
Theater: Medea (O. B.); Black Visions; The Cherry Orchard (O. B.);
        In White America (O. B.) 1963; A Hand Is on the Gate 1966;
        Yerma (Lincoln Center Repertory) 1966; Hippolyta in A Mid-
        Summer Night's Dream (O. B.) 1967; Agamemnon (NYSF) 1977.
Relationships: Wife of Clarence Williams III, actor.

FOXX, INEZ
        (Singer)
b.   September 9, 1942, Greensboro, S. C.
Special Interests: Songwriting.
Honors: Gold record.
Clubs: ABC.
Musical Compositions: I Love You 1, 000 Times.
Records: Inez Foxx in Memphis (Stax); Mockingbird (Symbol) 1963;
        Hi Diddle (Symbol) 1963; Ask Me (Symbol) 1964; Hurt by Love
        (Symbol) 1964; A Feeling (Brunswick); Jaybird; I Had a Talk
        with My Man; Cross Over the Bridge; I Love You 1, 000 Times.

FOXX, REDD (John Elroy Sanford)
        (Comedian)
b.   December 9, 1922, St. Louis, Mo.
Address: c/o National Broadcasting System, 3000 W. Alameda
        Avenue, Burbank, Calif. 91505.
Honors: NAACP Image award.
Career Data: Teamed with Slappy White 1951-55.
Clubs: Fontainebleau (Miami); Alabam; Stadium Club (L. A.); Oasis;
        Basin St. East 1959; Castaways (Las Vegas) 1960; Aladdin
        (Las Vegas) 1961; Summit (Hollywood) 1962; Sugar Hill (San
        Francisco) 1964; Caesar's Palace (Las Vegas) 1968; Hilton
        International (Las Vegas) 1970.

Films: Cotton Comes to Harlem 1970; Norman, Is That You? 1976.
Publications: The Redd Foxx Encyclopedia of Black Humor, Ward
      Ritchie Press, 1977.
Records: Naughties Goodies; Jokes I Can't Tell on Television;
      Adults Only; Shed House Humor; Funky Tales from a Dirty
      Old Junkman; Redd Foxx at Home; Pryor Goes Foxx Hunting
      (with Richard Pryor); Laff of the Party 1955; You Gotta Wash
      Your Ass (Atlantic); On the Loose (Loma); Both Sides (Loma);
      Foxx-a-Delic (Loma); Live-Las Vegas! (Loma); Up Against the
      Wall War (Warner Bros.).
Television: Addams Family; Virginia Graham Show; Steve Allen
      Show; Flip Wilson Show; The Tonight Show; A Time for Laugh-
      ter (special); Today Show 1964; Here's Lucy 1965; Mister Ed
      1965; Green Acres 1966; Soul 1968; Fred Sanford in Sanford
      and Son (series) 1972-77; Midnight Special 1974; Salute to Redd
      Foxx 1974; Cotton Club '75 (special) 1974; First Annual Comedy
      Awards 1975; American Sportsman 1975; Mike Douglas Show
      1975; Merv Griffin Show 1975; Hollywood Squares 1975; Smo-
      thers Brothers Show 1975; Saturday Night Live with Howard
      Cosell 1975; Cher 1975; Sammy and Company 1975; Jerry
      Visits 1975; Dinah! 1975; Ball Park Beef Franks commercial
      1975; Bob Hope's Christmas Party 1975; created Grady (series)
      1975; Lola (special) 1976; Clifton Davis (special) 1976; Second
      Annual Comedy Awards 1976; Take My Advice 1976; Bunny of
      the Year Pageant 1976; The Captain & Tennille 1976.
Theater: Hubert's Flea Circus 1941; appearances at Palace Theatre;
      Apollo Theatre 1969, 1975; Carnegie Hall 1975; Nanuet Star
      Theatre 1975; Westbury Music Fair 1975; produced Selma
      (Los Angeles) 1975; 3rd Annual Memorial Concert, Louis Arm-
      strong Memorial Stadium 1976.

FRANCIS, PANAMA (David Albert Francis)
      (Musician/Drummer)
b.   December 21, 1918, Miami, Fla.
Career Data: Played with bands of Teddy Wilson, Sy Oliver, Roy
      Eldridge 1939; Lucky Millinder 1940; Willie Bryant 1946; Cab
      Calloway 1947-52; member, N. Y. Jazz Repertory Company.
Clubs: Michael's Pub 1975; Thwaites Inn (Virgin Islands) 1975.
Records: Castle Rock, Messin' Around, Jazz at Town Hall.
Theater: Never Live Over a Pretzel Factory (played with quartet)
      1964; appeared at Carnegie Hall (Newport Jazz Festival) 1975.

FRANKLIN, ARETHA "Queen of Soul"
      (Singer)
b.   March 25, 1942, Memphis, Tenn.
Special Interests: Composing.
Address: c/o Queen Booking Corp. , 1650 Broadway, New York,
      N. Y. 10019.
Honors: Golden Mike award; 10 Grammy awards; 13 gold albums;
      Cashbox Magazine Top Female Vocalist 1967; Number One
      Female Singer 1968; Radio Artists Best Female Vocalist 1974;

Ebony Magazine Black Music Poll Hall of Fame and Music
Award 1975.
Career Data: Appeared at Newport Jazz Festival; Lower Ohio Jazz
Festival; opened National Democratic Convention with soul ver-
sion of "Star Spangled Banner" 1968.
Musical Compositions: Dr. Feelgood; Don't Let Me Lose This
Dream; Spirit in the Dark; Day Dreaming.
Records: On Columbia: Beginning World of ...; First 12 Sides;
Greatest Hits; Won't Be Long 1961; Don't Cry Baby 1962;
Runnin' Out of Fools 1964; Can't You Just See Me 1965; Take
a Look 1967; The Electrifying Aretha Franklin; Unforgettable;
Laughing on the Outside; Soft and Beautiful.   On Atlantic: I
Never Loved a Man (The Way I Love You) 1967; Respect 1967;
A Natural Woman 1967; Ain't No Way 1968; The House That
Jack Built 1968; I Say a Little Prayer 1968; Bridge Over
Troubled Water 1971; Real Thing; Spirit in the Dark; Let Me
in Your Life; Amazing Grace; With Everything I Feel in Me;
You; Today I Sing the Blues; Something He Can Feel; Aretha
Live at Fillmore West; Aretha's Gold; Aretha's Greatest Hits;
Soul Sister; Take It Like You Give It; Aretha Sings the Music
from Sparkle; Young, Gifted and Black; Aretha Arrives; Aretha
in Paris; Lady Soul; Aretha Now; The Tender, the Moving,
the Swinging; Best; Hey Now Hey (Atlantic); Gospel Soul
(Checker).
Television: Jonathan Winters Show; Kraft Music Hall; Room 222;
What's My Line? 1974; Midnight Special 1975; Mac Davis Show
1975; Academy Awards Show 1975; Bob Hope (special) 1975;
Dinah! 1975; co-host, Ebony Music Awards 1975; Muhammad
Ali Variety Special 1975; The Tonight Show 1975, 1976; Ameri-
can Bandstand 1976; Hollywood Squares 1976; American Music
Awards 1976.
Theater: Appeared at Westbury Music Fair; Fillmore West; Apollo
Theatre 1974; Radio City Music Hall 1974; Coliseum (Rich-
mond, Va.) 1975; Westchester Premier Theatre 1975; Carnegie
Hall 1975; Shubert Theatre (L.A.) 1976.

FRANKLIN, CARL (Mikal)
    (Actor)
b.   c. 1930.
Education: University of California at Berkeley.
Special Interests: Poetry.
Address: Rifkin-David Artists Management, 9615 Brighton Way,
Beverly Hills, Calif.
Films: The Laughing Policeman, Five on the Black Hand Side 1973.
Publications: Portrait of Man (poems), Exposition Pr., 1952.
Television: Streets of San Francisco 1974; Cannon 1974, 1975; Mark
Walters in Caribe (series) 1975; Barnaby Jones 1975; Good
Times; Most Wanted 1976; Monkey in the Middle 1976; Fan-
tastic Journey 1977.

FRANKLIN, J. E. (Jenny)
    (Playwright)
b. Houston, Texas.
Education: University of Texas B. A.
Career Data: Lectured at Herbert Lehman College.
Films: Black Girl 1972.
Theater: Four Women; Prodigal Daughter 1960; Two Flowers 1960;
    Mau-Mau Room 1960; A First Step to Freedom 1964; The In-
    Crowd (produced at Montreal Expo) 1967; Black Girl 1971; Cut
    Out the Lights and Call the Law 1972; The Prodigal Sister
    1974.

FRANKLIN, WENDELL JAMES
    (Director)
b. Los Angeles, Calif.
Education: Washington and Lee University (Lexington, Va.).
Address: 5526 W. Olympic Blvd., Los Angeles, Calif. 90036.
Honors: San Francisco International Film Festival award 1972.
Career Data: Co-founder, K-CALB (black spelled backwards) Pro-
    ductions 1970; staged shows at Mark Hopkins Hotel (San Fran-
    cisco); produced operas and concerts for Los Angeles Board
    of Education.
Films: Assistant director on Kitten with a Whip 1964; Strange Bed-
    fellows, The War Lord, The Greatest Story Ever Told 1965;
    Gambit, Madame X, 3 on a Couch 1966; Enter Laughing 1967;
    Funny Girl 1968; Medium Cool, Gaily Gaily, Model Shop 1969;
    directed The Bus Is Coming 1971; produced Tough 1974.
Memberships: Directors Guild of America.
Television: Stage manager for NBC; worked on Queen for a Day,
    George Gobel Show, Truth or Consequences, This Is Your
    Life, Eddie Fisher Show; assistant director for The Monroes,
    Name of The Game, Peyton Place, Bill Cosby Show.
Theater: Carmen Jones 1944-45; staged black cast productions in
    Civic Auditorium (Oakland, California).

FRAZIER, CLIFF
    (Producer/Actor)
b. August 27, 1934, Detroit, Mich.
Education: Wayne State University B. A. (Theatre) 1957; Will-O-Way
    Playhouse School of Theatre (Bloomfield Hills, Mich); studied
    theatre arts with Harold Clurman.
Special Interests: Teaching, directing.
Address: 62 West 45 Street, New York, N. Y. 10036.
Honors: Judge, Martin Luther King Film Festival; judge, council
    of Churches Broadcast Awards; panelist, Emmy Awards.
Career Data: Co-founder & artistic director, Stables Theatre, De-
    troit, 1960-63; co-founder & artistic director, The Concept
    East Theatre, Detroit, 1962-64; associate director, Theatre
    of Latin America Inc. 1968; executive director, Community
    Film Workshop Council, Inc. 1968-date; administrator, Third
    World Cinema Productions Inc. 1972-date; taught and lectured

at colleges and universities including Howard University, Temple University, Clark College, Brooklyn College.

Films: Executive producer: No Place to Go, A Day for Shooting, In Your Blood, Jive, Coalminer--Frank Jackson, Message from a Black Man, Line Fork Falls and Caves, Loco Race, Whitesburgh Epic, Catfish, Hog Killing, Turkey Treasure.

Memberships: AEA; AFTRA; SAG; N. Y. Film Council (Bd. of Dir.); National Academy of Television Arts and Sciences; International Radio and Television Society; N. Y. Motion Picture and Television Council (Exec. Bd.).

Publications: Discovery in Drama (co-author), Paulist Press, 1969; Film and the Ghetto; The Complete Guide to Film Study, National Council of Teachers of English, 1972.

Radio: The Urban Forum (WKCR-FM) 1968; The Movies (WBAI-FM) 1969, 1970; Barry Farber (WOR-AM) 1970, 1971.

Television: The Today Show; Positively Black; N. Y. P. D. ; The Nurses; The Frank Blair Show; The Negro Experimental Theatre; Like It Is 1970, 1976; Exec. producer of A World in View (CATV News Show) 1975.

Theater: Day of Absence (O. B.); Benito Cereno (O. B.); An Evening with Garcia Lorca (O. B.); Litany for the Man (O. B.); Weary Blues (O. B.); Lorenzaccio (ELT).

FRAZIER, JAMES JR.
  (Conductor/Pianist)
b. May 9, 1940, Detroit, Mich.

Education: Detroit Conservatory of Music 1958; Wayne State University B. S. 1962; University of Michigan M. Mus. 1965; National Music Camp (Interlochen, Mich.) 1964; Berkshire Music Center (Tanglewood).

Special Interests: Composing, teaching.

Address: 1 Sherman Square, New York, N. Y. 10023.

Honors: 1st prize National Assn. of Negro Musicians Piano competition 1962; 1st Prize Guido Cantelli International Conductors' competition (La Scala) 1969.

Career Data: Discovered by Eugene Ormandy and conducted Strauss' Don Juan and Rachmaninoff's Second Symphony with Detroit Symphony Orchestra (debut) 1964; appointed asst. conductor, Detroit Symphony Orchestra; other orchestras conducted: Los Angeles Philharmonic, Indianapolis Symphony, New Philharmonia of London, Leningrad Philharmonic (U. S. S. R.), La Scala opera (Milan), Spanish National Radio and TV Symphony, Royal Liverpool Philharmonic Symphony (England), Symphony of the New World, Byelo-Russian Statt Philharmonic and Academy choir (Minsk); appointed asst. conductor of the Philadelphia Orchestra for the Robin Hood Dell season 1974; toured Soviet Union 1972, 1975.

Musical Compositions: 12th Street: A Soul Opera; Martin Luther King Requiem; Twenty-Third Psalm.

Television: Soul and Symphony (NBC special) 1975; Symphonic Soul (PBS) 1976.

FRAZIER, SHEILA (E.)
    (Actress)
b. November 13, 1948, New York, N. Y.
Education: Dwight Morrow High School (Englewood, N. J.).
Special Interests: Modeling.
Career Data: Worked with Negro Ensemble Company and New Fed-
    eral Theatre.
Films: Super Fly 1972; Super Fly T. N. T. 1973; The Super Cops,
    Three the Hard Way 1974.
Memberships: SAG.
Television: Firehouse 1972.

FREEMAN, AL JR. (Albert Cornelius Freeman Jr.)
    (Actor)
b. March 21, 1934, San Antonio, Texas.
Education: Los Angeles City College.
Honors: Outstanding Drama Student, Los Angeles City College 1957;
    John Russwurm award; Emmy nominee; Emmy award.
Films: The Rebel Breed 1960; Ensign Pulver, Black Like Me, The
    Troublemaker 1964; Clay in The Dutchman 1967; The Detective,
    Finian's Rainbow 1968; Castle Keep, Lost Man 1969; My Sweet
    Charlie 1970; Thermidor; directed and acted in A Fable (from
    LeRoi Jones' Slave) 1971; co-authored Countdown at Kusini
    1976.
Memberships: AEA; SAG.
Television: Look Up and Live; Lt. Ed Hall in One Life to Live
    (series) 1968; New York Illustrated; Defenders 1965; Slattery's
    People 1965; The FBI 1968; Judd for the Defense 1969; title
    role in My Sweet Charlie 1970; Mod Squad 1972; To Be Young,
    Gifted and Black (NET Playhouse) 1972; Maude 1974; narrated
    The Harlem 28 1974; Bingham in Hot L Baltimore (series);
    The Chicago Conspiracy Trial (Hollywood Television Theatre)
    1975; Celebrity Tennis 1976; Kup's Show 1976; Kojak 1976.
Theater: The Long Dream 1960; This Property Is Condemned (UCLA)
    1960; Kicks and Company 1961; Tiger, Tiger, Burning Bright
    1962; Living Premise 1963; Trumpets of the Lord (O. B.) 1963;
    The Slave (O. B.) 1964; Conversations at Midnight 1964; Blues
    for Mr. Charlie 1964; Dutchman (O. B.) 1965; Golden Boy 1965;
    Medea (O. B.), Sisyphus and the Blue-Eyed Cyclops (NEC);
    Measure for Measure (NYSF) 1966; All's Well that Ends Well
    (NYSF) 1966; Camino Real (O. B.) 1968; The Dozens 1969;
    Homer Smith in Look to the Lilies 1970; Sweet-Talk (Shake-
    speare Festival Theatre Workshop) 1974; The Great MacDaddy
    (NEC) 1974; Kennedy's Children (tour) 1976.

FREEMAN, BEE "The Sepia Mae West"
    (Actress)
b. Boston, Mass.
Special Interests: Modeling.
Address: 120 West 3 Street, New York, N. Y. 10012.
Honors: Black Filmmakers Hall of Fame award 1977.

Career Data: Appeared in many all-black silent films.
Films: Harlem After Midnight 1934; Lem Hawkins' Confession 1935;
Temptation 1936; The Underworld 1937.
Theater: Shuffle Along 1921; Liza 1922; Runnin' Wild 1923; Anna
Lucasta 1944.
Relationships: Mother of Kenn Freeman, actor.

FREEMAN, KENN
(Actor)
b. Dorchester, Mass.
Special Interests: Dancing, directing, producing, singing, writing.
Address: c/o Negro Actors Guild, 1674 Broadway, New York, N. Y.
10019.
Clubs: Ciro's (L. A.); Circus Bar (Atlanta); Mocambo (Canada);
Monte Carlo Hotel (Florida).
Films: Appeared in Oscar Micheaux productions; Toddy films; Gold-
berg Productions; What a Guy 1947; Miracle in Harlem 1948.
Memberships: AEA; NAG (historian); SAG; Harlem Cultural Council.
Theater: Wrote Tis Cricket (a revue); acted in Anna Lucasta (Lon-
don, Scotland, Wales); Because I Am Black (Birmingham
Repertory Company) England.
Relationships: Son of Bee Freeman, actress.

FRENCH, ARTHUR
(Actor)
b. New York, N. Y.
Education: Brooklyn College.
Career Data: Production consultant, American Community Theatre.
Films: The Stone Killer, Gordon's War 1973; The Super Cops 1974;
Three Days of the Condor 1975.
Memberships: AEA; AFTRA; NEC (1967-73); SAG.
Television: Our Street (series); Emergency; Madigan; Bill Cosby
Show; If You Give a Dance, You Gotta Pay the Band; Legacy
of Blood (Wide World Mystery) 1974; Black News 1977; Kojak
1977.
Theater: The Hostage 1961; Raisin' Hell in the Son (O. B. debut)
1962; Mister Johnson (O. B.) 1963; Ballad for Bimshire (O. B.)
1963; Day of Absence (NEC) 1966; Happy Ending (NEC) 1966;
God Is a (Guess What?) (NEC) 1968; Song of the Lusitanian
Bogey (NEC) 1968; Perry's Mission (O. B.); Man Better Man
(NEC) 1969; Ceremonies in Dark Old Men (NEC) 1969; Brotherhood (O. B.) 1970; Jonah (O. B.); Black Girl (O. B.) 1971, Ain't
Supposed to Die a Natural Death 1971; The River Niger (NEC)
1973; The Iceman Cometh 1973; Show Down (New Federal
Theatre) 1976, Brownsville Raid (NEC) 1976; Macbeth (O. B.)
1977.

FRIERSON, ANDREW
(Singer)
b. Louisville, Ky.

Education: Juilliard School of Music B. S.
Address: 319 East 24 Street, New York, N. Y. 10011.
Career Data: Member, Belafonte Folk choir; formed group The
Frierson Ensemble which presented Musical Echoes of Africa
program in N. Y. C. public schools; lectured on African Music
at New York University and Shaw University, Raleigh, N. C.;
member, New York City Opera Company 1957-65; director,
Henry Street Music School 1969; taught voice at Southern Uni-
versity, Baton Rouge; soloist, East Orange, N. J. Symphony;
recitals throughout U. S. and West Indies.
Records: Cal in Blitzstein's Regina.
Theater: Sang at Carnegie Recital Hall 1949; Times Hall 1950;
Town Hall 1955; Annie Get Your Gun (City Center) 1958; Finian's Rainbow (City Center) 1960; Show Boat (City Center)
1961; Porgy and Bess (City Center) 1965; sang at Alice Tully
Hall 1975.

FULLER, CHARLES H. JR.
(Playwright)
b. March 5, 1939, Philadelphia, Pa.
Education: Villanova University.
Honors: Rockefeller grant for playwriting.
Career Data: Co-founder and co-director, Afro-American Arts
Theatre (Philadelphia) 1967-71.
Memberships: Dramatists Guild.
Radio: Writer/director, The Black Experience (WIP Philadelphia)
1970-71.
Television: Roots, Resistance and Renaissance (series) WHYY Phila-
delphia 1967; Mitchell (teleplay) WCAU Philadelphia 1968; Black
America (WKYW Philadelphia) 1970-71; consultant and format
designer, Speak Out (WKYW Philadelphia) 1971; story editor,
J. T. (pilot) ABC 1972; Positively Black 1977.
Theater: Wrote In My Many Names and Days; First Love; The
Candidate; Emma; In the Deepest Part of Sleep; Love Song for
Robert Lee 1967; The Rise 1967; The Layout (The Sunflowers)
1968; Ain't Nobody Sarah But Me (The Sunflowers) 1969; Cabin
(The Sunflowers) 1969; Indian Giver (The Sunflowers) 1969;
J. J. 's Game (The Sunflowers) 1969; Majorette (The Sunflowers)
1969; The Perfect Party (The Village: A Party) 1969; The
Conductor 1969; The Brownsville Raid 1976.

FURMAN, ROGER
(Actor/Director)
Education: American Negro Theatre.
Special Interests: Playwriting, designing, producing, teaching.
Address: 43 East 125 Street, New York, N. Y. 10035.
Career Data: Taught black theatre at New York University and Rut-
gers University; founding member, Black Theatre Alliance;
artistic director, New Heritage Theatre; field supervisor,
HARYOU Act Cultural Program 1963-71.
Films: Acted as Herbert in Georgia, Georgia 1972; acted in The
Long Night 1976.

Publications: Co-author, The Black Book, Random House, 1974.
Theater: Wrote Fool's Paradise (one act) 1952; wrote the Quiet Laughter (one act) 1952; wrote Three Shades of Harlem (with Doris
Brunson) 1964; wrote The Gimmick 1970; wrote To Kill a Devil
1970; wrote The Long Black Block 1972; directed The Threepenny Opera (O. B.) 1972; directed Madame Odum (O. B.) 1973;
directed Harlem Heyday (Voices Inc. production tour) 1973-74;
directed Striver's Row (O. B.) 1974; directed Truckin (O. B.)
1974; wrote (with Dee Dee Robinson) and produced Fat Tuesday
1975; directed The Man in the Family (Albany, N. Y.) 1977.

GAILLARD, SLIM (Bulee Gaillard)
(Singer/Musician)
b. January 4, 1916, Detroit, Mich.
Special Interests: Acting, guitar, piano, vibes, tenor saxophone,
composing.
Career Data: Appeared with Slam Stewart as team Slim and Slam;
formed own quintet Chicago 1940; performed at Monterey Jazz
Festival 1970.
Clubs: Billy Berg's (L. A.); The Swing Club (L. A.).
Films: Hellzapoppin' 1941; Almost Married, Star Spangled Rhythm
1942; Sweetheart of Sigma Chi 1943; O'Voutie O'Rooney 1946;
Go Man Go 1954.
Musical Compositions: Flat Foot Floogie 1938; Cement Mixer; Tutti
Frutti; Vol Vist Du Gaily Star; Chicken Rhythm.
Radio: WNEW series.
Records: Opera in Vout (Clef).
Television: Then Came Bronson 1969.

GAINES, JAMES E. "Sonny Jim"
(Playwright)
b. 1928.
Special Interests: Acting, directing.
Address: 2349 Seventh Avenue, New York, N. Y. 10030.
Honors: Drama Desk award nominee and Variety Poll nominee (for
Don't Let It Go to Your Head); Obie (for What If It Had Turned
Up Heads?); Obie (for acting in The Fabulous Miss Marie)
1971.
Career Data: Member of New Lafayette Theatre acting company.
Films: Acted in The Long Night 1976.
Television: Acted in Good Times 1976; acted in Just an Old Sweet
Song (General Electric Theatre) 1976; acted in Sanford and
Son 1977.
Theater: Wrote It's Colored, It's a Negro, It's a Blackman? 1970;
wrote Don't Let It Go to Your Head 1970; wrote What If It
Had Turned Up Heads 1970; acted in The Fabulous Miss Marie
(O. B.) 1971; wrote Sometimes a Hard Head Makes a Soft Be-
hind 1972; directed The Corner (O. B.) 1972; acted in The
Psychic Pretenders (O. B.) 1972; acted in What If It Had Turned
Up Heads (O. B.) 1972; wrote Heaven and Hell's Agreement
1974; acted in What the Winesellers Buy (O. B.) 1973.

GARNER, ERROLL (Louis)
     (Pianist/Composer)
b.   June 15, 1923, Pittsburgh, Pa.
d.   January 2, 1977 Los Angeles, Calif.
Honors: Metronome poll winner; Playboy poll winner; Esquire Mag-
     azine new star award 1946; Down Beat Magazine poll winner
     1949, 1957; Grand Prix Du Disque, France 1957; Man of the
     Year in Music 1966; Postage Stamp (Republic of Mali) issued
     in his honor 1971; Pittsburgh Press Club award 1972.
Career Data: Performed with symphony orchestras of Honolulu,
     Washington, Louisville, Detroit, Indianapolis and National
     Symphony orchestra; appeared at Paris Jazz Festival 1948;
     toured France, Switzerland, Hawaii, Japan, Australia and New
     Zealand.
Clubs: Stork Club (Miami); Empire Room-Waldorf Astoria; Mr.
     Kelly's (Chicago); Hyatt Regency Hotel (Atlanta); Great Ameri-
     can Music Hall. (San Francisco); Beef n' Boards (Cincinnati);
     Tondelayo's; Three Deuces; Mark Plaza Hotel (Milwaukee);
     Maisonette-St. Regis 1971.
Films: A New Kind of Love (score) 1963; Play Misty for Me (score)
     1971.
Memberships: ASCAP 1954; American Federation of Musicians.
Musical Compositions: Misty; Dreamy; Solitaire; Dreamstreet; That's
     My Kick; Feeling Is Believing; Blues Garni; Trio; Turquoise;
     Other Voices; No More Shadows; Passing Through; Errol's
     Bounce; Paris Mist; Play Play Play; Gaslight.
Radio: Played piano on KDKA (Pittsburgh).
Records: Deep Purple (Pickwick); Feeling Is Believing (Mercury);
     Gemini (London); Misty (Mercury); Errol Garner (Archive of
     Folk & Jazz Music); Garnering (Trip); Greatest Garner (At-
     lantic); Other Voices (Columbia); Magician (London); The Elf
     (Savoy); That's My Kick; Concert by the Sea (Columbia) 1956;
     Play It Again Errol (Columbia) 1975.
Television: Merv Griffin Show; Mike Douglas Show; Tonight Show;
     Perry Como Show; Ed Sullivan Show; Jackie Gleason Show;
     Ernie Ford Show; Arthur Godfrey Show; Bell Telephone Show;
     Today Show; A Sister From Napoli (Name of the Game) 1971.
Theater: Appearances at Apollo Theatre; Music Hall (Cleveland)
     1950; Carnegie Hall (debut) 1959.

GAYE, MARVIN
     (Singer)
b.   April 2, 1939, Washington, D. C.
Education: Cardoza High School (Washington, D. C.).
Special Interests: Organ, producing, songwriting.
Honors: NAACP Image award 1973; N. Y. Amsterdam News Enter-
     tainer of the Year 1974; UNESCO award 1975; Humanitarian
     award of Universal Leadership Foundation 1976.
Career Data: Member, The Moonglows singing group 1960s.
Films: Chrome and Hot Leather 1971; Trouble Man (score) 1972;
     Save the Children 1973.
Musical Compositions: I'll Be Doggone; Can I Get a Witness; Pride

and Joy; How Sweet It Is; Inner City Blues; Wonderful One;
Stubborn Kind of Fella; What's Going On; Mercy Mercy Me;
Hitch Hike Wide.

Records: I'm Coming Home; My Distant Lover; Marvin Gaye Live!
(Tamla); Marvin Gaye Super Hits (Tamla); Anthology (Motown).
For Tamla: I Want You; One More Heartache; Stubborn Kind
of Fellow 1962; How Sweet It Is to Be Loved by You 1964;
What Good Am I Without You (with Kim Weston) 1964; It Takes
Two (with Kim Weston) 1967; Your Precious Love 1967; I
Heard It Through the Grapevine 1968; What's Going On 1971;
Mercy Mercy Me 1971; Inner City Blues 1971; Let's Get It
On 1973; Live at the London Palladium (Motown) 1977.

Television: Soul Train; Midnight Special; The Ballad of Andy Crocker
1969; The American Music Awards 1975; Celebrity Sweepstakes
1975.

Theater: Appeared at Apollo Theatre; Nassau Coliseum 1974; Radio
City Music Hall 1974, 1975; Capital Centre Arena (Washington,
D. C.) 1974; Braves Stadium (Atlanta) 1974; Cow Palace (San
Francisco) 1975; Westchester Premier Theatre 1976.

GAYNOR, GLORIA
     (Singer)
b.   c. 1950, Newark, N. J.
Special Interests: Song writing.
Honors: Gold record (France); silver record (England); elected The
Queen of Disco by National Association of Discotheque Disc
Jockeys.
Career Data: Joined The Soul Satisfiers, a singing group; toured
Europe 1976.
Clubs: Cliche (Newark); Magic Carpet; Speak Easy; 2001 Odyssey
1975; Jupiter's (Long Island) 1976; Penthouse (Brooklyn) 1976;
Zero's II (Long Island) 1976.
Musical Compositions: We Just Can't Make It.
Records: Honeybee (Columbia). On M. G. M. : Experience Gloria
Gaynor; Never Can Say Goodbye; Do It Yourself; Real Good
People; Walk On By; We Just Can't Make It; I'm Still Yours;
Come Tonight; How High The Moon; Reach Out, I'll Be There.
Television: Mike Douglas Show 1975; Disco 1976; Don Kirshner's
Rock Concert 1976.
Theater: Madison Square Garden 1975.

GENTRY, MINNIE (Minnie Lee Watson)
     (Actress)
b.   December 2, 1915, Norfolk, Va.
Education: Studied piano at Phillis Wheatley School of Music (Cleveland); drama at Karamu Playhouse (Cleveland) 1931-60 on and
off.
Special Interests: Writing, composing, poetry, singing.
Address: 10 West 66 Street, New York, N. Y. 10023.
Honors: Tony Award (for Ain't Supposed to Die a Natural Death)
1972.

Career Data: Member, Sam Wooding Singers 1947-49; Karamu
   House Players (Cleveland).
Films: Georgia, Georgia 1972; Come Back Charleston Blue 1972;
   Black Caesar 1973; Claudine 1974.
Memberships: AEA; AFTRA; SAG.
Musical Compositions: This Road Leads Home (musical in prepara-
   tion).
Publications: My House Is Falling Down (a play in 2 acts) 1974.
Radio: Land O' Lakes Butter commercial 1974; Public Service ad:
   Jobs for Youth 1974.
Records: The Search (Scholastic Magazine Inc.) 1971; Black Per-
   spectives (Scholastic Magazine Inc.) 1971.
Television: Shell Oil commercial 1968; Frito Lay Potato Chip com-
   mercial 1969; On Being Black (series) 1969; Barney's Clothes
   commercial 1970; Soul 1971; Madigan 1972; Tony Award Show
   1972; Salty 1974; American Heart Assn. spot 1975; Sojourner
   (American Parade) 1975; Feeling Good 1975; Just an Old Sweet
   Song (General Electric Theater) 1976.
Theater: Carnegie Hall (appeared with Wooding singers) 1947-48;
   The Blacks (O. B.) 1961; Purlie Victorious (Pennsylvania) 1962;
   A Raisin in the Sun (Ohio State University) 1963; The Blacks
   (Washington, D. C. Theater Club) 1964; The Amen Corner
   (European tour) 1965; Wedding Band (Ann Arbor, Mich.) 1966;
   June Bug Graduates Tonight (O. B.) 1967; Black Quartet (O. B.)
   1969-70; Who's Got His Own (Center Stage, Baltimore) 1970;
   Black Girl (O. B.) 1971; Ain't Supposed to Die a Natural Death
   1971; Sunshine Boys 1972; Mady in God's Favorite (summer
   stock) 1975; All God's Chillun Got Wings 1975; Livin' Fat (NEC)
   1976; The Man in the Family (Albany, N. Y.) 1977.

GEORGE, NATHAN (Nathaniel George)
      (Actor/Director)
Education: Dramatic Workshop 1960-62.
Honors: Obie (for No Place to Be Somebody) 1969.
Career Data: Performed with New York Shakespeare Festival Com-
   pany.
Films: Klute 1971; The Taking of Pelham 1-2-3 1974; One Flew
   over the Cuckoo's Nest 1975; Short Eyes 1977.
Memberships: AEA; AFTRA; SAG.
Television: The Defenders; East Side, West Side; Madigan 1973.
Theater: Acted in: The Blacks (O. B.) 1961; The Great White Hope
   1969; Johnny Williams in No Place to Be Somebody 1969; The
   Anniversary (O. B.) 1973; directed: The Black Terror; Who's
   Got His Own (Center Stage, Baltimore) 1970; Natural Affection
   (O. B.) 1973; Overnight (O. B.) 1974; Daddy (O. B.) 1977.

GILLESPIE, DIZZY (John Birks Gillespie)
      (Jazz Musician)
b.   October 21, 1917, Cheraw, S. C.
Education: Laurenberg Institute, N. C.
Special Interests: Trumpet, conducting, composing, Bahai religion.

Address: c/o Associated Booking Corp. , 445 Park Avenue, New
          York, N. Y. 10022.
Honors: Esquire new star award 1945 (silver) 1947; Metronome
          Poll 1947-50; Berlin Film Festival First Prize 1962; N. Y. C.
          Handel award 1972; Grammy 1976.
Career Data: Performed and toured with bands of Teddy Hill 1937-
          39, Earl Hines, Billy Eckstine, Cab Calloway, Benny Carter,
          Charlie Barnet and others 1930-44; his own bands and groups
          1946-56; toured Scandinavia 1948, Iran, Pakistan, Lebanon,
          Turkey, Greece, Syria, Yugoslavia 1956-58, Argentina 1961;
          appearances at Juan-Les-Pins (France) Festival; Monterey
          1962-74; Montreux 1973; Newport 1973-76; co-founded "The
          Bop" movement and popularized songs including Round Mid-
          night, Oops Papa Da, Salt'n Peanuts, and I Can't Get
          Started.
Clubs: Ratzo's (Chicago); Three Deuces; Mintons and Monroes;
          Village Vanguard; Half Note 1974; Buddy's Place 1975.
Films: Jivin' in Be-Bop 1947; The Cool World (score) 1964.
Memberships: ASCAP 1957; Masons.
Musical Compositions: A Night in Tunisia; Cool World; Swing Low
          Sweet Cadillac; Woody'n You; Groovin' High; Tour de Force;
          Something Old, Something New; This Is the Way; Diddywa;
          Oliwaga; Passport; Jessica's Day; Dizzy Atmosphere; Leap
          Frog; Hot House; Algo Bueno; Salt'n Peanuts; Anthropology.
Records: The Be Bop Era; Oscar Peterson and Dizzy Gillespie;
          The Greatest of Dizzy Gillespie; Dizzy Gillespie's Big 4 (Pablo);
          Echoes of an Era (Roulette); The Giant (Prestige); At Village
          Vanguard (Solid State); Bahiana (Pablo); Big 7 Montreux '75
          (Pablo); My Way (Solid State); Newport Years (Verve); Some-
          thing Old, Something New (Trip); Swing Low, Sweet Cadillac
          (Impulse); Dizzy Gillespie and His Big Band (GNP Crescendo);
          At Salle Pleyel '48 (Prestige); Big Bands 1942-6 (Phoenix);
          Dizzy Gillespie (Archive of Folk & Jazz Music); In the Begin-
          ning (Prestige); Paris Concert (GNP Crescendo); The Small
          Groups 1945-46 (Phoenix); Sonny Rollins/Sonny Stitt Sessions
          '57 (Verve).
Television: What's My Line?; A. M. America 1975; Kup's Show 1975;
          Sammy and Company 1975; Like It Is 1976; Performance at
          Wolf Trap 1976; Soundstage 1977.
Theater: Appeared at Apollo Theatre; Carnegie Hall 1975, 76;
          Basilica di Massenzio (Rome) 1975; Avery Fisher Hall 1975;
          Radio City Music Hall 1976; City Center 1976.

GILLIAM, STU
          (Actor)
b. 1943, Detroit, Mich.
Special Interests: Comedy, ventriloquism.
Address: Ernestine McClendon Enterprises, 8440 Sunset Blvd. , Los
          Angeles, Calif. 90069.
Career Data: Performed comedy night club act 1970.
Clubs: Top Hat (Windsor, Ontario).
Films: The $1,000,000 Duck 1971; The Mack 1973; Farewell, My
          Lovely 1975; Dr. Black Mr. Hyde 1976; Brothers 1977.

Memberships: SAG.
Television: Harlem Globetrotters (cartoon voice); Hollywood Squares;
     The Hound Cats (cartoon voice); Golddiggers 1968; Ed Sullivan
     Show; I Spy; Get Smart; Laugh-In (series), Adam-12 1971;
     Cpl. "Sweet" Williams in Roll Out (series) 1973; Masquerade
     Party 1975; Celebrity Pleasure Hunt 1975; Rhyme and Reason
     1975; American Bandstand 1975; Cross-Wits 1976; Freeman
     (pilot) 1976; Celebrity Revue 1976; Quincy 1977; What's Happen-
     ing 1977; Love, American Style.

GILPIN, CHARLES (Sidney)
     (Actor)
b.   November 20, 1878, Richmond Va.
d.   May 6, 1930, Eldredge Park, N. J.
Special Interests: Playwriting.
Honors: Drama League award 1921; Spingarn medal 1921; Crisis'
     Man of the Month 1921.
Career Data: Lincoln Theatre (Harlem) 1910-17; dir., Lafayette
     Theatre Co. (Harlem) 1916; Pekin Players (Chicago); toured
     with Pan American Octette.
Films: Ten Nights in a Barroom 1926.
Theater: Appeared with Perkus and Davis Great Southern Minstrel
     Barn Storming Aggregation 1896; Gilmore Canadian Jubilee
     Singers 1903-04; Williams and Walker's The Smart Set 1905;
     Big Ann's Boy; The Girl at the Fort 1915; William Custis in
     John Drinkwater's Abraham Lincoln 1919; title role in Emperor
     Jones 1920-24.

GLANVILLE, MAXWELL
     (Actor/Director)
b.   February 11, 1918, Antigua, West Indies.
Education: New School for Social Research.
Special Interests: Producing, writing.
Career Data: The Committee for the Negro in the Arts; American
     Negro Theatre; founder and director, American Community
     Theatre.
Films: Cotton Comes to Harlem, The Out of Towners 1970; Come
     Back Charleston Blue 1972.
Memberships: AEA.
Television: N. Y. P. D.
Theater: Wrote Dance to a Nosepicker's Drum, The Fairy Tale Is
     Cindy; produced Soul Gone Home at Club Baron and 3 plays
     (Alice in Wonder, The Other Foot, A World Full of Men) 1951;
     stage manager for The Blacks (O. B.) 1961; acted in Home Is
     The Hunter (ANT) 1945; Walk Hard (Bway debut) 1946; Anna
     Lucasta 1946-47; How Long Till Summer 1949; Freight 1950;
     Autumn Garden 1951; Take a Giant Step 1953; Cat on a Hot
     Tin Roof 1955; The Shrike 1955; Interlock 1958; Simply Heaven-
     ly 1959; Nat Turner (O. B.) 1960; The Cool World 1960; Golden
     Boy 1964; We Bombed in New Haven 1968; Zelda 1969; Simple
     (O. B.); Lady Day (O. B.); Spring Beginning (O. B.); Penance
     (O. B.); directed Light in the Cellar (O. B.) 1975.

GLASS, RON
(Actor)
b. c. 1945, Evansville, Ind.
Education: B. A. University of Evansville; studied drama at Tyrone
      Guthrie Theater, Minnesota.
Address: 1121 Gordon Street, Los Angeles, Calif. 90038.
Television: Hawaii Five-O; Bob Newhart Show; All in the Family;
      Griff 1973; The New Perry Mason 1973; Sanford and Son 1974;
      Maude 1974; Good Times 1974; The Crazy World of Julius
      Vrooder 1974; Harris on Barney Miller (series) 1975; When
      Things Were Rotten 1975; Showoffs 1975; The Streets of San
      Francisco 1976; $20,000 Pyramid 1977.
Theater: Sergeant Musgrave's Dance (O. B.) 1968; The Rise of
      Arturo Ui (O. B.) 1968.

GLENN, ROY E.
(Actor)
b. c. 1914, Pittsburgh, Kan.
d. March 11, 1971, Los Angeles, Calif.
Films: Dark Manhattan 1937; Lydia Bailey, Bomba and the Jungle
      Girl 1952; Royal African Rifles 1953; The Golden Idol, Riot in
      Cell Block 11, Jungle Gents, Killer Leopard, Carmen Jones
      1954; Man Called Peter 1955; The Man in the Gray Flannel
      Suit, Written on the Wind 1956; Tarzan's Fight for Life 1958;
      Porgy and Bess; The Sound and the Fury 1959; A Raisin in
      the Sun 1961; Sweet Bird of Youth 1962; Dead Heat on a Merry-
      Go-Round 1966; The Way West, Father in Guess Who's Coming
      to Dinner? 1967; Hang'Em High 1968; The Great White Hope,
      Tick... Tick... Tick... 1970; Escape from the Planet of the
      Apes, Support Your Local Gunfighter 1971.
Memberships: AFTRA (national secretary).
Radio: Beulah (series).
Television: Beulah; Sam Benedict; Peter Gunn; Rawhide; Jack Benny
      Show; Amos 'n' Andy (series); The Pigeon 1969.
Theater: Jump for Joy (Hollywood) 1941; Run Lil' Chillun (Los
      Angeles); Anna Lucasta 1946; Desperate Hours (stock); The
      Blacks (O. B.) 1961; Golden Boy 1964.

GLENN, TYREE (Evans Tyree Glenn)
(Jazz Musician/Composer)
b. November 23, 1912, Corsicana, Texas.
d. May 18, 1974, Englewood, N. J.
Special Interests: Trombone, vibraharp.
Career Data: Played with bands of Benny Carter 1937-39, Cab Cal-
      loway 1940-46, Don Redman 1946, Duke Ellington 1947-51 and
      Louis Armstrong all stars 1964-71.
Clubs: Paradise (Los Angeles); Cotton Club; Royal Box-Hotel Ameri-
      cana; Roundtable 1969.
Memberships: ASCAP 1956.
Musical Compositions: Waycross Walk; Sterling Steel; After the Rain.
Radio: Jack Sterling Show (CBS) 1953.

Records: Liberian Suite (Columbia); Seven Ages of Jazz (Metro
      Jazz).
Television: Staff musician and actor (WPIX) 1952.

GOODWIN, ROBERT L.
      (Producer/Director)
Special Interests: Writing.
Career Data: Founder of Robert L. Goodwin Productions 1970.
Films: Wrote, produced and directed Black Chariot 1971.
Television: Wrote scripts for Bonanza; Love, American Style;
      Julia; And Then Came Bronson; The Outcasts; Dundee; Insight.

GORDON, CARL (Rufus)
      (Actor)
b.   January 20, 1932, Richmond, Va.
Education: Brooklyn College 1957-59; studied at Gene Frankel
      Theatre Workshop 1965-69.
Special Interests: Directing, teaching.
Address: 70 East 8th Street, Brooklyn, N. Y. 11218.
Films: Luther in Gordon's War 1973; The Bingo Long Traveling
      All-Stars and Motor Kings 1976.
Memberships: AEA; AFTRA; SAG.
Radio: Station WDET (Detroit) 1972.
Television: Charlie in One Last Look 1970; Harry in Man in the
      Middle 1970; Ed Sullivan Show (with cast of The Great White
      Hope) 1970; Love Is a Many Splendored Thing 1970; Where
      The Heart Is.
Theater: Day of Absence/Happy Ending (Chicago and O. B.) 1966-
      67; Kongi's Harvest (NEC) 1968; Trials of Brother Jero (O.
      B.) 1968; Strong Breed (O. B.) 1968; Charlie in One Last Look
      (NEC) 1968; The Great White Hope 1968; Black Girl (O. B.)
      1971; Ain't Supposed to Die a Natural Death 1971; The River
      Niger (NEC) 1973-74.

GORDONE, CHARLES
      (Playwright/Actor)
b.   October 12, 1925, Cleveland, Ohio.
Education: California State College B. A. (drama) 1952.
Honors: For No Place to Be Somebody: Drama Desk award 1969,
      Obie, Los Angeles Critics Circle award, Pulitzer Prize 1970;
      National Institute of Arts and Letters award 1971.
Career Data: Founder, Committee for the Employment of Negro
      Performers; director of plays, Bordentown, N. J. Youth Cor-
      rectional Institution 1975.
Films: Casting director for Black Like Me; associate producer
      for Nothing But a Man 1964; cartoon voice in Coonskin 1975.
Television: Sunday 1975.
Theater: Acted in: Judson Poets' Faust (O. B.) 1959; The Blacks
      (O. B.) 1961; Of Mice and Men (O. B.); title role in The Trials
      of Brother Jero (O. B.); wrote: Gordone Is a Muthah; Out of

Site; The Thieves; No Place to Be Somebody 1969; Worl's
Champeen Lip Dansuh An' Wahtah Mellon Jooglah 1969; Baba-
chops 1974; The Last Chord (directed production at Billie
Holiday Theatre, Brooklyn) 1976.

GORDY, BERRY, JR.
      (Producer/Composer)
b.   1929, Detroit, Mich.
Special Interests: Directing.
Address: 6464 W. Sunset Blvd., Los Angeles, Calif. 90028.
Career Data: Formed his own record company (Tamla label) 1959;
      formed Motown Record Corp. (developed and promoted talents
      including Diana Ross, Smokey Robinson, Stevie Wonder, Gladys
      Knight, Marvin Gaye); president and chairman of the board,
      Motown Industries, Inc.
Films: Produced Lady Sings the Blues 1972; directed and produced
      Mahogany 1975; produced The Bingo Long Traveling All-Stars
      and Motor Kings 1976.
Musical Compositions: Reet Petite; You Made Me So Very Happy;
      To Be Loved; Got a Job 1958; Bad Girl 1959; Shop Around 1960.
Television: Produced Jackson Five cartoon; appeared on American
      Music Awards 1975.

GORE, ALTOVISE
      (Singer/Actress)
b.   August 30, 1935.
Education: Studied with Lee Strasberg.
Special Interests: Dancing.
Career Data: Member, Alvin Ailey Dance Co.
Films: Welcome to Arrow Beach 1974; Pipe Dreams 1976.
Memberships: SAG.
Television: NBC Follies Show; Tonight Show; McMillan and Wife;
      Merv Griffin Show 1974; Dean Martin Comedy Hour (roasting
      of Sammy Davis Jr.) 1975; Sammy and Company 1975; Tattle-
      tales 1975; Bert D'Angelo/Superstar 1976.
Theater: Golden Boy (London) 1968.
Relationships: Wife of Sammy Davis Jr., entertainer.

GOSS, CLAY
      (Playwright)
b.   May 26, 1946, North Philadelphia, Pa.
Career Data: Playwright-in-residence, Howard University.
Theater: Wrote: Bird of Paradise; Space in Time; Ornette; Our-
      sides; Mars; (on) Of Being Hit 1970; Homecookin' 1972; Andrew
      1972.

GOSSETT, LOU (Louis Gossett Jr.)
      (Actor)
b.   May 27, 1936, Brooklyn, N.Y.

Education: New York University B. A. 1959; studied acting with
    Frank Silvera, Lloyd Richards.
Special Interests: Guitar, singing, teaching.
Career Data: Teacher, Inner City Institute for Performing Arts.
Clubs: Ciro's (L. A.); Purple Onion (L. A.); Sherry's (L. A.).
Films: George Murchison in A Raisin in the Sun (debut) 1961; The
    Bushbaby, The Landlord 1970; Skin Game 1971; Travels with
    My Aunt 1972; The White Dawn, The Laughing Policeman
    1974; River Niger 1975; J. D's Revenge 1976; Choirboys 1977.
Honors: Emmy award 1977.
Memberships: AEA; AFM; AFTRA; AGVA; NAG; SAG.
Television: The Big Story 1954; Philco Television Playhouse 1954;
    The Day They Shot Lincoln 1955; The Nurses 1962; The De-
    fenders 1964; The Best of Broadway 1964; The Ed Sullivan
    Show 1964; Omnibus; Suspicion; Kraft Theatre; Robert Her-
    ridge Theatre; East Side/West Side; Mod Squad; Daktari; You
    Are There; The Partridge Family; The Bill Cosby Show; Long-
    street; Companions in Nightmare 1968; The Young Rebels 1970;
    It's Good to Be Alive 1974; Sidekicks 1974; Celebrity Sweep-
    stakes 1974; Good Times 1974; McCloud 1974; Petrocelli 1974;
    Caribe 1975; Black Bart (special) 1975; Lucas Tanner 1975;
    Delancey Street 1975; Harry O 1975; Police Story (series)
    1975-76; Six Million Dollar Man 1975; The Jeffersons 1975;
    Little House on the Prairie 1976; Rockford Files 1976; Rookies
    1976; Insight 1976; Little Ladies of the Night 1977; Merv Grif-
    fin Show 1977; Fiddler in Roots 1977.
Theater: Spencer Scott in Take a Giant Step (debut) 1953; The Desk
    Set 1955; Take a Giant Step (O. B.) 1956; Absalom Kumalo in
    Lost in the Stars (City Center) 1957; George Murchison in A
    Raisin in the Sun 1959; Deodatus Village in The Blacks (O. B.)
    1961; Big-Eyed Buddy Lomax in Tambourines to Glory (O. B.)
    1963; Telemachus Clay (O. B.) 1963; The Blood Knot (O. B.)
    1964; Paulus in The Zulu and the Zayda 1965; My Sweet Char-
    lie 1966; Carry Me Back to Morningside Heights 1968; Tell
    Pharaoh 1972.

GRAINGER, PORTER
    (Playwright/Composer)
Special Interests: Composing, writing lyrics.
Musical Compositions: Cotton.
Theater: Lucky Sambo (with Freddie Johnson) 1925; De Board
    Meetin' (with Leigh Whipper) 1925; We's Risin: A Story of
    the Simple Life in the Souls of Black Folk (with Leigh Whip-
    per) 1927; Brown Buddies 1930; Hot Rhythm 1939.

GRANT, EARL
    (Singer/Organist)
b.   1931, Oklahoma City, Okla.
d.   June 19, 1970, Lordsburg, N. Mex.
Education: Kansas City Conservatory of Music; University of
    Southern California; De Paul University (Chicago); New Ro-
    chelle (N. Y.) Conservatory.

Films: Juke Box Rhythm, Imitation of Life (sang theme) 1959;
        Tender Is the Night 1961.
Records: For MCA: Winter Wonderland; Beyond the Reef; Best;
        Ebb Tide; Greatest Hits; Just for a Thrill; Spanish Eyes;
        Time for Us; It's So Good (Vocalion). For Decca: The End
        1958; Evening Rain 1959; House of Bamboo 1960; Swingin'
        Gently 1962; Sweet Sixteen Bars 1962; Stand By Me 1965.
Television: The Ed Sullivan Show.

GRANT, MICKI
        (Composer/Singer)
b. June 30, Chicago, Ill.
Education: University of Illinois, Roosevelt and DePaul University.
Special Interests: Writing lyrics, acting.
Address: c/o Mercury Records, 35 East Wacker Drive, Chicago,
        Ill. 60601.
Honors: Grammy 1972; NAACP Image award 1972; Obie award
        1972; Drama Desk award 1972; Outer Circle award 1972;
        Mademoiselle achievement award 1972; 2 Tony nominations
        1972.
Career Data: Artist in residence, Urban Arts Corps 1970.
Memberships: AEA; Dramatists Guild.
Television: Vibrations in Encore; Peggy Nolan in Another World
        (series).
Theater: The Cradle Will Rock (O. B.); Leonard Bernstein's Theatre
        Songs (O. B.); Brecht on Brecht; wrote Step Lively (based on
        Irwin Shaw's Bury the Dead); wrote music and lyrics for
        Croesus and the Witch; The Blacks (O. B.) 1961; Fly Blackbird
        (O. B.) 1962; Tambourines to Glory (Bway debut) 1963; Funny-
        house of the Negro (O. B.) 1964; Jerico-Jim Crow (O. B.) 1964;
        The Gingham Dog (Washington, D. C.) 1964; Tell Pharaoh (O.
        B.) 1967; To Be Young, Gifted and Black (O. B.) 1969; wrote
        and performed in Don't Bother Me I Can't Cope 1971-72;
        wrote music and lyrics for The Prodigal Sister 1974; wrote
        music and lyrics for The Ups and Downs of Theophilus Mait-
        land 1974; appeared at Town Hall (Interlude 5:45 series) 1976;
        I'm Laughing, But I Ain't Tickled (O. B.) 1976.

GRAVES, TERESA
        (Actress)
b. c. 1949, Houston, Texas.
Education: Washington High School (L. A.).
Special Interests: Singing.
Career Data: Former member, The Young Americans, and Doodle-
        town Pipers, vocal groups.
Films: That Man Bolt 1973; Black Eye 1974; Old Dracula 1976.
Memberships: SAG.
Records: Meet Teresa Graves (RCA) 1968.
Television: Our Place; The Funny Side 1971; Turn On; Keeping Up
        with the Joneses (pilot); Laugh-In (series) 1968; title role in
        Get Christie Love (series) 1974-75; Dinah! 1975; Emmy Awards
        Show 1975.

GRAYSON, JESSIE
   (Actress)
Special Interests: Singing.
Career Data: Member of Hall Johnson Choir.
Films: Addie in The Little Foxes 1941; Syncopation 1942; The
   Youngest Profession, Claudia 1943; Cass Timberlane 1947;
   Violet in Our Very Own 1950.
Memberships: AEA.

GREAVES, WILLIAM
   (Producer/Actor)
b. October 8, 1926, New York, N. Y.
Education: City College of New York 1949-51, studied at Actors
   Studio with Lee Strasberg, Elia Kazan and Daniel Mann 1948.
Special Interests: Directing, writing, Afro-American history and
   culture.
Address: 1776 Broadway, New York, N. Y. 10019.
Honors: Winner of 16 International film festival awards 1970-73;
   Emmy winner (for Black Journal) 1970; 3 Emmy nominations
   (for La Raza) 1973; John Russwurm award (for Black Journal)
   from National Newspaper Publishers Assn. of America 1970.
Career Data: Started theatrical career as an African dancer with
   Sierra Leonian Asadata Dafora Dance Co.; joined the Pearl
   Primus Dance Troupe; member, American Negro Theatre;
   acted from 1943-52; writer, editor, director, National Film
   Board of Canada 1952-60; founded Canadian Drama Studio with
   branches in Montreal, Toronto and Ottawa 1953-63; staff of
   U. N. Television 1963-64; executive producer, NET's Black
   Journal 1968-70; president, William Greaves Productions Inc.;
   teacher, Lee Strasberg Theatre Institute 1974; vice pres.,
   AMAS Repertory Theatre Inc.
Films: Acted in Miracle in Harlem 1948; acted in Lost Boundaries
   1949; produced over 200 documentary films since 1952 including
   Voice of La Raza 1971; In the Company of Men; From These
   Roots 1974; The Fighters 1974; The Marijuana Affair 1975.
Memberships: SAG; Directors Guild; Writers Guild; Nat. Assn. of
   Black Media Producers (Founder) 1970.
Musical Compositions: Composed over 100 popular songs including
   African Lullaby.
Television: Black Journal (NET); Black News 1975.
Theater: Three's a Family (ANT) 1943; Henri Christophe (ANT)
   1945; A Young American 1946; Finian's Rainbow 1946; John
   Loves Mary (black cast) 1948; Lost in the Stars 1949; Arsenic
   and Old Lace (black cast).

GREEN, AL
   (Singer)
b. April 13, 1946, Forrest City, Ark.
Special Interests: Composing.
Honors: Voted top male vocalist by Billboard, Cash Box and Record
   World; Rolling Stone Rock n' Roll Star of the year; seven gold
   singles and four gold albums.

Records: Back Up Train 1967; Tired of Being Alone; Call Me (Hi);
    I'm Still in Love with You (Hi); Let's Stay Together (Hi); Livin'
    for You (Hi); Al Green Is Blues (Hi); Al Green Gets Next to
    You (Hi); Al Green Explores Your Mind; Al Green's Greatest
    Hits (London); Al Green Is Love; Full of Fire (London); Have
    a Good Time.
Television: Soul Train; Hollywood Palladium 1975; Midnight Special
    1974; The American Music Awards 1975; Dinah! 1975; Mike
    Douglas Show 1975, 1976; Merv Griffin Show 1976; Sammy and
    Company 1976; The Tonight Show 1976.
Theater: Appeared at Apollo Theatre; Westbury Music Fair 1974,
    1977; Nanuet Theatre-Go-Round 1974; Circle Star Theatre (San
    Francisco) 1975; Westchester Premier Theatre 1975; Felt
    Forum 1975; In Concert, Uris Theatre 1976.

GREEN, EDDIE
    (Comedian)
b.   c. 1901, Baltimore, Md.
d.   September, 1950, Los Angeles, Calif.
Special Interests: Singing, writing, vaudeville.
Career Data: Teamed in comedy act with Dick Campbell; formed
    Sepia Art Picture Company 1938.
Clubs: Paradise (Atlantic City, N. J.).
Films: Dress Rehearsal 1939; Duffy's Tavern 1945; One Punch
    Jones, Mantan Messes Up 1946; produced Mr. Atom's Bomb
    1949.
Radio: The Rudy Vallee Show (a. k. a. The Fleischmann Hour) 1930-
    31; Stonewall the lawyer in Amos 'n' Andy (series); Eddie the
    waiter in Duffy's Tavern (series).
Theater: Appeared at Apollo Theatre; Hot Chocolates 1929; The Hot
    Mikado 1939.

GREENE, LORETTA
    (Actress)
b.   New York, N. Y.
Education: High School of Performing Arts; B. F. A. (Speech and
    drama) Howard University.
Special Interests: Teaching.
Honors: Obie and Drama Desk Award (for The Sirens) 1974.
Films: Black Girl 1972; Leadbelly 1976.
Memberships: AEA; NAG.
Theater: The Black Quartet (O. B.) 1969; Ruth Ann in Black Girl
    (O. B.) 1971; The Sirens (O. B.) 1974; What the Winesellers
    Buy (Chicago) 1975; In the Wine Time (O. B.) 1976.
Relationships: Niece of Stanley Greene, actor.

GREENE, REUBEN
    (Actor)
b.   November 24, 1938, Philadelphia, Pa.
Films: Bye Bye Braverman 1968; Bernard in The Boys in the Band
    1970.

Memberships: AEA; AFTRA; SAG.
Television: N. Y. P. D.; Jerico-Jim Crow; Dr. Jim Hudson on Where
    the Heart Is (series); All My Children (series).
Theater: War and Peace (APA); You Can't Take It with You (APA);
    Pantagleize (APA); The Brig (O. B.); Othello (O. B.); Jerico-
    Jim Crow (O. B.) 1964; Happy Ending (O. B.) 1966; To Be
    Young, Gifted and Black (O. B.) 1967; The Boys in the Band
    (O. B.) 1968.

GREENE, STANLEY (N.)
    (Actor)
b.   May 17, 1911, New York, N. Y.
Education: New York University (film-making).
Special Interests: Directing, modeling, producing.
Address: P. O. Box 1196, New Rochelle, N. Y. 10802.
Career Data: Co-founder, American Negro Theatre (worked as actor,
    director, producer, stage manager).
Films: Il Mondo Di Notte (Ital.); Playground; The Last Angry Man
    1959; The Rat Race 1960; Nothing But a Man 1964; For Love
    of Ivy 1968; The Landlord, Cotton Comes to Harlem, The
    Kremlin Letter 1970; Harry and Tonto, Death Wish 1974.
Memberships: AEA; AFTRA; SAG; National Academy of Television
    Arts and Sciences (Bd. of Governors, N. Y. Chapter).
Radio: Produced and directed These Are Americans Too (WEVD);
    acted on Sounds of the City (WWRL).
Television: The Guiding Light; A Case of Libel; The Defenders;
    Naked City; The Nurses; Edge of Night; Somerset; The Doctors;
    Member of the Wedding; That's Life; On Being Black; N. Y.
    Television Theatre; Calucci's Department; Search for Tomorrow.
Theater: Produced The Big Deal (O. B.); produced and directed The
    Left Hand Mirror (O. B.); The King and the Duke (O. B.); In
    Abraham's Bosom 1926; Porgy 1929; Natural Man 1941; On
    Striver's Row (ANT) 1946; Another Part of the Forest 1946;
    Take a Giant Step (O. B.) 1956; Simply Heavenly 1957; pro-
    duced Wedding in Japan (O. B.) 1957; produced and directed
    Land Beyond the River (O. B.) 1957; and the Wind Blows (O.
    B.) 1959; The Long Dream 1960; Weekend 1968; stage-managed
    and acted in Zelda 1969; Contributions (O. B.) 1970.
Relationships: Uncle of Loretta Greene, actress.

GREGORY, DICK (Richard Claxton Gregory)
    (Comedian/Actor)
b.   October 12, 1932, St. Louis, Mo.
Education: Southern Illinois University 1951-53, 1955-56.
Special Interests: Civil rights, lecturing.
Address: 79 W. Monroe Street, Chicago, Ill. 60603.
Career Data: Peace and Freedom Party candidate for U. S. Presi-
    dency 1968.
Clubs: Mr. Kelly's (Chicago); Village Gate; Club Apex (Robbins,
    Ill.); Esquire Club (Chicago); Roberts Show Club (Chicago)
    1959-60; Playboy Club (Chicago) 1961.

Films: Sweet Love; Bitter (a. k. a. It Won't Rub Off Baby) 1967.
Publications: Nigger, Dutton, 1964; What's Happening, Dutton, 1965;
From the Back of the Bus, Avon, 1971.
Records: Dick Gregory in Living Black and White; Dick Gregory;
The Light Side-Dark Side; Dick Gregory Live at The Village
Gate.
Television: Phil Donahue Show; Jack Paar Show; Nancy Wilson
Show; Today Show; Old Is Somebody Else 1974; Black Journal
1975, 1976; Wide World Special 1975; Gettin' Over 1975; As-
sassination: An American Nightmare (special) 1975; Second
Annual Comedy Awards Show 1976; Good Morning America
1976; Dinah! 1976.
Theater: Appeared at Apollo Theatre; Carnegie Hall, 1974.

GRICE, WAYNE
(Actor)
Memberships: NAG.
Television: Hawk (series) 1966.
Theater: Moon on a Rainbow Shawl (O. B.) 1962.

GRIER, PAM (Pamela Suzette)
(Actress)
b. c. 1950, Winston Salem, N. C.
Education: Metropolitan State College (Denver); University of Cali-
fornia at Los Angeles.
Address: Agency For Performing Arts, 9000 Sunset Blvd. , Los
Angeles, Calif. 90069.
Career Data: Formed Brown Sun (film) productions.
Films: Beyond the Valley of the Dolls 1969; The Big Doll House
1971; Hit Man, Cool Breeze, Women in Cages 1972; title role
in Coffey, Black Mama, White Mama, Scream Blacula, Scream
1972; title role in Foxy Brown 1974; Sheba Baby, The Arena,
Bucktown, title role in Friday Foster 1975; panther woman in
Twilight People, Drum, Greased Lightning 1976.
Memberships: SAG.
Television: Midday Live; Mike Douglas Show 1975; Celebrity Sweep-
stakes 1975; Tonight Show 1975, 1976; Merv Griffin Show 1976;
Hollywood Squares 1976.
Relationships: Cousin of Roosevelt Grier, entertainer.

GRIER, ROOSEVELT "Rosey"
(Entertainer)
b. July 14, 1932, Cuthbert, Ga.
Education: Pennsylvania State University B. S. 1955.
Special Interests: Football, public relations, singing.
Address: c/o Gershenson, Dingilian and Jaffe, 120 El Camino
Drive, Beverly Hills, Calif. 90212.
Career Data: Pro-football player N. Y. Giants 1955-62; L. A. Rams
1961-68; public relations director, National General Corp. ; per-
formed with The Real Thing, a singing group.

Clubs: Hong Kong Bar-Century Plaza Hotel (Beverly Hills) 1970.
Films: In Cold Blood 1968; The Liberation of L. B. Jones 1970;
    Skyjacked, The Thing with Two Heads 1972; Evil in the Deep
    1977.
Publications: Rosey Grier Needlepoint Book for Men, Walker, 1973.
Television: Daniel Boone; Bob Hope Show; I Dream of Jeannie; Wild
    Wild West; Jonathan Winters Show; Hollywood Palace; Celebrity
    Tennis; Steve Allen Show; Kraft Music Hall; Joey Bishop Show;
    McMillan and Wife; Mike Douglas Show; Fat of the Land (spe-
    cial); Mr. Novak 1964; Man from U. N. C. L. E. 1964; Shindig
    1964; Hullabaloo 1964; Rosey Grier Show (series) 1969; Car-
    ter's Army 1970; The Golddiggers 1971; Make Room for Grand-
    daddy 1971; Captain Kangaroo 1974; Dinah! 1974; Cotton Club
    '75 1974; Tomorrow 1974; Merv Griffin Show 1974, 1975;
    Marlo Thomas and Friends (special) 1975; Movin' On 1975;
    Masquerade Party 1975; Tony Orlando and Dawn 1975; Celeb-
    rity Pleasure Hunt 1975; Benjy in Movin' On 1975; Benjy in
    Once Upon a Tour 1976; Kojak 1976; Break the Bank 1976;
    Almost Anything Goes 1976; Lite Beer and Burger King com-
    mercials 1976.
Theater: Sang at Carnegie Hall 1963; musical version of Othello
    (tour) 1966.
Relationships: Cousin of Pam Grier, actress.

GRIST, RERI
    (Opera Singer)
b. New York, N. Y.
Education: H. S. of Music and Art; Queens College B. A.
Address: c/o Metropolitan Opera Assn., Lincoln Center Plaza,
    New York, N. Y. 10023.
Honors: Blanche Thebom Award for Voice 1958.
Career Data: Sang with Santa Fe Opera Co. 1959; debut with N. Y.
    C. Opera Co. 1959; Cologne Germany Opera Co.; N. Y. Metro-
    politan Opera Co.; repertoire includes: Queen of the Night in
    Magic Flute; The Nightingale; Zerbinetta in Ariadne auf Naxos;
    Blonda in Abduction from the Seraglio; Marriage of Figaro.
Theater: Jeb 1946; The Wisteria Trees 1950; The Barrier 1951;
    Cindy Lou in Carmen Jones 1956; Shinbone Alley 1957; West
    Side Story 1957; appeared at Covent Garden (London); La
    Scala (Milan); Vienna State Opera.

GUILLAUME, ROBERT (Robert Williams)
    (Actor)
b. November 30, 1927, St. Louis, Mo.
Address: 365 West End Avenue, New York, N. Y. 10024.
Honors: Joseph Jefferson Award.
Career Data: Former member, Karamu Theatre (Cleveland); artis-
    tic director, Afro-American Theatre; wrote Music, Music;
    wrote Montezuma's Revenge 1971.
Films: Super Fly T. N. T. 1973.
Records: Big Man.

Television: Marcus Welby, M. D. 1974; All in the Family 1975; Sanford and Son 1975; The Jeffersons 1975; Black News 1976, Positively Black 1976; Soap (series) 1977.

Theater: Babu in Benito Cereno (Goodman Theatre production); Johnny Williams in No Place to Be Somebody (Arena Stage); title role in Othello (WSF); Charlie Was Here and Now He Is Gone (O. B.); Music and Music (O. B.); Miracle Play (O. B.); Finian's Rainbow (City Center) 1960; Kwamina (Bway debut) 1961; Porgy and Bess (tour and City Center) 1961, 64; Tambourines to Glory (O. B.) 1963; Golden Boy 1964; Life and Times of J. Walter Smintheus (O. B.) 1970; title role in Purlie (replacing Cleavon Little 1970, and at Kennedy Center for Performing Arts, Washington, D. C. 1975); Jacques Brel Is Alive and Well and Living in Paris (O. B.) 1971; wrote Montezuma's Revenge 1971; Apple Pie (NYSF) 1976; Guys and Dolls 1976.

GUNN, BILL (William Harrison Gunn)
    (Playwright/Actor/Director)
b.   July 15, 1934, Philadelphia, Pa.
Address: Nyack, N. Y.
Honors: Emmy for best teleplay 1972; AUDELCO Black Theatre Recognition award 1975.
Films: Acted in: The Sound and the Fury 1959; The Interns 1962; Penelope, The Spy with My Face 1966; wrote and/or co-wrote: The Angel Levine, The Landlord 1970; wrote, directed and acted in Ganja and Hess (a. k. a. Blood Couple) 1973.
Television: acted in: Studio One; Danger; Route 66; The Interns; The Fugitive; Outer Limits; Stoney Burke; Tarzan; wrote Joannas 1968; acted in Sojourner (American Parade) 1975.
Theater: Acted in: Member of the Wedding 1950; The Immoralist 1954; Take a Giant Step (O. B.) 1956; Moon on a Rainbow Shawl (O. B.) 1962; Antony and Cleopatra (NYSF) 1963; A Winters Tale (NYSF) 1963. Wrote: The Celebration; The Owlight; That's Gustavo; Marcus in the High Grass 1958; Black Picture Show (and directed production for NYSF) 1974.

GUNN, MOSES
    (Actor)
b.   October 2, 1929, St. Louis, Mo.
Education: Tennessee State University B. A. 1959; University of Kansas, Graduate work in Speech and Drama 1959-61.
Special Interests: Directing.
Address: 395 Nut Plains Road, Guilford, Conn. 06437.
Honors: Obie (for Titus Andronicus) 1967-68; Obie (for The First Breeze of Summer) 1975; Lola D'Annunzio Award 1967-68; Jersey Journal Award 1967-68; Tony nomination best actor (for Poison Tree) 1976.
Career Data: Professor of Speech, Grambling College (La.); Member, Negro Ensemble Company; Karamu House Players, Cleveland.

Films: Nothing but a Man 1964; The Great White Hope 1970; Shaft,
        W. U. S. A. , Wild Rovers 1971; Hot Rock, Shaft's Big Score,
        Eagle in a Cage 1972; The Iceman Cometh 1973; Amazing
        Grace, The Pond 1974; Rollerball; Cornbread, Earl and Me
        1975; Aaron Loves Angela 1975.
Memberships: AEA; AFTRA; SAG.
Records: A Hand Is on the Gate; In White America.
Television: Armstrong Circle Theatre; N. Y. P. D. ; East Side, West
        Side; Of Mice and Men; Kung Fu; Nothing But Biography; Chase;
        The Borgia Stick; The Talking Drum (series); The FBI 1969;
        Carter's Army 1970; Love, American Style 1971; The Sheriff
        1971; Hawaii Five-O 1971; Haunts of the Very Rich 1972; Mc-
        Cloud 1972; If You Give a Dance You Gotta Pay the Band (ABC
        Theatre) 1972; The Cowboys (series) 1972-73; Moving Target
        1973; Legacy of Blood (Wide World Mystery) 1974; The Jef-
        fersons 1975; Positively Black 1975; Movin' On 1975; The Bi-
        centennial: A Black Perspective 1975; Black News 1976; The
        First Breeze of Summer (PBS) 1976; Law of the Land 1976;
        Kup's Show 1976; Switch 1976; Roots 1977; Good Times (series)
        1977; Quincy 1977.
Theater: The Perfect Party; Bohikee Creek; Measure for Measure;
        Romeo and Juliet; The Tempest; As You Like It; Macbeth;
        Hamlet; Twelfth Night; Henry IV Pt. 1; Cities of Bezique (in-
        cludes The Owl Answers and The Beast Story); Baal (O. B.);
        The Blacks (O. B.) 1961; In White America (O. B.) 1963; A
        Hand Is on the Gate 1966; Day of Absence (NEC) 1966; June
        Bug Graduates Tonight (O. B.) 1967; Aaron the Moor in Titus
        Andronicus (NYSF) 1967; Kongi's Harvest (NEC) 1968; Song of
        the Lusitanian Bogey (NEC) 1968; Summer of the Seventeenth
        Doll (NEC) 1968; Daddy Goodness (NEC) 1968; Othello (ASF)
        1970; directed Contributions (O. B.) 1970; Sty of the Blind Pig
        (NEC) 1972; A Wedding Band (O. B.) 1973; The First Breeze
        of Summer (NEC) 1975; The Poison Tree 1976; Martin Luther
        King in I Have a Dream (replacing Billy Dee Williams) 1976.

GUYSE, SHEILA
        (Actress/Singer)
b. Forest, Miss.
Clubs: Zombie (Detroit).
Films: Boy, What a Girl! 1946; Sepia Cinderella 1947; Miracle in
        Harlem 1948.
Records: This Is Sheila (MGM).
Theater: Memphis Bound 1945; Lost in the Stars 1949.

HAIRSTON, JESTER (Joseph)
        (Actor/Composer)
b. July 9, 1901.
Education: Tufts University 1929; Juilliard School of Music.
Special Interests: Arranging, conducting.
Address: 5047 Valley Ridge Avenue, Los Angeles, Calif. 90043.
Career Data: Assistant conductor, Hall Johnson choir; director,

Federal Theatre Project; U. S. O. Show 1945; toured Europe for
U. S. State Dept. 1961.
Films: Green Pastures 1936; arranger and conductor, Lost Horizon
1937; Duel in the Sun 1946; arranger and conductor, Portrait
of Jennie 1948; acted in Road to Zanzibar 1941; Tarzan's Hid-
den Jungle 1955; arranger and conductor, Friendly Persuasion
1956; Raymie, The Alamo 1960; acted in In the Heat of the
Night 1967; Lady Sings the Blues 1972.
Memberships: ASCAP 1956.
Musical Compositions: Mary's Boy Child; Elijah Rock; Poor Man
Lazrus; Amen; Gossip, Gossip; In Dat Great Gittin' Up Mor-
nin'.
Radio: Leroy on Amos 'n Andy (series); Beulah (series).
Television: Wildcat in That's My Mama (series) 1974, Harry O
1975.
Theater: Hello Paris 1930.

HAIRSTON, WILLIAM
        (Playwright)
Theater: Acted in Ride the Right Bus (People's Showcase Theatre)
1951; wrote Walk in Darkness 1963; The World of Carlos
1967; The Honeymooners 1967.

HAIZLIP, ELLIS
        (Producer)
b.   1932.
Address: c/o WNET, 356 West 58 Street, New York, N. Y. 10019
and 431 West 54 Street, New York, N. Y. 10019.
Career Data: Board of Directors, Symphony of the New World;
member, Howard University Players; organized conference for
minority writers for television co-funded by N. Y. State Council on the Arts and Corporation for Public Broadcasting (Tarry-
town) 1976.
Television: Executive producer and host of Soul (WNET series)
1968-7?; Positively Black 1976; produced Sixty Period (WNET
series) 1976.
Theater: Staged Black Nativity 1961; Trumpets of the Lord 1963;
The Amen Corner (European production) 1965; co-host of
Truckin' (Black Theatre Alliance production at Harlem Cultural Council) 1974.

HALL, ADELAIDE
        (Actress/Singer)
b.   October 20, 1910, Brooklyn, N. Y.
Special Interests: Guitar, painting.
Address: 1A Collingham Road, London S. W. 5, England.
Clubs: Owned The Big Apple (Paris); owned The New Florida (Lon-
don) 1939; performed at The Alhambra, Les Ambassadeurs, The
Lido, Le Moulin Rouge (Paris) 1934-38; The Cotton Club and
The Savoy 1937; The Savoy (London) 1938.

Films: The All-Colored Vaudeville Show; The Thief of Bagdad
‾‾‾‾‾1940; Night and the City 1950.
Memberships: AEA; AFTRA; BAEA.
Records: Creole Love Call (with Duke Ellington) 1927; Digga Digga
‾‾‾‾‾Doo.
Television: Paris Soir (1st TV show in Paris).
Theater:‾‾Shuffle Along 1922; Runnin Wild (N. Y. C. debut) 1923;
‾‾‾‾‾Chocolate Dandies 1925; Blackbirds of 1928 1928; Brown Bud-
dies 1930; Fitema in The Sun Never Sets (London) 1938; Hattie
in Kiss Me, Kate (London) 1951; Love from Judy (London)
1952; Someone to Talk To (London) 1956; Grandma Obeah in
Jamaica 1957; Janie Jackson (London) 1968; Paul Robeson an-
niversary concert at Royal Festival Hall (London) 1968; appeared at Palladium (London).

HALL, ALBERT (P.)
     (Actor)
b.   November 10, 1937, Boothton, Ala.
Education: Columbia University.
Special Interests: Pantomime.
Films: Shamus 1973; Willie Dynamite 1974; Leadbelly 1976.
Memberships: AEA.
Television: If You Give a Dance You Gotta Pay the Band; Wedding
‾‾‾‾‾Band; Sanford and Son 1975; Monkey in the Middle 1976.
Theater: Richard III (NYSF); Henry IV Pts. I and II (NYSF); As
‾‾‾‾‾You Like It (NYSF); Miss Julie; Les Femmes Noires; The
Dutchman (O. B.) 1965; The Basic Training of Pavlo Hummel
(O. B.) 1971; Ain't Supposed to Die a Natural Death 1971; The
Duplex (O. B.) 1973; A Wedding Band (O. B.) 1973; Black Pic-
ture Show 1974; We Interrupt This Program ... 1975; Rubbers
(O. B.) 1975; Yanks 3 Detroit 0 Top of the Seventh (O. B.) 1975.

HALL, ED
     (Actor)
b.   January 11, 1931, Roxbury, Mass.
Education: Howard University (drama); studied at American Shake-
‾‾‾‾‾speare Festival Academy; studied acting with Lloyd Richards.
Address: c/o Norah Sanders Agency, 9301 Wilshire Blvd. , Beverly
‾‾‾‾‾Hills, Calif. 90212.
Career Data: Performed with repertory theatre companies including
‾‾‾‾‾Center Theatre Group (Los Angeles): Henry IV Pt. I, Arena
Stage (Washington D. C.); Trinity Square Repertory Co. (Provi-
dence, R. I.): The Dutchman, Tooth of Crime, Peer Gynt and
many other productions.
Memberships: AEA; AFTRA; ACTRA; AGMA; SAG.
Radio: Phillip Morris Playhouse.
Television: U. S. Steel Hour; Omnibus; Naked City; The Climate of
‾‾‾‾‾Eden (Play of the Week); Solomon in The Road (presented in
4 parts); Dr. Stan Bricker in Medical Center (series); The
F. B. I. ; Courtship of Eddie's Father; The Nurses; The Defenders;
East Side, West Side; Mannix; Young Dr. Kildare; The Heist

(Movie of the Week); McCloud; Streets of San Francisco; Barnaby Jones 1976.

Theater: The Climate of Eden; No Time for Sergeants; Wilson in The Promised Land; Emanuel XOC (Canada); Death of Bessie Smith (O. B.); Trumpets of the Lord (O. B.); Black Nativity (tour); A Raisin in the Sun 1960; Blues for Mister Charlie 1964; The Zulu and the Zayda 1965; The World of Sholom Aleichem (O. B.) 1976.

HALL, JUANITA (Juanita Long)
       (Actress/Singer)
b. November 6, 1902, Keyport, N. J.
d. February 28, 1968, Bayshore L. I.
Education: Juilliard School of Music.
Special Interests: Arranging, composing.
Honors: Tony award and Donaldson award (for South Pacific) 1950; Bill "Bojangles" acting award, 20th Century-Fox appreciation award and Box Office Film Assn. award (for film South Pacific) 1958; The Laurel award as best actress 1962.
Career Data: Asst. dir. Hall Johnson Choir 1931-36; dir. , W. P. A. choral group 1936-41; musical dramatic activities, Westchester Negro Choral and Dramatic Assn. 1941-42; founder and dir. , Juanita Hall Choir.
Clubs: Shelbourne Lounge; Cafe Society; St. Moritz; Flamingo (Las Vegas); Black Orchid (Chicago); Latin Quarter (Boston); Town and Country (St. Louis); Elmwood Casino (Windsor, Canada); Town Casino (Buffalo); The Flame (Detroit); Le Cupidon, Five O'Clock Club (Miami); Thunderbird Hotel (Las Vegas).
Films: Miracle in Harlem 1948; South Pacific 1958; Flower Drum Song 1961.
Memberships: AEA; AFTRA; AGVA; SAG.
Radio: Ruby Valentine (series) 1954.
Television: This Is Show Business, Philco Television Playhouse, The Ed Sullivan Show, Perry Como Show, Today Show, Coca Cola Hour, Mike Wallace-P. M. East, Schlitz Playhouse of Stars 1952.
Theater: Show Boat 1928; The Green Pastures 1930; mango seller in The Pirate 1942; Sing Out Sweet Land 1944; Deep Are the Roots 1945; The Secret Room 1945; Leah in St. Louis Woman 1946; Mr. Peebles and Mr. Hooker 1946; Street Scene 1947; S. S. Glencairn (City Center) 1948; Moon of the Caribees (City Center) 1948; Bloody Mary in South Pacific 1949, (City Center) 1957; Singing the Blues (Apollo Theatre) 1953; Madame Tango in House of Flowers 1954; The Ponder Heart 1956; Madame Liang in The Flower Drum Song 1958, (tour) 1960; Mardi Gras (Jones Beach).

HAMILTON, BERNIE
       (Actor)
Honors: Black Filmmakers Hall of Fame 1976.
Films: The Jackie Robinson Story 1950; Jungle Man Eaters 1954;

Let No Man Write My Epitaph 1959; The Young One 1960; The
Devil at 4 O'Clock 1961; 13 West Street 1962; One Potato Two
Potato 1964; Synanon 1965; The Swimmer 1968; The Lost Man
1969; The Losers 1970; The Organization 1971; Hammer 1972;
Scream, Blacula, Scream 1973; Bucktown 1975.

Memberships: SAG.

Television: Alfred Hitchcock Presents; Ironside; The Dick Van Dyke
Show; Police Story; Six Million Dollar Man; The Name of the
Game 1968; A Clear and Present Danger 1970; That's My
Mama 1975; Captain Dobey in Starsky and Hutch (series) 1975;
Celebrity Sweepstakes 1976.

HAMILTON, CHICO (Foreststorn Hamilton)
   (Musician)
b.   September 21, 1921, Los Angeles, Calif.
Education: Studied with Jo Jones.
Special Interests: Clarinet, drums.
Career Data: Worked with Illinois Jacquet, Charlie Mingus, Count
Basie, Charlie Barnet, Lionel Hampton 1940, Lester Young
1941, Lena Horne 1948-52, 1954-55, Jerry Mulligan 1952; or-
ganized his own band; performed at Montreux Jazz Festival
1970.
Clubs: Mikell's; Billy Berg's (Hollywood); Village Gate 1976.
Films: Drummer in Road to Bali 1953; music and appearance in
Sweet Smell of Success 1957; Jazz on a Summer's Day (doc.)
1960; Repulsion (score) 1965; The Confession 1974.
Records: Chase and Steeple Chase; Bernie's Tune; Peregrinations
(Blue Note); Best (Impulse); Chic Chic Chico (Impulse); Dealer
(Impulse); El Chico (Impulse); Head Hunter (Solid State); Man
from 2 Worlds (Impulse); Passin' Thru (Impulse).
Television: Jazz a La Montreux.
Theater: Appearances at Felt Forum 1975; Carnegie Hall 1975;
Symphony Hall (Newark) 1975; Town Hall 1976.

HAMILTON, KIM
   (Actress)
b.   Los Angeles, Calif.
Education: Los Angeles City College.
Address: Marvin Moss 9200 Sunset Blvd., Los Angeles, Calif.
90069.
Films: Odds Against Tomorrow 1959; The Leech Woman 1960; The
Wizard of Bagdad 1960; The Wild Angels 1966.
Memberships: SAG.
Television: Amos 'n' Andy; Dr. Tracey Adams in General Hospital
(series); Clear Horizons (series); Mod Squad; Rookies; All in
the Family; Kojak; That's My Mama; Mannix; Adam-12; Ben
Casey 1963; Marcus Welby, M.D. 1975; Sanford and Son 1975;
Emergency 1975; Good Times 1975; Bronk 1975; Adam-12
1976.
Theater: Raisin in the Sun (London) 1959-60.

HAMILTON, LYNN
    (Actress)
b. Chicago, Ill.
Education: Goodman Memorial Theatre (Chicago).
Career Data: U. S. Cultural Exchange Program tours of Europe,
    Near East, South America with Theatre Guild Repertory Co. ;
    Seattle Repertory Theatre 1967.
Films: The New Girl (doc.); That Kind of Woman, Middle of the
    Night 1959; Shadows 1961; The Seven Minutes, Brother John
    1971; Buck and the Preacher 1972; Super Dude 1975; Leadbelly
    1976.
Memberships: AEA; AFTRA; SAG.
Television: Car 54 Where Are You?; The Naked City; Edge of
    Night; The Nurses; Look Up and Live; Cxydol and Scott Tis-
    sue commercials; The Green Pastures (Hallmark Hall of Fame);
    The Doctors (series); Insight; Donna in Sanford and Son (series)
    1973-; A Dream for Christmas 1973; Waltons 1973; Starsky
    and Hutch 1975; Rockford Files 1976.
Theater: Shaw's Black Girl in Search of God (YMHA); The Irregu-
    lar Verb to Love (tour); Climate of Eden (ELT); No Exit (O.
    B.); Land Beyond the River 1957; Only in America (O. B.)
    1959; The Cool World 1960; Face of a Hero 1960; Tambourines
    to Glory (O. B.) 1963; The Blacks (O. B.) 1963; A Midsummer
    Night's Dream (NYSF) 1964; Macbeth (NYSF) 1966; The Wed-
    ding Band.

HAMILTON, ROY
    (Singer)
b. April 16, 1929, Leesburg, Ga.
d. July 20, 1969, New Rochelle, N. Y.
Education: Lincoln High School (Jersey City, N. J.).
Career Data: Formerly amateur boxer who became popular record-
    ing star.
Records: I Believe; You'll Never Walk Alone 1954; If I Loved You
    1954; Ebb Tide 1954; Unchained Melody 1955; Without a Song
    1955; Multi-talented Roy Hamilton 1957; Don't Let Go 1958.
Television: American Bandstand; Ed Sullivan Toast of the Town
    1955.
Theater: Appeared at Apollo Theatre, 1958, 1959, 1960, 1961.

HAMPTON, LIONEL (Leo)
    (Conductor/Musician)
b. April 20, 1913, Louisville, Ky.
Education: U. C. L. A.
Special Interests: Composing, drums, piano, harp, vibraphones.
Address: 165 West 46 Street, New York, N. Y. 10036 and 1 Lin-
    coln Plaza, New York, N. Y. 10023.
Honors: Metronome Poll 1944-46; Esquire New Star Band award
    1945; Down Beat Critics Poll 1954; Medal from Pope Paul VI;
    Handel cultural award 1966.
Career Data: Played with Les Hite band 1932-36, Benny Goodman

band and small groups 1936-40; formed his own band 1940;
president Lionel Hampton Enterprises Inc.; London's Jazz
Expo 1969; Newport Jazz Festival; toured Europe, Japan,
Africa, Australia, the Middle East; organized Swing and Tempo Music Publishing Co.

Clubs: Sebastian's Cotton Club (Culver City, Calif.); Rainbow Grill;
Palm Gardens (Bronx); Paradise Café (Hollywood) 1936; Riverboat 1974; Jupiter's (Franklin, L. I.) 1975; Buddy's Place
1975; Host Farm Cabaret (Lancaster, Pa.) 1975.

Films: Depths Below; Pennies from Heaven 1936; Hollywood Hotel
1938; A Song Is Born 1948; Rock and Roll Revue 1955; The
Benny Goodman Story 1956; Mister Rock and Roll 1957.

Memberships: Friars; Masons.

Musical Compositions: Hamp's Boogie Woogie; Air Mail Special;
Ambulance Special; Flying Home.

Records: Lionel Hampton All-Stars; The Works!; Vibraphone Blues;
Golden Favorites (MCA); Best of ... (MCA); Jazz Man for All
Seasons (Folkways); Just Jazz All Stars (GNP Crescendo);
Original Star Dust (MCA).

Television: One Night Stand 1971; Kup's Show 1975; Positively
Black 1975; Mike Douglas Show 1975; Black Pride 1975; Sunday 1975; Dinah! 1976; Festival of Lively Arts for Young
People 1976.

Theater: Swinging the Dream 1939; Apollo Theatre 1955; Olympia
Theatre (Paris); Royal Festival Hall (London) 1957; Carnegie
Hall 1974; Avery Fisher Hall 1975; Clams on the Half Shell
Revue (with Bette Midler at Uris Theatre) 1975; Town Hall
1976.

HANCOCK, HERBIE (Herbert Jeffrey Hancock)
      (Pianist/Composer)
b.   April 12, 1940, Chicago, Ill.

Education: Grinnell College 1956-60; Roosevelt University 1960;
Manhattan School of Music 1962; New School for Social Research 1967.

Special Interests: Publishing.

Address: 202 Riverside Drive, New York, N. Y. 10025.

Honors: Citation of Achievement, Broadcast Music Inc. 1963; Jay
award, Jazz Magazine 1964; Down Beat critics poll 1967;
Record World all-star brand new artist award 1968; Down Beat
1st place piano award 1968-70, composer award 1971.

Career Data: Played with Chicago Symphony Orchestra 1952; performed with Coleman Hawkins 1960, Donald Byrd 1960-63,
Miles Davis 1963-68; formed his own septet; owner-publisher,
Hancock Music Company; Newport Jazz Festival 1976; president, Harlem Jazz Music Center.

Films: Something to Build On (doc.); Blow Up (score) 1966; Watermelon Man (score) 1970; Death Wish (score) 1974.

Memberships: Jazz Musicians Assn.; NARAS; NATAS.

Records: Crossings (Warner Bros.); Empyrean Isles (Blue Note);
Fat Albert Rotunda (Warner Bros.); Herbie Hancock (Blue
Note); Maiden Voyage (Blue Note); Mwandishi (Warner Bros.);

My Point of View (Blue Note); Prisoner (Blue Note); Secrets
(Columbia); Sextant (Columbia); Speak Like a Child (Blue Note);
Succotash (Blue Note); Takin' Off (Blue Note); Chameleon;
Treasure Chest (Warner Bros.); Thrust (Columbia); Head
Hunters (Columbia); Man-Child (Columbia); V. S. O. P. (Colum-
bia).

Television: Hey Hey Hey It's Fat Albert 1967; Soul Train 1974;
 Wide World Special; Soundstage 1975; Midnight Special 1975;
 Don Kirshner's Rock Concert 1976; Festival of Lively Arts
 for Young People 1976.

Theater: Appeared at Carnegie Hall (An Evening with Herbie Hancock) 1974, 1975; The Felt Forum; Music Center (Commack,
 L. I.) 1975; City Center 1976; Radio City Music Hall 1976.

HANDY, W. C. "Father of the Blues" (William Christopher Handy)
 (Composer)
b.   November 16, 1873, Florence, Ala.
d.   March 28, 1958, New York, N. Y.
Education: Alabama's A & M College, Fisk University.
Special Interests: Cornet.
Career Data: Organized a quartet in Birmingham and played at
 Chicago World's Fair 1893; bandmaster, Mahara's Minstrels
 1896-1900; music instructor, A & M College, Normal, Alabama 1900-02; formed Pace and Handy Music Co. (publisher)
 1913-21; President, Handy Brothers Music Co. 1949.
Films: Satchmo the Great (doc.) 1958.
Memberships: ASCAP 1924; NAG; National Assn. of Negro Musi-
 cians.
Musical Compositions: Memphis Blues (a. k. a. Mr. Crump) 1912;
 Jogo Blues 1913; St. Louis Blues 1914; Yellow Dog Blues
 1914; Joe Turner Blues 1915; Beale Street Blues 1916; Care-
 less Love (a. k. a. Loveless Love) 1921; Aunt Hager's Blues
 1922; Chantez Les Bas; East St. Louis Blues; John Henry;
 Annie Love; Hail to the Spirit of Freedom; Big Stick Blues
 March; Atlanta Blues; Wall Street Blues; Blue Destiny; Hesi-
 tation Blues Old Miss; Aframerican Hymn; Harlem Blues;
 Basement Blues; Symphony for Orchestra 1945.
Publications: Blues: An Anthology, 1926; Negro Authors and Com-
 posers of the U. S. , 1936; Father of the Blues (autobiography),
 Macmillan, 1941; Unsung Americans Sung; A Treasury of the
 Blues 1949.
Records: Blues Revisited (Heritage).
Theater: Appeared at Carnegie Hall (History of Music Concert)
 1928; Harlem Opera House; Apollo Theatre 1936.

HANSBERRY, LORRAINE (Vivian)
 (Playwright)
b.   May 19, 1930, Chicago, Ill.
d.   January 12, 1965, New York, N. Y.
Education: Art Institute of Chicago; University of Wisconsin; New
 School for Social Research.

Honors: Drama Critics Circle award 1960; Cannes Film Festival
        award 1961; Black Filmmakers Hall of Fame (posthumously)
        1975.
Films: A Raisin in the Sun 1961.
Records: Lorraine Hansberry Speaks Out (Caedmon); Art and the
        Black Revolution (Caedmon).
Television: Follow the Drinking Gourd (unproduced) 1960.
Theater: A Raisin in the Sun 1959; The Sign in Sidney Brustein's
        Window 1965; To Be Young, Gifted and Black (produced posthu-
        mously) 1969; Les Blancs (produced posthumously) 1970.

HAREWOOD, DORIAN
        (Actor/Singer)
b.   August 6, c. 1950, Dayton, Ohio.
Education: Cincinnati's Conservatory of Music.
Special Interests: Piano, song writing.
Films: Sparkle 1976.
Memberships: AEA.
Television: Gregory Foster in Foster and Laurie 1975.
Theater: Judas in Jesus Christ Superstar (tour); Two Gentlemen of
        Verona 1972; Miss Moffat (pre-Broadway tour) 1974; Don't
        Call Back 1975; Carlyle in Streamers (NYSF) 1976.

HARPER, KEN
        (Producer)
b.   c. 1939, Bronx, N. Y.
Address: Emanuel Azenberg, 165 West 46 Street, Room 914, New
        York, N. Y. 10036.
Honors: Tony award (for The Wiz) 1975.
Radio: Disc jockey, music director, program affairs director,
        WPIX-FM.
Television: Host, Call Back; acted in Another World (series);
        Black News 1975; Positively Black 1975; CBS News 1976; Pat
        Collins Show 1976.
Theater: Produced The Wiz 1975.

HARRIS, EDDIE
        (Jazz Musician)
b.   October 20, 1934.
Special Interests: Tenor saxophone.
Films: Soul to Soul 1971.
Memberships: NAG.
Records: Shades of ... (Trip); Genius (Tradition); Black Sax (GNP
        Crescendo); Cool Sax (Columbia). On Atlantic: This Is Why
        You're Overweight; E. H. in the U. K.; Electrifying; Excursions;
        High Voltage; Is It In; Second Movement; Exodus (Vee Jay)
        1961; I Need Some Money; Listen Here 1968; Bad Luck Is All
        I Have 1975; The Best of Eddie Harris; This Is Soul; How Can
        You Live Like That (Atlantic).
Television: Ebony Music Award Show 1975; Soul Train 1975.

HARRIS, EDNA MAE
    (Actress)
b.   c. 1914, New York, N. Y.
Career Data: Vocalist with Noble Sissle orchestra and Benny Car-
    ter band.
Films: Lying Lips; Zeba in The Green Pastures, Garden of Allah,
    Bullets or Ballots, Private Number 1936; Spirit of Youth 1938;
    Paradise in Harlem 1939; The Notorious Elinor Lee 1940;
    Murder on Lenox Avenue, Sunday Sinners 1941; Rhythm on the
    Run 1942.
Memberships: NAG.
Theater: The Green Pastures 1930, (revival) 1935; appeared at
    Apollo Theatre 1939; Good Neighbor 1941; Run Little Chillun
    1943; A Long Way from Home 1938.

HARRIS, JULIUS (W.)
    (Actor)
b.   c. 1924, Philadelphia, Pa.
Education: Studied with Herbert Berghof.
Address: c/o Ronald Muchnick-Yvette Schumer, 1697 Broadway,
    New York, N. Y. 10019.
Films: Nothing But a Man 1964; Slaves 1969; Trouble Man, Shaft's
    Big Score, Super Fly 1972; Black Caesar, Hell Up in Harlem,
    Live and Let Die 1973; The Taking of Pelham 1-2-3 1974;
    Let's Do It Again, Friday Foster 1975; Islands in the Stream
    1977.
Memberships: AEA; SAG.
Television: N. Y. P. D. ; Bob Newhart Show; Late Night Thriller;
    Salty (series) 1974; A Cry for Help 1975; Harry O 1975; Doc-
    tors Hospital 1975; Idi Amin in Victory at Entebbe 1976; San-
    ford and Son 1977.
Theater: The Amen Corner (tour) 1965; Bohikee Creek (O. B.) 1966;
    God Is a (Guess What?) (NEC) 1968; String (NEC) 1969; No
    Place to Be Somebody 1971.

HARRIS, THERESA
    (Actress)
Education: University of Southern California (music).
Honors: Black Filmmakers Hall of Fame 1974.
Career Data: Noted for appearances as Eddie "Rochester" Ander-
    son's girl friend in numerous films.
Films: Hold Your Man, Blood Money, Professional Sweetheart,
    Baby Face 1933; Jezebel, The Toy Wife 1938; Man About Town,
    Tell No Tales 1939; Buck Benny Rides Again, Love Thy Neigh-
    bor 1940; Flame of New Orleans, Our Wife, Blossoms in the
    Dust 1941; The Cat People 1942; I Walked with a Zombie,
    What's Buzzin Cousin? 1943; Three Little Girls in Blue,
    Smooth As Silk 1946; Miracle on 34th Street 1947; Thelma
    Jordan 1950; Grounds for Marriage, Al Jennings of Oklahoma
    1951.
Memberships: SAG.

HARRISON, PAUL CARTER
    (Playwright)
b. 1936.
Education: Actor's Studio (Playwrights unit).
Special Interests: Directing, teaching.
Address: 172 West 79 Street, New York, N.Y. 10024 or Amsterdam,
    Holland.
Honors: Obie award (for The Great MacDaddy) 1974; Obie nominee
    (for Tabernacle) 1974.
Career Data: Taught at the University of Massachusetts 1974.
Publications: The Drama of Nommo-Black Theater in the African
    Continuum, Grosset & Dunlap, 1972; Kuntu Drama-Plays of the
    African Continuum, Grove Press, 1974.
Theater: Wrote the Adding Machine; wrote Pavane for a Dead Pan
    Minstrel 1965; wrote Pawns (one act) (O. B.) 1966; wrote The
    Experimental Leader; directed Junebug Graduates Tonight (O.
    B.) 1967; wrote Tabernacle 1969; wrote Brer Soul 1970; di-
    rected his own play Top Hat (NEC) and Clay Goss' Home Cook-
    ing (NEC) 1971; directed Lady Day: A Musical Tragedy (Brook-
    lyn) 1972; wrote The Great MacDaddy 1972; wrote Dr. Jazz
    1975.

HARRISON, RICHARD (Berry)
    (Actor)
b. September 28, 1864, London, Ontario.
d. March 14, 1935, New York, N. Y.
Education: Training School of Art, Detroit.
Special Interests: Lecturing, elocution.
Honors: Spingarn medal 1931.
Career Data: Founded Dramatic School, North Carolina A & T State
    University, Greensboro, 1922-29.
Films: How High Is Up 1923; Easy Street 1930.
Theater: Macbeth (one man version); Julius Caesar (one man ver-
    sion); Pa Williams' Gal (Lafayette Theatre); Shylock in The
    Merchant of Venice (tour); title role in Othello (tour); De Lawd
    in The Green Pastures (Bway debut) 1930.

HARTMAN, ENA
    (Actress)
Address: Moss Agency, Ltd. , 113 N. San Vicente Blvd. , Beverly
    Hills, Calif. 90211.
Films: The New Interns 1965; Our Man Flint 1966; Airport 1970.
Memberships: SAG.
Television: Ironside; Bonanza; Name of the Game; Adam-12; It
    Takes a Thief 1968; Katie in Dan August (series) 1970-71.

HARTMAN, JOHNNY
    (Singer)
Career Data: Vocalist with bands of Earl Hines and Dizzy Gillespie.
Clubs: Parisian Room (L. A.); Cafe Society 1949; Copacabana (Philad.)

1949; Playboy Club 1972; Half Note Cafe 1973; Seafood Play-
house 1975; Across 110th Street 1975; The New Barrister
1975; Michael's Pub 1976, 1977.
Records: On RCA: Worrybird 1951, Out of the Night 1951. On
Impulse: John Coltrane and Johnny Hartman; I Just Dropped
By to Say Hello; Voice That Is.
Television: Arthur Godfrey's Talent Scouts 1950; Positively Black
1975.
Theater: Appearances at Paramount Theatre; Avery Fisher Hall
(Newport Jazz Festival) 1975.

HAVENS, RICHIE (Richard P. Havens)
     (Folk Singer)
b. January 21, 1941, Brooklyn, N. Y.
Education: Franklin K. Lane High School (Brooklyn).
Special Interests: Guitar, songwriting, sketching, poetry, writing
lyrics.
Career Data: Accompanied Nina Simone and Steve De Pass on Ford
Foundation tour; appeared at Expo' 67; formed Stormy Forest
Production Co. (records); member, Fresh Flavor (singing
group) 1973.
Clubs: Night Owl Cafe; Village Gate; Second Frett (Philadelphia);
The Bottom Line 1976; Smucker's (Brooklyn) 1977.
Films: Woodstock 1970; Catch My Soul 1974; Ali the Man 1975;
Santa Fe Satan 1976; Greased Lightening 1977.
Musical Compositions: Younger Men Grow Older.
Records: Mixed Bag (Verve) 1967; Somethin' Else Again 1968;
Richie Havens Record; Electric Richie Havens 1968; Richard
P. Havens, 1983 1968; 3 Day Eternity 1968; Alarm Clock
(STF); Great Blind Degree (STF); Richie Havens on Stage (STF);
Mixed Bag II (STF); Portfolio (STF); Stonehenge (STF); Tommy
(Ode); Indian Rope Man; Tribute to Woody Guthrie v. 1 (Colum-
bia); Tribute to Woody Guthrie v. 2 (Warner Bros.); Sesame
Song; Mirage (A&M) 1977.
Television: Merv Griffin Show; Tonight Show.
Theater: Appeared at Fillmore East 1968; Philharmonic Hall 1968,
1969, 1971; Fillmore West 1968; Woodstock; Avery Fisher Hall
1973; Carnegie Hall and concert at Museum of Modern Art
1968; Bohikee Creek (O. B.) 1966; produced Safari Zoo 1972;
Wollman Theatre, Central Park (Schaefer Music Festival) 1973,
1975; appeared at South Mountain Arena (N. J.) 1976.

HAWKINS, COLEMAN "Bean"; "Hawk"
     (Jazz Musician)
b. November 21, 1904, St. Joseph, Mo.
d. May 19, 1969, New York, N. Y.
Education: Washburn College (Topeka, Kansas).
Special Interests: Tenor saxophone.
Honors: Down Beat award 1939; Esquire (gold) award 1944-47;
Metronome award 1945-47.
Career Data: Played with Fletcher Henderson orchestra 1924-34;

led his own big band 1939-41, small band 1941-43, sextet
1945; Paris Jazz Festival 1948; participated in National Jazz
at the Philharmonic tours; co-led quintet with Roy Eldridge;
toured Europe 1934-39, 1948-50, 1957, 1967; Seven Ages of
Jazz presentations, Canada.

Clubs: White Horse Tavern (Kansas City); Kelly's Stables; Savoy
Ballroom; Golden Gate Ballroom; Arcadia Ballroom; Café Society; Terrassi's; Metropole; Village Gate; Village Vanguard.

Films: In Town Tonight (Brit. short); Stormy Weather 1943; The
Crimson Canary 1945.

Records: Desafinado (Impulse); Blues Groove (Prestige); Coleman
Hawkins (Archive of Folk & Jazz Music); Hawk Eyes (Pres-
tige); Night Hawk (Prestige); Pioneers (Prestige); Today and
Now (Impulse); Very Saxy (Prestige); Wrapped Tight (Impulse);
The Boys (Prestige); ... And the Trumpet Kings (Trip); In
Concert (Phoenix); In Holland (GNP Crescendo); Originals with
Hawkins (Stinson); Hollywood Stampede (Capitol); Coleman
Hawkins and Lester Young (Zim); Classic Tenors (Flying
Dutchman); Body and Soul (Bluebird); The Hawk Flies (Mile-
stone); On Tenor; Sirius (Pablo); The High and Mighty Hawk
(Master Jazz).

Theater: Appeared at Apollo Theatre.

HAWKINS, ERSKINE "The Hawk" (Ramsey)
(Musician/Conductor)
b. July 26, 1914, Birmingham, Ala.
Education: Alabama State University 1931-34.
Special Interests: Composing, trumpet.
Address: 257 West 131 Street, New York, N. Y. 10027.
Honors: Pittsburgh Courier award (contribution to Modern Music)
1949; City of Birmingham Award from Mayor 1972; Alabama
State University (certificate of accomplishment in Music,
plaque) 1973; inducted into Birmingham's Hall of Arts 1973.
Career Data: Made debut as orchestra leader at Harlem Opera
House; with orchestra toured all major clubs throughout U. S.
and Canada; performed at Newport Jazz Festival 1972-74.
Clubs: Concord Hotel (Kiamesha Lake) 1967-date; Lincoln Hotel;
Savoy Ballroom; Jazz Museum.
Memberships: ASCAP 1945.
Musical Compositions: Tuxedo Junction (theme); Gin Mill Special;
You Can't Escape from Me.
Records: Tuxedo Junction (Bluebird) 1939; After Hours 1940; Tippin'
In 1945.
Theater: Apollo Theatre.

HAYES, ISAAC "Black Moses"
(Musician)
b. August 20, 1942, Covington, Tenn.
Special Interests: Composing, scoring, singing, piano, saxophone.
Address: c/o Stax Records, 98 North Avalon, Memphis, Tenn.
38104.

Honors: Oscar winner (for Shaft, best song); Oscar nomination
(best score); Grammy for Shaft.
Career Data: Sang with gospel and rhythm and blues groups as a
youth; established Isaac Hayes scholarship fund in Drama
Department, Memphis State; made concert debut, Detroit 1969;
vice-president, Stax Records.
Clubs: Sahara (Tahoe).
Films: Shaft (score) 1971; The Black Moses of Soul, Save the
Children, Wattstax 1973; title role in Truck Turner, Three
Tough Guys 1974.
Musical Compositions: Hold on I'm Coming; Soul Man; Baby;
Black Moses.
Records: Hot Buttered Soul; Tough Guys (Enterprise); Live at the
Sahara Tahoe; Chocolate Chip (ABC); Black Moses; To Be
Continued; Truck Turner; Joy Groove-a-Thon (ABC); Disco
Connection; Juicy Fruit (ABC); A Man and a Woman (ABC).
Television: Midnight Special; Academy Award Show 1972; The Os-
monds special 1974; Merv Griffin Presents 1974; Salute to
Dr. Martin Luther King 1974; The American Music awards
1975; Celebrity Superstars 1975; Tonight Show 1975; Today
1975; Rockford Files 1976; Canada Dry commercial 1976;
Dean Martin Celebrity Roast 1976.
Theater: Appearances at Westbury Music Fair 1974, 1976; Nanuet
Theatre-Go-Round 1974; The Felt Forum 1975; Apollo Theatre
1975; Albemarle Theatre (Brooklyn) 1976; Mill Run Theatre
(Chicago) 1976; Garden State Arts Center 1976.

HAYES, ROLAND (W.)
(Concert Singer)
b.   June 3, 1887, Curryville, Ga.
d.   December 31, 1976, Boston, Mass.
Education: Fisk University 1905; Harvard University Extension
School; studied voice with Arthur J. Hubbard and Sir George
Henschel.
Special Interests: Teaching, lieder, folk songs.
Honors: NAACP Spingarn Medal 1924; French Government Palmes
d'officer 1949; American Missionary Assn's 1st Amistad award
1962.
Career Data: Member, Fisk Jubilee singers 1911; U. S. concert
tour 1916-20; command performance for King George V 1921;
sang at Constitution Hall (Washington, D. C.); performed with
symphony orchestras: Boston, Philadelphia, Detroit, San
Francisco, New York; faculty, Boston University School of
Music 1950.
Memberships: American Academy of Arts & Letters (Fellow).
Musical Compositions: Life of Christ.
Theater: Boston Symphony Hall (1st Black Soloist) 1917; Aeolian
Hall (London) 1920; Beethovensaal (Berlin) 1924; Carnegie Hall
(Farewell Concert) 1962.

HAYMAN, LILLIAN
      (Actress/Singer)
b. Baltimore, Md.
Education: Edward Waters College; Wilberforce University; Vir-
      ginia Union University.
Special Interests: Opera.
Address: 109-39 191 Street, Hollis, L. I. , 11412.
Honors: Tony (for Hallelujah Baby) 1968.
Clubs: Village Gate.
Films: Gone Are the Days 1963; The Night They Raided Minsky's
      1968; Mandingo 1975.
Records: My Prayer; Imitation of Life.
Television: The New Yorker; Love, American Style; Leslie Uggams
      Show; Mike Douglas Show; Mod Squad; One Life to Live (series)
      1969.
Theater: Dream About Tomorrow (O. B.); Tough to Get Help; Our
      Lan' (O. B.) 1947; Kiss Me Kate (City Center) 1956; Shinbone
      Alley 1957; Simply Heavenly (O. B.) 1957; Show Boat (City
      Center) 1961; Porgy and Bess (tour and City Center) 1961;
      Kwamina 1961; Along Came a Spider (O. B.) 1963; The Amen
      Corner (tour) 1965; Mother in Hallelujah Baby 1967; 70 Girls
      70 1971; No No Nanette 1972; Dr. Jazz 1975.

HAYNES, DANIEL L.
      (Actor)
b. 1894, Atlanta, Ga.
d. July 29, 1954, Kingston, N. Y.
Education: Atlanta University; University of Chicago; Turner Theo-
      logical Seminary; City College of New York.
Special Interests: Theology (Clergyman), painting.
Films: Zeke in Hallelujah (first all-Negro film) 1929; The Last
      Mile 1932; So Red the Rose 1935; Escape from Devil's Island
      1935; The Invisible Ray 1936.
Memberships: Art Students League of New York.
Theater: Bottom of the Cup; Brother Elijah in Earth 1927; Rang
      Tang 1927; Show Boat (understudy) 1929; The Green Pastures
      1930, 1935; Ferrovius in Androcles and the Lion (Lafayette
      Theatre in Harlem) 1938.

HAYNES, HILDA (Hilda Mocile Lashley)
      (Actress)
b. May 21, 1912, New York, N. Y.
Education: Braithwaite Business School (diploma) 1933; studied at
      American Theatre Wing 1950; The American Shakespeare Fes-
      tival Academy 1959; The New Theatre School; The Urban
      League Players.
Special Interests: Directing.
Address: 173 West 151 Street, New York, N. Y. 10039.
Honors: YMCA (Harlem Branch) award of honor 1969; Scitamard
      Players (Providence, R. I.) award of honor 1969; Camp Mini-
      sink Mini cultural award 1970.

Career Data: Worked with American Negro Theatre 1941-47; at-
tended World Theatre Festival (London) 1965; director, Cul-
tural Enrichment Program in the Virgin Islands 1966; worked
with Seattle Repertory Theatre 1971.
Films: Taxi 1953; A Face in the Crowd 1957; Stage Struck 1958;
Key Witness, Home from the Hill 1960; Gone Are the Days
1963; The Pawnbroker 1965; Diary of a Mad Housewife 1970;
Across 110th Street 1972; Let's Do It Again 1975; The River
Niger 1976.
Memberships: AEA; AFTRA; NAG; NAACP; SAG.
Television: Brown Girl Brownstones; Frontiers of Faith; Phil Sil-
vers Show; Studio One; Car 54 Where Are You; The Hawk;
Our American Heritage; The Defenders; The Doctors; Edge of
Night; The Nurses; The Guiding Light; The Secret Storm; Look
Up and Live; The Rookies; The Green Pastures (Hallmark Hall
of Fame) 1957; Mary McLeod Bethune in Light in the Southern
Sky 1958; Ed Sullivan Show 1969; All My Children 1971; That's
My Mama 1974; Sanford and Son 1974; Screen Test 1974; Good
Times 1975; The Jeffersons 1975; Starsky and Hutch 1975;
Sarah T. ... Portrait of a Teenage Alcoholic 1975; Ellery
Queen 1975; F. Scott Fitzgerald in Hollywood 1976; The Boy in
the Plastic Bubble 1976.
Theater: Three's a Family (ANT) 1943; On Strivers Row (ANT)
1946; Deep Are the Roots 1946; Anna Lucasta (tour) 1947-48;
A Street Car Named Desire 1948-50; Monday Heroes (O. B.)
1953; King of Hearts 1954; Trouble in Mind (O. B.) 1955-56;
Take a Giant Step (O. B.) 1956-57; Wisteria Trees (City Cen-
ter) 1955; Lost in the Stars 1958; The Long Dream 1960; The
Irregular Verb to Love 1963; Blues for Mr. Charlie 1964,
(London) 1965; Golden Boy (London) 1968; The Great White
Hope 1968-70; Wedding Band (O. B.) 1972-73; The River Niger
(tour) 1973-74.

HAYNES, LLOYD (Samuel Lloyd Haynes)
(Actor)
b. October 19, 1934, South Bend, Ind.
Education: University of Indiana; Oceanside-Carlsbad College; Los
Angeles City College; San Jose State College; studied at
Actors Workshop.
Special Interests: Music, painting, guitar, singing.
Address: International Creative Management, 1301 Avenue of the
Americas, New York, N. Y. 10019.
Career Data: Teacher at Film Industry Workshop Inc. ; former
pilot and Lieut. Commander U. S. Naval Reserves.
Films: Ice Station Zebra, Madigan 1968; The Mad Room 1969; The
Greatest 1977.
Television: Production manager on Celebrity Game; PDQ; Hollywood
Squares: Double Exposure and Video Village; acted in: Lancer;
Felony Squad; the F. B. I. ; Star Trek; Batman; The Fugitive; 12
O'Clock High; Green Hornet; Chrysler Theatre; Man from
U. N. C. L. E. ; CBS Playhouse; Tarzan; Julia 1968; Pete Dixon
in Room 222 (series) 1969-74; Assault on the Wayne 1970;

Masquerade Party 1974; Emergency 1975; Marcus Welby, M. D.
1975; Look What's Happened to Rosemary's Baby 1976; 79 Park
Avenue 1977.
Theater: Hollywood Shakespeare Festival.

HAYNES, TIGER
    (Entertainer)
b. December 13, 1907, St. Croix, Virgin Islands.
Special Interests: Acting, dancing, singing.
Career Data: Formerly with The Three Flames (Open the Door
    Richard fame).
Clubs: Bon Soir.
Films: George Washington Is Alive and Well.
Memberships: AEA.
Television: Merv Griffin Show; Mike Douglas Show 1976.
Theater: New Faces of 1956 (debut) 1956; Arthur Kopit's Mhie
    Dhai Im (Actors Studio); Finian's Rainbow (City Center) 1960;
    Kiss Me, Kate (City Center); Fade Out, Fade In 1964; The
    Great White Hope (tour) 1969; Pajama Game 1973; The Tin
    Man in The Wiz 1975.

HEATH, GORDON (Seifield Gordon Heath)
    (Actor)
b. September 20, 1918.
Education: City College of New York.
Special Interests: Directing, violin and guitar, writing, singing.
Address: 45 rue Sevres, Paris, France.
Career Data: Worked with American Negro Theatre 1948; divided
    professional activities between France and U. S.; founder and
    executive, Studio Theatre (Paris).
Clubs: Performer and co-partner since 1949 in L'Abbaye (Paris).
Films: Passionate Summer (Brit.) 1958; Sapphire (Brit.), Heroes
    and Sinners (a. k. a. Les Héros Sont Fatigues) 1959; Les
    Laches Vivant D'Espoir a. k. a. My Baby Is Black (Fr.) 1961;
    Mon Oncle du Texas (Fr.) 1962; The Last Command 1966.
Memberships: AEA; ANT.
Radio: Celebrity Hour 1976.
Television: Title role in Emperor Jones (Brit.) 1953; Troubled Air
    (Brit.) 1953; Halcyon Days (Brit.) 1954; The Concert (Brit.)
    1954; title role in Othello (Brit.) 1955; For the Defense (Brit.)
    1956; Cry the Beloved Country (Brit.) 1958.
Theater: Narrated Pearl Primus concert (Belasco Theatre) 1944;
    Brett Charles in Deep Are the Roots (Bway debut) 1945; and
    (London debut) 1947; Troll King in Peer Gynt (ELT) 1947; title
    role in Hamlet (Hampton Institute) 1947; The Washington Years
    (ANT) 1948; Death in Death Takes a Holiday (YMHA) 1948;
    Demoiselle de Petite Vertu (Paris) 1949; title role in Othello
    (England) 1951; Cranks (London) 1955; The Expatriate (London)
    1961; La Respecteuse (Paris) 1962; Petits Renards (Paris)
    1963; Oedipus (O. B.) 1969; directed In White America (Paris);
    After the Fall (Paris); Telemachus Clay (Paris); Skin of Our

Teeth (Paris); The Glass Menagerie (Paris); and Kennedy's
Children (Paris); Endgame (O. B.) 1977.

HEMSLEY, ESTELLE
(Actress)
b. May 5, 1887, Boston, Mass.
d. November 4, 1968, Los Angeles, Calif.
Career Data: Vaudeville Coney Island (debut) 1912; Keith Vaudeville
    Circuit; danced with Yank Yanna Girls; Archer's Chocolate
    Drops; Black Patti's Troubadours; member, Federal Works
    Theatre Project (WPA).
Films: Harvey 1950; Edge of the City 1957; Green Mansions 1959;
    The Leech Woman 1960; Take a Giant Step 1961; America,
    America 1963; Baby, the Rain Must Fall 1965.
Memberships: AEA; SAG.
Radio: Pretty Kitty Kelly.
Theater: Darktown Follies; Tobacco Road; Frimbo; Two Blind Mice;
    Macbeth (Lafayette Theatre) 1936; Turpentine Haiti (Lafayette
    Theatre) 1938; Harvey 1944-47; Detective Story 1949; Grand-
    mother in Take a Giant Step 1953; Mrs. Patterson 1954; Too
    Late the Phalarope 1956.

HEMSLEY, SHERMAN
(Actor)
b. February 1, 1938, Philadelphia, Pa.
Education: Philadelphia Academy of Dramatic Arts; studied acting
    with Lloyd Richards.
Honors: NAACP Image award as comedy actor on television (The
    Jeffersons) 1976.
Career Data: Formerly member, Urban Corps and Negro Ensemble
    Co.
Clubs: Act (with Andre Pavon) 1976.
Television: George Jefferson in All in the Family (series) 1973-75;
    George Jefferson in The Jeffersons (series) 1975-; New England
    Journal 1975; Merv Griffin Show 1975; Dinah! 1975; You Don't
    Say 1975; Joey [Heatherton] and Dad 1975; Dean's [Martin]
    Place 1975; Mike Douglas Show 1975; Thanksgiving Day Parade
    1975; Rich Little Show 1976; Dean Martin (Roasting of Muham-
    mad Ali) 1976.
Theater: The Blacks (Philadelphia); Friends (O. B.); Don't Bother
    Me I Can't Cope (tour); Mad Hatter in Alice in Wonderland
    (O. B.); The People vs. Ranchman (O. B. debut) 1958; Gitloe
    in Purlie 1970; The Odd Couple (Chicago) 1977.

HEMSLEY, WINSTON DEWITT
(Actor/Dancer)
Address: 1903 Talmadge Street, Los Angeles, Calif. 90028.
Career Data: Teamed for club act with Alan Weeks.
Clubs: Hallelujah Hollywood Show at M. G. M. Grand Hotel (Las
    Vegas).

Films: The Pawnbroker 1965.
Television: The Ed Sullivan Show; The Johnny Carson Show; Hulla-
          baloo; The Swinging World of Sammy Davis.
Theater: Golden Boy (debut) 1964; A Joyful Noise 1966; Hallelujah
          Baby 1967; The People vs. Ranchman (O. B.) 1968; Hello,
          Dolly! 1969; Purlie 1970-71; Don't Bother Me I Can't Cope
          1972; The Charlatan (Los Angeles) 1975; Rockabye Hamlet
          1976; Chorus Line 1976; appeared at Palais de Congress
          (Paris).

HENDERSON, FLETCHER "Smack" (James Fletcher Henderson)
          (Conductor/Musician)
b.   December 18, 1898, Cuthbert, Ga.
d.   December 29, 1952, New York, N. Y.
Education: Atlanta University, City College of New York.
Special Interests: Piano, arranging.
Honors: Down Beat poll winner as arranger 1938-40.
Career Data: Played with and for W. C. Handy, Ethel Waters, Bes-
          sie Smith; wrote arrangements for Dorsey Brothers, Benny
          Goodman 1933; led own band 1923, 1944-47; toured as accom-
          panist for Ethel Waters 1948-49, led sextet 1950.
Clubs: Club Alabam 1923; Roseland 1924; Club de Lisa (Chicago)
          1944-45; Cafe Society 1950.
Musical Compositions: Arrangements for Sometimes I'm Happy;
          When Buddha Smiles; King Porter Stomp; Blue Skies; Down
          South Camp Meeting; Wrapping It Up; Bumble Bee Stomp; No,
          Baby, No; Stampede; It's Wearing Me Down.
Records: Stealin' Apples; The Birth of Big Band Jazz (Riverside);
          Goodman Plays Henderson (Columbia); Benny Goodman Presents
          Fletcher Henderson Arrangements (Columbia); A Study in Frus-
          tration (Columbia); Complete 1927-36 (Bluebird); Immortal
          (Milestone); 1924-41 (Biograph); 1923-27 (Biograph).
Theater: Wrote score for The Jazz Train (produced at Bop City,
          1950).

HENDERSON, LUTHER JR.
          (Musician/Composer)
b.   March 14, 1919, Kansas City, Mo.
Education: Juilliard School of Music B. S. 1942; City College of
          New York 1935-38; New York University 1946; studied piano
          with Sonoma Talley 1925-38; Shillinger system with Rudolph
          Schramm.
Special Interests: Arranging, directing, piano.
Honors: Harlem amateur show winner 1934.
Career Data: Played with bands of Leonard Ware, Mercer Elling-
          ton; appeared with, arranged, conducted night club acts for
          Lena Horne (1947-50), Polly Bergen, Carol Haney and Anita
          Ellis; orchestrated and arranged for Teresa Brewer, Nancy
          Wilson, Carol Lawrence, Eartha Kitt, Marge and Gower Cham-
          pion and Duke Ellington; served on the arrangers and orches-
          trators staff at USN School of Music (Wash. , D. C.) 1944-46.

Memberships: ASCAP 1956; AFM.
Musical Compositions: Hold On; Solitaire; Ten Good Years.
Radio: The Story of Ruby Valentine (series) 1955.
Records: Conducted, arranged or orchestrated: Clap Hands; The
    Greatest Sounds Around; Pop! Goes the Western; The Luther
    Henderson Sextet; The Flower Drum Song; Do Re Mi, Theatre
    Party; Bravo Giovanni; Funny Girl; The Columbia Album of
    Richard Rogers.
Television: Musical director for The Helen Morgan Story (Play-
    house 90) 1957; The Victor Borge Show 1958, 1961; The Phil
    Silvers Special; Summer in New York; Polly and Me 1960;
    prepared dance arrangements and orchestrations for Home for
    the Holidays 1961; arranged and orchestrated The Broadway of
    Lerner and Lowe 1961; orchestrations, dance and vocal arrange-
    ments for The Ed Sullivan Show, The Garry Moore Show, The
    Perry Como Show, The Bell Telephone Hour.
Theater: Performed in, arranged and orchestrated Tropical Re-
    view (Toronto) 1943; orchestrated Beggar's Holiday 1946; dance
    arrangements for Flower Drum Song 1958; orchestrations for
    Do Re Mi 1960; dance arrangements and orchestrations for
    Bravo Giovanni 1962; orchestrations for Hot Spot 1963; dance
    orchestrations and arrangements for Funny Girl 1964; Hallelujah
    Baby 1967; Purlie 1969; No No Nanette 1971; Dr. Jazz 1975.

HENDERSON, TY
    (Actor)
Television: Mod Squad; Apple's Way 1974; It's Good to Be Alive
    1974; Harry O 1974; Lucas Tanner 1975; Emergency 1975;
    Rookies 1975; Marcus Welby, M. D. 1975.

HENDRIX, JIMI
    (Singer)
b. November 27, 1942, Seattle, Wash.
d. September 18, 1970, London, England.
Special Interests: Guitar, composing.
Honors: Billboard's Artist of the Year 1968; Playboy Magazine
    Artist of the Year 1969; Playboy Music Hall of Fame 1971.
Career Data: Worked with Band of Gypsies; played at Monterey
    Pop Festival; formed Jimi Hendrix Experience (vocal group)
    1966; performed at Woodstock Festival 1969.
Clubs: The Scene 1967.
Films: Pop Corn, Monterey Pop, Woodstock 1970; Jimi Plays
    Berkeley, Jimi Hendrix 1973.
Records: The Cry of Love (Reprise); Rare (Trip); Roots of Hendrix
    (Trip); Hey, Joe; Purple Haze; Woodstock Two; Hendrix in the
    West; War Heroes; Are You Experienced? (Reprise); Band of
    Gypsies (Capitol); Smash Hits (Reprise); Crash Landing (Re-
    prise) 1975; Midnight Lightning (Reprise) 1975; Genius of ...
    (Trip); Superpak (Trip); World of ... (United Artists); Jimi
    (Pickwick); At Monterey (Reprise); Axis (Reprise); Electric
    Landlady (Reprise); Smash Hits (Reprise).

Theater: Tivoli (Stockholm); Saville (London); Hollywood Bowl;
            Sports Arena (Copenhagen).

HENDRY, GLORIA
       (Actress)
b.   1949, Jacksonville, Fla.
Education: Warren Robertson's Workshop.
Special Interests: Singing, modeling, teaching.
Address: c/o Charter Management, 900 Sunset Blvd. , Los Angeles,
            Calif. 90069.
Career Data: Former Playboy Bunny.
Films: For Love of Ivy 1968; The Landlord 1970; Across 110th
            Street 1972; Slaughter's Big Ripoff, Black Caesar, Rosie Car-
            ter in Live and Let Die, Hell Up in Harlem 1973; Savage
            Sisters, Black Belt Jones 1974.
Memberships: AEA; AFTRA; AGVA; SAG.
Television: Blue Knight 1976.

HEPBURN, DAVID (Andrew)
       (Producer)
b.   September 12, 1924, Castries, St. Lucia.
Education: St. Mary's College, St. Lucia, B. A. (English Lit.);
            Columbia University School of Journalism M. S. 1946.
Address: 14 Madison Place, White Plains, N. Y. 10603.
Honors: Emmy 1970; Special Citation Award from National Academy
            of Television Arts and Sciences 1972.
Career Data: Public relations agent for performing artists including
            Virginia Capers, Alyce Webb, Arthur Prysock, Dinah Washing-
            ton and Mae Barnes; Vice President and Director of Commu-
            nity Relations, WNEW-TV (Metromedia); former press repre-
            sentative, WCBS.
Memberships: National Academy of Television Arts and Sciences
            1956-date.
Television: Co-founder, Black News (WNEW Channel 5), executive
            producer 1970-73; executive producer, Which Way Guyana
            (doc.) 1973; People of Paradise (doc.) 1974.
Relationships: Husband of Mildred Joanne Smith, actress.

HEPBURN, PHILIP
       (Actor)
b.   c. 1941, New York, N. Y.
Special Interests: Dancing.
Films: Bright Road 1953.
Memberships: AEA.
Theater: Finian's Rainbow 1947; Regina 1949; Peter Pan 1950;
            Twilight Walk 1951; The Green Pastures 1951; Pip in Moby
            Dick (O. B.) 1955; The World's My Oyster 1956; Mr. Johnson
            1956; The Cool World 1960; Shakespeare in Harlem (O. B.)
            1962.

HERNANDEZ, JUANO (Juan G. Hernandez)
    (Actor)
b. 1896, San Juan, Puerto Rico.
d. July 17, 1970, San Juan, Puerto Rico.
Special Interests: Boxing, acrobatics, singing.
Career Data: Professor, School of Dramatic Arts, University of
    Puerto Rico.
Clubs: Cotton Club.
Films: The Girl from Chicago 1932; The Notorious Elinor Lee
    1940; Intruder in the Dust, The Accused 1949; Stars in My
    Crown, The Breaking Point, Young Man with a Horn 1950;
    Kiss Me Deadly, The Trial 1955; Ransom 1956; Something of
    Value 1957; The Roots, St. Louis Blues, Machete, The Mark
    of the Hawk 1958; Sergeant Rutledge 1960; Sins of Rachel Cade,
    Two Loves 1961; Hemingway's Adventures of a Young Man
    1962; The Pawnbroker 1965; The Reivers, The Extraordinary
    Seaman 1969; They Call Me Mister Tibbs 1970.
Radio: Adapted and co-directed John Henry; Cavalcade of America;
    Jungle Jim; Counter Spy; Young Dr. Malone; Grand Central
    Station; Ford Theater; African Trek 1939; Amanda of Honey-
    moon Hill 1940; Lothar in Mandrake and the Magician 1940;
    We Love and Learn 1942; Tennessee Jed 1945.
Television: The Goodwill Ambassadors (Studio 57) 1957; Studio One
    1957; Black Monday (Play of the Week) 1961; Adventures in
    Paradise 1961; Good Night, Sweet Blues (Route 66) 1961; Safari
    (Dick Powell Theater) 1962; Defenders 1962; Naked City 1963.
Theater: Show Boat (chorus) 1927; Blackbirds (chorus); Strange Fruit
    1945; Set My People Free 1948; Othello (toured South America)
    1949.

HEWLETT, JAMES
    (Actor)
Special Interests: Singing, pantomime, Shakespeare.
Career Data: Founder of The African Company of New York (first
    American Black drama group) and The African Grove Street
    Theatre.
Theater: Title role in Othello and Richard III 1821; title role in
    The Drama of King Shotaway 1823; performed in The Assembly
    Room, Military Garden (Brooklyn) 1825-26; appeared on London
    stage 1827-30; performed at Columbian Hall 1831.

HIBBLER, AL (Albert)
    (Singer)
b. August 16, 1915, Little Rock, Ark.
Education: Arkansas State School for the Blind.
Honors: Esquire new star award as male singer 1947; Down Beat
    award as band vocalist 1948-49; participated in Newport Jazz
    Festival 1976.
Career Data: Worked with Andy Kirk band, Duke Ellington orchestra
    1943-51.
Clubs: New Barrister (Bronx) 1976; Riverboat 1976.

Records: For Decca: Unchained Melody 1955; He 1955; 11th Hour
    Melody 1956; Never Turn Back 1956; After the Lights Go Down
    Low 1956; Trees 1957; Here's Hibbler; Al Hibbler's Greatest
    Hits; Starring Al Hibbler.
Theater: Appeared at Apollo Theatre; Seafood Playhouse 1975;
    Carnegie Hall 1976.

HICKS, HILLY
    (Actor)
b. 1950.
Address: 3464 Troy Drive, Los Angeles, Calif. 90068.
Films: They Call Me Mr. Tibbs; Halls of Anger 1970; The New
    Centurions 1972.
Television: The Bill Cosby Show; Mod Squad 1971; Night Gallery
    1971; Adam-12 1972; The Rookies 1972, 1973; Toma 1973; Pfc.
    Jed Brooks in Roll Out (series) 1973; M*A*S*H 1975; That's
    My Mama 1975; The FBI vs. The Ku Klux Klan (Attack on
    Terror) 1975; Cannon 1975; Mobile One 1975; Barnaby Jones
    1975; Roots 1977.

HIGGINSEN, VY (Violet Higginson)
    (Disc Jockey)
b. New York, N.Y.
Education: Fashion Institute of Technology; N.Y.U.
Special Interests: Poetry, fashion, children's programming.
Address: c/o WNBT, 30 Rockefeller Plaza, New York, N.Y. 10020.
Honors: Blackfrica Cup.
Career Data: Formerly contributor to Essence magazine and account
    representative for Ebony magazine; publisher, Unique N.Y. (an
    entertainment guide).
Films: That's the Way of the World.
Radio: Host, Saturday Night Special WRVR-FM; disc jockey WBLS
    (Inner City Broadcasting Corp.) 1971-75; disc jockey, DRBR.
Television: Like It Is; commercial for Korvette's; Black Pride
    1975; co-host of Positively Black 1976.
Theater: Emcee for choreographers show at Paladium 1975.

HILL, ABRAM (Barrington)
    (Playwright)
b. January 20, 1911, Atlanta, Ga.
Education: City College of New York, 1930-32; Columbia University,
    Lincoln University B.A. 1937; New School for Social Research,
    Atlanta University.
Special Interests: Teaching, directing.
Career Data: Asst. N.Y. State supervisor C.C.C. dramatic activi-
    ties; co-founder, American Negro Theatre; former drama
    critic, Amsterdam News (N.Y.); faculty member and director
    of dramatics, Lincoln University 1938; researcher and con-
    sultant to Federal Writers Project and Federal Theatre.
Theater: Assistant director of Starlight; wrote Liberty Deferred

(with John Silvera) 1936; wrote Stealing Lightning (one act)
1937; wrote Hell's Half Acre 1938; wrote So Shall You Reap
1938; wrote On Striver's Row: A Comedy about Sophisticated
Harlem 1940; assistant director of Natural Man 1941; staged
all black cast production of Three's a Family 1943; wrote and
directed Walk Hard 1944; staged all black cast production of
Anna Lucasta 1945; directed Home Is the Hunter 1945; staged
all black cast production of John Loves Mary 1947; directed
and adapted (from Tolstoi) Power of Darkness 1948; wrote
Miss Mabel 1951; directed (for J. H. S. 178) student production
of The King and I 1960; wrote Split Down the Middle 1970.

HILL, ERROL (Gaston)
    (Playwright)
b. August 5, 1921, Trinidad.
Education: Royal Academy of Dramatic Art (England) 1951; Univer-
        sity of London; Yale University B. A. , M. F. A. 1962, D. F. A.
        1966.
Special Interests: Acting, directing, teaching.
Address: Drama Dept. , Dartmouth College, Hanover, N. H. 03755.
Honors: British Council Scholarship 1949-51; Rockefeller Foundation
        Fellowship 1958-60; Theatre Guild of America Playwrighting
        Fellowship 1961-62; Hummingbird Gold Medal, Govt. of Trini-
        dad & Tobago 1973.
Career Data: Tutor creative arts, University of West Indies 1953-
        58, 1962-65; teaching fellow, University of Ibadan, Nigeria
        1956-67; associate prof. of Drama, prof. of Drama, Dartmouth
        College, 1971-date.
Radio: Announcer/actor B. B. C. (London) 1951-52.
Theater: Wrote The Ping-Pong 1958; Man Better Man (folk musical)
        1964; Dance Bongo 1965; Dilemma 1966; Oily Portraits 1966;
        Strictly Matrimony 1966; Wey-Wey 1966.

HILL, RUBY
    (Singer/Actress)
b. 1922, Danville, Va.
Career Data: Vocalist with Noble Sissle band 1939; performed in
        U. S. O. show in Hollywood.
Clubs: Ubangi 1936; Le Ruban Bleu 1946; Riverboat 1976.
Films: Ebony Parade 1947.
Memberships: AEA; NAG.
Theater: Appeared at State Theatre 1939; St. Louis Woman (Bway
        debut) 1946; Anna Lucasta 1946.

HILLMAN, GEORGE
    (Dancer)
b. September 21, 1906, New York, N. Y.
Education: Lincoln University.
Career Data: Member, Hillman Brothers Dance Team (35 years).
Memberships: AEA; NAG.

Theater: Curly McDimple (O. B. debut) 1968; On Toby Time (O. B.)
     1977.

HINDERAS, NATALIE
     (Pianist)
b. Oberlin, Ohio.
Education: Oberlin College; Juilliard School of Music; Philadelphia
     Conservatory.
Special Interests: Teaching.
Address: c/o Joanne Rile Artists Representative, 424 West Upsal
     Street, Philadelphia, Pa. 19119.
Career Data: Played concerts with Philadelphia and Los Angeles
     Philharmonic Orchestras 1972 and Cleveland, Atlanta and N. Y.
     Symphony Orchestras 1973; toured Europe and United States;
     professor of music, Temple University.
Records: Natalie Hinderas Plays Music by Black Composers (DES-
     TO).
Television: Natalie Hinderas Concert (WNBK, Cleveland) 1953.
Theater: Avery Fisher Hall (with N. Y. Philharmonic) 1975.

HINES, EARL "Fatha" (Kenneth)
     (Conductor/Musician)
b. December 28, 1905, Duquesne, Pa.
Education: Schenley H. S. (Pittsburgh).
Special Interests: Composing, piano.
Address: c/o Stanley Dance, 12 Oakley Court, Rowayton, Conn.
     06853.
Honors: Esquire (silver) award 1944; Down Beat's International
     Critics' Hall of Fame 1966; Honorary Pres. , Overseas Jazz
     Club 1970; Down Beat's International Critics Poll nomination as
     world's no. 1 Jazz pianist; Newport Hall of Fame 1975.
Career Data: Appeared with his own band in major night clubs and
     theaters in U. S. from 1929-48; worked with Louis Armstrong
     band 1948-51; since 1951 has led small groups (currently a
     quartet); toured Europe (with Jack Teagarden) 1957; Soviet Union
     1966; South America 1968; Japan and Australia 1972; appeared
     at Pres. Nixon's White House party for Duke Ellington 1968;
     appeared at all major jazz festivals including Monterey, New-
     port, New Orleans, Nice, Berlin and Montreux (1974).
Clubs: Grand Terrace (Chicago) 1928-41; Sunset Café (Chicago);
     Apex (Chicago); Rainbow Grill 1975; Michael's Pub 1976.
Memberships: ASCAP 1949; American Federation of Musicians.
Musical Compositions: Deep Forest (theme); Jelly, Jelly; Mad House;
     The Earl; Everything Depends on You; Dancing Fingers; My
     Monday Date; Rosetta; Tantalizing a Cuban; Piano Man; Close
     to Me.
Records: Stormy Monday Blues; Boogie Woogie on St. Louis Blues;
     The Fatha Jumps (Bluebird); Second Balcony Jump; I Got It
     Bad; At Home (Delmark); Blues and Things (Master Jazz);
     Evening with Hines (Chiaroscuro); Fatha and His Flock on Tour
     (BASF); Grand Reunion (Trip); Hines '65 (Master Jazz); In-

comparable (Fantasy); Live at Buffalo (Improv); The Might
Fatha (Flying Dutchman); Once Upon a Time (Impulse); Earl
Hines Plays Duke Ellington (Master Jazz); Quintessential Re-
cording Sessions (Chiaroscuro); Tea for Two (Black Lion);
Tour de Force (Black Lion); Earl "Fatha" Hines (Archives of
Folk & Jazz Music); All-Star Session (Trip); Another Monday
Date (Prestige); Earl Hines (GNP Crescendo); Monday Date
1928 (Milestone).
Television: Johnny Carson Show; Merv Griffin Show; Mike Douglas
Show; David Frost Show; Performance at Wolf Trap 1976.
Theater: Appearances at Little Theatre; Carnegie Hall; Town Hall;
Avery Fisher Hall 1975; Bubbling Brown Sugar (score) 1976;
R. K. O. Albee (Brooklyn).

HODGES, JOHNNY "Rabbit" (John Cornelius Hodges)
      (Jazz Musician)
b.   July 25, 1907, Cambridge, Mass.
d.   May 11, 1970, New York, N. Y.
Education: Instructed by Sidney Bechet.
Special Interests: Composing, alto and soprano saxophone, con-
      ducting.
Honors: Down Beat poll winner 1940-49, Esquire (silver) 1944,
      46 (gold) 1945 awards, Metronome poll 1945-47.
Career Data: Played with Sidney Bechet 1925, Chick Webb 1927,
      Duke Ellington orchestra 1928-51; formed own band in 1951
      then a septet until 1955; rejoined Duke Ellington 1955-70;
      worked with Billy Strayhorn in 1958; toured Europe 1961.
Clubs: Rhythm Club 1924; Club Basha 1925; Paddock Club 1927;
      Savoy Ballroom 1927.
Memberships: ASCAP 1945.
Musical Compositions: The Hodge Podge, I'm Beginning to See the
      Light, Jepp's Blues, Jitterbug's Lullaby, Wanderlust, Mood to
      Be Wooed, Wonder of You, Crosstown, Squatty Roo, It Shouldn't
      Happen to a Dream, Harmony in Harlem, Shady Side, What's
      It All About?
Television: Ted Steele Show 1955.

HOLDER, GEOFFREY (Lamont)
      (Dancer/Choreographer)
b.   August 1, 1930, Port of Spain, Trinidad.
Education: Queens Royal College (Trinidad) 1948.
Special Interests: Painting, costume design, singing, writing, di-
      recting.
Address: 215 West 92 Street, New York, N. Y. 10025.
Honors: Guggenheim Fellowship in Painting 1957; United Caribbean
      Youth Award 1962; Clio 1970 (British West Indies Airways com-
      mercial); Clio 1971 (7-Up commercial); Tony as Best Director
      and Tony as Best Costume Designer (The Wiz) 1975; Harold
      Jackman Memorial award.
Career Data: Taught at Katherine Dunham School, New York; for-
      mer visiting prof., Yale University; formed own dance company

appearing in Caribbean and United States 1953; exhibited paintings Barone Gallery 1955-59, appeared at Theatre under the
Stars (Central Park) 1957; appeared at Radio City Music Hall
1957; appeared with John Butler Dance Theatre 1958; appeared
at Festival of Two Worlds (Spoleto) 1958; danced at Vancouver
(B. C.) Festival 1960; exhibited paintings Gropper Gallery (Cambridge Mass.) 1961; solo dancer at International Festival,
Lagos, Nigeria 1962; exhibited paintings Griffin Gallery 1963,
exhibited paintings Grinnel Galleries (Detroit) 1964.

Clubs: Coconut Grove (L. A.) 1957; Hotel Americana (Miami Beach)
1957; Village Gate 1959-60; The Arpeggio 1960.

Films: All Night Long (Brit.) 1961; William Shakespeare in Doctor
Dolittle 1967; Krakatoa East of Java 1969; Everything You
Wanted to Know About Sex But Were Afraid To Ask 1972;
Baron Samedi in Live and Let Die 1972; Death Is My Pardon,
The Noah (voice) 1975; Swashbuckler 1976.

Memberships: AEA; AFTRA; AGMA; AGVA; SAG.

Publications: Black Gods, Green Islands, Negro Universities Press,
1959; Geoffrey Holder's Caribbean Cookbook, Viking, 1973.

Television: 7-Up commercial; British West Indian Airways commercial; Star Burst commercial; Wisk (ring around the collar)
commercial; Drama Critic WNBC News; Jamaica Tourist Board
commercial; It Takes a Thief; Androcles and the Lion; Stage
Your Number 1953; Aladdin 1958; The Bottle Imp 1958; A Man
Without a Country 1973; Tonight Show 1975; A. M. America
1975; Dinah! 1975; Midday Live 1975; Good Morning, America
1976; The American Spirit 1976; Straight Talk 1976.

Theater: Jeux des Dieux for Harkness Ballet; Douglass for Dance
Theatre of Harlem; Ballet for Rite of Spring for Ballet Theatre;
House of Flowers (debut) 1954; Premier Danseur in Aida and
La Perichole (Metropolitan Opera) 1955-56; Lucky in Waiting
for Godot 1957; Show Boat (Jones Beach) 1957; Acted Twelfth
Night (Cambridge Dance Festival, Mass.) 1960; choreographed
Brouhaha 1960; danced with Josephine Baker and Her Company
1964; choreographed Mhil Daiim (Actors Studio Prod.) 1964;
I Got a Song 1974 (closed Buffalo); directed The Wiz (black
version of Wizard of Oz) 1975.

Relationships: Husband of Carmen de Lavallade, dancer/actress.

HOLDER, RAM JOHN (Wesley)
     (Actor)
b.   c. 1940 Guiana.
Special Interests: Guitar, singing, composing.
Films: Two Gentlemen Sharing 1969; Leo the Last 1969; The Edu-
cation of Sonny Carson 1974.
Memberships: BAEA.
Records: Black London Blues (Beacon); Bootleg Blues (Beacon).
Television: Rainbow City (BBC); Strange Report (London) 1968;
Friday in Robinson Crusoe 1974.
Theater: God Bless America (Royal Shakespeare Company, London)

HOLIDAY, BILLIE "Lady Day" (Eleanora Holiday)
    (Singer)
b. April 17, 1915, Baltimore, Md.
d. July 17, 1959, New York, N. Y.
Honors: Esquire award (gold) 1944-47, (silver) 1945, 1946; Metro-
    nome award 1945-46; Ebony Music award (posthumously) 1975.
Career Data: Vocalist with Eddie Condon, Benny Goodman 1933,
    Count Basie 1937, Artie Shaw 1938; recorded with Teddy Wil-
    son 1935-39.
Clubs: Gray Dawn (L. I.); Monette's Supper Club; Pod's and Jerry's;
    Onyx; Café Society; The Yeah Man.
Films: Symphony in Black 1935; New Orleans, 1947; Malcolm X
    (clips), Lady Sings the Blues (subject) 1972.
Publications: Lady Sings the Blues (autobiography), Doubleday, 1956.
Radio: Voice of America 1956.
Records: Billie Holiday's Greatest Hits (Columbia); The Billie Holi-
    day Story; Lady Day (Columbia); I Cover the Waterfront; Lover
    Man; Fine and Mellow; I Got a Right to Sing the Blues; Them
    There Eyes; Golden Years (Columbia); All or Nothing at All
    (Verve); Archetypes (MGM); Billie Holiday (Archive of Folk &
    Jazz Music); Easy to Remember (CMS Saga); Essential Carne-
    gie Hall Concert (Verve); First Verve Sessions (Verve); Gal-
    lant Lady (Monmouth Evergreen); God Bless the Child (Colum-
    bia); History (Verve); Lady Lives (ESP-Disk); Lady Love (Uni-
    ted Artists); Live (Trip); Original Records (Columbia); Real
    Lady Sings the Blues (Super Majestic); ... Sings the Blues
    (Pickwick); Solitude (Verve); ... Story (Columbia); Strange
    Fruit (Atlantic).
Television: Art Ford Jazz Show (Newark).
Theater: Appeared at Strand Theatre; Apollo Theatre; Carnegie
    Hall; Howard Theatre (Washington, D. C.).

HOLLAR, LLOYD
    (Actor)
b. New York, N. Y.
Education: New York University 1953-54; studied at Herbert Berghof
    Studio with Milton Katselas.
Address: 551 Hudson Street, New York, N. Y. 10014.
Films: The Crazies (Cambist Films); Code Name Trixie 1973.
Memberships: AEA; AFTRA; SAG.
Television: CBS Repertoire Workshop; Animal Keepers; Hidden
    Faces (series); The Best of Everything (series); A World
    Apart (series); Secret Storm; Good Times; Thurgood Marshall
    in With All Deliberate Speed 1976.
Theater: Wrong Way Bulb; Captain Brassbound's Conversion; The
    Brig (O. B.); Othello (O. B.); Baal (O. B.); Animal Keepers (O.
    B.); Assembly Line (O. B.); Tiger at the Gate (O. B.); Cyrano
    de Bergerac (O. B.); An Ordinary Man (O. B.); Pequod (O. B.);
    The Anvil (The Trial of John Brown) (O. B.) 1962; We Interrupt
    This Program ... 1975.

HOLLY, ELLEN (Virginia)
  (Actress)
b.   January 17, 1931, New York, N. Y.
Education: Hunter College B. A. 1952; Perry Mansfield School of
    the Theater, Colorado and New York City, 1952-53; studied
    acting with Uta Hagen, Mira Rostova.
Special Interests: Playwriting, modeling.
Address: 83-37 118th Street, Richmond Hill, N. Y. 11418.
Career Data: Member, Greenwich Mews Repertory Theatre and
    Joseph Papp's New York Shakespeare Company; first stage
    appearance as Electra in Daughters of Atreus (Hunter College
    Playhouse) 1953.
Films: Take a Giant Step 1961; Cops and Robbers 1973.
Memberships: AEA; AFTRA; SAG.
Publications: Unproduced screenplay about Henri Christophe.
Television: Sally Travers in Love of Life (series); The Nurses;
    The Defenders; Tituba in Salem Witch Trial Drama (Odyssey)
    1957; The Big Story 1957; Confidential File 1957; Two Black
    Candles 1962; Man Against Himself 1962; Sam Benedict 1963;
    Look Up and Live 1963; The Unwanted 1963; Dr. Kildare 1964;
    Carla Hall in One Life to Live (series) 1969-72; King Lear
    1975.
Theater: Cherry Orchard (O. B.); Taming of the Shrew (NYSF);
    Henry V (NYSF); 2 for Fun (O. B. debut) 1955; Salome (O. B.)
    1955; A Florentine Tragedy (O. B.) 1955; Too Late the Phala-
    rope (debut) 1956; Tevya and His Daughters (O. B.) 1957;
    Desdemona in Othello (O. B.) 1958; Fall of a Hero 1960;
    Twelfth Night (NYSF) 1961; Moon on a Rainbow Shawl (O. B.)
    1962; Tiger, Tiger Burning Bright 1962; Antony and Cleopatra
    (NYSF) 1963; Funny House of a Negro (O. B.) 1964; Titania in
    A Midsummer Night's Dream (NYSF) 1964; A Hand Is On the
    Gate 1966; Lady Macbeth in Macbeth (NYSF) 1966; Regan in
    King Lear (NYSF) 1973.

HOLT, NORA
  (Composer/Critic)
b.   c. 1895, Kansas City, Kan.
d.   January 25, 1974, Los Angeles, Calif.
Education: Western University (Quindaro, Kansas) Kansas State
    College B. S. 1915; Chicago Musical College M. M. 1918; Uni-
    versity of Southern California 1938-39; Columbia University
    1945.
Career Data: First music critic, Chicago Defender 1917-21; music
    editor & critic, Amsterdam News (N. Y.) 1943; Music Critics
    Circle of N. Y.
Clubs: Little Club (Shanghai).
Memberships: NAG; National Assn. of Negro Musicians Inc. (founder
    1919).
Musical Compositions: Rhapsody on Negro Themes 1918 (masters
    theme).
Radio: Nora Holt Concert Showcase (WLIB) 1953-64.

HOOKS, KEVIN
(Actor)
b.   September 19, 1958.
Address: 2240 Anvil Lane, Hillcrest Heights, Md. 20031.
Films: Sounder 1972; Aaron in Aaron Loves Angela 1976.
Television: N. Y. P. D.; J. T. 1970; Black Journal 1976; Rookies
      1976; Just an Old Sweet Song (General Electric Theater) 1976.
Relationships: Son of Robert Hooks, actor.

HOOKS, ROBERT (Bobby Dean Hooks)
(Actor)
b.   April 18, 1937, Washington, D. C.
Education: Temple University 1956-57; Bessie V. Hicks School of
      Theatre (Philad.) 1958-59; Actors Studio 1960.
Address: 2240 Anvil Lane, Hillcrest Heights, Md. 20031.
Honors: Theatre World award (for Where's Daddy?) 1966.
Career Data: Co-founder and executive director, Negro Ensemble
      Company, 1967 (with Douglas Turner Ward); founder and ex-
      ecutive producer, D. C. Black Repertory Co. (Washington, D. C.).
Films; Hurry Sundown, Sweet Love Bitter (a. k. a. It Won't Rub Off,
      Baby) 1967; The Last of the Mobile Hot Shots 1970; Mr. T. in
      Trouble Man 1972; Aaron Loves Angela 1975; Airport '77 1977.
Television: Black Journal; Marcus Welby, M. D. ; McMillan and
      Wife; Rookies; Streets of San Francisco; Profiles in Courage
      1965; The Cliff Dwellers 1966; Jeff Ward in N. Y. P. D. (series)
      1967-69; Mannix 1969; The F. B. I. 1969; Then Came Bronson
      1969; Carter's Army 1970; Bold Ones 1970; Cross Current
      1970; Vanished 1971; Man and the City 1971; The Cable Car
      Mystery 1971; Two for the Money 1972; Trapped 1973; Cere-
      monies in Dark Old Men 1975; Phil Donahue Show 1975; Police
      Story 1975; Petrocelli 1975; The Killer Who Wouldn't Die 1976,
      Just an Old Sweet Song (General Electric Theater) 1976.
Theater: Where's Daddy?; Henry V (O. B.); A Raisin in the Sun
      (debut) 1959; A Taste of Honey 1961; Tiger, Tiger Burning
      Bright 1962; The Blacks (O. B.) 1962; Arturo Ui 1963; Ballad
      for Bimshire (O. B.) 1963; Dutchman (O. B.) 1964; The Milk
      Train Doesn't Stop Here Anymore 1964; Happy Ending (NEC)
      1966; Day of Absence (NEC) 1966; Hallelujah Baby 1967; Kongi's
      Harvest (NEC) 1968; The Harangues (NEC) 1970; The Great
      McDaddy (NEC) 1974.
Relationships: Father of Kevin and Eric Hooks, actors.

HOPKINS, LINDA (Linda Mathews)
(Singer)
b.   December 14, 1925, New Orleans, La.
Education: Studied acting with Stella Adler.
Special Interests: Gospel, blues, jazz.
Honors: Nominee, Drama Desk award; Tony award winner (for Inner
      City) 1972; Catholic Actors Guild Woman of the Year 1976.
Career Data: Member (11 years), Southern Harp Spiritual singers.
Clubs: Bitter End; Copacabana; Brown Derby (Honolulu); Palmer

House (Chicago); El San Juan Hotel (Puerto Rico); Slim Junkins
(San Francisco); Baby Grand 1955.
Films: The Education of Sonny Carson 1974.
Memberships: AEA.
Records: Linda Hopkins (R. C. A.); Me and Bessie (Columbia).
Television: Dick Cavett Show; One to One Telethon 1974; Dinah!
    1974; Drink, Drank, Drunk 1974; The Tonight Show 1974-75;
    Black News 1975; A. M. America 1975; Positively Black 1975;
    Merv Griffin Show 1975; Sammy and Company 1976; Black
    Journal 1976; Mike Douglas Show 1976; Mitzi ... Roarin' in
    the 20's (special) 1976; Pat Collins Show 1976; Joe Franklin
    Show 1976.
Theater: Appearances at Apollo Theatre; Radio City Music Hall;
    Avery Fisher Hall; Jazz Train (European tour) 1960; Purlie
    (Bway debut) 1970; Inner City 1971; Philharmonic Hall (New-
    port Jazz Festival) 1974; Me and Bessie 1975-76; 5:45 Inter-
    lude Series at Town Hall 1975.

HORNE, LENA
    (Singer/Actress)
b. June 30, 1917, Brooklyn, N. Y.
Education: Girls High School 1933.
Special Interests: Civil rights.
Address: 45 East 89 Street, New York, N. Y. 10028.
Honors: Page One Award, N. Y. Newspaper Guild 1943; Black Film-
    makers Hall of Fame award 1975.
Career Data: Toured as vocalist with Noble Sissle orchestra 1935-
    36, Charlie Barnet orchestra 1940-41; served with U. S. O.
    Hollywood victory committee World War II; advisory council on
    Motion Pictures and Television (N. Y. C.).
Clubs: Cotton Club (chorus) 1933; Café Society Downtown 1941; Bill
    Miller's Riviera (N. J.); Club des Champs Elysees (Paris)
    1947; Copacabana; Mocambo (L. A.); Trocadero (L. A.); Empire
    Room-Waldorf Astoria; Caesar's Palace (Las Vegas); Lido
    (Paris); Moulin Rouge (Paris); Savoy Hotel (London) 1959; Talk
    of the Town (London); Salute to Fabulous Forties at Roseland
    1972; Fairmont Hotel (San Francisco); Hamburger Bors (Stock-
    holm); Loews Monte Carlo Hotel (Monaco) 1975; Diplomat
    (Hollywood-by-the-Sea, Fla.) 1976; Sahara (Las Vegas) 1976.
Films: The Duke is Tops (a. k. a. Bronze Venus) 1940; Panama
    Hattie 1942; Georgia Brown in Cabin in the Sky, I Dood It,
    Swing Fever, Thousands Cheer, Stormy Weather 1943; Boogie
    Woogie Dream, Broadway Rhythm, Two Girls and a Sailor
    1944; Ziegfeld Follies, Till the Clouds Roll By 1946; Words
    and Music 1948; Duchess of Idaho 1950; Meet Me in Las Vegas
    1956; Death of a Gunfighter 1969; That's Entertainment 1974.
Memberships: AEA; AFTRA; AGMA; AGVA; NAACP.
Publications: In Person, Lena Horne (autobiography), Greenberg,
    1950; Lena (autobiography), Doubleday, 1965.
Radio: Duffy's Tavern; Strictly from Dixie 1941; The Cats n'
    Jammers Show 1941.
Records: Birth of the Blues (RCA) 1940; Moanin' Low (RCA); Little

Girl Blue (RCA); Classics in Blue (RCA); Porgy and Bess
(RCA); Lena Horne Sings (MGM); At the Waldorf (Victor) 1958;
Lovely and Alive (Victor) 1962; On the Blue Side (Victor) 1962;
Like Latin (Charter) 1963; Sings Your Requests (Charter) 1963;
Lena and Michel (RCA); Stormy Weather (Stanyan).
Television: Ed Sullivan's Toast of the Town 1950; Perry Como Show
1959, 1962; The Lena Horne Show (London) 1959; Here's to the
Ladies 1960; Lena Horne's Grapevine; Flip Wilson Show; Lena
(special) 1964; Harry and Lena (special with Belafonte) 1969;
Sanford and Son; Tony and Lena (special with Tony Bennett)
1972; Englebert Humperdinck Show 1974; Jubilee 1976; America
Salutes Richard Rodgers: The Sound of His Music 1976.
Theater: Dance with Your Gods (debut) 1934; Lew Leslie's Black-
birds 1939; concert at Carnegie Hall 1941; appearance at Capi-
tal Theatre (with Duke Ellington) 1943; appearances at China
Theatre (Stockholm); Olympia Music Hall (Paris); Palladium
(London); ANTA album show 1955; Savannah in Jamaica 1957;
Nine O'Clock Revue (tour) 1961; performed with Billy Eckstine
at Circle Star Theatre (San Francisco) 1972; Westbury Music
Fair 1974; Garden State Arts Center (N. J.) 1974; Minskoff
Theatre Broadway (with Tony Bennett) 1974; Philadelphia Aca-
demy of Music (with Tony Bennett) 1975; Westchester Premier
Theatre 1975.

HORTON, JOHN WARNER see DAFORA, ASADATA

HOSKINS, ALLEN CLAYTON "Farina"
        (Actor)
b.   August 9, 1920, Chelsea, Mass.
Education: Supervised by Los Angeles Board of Education on Hal
        Roach lot.
Special Interests: Dancing, violin.
Clubs: Night club revue (tour) 1955.
Films: Farina in Our Gang (series) 1922-33; You Said a Mouthful
        1932; The Life of Jimmy Dolan, The Mayor of Hell, Reckless
        1935.
Memberships: SAG.

HOUSTON, THELMA
        (Singer/Musician)
b.   Mississippi.
Special Interests: Flute.
Career Data: Worked with Art Reynold's gospel group.
Clubs: Royal Box-Americana Hotel.
Films: The Bingo Long Traveling All-Stars and Motor Kings (sound-
        track) 1976.
Records: Sunshower (Dunhill); Thelma Houston (MOW); I've Got the
        Music in Me (Sheffield); The Bingo Long Song (Tamla); Any
        Way You Want It (Motown); Thelma and Jerry (Motown) 1977.
Television: Emcee on Ebony Music Awards 1975; Dinah! 1975;

American Music Awards 1975; Johnny Mathis Session 1975;
Death Scream 1975; Midnight Special 1976; Soul Train 1976;
Merv Griffin 1977.
Theater: Appearance at Carnegie Hall 1975.

HOWARD, GERTRUDE
       (Actress)
b.   October 13, 1892, Hot Springs, Ark.
d.   September 30, 1934, Los Angeles, Calif.
Career Data: Entered films in 1914.
Films: The Circus Cyclone 1925; River of Romance, Easy Pickings,
       South Sea Love, Uncle Tom's Cabin 1927; On Your Toes 1928;
       Hearts in Dixie, His Captive Woman, Synthetic Sin, Mississippi
       Gambler, Show Boat 1929; Great Day (with Joan Crawford),
       Guilty, Conspiracy 1930; Father's Son, The Prodigal 1931;
       Strangers in Love, The Wet Parade 1932; I'm No Angel 1933;
       Carolina, Peck's Bad Boy 1934; Uncle Tom's Cabin (rerelease
       of 1927 film) 1959.

HUBBARD, FREDDIE (Frederick Dewayne Hubbard)
       (Musician)
b.   April 7, 1938, Indianapolis, Ind.
Special Interests: Trumpet, piano, flugelhorn, mellophone.
Education: Jordan College of Music, Butler University, Indianapolis,
       Indiana.
Address: c/o John Levy Entertainments Inc. , 119 West 57 Street,
       New York, N. Y. 10019.
Honors: Down Beat new star award for trumpet 1961; Grammy
       award (best jazz performance).
Career Data: Performed with Sonny Rollins, J. J. Johnson, Quincy
       Jones and others; toured Europe, Japan, Austria; member,
       Art Blakey's Jazz Messengers 1961; participated Berlin Jazz
       Festival 1965, Newport Jazz Festival 1972, 1975, 1976.
Clubs: Village Vanguard, Village Gate.
Films: The Pawnbroker (soundtrack) 1965; Blow Up 1966; The Bus
       is Coming 1971; Shaft's Big Score 1972.
Records: Art (Atlantic); Artistry (Impulse); Backlash (Atlantic);
       Blue Spirits (Blue Note); Body and Soul (Impulse); Breaking
       Point (Blue Note); Echoes of Blue (Atlantic); First Light (CTI);
       Freddie Hubbard (Blue Note); Goin' Up (Blue Note); The Hub
       of Hubbard (BASF); Hub-Tones (Blue Note); Keep Your Soul
       (CTI); Night of the Cookers (Blue Note); Ready for Freddie
       (Blue Note); Red Clay (CTI); Sky Dive (CTI); Straight Life
       (CTI); Windjammer (Columbia); Open Sesame; The Soul Experi-
       ment (Atlantic); Polar AC (CTI); High Energy (Columbia); The
       Baddest Hubbard (CTI); Liquid Love (Columbia).
Television: Look Up and Live; Dick Cavett Show 1970; Soundstage
       1976; At the Top 1976; Club Date 1976.
Theater: Appearances at Billie Holiday Theatre (Brooklyn); Avery
       Fisher Hall 1975; Carnegie Hall 1975, 1976; Beacon Theatre
       1975, 1976; Radio City Music Hall 1976.

HUGHES, LANGSTON (James Langston Hughes)
(Playwright)
b. February 1, 1902, Joplin, Mo.
d. May 22, 1967, New York, N. Y.
Education: Columbia College 1921-22; Lincoln University (Pa.) B. A.
1929.
Special Interests: Poetry.
Honors: National Urban League 1st Opportunity Poetry Prize 1925;
The Harmon Gold Medal for Literature 1931; Guggenheim Fellowship 1935; Rosenwald Fellowship 1942; American Academy
of Arts Letters Grant 1947; Anisfield-Wolf award 1953; Spingarn Medal 1960.
Career Data: Karamu Playhouse, Cleveland 1936, 1939; correspondent, Afro-American (Baltimore) 1937; founder, Harlem
Suitcase Theatre 1938; founder, New Negro Theatre (L. A.)
1939; Skyloft Players (Chicago) 1942; columnist, Chicago Defender 1943-67; instructor, Atlanta University 1947; poet in
residence, University of Chicago 1949; elected to National Institute of Arts & Sciences 1961; toured Europe and Middle East
1962; columnist, N. Y. Post 1962-67.
Films: Co-authored (with Clarence Muse) Way Down South 1939.
Memberships: AAAS; AFTRA; Authors Guild; Dramatists Guild;
NAG; PEN; WGA East.
Publications: The Big Sea; An Autobiography, Knopf, 1940; I Wonder As I Wander: An Autobiographical Journey, Rinehart,
1956; Black Magic: A Pictorial History of the Negro in Amer-
ican Entertainment, Prentice-Hall, 1967.
Radio: Luncheon at Sardi's; Monitor; The Barry Gray Show; This
Is New York; Young Book Reviewers; Booker T. Washington
in Atlanta (script).
Records: Simple Speaks His Mind (Folkways) 1952; Story of Jazz
(Folkways) 1954; The Glory of Negro History (Folkways) 1955;
Rhythms of the World (Folkways) 1955; Simply Heavenly (Colum-
bia) 1957; The Weary Blues (M. G. M.) 1958; Something in Com-
mon and Other Stories 1963.
Television: Lamp Unto My Feet; Look Up and Live; The Mike Wal-
lace Show; Strollin' Twenties (Belafonte special) 1966.
Theater: The Gold Piece 1921; The Scottsboro Unlimited 1932;
Mulatto 1935; At an Air Raid Over Harlem: Scenario for a
Little Black Movie 1936; Little Ham 1936; When the Jack Hol-
lers 1936; Soul Gone Home 1937; Joy to My Soul 1937; Don't
You Want to Be Free? 1937; Emperor of Haiti (a. k. a. Drums
of Haiti) 1938; Limitations of Life 1938; Em-Fuehrer Jones
1938; The Organizer 1938-39; Front Porch 1939; The Sun Do
Move 1942; Freedom's Plow 1943; For This We Fight 1943;
Street Scene (lyrics) 1947; Troubled Island (musical version of
Emperor of Haiti) 1949; The Barrier (musical version of Mulatto) 1950; Just Around the Corner (lyrics) 1951; Simply
Heavenly 1957; Esther (book) 1957; Shakespeare in Harlem
1959; Port Town (book) 1960; The Ballad of the Brown King
(cantata) 1960; Black Nativity 1961; The Gospel Glow: A Passion Play 1962; Tambourines to Glory 1963; appearance at Philharmonic Hall 1963; Jerico-Jim Crow 1964; Mule Bone 1964;

The Prodigal Son 1965; The Weary Blues 1966; Mother and
Child 1966; Simple Blues 1967.

HUMPHREY, BOBBI (Barbara Ann Humphrey)
        (Musician)
b. Dallas, Texas.
Education: Texas Southern University 1968-70; Southern Methodist
        University; studied with Hubert Laws.
Special Interests: Flute.
Honors: Record World Magazine Female Jazz Performer of the
        Year; Ebony Magazine Best Flutist of the Year; Billboard
        Magazine Best Female Instrumentalist.
Career Data: Montreux Jazz Festival.
Clubs: Munk's Park After Dark 1975; Village Gate 1976.
Records: Blacks and Blues (Blue Note); Flute In (Blue Note) 1971;
        Dig This (Blue Note) 1972; Satin Doll (Blue Note) 1974; Fancy
        Dancer (Blue Note) 1975; Tailor Made (Blue Note) 1977.
Television: Today Show; Like It Is; Tonight Show 1971; Ebony Mu-
        sic Awards Show 1975; Positively Black 1976.
Theater: Appeared at Apollo Theatre (Amateur Show) 1971; Beacon
        Theatre 1975; Felt Forum 1975; Avery Fisher Hall (Newport
        Jazz Festival) 1975.

HUNTER, EDDIE
        (Playwright/Actor)
b. February 4, 1888, New York, N.Y.
Career Data: Known as "The Fighting Comedian"; numerous vaude-
        ville tours teamed with other comics.
Memberships: NAG.
Theater: Wrote The Battle of Who Run 1909, Going to the Races
        1909, How Come? 1923, The Lady 1944, My Magnolia (musi-
        cal with Alex Rogers) 1926; performed in Blackbirds (London);
        appeared at Alhambra Theatre.

HURSTON, ZORA NEALE
        (Playwright)
b. January 7, 1903, Eatonville, Fla.
d. January 28, 1960, Fort Pierce, Fla.
Education: Howard University 1921-24; Barnard College B.A. 1928;
        Morgan College.
Honors: Rosenwald Foundation Fellowship; Guggenheim Fellowship
        1936, 1938; Honorable Mention for Spears, Opportunity contest
        1925.
Career Data: Head, Drama Dept., North Carolina College (Durham).
Films: Served as technical adviser, Paramount Pictures 1941-42.
Publications: Compiler, Collection of Bahamian Folk Songs (with
        William Grant Still), 1937; Dust Tracks on a Dirt Road (auto-
        biography), Lippincott, 1942.
Theater: Wrote Color Struck: A Play in Four Scenes; The First
        One (one act) 1927; Great Day 1927; Mule Bone: A Comedy of

Negro Life in Three Acts (written with Langston Hughes) 1931;
Polk County 1944; Fast and Furious (a musical written with
Tim Moore) 1931; wrote and produced From Sun to Sun (pro-
gram of Negro spirituals and work songs) 1932.

HURT, MISSISSIPPI JOHN (Smith)
      (Singer)
b.   March 8, 1892, Teoc (Carroll County), Miss.
d.   November 2, 1966, Grenada, Miss.
Special Interests: Guitar, blues.
Career Data: Itinerant performer in Avalon, Miss.; lived in seclu-
      sion between 1928 and 1963; returned to limelight with ap-
      pearance at Newport Folk Festival 1963.
Clubs: Ontario Place Coffee House 1963.
Musical Compositions: Louis Collins (a ballad).
Records: Vol. 1 of a Legacy (Piedmont); 1928 (Biograph); Best
      (Vanguard); Last Sessions (Vanguard); Immortal (Vanguard).
      On Okeh: Frankie; Nobody's Dirty Business; Louis Collins
      1928; Candy Man 1928; Spike Driver Blues 1928; Stagger Lee
      Blues 1928; Avalon Blues 1928. On Piedmont: Presenting
      Mississippi John Hurt: Folk Songs and Blues 1963; Worried
      Blues 1964.
Theater: Appearances at Carnegie Hall, Town Hall.

HYMAN, EARLE
      (Actor)
b.   October 11, 1926, Rocky Mount, N. C.
Education: New School of Social Research; studied acting with Eva
      Le Gallienne at American Theatre Wing; studied at Actors
      Studio since 1956.
Special Interests: Languages, fencing, teaching.
Address: 109 Bank Street, New York, N. Y. 10014.
Honors: Canada Lee Foundation Award 1953; Theatre World Award
      (for No Time for Sergeants) 1956; Norwegian State Award as
      Best Actor (for Emperor Jones).
Career Data: Worked with American Shakespeare Festival (Strat-
      ford, Conn.) 5 sessions; teacher at Herbert Berghof Studio
      1961-date; toured Scandinavia for Norwegian Travelling Theatre
      1964.
Films: The African (Norwegian); The Bamboo Prison 1955; The Pos-
      session of Joel Delaney 1972; Super Cops 1974.
Memberships: AEA; AFTRA; SAG.
Radio: Story of Ruby Valentine (series) 1955; New York: A Por-
      trait in Sound (WOR) 1976.
Television: Jim in Huckleberry Finn; The Shepherd in Emmanuel;
      Macbeth; Sesame Street; Neil Davenport in The Edge of Night
      (series); Adam Hezdrel in The Green Pastures (Hallmark Hall
      of Fame) 1957.
Theater: Three's a Family (ANT) 1943; Run Little Chillun (Bway
      debut) 1943; Anna Lucasta 1944; London 1947; A Lady Passing
      Fair (pre-Bway run) 1947; Sister Oakes (O. B.) 1949; Ride the

Right Bus (People's Show Case Theatre) 1951; The Climate of
Eden 1952; The Prince of Morocco in The Merchant of Venice
(City Center) 1953, (ASF) 1957; title role in Othello (O. B.)
1953, (ASF) 1957, (Norway) 1964; Soothsayer in Julius Caeser
(ASF) 1955; Boatswain in The Tempest (ASF) 1955; Lieutenant
in No Time for Sergeants 1955; title role in Mister Johnson
1956; Melun in King John (ASF) 1956; Saint Joan (O. B.) 1956;
Hamlet (O. B.) 1957; Vladimir in Waiting for Godot 1957; An-
tonio in The Duchess of Malfi 1957; The Infernal Machine (O.
B.) 1958; The Cherry Orchard (O. B.); The Winter's Tale
(ASF) 1958; A Midsummer Night's Dream (ASF) 1958; Horatio
in Hamlet (ASF) 1958; Moon on a Rainbow Shawl (London) 1958;
Walter Lee Younger in A Raisin in the Sun (London) 1959-60;
Caliban in The Tempest (ASF) 1960; Alexas in Antony and
Cleopatra (ASF) 1960; title role in Mister Roberts (ELT) 1962;
The Worlds of Shakespeare (O. B.) 1963; The White Rose and
the Red (O. B.) 1964; title role in Emperor Jones (Norway)
1964; Orrin (O. B.); Jonah (O. B.); Life and Times of J. Walter
Smintheus (O. B.) 1970; House Party (American Place Theatre)
1974; As to the Meaning of Words (Stamford, Conn.) 1977;
Agamemnon (NYSF) 1977.

IGLEHART, JAMES
          (Actor)
Films: Beyond the Valley of the Dolls 1970; The Seven Minutes
          1971; Savage 1973; Bamboo Gods and Iron Men 1974.
Memberships: SAG.

INGRAM, REX
          (Actor)
b.   October 20, 1895, Cairo, Ill.
d.   September 19, 1969, Los Angeles, Calif.
Education: Northwestern University M. D. 1919.
Special Interests: Boating, building furniture.
Honors: Cited by U. S. Treasury Dept. for his broadcasts for na-
          tional defense 1941; Black Filmmakers Hall of Fame (posthu-
          mously) 1975.
Films: Tarzan of the Apes, Salome 1918; Scaramouche, The Ten
          Commandments 1923; Lord Jim 1925; The Big Parade, Beau
          Geste 1926; King of Kings 1927; Hearts in Dixie 1929; The Four
          Feathers 1929; Trader Horn 1931; Sign of the Cross 1932; King
          Kong, The Emperor Jones, Love in Morocco 1933; Harlem
          After Midnight 1934; Captain Blood 1935; De Lawd in The Green
          Pastures 1936; Let My People Live (doc.) 1938; Adventures of
          Huckleberry Finn 1939; The Thief of Bagdad 1940; The Talk of
          the Town 1942; Fired Wife, Sahara, Cabin in the Sky 1943;
          Dark Waters 1944; A Thousand and One Nights 1945; Moonrise
          1948; King Solomon's Mines 1950; Tarzan's Hidden Jungle 1955;
          The Ten Commandments, Congo Crossing 1956; Hell on Devil's
          Island 1957; God's Little Acre, Anna Lucasta 1958; Escort West,
          Watusi 1959; Elmer Gantry, Desire in the Dust 1960; Your

Cheatin' Heart 1965; Hurry Sundown, Journey to Shiloh, How to Succeed in Business Without Really Trying 1967.

Memberships: AEA; AFTRA; SAG (two terms, Board of Directors); NAG.

Radio: Against the Storm 1936-1937; adapted & presented Deep River Boys 1937; Kate Smith Show 1940.

Television: Playhouse 90; I Spy; Bill Cosby Show; Ramar of the Jungle 1953; Captain Midnight 1954; The Emperor Jones (Kraft Theatre) 1955; The Intolerable Portrait (Your Playtime) 1955; Black Saddle 1959; Law and Mr. Jones 1960; The Rifleman 1961; Sea Hunt 1962; Dick Powell Theatre 1962; Gentlemen in Blue (Lloyd Bridges Theatre) 1962; Sam Benedict 1962; The Brighter Day 1963; Mr. Novak 1963; The Breaking Point 1964; Daktari 1967, 1968; Cowboy in Africa 1968; Gunsmoke 1969.

Theater: Beale Street; Freedom Road; Lulu Belle (San Francisco) 1929; Once in a Lifetime; Crown in Porgy (San Francisco); Harlem (Hollywood); Lucky Days (San Francisco) (all these between 1929 and 1932); Satan in Ol' Man Satan 1932; Theodora the Queen 1931, Stevedore 1934; Dance with Your Gods 1934; Buttinhead Adams in Stick in the Mud 1935; wrote, produced and acted in Drums of the Bayou 1935; Marching Song 1937; title role in The Emperor Jones (Stock) 1937; Big Boy in How Come Lawd? (Negro Theatre Guild Prod.) at Ann Arbor Mich. Festival 1937; Prince of Morocco in the Merchant of Venice 1937; King Christophe in Haiti (W. P. A. project Prod. at La-fayette Theatre, N. Y. C.) 1938; Franklin D. Jones in Sing Out the News 1938; Lucifer Jr. in Cabin in the Sky 1940; Frank in Anna Lucasta 1944; St. Louis Woman 1946; Lysistrata 1946; Waiting for Godot 1957; Kwamina 1961.

JACKSON, ERNESTINE
          (Actress)
b.   September 18, Corpus Christi, Texas.
Education: Hunter College; New School for Social Research; The Opera Workshop; Butleroff School of Dance; Del Mar Junior College (Corpus Christi, Texas); Juilliard School of Music.
Honors: Theatre World award (for Raisin) 1974; Tony nominee 1974.
Clubs: The Grand Finale 1977.
Films: The Out of Towners 1970; Aaron Loves Angela 1975.
Memberships: AEA; NAG.
Television: Geritol commercial; Musical Chairs 1975; Black News 1976; Positively Black 1976.
Theater: Storyville; Finian's Rainbow (City Center); Tricks; Jesus Christ Superstar; Showboat (Lincoln Center) 1966; Mrs. Malloy in Hello, Dolly! 1969; Applause 1970; Ruth Younger in Raisin 1973; A Musical Jubilee (standby) 1976; Sister Sarah in Guys and Dolls 1976.

JACKSON, HAL (Harold Jackson)
          (Producer/Broadcaster)
b.   November 3, 1922, Charleston, S. C.

Education: Howard University.
Honors: Disc jockey of the year; Man of Year award.
Career Data: Vice-president, Inner City Broadcasting (WBLS-FM and WLIB-AM); executive producer, Miss U. S. Talented Teen Pageant; executive, Hal Jackson Productions.
Memberships: AFTRA.
Radio: The House That Jack Built (Wash. D. C.) 194?; Hal Jackson Show (WMCA) 1952; ABC network program.
Television: Guest host Soul (NET); African American Day Parade 1975.

JACKSON, LEONARD (L. Errol Jaye)
    (Actor)
b.   February 7, 1928, Jacksonville, Fla.
Education: Fisk University B. A. 1952; studied acting at Herbert Berghof Studio with Uta Hagen; studied acting with Philip Burton.
Address: 400 Central Park West, New York, N. Y. 10025.
Honors: Johnnie Walker Golden Monacle award for outstanding contributions in the field of entertainment.
Films: Up Tight 1968; Pound 1970; Mr. Brooks in Five on the Black Hand Side, Ganja and Hess (a. k. a. Blood Couple), Together for Days 1973; Super Spook 1975.
Memberships: AEA; AFTRA; SAG.
Television: Caught in the Middle; Saroyan Plays (NET); Love Is a Many Splendored Thing (series); Blind Man's Bluff (Hawk); commercials for Bagatelle (Toni), Standard Oil, Great American Soups, American Air Lines, Doral and Stroh's Beer, Scope.
Theater: Phil Crown in Together for Days; Henry V (O. B.); Murderous Angels (O. B.); Chickencoop Chinaman (O. B.); The Karl Marx Play (O. B.); Coriolanus (NYSF); Moon on a Rainbow Shawl (O. B.) 1962; Troilus and Cressida (O. B. debut for NYSF) 1965; Happy Ending (O. B.) 1966; Day of Absence (O. B.) 1966; Who's Got His Own (O. B.) 1966; Great White Hope (Bway debut) 1968; Electronic Nigger and Others (O. B.) 1968; Black Quartet (O. B.) 1969; Mr. Brooks in Five on the Black Hand Side (O. B.) 1970; Boesman and Lena (O. B.) 1970; Lost in the Stars 1972; The Prodigal Sister 1974; Macbeth (O. B.) 1977.

JACKSON, MAHALIA "Queen of the Gospel Singers"
    (Gospel Singer)
b.   October 26, 1911, New Orleans, La.
d.   January 27, 1972, Evergreen Park, Ill.
Honors: Grammy awards 1961, 1962; National Academy of Recording Arts and Sciences 1961-65; 5 gold records.
Career Data: Participated Newport Jazz Festival 1958, 1970; sang at U. S. Presidential Inauguration 1961; popularized Trouble of the World, He's Got the Whole World in His Hands, Move on Up a Little Higher, The Lord's Prayer, Go Tell It on the Mountain, Down by the Riverside, Didn't It Rain and numerous others.

Films: St. Louis Blues 1958; Imitation of Life 1959; Jazz on a
        Summer's Day (doc.) 1960; The Best Man 1964; Newport Jazz
        Festival (doc.) 1970; Mahalia (doc.) 1975 (posthumously).
Publications: Moving On Up (autobiography), Hawthorn Bks., 1966.
Radio: CBS (series) 1954.
Records: In The Upper Room (Kenwood); Just As I Am (Kenwood);
        Mahalia (Kenwood); World's Greatest Gospel Singer (Columbia);
        Bless This House (Columbia); Every Time I Feel the Spirit
        (Columbia); When We Were Young; Newport 1958 (Columbia);
        Sweet Little Jesus Boy; Silent Night (Columbia); Christmas
        (Columbia); The Life I Sing About (Caedmon); Best (Kenwood);
        Best Loved Hymns of Dr. King (Columbia); Garden of Prayer
        (Columbia); Great ... (Columbia); Great Gettin' Up Morning
        (Columbia); Greatest Hits (Columbia); How I Got Over (Colum-
        bia); I Believe (Columbia); In Concert (Columbia); Mighty For-
        tress (Columbia); My Faith (Columbia); Power and the Glory
        (Columbia); Recorded in Europe (Columbia); Right Out of the
        Church (Columbia); What the World Needs Now (Columbia).
Television: Studs Terkel Show (Chicago) 1950; Ed Sullivan Show;
        Got to Tell It: A Tribute to Mahalia (posthumously) 1975.
Theater: Appearances at Carnegie Hall 1950; Randalls Island Stadium
        1962; Philharmonic Hall 1967.

JACKSON, MILLIE
        (Singer)
b.   Georgia.
Honors: Cashbox Best Female R & B Vocalist 1973; NATRA Most
        Promising Female Vocalist 1973; Grammy nominee 1974; gold
        record.
Clubs: Zanzibar (Hoboken); Barney Google's 1975.
Records: Caught Up (Spring); Still Caught Up (Spring); Free and in
        Love (Spring); My Man Is a Sweet Man; If Loving You is Wrong;
        It Hurts So Good (Spring); I Don't Want to Be Right; Millie
        (Spring); Lovingly Yours.
Television: Positively Black 1975; Ebony Music Awards Show 1975;
        Soul Train 1975; Ebony Affair 1975; Dinah! 1976; Don Kirsh-
        ner's Rock Concert 1976.
Theater: Appearances at Apollo Theatre 1975; Westbury Music Fair
        1975.

JACKSON, MILT(ON) "Bags"
        (Jazz Musician)
b.   January 1, 1923, Detroit, Mich.
Education: Michigan State.
Special Interests: Vibraharp, piano, guitar.
Address: 192-12 105 Avenue, Hollis, New York 11412.
Honors: Esquire New Star Award 1947; Metronome Poll winner
        1956-60; Down Beat Poll winner 1955-59; Down Beat Critics
        Poll Winner 1955-59; Playboy All Stars award 1959-60; Ency-
        clopedia of Jazz Poll as "Greatest Ever" 1956.
Career Data: Played with Woody Herman band 1949-50 and Dizzy
        Gillespie 1950-52; joined Modern Jazz Quartet 1953-60.

Clubs: Buddy's Place 1975; Village Vanguard 1975.
Films: Odds Against Tomorrow (played score) 1959.
Records: Howard McGhee and Milt Jackson (Savoy); Soul Brothers
(Atlantic); Opus De Funk (Prestige); Second Nature (Savoy);
Art (Atlantic); Bags and Flute (Atlantic); Bags and Trane (At-
lantic); Big Band Bags (Milestone); Big 4 Montreux '75 (Pablo);
Complete (Prestige); Feelings (Pablo); Goodbye (CTI); Impulse
Years (Impulse); Jazz 'n' Samba (Impulse); Live at the Mu-
seum of Modern Art (Trip); Olinga (CTI); Plenty Plenty Soul
(Atlantic); Statements (Impulse); Sunflower (CTI); That's the
Way (Impulse); Milt Jackson (GNP Crescendo).
Theater: Appeared at Avery Fisher Hall 1975; Carnegie Hall (New-
port Jazz Festival) 1975.

JACOBS, LAWRENCE-HILTON
     (Actor)
b.   September 4, 1953, New York, N. Y.
Education: H. S. of Art and Design 1971.
Special Interests: Writing songs and scripts.
Address: Dickens-Held, 9255 Sunset Blvd. , Suite 705, Los Angeles,
     Calif. 90069.
Honors: Terry Tune cartoon award.
Career Data: Former member, Al Fann Theatrical Ensemble (ap-
     pearing in: The Exterminator, Cora's Second Kiss, Masks in
     Black); former member, NEC.
Films: Serpico 1973; Super Cops, The Gambler, Claudine, Death
     Wish 1974; Cooley High 1975.
Memberships: SAG.
Television: Commercials for Nathan's and United Negro College
     Fund 1975; Merv Griffin Show 1975; Soul Train 1975; Freddie
     "Boom Boom" Washington in Welcome Back, Kotter (series)
     1975-; American Bandstand 1976; Rich Little Show 1976; Donny
     and Marie 1976; Break the Bank 1976; Positively Black 1976;
     Roots 1977; Tonight Show 1977.

JACQUET, ILLINOIS (Jean Battiste Illinois Jacquet)
     (Conductor/Jazz Musician)
b.   October 31, 1922, Broussard, La.
Special Interests: Tenor, alto and soprano saxophone.
Address: 112-44 179th Street, St. Albans, N. Y. 11433.
Career Data: Played with bands of Lionel Hampton, Cab Calloway
     1943-44, Count Basie 1945-46; then his own band and Jazz at
     the Philharmonic units; participated in Monterey Jazz Festival
     1974; popularized Flying Home.
Clubs: Metropole 1959; Buddy's Place 1975; Storyville 1977.
Films: Jammin' the Blues 1944.
Records: Then Came Swing (Capitol); Great Tenor Sax Artists (RCA);
     Port of Rico (Verve); Swing's the Thing (Verve); Groovin'
     (Verve); Jazz Moods (Verve); Birthday Party (JRC); Blues That's
     Me (Prestige); Bottoms Up (Prestige); Genius at Work (Black
     Lion); How High the Moon (Prestige); King! (Prestige); Message
     (Cadet); Soul Explosion (Prestige).

Theater: Appeared at Apollo Theatre 1950, 1955; Radio City Music
Hall 1976.

JAMAL, AHMAD (Fritz Jones)
(Jazz Musician)
b. July 2, 1930, Pittsburgh, Pa.
Education: Studied with Mary Caldwell Dawson and James Miller.
Special Interests: Piano.
Career Data: Played with George Hudson orchestra, Four Strings
1950, The Caldwells; formed his own trio 1951; appeared at
Newport Jazz Festival 1975.
Clubs: Blue Note (Chicago); Rainbow Grill-Waldorf Astoria; The
Embers 1952; Village Gate 1975; Top of the Gate 1975; New
Barrister 1976.
Records: At the Pershing--But Not for Me (Cadet); Alhambra (Ca-
det); All of You (Cadet); At the Blackhawk (Cadet); At the
Penthouse (Cadet); At Top--Poinciana Revisited (Impulse);
Awakening (Impulse); Bright, Blue and the Beautiful (Cadet);
Cry Young (Cadet); Extensions (Cadet); Freelight (Impulse);
Heat Wave (Cadet); Inspiration (Cadet); Jamaica (20th Century);
Jamal Plays Jamal (20th Century); Live at Oil Can Harry's
(Catalyst); Naked City Theme (Cadet); Poinciana (Cadet); Rhap-
sody (Cadet); '73 (20th Century); Steppin' Out with a Dream
(20th Century); Tranquility (Impulse); Count 'Em 88 (Cadet);
But Not for Me 1958.
Television: Mark of Jazz 1976.
Theater: Appearances at Apollo Theatre 1950; Town Hall 1975;
Billie Holiday Theatre (Brooklyn) 1975.

JAMES, OLGA
(Actress/Singer)
Education: Juilliard School of Music 1952.
Special Interests: Languages.
Career Data: Instructor at Los Angeles City College and San Fer-
nando Valley College, Northridge, Calif.; worked on productions
for Inner City Cultural Workshop.
Clubs: Le Cupidon 1956.
Films: Cindy Lou in Carmen Jones 1954.
Television: Verna in The Bill Cosby Show (series) 1969-71; Young
Doctor Kildare 1972; Sealab 2020 (voice) 1972-73; Positively
Black 1976.
Theater: Ethel in Mr. Wonderful 1956-57.
Relationships: Wife of Julian "Cannonball" Adderley, jazz musician.

JAMISON, JUDITH
(Dancer)
b. May 10, 1943, Philadelphia, Pa.
Education: Fisk University; Philadelphia Dance Academy; Judimar
School of Dance (Philadelphia).
Address: Alvin Ailey American Dance Theater, 229 East 59 Street,
New York, N.Y. 10022.

Honors: Dance Magazine Annual Citation 1972.
Career Data: Danced with San Francisco Ballet; American Ballet
      Theatre 1965; lead dancer, Alvin Ailey American Dance Theater
      1965-date; Harkness Ballet 1966-67; participated in Harper
      Festival, Chicago 1965; Festival of Negro Arts, Dakar, Sene-
      gal 1966; Edinburgh Festival 1968.
Memberships: National Council of the Arts (board member).
Television: Midday Live 1975.
Theater: Danced Mary Seaton in Agnes De Mille's The Four Marys
      (Lincoln Center) 1965; Voudoun in Geoffrey Holder's The Prodi-
      gal Prince 1968; the Mother in Ailey's Knoxville: Summer of
      1915; danced roles in Caravan; Portrait of Billie; Revelations;
      Seven Deadly Sins; Carmina Burana; Cry, Fanga; The Wedding
      Blues Suite; The Black Belt; The Mooche; Reflections in D;
      Pas de Duke; Facets, Fix Me Jesus; Wading in the Water;
      According to Eve; Blood Memories 1976.

JARBORO, CATERINA (Catherine Yarborough)
      (Opera Singer)
b.   July, 1903, Wilmington, N. C.
Education: Studied music in Europe.
Honors: Caterina Jarboro Company named in her honor.
Career Data: Sang in opera houses in Italy, France, Belgium, Hol-
      land, Switzerland; operatic repertoire included title role in
      Aida, Inez in L'Africaine; Balkis in Gounod's La Reine de Saba
      (Queen of Sheba); sang with Alfredo Salmaggi's Chicago Opera
      Co.
Theater: Shuffle Along 1921; Runnin' Wild 1923; Puccini Theatre
      (Milan) 1930; Hippodrome 1933, 1934; Academy of Music (Brook-
      lyn) 1939; Town Hall 1942; Carnegie Hall 1944.

JEANETTE, GERTRUDE
      (Actress)
b.   November 28, 1918, Little Rock, Ark.
Education: New School of Social Research.
Special Interests: Writing, producing.
Career Data: Worked with American Negro Theatre.
Films: Cry of the City 1948; Nothing But a Man 1964; Cotton Comes
      to Harlem 1970; Shaft 1971; Legend of Nigger Charley, Black
      Girl 1972.
Television: Fred Waring Show.
Theater: 417 (O. B.); wrote This Way Forward (O. B.) 1951; wrote
      A Bolt from the Blue 1952; acted in Lost in the Stars (O. B.)
      1949; The Long Dream 1960; Deep Are the Roots (O. B.) 1960;
      Moon on a Rainbow Shawl (O. B.) 1962; Nobody Loves an Alba-
      tross 1963; The Amen Corner 1965; To Be Young, Gifted and
      Black (O. B.) 1969; The Skin of Our Teeth 1975; wrote and pro-
      duced Light in the Cellar (O. B.) 1975; directed The Yellow
      Pillow (Harlem Performance Center) 1976; Vieux Carré 1977.

JEFFERSON, "BLIND LEMON"
    (Guitarist/Singer)
b. 1897, Wortham, Texas.
d. October 10, 1930, Chicago, Ill.
Special Interests: Blues, folk.
Career Data: Recorded Paramount "Race Records" reissued on River-
    side Records.
Records: Piney Woods; Money Mama; Classic Folk Blues (Riverside);
    Master of Blues (Biograph); Black Snake Man (Milestone); Blind
    Lemon Jefferson 1926-9 (Milestone); Immortal (Milestone);
    1926-29 (Biograph).

JEFFERSON, HERBERT JR.
    (Actor)
b. September 28, 1946, Sandersville, Ga.
Education: Rutgers University.
Address: Goldstein Shapira, 9171 Wilshire Blvd., Beverly Hills,
    Calif.
Films: Chrome and Hot Leather 1971; Black Gun 1972; Detroit 9000
    1973.
Memberships: SAG.
Television: The Partridge Family; Marcus Welby, M. D. 1974; For
    Good or Evil episode on Streets of San Francisco 1974; Mc-
    Cloud 1975; Columbo 1975; Caribe 1975; Get Christie Love
    1975; Popi 1975; Rich Man, Poor Man 1976; Bionic Woman
    1976; Delvecchio 1976; Szysznyk 1977.
Theater: Damn Yankees (O. B. debut); Black Electra (O. B.); Mur-
    derous Angels (O. B.); The Blacks (O. B.) 1961; The Great
    White Hope 1968; Dream on Monkey Mountain (O. B.) 1971;
    The Last of Mrs. Lincoln 1973; Streamers (New Haven, Conn.)
    1976.

JEFFRIES, HERB(ERT) a. k. a. Herb Jeffrey
    (Actor/Singer)
b. September 24, 1916, Detroit, Mich.
Education: Paris Conservatory.
Special Interests: Composing.
Career Data: Sang with bands of Earl Hines, Duke Ellington 1940-
    42; popularized songs "Flamingo" and "Cocktails for Two";
    toured with Four Tones 1939.
Clubs: Alabam (L. A.) 1937.
Films: Bronze Buckaroo 1938; Harlem on the Prairie; Two Gun
    Man from Harlem, Harlem Rides the Range 1939; Flamingo
    1947; Calypso Joe 1957.
Musical Compositions: The Singing Prophet (Adam and Earl Blues);
    Deep Down in the Middle of Your Heart; Don't You Weep Little
    Children; Which Way Does the Wind Blow?; The Guru--and the
    Theme Is Love 1974.
Television: Showtime at the Apollo 1954; Name of the Game 1968.
Theater: Jump for Joy (L. A.) 1941.

JENKINS, CAROL (Ann)
    (Broadcaster)
b.   November 30, 1944, Montgomery, Ala.
Education: Boston University B. S. 1966, New York University M. A.
    1968.
Special Interests: Speech therapy.
Address: 30 Rockefeller Plaza, New York, N. Y. 10020.
Memberships: AFTRA; American women in Radio & TV; International
    Radio and TV Society; National Association of Media Women;
    National Academy of Arts and Sciences; Writers Guild of Amer-
    ica East.
Radio: WNYC; WHBI.
Television: News correspondent (including News Center 4 feature,
    How to Beat the System) WNBC-TV 1973-date; correspondent,
    ABC-TV (including Reasoner/Smith Report, Eyewitness News)
    1972-73; moderator, co-host, Straight Talk WOR-TV 1971-72;
    co-anchor person (with Bill Ryan), reporter, News Report
    WOR-TV, 1970-71.

JESSYE, EVA (Alberta)
    (Conductor/Composer)
b.   January 20, 1895, Coffeyville, Kan.
Education: Western University (Quindaro, Kansas) 1914; Wilber-
    force University M. A.; Allen University D. Mus.
Special Interests: Acting, arranging.
Honors: Eva Jessye Collection established at University of Michigan
    Library.
Career Data: Head, Music Department, Morgan State College 1919-
    20; director, original Dixie Jubilee Singers and Eva Jessye
    Choir; artist-in-residence, Glassboro (New Jersey) State Col-
    lege.
Films: Hallelujah (director of music) 1930; Porgy and Bess 1959;
    Black Like Me 1964; Slaves 1969; Cotton Comes to Harlem
    1970; Hot Rock, The Possession of Joel Delaney 1972.
Musical Compositions: Arrangements for An' I Cry; Who Is That
    Yondah?; The Spirit o' the Lord Done Fell on Me.
Radio: Creator of Aunt Mamy's Chillun and Four Dusty Travellers.
Theater: Porgy and Bess (choral director all productions 1935-58);
    Paradise Lost and Regained; Lost in the Stars 1950; Four
    Saints in Three Acts 1952.

JOHN, ERROL
    (Actor/Playwright)
b.   Trinidad.
Honors: Guggenheim Fellowship.
Films: Simba 1955; The Nun's Story 1959; The Sins of Rachel Cade
    1961; PT 109 1963; Man in the Middle, Guns at Batasi 1964;
    Assault on a Queen 1966; Buck and the Preacher 1972.
Memberships: BAEA.
Television: Secret Agent.
Theater: Wrote Moon on a Rainbow Shawl 1962; appeared in London

in: Anna Lucasta, The Respectful Prostitute, Cry the Beloved
Country, Member of the Wedding 1957, Othello 1962.

JOHNSON, ARNOLD
     (Actor)
Films: Title role in Putney Swope 1969; Shaft 1971; Pipe Dreams
     1976.
Memberships: SAG.
Television: Sanford and Son 1975, Good Times 1975; The Richard
     Pryor Special? 1977.
Theater: Shark 1975.

JOHNSON, DOTTS (Hyland Montague Johnson)
     (Actor)
b. February 3, 1913, Baltimore, Md.
Special Interests: Poetry, music, Afro-American culture, singing.
Address: 420 West 130 Street, New York, N. Y. 10027.
Honors: Received best performance nomination (for Paisan) 1958.
Career Data: Began at 8 years of age as lead singer with The Mt.
     Winons Four; performed with American Negro Theatre.
Films: Tall, Tan and Terrific 1946; Paisan 1948; No Way Out
     1950; The Joe Louis Story 1953; The Grissom Gang 1971.
Memberships: AEA; AFTRA; AGVA; NAG; SAG.
Musical Compositions: Kill the Hard Drugs Pusher; No Note Blue.
Radio: The World's Great Novels; Sometime Before Morning.
Records: Street of Dreams/Paradise (MGM) 1958; Art for Arts
     Sake (Earth) 1975.
Television: Playhouse 90; Alcoa Presents; Pontiac Hour; title role
     in The Candidate (WGBH); If You Give a Dance, You Gotta
     Pay the Band (ABC Theatre) 1972.
Theater: Freeman (O. B.); Three's a Family (U. S. O. tour); Blos-
     som in The Hasty Heart (tour); Freight (Bway debut); Anna
     Lucasta; Death of a Salesman 1975.

JOHNSON, GEORGE PERRY
     (Producer)
b. February, 1887.
Address: 2455 S. St. Andrews Place, Los Angeles, Calif. 90018.
Honors: Black Film collection in Bancroft Library, U. C. L. A. ,
     named in his honor.
Career Data: General Booking Manager, Lincoln Motion Picture
     Company, Inc. 1916.
Films: Wrote By Right of Birth 1921.
Relationships: Brother of Noble P. Johnson, actor/producer.

JOHNSON, HALL
     (Musician/Conductor)
b. March 12, 1888, Athens, Ga.
d. April 30, 1970, New York, N. Y.

Education: Knox Institute (Athens, Ga.) 1903, Allen University
        (Columbia, S. C.) 1908, Hahn School of Music (Philadelphia)
        1970, University of Pennsylvania B. Mus. 1910, N. Y. Insti-
        tute of Musical Art 1923-24, Juilliard School of Music, Phila-
        delphia Music Academy D. Mus. 1934.
Special Interests: Composing.
Honors: Simon Haessler prize for competition 1910; Harmon award
        1931; Black Filmmakers Hall of Fame (posthumously) 1975.
Career Data: Organized Hall Johnson choir 1925; member, Vernon
        and Irene Castle Dance orchestra; organized Festival Negro
        Chorus of Los Angeles 1936; organized Festival chorus of New
        York City 1946.
Films: Music for: Green Pastures, Hearts Divided 1936; Lost
        Horizon 1937; Way Down South, Swanee River 1939; Lady for
        a Night, Meet John Doe 1941; Tales of Manhattan 1942; Cabin
        in the Sky 1943.
Memberships: ASCAP 1952.
Musical Compositions: Son of Man (cantata) 1946; Fi-Yer 1949; Way
        Up in Heaven; Sonata; Banjo Dance.
Radio: New World a-Coming (WMCA) 1944.
Theater: Shuffle Along (tour) 1922; arranged and directed music,
        The Green Pastures 1930; wrote book and music, Run Little
        Chillun 1933; appeared at Pythian Temple 1928; Town Hall
        1928; Lewisohn Stadium 1928, 1938; Blue Holiday 1945.

JOHNSON, J. J. (James Louis Johnson)
        (Musician/Composer)
b.   January 22, 1924, Indianapolis, Ind.
Special Interests: Trombone, conducting, arranging.
Address: 131 Garden Street, Teaneck, N. J. 07666.
Honors: Esquire New Star award 1946; Down Beat Critics' Poll
        Winner 1955-59; Metronome Poll winner 1956-60; Playboy Poll
        winner 1957-60; Musicians' Musicians Poll winner (Encyclo-
        pedia Yearbook of Jazz) 1956; Ebony Music award winner 1975.
Career Data: Played with bands of Benny Carter 1942-45, Count
        Basie 1945-46; toured with Illinois Jacquet 1947-49; worked
        with Woody Herman, Dizzy Gillespie; toured Korea and Japan
        for U. S. O. 1951; toured as part of Jay and Kay Quintet (with
        Kai Winding) 1956; toured Europe 1957, 58; performed at
        Monterey Jazz Festival 1959.
Films: Scores for Shaft 1971; Across 110th Street, Top of the Heap,
        Man and Boy 1972; Cleopatra Jones 1973; Willie Dynamite 1974.
Records: J Is for Jazz (Columbia); Dial J. J. 5 (Columbia); J. J. in
        Person (Columbia); Eminent J. J. Johnson v. 1 & 2 (Blue Note);
        Blue Trombone (Columbia); First Place (Columbia); Proof Posi-
        tive (Impulse); Finest of ... (Bethlehem).
Television: Appeared on Ebony Music Awards Show 1975; Sammy
        and Company 1975; wrote music for Street Killing 1976.

JOHNSON, JAMES WELDON
        (Lyricist)
b.   June 17, 1871, Jacksonville, Fla.

d.   June 26, 1938, Wiscasset, Maine.
Education: Atlanta University 1894.
Honors: Spingarn medal 1925.
Career Data: U. S. consul in Venezuela 1906 and Nicaragua 1909;
        field secretary and secretary, NAACP 1920-30; professor,
        Fisk University 1930-38.
Musical Compositions: Wrote songs for vaudeville, stage, minstrel
        shows and light opera including Lift Every Voice and Sing
        (a. k. a. The Black National Anthem); The Young Warrior 1916.
Relationships: Brother of J. Rosamond Johnson, musician/composer.

JOHNSON, JOHN
        (Broadcaster)
b.   June 20, 1938, New York, N. Y.
Education: High School of Art and Design 1956; City University of
        New York; Lincoln University (Pa.); Indiana University.
Special Interests: Film-making, teaching, directing, producing,
        writing.
Address: WABC-TV, 77 West 66 Street, New York, N. Y. 10023.
Honors: Christopher award (for directing To All the World's
        Children); NATAS citation of merit 1977.
Career Data: Associate Professor (Fine Arts), Lincoln University;
        Teacher, Chairman of Arts Department, Dean of Students,
        Asst. Principal, New York City Board of Education 1963-68.
Television: Correspondent, producer, director, writer, WABC-TV
        (includes assignments with Evening News; Eye Witness News;
        People, Places and Things) 1968-date.

JOHNSON, J(OHN) ROSAMOND
        (Musician/Composer)
b.   August 11, 1873, Jacksonville, Fla.
d.   November 11, 1954, New York, N. Y.
Education: New England Conservatory of Music.
Special Interests: Conducting.
Career Data: Vaudeville tour, U. S. and Europe 1896-98; music
        director, Hammerstein's Opera House (London) 1912-13; played
        Orpheum Keith vaudeville circuit with his own quintet; taught
        music, N. Y. Music School Settlement for Colored Pupils 1914-
        17.
Films: Emperor Jones (score) 1933.
Memberships: ASCAP 1927; The Frogs (a theatrical assn.).
Musical Compositions: Under the Bamboo Tree; Since You Went
        Away; My Castle on the Nile; The Maiden with the Dreamy
        Eyes; Li'l Gal; Lift Every Voice and Sing (a. k. a. The Black
        National Anthem); The Awakening; Two Eyes; Morning Noon
        and Night; Oh, Didn't He Ramble; Song of the Heart; The Old
        Flag Never Touched the Ground; When the Band Plays Rag-
        time; Bon Bon Buddy; I Told My Love to the Roses; Walk To-
        gether, Children.
Publications: Book of American Negro Spirituals, 1925; Second Book
        of Negro Spirituals, 1926; Shout Songs, 1936; Rolling Along in
        Song, 1937.

Theater: Wrote scores for The Sleeping Beauty; Humpty Dumpty;
        Shoo-Fly Regiment 1906; Mr. Lode of Koal 1909; Emperor
        Jones 1933. Performed: Red Moon 1909; New Standard
        Theatre (Philadelphia); Hippodrome (Bristol, England) 1927;
        Carnegie Hall (history of music concert) 1928; Porgy and Bess
        1936-37; Preacher in Mamba's Daughters 1939; Cabin in the
        Sky 1940.
Relationships: Brother of James Weldon Johnson, lyricist.

JOHNSON, KYLE
        (Actor)
Career Data: Concert, Inner City Cultural Center (L. A.)
Films: The Learning Tree 1969; Brother on the Run 1973.
Memberships: SAG.
Television: The Sheriff 1971.

JOHNSON, LOUIS
        (Dancer/Choreographer)
b.   March 19, 1933, Stateville, N. C.
Education: School of American Ballet; Katherine Dunham School of
        Dance; Ballet Russe.
Special Interests: Directing.
Honors: Tony nomination 1970; A. M. Schaefer award 1970.
Career Data: Choreographed and worked with Cincinnati Ballet, The
        Washington Ballet, Alvin Ailey Dance Co. , Dance Theatre of
        Harlem, Ballet Theatre, Metropolitan Opera Ballet; founder
        and director, Louis Johnson Dance Theatre; head, dance dept. ,
        Howard University; presented HAR-YOU Dancers at YMHA 1965;
        choreographed acts for stars including Aretha Franklin, Alexis
        Smith.
Films: Damn Yankees 1958; Cotton Comes to Harlem 1970.
Television: Choreographed dances for The Ed Sullivan Show, The
        Strollin Twenties (special) 1966, Lauren Bacall Special; ap-
        peared on Positively Black.
Theater: Danced Ballade (debut, N. Y. C. Ballet Co.) 1952; choreo-
        graphed Forces of Rhythm, Fete Noire, Lament 1953; danced
        in Damn Yankess 1955; choreographed Jamaica 1957; directed
        Miss Truth (Newport Jazz Festival); dance director for NEC
        productions: Kongi's Harvest, God Is a (Guess What?), Song
        of the Lusitanian Bogey 1968-69; choreographed Les Blancs
        1970; choreographed Purlie 1970; choreographed Mahagonny;
        choreographed Lost in the Stars 1972; choreographed Tree-
        monisha 1975; choreographed Aida and Dance of the Hours
        Ballet for La Gioconda (N. Y. Metropolitan Opera) 1975; choreo-
        graphed When Malindy Sings 1976.

JOHNSON, NOBLE M.
        (Actor/Producer)
b.   April 18, 1881, Colorado Springs, Colo.
d.   c. 1957.

Special Interests: Directing.
Career Data: Founder and President, Lincoln Motion Picture Co.,
Inc. 1915.
Films: Charmer, Gold Hunters 1915; The Realization of a Negro's
Ambition, The Trooper of Company K 1916; The Bull's Eye
(serial), The Law of Nature 1918; The Lure of the Circus
(serial), Fighting for Love 1919; The Leopard Woman, Adorable
Savage, Under Crimson Skies 1920; The Conquering Power,
The Bronze Bell, The Four Horsemen of the Apocalypse, Sere-
nade, Homeward Trail, The Wallop, The Girl He Left Behind
1921; Adventures of Robinson Crusoe, Ghost Breaker, Cowboy
and the Lady, Blackie Lopez in The Loaded Door, Tracks
1922; The Courtship of Miles Standish, The Ten Command-
ments, Drums of Fate, Burning Words, In the Palace of the
King, Cameo Kirby 1923; The Navigator, The Thief of Bagdad,
A Man's Mate, Midnight Express, Friday in Little Robinson
Crusoe 1924; Everlasting Whisper, Adventure, The Dancers,
The Gold Hunters 1925; Chief Sitting Bull in The Flaming
Frontier, Manon Lescaut, Lady of the Harem, Law of the
Snow Country, Hands Up, The Bells, Last Frontier, Skyrocket,
Aloma of the South Seas 1926; Soft Cushions, The King of
Kings, Upstream, Topsy and Eva, Red Clay, Ben Hur, When a
Man Loves, Vanity 1927; Gateway of the Moon, The Black Ace,
Manhattan Knights, Something Always Happens, Why Sailors Go
Wrong, Diamond Handcuffs, Yellow Contraband 1928; The
Apache, West of Zanzibar, Redskin, Black Waters, Sal of
Singapore, Four Feathers, The Mysterious Dr. Fu Manchu,
Noah's Ark 1929; Isle of Escape, Mamba, Moby Dick, Kismet
1930; East of Borneo, Son of India, Safe in Hell 1931; Mur-
ders in the Rue Morgue, Mystery Ranch, The Most Dangerous
Game 1932; The Mummy, native chief in King Kong, Son of
Kong, White Woman, Nagana 1933; Murder in Trinidad 1934;
Lives of a Bengal Lancer, She, Escape from Devil's Island
1935; Conquest 1937; Juarez, Tropic Fury, Frontier Pony Ex-
press 1939; The Ghost Breakers, The Cowboy and the Lady
1940; Hurry, Charlie, Hurry, Aloma of the South Seas 1941;
Jungle Book, Shut My Big Mouth, Night in New Orleans, Ten
Gentlemen from West Point, The Mad Doctor of Market Street
1942; The Desert Song 1943; A Game of Death 1945; Hard-
Boiled Mahoney, Unconquered 1947; She Wore a Yellow Ribbon
1949; North of the Great Divide 1950.
Memberships: SAG.
Relationships: Brother of George P. Johnson, producer.

JOHNSON, RAFER
        (Actor)
b. August 18, 1935, Hillsboro, Texas.
Education: U.C.L.A. B.A. 1959.
Address: The Mishkin Agency, 9255 Sunset Blvd., Los Angeles,
Calif. 90069.
Honors: Pan Am Games Gold Medal 1955; Olympics in Australia
Silver Medal 1956; Olympic Decathlon Champion 1960.

Films: Sergeant Rutledge 1960; The Sins of Rachel Cade, Pirates
         of Tortuga, The Fiercest Heart, Wild in the Country 1961;
         The Lion 1963; None But the Brave 1965; Tarzan and the
         Great River 1967; Tarzan and the Jungle Boy 1968; Grigsby
         1969; The Games, The Last Grenade 1970; Soul Soldier 1972.
Television: Pro-Celebrity Tennis; Saturday Night Live With Howard
         Cosell 1975; Six Million Dollar Man 1975.

JONES, DUANE
    (Actor)
Career Data: Executive Director, Black Theatre Alliance.
Films: Night of the Living Dead 1968; Ganja and Hess (a. k. a.
         Blood Couple) 1973; Double Possession 1975.
Memberships: SAG.

JONES, JAMES EARL
    (Actor)
b.   January 17, 1931, Arkabutla, Miss.
Education: University of Michigan B. A. 1953; American Theatre
         Wing 1957; Studied acting with Lee Strasberg.
Address: 458 West 20 Street, New York, N. Y. 10011.
Honors: Obie awards (for Clandestine on the Morning Line, The
         Apple, Moon on a Rainbow Shawl) 1962; Theatre World award
         (for Moon on a Rainbow Shawl) 1962; Emmy and Golden Nymph
         (for East Side West Side) 1963; Obie award (for NYSF Othello)
         1965; Tony award (for Great White Hope) 1969; Oscar nomina-
         tion (for Great White Hope) 1971; Black Filmmakers Hall of
         Fame award 1977.
Career Data: Member, Joseph Papp's New York Shakespeare Festi-
         val 1955-67; Bd. of Governors, Academy of Motion Picture
         Arts and Sciences; Advisory Bd. , National Council of the Arts.
Films: Dr. Strangelove 1964; The Comedians 1967; The End of the
         Road, The Great White Hope 1970; The Man 1972; Claudine
         1974; River Niger, The Bingo Long Traveling All-Stars and
         Motor Kings, Swashbuckler, Deadly Hero 1976; Jesus of Naza-
         reth, The Greatest, Star Wars (voice), The Last Remake of
         Beau Geste, A Piece of the Action 1977.
Memberships: AEA; AFTRA; SAG.
Television: Lamp Unto My Feet; Dr. Turner in As the World Turns
         (series); Today Show; host for Black Omnibus (series); Detec-
         tive Andrews on The Defenders (series) 1962; Catholic Hour
         1962; Camera 3 1963; Look Up and Live 1963; Joe in Who Do
         You Kill? (East Side West Side) 1963; Channing 1964; A Cry
         from the States (Dr. Kildare) 1966; The Guiding Light (series)
         1967; Tarzan 1967, 1968; Trumpets of the Lord (N. E. T. Play-
         house) 1968; N. Y. P. D. 1969; Mike Douglas Show 1974, 1975;
         Merv Griffin Show 1974; Filmmakers on Filmmaking 1974;
         The Cay 1974; narrated Sojourner (American Parade) 1975;
         Roundtable 1975; The People 1975; Directions 1975; title role
         in King Lear 1975; Happy Endings (special) 1975; voice on
         Vegetable Soup 1975; The U. F. O. Incident 1975; Day Without

Sunshine 1976; Sunday 1976; Dinah! 1976; Pat Collins Show 1976; Celebrity Revue 1976.

Theater: Gregory in Romeo and Juliet (NYSF) 1955; understudy for The Egghead 1957; Wedding in Japan (O. B.) 1957; Sunrise at Campobello 1958; The Pretender 1959; Harrison in The Cool World 1960; Williams in King Henry V (NYSF) 1960; Dark of the Moon (ELT) 1960; Abhorson in Measure for Measure (NYSF) 1960; Deodatus Village in the Blacks (O. B.) 1961; Oberon in A Midsummer Night's Dream (NYSF) 1961; Romeo and Juliet (NYSF) 1961; Lord Marshall in King Richard II (NYSF) 1961; Clandestine on the Morning Line (O. B.) 1961; The Apple (O. B.) 1961; Ephraim in Moon on A Rainbow Shawl (O. B.) 1962; Infidel Caesar 1962; Prince of Morocco in Merchant of Venice (NYSF) 1962; Caliban in The Tempest (NYSF) 1962; Henry in Toys in the Attic (stock) 1962; P. S. 193 (O. B.) 1962; Macduff in Macbeth (NYSF) 1962; The Love Nest (O. B.) 1963; The Last Minstrel (O. B.) 1963; title role in Othello (stock) 1963; Camillo in The Winter's Tale (NYSF) 1963; title role in Mr. Johnson (ELT) 1963; Next Time I'll Sing to You (O. B.) 1963; Zachariah in Blood Knot (O. B.) 1964; title role in Othello (NYSF) 1964; A Midsummer Night's Dream (NYSF) 1964; Danton's Death (LCR); Baal (O. B.) 1965; title role in Macbeth (NYSF) 1966; Bohikee Creek (O. B.) 1966; A Hand Is on the Gate 1966; The Cherry Orchard; Jack Jefferson in The Great White Hope 1968; Boesman and Lena (O. B.) 1970; Les Blancs 1970; title role in King Lear (NYSF) 1973; Hickey in The Iceman Cometh 1973; Lennie in Of Mice and Men 1974; title role in Emperor Jones (Boston Arts Festival); Claudius in Hamlet 1975; Oedipus Rex (O. B.) 1977.

Relationships: Son of Robert Earl Jones, actor.

JONES, JONAH (Robert Elliott Jones)
    (Musician)
b.   December 31, 1909, Louisville, Ky.
Special Interests: Trumpet.
Career Data: Played with bands of Jimmie Lunceford 1931, McKinney's Cotton Pickers 1935, Fletcher Henderson 1940, Benny Carter 1940-41, Cab Calloway 1941-52, Earl Hines Combo 1952-53.
Clubs: The Embers 1952; L'Onyx 1953; St. Regis Maisonette 1974; Rainbow Room 1975.
Records: Jonah Wails (Angel); Holiday in Trumpet (Emarcy).

JONES, KEVA (Angela Keva Jones)
    (Actress)
b.   August 16, 1948, Bronx, N. Y.
Education: City College of New York; Studied at Afro-American Studio for Acting and Speech (Ernie McClintock); studied at Weist-Barron School of TV.
Address: 1695 Madison Avenue, New York, N. Y. 10019.
Films: Gordon's War 1973; Supercops, Education of Sonny Carson 1974.

Theater: Johannas; Experimental Death Unit   1; Sister Son/ji; Moon
       on a Rainbow Shawl; The Amen Corner; Raisin in the Sun;
       First in War.

JONES, LAUREN
       (Actress)
b.   September 7, 1942, Boston, Mass.
Honors: Theatre World award 1969.
Films: The Liberation of L. B. Jones 1970; Lipstick, Car Wash
       1976.
Memberships: AFTRA.
Television: Movin' On 1975, Sanford and Son 1976.
Theater: Skyscraper; Does a Tiger Wear a Necktie?; Ballad for
       Bimshire (O. B.) 1963; Ben Franklin in Paris (debut) 1964;
       Trials of Brother Jero (O. B.) 1968; The Strong Breed (O. B.)
       1968.
Relationships: Wife of Michael A. Schultz, director.

JONES, LEROI   see   BARAKA, IMAMU AMIRI

JONES, QUINCY   (Delight)
       (Composer/Musician)
b.   March 14, 1933, Chicago, Ill.
Education: Berklee College of Music; Boston Conservatory of Mu-
       sic; Seattle University.
Special Interests: Arranging, conducting, jazz, producing, singing,
       trumpet.
Address: c/o A & M Records, 1416 La Brea, Hollywood, Calif.
       90028.
Honors: Academy award nominee (Banning) 1968; winner (In Cold
       Blood) 1968; winner (For Love of Ivy) 1969; Emmy nominee
       (Bill Cosby Show); Grammy winner, best instrumental 1963,
       1969, 1972, 1973 (plus over 30 nominations); Image award as
       jazz artist of the year 1975; Black Filmmakers Hall of Fame
       award 1975; winner of 5 Ebony music awards 1975.
Career Data: President, A & M Records and Quincy Jones Pro-
       ductions; executive vice-president, Mercury Records 1964;
       played, composed and/or arranged for Count Basie, Frank
       Sinatra, Billy Eckstine, Dinah Washington, Sarah Vaughan,
       Roberta Flack, Aretha Franklin, Dizzy Gillespie, Lionel Hamp-
       ton and others; formed Institute for Black American Music
       (IBAM).
Clubs: Birdland 1961.
Films: Composed music for over 50 films including: Boy in the
       Tree (Swedish), The Pawnbroker, The Slender Thread, Mirage
       1965; The Deadly Affair, Made in Paris, Walk Don't Run 1966;
       Enter Laughing, In the Heat of the Night, Banning, In Cold
       Blood 1967; A Dandy in Aspic, The Split, For Love of Ivy
       1968; The Lost Man, John and Mary, MacKenna's Gold 1969;
       The Last of the Mobile Hot Shots, The Out of Towners, Bob

& Carol and Ted & Alice, They Call Me Mr. Tibbs 1970;
Brother, John, The Anderson Tapes, $, Cactus Flower 1971;
The New Centurions, The Getaway, The Hot Rock 1972; Save
the Children 1973.
Memberships: ASCAP 1955.
Musical Compositions: I Needs to Bee'd With; Blues Bittersweet;
    Soul; Pleasingly Plump; Rat Race; Muttnik; Plenty Plenty; Lil'
    Ol' Groovemaker; Jessica's Day; Kingfish; Stockholm Sweetnin';
    The Midnight Sun Will Never Set; Every Now and Then (ballet
    for Dance Theatre of Harlem) 1975.
Records: Live at Newport '61 (Trip); Great Wide World of ... (Trip);
    Mode (ABC); Quintessence (Impulse); You've Got It (A & M);
    The Black Requiem; Walking in Space (A & M); Body Heat (A
    & M); Mellow Madness (A & M); It Might As Well Be Swing
    (Reprise); Gula Matari (A & M) 1970; Smackwater Jack (A &
    M) 1971; Ndeda (Mercury) 1972; You've Got It Bad Girl (A &
    M) 1973; I Heard That (A & M) 1976; Roots (A & M) 1977.
Television: The Bill Cosby Show (music); Sanford and Son (music);
    acted in Ironside; Merv Griffin Presents Quincy Jones (special)
    1971; co-produced Duke Ellington We Love You Madly 1973;
    Salute to Redd Foxx 1974; Ebony Music Awards 1975; Soul
    Train 1975; Tonight Show 1975; Positively Black 1975; Sound-
    stage 1976; Roots (score) 1976.
Theater: Musical director for Free and Easy (Europe) 1959-60;
    appeared at Cow Palace (San Francisco); Paramount Theatre
    (Oakland); appeared at Greek Theatre (L. A.) 1971; Felt Forum
    1973, 1976.

JONES, ROBERT EARL
    (Actor)
b.   February 3, 1900, Coldwater, Miss.
Education: Actors Studio.
Special Interests: Teaching.
Honors: Black Filmmakers Hall of Fame 1975.
Career Data: Director, Accent on Haiti Cric-Crac Workshop, Brook-
    lyn; taught at Wesleyan University and The City University of
    New York.
Films: Lying Lips 1939; The Notorious-Elinor Lee 1940; Odds
    Against Tomorrow 1959; Wild River 1960; One Potato Two Po-
    tato 1964; Terror in the City 1966; Mississippi Summer 1971;
    The Sting, Willie Dynamite 1974.
Memberships: AEA (its Paul Robeson Citation Committee); AFTRA;
    SAG.
Television: The Defenders; Today Show 1976; Kojak 1976.
Theater: Title role in Othello (O. B.); title role in The Emperor
    Jones (O. B.); Of Mice and Men (O. B.); Don't You Want to Be
    Free? (Harlem Suitcase Theatre) 1936; Herod and Marianne
    (pre-Bway) 1938; Walk Hard (ANT) 1944; Strange Fruit 1945;
    Blossom in The Hasty Heart 1945; The Eagle Has Two Heads
    1947; Caesar and Cleopatra 1949; Fancy Meeting You Again
    1952; Winkelberg (O. B.) 1958; The Moon Besieged 1962; Moon
    on a Rainbow Shawl (O. B.) 1962; The Displaced Person (O. B.)

1967; The Iceman Cometh 1974; All God's Chillun Got Wings
1975; Unexpected Guests (O. B.) 1977.
Relationships: Father of James Earl Jones, actor.

JONES, ROBERT G.
    (Publicist)
b.   July 4, 1936, Ft. Worth, Texas.
Education: University of Southern California.
Special Interests: Writing.
Address: 6464 Sunset Blvd. , Los Angeles, Calif. 90028.
Career Data: Publicity manager, Motown Record Corp. 1975-date;
    entertainment editor, Hollywood columnist, L. A. Herald Dis-
    patch; account executive, Rogers & Cowan Public Relations;
    clients include The Jackson Five, Lou Rawls, James Brown,
    Stevie Wonder, Temptations, Marvin Gaye, Smokey Robinson,
    Thelma Houston, Syreeta, Eddie Kendricks and others; chair-
    man, NAACP Image Awards (L. A.) 1973, 1974.

JONES, SISSERETTA "Black Patti" (Matilda S. Joyner)
    (Singer)
b.   January 5, 1869, Portsmouth, Va.
d.   1933.
Education: Academy of Music (Providence, R. I.); New England Con-
    servatory of Music (Boston).
Special Interests: Opera.
Career Data: Toured country with her troubadours in shows includ-
    ing Captain Jasper, In the Jungles, A Trip to Africa; sang at
    White House reception invited by President Benjamin Harrison
    1892; participated at Pittsburgh Exposition 1892, 1893; toured
    South America and West Indies; associated with songs Swanee
    River, I Dreamt I Dwelt in Marble Halls, Home Sweet Home;
    sang in capitals of the world including Paris, Berlin, London
    and St. Petersburg.
Theater: Appeared at San Souci Gardens; Covent Garden (London);
    Wallack's Theater (Boston); Madison Square Garden 1886; Bijou
    Theatre 1907; Grand Opera House 1912; Orpheum Theatre (Bal-
    timore) 1914.

JONES, THAD (Thaddeus Joseph Jones)
    (Jazz Musician)
b.   March 28, 1923, Pontiac, Mich.
Special Interests: Trumpet, flugelhorn.
Career Data: Played with bands of Billy Mitchell, Count Basie
    1954.
Clubs: Village Vanguard 1975; Buddy's Place 1975.
Records: Suite for Pops (Horizon); Thad Jones/Mel Lewis (Blue
    Note); Potpourri (Philadelphia International); Consummation
    (Blue Note); Live at Village Vanguard (Solid State); Monday
    Night (Solid State); New Life (Horizon); Presenting Thad Jones
    (Solid State); Central Park North (Solid State).

Television: At the Top 1975.
Theater: Satchmo '76 at Beacon Theatre 1976.

JOPLIN, SCOTT "King of Ragtime"
      (Composer/Musician/Pianist)
b. November 24, 1868, Texarkana, Texas.
d. April, 1917, New York, N.Y.
Education: George Smith College (Sedalia, Missouri).
Special Interests: Piano.
Honors: Pulitzer Prize (posthumously) 1976.
Career Data: Performed at World's Fair 1893; toured vaudeville
      circuit 1906-09.
Films: The Sting (score based on his The Entertainer) 1974.
Musical Compositions: Sugar Cane Rag; Wall Street Rag; Bethena--
      A Concert Waltz; Eugenia; Leola--Two Step; Gladiolus Rag;
      Rose Leaf Rag--A Rag Time Two Step; Fig Leaf Rag; Pine-
      apple Rag; Paragon Rag; Euphonic Sounds--A Syncopated Novel-
      ty; The Prodigal Son (ballet); Combination March 1896; Har-
      mony Club Waltz 1896; Maple Leaf Rag 1899; Swipesy Cake
      Walk 1900; Sunflower Slowdrag 1901; Peacherine Rag 1901;
      Elite Syncopation 1902; The Entertainer--A Rag Time Two
      Step 1902; Palm Leaf Rag 1903; The Rag-Time Dance (folk
      ballet) 1903; A Guest of Honor (A Ragtime Opera) 1903; The
      Crysanthemum--An Afro Intermezzo 1904; The Cascades 1904;
      Non Pareil (None to Equal) 1907; Solace--A Mexican Serenade
      1908; Pleasant Moments 1909; Treemonisha (opera) 1911.
Records: Scott Joplin: His Complete Works v. I & II; Scott Joplin
      1916; Piano Rags (Nonesuch) 1970; More Rags 1972.

JORDAN, JACK
      (Producer)
b. August 21, 1929, New York, N.Y.
Education: High School of Performing Arts; Columbia University.
Address: Kelly-Jordan Enterprises, 342 Madison Avenue, New York,
      N.Y. 10002.
Career Data: Formed all-black girl orchestra 1961; formed Kelly-
      Jordan (with Quentin Kelly) Enterprises, a production company.
Films: Rhapsody in Black (Swedish doc.); Georgia, Georgia 1972;
      Honey Baby Honey Baby 1974; Blood Couple (a. k. a. Ganja and
      Hess) 1975.
Theater: Josephine Baker and Her International Revue 1973.

JORDAN, LOUIS
      (Musician/Conductor)
b. July 8, 1908, Brinkley, Ark.
d. February 4, 1975, Los Angeles, Calif.
Education: Arkansas Baptist College (Little Rock).
Special Interests: Alto saxophone, clarinet.
Honors: 5 gold records.
Career Data: Played with bands of Ruby Williams 1927, Chick Webb

1936-38; formed his own group, The Tympany Five 1938; hits
include Caldonia, Choo Choo Boogie, Knock Me a Kiss, Is You
Is or Is You Ain't My Baby.

Clubs: Café Society; The Capitol Lounge (Chicago); Savoy Ballroom;
Billy Berg's (L. A.); Latin Casino (Philadelphia); Elks Club;
Trocadero (Hollywood).

Films: Follow the Boys 1944; Caldonia 1945; Swing Parade of 1946,
Toot That Trumpet, Beware 1946; Reet Petite and Gone 1947;
Look Out Sister 1948.

Records: Oldies But Goodies.

Theater: Appeared at Apollo Theatre.

JULIEN, MAX
(Actor)

b. Washington, D. C.

Special Interests: Writing, producing.

Address: Allen Susman, 9601 Wilshire Blvd. , Beverly Hills, Calif.

Films: Psych-Out, The Savage Seven, Uptight 1968; Getting Straight
1970; The Mack, co-produced and wrote Cleopatra Jones 1973;
wrote, co-produced and starred in Thomasine & Bushrod 1974.

Memberships: SAG.

Television: Mod Squad; Deadlock 1969; The Time Is Now (Name of
the Game) 1970; Tattletales 1974.

KAY, ULYSSES SIMPSON
(Composer)

b. January 7, 1917, Tucson, Ariz.

Education: University of Arizona B. A. 1938; Eastman School of
Music; University of Rochester M. A. 1940; Yale University
1941-42; Columbia University 1946-48; Berkshire Music Center.

Special Interests: Piano, violin, flute, piccolo, saxophone.

Address: c/o Herbert H. Lehman College, CUNY, Bedford Park
Boulevard West, Bronx, N. Y. 10468.

Honors: Ditson Fellowship; Rosenwald Fellowship 1947-49; Prix di
Rome 1949-52; Fulbright Scholarship 1950-51; Guggenheim Fellowship 1964-65; Academy of Arts and Letters and National
Institute of Arts and Letters grants; Broadcast Music Inc.
prize; Gershwin Memorial prize; American Broadcasting Co.
prize.

Career Data: Music consultant, Broadcast Music Inc. 1953-66; U. S.
State Dept. Cultural Exchange Tour of U. S. S. R. 1958; visiting
professor of music, Boston University (summer 1965) and
University of California at Los Angeles 1966-67; professor of
music, Herbert H. Lehman College 1968-date, distinguished
professor 1972-date.

Films: The Quiet One (score) 1948.

Memberships: American Federation of Musicians.

Musical Compositions: A Short Overture; Aulos; Portrait Suite;
Presidential Suite; Reverie & Rondo; Suite from The Ballet:
Danse Calinda; Symphony; Trigon; Stephen Crane Set; Ancient
Saga; Brief Elegy; Pieta; Six Dances; A Lincoln Letter; A New

Song; A Wreath for Watts; Christmas Carol; Come Away, Come
Away Death; Emily Dickinson Set; Flowers in the Valley; Four
Hymn-Anthems; Grace to You, and Peace; How Stands the Glass
Around? Hymn-Anthem on Hanover; Tears, Flow No More;
The Birds; The Epicure; To Light That Shines; Triumvirate;
Two Dunbar Lyrics; What's In a Name?; Concert Sketches;
Forever Free; Short Suite for Concert Band; Partita in A;
Serenade No. 2; String Quartet No. 2; String Quartet No. 3;
Suite for Flute and Oboe; Triptych on Texts of Blake; Trumpet
Fanfares; Four Inventions; Ten Essays for Piano; Two Short
Pieces for Piano; Organ Suite; Two Meditations; The Boor (an
opera); Overture of New Horizons 1944; Suite for Orchestra
1947; Song of Jeremiah 1947; Suite for Strings 1947; Solemn
Prelude 1948; Concerto for Orchestra 1948; Three Pieces After
Blake 1952; Brass Quartet 1952; Serenade for Orchestra 1954;
The Juggler of Our Lady (an Opera) 1956; Phoebus Arise 1959;
Choral Triptych 1962; Umbrian Scene 1963; Inscriptions from
Whitman 1963; Fantasy Variations 1964; Markings 1966; Parables
1970; Facets 1971; Visions 1975.
Records: Brass Quartet (Folkways); Choral Triptych (Cambridge);
    Fantasy Variations; How Stands the Glass Around?; What's in a
    Name?; Round Dance and Polka; Serenade for Orchestra; Sin-
    fonia in E; Umbrian Scene.
Television: An Essay on Death 1964.

KELLY, JIM
    (Actor)
b. Paris, Ky.
Education: University of Louisville 1964-65; studied with Lee Stras-
    berg.
Special Interests: Karate.
Honors: International Middleweight Karate Championship 1971.
Films: Melinda 1972; Enter the Dragon 1973; title role in Blackbelt
    Jones, Three the Hard Way, Golden Needles 1974; Take a Hard
    Ride 1975; Hot Potato 1976; Black Samurai 1977.
Memberships: SAG.
Television: Viewpoint on Nutrition 1976.

KELLY, PAULA
    (Actress/Singer/Dancer)
b. c. 1944.
Education: H. S. of Performing Arts; Juilliard School of Music.
Special Interests: Singing, choreography.
Address: Smith-Stevens Representation, 434 N. Rodeo Drive,
    Beverly Hills, Calif.
Honors: Variety award (England) best supporting actress in a musi-
    cal (Sweet Charity) 1968.
Career Data: Danced with companies of Pearl Lang, Donald McKayle,
    Alvin Ailey, Tally Beatty.
Clubs: Caesar's Palace (Las Vegas).
Films: Sweet Charity 1969; The Andromeda Strain 1971; Trouble

Man, Top of the Heap 1972; The Spook Who Sat by the Door,
Soylent Green 1973; Three Tough Guys, Lost in the Stars, Up-
town Saturday Night 1974; Drum 1976.
Memberships: SAG.
Television: Gene Kelly's New York, New York (special); History of
Jazz and Dance (NET); The Strollin' Twenties (special) 1966;
Medical Center 1974; Sammy and His Friends (special); The
Company (Police Woman) 1975; Cannon 1975; Streets of San
Francisco 1976; The Richard Pryor Show 1977.
Theater: Something More (debut); Sweet Charity (London) 1967;
Your Own Thing (tour) 1969, The Dozens 1969; Story Theater's
Metamorphoses 1971; Don't Bother Me I Can't Cope (L.A.)
1972.

KENDRICKS, EDDIE (J.)
(Singer)
b. December 17, 1940, Union Springs, Ala.
Address: c/o J.S.F. Productions, 8732 Sunset Blvd., Los Angeles,
Calif. 90069.
Honors: Grammy award 1970; singer of the year awards, Cashbox,
Record World, Billboard 1973.
Career Data: Tenor with Temptations 11 years.
Clubs: Community Gardens 1974; Paul's Mall (Boston) 1975; Folk
City 1976.
Records: For You (Tamla); The Hit Man (Tamla); He's A Friend
(Tamla); Goin' Up in Smoke; Boogie Down! (Tamla); All by
Myself (Tamla); People ...! Hold On (Tamla).
Television: Rockin' in the U.S.A. Ebony Affair 1975; Soul Train
1975; Don Kirshner's Rock Concert 1976; Midnight Special
1976; American Bandstand 1976.
Theater: Appeared at Nanuet Theatre Go Round 1974; Carnegie Hall
1974; Felt Forum 1975, 1976; Apollo Theatre 1976; Auditorium
Theatre (Chicago).

KENNEDY, ADRIENNE (L.)
(Playwright)
b. September 13, 1931, Pittsburgh, Pa.
Education: Ohio State University B.S. 1953; Actor's Studio 1962-64;
Circle in the Square Theatre School; American Theatre Wing;
Columbia University; Edward Albee's Workshop 1962.
Honors: The Stanley award for playwriting 1963; Obie (for Funny-
house of a Negro) 1964; Rockefeller grant 1965, 1968, 1974;
Guggenheim grant for creative writing 1967; National Endow-
ment for the Arts grant 1972.
Career Data: Lecturer (playwriting), Yale University 1972-74.
Memberships: P.E.N.; National Society of Literature & Arts 1975.
Theater: Wrote Funnyhouse of a Negro 1962; The Owl Answers
1963; A Lesson in Dead Language 1964; A Rat's Mass 1965;
A Beast's Story 1966; The Son 1970; In His Own Write (adapta-
tion of a book by John Lennon) 1971.

KENNEDY, SCOTT (James Scott Kennedy)
    (Producer)
b.   1927, Knoxville, Tenn.
Education: B. A. , M. A. , Ph. D. New York University; studied in
    Heidelberg, London and Paris.
Special Interests: Acting, dancing, playwriting.
Address: c/o Theater Department, Brooklyn College, Brooklyn,
    N. Y. 11210.
Honors: Rockefeller Foundation Grant.
Career Data: Instructor, Speech-Theatre, Long Island University;
    director of radio and television, Morgan State College; formed
    Scott Kennedy Players Workshop (which performed at Town Hall,
    Carnegie Hall and Off Bway) 1958; professor, theater dept. ,
    Brooklyn College 1959-date; attended First World Festival of
    Negro Arts, Dakar, Senegal 1966; participated in First World
    Pan-African Cultural Festival, Algiers 1969; formed The Amis-
    tad Players (Brooklyn College).
Publications: In Search of African Theatre, Scribner's, 1973.

KENNY, BILL
    (Singer)
Career Data: Original member of famed Ink Spots, vocal group.
Records: The Best of the Ink Spots (RCA); If I Didn't Care; Do I
    Worry; Are You Lonesome Tonight?; Maybe.
Television: Merv Griffin Show.

KEYES, JOHNNY
    (Actor)
Career Data: Noted for work in X-rated pornography films.
Films: Sodom and Gomorrah, Teenage Trouble, Magic Finger,
    Double Threat, Sex Satisfaction, Behind the Green Door 1972,
    Lacy Bodine 1975, Too Much to Handle 1975.
Memberships: SAG.

KILLENS, JOHN OLIVER
    (Playwright)
b.   1916, Macon, Ga.
Education: Edward Waters College; Morris Brown College; Howard
    University; New York University.
Address: 1492 Union Street, Brooklyn, New York 11213.
Honors: Black Filmmakers Hall of Fame 1976.
Career Data: Writer-in-residence, Howard University; writer-in-
    residence, Fisk University; founder/chairman, Harlem Writers
    Guild Workshop; adjunct professor/head, creative writers work-
    shop, Columbia University.
Films: Odds Against Tomorrow 1959; Slaves 1969.
Theater: Wrote Lower Than the Angels 1965; Ballad of the Winter
    Soldiers (with Loften Mitchell) 1965; Cotillion (produced at New
    Federal Theatre) 1975.

KILPATRICK, LINCOLN
    (Actor)
b. c. 1932, St. Louis, Mo.
Education: Lincoln University (Missouri); American Theatre Wing.
Address: International Creative Management, 8899 Beverly Blvd.,
    Los Angeles, Calif. 90048.
Career Data: Member, Lincoln Center Repertory Co. 1965-66; co-
    founder, Kilpatrick-Cambridge Theatre Arts School (L. A.).
Films: The Last Angry Man, Odds Against Tomorrow 1959; A
    Lovely Way to Die, What's So Bad About Feeling Good? 1968;
    Stiletto, The Lost Man, Generation 1969; Brother John, Honky,
    The Omega Man 1971; Soul Soldiers, Cool Breeze 1972; Soylent
    Green 1973; Chosen Survivors, Together Brothers, Uptown
    Saturday Night 1974; The Master Gunfighter 1975.
Memberships: SAG.
Television: Naked City; Armstrong Circle Theatre; The Bold Ones;
    Medical Center; Six Million Dollar Man; Ironside; N. Y. P. D. ;
    Name of the Game; Love of Life (series) 1968; Leslie Uggams
    Show 1969; Dead Men Tell No Tales 1971; Mannix 1974; Harry
    O 1975; Baretta 1975; Just An Old Sweet Song (General Electric
    Theater) 1976; The Money Changers 1976.
Theater: Take a Giant Step (O. B.) 1956; A Raisin in the Sun 1959;
    The Ballad of Jazz Street (O. B.) 1959; Deep Are the Roots
    (O. B.) 1960; The Blacks (O. B.) 1963; One Flew Over the
    Cuckoo's Nest 1963; Blues for Mister Charlie 1964; Hallelujah
    Baby 1967; Danton's Death (LCR); The Country Wife (LCR).

KING, ALDINE
    (Actress)
Films: Slaves 1969; Airport 1975 1974.
Memberships: SAG.
Television: Ironside; The Strange and Deadly Occurrence (Marcus
    Welby, M. D.) 1974; McCloud 1975; Cissy in Karen (series)
    1975; Most Wanted 1976.

KING, B. B. (Riley B. King)
    (Singer/Musician)
b. September 16, 1925, Itta Bena, Miss.
Special Interests: Guitar, blues.
Address: 1414 Avenue of the Americas, New York, N. Y. 10019.
Honors: Grammy 1970; B'nai B'rith music award 1973; Gallery of
    the Greats & Best Guitarist of 1974; Guitar Player Magazine
    1974; Artist of Decade, Record World Magazine 1974; Best
    Blues Singer, NATRA 1974; Best Blues Vocalist and Guitarist,
    and Hall of Fame, Ebony Magazine 1974.
Career Data: Founding member, John F. Kennedy Performing Arts
    Center 1971; Schaefer Music Festival 1975.
Clubs: Shady Grove (Maryland); El San Juan Hotel (Puerto Rico)
    1973; Hilton (Las Vegas) 1975; Latin Casino (Cherry Hill,
    N. J.) 1975.
Films: Medicine Ball Caravan; Seven Minutes (sang theme song)
    1971.

Publications: B. B. King Blues Guitar, 1970; B. B. King Songbook, 1971; B. B. King: The World's Greatest Living Blues Artist; Blues Guitar, A Method by B. B. King, 1973.

Records: Back in the Alley (ABC); Lucille Talks Back (ABC); Friends (ABC); Blues Is King (ABC); Blues on Top of Blues (ABC); Completely Well (ABC); Confessin' the Blues (ABC); ... In London (ABC); Indianola Mississippi Seeds (ABC); L. A. Midnight (ABC); Live and Well (ABC); Live at Cook County Jail (ABC); Live at the Regal (ABC); Mr. Blues (ABC); Paying the Cost to Be the Boss (Pickwick); Together for the First Time Live with Bobby Bland (ABC); His Best--The Electric B. B. King (ABC); Why I Sing the Blues (Bluesway) 1969; Get Off My Back Woman (Bluesway) 1969; The Thrill Is Gone (Bluesway) 1970; Guess Who (ABC) 1972; To Know You Is to Love You (ABC) 1973.

Television: One Night Stand 1971; Feeling Good 1974; Soul Train 1975; Ebony Music Awards 1975; A. M. America 1975; Mike Douglas Show 1975; Superstars of Rock 1975; Midnight Special 1975, 1976; Merv Griffin Show 1975, 1976; Sammy and Company 1976; Sanford and Son 1977.

Theater: Appeared at Apollo Theatre; Avery Fisher Hall (Newport Jazz Festival) 1974; Westchester Premier Theatre 1975; Nassau Coliseum (Newport Jazz Festival) 1975; Beacon Theatre 1976.

KING, BEN E. (Benjamin Nelson)
    (Singer)
b.   September 28, 1938, Henderson, N. C.
Career Data: Former member The Crowns 1958, later The Drifters 1959-60.
Clubs: Barney Google's 1975; Stardust Ballroom (Bronx) 1975.
Records: On ATCO: Spanish Harlem 1961; Stand By Me 1961; Amor 1961, Young Boy Blues 1961; Ecstasy 1962; Don't Play That Song 1962; I Who Have Nothing 1963; It's All Over 1964; The Record 1965; Goodnight, My Love 1966; Tears Tears Tears 1967; Dance with Me; The Magic Moment; There Goes My Baby; Supernatural (Atlantic); I Had a Love (Atlantic).
Television: Soul Train 1975; American Bandstand 1975; Midnight Special 1975; Dinah! 1975; Positively Black 1975; Black News 1976.
Theater: Apollo Theatre.

KING, MABEL
    (Actress)
Special Interests: Singing.
Films: Cotton Comes to Harlem, Angel Levine 1970; They Might Be Giants 1971; Hot Rock 1972; Blood Couple (a. k. a. Ganja and Hess) 1975; Bingo Long Traveling All-Stars and Motor Kings 1976; Mrs. Bowser in Don't Play Us Cheap.
Television: What's Happening! (series) 1976; Mike Douglas Show 1977.

Theater: Maria in Porgy and Bess (tour); A Race with the Wind;
           Anna Lucasta; Ernestine in Hello, Dolly! 1969; Mrs. Bowser
           in Don't Play Us Cheap 1972; The Women; La Dispute de Mari-
           vaux (Paris) 1976; The Wiz 1977.

KING, TONY
       (Actor)
Career Data: Former professional football star.
Films: Shaft 1971; Gordon's War, Hell Up in Harlem 1973; Report
         to the Commissioner, Bucktown, Super Spook 1975; Sparkle
         1976.
Television: John Webber in Bronk (series) 1975.

KING, WOODIE JR.
       (Producer/Director)
b.   July 27, 1937, Mobile, Ala.
Education: Wayne State University 1961; Will-O-Way School of
         Theatre (Bloomfield Hills, Mich.) 1958-62.
Special Interests: Acting, consulting, writing.
Address: 417 Convent Avenue, New York, N. Y. 10031.
Honors: John Hay Whitney Fellowship (for directing 1965-66); AUDEL-
         CO Black Theatre Recognition Award 1973, 1975.
Career Data: Model 1955-68; drama critic, Detroit Tribune 1960-
         63; co-founder and manager, Concept East Theatre (Detroit)
         1960-63; Rockefeller Foundation consultant, arts and humanities
         (including Black Theatre Survey of 1969) 1968-70; artistic di-
         rector, Henry Street Settlement and co-director of New Federal
         Theatre 1970-date; associate producer Lincoln Center; presi-
         dent, Woodie King Associates.
Films: Produced The Game, Ghetto, Where We Live, You Dig It?,
         Epitaph; co-produced Right On! 1971; acted in Serpico, To-
         gether for Days 1973; directed, co-scripted, co-produced The
         Long Night 1976.
Publications: Black Drama Anthology (with Ron Milner), New Ameri-
         can Library, 1971; Black Spirits, Random House, 1972.
Records: Produced New Black Poets in America (Motown); produced
         Nation Time (Motown) 1972.
Television: Wrote episode of Sanford and Son 1974; produced and
         wrote episode of Hot L Baltimore 1975; acted in N. Y. P. D.;
         Pat Collins Show 1976.
Theater: Produced: A Black Quartet; Day of Absence (O. B.) 1966;
         Slaveship (O. B.) 1969; In New England Winter (O. B.) 1971;
         Black Girl (O. B.) 1971; The Fabulous Miss Marie (O. B.) 1971;
         Cometh the Vanderkellans (NEC) 1972; What the Winesellers
         Buy 1973; The Prodigal Sister 1974; The First Breeze of Sum-
         mer 1975; The Taking of Miss Janie 1975; Gilbeau (New Fed-
         eral Theatre) 1976; The Mystery of Phillis Wheatley 1976.
         Directed: Cut Out the Lights and Call the Law; Who Got His
         Own (O. B.) 1966; Busting Candidate; Study in Color; The Warn-
         ing: A Theme for Linda 1969; Aid to Dependent Children 1975.
         Acted in: Benito Cereno (O. B.); Displaced Person (O. B.) 1966;

The Great White Hope 1968. Wrote: The Weary Blues (adapted
from Langston Hughes) 1966; Simple Blues (adapted from Langston Hughes) 1967; produced Gilbeau (New Federal Theatre)
1976; produced The Mystery of Phillis Wheatley 1976; directed
Daddy (New Federal Theatre) 1977.

KIRBY, GEORGE
        (Entertainer)
b.   June 8, 1924, Chicago, Ill.
Special Interests: Comedy, impressions, singing.
Address: c/o Kircha Enterprises Inc., 15 West 72nd Street, New
        York, N. Y. 10023 and College Inn, 1 IBM Plaza, Chicago, Ill.
        60611.
Career Data: Honored by "Friars Roast" 1970.
Clubs: Shamrock (Houston); Shoreham Hotel (Washington, D. C.);
        Mister Kelly's (Chicago); Americana Royal Box; Sherman
        House (Chicago); Caesar's Palace (Las Vegas); Harrah's (Reno);
        Palmer House (Chicago); 845 Club (Bronx); London Casino;
        Grossingers; Playboy (Chicago); Playboy (Mc Afee, N. J.); De
        Lisa (Chicago); Riviera (Las Vegas) 1975; St. Francis Hotel
        (San Francisco) 1976; Tamiment (Pa.) 1976.
Films: A Man Called Adam 1966; Oh Dad, Poor Dad, Mama's Hung
        You in the Closet and I'm Feelin' So Sad 1967.
Memberships: Friars Club; Grand Street Boys; NAACP.
Records: The Real George Kirby.
Television: Perry Como Show; Koppy Kats (series); Match Game;
        Celebrity Sweepstakes; Tonight Show; George Kirby Special;
        Ed Sullivan Show (debut) 1948; Your First Impression (series)
        1962-64; Strollin' Twenties (special) 1966; Half the George
        Kirby Comedy Hour 1972-73; Jack Jones (special) 1974; Rosen-
        thal and Jones (comedy special) 1975; Sound Stage 1975; Alan
        King: Comedy in Las Vegas (Wide World of Entertainment)
        1975; Captain Kangaroo 1975; Dinah! 1975; Musical Chairs
        1975; Merv Griffin Show 1975, 1976; Mike Douglas Show 1975,
        1976; N. Y. Emmy award show 1976; Sammy and Company
        1976; Apollo (special) 1976; Joys (Bob Hope special) 1976.
Theater: Appearance at Nanuet Theatre-Go-Round; Apollo Theatre
        1960.

KIRK, ANDY (Andrew Dewey Kirk)
        (Jazz Musician)
b.   May 28, 1898, Newport Ky.
Special Interests: Saxophone, conducting, composing.
Address: 555 Edgecombe Avenue, New York, N. Y. 10032.
Career Data: Played with George Morrison's Jazz Band 1924; led
        his own band Clouds of Joy from 1929-48.
Clubs: Tic Toc (Boston); Roseland; Savoy Ballroom; Cotton Club;
        Tunetown Ballroom (St. Louis).
Memberships: ASCAP 1963; NAG.
Musical Compositions: Cloudy; Wednesday Night Hop; Mind If I
        Remind You.

KIRK, RAHSAAN ROLAND
    (Musician)
b.   August 7, 1937, Columbus, Ohio.
Education: Columbus School for Blind.
Special Interests: Tenor Saxophone, flute, harmonica, lyricon.
Address: East Orange, N. J.
Honors: 1st Place award Down Beat magazine 1962-65; Musician of
    the Year, Melody Maker Magazine 1964, 1966.
Career Data: Toured U. S. , Europe and Japan; Leader, Roland Kirk
    Quartet 1954-date; writer, Broadcast Music Inc. 1962-date;
    president, Rakir Music Corp. 1964-date.
Clubs: Mediterranee (Guadeloupe) 1976; Sparky J's (Newark) 1976.
Memberships: American Federation of Musicians.
Records: Here Comes the Whistleman (Atlantic); Please Don't Cry
    Beautiful Edith (Atlantic); The Return of the 5, 000 lb. Man
    (Warner Bros.); Art (Atlantic); Best (Atlantic); Blacknuss (At-
    lantic); Bright Moments (Atlantic); Domino (Trip); Funk Under-
    neath (Prestige); Inflated Tear (Atlantic); Kirk in Copenhagen
    (Trip); Other Folks' Music (Atlantic); 3-Sided Dream (Atlantic);
    Volunteered Slavery (Atlantic); We Free Kings (Trip).
Television: Soundstage 1976.
Theater: Appeared at Radio City Music Hall 1976; Beacon Theatre
    (First Latin Summer Festival) 1976; Salle Wilfrid-Pelletier
    (Montreal) 1976; Town Hall 1977.

KITT, EARTHA (Mae)
    (Singer/Actress)
b.   January 26, 1928, North, S. C.
Education: H. S. of Performing Arts; studied drama with Edith
    Banks.
Special Interests: Dance, languages, teaching, writing.
Address: 1230 La Collina Drive, Beverly Hills, Calif. 90210.
Honors: France Soir, second place acting award of France (for
    Faust) 1951; Golden Rose of Montreux for Performance on
    Swedish Television 1962; Emmy nomination 1966; National
    Assn. of Negro Musicians Woman of the Year Award 1968;
    Black Filmmakers Hall of Fame 1975.
Career Data: Katherine Dunham Dance Troup 1946-48; teaches
    modern dance at Jordan Downs Center, Watts, Calif. ; made
    tour of South Africa 1972; founder, Kittsville Youth Foundation
    Dance School (L. A.).
Clubs: Karavansarey (Istanbul) 1951; Village Vanguard 1952; Mo-
    cambo (Hollywood) 1953; La Vie En Rose 1954; Latin Quarter
    (Boston) 1955; Blinstrub's (Boston) 1956; Latin Quarter 1957;
    Empire Room 1957; Persian Room 1958-76; Latin Quarter
    (Philad.) 1960; Palmer House (Chicago) 1962; Blue Angel; Bon
    Soir; Jack's; Carroll's (Paris); El Rancho (Las Vegas).
Films: New Faces 1954; St. Louis Blues, Mark of the Hawk 1958;
    title role in Anna Lucasta 1959; The Saint of Devil's Island
    1961; Portrait of a Lady (doc.) 1962; Synanon 1965; Up the
    Chastity Belt (Brit.) 1971; Friday Foster 1975.
Memberships: AEA; AGVA; SAG.

Publications: Thursday's Child (autobiography), Duell, Sloan & Pearce, 1956; Alone with Me (autobiography), Henry Regnery, 1976.

Records: New Faces of 1952 (RCA); Fabulous (Kapp); That Bad Eartha (RCA); Bad, But Beautiful (MGM); Revisited (Kapp); Down to Eartha (RCA); Eartha Kitt (RCA); Somebody Bad Stole de Wedding Bell (RCA) 1959; Thursday's Child (RCA); Folk Tales of the Tribes of Africa (Caedmon); Santa Baby (RCA) 1953; I Want to Be Evil; C'est Si Bon (RCA) 1953; Monotonous; Best of All Possible Worlds (Stanyan); For Always (Stanyan); At the Plaza (GNP Crescendo).

Television: Ed Sullivan Show; Today Show 1953; All Star Review 1953; Colgate Comedy Hour 1954; Your Show of Shows 1954; Ed Murrow's Person to Person 1954; Jinx's Diary 1955; title role in Salome (Omnibus) 1955; Heart of Darkness (Playhouse 90) 1958; The Wingless Victory (Play of the Week) 1961; Kaskade (Swedish) 1962; I Spy 1965; Ben Casey 1965; Catwoman in Bat Man (series) 1967; Mission: Impossible 1967; Johnny Carson Show; Mike Douglas Show; Burke's Law; The Protectors; Lieutenant Schuster's Wife 1972; Masquerade Party 1974; Kup's Show 1974, 1976; Merv Griffin Show 1975; Sunday 1976; Pat Collins Show 1976; Today Show 1976; Black Conversations 1976.

Theater: Blue Holiday (Bway debut) 1945; Bal Negre 1946; Helen of Troy in Faust (France, Belgium, Germany) 1951; New Faces of 1952; Teddy Hicks in Mrs. Patterson 1954; Mehitabel in Shinbone Alley 1957; Jolly in Jolly's Progress 1959; The Owl and the Pussycat (tour) 1964; Yesterday, Today and Tomorrow (one woman show) and Bread, Beans and Things (one woman show, L. A.) 1974; A Musical Jubilee (Miami Beach) 1976.

KITZMILLER, JOHN
        (Actor)
b.   1913, Battlecreek, Mich.
d.   February 23, 1965, Rome, Italy.
Honors: Cannes Film Festival Best Acting Award (for Dolina Mira) 1957.
Films: Paisan 1946; To Live in Peace 1947; Senza Pieta (a. k. a. Without Pity 1950) 1948; Lieutenant Craig-Missing 1951; Dolina Mira 1957; The Naked Earth 1958; The Island Sinner 1960; Doctor No 1963; Luci del Varieta (Variety Lights); Uncle Tom's Cabin; Cave of the Living Dead (German) 1965.

KNIGHT, GLADYS
        (Singer)
b.   May 28, 1944, Atlanta, Ga.
Honors: Won Ted Mack's amateur hour (age 8); Grammys; 3 gold albums; 5 gold singles; Bill Board Award; Cash Box Award; National Assn. of Record Merchandisers' Best Selling Female Soul Artist award; Ebony Music Award 1975.
Career Data: Performs with support of The Pips, a vocal group consisting of brother and two cousins.

Clubs: Shady Grove (Maryland); Empire Room-Waldorf Astoria
        1974; Hilton (Las Vegas) 1974; Painter's Mill Theater Club
        (Baltimore) 1977.
Films: Save the Children 1973; Claudine (sang theme) 1974; Pipe
        Dreams 1976.
Records: World of ... (United Artists); Anthology (Motown); It Hurt
        Me So (Pickwick); A Little Knight Music (Motown); Claudine;
        I Feel a Song in My Heart (Motown); Every Beat of My Heart
        (Fury) 1961. On Soul: Knight Time; Standing Ovation; I
        Heard It Through the Grapevine 1967; The Nitty Gritty 1969;
        Friendship Train 1969; If I Were Your Woman 1970; I Don't
        Want to Do Wrong 1971; Help Me Make It Through the Night
        1972; Neither One of Us 1973, All I Need Is Time 1973.   On
        Buddah: Midnight Train to Georgia 1973; Second Anniversary;
        Imagination; Bless This House; Best of ...; Still Together
        (Columbia) 1977.
Television: Ted Mack's Amateur Hour; Soul Train; Hollywood
        Squares; $25,000 Pyramid; The Tonight Show 1974; Soul! 1974;
        Midday Live 1974; hosted "Ailey Celebrates Ellington" (Festi-
        val of the Arts for Young People) 1974; Midnight Special 1974;
        Mac Davis Show 1974; $10,000 Pyramid 1975; Entertainer of
        the Year Award 1975; Gladys Knight and The Pips (Variety)
        1975; The Grammy Awards 1975, 1976; Superstars and Rock
        1975; Mike Douglas Show 1975; Celebrity Sweepstakes 1975;
        Don Kirshner's Rock Concert 1976.
Theater: Appeared at Nanuet Theatre-Go-Round; Melody Fair (Buf-
        falo); Westbury Music Fair 1975; Apollo Theatre 1975; Felt
        Forum 1975; Westchester Premier Theater 1975.

KOTTO, YAPHET
        (Actor)
b.   November 15, 1937, New York, N.Y.
Education: American Conservatory Theater (Pitts.).
Address: Contemporary-Korman, 132 Lasky Drive, Beverly Hills,
        Calif.
Honors: Cowboy Hall of Fame award; National Assn. of Media
        Women's Man of the Year Award.
Career Data: Co-founder, Watts Actors' Workshop (L.A.).
Films: Nothing But a Man 1964; Five Card Stud 1968; Thomas
        Crown Affair 1968; The Liberation of L.B. Jones 1970; Across
        110th Street 1972; Man and Boy 1972; acted and directed The
        Limit 1972; Live and Let Die 1973; Crunch in Report to the
        Commissioner 1975; Sharks' Treasure 1975; Friday Foster
        1975; Drum, The Shootist, Monkey Hustle 1976.
Memberships: SAG.
Television: Losers Weepers 1967; Big Valley 1967; The Buffalo
        Soldiers (High Chaparral) 1968; Daniel Boone 1968; Hawaii
        Five-O 1969; Mannix 1969; The Time Is Now (Name of the
        Game) 1970; Gunsmoke 1970; Night Chase 1970; Doctors Hos-
        pital 1975; Idi Amin in Raid on Entebbe 1977.
Theater: A Good Place to Raise a Boy (O.B.); title role in Othello
        (stock); Walter Younger in Raisin in the Sun (stock); Great

Western Union (O. B.); Cyrano de Bergerac (O. B.); Black Mon-
day (O. B.) 1962; In White America (O. B.) 1964; Blood Knot
(O. B.) 1964; The Zulu and the Zayda (debut) 1965; succeeded
James Earl Jones in The Great White Hope 1969.

KYA-HILL, ROBERT (Robert Hill)
    (Actor)
b.   December 4, 1930, Whitaker, N. C.
Education: City College of New York; New York College of Music;
    studied with Vinnette Carroll.
Special Interests: Directing, guitar, music composition, teaching,
    singing, writing.
Address: 463 West Street, New York, N. Y. 10014.
Honors: Show Business Best actor of the year 1969; National Evan-
    gelical Film Assn. best actor of the year in a religious film.
Career Data: Worked with American Shakespeare Company (Strat-
    ford, Conn.), Morris Repertory Theatre (Morristown, N. J.),
    The Centaur Theatre (Montreal), The Vanguard Theatre (Pitts-
    burgh); drama consultant to New Jersey public schools; developed
    Black Theatre course at Hunter College; artist-in-residence,
    Western Australian Institute of Technology 1975.
Films: Dark Valley; Slaves 1969; Shaft's Big Score, Rivals 1972;
    Death Wish 1974.
Memberships: AEA; AFTRA; Australian Actors' Equity; National
    Academy of Television Arts and Sciences; SAG.
Musical Compositions: T. D. M. (an opera).
Television: Another World (series); Bay City.
Theater: Fiorello! (City Center) 1962; Abe Lincoln in Illinois (ELT)
    1963; The Merchant of Venice (ASF) 1967; Lost in the Stars;
    Purlie Victorious (O. B.); Young Martin Luther King (O. B.);
    Kafka's The Trial (O. B.); title role in Othello (Australia) 1975.

LAINE, CLEO (Clementine Dinah Campbell)
    (Singer)
b.   October 27, 1927, Southall, Middlesex, England.
Special Interests: Acting.
Address: The Old Rectory, Wavendon, Bletchley, Bucks. , England
    and International Artistes Representation, 235 Regent Street,
    London, England W. 1.
Career Data: Sang with John Dankworth band; popularized Gimme
    a Pigfoot and It's a Pity to Say Goodnight (concluding theme).
Clubs: Working men's clubs (Middlesex) 1950s; St. Regis Maisonette;
    Rainbow Grill.
Films: The Roman Spring of Mrs. Stone 1961.
Records: A Beautiful Theme (RCA); Pierrot Lunaire (RCA); All
    About Me!; The Unbelievable Miss Cleo Laine; Woman Talk;
    Shakespeare and All That Jazz; Soliloquy and Portrait; Born on
    a Friday (RCA); Live at Carnegie Hall (RCA); I Am a Song
    (RCA); Day by Day (Buddah and Stanyan); Easy Livin' (Stanyan);
    Cleo's Choice (GNP Crescendo); Porgy and Bess (RCA) 1976;
    Best Friends (RCA) 1977.

Television: One Man's Music (England); Marvelous Party (England);
Talk of the Town (England); Not So Much a Programme (England); The Sammy Davis Show; Merv Griffin Show 1974; Cotton Club '75 (special) 1974; Dinah! 1974; Mike Douglas Show 1974, 1976; Tonight Show 1974, 75; Today Show 1975; Pat Collins Show 1976; Sammy Meets the Girls; Sammy and Company 1976; In Performance at Wolf Trap (PBS) 1976.
Theater: Brecht-Weill's Seven Deadly Sins; Titania in A Midsummer Night's Dream; title role in Hedda Gabler (Canterbury); Julie in Show Boat (London) 1971; appearances at Hollywood Bowl, Alice Tully Hall 1972; Westbury Music Fair 1974; Carnegie Hall 1974, 1975; Nassau Coliseum 1975; Avery Fisher Hall (Newport Jazz Festival) 1975.
Relationships: Wife of John Dankworth, musician.

LAMONT, BARBARA
(Newscaster)
b. November 9, 1939, Bermuda.
Education: Sarah Lawrence College B. A. 1960; Hunter College 1974-76.
Special Interests: Acting, singing, writing.
Address: 205 East 67 Street, New York, N. Y. 10021.
Honors: Newswomans Club Front Page award 1973.
Career Data: Actress/singer 1960-69.
Publications: City People, Macmillan, 1975.
Radio: WINS Reporter 1970-75.
Television: Host, Voice of Germany 1965-67; associate producer WNET 1970; producer, Guyana (doc.) 1973 and Brownstone Fever (doc.) 1974; guest hostess, Midday Live 1974, 1975; co-host, Black News (WNEW series).
Theater: Tambourines to Glory 1963.

LANCELOT see SIR LANCELOT

LANEUVILLE, ERIC
(Actor)
b. July 14, 1952, New Orleans, La.
Address: Iris Burton, 1450 Belfast, Los Angeles, Calif. 90069.
Films: Blackbelt Jones 1974.
Memberships: SAG.
Television: Room 222; Insight; Saturday Night Adoption; Murder and the Computer (Mystery of The Week) 1972; Twice in a Lifetime (pilot for Flo's Place); Foster and Laurie 1975; Police Story 1975; Popi 1976; Kraft commercial; What's Happening 1976; Sanford and Son (series) 1976.
Theater: Raisin in the Sun (Inner City Repertory, L. A.).

LANGE, TED
(Actor)
b. c1947, Oakland, Calif.

Education: San Francisco City College 1967.
Special Interests: Directing, playwriting.
Address: Arnold Soloway Associates, 118 So. Beverly Drive, Bever-
      ly Hills, Calif.
Films: Wrote several screenplays: Booker's Back; Boss Rain Bow;
      Little Brother; Tuned In; Passing Thru (produced by U. C. L. A.)
      1973; appeared in Wattstax, Blade 1973; Friday Foster
      1975.
Memberships: SAG.
Television: Junior in That's My Mama (series) 1974; Rhyme and
      Reason 1975; Mr. T. and Tina (series) 1976; Love Boat (series)
      1977.
Theater: Wrote: Day Zsa Voo; A Foul Movement; Pig, Male and
      Young; Sounds from a Flute; appeared in: Golden Boy 1964;
      Big Time Buck White 1969; Rhinoceros; Hair 1969; Ain't Sup-
      posed to Die a Natural Death 1971; The Bald Soprano; Visigoths;
      Soul Gone Home; Integration; directed: Medea (for Zodiac
      Theatre, L. A.).

LARKINS, ELLIS (Lane)
      (Pianist)
b.   May 15, 1923, Baltimore, Md.
Education: Peabody Conservatory of Music; Juilliard School of
      Music 1940.
Career Data: Played with Edmond Hall sextet; formed own trio.
Clubs: Blue Angel; Café Society 1945-46; Tangerine 1975; Shepheards
      in the Drake Hotel 1975; Larson's 1977.
Films: The Joe Louis Story 1953.
Records: Ella Fitzgerald Sings Gershwin (Decca); The Talk of the
      Town (Columbia) 1975.
Television: Positively Black 1975.
Theater: Pousse Café 1966; appeared at Avery Fisher Hall (New-
      port Jazz Festival) 1975.

LATEEF, YUSEF (Bill Evans)
      (Jazz Musician)
b.   October 9, 1920, Chattanooga, Tenn.
Education: B. M. , M. M. , Manhattan School of Music; Ph. D. ,
      University of Massachusetts 1975.
Special Interests: Composing, teaching.
Career Data: Led quartet 1960; worked with Charles Mingus 1960-
      61, Babatundi Olatunji 1961-62, with Cannonball Adderley, Stan
      Kenton 1963 and Roy Eldridge; associate professor, Borough of
      Manhattan Community College, 1971-76.
Clubs: Village Vanguard; The Bottom Line 1976.
Musical Compositions: Nocturne (ballet) 1974; Yusef's Mood.
Publications: Yusef Lateef's Flute Book of the Blues.
Records: Part of the Search (Atlantic); Morning (Savoy); The Cen-
      taur; A♭ G♭ & C (Impulse); Best (Atlantic); Blue (Atlantic);
      Blues for the Orient (Prestige); Club Date (Impulse); Complete
      (Atlantic); Cry-Tender (Prestige); Doctor Is In ... & Out (At-

lantic); Eastern Sounds (Prestige); Expression (Prestige); Gen-
tle Giant (Atlantic); Golden Flute (Impulse); Hush'n' Thunder
(Atlantic); Imagination (Prestige); Into Something (Prestige);
Jazz Round the World (Impulse); Live at Pep's (Impulse);
Many Faces of ... (Milestone); 1984 (Impulse); Outside Blues
(Trip); ... Plays for Lovers (Prestige); Psychicemotus (Im-
pulse); Sounds (Prestige); Yusef Lateef (Cadet, Prestige and
Archive of Folk & Jazz Music); Ten Years Hence (Atlantic)
1975.
Television: Like It Is.
Theater: Appeared at Symphony Hall.

LATHAN, STAN
    (Director)
b. c. 1944, Philadelphia, Pa.
Education: Pennsylvania State University B. A. (Theatre); Boston
    University.
Honors: Jamaica's First Black Film Director Award 1974.
Career Data: New Lafayette Theatre Workshop.
Films: Save the Children 1973; Amazing Grace 1974.
Television: Workshop (WGBH Boston); Say Brother; Feeling Good;
    Soul!; Sesame Street; Sanford and Son; Black Journal 1969,
    1976; In Performance at Wolf Trap (special) 1974; That's My
    Mama 1975; Flip Wilson (special) 1975; Almos' a Man 1977.
Theater: Riot (Boston and O. B.) 1968-69.
Relationships: Brother of William Lathan, actor/director.

LAWS, HUBERT
    (Musician)
b. November 10, 1939, Houston Texas.
Education: Juilliard School of Music 1964.
Special Interests: Flute, composing.
Address: 66 West 94 Street, New York, N. Y. 10025.
Honors: Down Beat poll winner 1971-74; Ebony Music award 1973;
    Grammy nomination 1973; Playboy poll winner 1974.
Career Data: Member, The Nite Hawks, The Jazz Crusaders;
    played with Berkshire Festival Orchestra and Orchestra U. S. A. ;
    played with N. Y. Metropolitan Opera orchestra 1968-73; alter-
    nate with N. Y. Philharmonic 1969-.
Records: In the Beginning (CTI); Wild Flower (Atlantic); Romeo
    and Juliet (Columbia); Carnegie Hall (CTI); Flute By-Laws (At-
    lantic); Laws of Jazz (Atlantic); The Chicago Theme (CTI);
    Morning Star (CTI); The Rite of Spring (CTI); Crying Song
    (CTI); Afro-Classic (CTI).
Television: David Frost Show; Positively Black; Soundstage 1975;
    Black News 1976.
Theater: Appearances at Felt Forum 1975 and Carnegie Hall 1976.

LAWS, SAM (Samuel)
    (Actor)
Special Interests: Singing.

Address: Ernestine McClendon Enterprises, 8440 Sunset Blvd. , Los
~~~~~~Angeles, Calif. 90069.
Films: The Pawnbroker 1965; Sweet Sweetback's Baadasss Song
~~~~~~1971; Hit Man, The Final Comedown, Cool Breeze 1972; Walk-
ing Tall, Sweet Jesus, Preacher Man 1973; Dirty O'Neil, Truck
Turner 1974; White Line Fever 1975; Mr. Billion 1977.
Memberships: SAG.
Television: Roll Out (series) 1973; That's My Mama 1975; Kojak
~~~~~~1975; The Practice (series) 1976; Jigsaw John 1976; The Richard
Pryor Show 1977.
Theater: Cabin in the Sky (O. B.) 1964; Who's Got His Own (O. B.)
~~~~~~1966.

LAWSON, RICHARD
~~~~~~(Actor)
Films: Scream Blacula Scream 1973; Willie Dynamite, Sugar Hill
~~~~~~1974; Bogard 1975.
Memberships: SAG.
Television: Medical Center 1975; Streets of San Francisco 1975;
~~~~~~Crossfire 1975; Get Christie Love 1975.

LEADBELLY "King of the Twelve-String Guitar" (Huddie Ledbetter)
~~~~~~(Singer)
b.   January 21, 1885, Mooringsport, La.
d.   December 6, 1949, New York, N. Y.
Special Interests: Guitar, folksinging, composing, accordion.
Career Data: Joined with "Blind Lemon" Jefferson as singing team
~~~~~~1917; served jail term for murder in Texas 1918-25; served
another jail term in Louisiana 1930-34; pardoned after singing
for Governor of Louisiana; recorded folk songs, ballads and
work songs for Library of Congress; toured France in 1949.
Clubs: The Village Vanguard.
Musical Compositions: Good Night Irene; On Top of Old Smoky;
~~~~~~Gray Goose; Good Morning Blues; The Midnight Special; Whoa
Black Buck; Easy Rider; Keep Your Hands Off Her; Fannin
Street; Rock Island Line.
Records: The Legendary Leadbelly (Tradition); The Midnight Special
~~~~~~(Folkways); The Solid South (Capitol); Early Leadbelly 1935-
1940 (Biograph); Leadbelly's Last Sessions 2 vols. (Folkways);
Folk Songs (Folkways); Leadbelly (Columbia); Huddie Ledbetter
(Fantasy); Leadbelly Memorial (Stinson); Ledbetter's Best (Capi-
tol); Play-Party Songs (Stinson); Shout On (Folkways); ... Sings
and Plays (Stinson); Take This Hammer (Folkways).
Theater: Apollo Theatre.

LEAGUE, JANET
~~~~~~(Actress)
Education: Loyola University; Goodman Memorial Theatre (Chicago).
Career Data: Resident, Lincoln Center Repertory Co. 1967-68.
Films: The Spook Who Sat by the Door 1973.

Memberships: AEA; AFTRA; NEC; SAG.

Television: Camera Three; On Being Black; The Secret Storm; The
Guiding Light; Our Street (series); Carol Gault in Where the
Heart Is (series); Positively Black 1976; The First Breeze of
Summer (PBS) 1976.

Theater: Don't Cry and Say No (O. B.); Tiger at the Gates (LCR)
1967; Cyrano de Bergerac (LCR) 1967; Romeo and Juliet (Wash-
ington D. C.) 1968; Love's Labour's Lost (ASF); To Be Young
Gifted and Black 1969; The Screens (O. B.) 1971; The First
Breeze of Summer (NEC) 1975; For Colored Girls Who Have
Considered Suicide/When the Rainbow Is Enuf (NYSF) 1976.

LEAKS, SYLVESTER
(Publicist)
b.   August 11, 1927, Macon, Ga.
Education: City College of New York 1950-57; Cambridge School of
Radio Broadcasting.
Special Interests: Acting, dancing, poetry, writing.
Address: 340 New York Avenue, Brooklyn, N. Y. 11213.
Career Data: Asadata Dafora Dance Co. (lead dancer) 1947-52;
Dramatic Workshop 1949-52; Elks Community Theatre 1950-56;
N. Y. editor, Muhammad Speaks, 1960-65; president, Sylvester
Leaks Associates Inc.
Memberships: Harlem Writers Guild (President).
Publications: Trouble, Blues, N' Trouble (play); My God, My God
Is Dead (screenplay).
Theater: Publicity for The World of Sholom Aleichem 1953; Raisin
1973.

LEE, CANADA (Leonard Lionel Cornelius Canegata)
(Actor)
b.   1907, New York, N. Y.
d.   May 8, 1952, New York, N. Y.
Special Interests: Prize fighting, music (former band leader).
Honors: Black Filmmakers Hall of Fame (posthumously) 1976.
Career Data: Worked with W. P. A. Negro Federal Theatre Unit.
Films: Henry Brown, Farmer (doc.) 1942; Joe the Steward in Life-
boat 1944; Body and Soul, The Roosevelt Story (doc.)
1947; Lost Boundaries 1949; Cry the Beloved Country 1952.
Radio: Narrated Unofficial Ambassadors; narrated Flow Gently
Sweet Rhythm; Tolerance Through Music; Mutual's Green Valley
U. S. A. ; narrated New World A-Coming (WMCA).
Television: The Final Bell (Tele Theatre) 1950.
Theater: Meek Mose (debut); Talking to You; Stevedore; Banquo in
Macbeth 1936; Haiti 1938; Mamba's Daughters 1939; Big White
Fog (Lincoln Theater Harlem) 1940; produced and acted as
Danny in South Pacific 1941; Bigger Thomas in Native Son
1941; Across the Board on Tomorrow Morning 1942; Anna
Lucasta 1944; Caliban in the Tempest 1945; Daniel de Bosola
in Dutchess of Malfi (in white face) 1946; co-produced and
acted in On Whitman Avenue 1946; Set My People Free 1948;

title role in Othello (stock) 1948; narrated Toll the Liberty
Bell at Madison Square Garden 1952.
Relationships: Father of Carl Lee, actor.

LEE, CARL (Carl Vincent Canegata)
    (Actor)
b. November 22, 1933, New York, N. Y.
Education: Neighborhood Playhouse; studied with Stella Adler.
Special Interests: Guitar, singing.
Honors: Emmy nominee (for The Nurses).
Career Data: The Living Theatre.
Films: The Connection 1962; acted and co-scripted The Cool World
    1964; A Man Called Adam 1966; The Landlord, Pound 1970;
    Super Fly 1972; Gordon's War 1973.
Memberships: SAG.
Television: Express Stop episode (The Nurses); Caribe 1975; Man-
    nix 1975; Good Times 1977.
Theater: Deep Are the Roots (tour); Decision (O. B.); The Respect-
    ful Prostitute (subway circuit tour); Wedding in Japan (O. B.)
    1957; title role in Othello (Cleveland); Black Hamlet; God
    Bless (Yale University); The Odd Couple (tour); No Time for
    Sergeants (tour); The Connection (O. B.) 1959; The Marrying
    Maiden (O. B.) 1960; Ceremonies in Dark Old Men (NEC) 1969.
Relationships: Son of Canada Lee, actor.

LEE, EVERETT
    (Conductor/Musician)
Address: 250 West 57 Street, New York, N. Y. 10019.
Career Data: Performed with N. Y. Philharmonic and N. Y. City
    Opera Co. ; introduced David Baker's Kosbro; music director/
    conductor, Symphony of the New World.
Theater: Performed at Avery Fisher Hall 1976; Carnegie Hall 1976.

LEE, LESLIE
    (Playwright)
b. c. 1935 Bryn Mawr, Pa.
Education: University of Pennsylvania B. A. , Villanova University
    M. A. (Theatre).
Address: 279 West 12 Street, New York, N. Y. 10014.
Honors: Rockefeller Foundation Playwriting Grant; Schubert Founda-
    tion Grant; Obie 1975; Obie award and Tony nomination (for
    The First Breeze of Summer) 1976.
Career Data: Instructor of playwriting, College at Old Westbury,
    N. Y. 1975-76; worked for Ellen Stewart's La Mama.
Television: Black Pride 1976; The First Breeze of Summer (PBS)
    1976.
Theater: Wrote: Elegy to a Down Queen; Cops and Robbers; The
    Night of the Moon; The War Party; Between Now and Then;
    The First Breeze of Summer 1975; The Book of Lambert 1977.

LEHMAN, LILLIAN
    (Actress)
Memberships: AFTRA.
Television: Emergency 1972; Tenafly (series) 1973; Kojak 1974;
    Letty on Fay (series) 1975; This Is the Life 1975; The Jeffer-
    sons 1977.

LE NOIRE, ROSETTA (Rosetta Olive Burton)
    (Actress)
b. August 8, 1911, New York, N. Y.
Education: Betty Cashman Dramatic School 1946; American Theatre
    Wing 1950; ASFTA Dramatic School 1955-58; studied singing
    with Reginald Beane, acting with Morris Carnovsky.
Special Interests: Dancing, directing, singing.
Address: 1037 East 232 Street, Bronx, N. Y. 10466.
Honors: Dallas Texas Blue Bonnet Musical Award (for Show Boat)
    1963; Harold Jackman Memorial award 1976.
Career Data: Founder, president and artistic director, AMAS Reper-
    tory Theatre Inc. (an actor's and playwright's workshop); nar-
    rator, film Dept. , Lincoln Center for the Performing Arts, Inc.
Films: Stella in Anna Lucasta 1959; Nurse in The Sunshine Boys
    1975.
Memberships: AEA; AFTRA; AGVA; NAG; SAG; Catholic Actors
    Guild of America; Actors Fund of America; Catholic Actors
    St. Malachys Discussion Group.
Radio: 21st Precinct (CBS); Counterspy (CBS); David Harding (CBS).
Records: A Streetcar Named Desire (Caedmon).
Television: The Reporter; Love of Life (series); Emma in Search
    for Tomorrow (series); Lamp Unto My Feet; Armstrong Circle
    Theatre; In the Dog House (series); The Nurses; The Doctors
    and the Nurses; Mrs. Noah in The Green Pastures (Hallmark
    Hall of Fame) 1957; A World Apart (series) 1969-70; Canada
    Dry commercial 1969-70; The Guiding Light 1971-72; Children
    Guidance Program 1971-72; Another World 1971-73; Calucci's
    Department 1973; Comet Cleanser commercial 1973; G. E. Tele-
    phone commercial 1973; Legacy of Blood (Wide World Mystery)
    1974; Tillie in Guess Who's Coming to Dinner? (pilot) 1975;
    Bell Telephone commercial 1977.
Theater: WPA production of Macbeth (debut) 1936; Bassa Moona
    1936; Bluebird 1937; The Hot Mikado 1939; Head of the Family
    (Westport summer theatre) 1941; You Can't Take It with You
    (U. S. O. tour) 1943; Janie (tour) 1943-44; Decision and Three's
    a Family (subway circuit) 1944; Stella in Anna Lucasta 1944;
    Annie in scenes from The Easiest Way (ANTA album produc-
    tion) 1949; Kiss Me Kate (Dallas summer theatre) 1950; Four
    Twelves Are 48 1951; O Distant Land (ELT) 1952; Carmen
    Jones (Westport summer theatre) 1952; Supper for the Dead
    (O. B.) 1954; Finian's Rainbow (City Center) 1955; The White
    Devil (O. B.) 1955; Mister Johnson 1956; Ceremonies of Inno-
    cence (ANTA) 1956; Christine in Take a Giant Step (O. B.) 1956;
    Lost in the Stars (City Center) 1958; Destry Rides Again 1959;
    Double Entry: The Bible Salesman and The Oldest Trick in

the World (O. B.) 1961; Bloody Mary in South Pacific (City
Center) 1961; Clandestine on The Morning Line (O. B.) 1961;
Sophie 1963; Tambourines to Glory (O. B.) 1963; Petunia Jack-
son in Cabin in the Sky (O. B.) 1964; Blues for Mr. Charlie
1964; I Had a Ball 1964; Great Indoors; Queenie in Show Boat
(LCR) 1966; Marching with Johnny; The Name of the Game
(Florida) 1967; Mrs. Kumalo in Lost in the Stars 1972; Mrs.
Holiday in Lady Day (O. B.) 1972; Streetcar Named Desire
(LCR) 1973; Nurse in The Sunshine Boys 1973; God's Favorite
1974; produced Bubbling Brown Sugar (AMAS Repertory) 1975;
The Royal Family 1976.

LEONARDOS, URYLEE
    (Singer/Actress)
b.   May 14, Charleston, S. C.
Education: Manhattan School of Music; Chicago Conservatory of
    Music; Roosevelt College; studied with Abbie Mitchell.
Address: 115-03 173 Street, St. Albans, N. Y. 11434.
Clubs: One Fifth Avenue.
Films: No Sad Songs for Me 1950; Porgy and Bess (voice) 1959;
    Klute 1971.
Television: Arthur Godfrey Show; Garry Moore Show; Ed Sullivan
    Show; Another World (series).
Theater: Mert in Carmen Jones (debut) 1943; Bess (alternating with
    Leontyne Price) in Porgy and Bess 1953; Bells Are Ringing
    1956; Shangri-La 1956; Wildcat 1960; Milk and Honey 1961;
    Sophie 1963; 110 in the Shade 1963; The King and I (Chicago)
    1963; Bajour 1964; To Broadway with Love (N. Y. World's Fair)
    1965; The Amen Corner 1966-67; Illya Darling 1967; Golden
    Boy (London) 1968-69; Dear World; Billy No Name (O. B.) 1970;
    The Last of Mrs. Lincoln 1971; Lost in the Stars 1972; Desert
    Song 1973; Nurse in The Sunshine Boys 1974; 1600 Pennsylvania
    Avenue 1976.

LESTER, KETTY (Roberta Frierson)
    (Singer/Actress)
b.   August 16, 1938, Hope, Ark.
Education: City College (San Francisco); San Francisco State College.
Address: Dorothy Day Otis Agency, 6430 Sunet Blvd. , Los Angeles,
    Calif.
Honors: Theatre World 1964.
Career Data: Sang with Cab Calloway's Orchestra.
Clubs: Purple Onion (San Francisco); Village Vanguard; Ye Little
    Club (Calif).
Films: Uptight 1968; Blacula 1972; Uptown Saturday Night 1974.
Memberships: SAG.
Records: For Era Label: Love Letters 1962; But Not for Me 1962;
    You Can't Lie to a Liar 1962; This Land Is Your Land 1962;
    In Concert (Sheffield).
Television: Groucho Marx You Bet Your Life; Sanford and Son; Bill
    Cosby Show; Secret deodorant commercial; Teri commercial;
    Marcus Welby, M. D. 1975; Streets of San Francisco 1975;

Harry O 1975; Adventurizing with the Chopper (pilot) 1976;
Days of Our Lives (series) 1977.

Theater: Raisin in the Sun (Inner City Repertory Co., L. A.); appeared at Apollo Theatre 1958; Cotton Club Revue 1959; Cabin
in the Sky (O. B. revival) 1964.

LEWIS, HENRY
(Conductor)
b. October 16, 1932, Los Angeles, Calif.
Education: University of Southern California.
Special Interests: Double bass.
Address: 1020 Broad Street, Newark, N. J. 07102.
Career Data: Conductor, Seventh Army Symphony Orchestra, Ger-
many/Holland, 1955-57; founder, Los Angeles Chamber Orches-
tra (formerly, String Society of Los Angeles) 1958; music
director, Los Angeles Opera Company, 1965-68; associate
conductor, Los Angeles Philharmonic Orchestra 1962-65; con-
ductor, Metropolitan Opera Company 1972; director, New Jersey
Symphony Orchestra, Newark 1968-date; guest conductor, Chi-
cago, Boston, American, Detroit, and London symphony orchestras and the San Francisco and La Scala Opera Company
Orchestras; led Chamber Music Outdoors Program, Washington
Square Park, N. Y.
Memberships: Black Academy of Arts & Letters (founder).
Theater: Performances at Kennedy Center for the Performing
Arts (Washington, D. C.); La Scala Opera House (Milan)
1965; Carnegie Hall 1967; Newark Symphony Hall 1971;
Brooklyn Academy of Music 1974; NHK Hall (Tokyo) 1975;
Metropolitan Opera 1972, 1974, 1975; directed Le Prophète
1977.

LEWIS, JOHN (Aaron)
(Composer/Musician)
b. May 3, 1920, La Grange, Ill.
Education: Manhattan School of Music B. Mus., M. Mus.; Univer-
sity of New Mexico.
Special Interests: Arranging, jazz trombone, teaching, conducting.
Address: Modern Jazz Quartet, 200 West 57 Street, New York, N. Y.
10019.
Career Data: Member, Modern Jazz Quartet; executive director,
School of Jazz, Lenox, Mass.; taught music at City College of
N. Y. and Harvard University (1975); participated in Newport
Jazz Festival 1954, 1975 and Monterey Jazz Festival 1958;
musical director, Orchestra U. S. A. 1962; trustee, Manhattan
School of Music; arranger with Dizzy Gillespie 1946-47 and
worked with Miles Davis; toured Europe 1964.
Films: L'Espoir de L'eau (French); Kemek; No Sun in Venice (a. k. a.
Sait-on Jamais) 1957; Odds Against Tomorrow 1959; A Milanese
Story 1962.
Musical Compositions: Toccata for Trumpet and Orchestra; Vendome
and Versailles; Concorde; Three Little Feelings; Django 1954;
Fontessa 1956; Original Sin (a ballet) 1961.

Television: Night Gallery (score).
Theater: Wrote music for Natural Affection 1963; appeared at Car-
     negie Hall 1975.

LEWIS, MARY RIO
     (Actress)
Address: 1026 East 219 Street, Bronx, N. Y. 10469.
Career Data: Katherine Dunham Dance Co.
Films: The Pawnbroker 1965; The Group 1966; Up the Down Stair-
     case 1967; The Hospital 1971.
Memberships: AEA; AFTRA; SAG.
Television: You Are There; Armstrong Circle Theatre; Philco Play-
     house; Guiding Light; As the World Turns; Love Is a Many
     Splendored Thing; Another World; Frontiers of Faith; The De-
     fenders; The Doctors and the Nurses; The Trials of O'Brien;
     For the People; A Place Called Today 1972.
Theater: Carib Song 1945; Memphis Bound 1945; Bal Negre 1946;
     Our Lan' 1947.

LEWIS, RAMSEY (Emanuel Jr.)
     (Pianist/Composer)
b.   May 27, 1935, Chicago, Ill.
Education: Chicago Music College 1947-54; University of Illinois
     1953-54; DePaul University 1954-55.
Special Interests: Producing.
Address: 119 West 57 Street, New York, N. Y. 10019 and c/o Rams
     L. Productions Inc., 30 N. La Salle Street, Chicago, Ill.
     60602.
Honors: Grammy award 1965.
Career Data: Manager, Record Dept., Hudson-Ross Inc., Chicago,
     1954-56; organized Ramsey Lewis Trio 1956; played Randalls
     Island Jazz Festival 1959, Saugatuck Michigan Jazz Festival
     1960, Newport Jazz Festival 1961-63; toured with Free Sounds
     of 1963; organized Rams L. Productions Inc. and Ramsel Pub-
     lishing Co., Chicago 1966.
Clubs: Bottom Line 1975; Brody's Place 1975; Boomer's 1975; The
     Rainbow Grill 1975.
Musical Compositions: Fantasia for Drums; Look-A-Here; Sound of
     Christmas; Sound of Spring.
Records: Hang on Sloopy (Cadet); Hard Day's Night; Sun Goddess
     (Columbia); Don't It Feel Good (Columbia); Another Voyage
     (Cadet); At Bohemian Caverns (Cadet); Back to the Blues (Ca-
     det); Back to the Roots (Cadet); Barefoot Sunday Blues (Cadet);
     Best (Cadet); Choice (Cadet); Dancing in the Street (Cadet);
     Funky Serenity (Columbia); Goin' Latin (Cadet); Greatest Hits
     (Columbia); Groover (Cadet); Hour (Cadet); In Crowd (Cadet);
     Inside Ramsey Lewis (Cadet); Maiden Voyage (Cadet); More
     Music from the Soil (Cadet); Mother Nature's Son (Cadet);
     Movie Album (Cadet); Never on Sunday (Cadet); The Piano
     Player (Cadet); Pot Luck (Cadet); Salongo (Columbia); Solar
     Wind (Columbia); Solid Ivory (Cadet); Stretching Out (Cadet);

Swingin' (Cadet); Them Changes (Cadet); Up Pops (Cadet);
Upendo Ni Pamoja (Columbia); Upendo/Funky Serenity (Colum-
bia); Wade in the Water (Cadet); Gentlemen of Jazz (Cadet);
Down to Earth (Trip); Love Notes (Columbia).
Television: Mark of Jazz; Soul Train 1975; Don Kirshner's Rock
    Concert 1975.
Theater: Appeared at Carnegie Hall 1975; Symphony Hall (Newark)
    1975; Nassau Coliseum 1976; Felt Forum 1977.

LINCOLN, ABBEY (Anna Marie Woolridge, a. k. a. Aminata Moseka,
    a. k. a. Gaby Lee)
    (Actress/Singer)
b. August 6, 1930, Chicago, Ill.
Special Interests: Writing.
Address: California State University, Northridge, Calif. 91324.
Honors: Black Filmmakers Hall of Fame 1975.
Career Data: Teacher, African-American Theatre, California State
    University, Northridge, Calif.; band vocalist, Michigan; club
    vocalist, California 1954-57.
Clubs: Astor (London) 1959.
Films: Girl Can't Help It 1957; Nothing But a Man 1964; Ivy in
    For Love of Ivy 1968; Short Walk to Daylight 1972.
Records: Straight Ahead.
Television: Marcus Welby M. D.; Name of the Game 1968.
Theater: Acted in Wine in the Wilderness; Jamaica (tour) 1959.
    Wrote: A Pig in a Poke; A Steak O'Lean.
Relationships: Former wife of Max Roach, jazz musician.

LITTLE, CLEAVON (Jake)
    (Actor)
b. June 1, 1939, Chickasha, Okla.
Education: San Diego State College B. A. 1965; American Academy
    of Dramatic Arts 1965-67.
Address: c/o William Morris Agency and Henderson Hogan Agency,
    200 West 57 Street, New York, N. Y. 10019.
Honors: American Broadcasting Company scholarship award; Tony
    for best actor in a musical 1970; N. Y. Critic Poll award 1970;
    Drama Desk award 1970; F & M Schaefer Brewing Company
    award 1970; NAACP Image award (dramatic actor) 1976.
Films: Three 1967; What's So Bad About Feeling Good? 1968; John
    and Mary 1969; Cotton Comes to Harlem 1970; Super Soul in
    The Vanishing Point 1971; Blazing Saddles 1974; Greased
    Lightening 1977.
Memberships: AEA; AFTRA; SAG.
Radio: Dick Richards (WHBI).
Television: Host, Night to Night (Los Angeles); David Frost Show;
    The Homecoming: A Christmas Story 1971; All in the Family
    1971; Dr. Jerry Noland in Temperature's Rising (series) 1972;
    Mod Squad 1972; Money to Burn 1973; The Day the Earth Moved
    1974; A. M. America 1975; Tonight Show 1975; Black Journal
    1975; Dinah! 1975; Positively Black 1975; Mike Douglas Show

1975; narrated Can You Turn a Neighborhood Around (N. Y.
Illustrated) 1975; Merv Griffin Show 1975; Not for Women Only
1975; Tony Awards Show 1975; $10,000 Pyramid 1975; Waltons
1975; Police Story 1975; Rookies 1975; Kup's Show 1975.
Theater: Macbeth (NYSF) 1966; Skin of Our Teeth (La Jolla, Calif.
Playhouse); Macbird (O. B.) 1967; Hamlet (NYSF) 1967; Scuba
Duba (O. B.) 1967; Jimmy Shine (Bway debut) 1968; The Ofay
Watcher 1969; Someone's Coming Hungry 1969; The Charlatan
(L. A.); title role in Purlie 1970; The Great MacDaddy (NEC)
1974; All Over Town 1975; The Poison Tree 1976; Joseph and
the Amazing Technicolor Dreamcoat (Brooklyn Academy of
Music) 1976; Same Time Next Year (L. A.) 1977.

LITTLE ANTHONY (Anthony Gourdine)
    (Singer)
b. January 8, 1940, Brooklyn, N. Y.
Career Data: Worked with various musical groups, The Duponts,
The Chesters and The Imperials.
Clubs: Jupiter's; Camelot Inn; Playboy Club Hotel (McAfee, N. J.)
1974; Empire Room-Waldorf Astoria 1975.
Records: Best (Veep); Hurt So Bad; Tears on My Pillow; On the
Outside Looking In.
Television: Host, Midnight Special 1974; Mike Douglas Show 1975;
Kingston Confidential 1976.
Theater: Appeared at Beacon Theater; Madison Square Garden 1976.

LITTLE RICHARD (Richard Penniman)
    (Singer)
b. December 25, 1935, Macon, Ga.
Education: Oakwood College.
Honors: Talent contest winner, Atlanta.
Career Data: Singer and dancer in Medicine show; organized his
own band.
Films: The Girl Can't Help It; Don't Knock the Rock; Mister Rock
and Roll 1957; Let the Good Times Roll 1973.
Records: Big Hits (GNP Crescendo); Very Best (United Artists);
Together (Pickwick); Roots (Archive of Folk & Jazz Music);
Greatest Hits (Okeh); Cast a Long Shadow (Epic); Greatest Hits
(Trip); Greatest Hits (Epic). On Specialty: Well Alright!;
Tutti Frutti 1955; Long Tall Sally 1956; True, Fine Mama
1958; Kansas City 1959. On Vee Jay: I Don't Know What
You've Got But It's Got Me 1965.
Television: Merv Griffin Show; Tonight Show; Midnight Special;
Rock'n'Roll Revival (Wide World Special) 1975; Night Dreams
1975; Dinah! 1976; Tomorrow 1976.
Theater: Rock & Roll Revival Spectacular 1974; appeared at Radio
City Music Hall 1975.

LOCKHART, CALVIN (Calvin Cooper)
    (Actor)
b. 1934, Nassau, Bahamas.

Education: Cooper Union.
Address: Natural Artists Enterprises, 8380 Melrose Avenue, Los
    Angeles, Calif. 90069.
Films: Contact (Uganda), Dark of the Sun, Joanna, Le Grabuge
    (Brazil), A Dandy in Aspic, Only When I Larf, The High Com-
    missioner, Salt and Pepper 1968; Halls of Anger, Cotton Comes
    to Harlem, Leo the Last, Myra Breckenridge 1970; Melinda
    1972; Honeybaby, Honeybaby, Uptown Saturday Night 1974; The
    Marijuana Affair, The Beast Must Die, Let's Do It Again 1975;
    Every Nigger Is a Star, Baron Wolfgang Von Tripps 1976.
Memberships: BAEA; SAG.
Television: Get Christie Love 1974.
Theater: A Taste of Honey; Dark of the Moon (E. L. T.) 1960; The
    Cool World 1960; The Pretender (O. B.) 1960; Dutchman (Lon-
    don); Royal Shakespeare Co. (London) 1973-74.

LONG, AVON
    (Actor/Singer/Dancer)
b.   June 18, 1910, Baltimore Md.
Education: New England Conservatory of Music (Boston) 1929; Allied
    Art Center (Boston) 1929; Sonya Koretna School of Dance (Bos-
    ton) 1929.
Special Interests: Songwriting.
Address: 790 Riverside Drive, New York, N. Y. 10026.
Honors: Variety award as Performer Most Likely to Succeed 1941;
    citation as Best Broadway Male Actor of the Year (Porgy and
    Bess) 1942; Henry Morgenthau Certificate for Entertaining the
    Armed Forces 1942; Tony nomination (for Don't Play Us Cheap)
    1972.
Career Data: Toured U. S. , Canada, and Trinidad with his own con-
    cert groups; entertained troops in U. S. O. tours during World
    War II; made Theatrical debut in 1932 at Lafayette Theatre.
Clubs: Cotton Club 1931; Connie's Inn.
Films: Manhattan Merry-Go-Round 1937; Centennial Summer, Zieg-
    feld Follies 1946; Romance on the High Seas 1948; Finian's
    Rainbow 1968; Harry and Tonto, The Sting 1974.
Memberships: AEA; AFTRA; AGVA; AGMA; SAG.
Television: Garroway-at-Large 1949, 1951; U. S. Steel Hour 1958;
    Jim on The Big Story 1959; The Green Pastures (Hallmark
    Hall of Fame) 1960; Positively Black 1976; Midday Live 1976.
Theater: Very Warm for May; Shuffle Along; Beggars Holiday; Car-
    men Jones; Kiss Me Kate; Arsenic and Old Lace (1st Black
    Prod.); Connie's Hot Chocolates 1934; Gentlemen Unafraid (St.
    Louis Opera House) 1938; La Belle Helene (Westport, Conn.)
    1939; Sportin' Life in Porgy and Bess (Bway debut) 1942;
    Bloomer Girl 1944; Carib Song, Memphis Bound 1945; Hotel
    Broadway 1949; Green Pastures 1951; Carnegie Hall Concert
    1953; Mrs. Patterson 1954; Ballad of Jazz Street (O. B.) 1959;
    Fly Blackbird (O. B.) 1962; Head of the Family (Westport, Conn.)
    and narrated The Threepenny Opera (Westport, Conn.) 1963;
    Don't Play Us Cheap 1972; Treemonisha 1974; Bubbling Brown
    Sugar (tour and Bway) 1975-76.

LORD OBSERVER (Lennox Clarke)
(Singer)
b. July 11, 1937, Port of Spain, Trinidad.
Education: Carvers College (Trinidad) 1954-58.
Special Interests: Calypso, composing, guitar.
Address: 99-20 24th Avenue, East Elmhurst, N. Y. 11369
Honors: Calypso ambassador (Toco-Trinidad Calypso Assn.) 1968.
Clubs: Oasis (Bridgetown, Barbados); No One Club (London); Club
    Inferno (Grand Cayman Island) 1966; Brandon Beach Club
    (Barbados) 1968; Waldorf Astoria Jade Room; Gobblers Nob;
    Jamaica Arms.
Films: The Calypso Traveler (Cinerama) 1962.
Memberships: The Performing Right Society Ltd. (London); The
    Toco-Trinidad Calypso Assn. (Pres. 1964-68).
Radio: Calling the Caribbean (BBC); ZIZ (St. Kitts); WEBE (St.
    Croix and St. Thomas); Focus (WRLB).
Records: On Cook Caribbean: Ban the Nuclear Weapons; Banana
    Man 1960; You Too Sweet 1961; Observer Don't Go 1961; Don't
    Buy 1962; Ring the National Guard 1968; Observer Goodbye
    1969; Eating Competition 1970; English Racing 1971; I Love
    New York City 1975; New York City Broke 1975.
Television: The B. B. C. Commonwealth Art Festival Show (London)
    1966; Clairol Shampoo commercial 1974; The Lord Observer
    Variety Show (cable television on channel D teleprompter) 1975;
    The Eddie Rain Show (cable television) 1975; The Lord Duncan
    Show (cable television) 1975; The Dick Roffman Show (cable
    television) 1975; The Joe Franklin Show 1975.
Theater: Extravaganza '72 at Manhattan Center 1972; Observer in
    Concert at Ward Theatre (Kingston, Jamaica) 1973; starred in
    Calypso Theatre (Port of Spain, Trinidad) 1974.

LOWE, JAMES B.
(Actor)
b. c. 1880.
d. May 18, 1963.
Films: Demon Rider 1925; Blue Blazes 1926; title role in Uncle
    Tom's Cabin 1927.

LUCAS, SAM (Samuel Mildmay)
(Actor)
b. 1840, Washington, Ohio.
d. January 11, 1916, New York, N. Y.
Special Interests: Comedy, composing, singing.
Honors: Appearance before Queen Victoria of England.
Career Data: Member, Boston Museum Stock Co. ; Calendar's Min-
    strels; performed with Sprague's Georgia Minstrels.
Films: A Trip to Coontown 1898; title role in Uncle Tom's Cabin
    1914.
Musical Compositions: Carve Dat Possum; Grandfather's Clock;
    Turnip Greens; Every Day Will Be Sunday By and By; Where
    Was Moses When the Light Went Out?

Theater: The Creole Show 1890; The Shoo-Fly Regiment 1907; The
        Red Moon 1909.

LUCIEN, JON
        (Singer)
b.   Tortola.
Special Interests: Guitar.
Career Data: Performed with Marty Clark.
Clubs: Top of the Gate; The Other End; Village Gate; Parkside
        Elegant (Bronx) 1976.
Records: Premonition (Rounder); I Am Now (RCA) 1970; Rashida
        (RCA) 1973; Mind's Eye (RCA) 1974; Song for My Lady (Co-
        lumbia) 1975.
Television: Positively Black 1975; Like It Is 1976; Diahann Carroll
        Show 1976.
Theater: Appeared at Philharmonic Hall; Carnegie Hall (Newport
        Jazz Festival) 1975, 1976; Felt Forum 1977.

LUNCEFORD, JIMMIE (James Melvin Lunceford)
        (Jazz Musician)
b.   June 6, 1902, Fulton, Mo.
d.   July 13, 1947, Seaside, Ore.
Education: Fisk University B. A. (music) 1926; studied at City Col-
        lege of New York.
Special Interests: Arranging, composing, conducting, flute, guitar,
        saxophone, teaching, trombone.
Career Data: Played with George Morrison's orchestra 1922; taught
        music in Memphis 1926-29; formed his own orchestra 1929
        which became most popular Negro band in 1935; toured Scan-
        dinavia 1937; taught music, Fisk University.
Clubs: Renaissance; Cotton Club 1934.
Films: Blues in the Night 1941.
Memberships: ASCAP 1942.
Records: Blues in Night (Pickwick); Lunceford Special (Columbia).
Musical Compositions: Rhythm Is Our Business (theme); Uptown
        Blues; Rhythm in My Nursery Rhymes; Dream of You.
Theater: Appeared at Empress Theatre (Denver) 1922; Lafayette
        Theatre 1933; Apollo Theatre.

LUTCHER, NELLIE
        (Singer/Pianist)
b.   October 15, 1915, Lake Charles, La.
Special Interests: Composing, jazz.
Career Data: Performed with Clarence Hart, Southern Rhythm Boys;
        popularized My Mother's Eyes and Come on to My House.
Clubs: Cafe Society; Dunbar Hotel Lounge (Hollywood); Bocage (Hol-
        lywood).
Memberships: AFTRA; AGAC; ASCAP; NAACP.
Musical Compositions: He's a Real Gone Guy; Hurry on Down.
Records: He's a Real Gone Guy.

Television: Ed Sullivan Show.
Theater: Appeared at Town Hall; Paramount Theatre; Apollo Theatre.

LYLES, AUBREY L.
    (Lyricist/Actor)
b.   c. 1884, Jackson, Tenn.
d.   July 28, 1932, New York, N. Y.
Education: Fisk University.
Career Data: Comedy teamed with Flournoy Miller.
Radio: CBS series 1931.
Theater: Wrote: Lazy Rhythm; Darkydom 1914-15; Shuffle Along
     1921; Runnin' Wild 1923; Rang Tang 1927-28; Keep Shufflin'
     1928; appeared in: Midnight Frolic; Charlot's Revue (London)
     1915; George White's Scandals 1925; Great Day 1929; Sugar
     Hill 1931.

LYMON, FRANKIE
    (Singer)
b.   September 30, 1942, New York, N. Y.
d.   February 27, 1968, New York, N. Y.
Career Data: Sang with The Teenagers, a vocal group.
Records: Why Do Fools Fall in Love (GEE) 1956; Goody Goody
     (GEE) 1957.

MABLEY, JACKIE "Moms" (Loretta Mary Aiken)
    (Comedienne)
b.   March 19, 1897, Brevard, N. C.
d.   May 23, 1975, White Plains, N. Y.
Special Interests: Singing.
Honors: Gold Record.
Clubs: Club Harlem (Atlantic City); The Cotton Club; Club 45; Copa-
     cabana; Beverly Hilton (Newport, Ky.); Connie's Inn 1923.
Films: Jazz Heaven (a. k. a. Boarding House Blues) 1929; Emperor
     Jones 1933; Killer Diller 1948; Amazing Grace 1974.
Memberships: AGVA; SAG.
Radio: Swingtime at the Savoy.
Records: Moms Mabley at the U. N. ; Moms Mabley at the Geneva
     Conference; Moms Mabley--The Funniest Woman in the World
     (Chess); Moms Live at Sing Sing; Now Hear This (Mercury);
     At the Playboy Club (Chess); Best (Mercury); One More Time
     (Chess); Young Men, Si-Old Men, No (Chess); Moms Mabley
     and Pigmeat Markham (Chess).
Television: Merv Griffin Show; Tonight Show; Bill Cosby Show; Pat
     Collins Show; Smothers Brothers; Flip Wilson Show; Mike
     Douglas Show; Grammy Awards Show; A Time for Laughter
     1967.
Theater: Appeared at Lafayette Theatre; appeared at Apollo Theatre
     (on and off since 1939); Blackbirds; Swinging the Dream 1939;
     appeared at Regal Theatre (Chicago); Carnegie Hall 1962; Ken-
     nedy Cultural Center (Washington, D. C.) 1972.

McBROOM, MARCIA (Leanne)
    (Actress)
b. August 6, 1947, New York, N. Y.
Education: Hunter College B. A. 1974; Katherine Dunham School
    1965-70; Herbert Berghof Studio; studied dance with Rod
    Rodgers and Jean Leon Destiné.
Special Interests: Dancing, modeling, teaching.
Address: 305 East 24 Street, New York, N. Y. 10010.
Honors: International Mannequin's Model of the Year award 1975.
Career Data: Worked as model for Black Beauty Model Agency;
    internship program with NBC; modeled several record album
    covers for Atlantic, AVCO and CTI labels; director of re-
    ligious education, The Community Church of New York 1976.
Clubs: Liborio; Cotton Club Revue/La Mama Annex.
Films: Beyond the Valley of the Dolls 1970; The Legend of Nigger
    Charley, Come Back Charleston Blue 1972; Jesus Christ Super
    Star 1973; Willie Dynamite 1974; Bingo Long Traveling All-
    Stars and Motor Kings 1976.
Memberships: AFTRA; AGVA; SAG.
Radio: Tim Grey Show 1973; Dyana Williams Show (Washington,
    D. C.) 1974.
Television: Michel Le Grand (Special) Paris 1975; Deux Anges Sont
    Venus (Special) Paris 1965; Harlem Cultural Festival 1966;
    Like It Is 1969; Julia Meade (Cable) 1970; Black Pride 1975;
    Joe Franklin Show 1975; Nick La Tour Show (Cable) 1975;
    Manhattan Skyline (Cable) 1975.
Theater: Danced in Aida (Metropolitan Opera House); Deux Anges
    Sont Venus (Paris) 1975; Blues for Mr. Charlie (O. B.) 1974;
    Moon of The Caribbees (O. B.) 1974.

McCANN, LES (Leslie Coleman)
    (Pianist/Composer)
b. September 23, 1935, Lexington, Ky.
Education: Westlake College of Music; Los Angeles City College.
Special Interests: Photography, teaching.
Address: 6248 Scenic St., Los Angeles, Calif. 90068.
Career Data: Formed 1st group 1959; leader, Les McCann quartet;
    toured Europe, Africa, Mexico, Jamaica, Tahiti; president,
    Jana Music; performed concerts in penal institutions; founder
    and instructor, Black American Music Division; Operation
    Bread Basket; photographs exhibited Montreux, Switzerland
    1970; Washington, Detroit, Studio Museum of Harlem 1975.
Clubs: Playboy (Phoenix) 1974; The Bottom Line 1975.
Films: Soul to Soul 1971.
Memberships: ASCAP 1960; African-American Cultural Exchange
    Board.
Musical Compositions: The Gospel Truth; It's Way Past Suppertime;
    The Shampoo; You Thought I Knew; The Shout; Dorene; Don't
    Cry; Somebody Stole My Chitterlings.
Records: Talk to the People (Atlantic); Layers (Atlantic); Comment
    (Atlantic); Invitation to Openness (Atlantic); Live at Montreux
    (Atlantic); Much Les (Atlantic); River High, River Low (Atlantic);

Swiss Movement (Atlantic); Another Beginning (Atlantic); The
    Truth (Pacific Jazz) 1960; Hustle to Survive (Atlantic) 1975.
Television: Ed Sullivan Show 1956; Positively Black; Black News
    1975; Interface 1975; Police Woman 1975.
Theater: Appeared at Apollo Theatre 1974; Carnegie Hall 1975;
    Avery Fisher Hall 1975; Felt Forum 1976.

McCLENDON, ERNESTINE (Ernestine Epps)
    (Actress)
b.   August 17, 1918, Norfolk, Va.
Education: Columbia University 1935-36; studied acting with Michael
    Howard.
Career Data: Became an artist's representative 1962; operates
    theatrical agency in Santa Monica, Calif.
Films: A Face in the Crowd 1957; The Last Angry Man 1959; The
    Apartment, The Rat Race 1960; The Young Doctors, The World
    by Night, The Young Savages 1961.
Memberships: AEA; AFTRA; AGVA; SAG.
Television: Clementine in No Time for Comedy (Celanese Theatre)
    1950; Lady with a Will (Schlitz Playhouse) 1950; The Skeptic
    (Lights Out); The Mother (Philco Television Playhouse); The
    Ed Sullivan Show (with Pigmeat).
Theater: Liz in Time Out for Ginger (Woodstock Playhouse) 1958;
    Millie in Anniversary Waltz (Newport, R. I.) 1959; Bella in
    Deep Are the Roots (New Jersey) 1959; Alley of the Sunset
    (O. B.) 1959; Berenice in The Member of the Wedding (E. L. T.)
    1959-60; The Goose (O. B.) 1960; Catherine Creek in The
    Grass Harp (E. L. T.) 1960-61; Lena Younger in A Raisin in
    the Sun (stock) 1961.

McCLENDON, ROSE
    (Actress)
b.   1885, New York, N. Y.
d.   July 12, 1936, New York, N. Y.
Education: American Academy of Dramatic Arts (with Frank Sar-
    geant).
Career Data: Ethiopian Art Theatre; organized the Negro People's
    Theatre.
Theater: Justice 1916; Deep River 1926; In Abraham's Bosom 1926;
    Porgy 1927; Earth 1927; Never No More 1932; Mulatto 1934.
    Wrote Taxi Fare.

McCLINTOCK, ERNIE
    (Director)
Address: 36 Greene Street, New York, N. Y. 10013.
Honors: AUDELCO Black Theatre Recognition award 1973.
Career Data: President, Black Theatre Alliance; executive director,
    Afro-American Total Theatre.
Theater: Repertory work includes direction of The Amen Corner;
    Acife and Pendabis; Tabernacle 1974; A Hand is on the Gate
    1974.

McCOY, VAN
  (Composer)
b. January 6, 1944, Washington, D. C.
Education: Howard University.
Special Interests: Arranging, conducting.
Address: 7825 Orchid Street N. W. , Washington, D. C. 20012.
Honors: Billboard, Cashbox and Record World awards (for The
     Hustle) 1975; Grammy Best Pop Instrumental (for The Hustle)
     1976.
Career Data: Member, Starlighters (singing group); created Soul
     City Symphony; formed a record production company 1967
     (producer for Stylistics, The Choice Four); popularized "The
     Hustle, " a dance.
Musical Compositions: Lean on Me; The Hustle.
Records: Mr. D. J.; From Disco to Love (Buddah); Nightime Is
     Lonely Time (Columbia); Disco Baby (AVCO); The Disco Kid
     (AVCO); This Is It (Buddah) 1976.
Television: Tonight Show; Merv Griffin Show 1976.
Theater: Appearance at Avery Fisher Hall (with his symphony) 1975;
     Nassau Coliseum 1976; Westchester Premier Theatre 1976.

McCREARY, BILL (William McCreary)
  (Broadcaster)
b. August 18, 1933, New York, N. Y.
Education: City College of New York; New York University.
Address: WNEW-TV, 205 East 67 Street, New York, N. Y. 10021.
Honors: Emmy award 1969-70; Citation of Merit 1971-72; NAACP
     achievement award (L. I. Chapter) 1975.
Radio: Staff engineer, co-producer and night program manager,
     WWRL 1960-62; newscaster WLIB 1963.
Television: Newscaster, Metro Media Broadcasting 1967; WNEW co-
     anchor man, 10 o'clock news; anchor man, Black News 1970;
     managing editor and executive director, 1973.

McCURRY, JOHN
  (Actor/Singer)
b. Anderson, S. C.
Address: 109 West 85 Street, New York, N. Y. 10024.
Career Data: Karamu Playhouse, Cleveland (acted Ferrovius in
     Androcles and the Lion; Lennie in Of Mice and Men; Husky
     Miller in Carmen Jones).
Films: The Last Mile 1959; The Pawnbroker 1965; The Landlord,
     Where's Poppa 1970; Little Murders 1971; Bingo Long Travel-
     ing All Stars and Motor Kings 1976.
Memberships: AEA; AFTRA; SAG.
Theater: Crown in Porgy and Bess (tour) 1952-1953; The Connection
     (O. B.) 1959; Finian's Rainbow (City Center) 1960; The Rocks
     Cried Out (San Francisco) 1960; The Death of Bessie Smith
     (O. B.) 1961; Blues for Mister Charlie 1964; Once in a Life-
     time (O. B.) 1964; Marco's Millions (O. B.) 1964; Macbeth
     (NYSF) 1966; Two Gentlemen of Verona (tour) 1972; Hallelujah
     (O. B.) 1973; The Man in the Glass Booth.

McDANIEL, HATTIE "The Colored Sophie Tucker"; "The Female
    Bert Williams"
    (Actress)
b. June 10, 1895, Wichita, Kans.
d. October 26, 1952, San Fernando Valley, Calif.
Education: East Denver High School.
Honors: First black recipient of an Oscar award (for best per-
    formance in a supporting role in Gone with the Wind) 1940;
    Black Filmmakers Hall of Fame (posthumously) 1975.
Clubs: Sam Pick's Suburban Inn (Milwaukee).
Films: The Golden West, Blonde Venus, Hypnotized, Washington
    Masquerade 1932; I'm No Angel, The Story of Temple Drake
    1933; Operator 13, Little Men, Judge Priest, Lost in the
    Stratosphere, Babbitt, Imitation of Life 1934; Music Is Magic;
    China Seas, Another Face, Alice Adams, The Little Colonel,
    The Travelling Saleslady 1935; Gentle Julia, The First Baby,
    High Tension, Star for a Night, Can This Be Dixie?, Reunion,
    Showboat, Postal Inspector, Hearts Divided, The Bride Walks
    Out, Big Time Vaudeville Reels (shorts), Valiant Is the Word
    for Carrie, Next Time We Love, Libeled Lady, The Singing
    Kid 1936; Don't Tell the Wife, Racing Lady, The Crime Nobody
    Saw, True Confession, Saratoga, Over the Goal, 45 Fathers,
    Nothing Sacred, The Wildcatter 1937; Battle of Broadway,
    Everybody's Baby, Shopworn Angel 1938; The Shining Hour,
    The Mad Miss Manton, Mammy in Gone with the Wind, Zenobia
    1939; Maryland 1940; Affectionately Yours, The Great Lie, They
    Died with Their Boots On 1941; The Male Animal, In This Our
    Life, George Washington Slept Here, Reap the Wild Wind 1942;
    Thank Your Lucky Stars, Johnny Come Lately 1943; Since You
    Went Away, Janie, Three Is a Family 1944; Hi Beautiful 1945;
    Margie, Never Say Goodbye, Janie Gets Married 1946; Song of
    the South 1947; The Flame, Mr. Blandings Builds His Dream
    House, Mickey 1948; Family Honeymoon, The Big Wheel 1949.
Memberships: SAG.
Radio: The Eddie Cantor Show; Amos 'n' Andy Show; title role in
    Hi Hat Hattie 1931; Mammy in Show Boat; title role in Beulah
    (series) 1947-51; The Billie Burke Show.
Television: Title role in Beulah (series) 1951.
Theater: Member, Prof. George Morrison's Colored Orchestra (Pan-
    tages Circuit) 1924-25.
Relationships: Sister of Sam McDaniel, actor.

McDANIEL, SAM "Deacon"
    (Actor)
b. c. 1896, Wichita, Kan.
d. September 25, 1962, Los Angeles, Calif.
Films: Belle of the Nineties, Polo Joe, Operator 13, The Lemon
    Drop Kid 1934; George White's Scandals of 1935, Unwelcome
    Stranger, Lady Tubbs, The Virginia Judge 1935; Hearts Di-
    vided 1936; Dark Manhattan, Captains Courageous, Bargain
    with Bullets 1937; Sergeant Murphy 1938; Gambling Ship, Pride
    of the Bluegrass 1939; Calling All Husbands, Am I Guilty 1940;

The Great Lie, South of Panama, Broadway Limited, Birth of
the Blues, New York Town, Bad Men of Missouri, Louisiana
Purchase 1941; All Through the Night, Johnny Doughboy, Sullivan's Travels, Mr. and Mrs. North, The Traitor Within, I
Was Framed, Mokey 1942; Dixie Dugan, The Ghost and the
Guest, Gangway for Tomorrow, Three Little Sisters 1943; Adventures of Mark Twain, Home in Indiana 1944; A Guy a Gal
and a Pal 1945; Joe Palooka-Champ, Gentleman Joe Palooka
1946; I Wonder Who's Kissing Her Now, The Egg and I, The
Foxes of Harrow 1947; Heart of Virginia, Secret Service In-
vestigator 1948; Flamingo Road 1949; Girl's School 1950.
Relationships: Brother of Hattie McDaniel, actress.

McEACHIN, JAMES (Elton)
     (Actor)
b.   May 20, 1930, Rennert, North Carolina.
Special Interests: Directing, writing.
Address: 100 Universal City Plaza, Universal City, Calif. 91608.
Honors: Purple Heart.
Career Data: Working at Universal Studios since 1969.
Films: Uptight, If He Hollers, Let Him Go 1968; True Grit, Hello
     Dolly, The Undefeated 1969; Play Misty for Me 1971; Buck
     and the Preacher, The Groundstar Conspiracy, Short Walk to
     Daylight, Fuzz 1972.
Memberships: AFTRA; SAG.
Television: The FBI; Hawaii Five O; Mannix; Marcus Welby, M. D. ;
     Ironside; O'Hara; Chase; Six Million Dollar Man; Petrocelli;
     Then Came Bronson 1969; The Time Is Now (Name of the
     Game) 1970; That Certain Summer 1972; The Judge and Jake
     Wyler 1972; title role in Tenafly (series) 1973; Emergency
     1974; Harry O 1974; Rockford Files 1974; Night Train to L. A.
     (McMillan and Wife) 1975; The Dead Don't Die 1975; Police
     Story 1975, 76; Invisible Man 1975; Adam-12 1975; Kingston
     Confidential 1977.

McFERRIN, ROBERT
     (Opera Singer)
b.   March 19, 1921, Marianna Ark.
Education: Fisk University 1940-41; Chicago Musical College 1941-
     42, 1946-48; B. M. Kathryn Turney Long School 1953.
Career Data: New England Opera Co. (Boston) 1950; first black
     male performer at Metropolitan Opera (debut) 1955; San Carlo
     Opera Co. (Naples) 1956; roles include: Orestes in Iphigenia
     in Tauris, Tonio in Pagliacci, Rigoletto, Faust, Amonasro in
     Aida; guest professor (voice), Sibelius Academy, Helsinki, Fin-
     land 1959; staff member, Nelson School of Fine Arts, Nelson,
     B. C. , Canada 1961; teacher, St. Louis (Mo.) conservatory;
     visiting prof. (voice), Roosevelt University (Chicago) 1976-77.
Films: Porgy and Bess (voice of Porgy) 1959.
Theater: Lost in the Stars 1949; Troubled Island (City Center) 1949;
     The Green Pastures 1951; My Darlin' Aida 1952; appeared at

Carnegie Hall; Teatro San Carlo (Naples); Lewisohn Stadium 1954.

McGEE, VONETTA (Lawrence Vonetta McGee Jr.)
(Actress)
b. San Francisco, Calif.
Education: San Francisco State College; University of California at Berkeley.
Special Interests: Buddhism.
Films: The Lost Man 1969; Blacula, Hammer, title role in Melinda 1972; Detroit 9000, Shaft in Africa 1973; Thomasine & Bushrod 1974; The Eiger Sanction 1975; Brothers 1977.
Memberships: SAG.
Television: Tonight Show; Tattletales; The Norliss Tapes 1973; Police Woman 1975; Ebony Music Awards Show 1975; Black News 1975.

McGREGOR, CHARLES
(Actor)
b. New York, N.Y.
Films: Fat Freddie in Super Fly, The French Connection 1972; Three the Hard Way, Blazing Saddles 1974; That's the Way of the World, Take a Hard Ride, Aaron Loves Angela 1975; Baron Wolfgang Von Tripps 1976.
Memberships: SAG.
Television: Mike Douglas Show 1974.

McIVER, RAY
(Playwright)
Theater: Wrote God Is a (Guess What?) 1968.

McKAYLE, DONALD (Cohen)
(Dancer/Choreographer)
b. July 6, 1930, New York, N.Y.
Education: City College of N.Y. 1947-49; New Dance Group Studio 1947; Martha Graham School of Contemporary Dance 1948; studied with Pearl Primus, Merce Cunningham.
Special Interests: Teaching, directing, designing.
Honors: 12th Annual Capezio Dance Award 1963; Tony nominee (for Raisin) 1973.
Career Data: Teacher at Juilliard School of Music, Sarah Lawrence College, Bennington College, Neighborhood Playhouse, New Dance Group, Martha Graham School; guest artist with Dudley-Maslow-Bales Dance Co. 1948-51 and Jean Erdman Dance Co. 1948-53; Anna Sokolow Dance Theatre 1954-55; advisor for cultural program of Tunisian Government 1964; Inner City Dance Company.
Clubs: Staged Rita Moreno's act at El Rancho Vegas (Las Vegas) 1957; Helen Gallagher's act at Hotel Plaza's Persian Room 1958; Belafonte Folk Choir Act at Village Gate 1960.

Films: Edge of the City 1957; Jazz on a Summer's Day 1959; On
the Sound 1960; Great White Hope 1970.
Memberships: AEA; AFTRA; AGMA; AGVA; ASCAP.
Musical Compositions: Black New World; Games 1951; Her Name
Was Harriet 1952; Nocturne 1953; Rainbow 'Round My Shoulder
1959; District Storyville 1962; Blood of the Lamb 1963.
Records: Co-authored and narrated Come and See the Peppermint
Tree (Wash. D. C.) 1959; sang in Sometime, Anytime (Wash.
D. C.) 1960.
Television: Bill Cosby Show; Fred Waring Show 1951-52; Folio
(CBC Canada) 1957; They Called Her Moses (Camera Three)
1960; Quest (CBC Canada) 1962; choreographed and danced
The Ghost of Mr. Kicks (Repertory Workshop) 1963; choreo-
graphed Baseball Ballet (Exploring) 1963; choreographed and
danced in Amahl and the Night Visitors (NBC Opera) 1963;
Strollin' Twenties (special) 1966; The Leslie Uggams Show
1969; Academy Awards Show 1971.
Theater: American Dance Festival (New London, Conn.) 1948-63;
danced and choreographed Just a Little Simple 1950; danced
with N. Y. C. Dance Theatre (City Center) 1950; danced in
Bless You All 1950; danced in The Dybbuk (City Center) 1952;
danced in B. de Rothschild Dance Festival (ANTA) 1953;
danced in repertoire of N. Y. C. Opera Co. (City Center) 1954;
danced in House of Flowers 1954; choreographed 1-2-3 Follow
Me (O. B.) 1957; Out of the Chrysallis (Juilliard Dance Theatre)
1957; danced in Show Boat (Jones Beach) 1957; dance captain
for West Side Story 1957; danced and choreographed Copper
and Brass 1957; stage director for An Evening with Belafonte
(tour) 1958; assoc. choreographer for Redhead 1959; choreographed Semele (summer) 1959; directed Album Leaves (Festival of the Two Worlds) Spoleto 1960; directed and choreographed
Free and Easy 1960; choreographer for Kicks and Co. (Chicago) 1961; choreographed The Tempest, Antony and Cleopatra,
As You Like It (NYSF) 1963; choreographed and danced in
August Fanfare (Philharmonic Hall) 1963; choreographed Reflections in the Park (for Modern Jazz Society) 1964; choreographed Golden Boy 1964; choreographed Daughters of the Garden (Israel) 1964; Trumpets of the Lord (O. B.) 1964; choreographed Raisin 1973; choreographed and directed Dr. Jazz
1975; choreographed 1600 Pennsylvania Avenue 1976; choreographed Blood Memories 1976.

MACKEY, WILLIAM WELLINGTON
(Playwright)
b. Miami, Fla.
Theater: Wrote Behold! Cometh the Vanderkellans 1965; Billy No
Name (musical) 1970; Homeboys; Death of Charlie Blackman;
Family Meeting 1973; Love Me, Love Me, Daddy or I Swear
I'm Gonna Kill You; Requiem for Brother X Saga (musical)
1973.

McKINNEY, NINA MAE
    (Actress)
b.   1913, Lancaster, S. C.
d.   May 3, 1967, New York, N. Y.
Clubs: Chez Florence (Paris).
Films: Chick in Hallelujah 1929; Safe in Hell 1931; Pie Pie Black-
      birds 1932; The Devil's Daughter, Kentucky Minstrels (a. k. a.
      Life Is Real) 1934; Sanders of the River, Reckless 1935;
      Black Network 1936; St. Louis Gal, Gang Smashers 1938;
      Straight to Heaven, Pocomania 1939; Dark Waters, Together
      Again 1944; Without Love 1945; Mantan Messes Up, Night
      Train to Memphis 1946; Danger Street 1947; Pinky 1949.
Theater: London Palladium 1928; Lew Leslie's Blackbirds 1928;
      appeared at Apollo Theatre 1939; Good Neighbor 1941; Sadie
      Thompson in Rain (Brooklyn) 1951.

MacLACHLAN, JANET (Angel)
    (Actress)
b.   New York, N. Y.
Education: Hunter College B. A. , studied acting with Lee Grant,
      Sidney Poitier and Herbert Berghof.
Address: c/o Global Business Management, 9601 Wilshire Blvd. ,
      Beverly Hills, Calif. 90210.
Career Data: Tyrone Guthrie Theatre, Minneapolis (appeared in
      Hamlet, The Miser, Death of a Salesman).
Films: Uptight 1968; Change of Mind 1969; Tick... Tick... Tick... ,
      Darker Than Amber, Halls of Anger 1960; school teacher in
      Sounder, The Man 1972; Maurie 1973.
Television: A Glow of Dying Embers (Love Story); Bill Cosby Show;
      The F. B. I. ; Longstreet; Streets of San Francisco; I Spy 1967;
      Ironside 1968; Mod Squad 1969; C. B. S. Playhouse 1969; Name
      of the Game 1970; Mary Tyler Moore Show 1971; Cutter 1972;
      Love Thy Neighbor (series) 1973; Trouble Comes to Town
      1973; Medical Center 1974; Rockford Files 1975; The Blue
      Knight 1975; Manhunter 1975; S. W. A. T. 1975; Six Million Dol-
      lar Man 1975; Ellery Queen 1976; Dark Victory 1976; Louis
      Armstrong-Chicago Style 1976; Barney Miller 1976; Chlorox
      commercial 1976; What's Happening 1976; Most Wanted 1977;
      Wonder Woman 1977; Rafferty 1977.
Theater: The Dollar (O. B.); Ivanov (O. B.); Paradise Lost (O. B.);
      The Devil and Daniel Webster (O. B.); Race with the Wind
      (O. B.); The Blacks (O. B.) 1961; Tiger, Tiger Burning Bright
      1962; Raisin' Hell in the Son (O. B.) 1962.

McNAIR, BARBARA (J.)
    (Singer/Actress)
b.   March 4, 1939, Racine, Wis.
Education: U. S. C. (L. A.).
Special Interests: Guitar.
Clubs: Caesar's Palace (Las Vegas); Coconut Grove (Las Vegas);
      Riviera (Las Vegas); Village Vanguard; Purple Onion; Plaza

Hotel Persian Room 1966, 75; Carlton Inn (Three Rivers,
Wisc.) 1975; Kutscher Stardust Room (Monticello, N. Y.) 1976.

Films: Spencer's Mountain (sang) 1962; If He Hollers Let Him Go
1968; Stiletto 1969; They Call Me Mr. Tibbs, Change of Habit,
Venus in Furs 1970; The Organization 1971.

Memberships: AEA; AFTRA; AGVA; SAG.

Publications: The Complete Book of Beauty for Black Women, Prentice-Hall, 1972.

Records: Bobby (Coral).

Television: Arthur Godfrey's Talent Scouts; Ed Sullivan Show; Danny Kaye Show; Password; Dr. Kildare; Celebrity Sweepstakes;
Mission: Impossible; Dean Martin Show; hosted Schaefer
Circle (series) 1960-61; Eleventh Hour 1964; Something Special
1966; The Most in Music 1966; I Spy 1967; Hogan's Heroes
1967; The Lonely Profession 1969; The Barbara McNair Show
(series) 1969; To Rome with Love 1970; McMillan and Wife
1972; Mod Squad 1972; Jack Paar Show 1973; Mike Douglas
Show 1974; Merv Griffin Show 1974; Hollywood Freeway 1974;
Tattletales 1975; You Don't Say 1975; All Stars 1975; The
American Freeway (special) 1975; Match Game 1975; Kup's
Show 1975; Vaudeville (Wide World Special) 1975; Rhyme and
Reason 1976; Celebrity Tennis 1976.

Theater: Guys and Dolls; The Body Beautiful (debut) 1958; The
Merry World of Nat King Cole (Philadelphia) 1961; No Strings
(replacing Diahann Carroll) 1963; Pajama Game 1973.

McNEIL, CLAUDIA
(Actress)
b. August 13, 1917, Baltimore, Md.
Education: Studied acting with Maria Ouspenskaya.
Special Interests: Singing, Yiddish.
Honors: Tony nomination (for Tiger, Tiger, Burning Bright) 1962
and Emmy nomination (for The Nurses episode) 1963.
Career Data: First stage appearance at Duxbury (Mass.) Playhouse;
appearances at Ann Arbor (Mich.) Drama Festival; vocalist
with Katherine Dunham Dance Co. tour of South America.
Clubs: Black Cat (debut) 1933; The Famous Door; The Onyx; The
Greenwich Village Inn.
Films: The Last Angry Man (debut) 1959; Lena Younger in A Raisin
in the Sun 1961; There Was a Crooked Man 1970; Black Girl
1972.
Memberships: AEA; AFTRA; SAG.
Radio: Program coordinator and entertainer, Jamaican Broadcasting
Co. (Kingston) 1951-52.
Television: Molly Goldberg Show; Camera Three; Personal Story;
Spotlight; Berenice in Member of the Wedding (Dupont Show of
the Month) 1958; Simply Heavenly (Play of the Week) 1959; Look
Up and Live 1959; Express Stop from Lenox Avenue (The Nur-
ses) 1963; Profiles in Courage 1965; Do Not Go Gentle into
That Good Night (CBS Playhouse) 1967; Incident in San Fran-
cisco 1971; To Be Young, Gifted and Black (NET Playhouse)
1972; Mod Squad 1972; Moon of the Wolf 1972; Cry Panic 1974;
Kup's Show 1975; American Woman: Portraits of Courage 1976.

Theater: Mamie in Simply Heavenly (debut O. B.) 1957; The Crucible
        (O. B.) 1958; Winesburg Ohio 1958; Lena Younger in A Raisin
        in the Sun 1959; Tiger, Tiger Burning Bright 1962; The Amen
        Corner (London) 1965; Something Different 1967; Her First
        Roman 1968; Wrong Way Light Bulb; Contribution (O. B.) 1970.

McPHATTER, CLYDE
        (Singer)
b.   1931, Durham, N. C.
d.   June 13, 1972, Teaneck, N. J.
Career Data: Member of The Dominoes 1950-53, The Drifters
        1953-54.
Records: On Atlantic: Seven Days 1955; Treasure of Love 1956;
        A Lover's Question 1958. On MGM: Let's Try It Again
        1959. On Mercury: Lover Please.
Theater: Appeared at Apollo Theatre.

McQUEEN, BUTTERFLY (Thelma McQueen)
        (Actress)
b.   January 8, 1911, Tampa, Fla.
Education: City College of New York B. A. 1975; C. C. L. A. 1946;
        U. C. L. A. (Westwood) 1946; Queens College 1952; studied
        dance with Katherine Dunham, Geoffrey Holder and Janet Col-
        lins; studied singing with Adelaide Hall.
Special Interests: The Classics, dancing, singing, teaching, Spanish.
Address: 405 West 147 Street, New York, N. Y. 10031.
Honors: Rosemary awards 1973; Black Filmmakers Hall of Fame
        award 1975.
Career Data: Performed "Butterfly" ballet with Venezuela Jones
        Negro Youth Group 1935; taught acting at Southern Illinois
        University, Mt. Morris Park Recreation Center.
Clubs: Sang at Blue Angel; Village Vanguard; Snookies.
Films: Prissy in Gone with the Wind, The Women 1939; Affection-
        ately Yours 1941; Cabin in the Sky, I Dood It 1943; Since You
        Went Away (scenes deleted) 1944; Mildred Pierce, Flame of
        the Barbary Coast 1945; Vashti in Duel in the Sun 1947; Killer
        Diller 1948; The Phynx 1970; Amazing Grace (Cameo) 1974.
Memberships: AEA; AFTRA; AGVA; SAG.
Publications: Prissy in C. Jew York, 1974.
Radio: The Goldbergs (debut); The Dinah Shore Show; The Jack
        Benny Show; Vivian in The Beulah Show (series); The Danny
        Kaye Show.
Records: Polly/Nature Fills World with Love (Butterfly) 1973.
Television: Mike Wallace Show; Virginia Graham Show; Dating Game;
        Give Us Our Dream (Studio One) 1950; Oriole in Beulah (series)
        1950; The Green Pastures (Hallmark Hall of Fame) 1957; Today
        Show 1968; Mike Douglas Show 1968; Black Pride 1975.
Theater: Brother Rat 1937; Brown Sugar 1937; What a Life 1938;
        Swingin' the Dream 1939; Harvey (black cast tour) 1946; One
        Woman Show (Carnegie Recital Hall) 1951; The World's My
        Oyster (O. B.) 1956; The Athenian Touch (O. B.) 1964; Curley

McDimple (O. B.) 1968; Butterfly McQueen and Friends (O. B.)
1969; Three Men on a Horse 1969; Concert (Alice Tully Hall)
1973; The Wiz (pre-Bway) 1975; Prissy in Person (Harlem)
1975; Town Hall (5:45 Interlude series) 1976.

McRAE, CARMEN
    (Singer)
b.   April 8, 1922, New York, N. Y.
Special Interests: Piano.
Address: c/o Mainstream Records, 1700 Broadway, New York,
    N. Y. 10019.
Honors: Down Beat's new star 1954.
Career Data: Performed with bands of Benny Carter 1944, Mercer
    Ellington 1946-47, Count Basie; co-owner (with Della Reese)
    of boutique.
Clubs: Minton's; Buddy's Place 1975; Dangerfield's 1976, 1977.
Films: Hotel 1967.
Records: Ms. Jazz; I Am Music; Live at the Dug; Alive (Main-
    stream); As Time Goes By (Catalyst); Can't Hide Love (Blue
    Note); Carmen McRae (Mainstream); Carmen's Gold (Main-
    stream); For Once in My Life (Atlantic); Great American Song-
    book (Atlantic); I Am Music (Blue Note); I Want You (Main-
    stream); Just a Little Lovin' (Atlantic); Live and Doin' It
    (Mainstream); Mad About the Man (Stanyan); Portrait (Atlantic);
    Sound of Silence (Atlantic); Velvet Soul (Groove Merchant);
    Take Five (Columbia Special Products); So Easy to Love (Beth-
    lehem).
Television: Soul 1974; Sammy and Company 1976.
Theater: Appearance at Avery Fisher Hall 1975.

MADAME SUL TE WAN see WAN, MADAME SUL TE

MAHAL, TAJ (Henry Fredericks)
    (Musician)
Education: University of Massachusetts.
Clubs: The Bottom Line 1975, 1976.
Films: Ike in Sounder 1972; Part 2 Sounder 1976; Brothers (score)
    1977.
Records: On Columbia: Recycling the Blues; Satisfied 'n Tickled
    Too; Mo' Roots; Music Keeps Me Together; Giant Step/De Ole
    Folks; Happy to Be Like; Natch'l Blues; Oooh So Good; Real
    Thing.
Television: Boarding House 1975; Mark of Jazz 1976; Apollo
    Theatre (special) 1976; At the Top 1976; Dinah! 1976.
Theater: Appeared at Carnegie Hall 1975; Beacon Theatre 1976.

MAJOR, TONY (Anthony Major)
    (Actor/Producer)
b.   November 20, 1939, Sarasota, Fla.

Education: City College of New York 1958; Hofstra University B. A.
       (Theatre Arts) 1964; New York University M. F. A. 1973; studied
       with Brett Warren at Actors Mobile Theatre.
Special Interests: Directing, music, teaching, writing.
Address: 400 Central Park West, New York, N. Y. 10025.
Honors: Distinguished Service Award from Mayor Lindsay, N. Y. C.
       (for Up the Down Staircase) 1966; Honorable mention, Balti-
       more Film Festival (for Off-Duty) 1973.
Career Data: Worked with New York Shakespeare Festival 1964;
       founder and director, The Tony Major Grassroots Theatre
       1965; served on bd. of dir. , Mayor Lindsay's Operation Youth
       Network (which trained youth in film, television and radio);
       advisor to Vice-President Humphrey's Youth Council 1968.
Films: Acted in No Way to Treat a Lady 1966; production asst.
       and acted in Up the Down Staircase 1967; acted in For Love
       of Ivy 1968; drama coach for Halls of Anger 1970; production
       asst. and acted in The Angel Levine 1970; production asst. ,
       asst. director and actor in The Landlord 1970; acted in Hitch
       1970; asst. dir. for The Pursuit of Happiness 1971; production
       asst. for The French Connection 1971; acted in Shaft's Big
       Score, Come Back Charleston Blue, Across 110th Street, Bang
       the Drum Slowly 1972; wrote, directed and edited Off-Duty
       (short) 1972; asst. director for Ganja & Hess (a. k. a. Blood
       Couple) 1973; wrote, directed and produced Super Spook 1975.
Memberships: AEA; SAG.
Radio: Community Coordinator, WWRL (Woodside, N. Y.).
Records: Writer and producer for The Sparks (M. G. M.) 1968 and
       Super Spook (sound track) 1975.
Television: Cast coordinator for Harry and Lena (special) 1969;
       production asst. for To Be Young, Gifted and Black 1971; pro-
       duction supervisor for J. T. (Pilot) 1973.
Theater: Hello Out There; Happy Ending (O. B.) 1967; A Raisin in
       the Sun (stock) 1968; Transfers (O. B.) 1970; In New England
       Winter (O. B.) 1971; Candidate (O. B.) 1974; We Interrupt This
       Program ... 1975.

MAKEBA, MIRIAM (Zensi Miriam Makeba)
       (Singer)
b.   March 4, 1934, Prospect Township, Johannesburg, Union of
       South Africa.
Education: Kilmerton Training Institute (Pretoria).
Special Interests: Black liberation, composing.
Honors: Grammy 1965; Guinea delegate to U. S. 1975.
Career Data: Vocalist with Black Mountain Brothers (touring South
       Africa, Rhodesia and Belgian Congo) 1954-57; Venice Film
       Festival 1959.
Clubs: Village Vanguard 1960; Blue Angel; Waldorf Astoria Empire
       Room; The Village Gate 1963; Basin Street East 1964; The
       Crescendo (L. A.); Ciro's (L. A.); Storyville (Boston).
Films: Come Back Africa 1958.
Memberships: ASCAP 1951.
Musical Compositions: Unhome; Amampondo Dubula; Pole Mze;
       Boot Dance; Mangwene Mpulele.

Records: The Voice of Africa; Popular Songs & African Folk Songs
          (RCA); Miriam Makeba (RCA); The World of Miriam Makeba
          (RCA); Makeba Sings (RCA); The Click Song (a. k. a. Qonqon-
          thwane); Wimoweh (a. k. a. Mbube); Back of the Moon; The
          Many Voices of Miriam Makeba (Kapp); Miriam Makeba in
          Concert (Reprise).
Television: Steve Allen Show (debut) 1959; Soul; Like It Is.
Theater: King Kong: a Jazz opera (South Africa) 1959; appearances
          at Carnegie Hall 1961; New York Philharmonic Hall 1964;
          Forest Hills Stadium (with Harry Belafonte) 1964.
Relationships: Former wife of Stokely Carmichael, civil rights leader;
          former wife of Hugh Masekela, musician; former wife of Sonny
          Pillay, ballad singer.

MAPP, JIM E.
     (Actor/Producer)
Education: Cambridge School of Radio Broadcasting; Wolter School
          of Speech and Drama, Carnegie Hall; Bown Adams Professional
          School.
Career Data: Founder, Playward Bus Theatre Repertory Co., Phila-
          delphia 1965.
Films: Trick Baby 1973.
Memberships: AEA.
Theater: Acted in Another Part of the Forest (ELT); Deep Are the
          Roots; You Can't Take It with You; Murder without Crime;
          The Last Seconds.

MARKHAM, DEWEY "Pigmeat"
     (Comedian)
b.   April 18, 1906, Durham, N. C.
Address: 100-20 Darrow Place, Bronx, N. Y. 10475.
Career Data: Toured as child star with Gilliscarnivals 1919.
Films: Hellcats; Junction 88; Swanee Showboat; The Wrong Mr.
          Right; Gang War 1939; Am I Guilty?, Mr. Smith Goes Ghost,
          One Big Mistake 1940; Fight That Ghost, Shut My Big Mouth,
          House Rent Party 1946; Pigmeat's Laugh Hepcats 1947.
Radio: Alamo in Eight to the Bar (Andrew Sisters series).
Records: Here Come de Judge; Crap Shootin' Reverend (Jewel);
          Would the Real Pig Meat Please Sit Down (Jewel); Moms
          Mabley and Pigmeat Markham (Chess).
Television: The Ed Sullivan Show.
Theater: Regal Theatre (Chicago); Paramount Theatre; Howard
          Theatre (Washington, D. C.); Lincoln Theatre (L. A.); Standard
          Theatre (Philadelphia); Alhambra Theatre 1928; Apollo Theatre
          (on and off since 1935); Hot Rhythm 1930; Cocktails of 1932.

MARRIOTT, JOHN
     (Actor)
b.   September 30, 1893, Boley, Okla.
d.   April 5, 1977, Jamaica, N. Y.

Education: Wilberforce University B. S.; Ohio State University.
Career Data: Karamu Players (Cleveland, Ohio) 1922-34.
Films: The Little Foxes 1941; The Joe Louis Story 1953; The
    Court Martial of Billy Mitchell 1955; The Cool World, Black
    Like Me 1964; Badge 373 1973; Dog Day Afternoon 1975.
Memberships: AEA; AFTRA; SAG.
Television: Love of Life; Omnibus; Kraft Theatre; Edge of Night;
    If You Give a Dance, You Gotta Pay the Band (ABC Theatre)
    1972.
Theater: Too Many Boats (debut) 1934; Sweet River 1936; Chalked
    Out 1937; Janie 1942; No Way Out 1944; The Iceman Cometh
    1946; How I Wonder 1947; The Respectful Prostitute 1948; The
    Small Hours 1951; The Green Pastures 1951; The Ponder
    Heart 1956; Season of Choice (O. B.) 1959; Bicycle Ride to
    Nevada (O. B.); Arturo Ui 1963; Death of the Well Loved Boy
    (O. B.); More Stately Mansions 1967; Weekend 1968; The Last
    Meeting of the Knights of the White Magnolia 1976.

MARRS, STELLA "Miss Soft Soul" (Stella Booker)
    (Jazz Singer)
b.   March 22, 1932, New York, N. Y.
Education: New Heritage Repertory Theatre Workshop.
Special Interests: Poetry, art, acting.
Address: 1700 Grand Concourse, Bronx, N. Y. 10457.
Honors: The Jazz at Home Club's jazz achievement award 1972;
    Westchester Jazz Society award 1975; Jazz Honor Citation Bi-
    centennial Jazz Program Kick-off.
Career Data: Toured as vocalist with Lionel Hampton band 1969,
    1972-73; toured colleges and universities in concert.
Clubs: Blue Coronet; Pier 83; Steer Inn (Freeport, L. I.); Executive
    Suite; The Cookery; Needle's Eye; Boomer's; Fiddlestix; Rain-
    bow Grill; Losers Club (Dallas); Stardust Lounge (Las Vegas);
    Shamrock Hilton (Houston); Jimmy Westons; Club Sanno; Car-
    mine's Copa (Bklyn.); Dunes (Las Vegas); Hotel Pontchartrain
    (Houston); Plaza Nine and All That Jazz; CBC (Ottawa); Jazz
    at Home (Philad.); Richie's Lounge (Lakewood, N. J.); Vin-
    cent's Place 1975; Seafood Playhouse 1975; Rust Brown's 1975.
Films: Cotton Comes to Harlem, Angel Levine, The Landlord,
    Where's Poppa 1970; Pursuit of Happiness 1971; Hot Rock,
    Come Back Charleston Blue 1972; Badge 373 1973.
Memberships: AFTRA; SAG.
Radio: Hosted Jazz with Stella Marrs (WRVR); disc jockey on WHBI;
    Arthur Godfrey Show; Perspective (WLIB); programs in Aus-
    tralia and Las Vegas.
Records: Anyone Can Whistle (Grenider).
Television: Hosted Applauds (teleprompter cable TV) 1972; The
    Stella Marrs Show (teleprompter cable TV on Channel D);
    Tommie Leonette Show (Sidney, Australia); Joe Delaney Show
    (Las Vegas) and other shows in Australia and Las Vegas; Posi-
    tively Black 1975.
Theater: Wrote, produced and acted in I a Black Woman; Emmet
    Till Story (O. B.); Collud Folks (O. B.); Community Kitchen

(O. B.).   Appearances at Brooklyn Academy of Music; Town
Hall; New York Jazz Museum; Avery Fisher Hall 1974; International Art of Jazz Ensemble Concert (Northport, N. Y.) 1976.

MARSHALL, DON
(Actor)
Films: Sergeant Ryker 1960; Dr. Williams in The Thing with Two
Heads 1972; Uptown Saturday Night 1974.
Memberships: SAG.
Television: Julia (series); Star Trek; Alfred Hitchcock Presents;
Great Gettin' Up Mornin' (Repertoire Workshop) 1964; Police
Story 1975; Good Times 1976; Benny and Barney: Las Vegas
Undercover 1977.

MARSHALL, WILLIAM
(Actor)
b. 1924, Gary, Ind.
Education: New York University; American Theater Wing.
Special Interests: Composing, directing, teaching.
Address: 11351 Dronfield Avenue, Pacoima, Calif. 91331.
Honors: Black Filmmakers Hall of Fame 1974.
Career Data: Toured U. S. with Mahalia Jackson 1966; professor
and director of Theatrecraft workshop, San Fernando Valley
College, Northridge, Calif. 1969-; lecturer, Brooklyn College
(Martin Luther King series) 1971.
Films: Lydia Bailey 1952; Demetrius and the Gladiators 1954;
Something of Value 1957; Sabu and the Magic Ring 1958; The
Boston Strangler, The Hell with Heroes 1968; Skullduggery
1970; Honky 1971; title role in Blacula 1972; Scream, Blacula
Scream 1973; Abby 1974; Twilight's Last Gleaming 1977.
Radio: Tallulah Bankhead Show; The Long Voyage Home (NBC's
Best Plays).
Television: Othello (Omnibus); Oedipus Rex (Omnibus); Rawhide;
Patterns for Living; Interpol (London); host and narrator, The
Black Frontier (doc. series); Tarzan; Ben Casey; Star Trek;
Bonanza; Harlem Detective (series) 1953-54; Zig Zag 1970;
directed and appeared in The Tragedy of King Christophe 1970;
Mike Douglas Show 1975; title role in Tragedy of King Chris-
tophe (KNBC, Los Angeles) 1976; Rosetti and Ryan: Men Who
Love Women 1977.
Theater: Trial by Fire; The Virtuous Island (O. B.); Time to Go;
When We Dead Awaken; Carmen Jones (debut) 1944; Jeb 1946;
Our Lan' (O. B.) 1947; Set My People Free 1948; Call Me
Mister 1948; Lost in the Stars 1949; De Lawd in Green Pas-
tures 1951; Peter Pan 1954; title role in Othello 1958; Toys
in the Attic 1960; The Bear and the Marriage Proposal (France)
1961; directed The Long Voyage Home (Paris) 1962; Javelin
(O. B.) 1966; narrated Copland's A Lincoln Portrait (Gary,
Indiana) 1967; Stravinsky's Oedipus Rex (Chicago) 1968; Sieg-
meister's I Have a Dream (Los Angeles) 1969; title role in
Othello (San Diego) 1976; Timbuktu (pre-Bway) 1977.

MARTIN, D'URVILLE
   (Actor)
b. February 11, 1939, New York, N. Y.
Education: Studied at American Community Theatre 1960.
Special Interests: Directing, producing.
Address: 1101 S. Alfred Street, Los Angeles, Calif. 90035.
Honors: Clio (for Join commercial) 1965.
Career Data: Co-founder, Abel/D'Urville Enterprises; artistic di-
   rector, Board of Afro-American Total Theatre.
Films: Co-produced and photographed Madame; grip for The Cool
   World, Black Like Me 1964; Guess Who's Coming to Dinner
   1967; Rosemary's Baby, A Time to Sing 1968; Cotton Comes
   to Harlem, Watermelon Man 1970; The Legend of Nigger Char-
   ley, Hammer, co-produced and acted in The Final Comedown
   1972; Booker T in Five on the Black Hand Side, Black Caesar,
   Book of Numbers, Hell Up in Harlem, The Soul of Nigger
   Charley 1973; The Zebra Killer 1974; Sheba Baby, Boss Nigger,
   directed and acted in Dolomite 1975; directed and acted in
   Black Samurai, Death Journey 1976.
Memberships: AEA; AFTRA; Directors Guild; SAG.
Radio: Satchmo (Armed Services) 1966.
Television: Man from U. N. C. L. E. 1965; Name of the Game 1968;
   The Bold Ones 1971; Joe and Sons 1975.
Theater: Staged The Blacks (benefit for Mfundi Institute); Sisyphus
   and the Blue-Eyed Cyclops (Studio-West, California); acted in
   Cabin in the Sky (O. B.) 1964; acted in The Toilet (O. B.) 1965.

MARTIN, HELEN (Dorothy)
   (Actress)
b. July 28, St. Louis, Mo.
Education: Fisk University; A & I State College; Paul Mann Work-
   shop.
Special Interests: Comedy, dialects, music (piano and singing).
Address: 50 Manhattan Avenue, New York, N. Y. 10025.
Honors: Rose McClendon scholarship 1959.
Career Data: Joined Rose McClendon players 1939; became original
   member of American Negro Theatre 1940.
Films: Phoenix City Story 1955; A Matter of Conviction 1960; Where's
   Poppa, Cotton Comes to Harlem 1970; The Anderson Tapes
   1971; Death Wish 1974.
Memberships: AEA; AFTRA; SAG.
Radio: Honey Turner in Deep Are the Roots (B. B. C.) 1947; disc
   jockey (WOV) 1953; The W. C. Handy Story (WBC); Sounds of
   the City (series).
Television: Big Daddy; On Being Black; The Green Pastures (Hallmark Hall of Fame) 1957; The Bitter Cup (Frontiers of Faith)
   1960; The Nurses 1964; The Defenders 1964; Maude 1973; J. T.
   1973; Good Times 1974; That's My Mama 1975; Scoop's Place
   1975; Police Woman 1975; What's Happening! 1976; Roots 1977;
   Starsky and Hutch 1977.
Theater: Stevedore (ELT); Hits, Bits and Skits 1940; Native Son
   (debut) 1941; Mamba's Daughters (N. Y. C. subway circuit) 1943;

Three's a Family (ANT) 1943; Chicken Every Sunday (stock)
1944; Honey Turner in Deep Are the Roots 1945; (London)
1947; On Striver's Row (ANT) 1946; The Little Foxes (stock);
The Royal Family (stock) 1951; The Petrified Forest (stock)
1951; Poppy in Take a Giant Step 1953; Major Barbara (O. B.)
1954; Reba in You Can't Take It with You (tour) 1954-55; Juno
and the Paycock (O. B.) 1955; Anniversary Waltz (stock) 1955;
King of Hearts (stock) 1956; A Land Beyond the River 1957;
Fever for Life (stock) 1957; The Ballad of Jazz Street (O. B.)
1959; The Long Dream 1960; Period of Adjustment 1960;
Felicity in The Blacks (O. B.) 1961; Missy in Purlie Victorious
1961; Critic's Choice (stock) 1962; My Mother, My Father and
Me 1963; Bobo in The Blacks (O. B.) 1963; The Amen Corner
1964; The Cat and the Canary (O. B.); Purlie 1970; Raisin
1973.

MARTINS, ORLANDO
(Actor)
b.   December 8, 1900, Lagos, Nigeria.
Education: Eko High School, Lagos, Nigeria.
Address: 14-16 Sanniadewali, Lagos, Nigeria.
Career Data: British films and stage.
Films: Seven Waves Away; In Judea; This Book Is News; Murder
    in Soho; Black Libel; If Youth But Knew; Tiger Bay 1933; San-
    ders of the River 1935; Frankie and Johnnie 1936; Jericho,
    Song of Freedom 1937; The Man from Morocco 1944; Men of
    Two Worlds (debut) 1946; End of the River 1947; Blossom in
    The Hasty Heart, Good Time Girl, American Guerilla in the
    Philippines 1950; Where No Vultures Fly, Cry the Beloved
    Country, Kisenga Man of Africa, The Ivory Hunters 1952; The
    Heart of the Matter 1954; Simba, West of Zanzibar 1955; Safari
    1956; Tarzan and the Lost Safari, Abandon Ship 1957; Naked
    Earth 1958; Nun's Story, Sapphire 1959; Killers of Kilimanjaro
    1960; Call Me Bwana 1963; Mister Moses, A Boy Ten Feet
    Tall (a. k. a. Sammy Going South) 1965; Bullfrog in the Sun
    1971.
Memberships: BAEA.
Theater: They Shall Not Die; Colony (alternating with Robert Adams);
    When Blue Hills Laughed 1930; Stevedore 1937; Toussaint L'-
    Ouverture 1938; The Hasty Heart 1945.

MASEKELA, HUGH (Ramapolo)
(Musician)
b.   1939, Johannesburg, South Africa.
Education: Royal Academy of Music (London), Guild Hall School
    (London), Manhattan School of Music.
Special Interests: Composing, trumpet.
Career Data: Led his own jazz quintet 1964; formed Chisa Records
    Company 1966.
Clubs: The East (Brooklyn) 1975; Village Gate 1976.
Films: Monterey Pop 1969.

Records: The Americanization of Ooga Booga; The Emancipation of
Hugh Masekela; The Boy's Doing It (Casablanca); Not Afraid;
Hugh Masekela's Latest--Hugh Masekela Is; Alive and Well at
The Whiskey; Home Is Where the Music Is (Blue Thumb);
Colonial Man (Casablanca); I Am Not Afraid (Blue Thumb);
Introducing Hedzoleh Sounds (Blue Thumb).

Theater: Appeared at King Kong; Carnegie Hall 1975.

Relationships: Former husband of Miriam Makeba, singer.

MASON, CLIFFORD (Lester)
(Playwright/Critic)
b.   March 5, 1932, New York, N. Y.
Education: Queens College B. A. 1958.
Special Interests: Directing, teaching.
Address: 800 West End Avenue, New York, N. Y. 10025.
Career Data: Taught at Manhattanville College and Rutgers Univer-
sity.
Memberships: AEA; Dramatists Guild; New Dramatists.
Publications: "Why Does White America Love Sidney Poitier So?"
in New York Times September 10, 1967; Black Drama Anthology,
Signet, 1970.
Radio: Clifford Mason on Black Theatre (WBAI-FM) 1967.
Television: Documentary on black religion (CBS) 1973.
Theater: Acted as stationmaster in Joseph Papp production of Chek-
hov's Cherry Orchard; wrote Sister Sadie 1970; Jimmy X (one
act) 1971; Gabriel; Midnight Special.

MATHIS, JOHNNY (Royce)
(Singer)
b.   September 30, 1935, San Francisco, Calif.
Education: San Francisco State College.
Address: c/o Rajon Productions, 6290 Sunset Blvd. , Hollywood,
Calif. 90028.
Honors: Second place (to Sinatra's first) in sale of popular music
albums; four albums on "top 100" simultaneously and one for
40 weeks; 18 gold albums.
Career Data: Former track and field athlete; participated in Newport
Jazz Festival 1974.
Clubs: Empire Room--Waldorf Astoria; 440 (San Francisco); Sahara
(Las Vegas); Fairmont (Dallas); Flambouyant (Puerto Rico);
Talk of the Town (London); Latin Casino (N. J.); Black Hawk
(San Francisco).
Films: Lizzie, Wild Is the Wind (sang theme) 1957; A Certain
Smile 1958; The Best of Everything (sang theme) 1959; Walking
Tall (sang theme) 1973.
Records: Tender Is the Night; The Shadow of Your Smile; What'll I
Do; Johnny's Greatest Hits (Columbia); This Is Love; Love Is
Everything; The Sweetheart Tree; Ole; Give Me Your Love for
Christmas (Columbia); Merry Christmas (Columbia); Heart of
Woman (Columbia); Heavenly/Faithfully (Columbia); I Only Have
Eyes for You (Columbia); Mahogany (Columbia); When Will I

See You Again (Columbia); Feelings (Columbia); All Time
Greatest Hits (Columbia); First Time Ever I Saw Your Face
(Columbia); Good Night Dear Lord (Columbia); I'm Coming
Home (Columbia); Impossible Dream (Columbia); In Person
(Columbia); Killing Me Softly; Love Is Blue; Love Story; Love
Theme from Romeo and Juliet; Me and Mrs. Jones; More
Greatest Hits; Music from Bacharach and Kaempfert; Newest
Hits; People; Raindrops Keep Falling; Song Sung Blue; Today
Hits; Warm/Open Fire; You've Got a Friend; Wonderful! Won-
derful 1957; It's Not for Me to Say 1957; Chances Are 1957;
Misty 1959; Maria 1960; On a Clear Day You Can See Forever
1965; Hold Me Thrill Me Kiss Me (Columbia) 1977.
Television: American Bandstand; What's My Line?; Merv Griffin
Show; Phil Donahue Show; Soul Train; Tonight Show; Celebrity
Sweepstakes; Tattletales; Match Game; The Most in Music
1966; Ice Palace 1971; Midday Live 1974; Feeling Good 1975;
The Johnny Mathis Session 1975; Dinah! 1975; Bobby Goldsboro 1975; Mike Douglas Show 1975, 1976; Johnny Mathis in
the Canadian Rockies 1975; Diahann Carroll Show 1976; Once
Upon a Time Is Now (sang theme) 1977.
Theater: Appeared at Garden State Arts Center 1974; Uris Theater
1974; Westbury Music Fair 1975; Westchester Premier Theatre
1975; Shubert Theatre (L. A.) 1976.

MAYFIELD, CURTIS
(Musician)
b. June 3, 1942, Chicago, Ill.
Special Interests: Singing, composing, producing.
Address: 5915 N. Lincoln Avenue, Chicago, Ill. 60659.
Honors: Nomination for Golden Globe and Oscar (for Claudine)
1975; NAACP Image award best musical score (for Let's Do
It Again) 1976.
Career Data: Singer with the Alphatones, the Roosters; lead singer,
the Impressions 1958-70; started his own record company
Curtom Record & Publishing Co. 1970.
Films: Super Fly (score) 1972; Save the Children 1973; Claudine
(score) 1974; Let's Do It Again (score) 1975; Sparkle (score)
1976; Short Eyes (acted and wrote score) 1977.
Musical Compositions: Gypsy Woman; Keep on Pushing; This Is My
Country; Amen; People Get Ready.
Records: Back to the World (Buddah); Sweet Exorcist (Buddah);
Kung Fu (Curtom); Got to Find a Way; America Today (Cur-
tom); Super Fly; Claudine; Let's Do It Again; Give, Get Take
and Have (Curtom); Early Years (ABC).
Television: Bobby Goldsboro; Don Kirshner's Rock Concert 1974,
1975; Soul Train 1975.

MAYFIELD, JULIAN (Hudson)
(Playwright/Actor)
b. June 6, 1928, Greer, S. C.
Education: Lincoln University (Pa.); studied at Paul Mann Actors
Workshop (with Paul Mann, Lloyd Richards) 1951-54.

Special Interests: Directing, teaching.
Address: 235 Gallatin Street, N. W. Washington, D. C. 20011.
Career Data: Actor/playwright, Group 20 Players (Unionville, Conn.)
    1949; playwright, Camp Unity, N. Y. 1962-63; aide to Pres.
    Kwame Nkrumah 1963-66; lecturer, Afro-American Studies,
    University of Maryland.
Films: Wrote and starred as Tank in Uptight 1968; wrote Children
    of Anger (doc.) 1970; wrote The Long Night 1975.
Memberships: AEA; AFTRA; Authors Guild of America; Screen-
    writers Guild of America; PEN.
Records: Leave Them Alone (lyrics) 1954.
Television: Wrote Johnny Staccato (series) 1961.
Theater: Wrote Fire 1949; acted as Brother Martin de Porres in
    City of Kings (Blackfriars Guild) 1949; acted as Absalom in
    Lost in the Stars 1949-50; directed Alice in Wonder (O. B.);
    wrote The Other Foot, World Full of Men 1952; wrote 417.

MAYNOR, DOROTHY
    (Concert Singer)
b.   September 3, 1910, Norfolk, Va.
Education: Studied music with J. Nathaniel Dett at Hampton Insti-
    tute; studied voice with Westminster Choir College (Princeton,
    N. J.).
Special Interests: Lieder, Negro folk songs.
Address: 409 West 141 Street, New York, N. Y. 10031.
Honors: Town Hall Endowment Series award 1939; soloist, U. S.
    President Eisenhower Inauguration 1953; Young Audience annual
    award 1976.
Career Data: Appeared at Berkshire Music Festival 1939; toured
    U. S. , Canada and Latin America; appeared with N. Y. Phil-
    harmonic and Boston, Philadelphia, Chicago, Cleveland, San
    Francisco, Los Angeles symphony orchestras; founder/execu-
    tive director, Harlem School of the Arts 1965-; board mem-
    ber, Metropolitan Opera Assn.
Records: The Art of Dorothy Maynor.
Theater: Appeared at Town Hall (debut) 1939; Constitution Hall
    (Washington, D. C.) 1952; Alice Tully Hall (conducting Heritage
    Society Chorus' An Evening of Negro Spirituals) 1975.

MAYO, WHITMAN (Blount)
    (Actor)
b.   November 15, 1930, New York, N. Y.
Education: Chaffey College (Ontario, Canada) 1950-51; Los Angeles
    City College 1954-55; Los Angeles State College 1956-58.
Address: 9000 Fifth Avenue, Inglewood, Calif. 90305.
Career Data: Organized a writer's agency; produced Holiday Jamaica
    (week festival in Jamaica 1975); president, NASABA Artists
    Management Inc.; president, Whitman Mayo Travel Agency;
    advisor and board of directors, Miss Black USA Beauty Pageant
    1976.
Films: The Black Klansman 1966; Hard Heads 1975.

Memberships: AEA; AFTRA.

Television: Grady on Sanford and Son (series) 1972-1975; Salute to
    Redd Foxx on Wide World Special 1974; Merv Griffin Show
    1975; Gladys Knight and the Pips 1975; Hollywood Squares
    1975; Dinah! 1975; title role in Grady (series) 1975; Celebrity
    Sweepstakes 1976; Baretta 1976; Tattletales 1976; A. E. S. Hud-
    son Street 1977.

Theater: The Amen Corner (Los Angeles) 1964; In the Wine Time
    1968; Goin' to Buffalo 1969; What If It Had Turned Up Heads
    (O. B.) 1972.

MELVIN, HAROLD
    (Singer)
b. Philadelphia, Pa.
Career Data: Performed with The Blue Notes, a vocal group, until
    1975.
Clubs: Playboy (L. A.) 1975; Jupiter's (Long Island) 1975; Barney
    Google's 1975; 2001 Odyssey (Bklyn.) 1975; Zero's II (Long
    Island) 1976.
Records: To Be True (Philadelphia International); I Don't Know
    What It Is (Brooke) 1959; My Hero (Value) 1960; I Miss You
    (Philadelphia International) 1972; If You Don't Know Me by Now
    (Philadelphia International) 1972; Yesterday I Had the Blues
    (Philadelphia International) 1973; The Love I Lost (Philadelphia
    International) 1973; Wake Up Everybody (Philadelphia Inter-
    national) 1975; Collector's Item (Philadelphia International);
    Black and Blue (Philadelphia International); Reaching for the
    World.
Television: Dinah! 1975; Ebony Music Awards 1975; Mike Douglas
    Show 1975; Midnight Special 1975; Soul Train 1975; Apollo
    Theatre (special) 1976.
Theater: Appeared at Nassau Coliseum (Newport Jazz Festival)
    1975; Apollo Theatre 1975; Felt Forum (Big Apple Jam '75)
    1976; Westchester Premier Theatre 1976.

MERCER, MABEL
    (Singer)
b. February 3, 1900, Burton-On-Trent, England.
Clubs: Bricktop's (Paris) 1931-38; Tony's on 52nd St. ; Byline Room;
    Downstairs at the Upstairs 1964; St. Regis Hotel 1975; Cleo
    1977; Playboy Club (London) 1977.
Films: The Sand Castle (voice) 1961.
Records: Mabel Mercer for Always (Decca); A Tribute to Mabel
    Mercer on the Occasion of Her 75th Birthday (Atlantic); The
    Art of Mabel Mercer (Decca); Merely Marvelous (Atlantic);
    The Art of Mabel Mercer (Atlantic); At Town Hall (Atlantic);
    Once in a Blue Moon (Atlantic); Second Town Hall (Atlantic).
Television: Mabel Mercer; Bobby Short and Friends 1974; Midday
    Live 1975; Lee Graham Show 1975; Black Pride 1975; People,
    Places and Things 1975; Mark of Jazz 1976.
Theater: Menotti's The Consul (recorded voice) 1950; appeared at
    Avery Fisher Hall (Newport Jazz Festival) 1975.

MERCER, MAE
(Actress)
Address: Moss Agency Ltd., 113 N. San Vicente Blvd., Beverly
Hills, Calif. 90211.
Films: The Hell with Heroes 1968; The Beguiled, produced Angela,
Portrait of a Revolutionary 1971; Frogs 1972.
Memberships: SAG.
Television: Kung Fu.

MERRITT, THERESA
(Actress)
b. September 24, 1922, Newport News, Va.
Education: Temple University; New York University; Juilliard
School of Music; Settlement School of Music (Philadelphia).
Special Interests: Singing.
Address: c/o Richard A. Bauman Agency, 1650 Broadway, New
York, N.Y. 10019 and 192-06 110 Road, Hollis, L. I., N.Y.
11412.
Career Data: Performed with Belafonte singers; toured Eastern
region as Aunt Jemima for Quaker Oats.
Films: They Might Be Giants 1971.
Memberships: AEA; AFTRA; AGMA; NAACP; SAG.
Television: J. T. (children's series); Midday Live; Mama in That's
My Mama (series) 1974; Password All Stars 1975; Merv Grif-
fin Show 1975; Police Story 1975; Hollywood Squares 1975;
Dinah!, Tattletales 1975; Say Brother 1975.
Theater: Frankie in Carmen Jones (tour) 1943-45; concert debut at
Town Hall 1961; South Pacific (City Center) 1961; Show Boat
(City Center) 1961; Tambourines to Glory (O. B.) 1963; Trum-
pets of the Lord (O. B. and Europe tour) 1963; Funny Girl
1964; The Amen Corner (Europe tour) 1965; F. Jasmine Addams
(O. B.); Hallelujah Baby 1967; Golden Boy 1968; Don't Play Us
Cheap 1972; The Crucible (City Center); Mammy in Gone with
the Wind (musical production, Los Angeles) 1974; The Wiz
1976.

MICHEAUX, OSCAR "Dean of Black Filmmakers"
(Producer/Director)
b. 1884, Metropolis, Ill.
d. April 1, 1951, Charlotte, N. C.
Special Interests: Novelist, publisher.
Career Data: Founder and president, Oscar Micheaux Corp. 1918-;
career spanned 30 years 1918-1948 (produced 44 films including
first all black silent film and first all black sound film).
Films: Phantom of Kenwood; Swing from The Story of Mandy; Dark
Princess; A Fool's Errand; Within Our Gates 1920; The Hypo-
crite, The Shadow, The Symbol of the Unconquered, Gunsaulus
Mystery 1921; The Homesteader, The Dungeon, Uncle Jasper's
Will 1922; Ghost of Tolston's Manor, Deceit, The Virgin of
the Seminole 1923; Son of Satan, Birthright 1924; Body and
Soul, Marcus Garland, The Brute 1925; The Devil's Disciple,

The Conjure Woman 1926; The Spider's Web, The Millionaire, The Broken Violin, The House Behind the Cedars 1927; Thirty Years Later, When Men Betray 1928; Wages of Sin 1929; Easy Street, Daughter of the Congo 1930; The Exile, Darktown Revue 1931; Veiled Aristocrats, Ten Minutes to Live, Black Magic 1932; The Girl from Chicago, Ten Minutes to Kill 1933; Harlem After Midnight 1934; Lem Hawkins' Confession 1935; Underworld, Temptation 1936; Miracle in Harlem, God's Step Children 1937; Lying Lips 1939; The Notorious Elinor Lee 1940; Betrayal 1948.

Publications: Wrote 5 novels: The Conquest, 1913; The Forged Note, 1915; The Homesteader, 1917; The Case of Mrs. Wingate, 1945; The Masquerade, 1947.

MILLER, FLOURNOY E.
    (Actor/Composer)
b.   April 14, 1887, Nashville, Tenn.
d.   June 6, 1971, Hollywood, Calif.
Education: Fisk University.
Special Interests: Comedy.
Career Data: Wrote songs for Pekin Theatre (Chicago) 1907; partner in vaudeville act with Aubrey Lyles and later with Mantan Moreland.
Films: That's the Spirit 1932; Mystery in Swing, The Bronze Buckaroo, Harlem Rides the Range 1938; Harlem on the Prairie, Double Deal 1939; Mr. Washington Goes to Town, Lady Luck 1940; Professor Creeps 1941; Stormy Weather 1943; Mantan Runs for Mayor 1946; She's Too Mean for Me 1948; Yes Sir, Mr. Bones 1951.
Memberships: ASCAP 1950.
Musical Compositions: Keep 'Em Guessing; Peace, Sister, Peace; Stay Out of the Kitchen; My Sweet Hunk O'Trash; No Labor in My Job; You Can't Lose a Broken Heart.
Radio: Wrote scripts for Amos 'n' Andy 1940.
Theater: Co-wrote The Oyster Man 1907; Darkydom 1915; Shuffle Along 1921; Runnin' Wild 1923; Rang Tang 1927; Brownskin Models 1927; Keep Shufflin' 1928; Blackbirds of 1930 1930; Lazy Rhythm 1931; wrote and appeared in Shuffle Along of 1933, 1952; Meet Miss Jones 1947; produced and appeared in Sugar Hill; appeared at Palace Theatre 1955.

MILLINDER, LUCKY (Lucius Millinder)
    (Jazz Musician)
b.   August 8, 1900, Anniston, Ala.
d.   September 29, 1966, New York, N. Y.
Special Interests: Arranging, conducting.
Career Data: Toured R. K. O. circuit 1931; toured Europe (Paris, Monte Carlo) 1933; led his own band 1940-51; popularized song, Sweet Slumber.
Films: Paradise in Harlem 1939.
Radio: Disc jockey, WNEW; Swingtime at the Savoy (NBC) 1948; emcee, Harlem Amateur Hour (WJZ).

Television: Modern Minstrels (a. k. a. Swingtime at the Savoy) 1948.
Theater: Staff band leader and arranger at Apollo Theatre; appeared
    at Loew's State 1939.

MILLS, FLORENCE
        (Singer)
b. January 25, 1895, Washington, D. C.
d. November 1, 1927, New York, N. Y.
Career Data: Member, Mills Trio (with her sisters) 1910; then
    member Panama Four; became associated with the song, I'm
    a Little Blackbird Looking for a Bluebird, Too.
Clubs: Plantation Club.
Theater: Sons of Ham 1900; Shuffle Along 1921; Plantation Revue
    1922; From Dover Street to Dixie 1923; Dixie to Broadway
    1924-25; La Revue Negre (Paris) 1925; Blackbirds 1926.

MILLS, STEPHANIE (Dorothea)
        (Singer/Actress)
b. March 22, 1959, Queens, N. Y.
Education: Boro Hall Academy (Bklyn.); Juilliard School of Music.
Special Interests: Dancing.
Address: 1534 President Street, Brooklyn, N. Y. 11213.
Clubs: Grand Finale 1977.
Films: Piece of the Action (doc.) 1974.
Records: I Knew It Was Love (Paramount) 1974; Moving in the
    Right Direction (ABC Dunhill) 1975; For the First Time (Mo-
    town) 1976; Stephanie 1976.
Television: The Electric Company (NET); Leon Bibb Show 1970;
    Mike Douglas Show 1974, 1975; Midday Live 1974; WNEW-TV
    News 1974; Eyewitness News 1974; Wonderama 1974, 1975;
    Black Journal 1975; The Tonight Show 1975; Feeling Good
    1975; Musical Chairs 1975; Saturday Night Live (with Howard
    Cosell) 1975; Dinah! 1975; Sammy and Company 1975; The
    Today Show 1975; Apollo (special) 1976; Kup's Show 1976; Sun-
    day 1977.
Theater: Pansie in Maggie Flynn 1968; String (NEC) 1969; appear-
    ances at Apollo Theatre 1971; Avery Fisher Hall; Albany Con-
    cert Hall (with the Temptations); Bill Cosby special at Lew
    Fisher Theatre, Buffalo; Oakdale Musical Festival (with The
    Spinners) 1974; Dorothy in The Wiz 1975.

MILNER, RONALD
        (Playwright)
b. May 29, 1938, Detroit, Mich.
Education: Highland Park Junior College, Detroit Institute of Tech-
    nology, Columbia University 1965.
Address: 16225 Kentucky Street, Detroit, Mich. 48221.
Honors: John Hay Whitney award 1962-63; Rockefeller Foundation
    grant 1965-66.
Career Data: Co-founder, Concept East Theatre (Detroit) 1960-63;
    Instructor, Wayne State University (Detroit); Michigan State

University; writer-in-residence Lincoln University (Pennsyl-
vania) 1966-68.
Publications: Black Drama Anthology (edited with Woodie King),
___ Columbia University Press, 1972.
Theater: Wrote: The Greatest Gift (children's play); Life Agony
___ 1963; These Three; Circus; Who's Got His Own 1966; The
Warning: A Theme for Linda 1968; M(Ego) and The Green
Ball of Freedom 1972; What the Winesellers Buy 1972; Season's
Reasons: Just a Natural Change 1975.

MINGUS, CHARLES
___ (Musician/Composer)
b. April 22, 1922, Nogales, Ariz.
Education: Studied with H. Rheinschagen.
Special Interests: Bass, arranging, piano, jazz, conducting.
Address: c/o Savoy Records, 56 Ferry Street, Newark, N. J. 17105.
Honors: Down Beat new star award 1953; Guggenheim Foundation
___ grant 1971-72.
Career Data: Appeared with Louis Armstrong 1941-43; Kid Ory,
___ Lionel Hampton 1946-48, Red Norvo 1950-51, Billy Taylor
1952-53, Duke Ellington, Charlie Parker, Stan Getz, Bud
Powell and Art Tatum; toured U. S. , Europe and Japan 1972;
participated in Newport Jazz Festival 1974, 1976; formed his
own jazz workshop quintet.
Clubs: Max's Kansas City; Village Vanguard 1974-75; Top of the
___ Gate 1975, 1976; The Bottom Line 1975; Village Gate 1975, 1976.
Films: Road to Zanzibar 1941; Higher and Higher 1944; Mingus
___ (doc.) 1968.
Publications: Beneath the Underdog, His World As Composed by
___ Mingus, Knopf, 1971.
Records: The Best of Charles Mingus (Atlantic); Mingus Plays
___ Piano (Impulse); A Man and His Bass; Jazz Composers Work-
shop (Fantasy); Modern Jazz Concert; Reevaluation (Impulse);
Art (Atlantic); At Carnegie (Atlantic); At Monterey (Fantasy);
Better Git It in Your Soul (Columbia); Black Saint and Sinner
Lady (Impulse); Blues and Roots (Atlantic); Changes One (At-
lantic); Changes Two (Atlantic); Charles Mingus (Prestige);
Chazz (Fantasy); Great Concert (Prestige); Let My Children
Hear Music (Columbia); Mingus Ah Um (Columbia); Mingus,
Mingus, Mingus (Impulse); Mingus Moods (Trip); Mingus Moves
(Atlantic); Mingus Revisited (Trip); My Favorite Quintet (Fan-
tasy); Oh Yeah (Atlantic); Quintet Plus Max Roach (Fantasy);
Reincarnation of a Lovebird (Prestige); Stormy Weather (Bar-
naby); Tia Juana Moods (RCA); Town Hall Concert (Solid
State); Trio & Sextet (Trip); Wonderland (United Artists); Char-
les & Friends in Concert (Columbia).
Television: CBS with Mel Torme; Midday Live 1975; Black News 1976.
Theater: Appeared at Philharmonic Hall 1972; Carnegie Hall 1974,
___ 1976; Avery Fisher Hall 1976; Radio City Music Hall 1976.

MITCHELL, ABBIE
   (Actress/Singer)
b. 1884, Baltimore, Md.
d. March 16, 1960, New York, N. Y.
Education: Studied voice with Harry T. Burleigh, Emila Serrano
    and Jean de Reszke (Paris).
Career Data: Member, Lafayette Players; head, music dept., Tus-
    kegee Institute; sang soprano roles in operas (Carmen, La
    Traviata); executive secretary, Negro Actors Guild; performed
    in In Dahomey before King Edward VII of England; performed
    in The Red Moon before Czar Nicholas II of Russia.
Films: The Scapegoat 1917.
Theater: Clorindy, The Origin of the Cake Walk (debut) 1898; con-
    cert with Nashville students at Proctor's Theatre 1905; Help
    Wanted 1914; In Abraham's Bosom 1926; Coquette 1927; Steve-
    dore 1934; Clara in Porgy and Bess 1935; Addie in The Little
    Foxes 1939; On Whitman Avenue 1946.
Relationships: Wife of Will Marion Cook, composer.

MITCHELL, ARTHUR
   (Dancer/Choreographer)
b. March 26, 1934, New York, N. Y.
Education: High School of Performing Arts 1952; School of American
    Ballet.
Address: 466 West 152 Street, New York, N. Y. 10031.
Honors: Certificate of Recognition, Harold Jackman Memorial Com-
    mittee 1969; Special Tribute, Northside Center For Child De-
    velopment Inc. 1969; The Changers Award, Mademoiselle Maga-
    zine 1960; North Shore Communication Arts Center Award 1971;
    20th annual Capezio Dance Award 1971.
Career Data: Joined dance companies of Donald McKayle and John
    Butler; premier danseur, New York City Ballet Co. 1955-59;
    Spoleto Festival of Two Worlds 1960, 1961; National Brazilian
    Ballet Co. 1966-68; director, Dance Dept., Harlem School of
    the Arts 1968; founder, Dance Theatre of Harlem 1969; created
    other companies in Brazil, Senegal; U. S. Dept. of State Dance
    Panel 1973; N. Y. State Council on the Arts, Dance Panel
    1973; roles include Puck in Balanchine's Midsummer Night's
    Dream, Mercutio in Romeo and Juliet, Jason in Medea, Cre-
    ation of the World, Arcade, title role in Othello, Orpheus,
    Nutcracker Suite, The Unicorn, The Gorgon and the Manticore,
    Bakuko, Interplay, Otis Agon; choreographed Manifestations,
    Every Now and Then 1975, Spiritual Suite 1976.
Films: Dance Theatre of Harlem (doc.), McGraw-Hill.
Memberships: National Society of Literature & the Arts 1975.
Television: To Tell the Truth; Positively Black 1974, 1976; Mike
    Douglas Show 1974; A. M. New York 1975; Christopher Close-
    up 1975; Kup's Show 1975; Sunday 1976.
Theater: Four Saints in Three Acts 1952, House of Flowers 1955,
    Sweet Potato 1968.

MITCHELL, DON
    (Actor)
Address: Herb Tannen & Associates, 6640 Sunset Blvd. Los
    Angeles, Calif. 90028.
Career Data: Director of Project Development, Bill Sargent's
    Theatre Television Corp. , 1975.
Films: Short Walk to Daylight 1972; Scream Blacula Scream 1973.
Memberships: SAG.
Television: The Fugitive; The Virginian; Innervision; Mark Sanger
    in Ironside (series); Medical Story 1976.
Theater: Mister Johnson (O. B.) 1963.
Relationships: Husband of Judy Pace, actress.

MITCHELL, GWENN
    (Actress)
b. July 6, Morristown, N. J.
Education: Studied acting with Lloyd Richards, Uta Hagen.
Address: Cunningham & Associates, 5900 Wilshire Blvd. , Los
    Angeles, Calif. 90036.
Career Data: Negro Ensemble Company.
Films: Recess 1970; Shaft 1971; Brother on the Run 1973; Chosen
    Survivors 1974.
Memberships: SAG.
Television: United Airlines commercial; As The World Turns; The
    Edge of Night; The Best of Everything (series); Mission: Im-
    possible; Rookies; Police Story 1975; Police Woman 1975; Amy
    Prentiss (series) 1975; Marcus Welby, M. D. 1975.

MITCHELL, LOFTEN
    (Playwright)
b. April 15, 1919, New York, N. Y.
Education: City College of New York; Talladega College B. A. 1943;
    Columbia University M. A. 1951.
Address: 3217 Burris Road, Vestal, N. Y. 13850.
Honors: Guggenheim award for creative writing in the drama 1958-
    59; Rockefeller Foundation grant 1961.
Career Data: Professor, State University of New York at Bingham-
    ton; guest lecturer, New School for Social Research.
Publications: Black Drama: The Story of the American Negro in
    the Theater, Hawthorn Bks. , 1967; Voices of the Black Theatre,
    James T. White & Co. , 1975.
Radio: The Later Years (WNYC series) 1950-52; Friendly Advisor
    (WWRL series) 1954.
Theater: Acted in: Having Wonderful Time (O. B.). Wrote: Horse's
    Play; Blood in the Night; The Cellar 1947; The Bancroft Dy-
    nasty 1948; Young Man of Williamsburg 1954; Land Beyond the
    River 1957; The Phonograph 1961; Integration: Report One
    1961; I'm Sorry 1962; Ballad for Bimshire (with Irving Burgie)
    1963; Star in the Morning (story of Bert Williams) 1964; Bal-
    lad of the Winter Soldiers (with John O. Killens) 1965; Tell
    Pharaoh 1967; Ballad of a Blackbird 1968; The World of a

Harlem Playwright 1968; The Walls Came Tumbling Down 1969;
The Final Solution of the Black Problem in the United States
of America or The Fall of the American Empire 1970; The
Afro-Philadelphian 1970; Come Back to Harlem (producer)
1972; The Vampires of Harlem 1973; Bubbling Brown Sugar
(with Rosetta Le Noire) 1975.

MITCHILL, SCOEY
    (Actor)
b.   March 12, 1930, Newburgh, N. Y.
Education: Virginia Union University (Richmond) 1948-50.
Career Data: President, Scomi Productions, Hollywood, Calif.
    1970-.
Memberships: SAG.
Television: The Smothers Brothers Show; The Hollywood Palace;
    The Steve Allen Show; The Carol Burnett Show; Ed Sullivan
    Show; Mothers-in-Law; That Girl; Password; What's It All
    About World? 1967-68; Paul in Barefoot in the Park (series)
    1970; The Voyage of the Yes 1973; Six Million Dollar Man;
    Match Game 1975; Tattletales 1974, 1975; Rhoda 1975; Police
    Story 1975; Joe Forrester 1975; Doc 1976; Cross-Wits 1976.
Theater: Appeared at Apollo Theater.

MONK, THELONIUS (Sphere)
    (Composer/Pianist)
b.   October 10, 1918, Rocky Mountain, N. C.
Special Interests: Jazz.
Address: 473 West End Avenue, New York, N. Y. 10024.
Honors: Paris Jazz Festival 1954; recipient, International Critics
    Award as Outstanding Jazz Pianist 1958, 1959, 1960; Time
    Magazine cover 1964.
Career Data: Played with bands of Lucky Millinder 1942, Coleman
    Hawkins 1944 and with Dizzy Gillespie and Charlie Parker;
    pioneered "bop movement" in jazz; participated in Newport
    Jazz Festival 1976.
Clubs: Village Vanguard; Minton's Play House.
Films: Jazz on a Summer's Day 1960.
Musical Compositions: Round Midnight; Ask Me Now; Pannonica;
    Off Minor; Brilliant Corners; Monk's Mood; Work; Ruby My
    Dear.
Records: Monk's Blues (Columbia); It's Monk's Time (Columbia);
    Third Stream Music; Jazz Ensemble; Featuring ...; Monk/
    Trane (Milestone); Brilliance (Milestone); Complete Genius
    (Bluenote); Blue Monk (Prestige); Criss-Cross (Columbia Spe-
    cial Products); Genius (Prestige); Golden ... (Prestige);
    Greatest Hits (Columbia); High Priest (Prestige); In Person
    (Milestone); The Man I Love (Black Lion); Misterioso (Colum-
    bia); Monk (Columbia); Monk (Blue Note); Monk's Dream (Co-
    lumbia Special Products); Pure Monk (Milestone); Reflections
    (Prestige); Solo (Columbia); Something in Blue (Black Lion);
    Straight No Chaser (Columbia); Underground (Columbia); Who's

Afraid of Big Band Monk (Columbia); Thelonius Monk (GNP Crescendo).

Theater: Appeared at Avery Fisher Hall (Newport Jazz Festival) 1975; Carnegie Hall 1976; Radio City Music Hall 1976.

MONTGOMERY, BARBARA
(Actress)

Address: c/o Kahn, Lifflander and Rhodes, 853 Seventh Avenue, New York, N. Y. 10019.

Honors: Obie and Black Theatre awards (for My Sister, My Sister) 1974, AUDELCO award.

Career Data: Member, La Mama's Jarboro and Serbian Companies; member, Negro Ensemble Company.

Memberships: AEA.

Television: Louise Johnson in The Guiding Light (series); Aunt Edna in The First Breeze of Summer (NET).

Theater: Black Vision (O. B.); Les Femmes Noires (O. B.); Thoughts (O. B.); The Blacks (tour); No Place to Be Somebody (tour) 1971; standby for Virginia Capers in Raisin 1973; Wedding Band (O. B.) 1973; My Sister, My Sister (O. B.) 1974; Waiting for Mongo (O. B.) 1975; The First Breeze of Summer (NEC) 1975; Wanda in Kennedy's Children 1975; Eden (NEC) 1976; Godsong (O. B.) 1977; The Great MacDaddy (O. B.) 1977; Lady Macbeth (O. B.) 1977.

MOODY, LYNNE
(Actress)

Films: Scream Blacula Scream 1973; Las Vegas Lady 1976.

Memberships: AFTRA; SAG.

Television: Tracey in That's My Mama (series) 1974-75; S. W. A. T. 1976; Nightmare in Badham County 1976; Roots 1977.

MOORE, ARCHIE (Archibald Lee Moore)
(Actor)

b. December 13, c1916, Benoit, Miss.

Special Interests: Playing cornet, photography.

Address: 3517 East Street, San Diego, Calif. 92102.

Career Data: Light Heavyweight Boxing Champion 1953-63.

Films: Jim in The Adventures of Huckleberry Finn 1960; The Carpetbaggers 1964; The Fortune Cookie 1966; The Outfit 1974; Hard Times 1975; Breakheart Pass 1976.

Memberships: NAACP; Urban League.

Publications: The Archie Moore Story (autobiography), McGraw-Hill, 1960.

Television: Cutter 1972; Archer 1975.

MOORE, CARMAN LEROY
(Composer)

b. October 8, 1936, Lorain, Ohio.

Education: Ohio State University B. S. (music) 1958; Juilliard School
_____of Music M. S. 1966; studied with Hall Overton.
Special Interests: Criticism, musicology, French horn, lyrics.
Address: 65 West 90 Street, New York, N. Y. 10024.
Honors: New York State Council on the Arts grant 1974.
Career Data: Music critic, Village Voice 1965-date; associate ar-
_____tistic director, Harlem Theatre workshop; teacher of music at
_____Manhattanville College, New School for Social Research, Yale
_____University, Queens College, New York University.
Memberships: ASCAP; The American Music Center; Society of
_____Black Composers (founder) 1968.
Musical Compositions: African Tears; Drum Major; Gospel Fuse;
_____Wild Fires and Field Songs.
Publications: Somebody's Angel Child: The Story of Bessie Smith,
_____Crowell, 1970.
Records: Lyricist on Felix Cavaliere (Bearsville) 1974; Fog Hat
_____(Bearsville) 1974; Destiny (Bearsville) 1975.
Theater: Gospel Fuse (premier with San Francisco Symphony) 1975;
_____Wild Fires and Field Songs (premier with N. Y. Philharmonic
_____Orchestra) 1975; performed with Columbus (Ohio) Symphony;
_____wrote music for Joe Anne 1976.

MOORE, CHARLES
_____(Dancer)
b.   May 22, 1928, Cleveland, Ohio.
Education: Karamu House, Cleveland, Ohio; studied dance with
_____Katherine Dunham, Pearl Primus, Geoffrey Holder, Jean Leon
_____Destiné, Donald McKayle, Talley Beatty, Alvin Ailey, Olatunji
_____and Prof. A. Opoku of the University of Ghana.
Special Interests: Acting, children's theatre, singing, drums, teach-
_____ing.
Address: 1043 President Street, Brooklyn, N. Y. 11225.
Career Data: Toured Far East and Australia for U. S. State Dept.
_____with the Alvin Ailey Co. ; performed at N. Y. World's Fair
_____1965; instructor at Clark Center YWCA, and schools and col-
_____leges throughout U. S. ; conducted dance workshops for N. Y.C.
_____Board of Education's Cultural Heritage Program, Head Start,
_____Bi-Lingual Center, HARYOU, Martin De Porres Community
_____Center, Brooklyn Academy of Music; performed at American
_____Museum of Natural History, Metropolitan Museum of Art,
_____The City University Mall and The Brooklyn Museum; toured
_____Europe with Katherine Dunham Company.
Films: Who Killed Teddy Bear 1965; You're a Big Boy Now 1967;
_____Where Were You When the Lights Went Out 1968.
Memberships: AEA; AFTRA; AGMA; AGVA; SAG.
Television: Du Pont-A. W. Ayers commercial; Look Up and Live;
_____On Being Black; F. Y. I. ; Swinging World of Sammy Davis;
_____Androcles and the Lion; The Light Fantastics (Stage '67);
_____Carol for Another Christmas 1964; A Time for Laughter (Bela-
_____fonte Special) 1967; Anne Bancroft Special 1970; Lauren Bacall
_____Special.

Theater: Around the World in 80 days (Jones Beach); Jamaica
1957; Kwamina 1961; Ballad for Bimshire (O. B.) 1963; The
Zulu and the Zayda 1965; House of Flowers (O. B.) 1968; Les
Blancs 1970; Billy No Name (O. B.) 1970; Emperor Jones
(Princeton Repertory Theatre); Dances and Drums of Africa at
Town Hall; Abul in Bomarzo (N. Y. C. Opera Company); Death
of a Salesman 1975; appeared at Billie Holiday Theatre (Brooklyn); choreographed Let the Big Drum Roll, Haitian Suite, Ballad Caribe.

MOORE, JUANITA
    (Actress)
b.   October 19, 1922, Los Angeles, Calif.
Education: Los Angeles City College, Actors Lab (Hollywood).
Special Interests: Singing, piano.
Address: Cunningham & Associates, 5900 Wilshire Blvd. , Los
    Angeles, Calif. 90036.
Honors: Oscar nominee, best performance by an actress in a sup-
    porting role (Imitation of Life) 1959; Black Filmmakers Hall
    of Fame 1974.
Career Data: President, Benevolent Variety Artists.
Clubs: Zanzibar; Moulin Rouge (Paris); Small's Paradise.
Films: Affair in Trinidad, Lydia Bailey 1952; Witness to Murder
    1954; Women's Prison 1955; Ransom, The Girl Can't Help It
    1956; Something of Value, A Band of Angels, The Green Eyed
    Blonde 1957; Annie Johnson in Imitation of Life 1959; Tammy
    Tell Me True, A Raisin in the Sun 1961; Walk on the Wild
    Side 1962; Papa's Delicate Condition, A Child Is Waiting 1963;
    The Singing Nun 1966; Rosie, Up Tight 1968; Skin Game 1971;
    The Mack 1973; Thomasine and Bushrod, Abby 1974; Deliver
    Us from Evil 1975.
Memberships: SAG.
Television: Climax; Soldiers of Fortune 1955; Insight; Alfred Hitch-
    cock Theatre 1963, 1964, 1965; Wagon Train 1963; Mr. Novak
    1964; Farmer's Daughter 1965; Slattery's People 1965; Gentle
    Ben 1968; The Outsider 1968; Bold Ones 1969; Fare Thee Well
    Rev. Taylor (On Being Black) 1969; Name of the Game 1969;
    Mannix 1970; Ironside 1971; Marcus Welby, M. D. 1972; A
    Dream for Christmas 1973; Adam-12 1975; Ex-Lax commercial
    1977.
Theater: Palladium (London) 1942; No Exit (Ebony Show Case Theatre)
    1951; A Raisin in the Sun (London) 1959-60; The Blacks (Los
    Angeles); The Amen Corner 1965.

MOORE, MELBA (Beatrice Melba Mooreman)
    (Singer/Actress)
b.   October 27, 1945, New York, N. Y.
Education: Montclair State Teachers College (B. A. music education).
Special Interests: Songwriting.
Address: c/o Charles Gallery, 315 West 125 Street, New York,
    N. Y. 10027.

Honors: Theatre World; Outer Circle; Drama Desk; Drama Critics; Variety and Tony awards (for Purlie) 1970; AGVA Rising Star of the Year award 1970.
Career Data: Member, Voices Inc.; Schaefer Festival 1976.
Clubs: Riviera (Las Vegas); Caesar's Palace (Las Vegas); Palmer House (Chicago); Fairmount Hotel (San Francisco); Empire Room--Waldorf Astoria; St. Regis Maisonette; Copacabana 1973; Grossingers 1975; Mr. Kelly's (Chicago) 1975; Bottom Line 1975.
Films: Cotton Comes to Harlem 1970; Pigeons 1971; Lost in the Stars 1974.
Records: Purlie 1970; Learning to Give 1970; Look What You're Doing to the Man (Mercury) 1971; Live! 1972; Peach Melba 1975; This Is It (Buddah) 1976; I Am His Lady; Melba (Buddah); I Got Love (Mercury).
Television: Ed Sullivan Show; David Frost Show; Comedy Is King; Mike Douglas Show; Flip Wilson Show; One to One; Black News; The Melba Moore-Clifton Davis Show (summer series) 1972; Clio Awards Show 1974; Scott Joplin's Rag Time 1974; Good Night America 1974; Tonight Show 1975; Vegetable Soup 1975; Bobby Vinton Show 1975; Not for Women Only 1975; Soul Train 1975; Pat Collins Show 1975; Cerebral Palsy Telethon 1975; Dinah! 1975; Merv Griffin Show 1975; Positively Black 1975; Midday Live 1975; A. M. America 1975; Kup's Show 1975; Black Journal 1975, 76; N. Y. Emmy Awards 1976; A. M. New York 1976; The American Woman-Portrait of Courage 1976; Lifestyles with Beverly Sills 1976; Disco '77 1977.
Theater: Hair 1968-70; Lutiebelle in Purlie 1970.
Relationships: Wife of Charles Huggins, owner of Charles Gallery.

MOORE, PHIL
      (Pianist)
b.   February 20, 1918, Portland, Ore.
Education: University of Washington Cornish Conservatory.
Special Interests: Piano, composing, arranging.
Career Data: Piano soloist with Portland Junior Symphony; formerly with music dept. , M. G. M. Studios; played with Les Hite and his own group, Phil Moore Four.
Clubs: Reno Sweeney's 1975; Café Society.
Films: The Duke Is Tops (a. k. a. Bronze Venus), Broadway Melody 1940; A Song Is Born 1948.
Memberships: ASCAP 1944.
Musical Compositions: Shoo-Shoo-Baby; I Feel So Smoochie; A Little on the Lonely Side; I'm Gonna See My Baby; Blow Out the Candle; Specie Americana (instrumental).
Radio: Mildred Bailey (series) CBS.
Records: Frankie & Johnny (arranger); Lotus Land (arranger); Misty Moon Blues.
Television: Cotton Club '75 (special) 1974; Clifton Davis Special 1976; The Sty of the Blind Pig (score) 1974.

MOORE, TIM (Harry R. Moore)
     (Actor)
b.   1888, Rock Island, Ill.
d.   December 13, 1958, Los Angeles, Calif.
Career Data: Former prize fighter.
Films: His Great Chance 1923; Boy, What a Girl! 1946.
Television: Kingfish in Amos'n'Andy (series) 1951-54.
Theater: Appeared at Alhambra Theatre; Rarin' to Go; Tim Moore's
     Chicago Follies (tour) 1921-25; Lew Leslie's Blackbirds 1928;
     Harlem Scandals 1932.

MOORE, UNDINE SMITH
     (Composer)
b.   1904, Jarrat, Va.
Education: Fisk University; Juilliard School of Music; Columbia
     University; Eastman School of Music (Rochester).
Special Interests: Piano, organ, arranging, teaching.
Career Data: Professor and co-director Black Music Center, Vir-
     ginia State College; lecturer at Carleton College (Northfield,
     Minnesota), Howard University, Fisk University, Indiana Uni-
     versity.
Musical Compositions: Afro-American Suite for Flute, Cello and
     Piano; We Give Thanks to Thee for These Thy Servants; Mo-
     ther to Son; Hail Warrior; Daniel, Daniel, Servant of the Lord;
     Let Us Make Man in Our Image; Striving After God; The Lamb;
     Long Fare You Well; Bound for Canaan's Land; Just Come
     from the Fountain; A Christmas Alleluia; Three Pieces for
     Flute and Piano; Love Let the Wind Cry.

MORELAND, MANTAN
     (Actor/Comedian)
b.   1902, Monroe, La.
d.   September 28, 1973, Hollywood, Calif.
Career Data: Played Birmingham, the chauffeur in Charlie Chan
     film series; made vaudeville tours with Tim Moore, Fluornoy
     Miller, then Ben Carter, later with Roosevelt Livingood.
Films: Condemned Man; Yeah Man, That's the Spirit 1932; Spirit
     of Youth, Next Time I Marry, Frontier Scout, There's That
     Woman Again, Gang Smashers 1938; Irish Luck, Harlem on
     the Prairie, Tell No Tales, One Dark Night (a. k. a. Night
     Club Girl), Two-Gun Man from Harlem, Riders of the Fron-
     tier 1939; Mr. Washington Goes to Town, Millionaire Playboy,
     Chasing Trouble, Pier 13, The City of Chance, The Man Who
     Wouldn't Talk, Four Shall Die, Lady Luck, While Thousands
     Cheer, Star Dust, Viva Cisco Kid!, On the Spot, Laughing at
     Danger, Drums of the Desert 1940; Birth of the Blues, Lucky
     Ghost, Ellery Queen's Penthouse Mystery, Cracked Nuts, Up
     in the Air, King of the Zombies, The Gang's All Here, Hello,
     Sucker!, Dressed to Kill, Four Jacks and a Jill, Footlight
     Fever, You're Out of Luck, Sign of the Wolf, Let's Go Col-
     legiate!, Sleepers West, Marry the Boss's Daughter, Up

Jumped the Devil, World Premiere 1941; Professor Creeps,
Andy Hardy's Double Life, The Strange Case of Dr. RX,
Treat 'Em Rough, Mexican Spitfire Sees a Ghost, Palm Beach
Story, Footlight Serenade, Phantom Killer, Eyes in the Night,
Girl Trouble, Tarzan's New York Adventure 1942; Hit the Ice,
Cabin in the Sky, Cosmo Jones-Crime Smasher, Sarong Girl,
Revenge of the Zombies, Melody Parade, She's for Me, My
Kingdom for a Cook, Slightly Dangerous, Swing Fever, You're
a Lucky Fellow, Mr. Smith, We've Never Been Licked 1943;
This Is the Life, The Mystery of the River Boat (series),
The Chinese Cat, Moon Over Las Vegas, Chip Off the Old
Block, Pin-up Girl, South of Dixie, Black Magic, Bowery to
Broadway, Charlie Chan in the Secret Service, See Here, Pri-
vate Hargrove 1944; She Wouldn't Say Yes, The Scarlet Clue,
Tall, Tan and Terrific, The Jade Mask, The Shanghai Cobra,
The Spider, Captain Tugboat Annie, Mantan Messes Up, Man-
tan Runs for Mayor, Come on Cowboy, Dark Alibi, Shadow
over Chinatown 1946; The Trap, What a Guy, The Chinese
Ring, Ebony Parade, Murder at Malibu Beach 1947; Docks of
New Orleans, The Dreamer, The Mystery of the Golden Eye,
The Feathered Serpent, She's Too Mean to Me, The Shanghai
Chest, Best Man Wins 1948; Sky Dragon 1949; Rockin' the
Blues, Rock'n'Roll Revue 1955; Rock'n'Roll Jamboree 1957;
Enter Laughing 1967; The Comic 1969; The Watermelon Man
1970.
Radio: Bob Burns Show 1944-45; Rudy Vallee Show.
Television: Adam 12; Love, American Style; Saturday Night at the
    Apollo; Merv Griffin Show; Midas Muffler commercial; The
    Green Pastures (Hallmark Hall of Fame) 1959; Bill Cosby
    Show 1970.
Theater: Appearances at Apollo Theatre; Loew's State Theatre;
    Harlem Scandals 1932; Estragon in Waiting for Godot 1957.

MORRIS, GARRETT
    (Actor)
b. February 1, 1937, New Orleans, La.
Education: Dillard University B. A.; Juilliard School of Music;
    Manhattan School of Music; Tanglewood Music Workshop.
Special Interests: Singing, composing.
Honors: Omega Psi Phi National Singing Contest winner.
Career Data: Arranger for Belafonte singers.
Films: Where's Poppa? 1970; The Anderson Tapes 1971; Cooley
    High 1975.
Memberships: ASCAP 1963.
Musical Compositions: If I Had-a My Way; Tell God All-a My
    Troubles.
Television: Roll Out (series) 1973; Saturday Night Live (series)
    1975; Mike Douglas Show 1977.
Theater: Authored and acted in The Secret Place; Ododo; (O. B.);
    Street Sounds; Basic Training of Pavlo Hummel (O. B.); The
    Great White Hope; Bible Salesman (O. B.) 1961; Porgy and
    Bess (City Center) 1964; Show Boat (L. C. R.) 1966; Hallelujah

Baby 1967; Finian's Rainbow (City Center) 1967; I'm Solomon
1968; Slave Ship (O. B.) 1969; Transfers (O. B.) 1970; Operation
Sidewinder (L. C. R.) 1970; Ain't Supposed to Die a Natural
Death 1971; In New England Winter (O. B.) 1971; What the
Winesellers Buy (L. C. R.) 1973.

MORRIS, GREG
    (Actor)
b. September 27, 1934, Cleveland, Ohio.
Education: Ohio State University; University of Iowa.
Address: c/o Frank Liberman & Associates Inc. , 9255 Sunset Blvd.
    Suite 510, Los Angeles, Calif. 90069.
Honors: Most promising newcomer to fashion on television (Cos-
    tume Designers Guild) 1968-69; Emmy Nominations 1969,
    1970, 1972; NAACP Image award 1971; nomination, Star of
    the Year, Hollywood Women's Press Club 1971; Angel of the
    Year, Girls Friday of Show Business 1971; TV Father of the
    Year (National Father's Day Committee) 1971.
Career Data: Board of directors, Center Theatre Group of Los
    Angeles 1972; board of trustees, Benedict College 1973.
Films: The New Interns, The Lively Set 1964; The Sword of Ali
    Baba 1965, Countdown at Kusini 1976.
Television: Twilight Zone; Ed Sullivan Show; Dean Martin Show;
    What's My Line; Mannix; Match Game; Tattletales; Celebrity
    Sweepstakes; Six Million Dollar Man; A Glow of Dying Embers
    (Love Story); Dr. Kildare 1963; Dick Van Dyke Show 1963,
    65; Ben Casey 1963; Fugitive 1965; Branded 1965; Barney Col-
    lier in Mission: Impossible (series) 1966-72; I Spy 1966;
    Love, American Style 1970; Killer by Night 1972; Password
    1974; Knowledge 1974; Lucas Tanner 1975; Masquerade Party
    1975; Mitzi and 100 Guys (special) 1975; Dionne Warwicke
    (Special) 1975; Jerry Visits 1975; Don Adams Screen Test
    1975; Cross-Wits 1975; Captain Kangaroo 1975; Streets of San
    Francisco 1975; Show-Offs 1975; You Don't Say 1975; Ameri-
    can Express Card commercial 1976; Sanford and Son 1976;
    Flight to Holocaust 1977.
Theater: A Raisin in the Sun (L. A.).

MORTON, BENNY (Henry Sterling Morton)
    (Jazz Musician/Conductor)
b. January 31, 1907, New York, N. Y.
Special Interests: Trombone, conducting.
Career Data: Played with Fletcher Henderson 1927, 1931-32, Count
    Basie 1937-39, Teddy Wilson 1940; formed his own band 1946;
    worked with pit bands for Broadway shows.
Clubs: Café Society; Roseland.
Radio: Worked with Raymond Scott (CBS) 1944.
Television: Soundstage 1975.
Theater: Worked with pit bands for Memphis Bound 1944; St. Louis
    Woman 1946; Lend an Ear 1948; Regina 1949; Guys and Dolls
    1950-53; Silk Stockings 1955; Shinbone Alley 1957; Jamaica
    1957; Whoop-Up; played in Radio City Music Hall orchestra 1959.

MORTON, JELLY ROLL (Ferdinand Joseph La Menthe)
    (Jazz Musician/Composer)
b.   September 20, 1885, Gulfport, La.
d.   July 10, 1941, Los Angeles, Calif.
Special Interests: Piano, conducting, singing, guitar.
Honors: Record Changer, All Time, All Star Poll Winner 1951.
Career Data: Led his own band, Morton's Red Hot Peppers, 1926-
    30.
Musical Compositions: Steamboat Stop; Sidewalk Blues; The King
    Porter Stomp; Tiger Rag; Milenburg Joys; Wolverine Blues;
    The Pearls; Shoe Shiner's Drag (a. k. a. London Blues); Wild
    Man Blues; Kansas City Stomps; The Miserere; Big Fat Home;
    Mamie's Blues; Chicago Breakdown; Superior Rag; Grandpa
    Spells.
Records: King of New Orleans Jazz (Victor); The Saga of Mr. Jelly
    Lord; Jelly Roll Morton: 1923/24 (Milestone); Jelly Roll Mor-
    ton Plays Jelly Roll; New Orleans Memories & Last Band
    Dates 1938; Immortal (Milestone); Jelly Roll Morton (Archive
    of Folk & Jazz Music); 1924-6 Rare Piano Rolls (Biograph);
    Piano Roles (Trip).

MORTON, JOE (Joseph Thomas Morton)
    (Actor)
b.   October 18, 1947, New York, N. Y.
Education: Hofstra University (drama).
Special Interests: Writing.
Address: 105 East 19 Street, New York, N. Y. 10003.
Honors: Theatre World Award 1974; Tony nomination 1974.
Films: Between the Lines 1977.
Memberships: AEA; AFTRA; SAG.
Television: Dr. James Foster in Search for Tomorrow (series)
    1972-74; Feeling Good (series) 1974; Not for Women Only 1974;
    Sanford and Son 1975; Grady (series) 1975; M*A*S*H 1976;
    What's Happening 1976.
Theater: Hair; Tricks (O. B.); Salvation; Charlie Was Here but Now
    He's Gone; Christophe (Chelsea Theatre Prod.); Jesus Christ
    Superstar (tour); Month of Sundays (O. B.) 1968; Valentine in
    Two Gentlemen of Verona 1972; Walter Lee Younger in Raisin
    1973-75; I Paid My Dues (O. B.) 1976.

MOSES, ETHEL "The Negro Harlow"
    (Actress)
Special Interests: Dancing.
Career Data: Entertained in night clubs; leading lady in silent and
    sound black films, now retired; toured with Lucky Millinder
    orchestra.
Clubs: Cotton Club; Ubangi Club; Connie's Inn.
Films: Lem Hawkins' Confession 1935; Temptation 1936; The Under-
    world 1937; God's Stepchildren, The Policy Man 1938; Birth-
    right, Gone Harlem 1939.
Theater: Dixie to Broadway 1924-1925; Blackbirds 1926; Show Boat
    1927; Keep Shufflin' 1928.

MOSES, GILBERT
        (Director)
b. August 20, 1942, Cleveland, Ohio.
Education: Oberlin College 1960-63; New York University 1966;
        Sorbonne; studied acting/playwriting with Lloyd Richards,
        Paul Sills, Kristin Linklater.
Special Interests: Acting, guitar, composing, writing.
Address: 463 West Street, New York, N.Y. 10014.
Honors: Obie (for Slave Ship) 1969; Tony nomination and Drama
        Desk award for (Ain't Supposed to Die a Natural Death) 1972;
        Obie (for Taking of Miss Janie) 1975; AUDELCO Theatre Rec-
        ognition award 1975.
Career Data: Co-founder and artistic director, The Free Southern
        Theatre, New Orleans 1963; productions include: In White
        America, East of Jordan, Slave Ship; director, Karamu Play-
        house, Cleveland.
Films: Wrote music and lyrics, scored 4 songs and directed Willie
        Dynamite 1974.
Memberships: Directors Guild of America.
Publications: Roots (1 act play) 1966; co-edited The Free Southern
        Theatre (a documentary of the South's Black Theatre), Bobbs-
        Merrill, n.d.; edited Fort Greene Drum, Brooklyn, n.d.
Television: Positively Black 1975; Roots 1977.
Theater: Rigoletto (San Francisco Opera); Mother Courage (Arena
        Stage, Wash. D.C.); No Place to Be Somebody (Arena Stage,
        Wash. D.C.); Blood Knot (American Conservatory Theatre),
        San Francisco; In New England Winter (Boston Theatre Co.);
        Slave Ship 1969; Don't Let It Go to Your Head (Henry Street
        Playhouse) 1972; The Duplex (LCR) 1972: Ain't Supposed to
        Die a Natural Death 1972; Rip Off 1974; Black Picture Show
        (LCR) 1974; The Wiz 1975; The Taking of Miss Janie 1975;
        Every Night When the Sun Goes Down (O.B.) 1976; co-directed
        and choreographed 1600 Pennsylvania Avenue 1976.

MOSLEY, ROGER E.
        (Actor)
b. Los Angeles, Calif.
Education: Trade Tech at California State.
Address: Aimee Entertainment, 14241 Ventura Blvd., Sherman Oaks,
        Calif.
Career Data: Member, Watts Writers Workshop; Head of Drama
        Dept., Mfundi Institute.
Films: Hit Man, The New Centurions 1972; The Mack, Sweet Jesus
        Preacher Man 1973; McQ 1974; Darktown Strutters 1975; title
        role in Leadbelly, The River Niger, Stay Hungry, Drum 1976;
        The Greatest 1977.
Memberships: SAG.
Television: Kung Fu; Sanford and Son; Streets of San Francisco;
        McCloud; Cannon; Kojak 1974; That's My Mama 1975; Like It
        Is 1975; Baretta 1975; Rookies 1975; Starsky and Hutch 1977.
Theater: Porgy and Bess (L.A.).

MOSLEY, SNUB (Lawrence Leo Mosely)
  (Jazz Musician)
b. December 29, 1909, Little Rock, Ark.
Education: Studied with Eugene Crook (Cincinnati).
Special Interests: Singing, slide-saxophone, trombone.
Address: 555 Edgecombe Avenue, New York, N.Y. 10032.
Career Data: Played with bands of Claude Hopkins 1934-36, Fats
     Waller 1935, Louis Armstrong 1938; led his own band since
     1938; U.S.O. tours in 1940s.
Clubs: Woodmere Country Club (L.I.) 1939; Queens Terrace (L.I.)
     1940; Stagecoach (N.J.); The Frolic Inn.
Television: Joe Franklin Show 1976.
Theater: Ken Murray's Blackouts.

MOTEN, BENNIE
  (Jazz Musician/Conductor)
b. November 13, 1894, Kansas City, Mo.
d. April 2, 1935, Kansas City, Mo.
Special Interests: Piano.
Career Data: Led his own band from 1922-35; Count Basie, Hot
     Lips Page, Ben Webster and others worked for him.
Theater: Appeared at Lafayette Theatre (Harlem) 1931.

MOTEN, ETTA
  (Singer/Actress)
b. San Antonio, Texas.
Education: Western University (Kansas City); University of Kansas
     (Lawrence, Kansas) A.B. (music and dramatic arts) 1931.
Special Interests: Teaching dramatics to children.
Address: Mrs. Claude Barnett, 3619 So. Martin Luther King Drive,
     Chicago, Ill. 60653.
Career Data: Toured Keith-Orpheum Theatre circuit throughout the
     U.S.; performed with Redpath Chatauqua circuit unit 1941;
     gave recitals in major cities throughout U.S.
Films: Dubbed singing for Barbara Stanwyck in Ladies of the Big
     House 1932; Gold Diggers of 1933; performed Carioca number
     in Flying Down to Rio 1933; dubbed singing for Ginger Rogers
     in 20 Million Sweethearts 1934.
Memberships: National Council of Negro Women.
Radio: Soloist with Meredith Wilson orchestra and the Kare Free
     Karnival (NBC); Variety Hour (CBS).
Theater: Appearances at The Palace Theatre; The N.Y. Academy
     of Music; The Paramount Theatre (Los Angeles); Fast and
     Furious 1931; Sugar Hill 1931; Zombie 1932; Replaced Anne
     Brown as Bess in Porgy and Bess 1944; title role in Lysistrata
     1946.

MURPHY, ROSE "Chi Chi Girl"
    (Singer)
b.   April 28, Xenia, Ohio.
Special Interests: Composing, piano.
Career Data: Performed at Newport Jazz Festival 1974.
Clubs: Café Society; Cookery 1977.
Films: A Wave, a Wac and a Marine 1944; George White's Scandals
    1945.
Memberships: ASCAP (1961).
Musical Compositions: What Good?; Whatcha Gotta Lose?
Television: Ed Sullivan Show.
Theater: Appearance at Palladium (London).

MURRAY, JAMES P.
    (Critic)
b.   October 16, 1946, Bronx, N.Y.
Education: Syracuse University B.A. (journalism) 1968.
Address: 30 Rockefeller Plaza, New York, N.Y. 10020.
Honors: First black elected to N.Y. Film Critics Circle 1972.
Career Data: Editor-in-chief, Black Creation Magazine 1972-74;
    arts & entertainment editor, Amsterdam News (N.Y.) 1973-75.
Memberships: Harlem Writers Guild 1971.
Publications: To Find an Image: Black Films from Uncle Tom to
    Super Fly, Bobbs-Merrill, 1973; "The Subject Is Money" in
    Lindsay Patterson's Black Films and Filmmakers, Dodd, Mead,
    1975.
Television: News trainee, ABC-TV News 1968-71; Black Pride 1973;
    press representative, NBC 1975-.

MURRAY, JOAN (E.)
    (Broadcaster)
b.   November 6, 1941, Ithaca, N.Y.
Education: Ithaca College; Hunter College; New School for Social
    Research; French Institute; Harvard University.
Address: 536 East 79 Street, New York, N.Y. 10021.
Honors: One of Foremost Women in Communications 1969-70;
    Mademoiselle award for outstanding achievement 1969; John
    Russwurm award; N.Y. Urban League's Certificate of Merit,
    Media Woman of the Year; Matrix award from N.Y. Women
    in Communications 1974; Links distinguished service award in
    field of communications; Mary McLeod Bethune achievement
    award.
Career Data: Founder and executive vice-president, Zebra Associ-
    ates, Inc. (black advertising agency) 1970.
Memberships: AFTRA; American Women in Radio & TV; Television
    Academy of Arts and Sciences.
Publications: A Week with the News (autobiography), McGraw-Hill
    (Young Pioneer Book Series), 1968.
Radio: Interviewer, The Joan Murray Show ... And There Are
    Women.

Television: Co-hostess, Two at One; production assistant and writer, Candid Camera; co-hostess, writer, production assistant,
Women on the Move (NBC series) 1963-65; News correspondent, (CBS) 1965-70; Opportunity Line, (CBS) 1971.

MUSE, CLARENCE E.
(Actor)
b. October 7, 1889, Baltimore, Md.
Education: LL.B. (International Law) Dickinson College, School of
Law, Carlyle, Pa. (1919).
Special Interests: Songwriting, directing.
Address: Good Hope Valley, Perris, Calif. 92370.
Honors: Black Filmmakers Hall of Fame 1973.
Career Data: Co-founder, Lafayette Players.
Films: Nappus in Hearts of Dixie 1929; Guilty?, Royal Romance,
Rain or Shine 1930; Dirigible, The Last Parade, Safe in Hell,
The Fighting Sheriff, Huckleberry Finn, Secret Witness, Ter-
ror by Night 1931; Woman from Monte Carlo, Prestige, Lena
Rivers, Night World, Wet Parade, Winner Take All, Attorney
for the Defense, Is My Face Red?, White Zombie, Hell's
Highway, Washington Merry-Go-Round, Cabin in the Cotton,
Man Against Woman 1932; Laughter in Hell, From Hell to
Heaven, The Mind Reader, The Wrecker 1933; Massacre, Fury
in the Jungle, Black Moon, The Personality Kid, The Count of
Monte Cristo, Broadway Bill 1934; Harmony Lane, Alias Mary
Dow, O'Shaughnessy's Boy, So Red the Rose, East of Java
1935; Laughing Irish Eyes, Muss'Em Up!, Showboat, Rainbow
on the River, Follow Your Heart, Daniel Boone 1936; Mysterious Crossing 1937; Spirit of Youth, The Toy Wife, Prison
Train, Secrets of a Nurse 1938; Way Down South (acted in and
wrote with Langston Hughes) 1939; Broken Strings (acted in
and wrote screenplay) Zanzibar, Maryland, Sporting Blood,
That Gang of Mine, Murder over New York 1940; The Flame
of New Orleans, Adam Had Four Sons, New York Town, Invisible Ghost, Love Crazy, Gentlemen from Dixie 1941; Tales
of Manhattan, The Black Swan 1942; The Sky's the Limit,
Watch on the Rhine, Shadow of a Doubt, Heaven Can Wait,
Flesh and Fantasy, Johnny Come Lately, Sherlock Holmes in
Washington 1943; Follow the Boys, In the Meantime Darling,
Jam Session 1944; The Racket Man, Scarlet Street 1945; Night
and Day 1946; Two Smart People, Joe Palooka in The Knock-
out 1947; Live Today for Tomorrow, An Act of Murder 1948;
The Great Dan Patch 1949; Riding High, County Fair 1950;
The Las Vegas Story, My Forbidden Past, Apache Drums 1951;
Caribbean, So Bright the Flame 1952; Jamaica Run 1953; Por-
gy and Bess 1959; Buck and the Preacher 1972; World's Great-
est Athlete 1973; Car Wash 1976.
Memberships: ASCAP 1940; SAG.
Musical Compositions: When It's Sleepy Time Down South; Weary
Feet; River of Freedom; Liberty Road; Deep and Mighty Is
the River; Have You Ever Been Down Yonder?

Publications: The Dilemma of the Negro Actor (pamphlet), 1934,
    Way Down South (story of a Negro vaudeville troupe) 1932.
Television: Bourbon Street (Four Star Playhouse) 1954; Casablanca
    (series) 1955; Kup's Show 1976.
Theater: Formed Clarence Muse Co. (New York); appeared with
    Lincoln Players, co-founder Lafayette Players; Lafayette Pro-
    ductions: Porgy, Trilby, The Servant in the House, Within
    the Law, Dr. Jekyll and Mr. Hyde, Run Little Chillun.

MYERS, PAULINE (Evelyn)
    (Actress)
b. November 9, Ocilla, Ga.
Career Data: Worked with American Negro Theatre.
Films: The Green Pastures 1936; Boomerang 1947; Tarzan's Fight
    for Life 1958; All the Fine Young Cannibals 1960; Take a
    Giant Step 1961; Fate Is the Hunter, Shock Treatment, Honey-
    moon Hotel 1964, The Lost Man, The Comic 1969; Tick...Tick
    ...Tick... 1970; Lady Sings the Blues 1972; Maurie 1973; The
    String Lost in the Stars 1974.
Memberships: AEA; AFTRA; NAG; SAG.
Radio: Theater Guild of the Air; The Ford Hour; Cavalcade of
    America; The Jack Benny Show.
Television: Days of Our Lives (series); Eddie Cantor Show; Big
    Story; Plain Clothesman; Starlight Theatre; Mannix; Silver
    Theatre; Stage Door; Alfred Hitchcock Presents; Room 222;
    Night Stalker; Train for Tecumseh (G.E. Theatre) 1959; Great
    Gettin' Up Mornin' (Repertoire Workshop) 1964; Then Came
    Bronson 1969; That's My Mama 1974; The Jeffersons 1975;
    This Is the Life 1975; All in the Family 1975; Police Woman
    1975; The F.B.I. vs. the Ku Klux Klan (Attack on Terror)
    1975; Good Times 1976; Ex-Lax commercial 1977.
Theater: Trial by Fire (Blackfriars Guild); Growing Pains (debut)
    1933; Kykunkor 1934; Plumes in the Dust; The Willow and I;
    The Naked Genius; Dear Ruth; Take a Giant Step 1953; The
    World of My America (one woman show O.B.) 1966.

NASH, JOHNNY
    (Singer/Actor)
b. August 19, 1940, Houston, Texas.
Education: School for Young Professionals.
Honors: Silver Sail (Locarno Motion Picture Festival).
Clubs: The Bottom Line 1974.
Films: Key Witness 1960; Take a Giant Step 1961.
Memberships: ASCAP 1961.
Musical Compositions: What Kind of Love Is This?; Let Me Cry;
    Lonesome Romeo.
Records: A Very Special Love (ABC) 1957; Hold Me Tight (JAD)
    1968; I Can See Clearly Now (Epic) 1972; Celebrate Life
    (Epic) 1974; Besame Mucho (Pickwick); Merry Go-Round
    (Epic); Teardrops in the Rain (Repeat).

Television: Arthur Godfrey Show; Matinee (KPRC-Houston) 1953-55;
    Don Kirshner's Rock Concert 1974; Soul Train 1974; Mike
    Douglas Show 1975.

NELSON, GAIL (Evangelyn)
    (Singer/Actress)
b. March 29, 1946, Durham, N.C.
Education: Oberlin College B.M. 1965; New England Conservatory
    M.M. 1967, Philadelphia Music Academy 1959-61; Mozarteum
    (Salzburg, Austria) 1963-64; Graz Summer Vocal Institute,
    (Graz, Austria) 1972.
Special Interests: Dancing.
Address: 401 West 44 Street, New York, N.Y. 10036.
Honors: Metropolitan Opera Studio Lucretia Bori award 1970-72.
Career Data: Lieder concert tours throughout U.S. and Europe;
    sang opera in Europe and U.S. 1963-73; Alvin Ailey Dance
    Concert 1975.
Clubs: Rodney Dangerfield's; The Brothers and Sisters.
Films: The Way We Live Now, Cotton Comes to Harlem 1970;
    I Never Sang for My Father 1971.
Memberships: AEA; AFTRA; AGMA; AGVA; SAG.
Records: Avez Vous Peanut Butter (Goober); That Healin' Feelin'
    (Blue Note); Ghetto Lights (Blue Note); Phase Three (Blue
    Note).
Television: The World of Kurt Weill; Someone New 1969; Callback
    1969; Kodak commercial.
Theater: Hello, Dolly! (understudy) 1968-70; Lost in the Stars
    (understudy) (ELT) 1968; Applause 1971; Six (O.B.) 1971; On
    the Town 1971; Music Music (City Center) 1974; appeared at
    City Center; Alice Tully Hall 1971; Radio City Music Hall
    1974; Avery Fisher Hall 1975; Duet (An Evening of Theatre
    in Song with Leon Bibb, Vancouver) 1975.

NELSON, NOVELLA (C.)
    (Singer/Actress)
b. December 17, 1939, Brooklyn, N.Y.
Education: Brooklyn College
Special Interests: Directing, producing.
Address: 425 Lafayette Street, New York, N.Y. 10003.
Career Data: Member, acting company of ACT, Alliance Theatre,
    Atlanta; Seattle Repertory Co.; Ju Ju Players; Harlem Chil-
    dren's Theatre, New Heritage Theatre; Resident Consultant,
    The Public Theatre; participated in Newport Jazz Festival.
Clubs: Reno Sweeney 1975; Village Vanguard 1975; The Bottom Line
    1975; The New Barrister (Bronx) 1976; Village Gate 1977.
Memberships: National Council of Negro Women; NEC.
Television: Soul; Black Pride; Positively Black 1975; Woman Alive
    1975; Express Yourself (public television) 1975.
Theater: Directed: Les Femmes Noires; Sister Sonjii; Nigger
    Nightmare (O.B.) 1971; Julius Caesar (NYSF); Sweet Talk
    (Shakespeare Festival Theatre Workshop) 1974; acted in:

House of Flowers (O.B.) 1968; Helly, Dolly! 1969; Purlie
1970; Gilbeau (New Federal Theatre) 1976; appearances at:
Avery Fisher Hall 1975; An Evening with Novella Nelson
(Vincent's Place) 1975; Ftatateeta in Caesar and Cleopatra
1977.

NELSON, OLIVER (Edward)
    (Jazz Musician)
b. June 4, 1932, St. Louis Mo.
d. October 27, 1975, Los Angeles, Calif.
Education: Washington Univ. 1954-57; Lincoln Univ. 1957-58.
Special Interests: Alto & tenor saxophone, flute, composing, ar-
    ranging.
Honors: Edison award (Amsterdam) 1965; Deutsche Grammophone
    award 1967; 12th International Jazz Critics Poll (Down Beat)
    winner; Grammy winner; Grand Gala du Disque award (Amster-
    dam).
Career Data: Played with Duke Ellington, Count Basie, Louis
    Jordan 1950-51, Erskine Hawkins, Louis Bellson; U.S. State
    Dept. tour of Africa 1969.
Clubs: Bottom Line.
Films: Walk on the Wild Side (score) 1962; Who's Afraid of Vir-
    ginia Woolf (score) 1966; Death of a Gunfighter (score) 1969;
    Skullduggery (score) 1970.
Musical Compositions: The Artists' Rightful Place; Black, Brown
    and Beautiful; The American Wind Symphony; Hobo Flats;
    African Sunset; Hoe Down; Miss Fine; Emancipation Blues;
    Goin' Out of My Head; Kilimanjar; Woodwind Quintet 1960;
    Song Cycle for Contralto and Piano 1961; Dirge for Chamber
    Orchestra 1962; Soundpiece for String Quartet and Contralto
    1963; Soundpiece for Jazz Orchestra 1964; Jazzhattan Suite
    1967.
Records: Blues and the Abstract Truth (Impulse); More Blues and
    the Abstract Truth (Impulse); Full Nelson; Fantabulous; Main
    Stem (Prestige); Afro-American Sketches (Prestige); Berlin
    Dialogue (Flying Dutchman); Black, Brown and Beautiful (Fly-
    ing Dutchman); Dream Deferred (Flying Dutchman); In London
    (Flying Dutchman); Images (Prestige); Kennedy Dream: A
    Musical Tribute (Impulse); Live from Los Angeles (Impulse);
    Michelle (Impulse); Skull Session (Flying Dutchman); Sound
    Pieces (Impulse); Swiss Suite (Flying Dutchman).
Television: Ironside (score); It Takes a Thief (score); The Name
    of the Game (score); Night Gallery (score); The Six Million
    Dollar Man (score); Positively Black 1975.

NICHOLAS, DENISE
    (Actress)
b. c.1944, Detroit, Mich.
Education: University of Michigan B.A.; Studied acting with Paul
    Mann, dance with Louis Johnson.
Special Interests: Guitar, singing, writing poetry.

Honors: NAACP Image award as motion picture actress (Let's Do
It Again) 1976 and dramatic role in television (Police Story)
1976.
Career Data: Negro Ensemble Co. 1967-68; member, Free Southern
Theatre (New Orleans) 1964-66.
Films: Blacula 1972; The Soul of Nigger Charley 1973; Mr. Ricco
1975; Let's Do It Again 1975; A Piece of the Action 1977.
Television: The F.B.I.; It Takes a Thief 1968; Liz in Room 222
(series) 1969-73; N.Y.P.D.; Rhoda; Dinah! 1975; Police Story
1975; Marcus Welby, M.D. 1975.
Theater: In White America (tour) 1964; Viet Rock (O.B.); Purlie
Victorious (tour) 1965; Waiting for Godot (tour) 1965; Three
Boards and a Passion (tour) 1966; Song of the Lusitanian
Bogey (NEC) 1968; Kongi's Harvest (NEC) 1968; Daddy Good-
ness (NEC) 1968; Ceremonies in Dark Old Men (O.B.) 1969.
Relationships: Former wife of Gil Moses, director and former
wife of Bill Withers, singer.

NICHOLS, NICHELLE
    (Actress)
b. c.1936, Robbins, Ill.
Special Interests: Singing.
Career Data: Toured U.S., Canada and Europe with bands of Duke
Ellington, Lionel Hampton; executive vice-president, The Wom-
an in Motion Production Co. (L.A.).
Clubs: Blue Angel 1962.
Films: Mister Buddwing 1966; Doctor You've Got to Be Kidding
1967; Truck Turner 1974.
Memberships: SAG.
Television: Uhura in Star Trek (series); The Lieutenant; Great
Gettin' Up Mornin' (Repertoire Workshop) 1964.
Theater: Kicks and Company 1961.

NOBLE, GIL (Gilbert E. Noble)
    (Broadcaster/Producer)
b. February 22, 1932, New York, N.Y.
Special Interests: Music (piano); black history and culture; media.
Address: c/o WABC TV, 77 West 66 Street, New York, N.Y. 10023.
Honors: John Russworm award from Urban League 1969; Emmy
award 1970; Emmy Nominee 1974; N.Y. Emmy award 1976.
Black Citizens for a Fair Media citation 1976.
Memberships: AFTRA.
Radio: Newsman/announcer WLIB 1962-67.
Television: Weekend News (ABC) 1971; Newsman, Eyewitness News
(ABC); host and producer, Like It Is (ABC) (includes specials:
El Hajj Malik El Shabazz; Paul Robeson: The Tallest Tree;
The Life and Times of Frederick Douglass).

NORFORD, GEORGE (E.)
    (Playwright/Producer)
b. January 18, 1918, New York, N.Y.

Education: Columbia University; New School for Social Re-
    search.
Address: 90 Park Avenue, New York, N.Y. 10016
Career Data: Vice-president, Westinghouse Broadcasting Co.;
    former editor, Negro Digest.
Memberships: NATAS.
Television: Press writer, The Today Show; produced network pro-
    gram at NBC 1957; produced The Subject Is Jazz 1958.
Theater: Wrote Joy Exceeding Joy 1938 and Head of the Family
    1950.

NORMAN, JESSYE
    (Concert Singer)
b.   September 15, 1945, Augusta, Ga.
Education: Howard University 1963-67 B. Mus.; studied with Alice
    Duschak at Peabody Conservatory; University of Michigan.
Special Interests: Lieder, opera.
Address: c/o Harry Beall Management, Inc., 119 West 57 Street,
    New York, N.Y. 10019.
Honors: National Society of Arts and Letters First Prize 1965;
    Munich International Music Competition First Prize 1968;
    Finalist in Montreux International Record Award Competition
    1971.
Career Data: Sang with Deutsche Oper Berlin 1970-73; appearances
    in Israel, Canada, Mexico, South America; U.S. State Depart-
    ment tour of South America 1968; appeared at following festi-
    vals: Two Worlds (Spoleto) 1970; Vienna, the Schwetzingen
    (Germany), Bath, Tours, Harrogate (England), Lucerne, Hel-
    sinki, Aldeburgh 1973; Israel 1974; Ravinia 1975.
Records: The Marriage of Figaro (Philips) 1971; Euryanthe (Angel)
    1975.
Theater: Sang Handel's Messiah at Constitution Hall (Washington,
    D.C.) 1968; Elizabeth in Tannhäuser, Deborah at Teatro Com-
    munale (Florence) 1970; Idamante in Idomeneo (Rome) 1971;
    title role of L'Africaine (Florence) 1971; Countess in Marriage
    of Figaro (Berlin) 1971; title role in Aida (Berlin) 1972; debut
    at La Scala 1972; debut at Hollywood Bowl 1972; Cassandra in
    Berlioz' The Trojans at Covent Garden (London) 1972; appear-
    ances at Alice Tully Hall and Kennedy Center for the Perform-
    ing Arts (Washington, D.C.) 1973; Marguerite in Damnation
    of Faust (Rotterdam) 1973; Donna Elvira in Don Giovanni at
    Hollywood Bowl 1973; Tove in Schoenberg's Gurrelieder (Israel)
    1974; appearance at Royal Albert Hall (London) 1974; appear-
    ance at Carnegie Hall 1975; Avery Fisher Hall 1975; Brooklyn
    Academy of Music 1975; debut with N.Y. Philharmonic 1976.

NORMAN, MAIDIE (R.)
    (Actress)
b.   October 16, 1912, Ga.
Education: Bennett College 1934; Columbia University 1937; Actors
    Lab (Hollywood) 1946-49.

Special Interests: Directing, teaching.
Address: c/o U.C.L.A., 405 Hilgard, Los Angeles, Calif. 90024.
Honors: Cabrillo award for acting achievement 1952; Negro Authors
   Study Club award for civic service 1957; L.A. Sentinel Woman
   of the Year award 1963; Black Filmmakers Hall of Fame 1977.
Career Data: Artist in Residence, Stanford University 1968-69;
   acting teacher, University of California, Los Angeles 1970-
   date.
Films: The Burning Cross 1948; The Well 1951; Bright Road,
   Torch Song 1953; About Mrs. Leslie, Susan Slept Here 1954;
   Tarzan's Hidden Jungle 1955; The Opposite Sex 1956; Written
   on the Wind 1957; Elvira in Whatever Happened to Baby Jane
   1962; The Final Comedown 1972; Maurie 1973; A Star Is Born
   1976; Airport '77 1977.
Memberships: ANTA; California Educational Theater Assn.; League
   of Allied Arts; Lullaby Guild.
Television: Mannix; Adam-12; Cannon; Ironside; Name of the Game
   1969; Days of Our Lives 1971; Another Part of the Forest
   (Hollywood Television Theatre) 1972; Say Goodbye Maggie
   Cole 1972; Sty of the Blind Pig 1974; Streets of San Francisco
   1974; Rhoda 1974; Lucas Tanner 1974; Kung Fu 1975; Good
   Times 1975; Night Stalker 1975; Harry O 1975; The Jeffersons
   1975; Police Story 1976.
Theater: The Amen Corner 1965.

ODETTA (Odetta Holmes Felious)
   (Folk Singer)
b. December 31, 1930, Birmingham, Ala.
Education: Los Angeles City College.
Special Interests: Guitar.
Career Data: Toured U.S. and Canada 1958-59; performer at New-
   port Folk Festival; toured Soviet Union 1974.
Clubs: Tin Angel (San Francisco); Blue Angel; Gate of Horn (Chi-
   cago); Reno Sweeney 1975.
Films: Cinerama Holiday; The Last Time I Saw Paris 1954; Sanc-
   tuary 1961; Festival 1967.
Records: Odetta Sings Ballads and Blues (Tradition); The Best of
   Odetta (Tradition); Odetta Sings Dylan; Essential Odetta (Van-
   guard); Ballad for Americans (United Artists); At Carnegie
   Hall (Vanguard); At the Gate of Horn (Tradition); At Town
   Hall (Vanguard); Folk Songs (RCA); Odetta (Archive of Folk
   & Jazz Music); Odetta (Fantasy); One Grain of Sand (Van-
   guard).
Television: TV Tonight (Belafonte special); Boboquivari 1974; The
   Autobiography of Miss Jane Pittman 1974; Black News 1975;
   Black Conversations 1976; Joe Franklin Show 1976.
Theater: Finian's Rainbow (L.A.) 1949; appearances at Town Hall
   1959; (5:45 Interlude series) 1976; Turnabout Theatre (L.A.);
   Carnegie Hall 1960, 1976; Brooklyn Academy of Music 1974;
   Lincoln Center 1975; Look! What a Wonder (Berkeley Com-
   munity Theater, Berkeley, Calif.) 1976.

OKPAKU, JOSEPH O. O.
   (Playwright)
b.   March 24, 1943, Lokoja (Northern Nigeria).
Education: Northwestern University B.S. 1965; Stanford University
   M.S. 1966.
Address: 444 Central Park West, New York, N.Y. 10025.
Honors: Second prize, BBC African Drama Competition (for Virtues
   of Adultery) 1966.
Career Data: Founder/president, The Third Press (Joseph Okpaku
   Publishing Co.).
Theater: Wrote Born Aside the Grave 1966; The Frogs on Capitol
   Hill (adaptation of Aristophanes' The Frogs); The Virtues of
   Adultery 1966.

OLATUNJI, MICHAEL BABATUNDE
   (Drummer)
b.   Nigeria.
Address: 875 West End Avenue, New York, N.Y. 10025.
Career Data: Director, Olatunji Center for African Culture.
Records: Drums of Passion; More Drums of Passion.
Television: Mike Douglas Show 1975; Say Brother 1975.
Theater: Appeared at Apollo Theatre; Klitgord Center (Brooklyn);
   Billie Holiday Theatre (Brooklyn); Harlem Performance Center
   1976.

OLIVER, KING (Joseph Oliver)
   (Jazz Musician)
b.   May 11, 1885, New Orleans, La.
d.   April 8, 1938, Savannah, Ga.
Special Interests: Cornet, conducting, composing.
Career Data: Played with several groups 1908-17; worked with
   Kid Ory 1917-19; led his own Creole Jazz Band 1922-25; his
   Syncopaters 1925-27; formed and led other bands on and off
   until 1937; known as the "Talking Trumpet" cornetist.
Clubs: Lincoln Gardens (Chicago); Dreamland (Chicago); Pekin
   Cabaret (Chicago); Deluxe Cafe (Chicago); Savoy Ballroom.
Musical Compositions: Sugar Foot Stomp (a.k.a. Dipper Mouth
   Blues); Canal Street Blues; Snag It; Chimes Blues; West End
   Blues; Doctor Jazz; Riverside Blues (a.k.a. Jazzin' Babies
   Blues).
Records: King Oliver in N.Y.; The King Oliver Creole Jazz Band;
   King Oliver "Papa Joe" 1926-1928; King Oliver's Jazz Band
   1923 (Smithsonian).

OLIVER, SY (Melvin James Oliver)
   (Jazz Musician)
b.   December 17, 1910, Battle Creek, Mich.
Special Interests: Arranging, composing, trumpet, conducting.
Address: 865 West End Avenue, New York, N.Y. 10025.

Honors: Down Beat poll winner 1941-45; Metronome poll winner
          1944; National Urban League award for contribution to world
          of music 1976.
Career Data: Played with Jimmy Lunceford 1933-39, Tommy Dor-
          sey 1939-42; led own band 1946; arranger for Ella Fitzgerald;
          musical director, Bethlehem Records 1954; Newport Jazz Fes-
          tival 1974.
Clubs: Zanzibar 1946; Music Box-Americana Hotel; Rainbow Room-
          Waldorf Astoria 1975, 76.
Musical Compositions: Easy Does It; Opus I; Swing High; Well Get
          It.
Radio: Endorsed by Dorsey.
Records: Above All 1977.
Television: Positively Black 1975; Black News 1977.
Theater: Scored: America Be Seated; Guys and Dolls; New Faces;
          Dr. Jazz 1975.

OLIVER, THELMA
          (Dancer/Actress)
b.   California.
Education: Studied with Herbert Berghof.
Special Interests: Piano, singing.
Honors: Lavinia Williams scholarship.
Career Data: Danced with Pearl Primus Dance Co. and Donald
          McKayle Dance Co.; participated in International Folk Festival
          (Los Angeles) 1959.
Films: South Pacific 1958; Pirates of Tortuga 1961; Black Like Me
          1964; The Pawnbroker 1965.
Television: The Doctors and the Nurses; Show Street; Merv Griffin
          Show; Cindy (Stage Two).
Theater: The Living Premise (O.B.); The Blacks (O.B.) 1961;
          Fly Blackbird (O.B.) 1962; Cindy (O.B.) 1964; Sweet Charity
          1966; The Tempest (NYSF); Three One Acts (O.B.); House of
          Flowers (O.B.) 1968.

O'NEAL, FREDERICK (Douglass)
          (Actor)
b.   August 27, 1905, Brooksville, Miss.
Education: New Theatre School 1936-40; American Theatre Wing;
          studied with Komisarjevsky, Lem Ward and others.
Special Interests: Civil rights, labor movement, teaching, inter-
          group relations, black history and culture, directing.
Address: 41 Convent Avenue, New York, N.Y. 10027, and 1500
          Broadway, New York, N.Y. 10036.
Honors: Clarence Derwent award and N.Y. Drama Critics award
          (for Anna Lucasta) 1944-45; Chicago Critics' award 1945-46;
          Motion Picture Critics' award (for Anna Lucasta) 1959; Ira
          Aldridge award (Assn. for the Study of Negro Life and History)
          1963; Hoey award (Catholic Interracial Council) 1964; David
          W. Petagorsky award for civic achievement (American Jewish

Congress) 1964; National Urban League E.O.D. award 1965;
Canada Lee Foundation award; N.Y.C. Central Labor Council
distinguished service award 1967; City of St. Louis award
1968; Frederick Douglass award (N.Y. Urban League) 1971;
Yiddish Theatrical Alliance 1971; League for Industrial Democ-
racy award 1973; Negro Trade Union Leadership Council Hu-
manitarian Award 1974; Black Filmmakers Hall of Fame 1975;
Audelco Recognition Award 1976.

Career Data: Founder, Aldridge players (St. Louis) 1927; co-
founder (with Abram Hill) of American Negro Theatre 1940;
helped organize British Negro Theatre (London) 1948; President Negro Actors Guild 1961-64; visiting professor, Southern
Illinois University 1962 and Clark College 1963; president
(first Black), Actors' Equity Association 1964-73; Vice President AFL-CIO 1969; chairman, AFL-CIO Civil Rights Committee 1970; international president, Associated Actors and Artistes of America 1970-date; secretary-treasurer, African-
American Labor Center 1974; advisory consultant, Federation
for the Extension and Development of the American Professional Theatre; commissioner, N.Y.C. Commission for Cultural
Affairs 1975; N.Y. State Council on the Arts 1976.

Films: Jake in Pinky (debut) 1949; No Way Out 1950; Tarzan's
Peril 1951; Something of Value 1957; Frank in Anna Lucasta
1959; Lem in Take a Giant Step 1961; The Sins of Rachel
Cade 1961; Free, White and 21 1963; Strategy of Terror 1969.

Memberships: AEA; AFI; AFTRA; ANTA; NAACP; NAG; NATAS;
SAG; Catholic Actors Guild; Actors Fund of America; Ohio
Community Theatre Assn.; Coordinating Council for Negro
Performers; Ira Aldridge Society; Episcopal Actors' Guild;
The Players; The Lambs; International Theatre Institute;
Harlem Cultural Council Advisory Board; A. Philip Randolph
Institute; Interamerican Federation of Entertainment Workers;
Board, Schomburg Collection of Black History; Literature and
Art Inc.; One Hundred Black Men.

Publications: "The Negro in the American Theatre," U.S. Information Service.

Television: Preacher in God's Trombones (Fred Waring Show);
Three's Company (pilot) 1954; Playwrights 1956; Phil Silvers
Show 1957; Trial of Diamonds (Armstrong Circle Theatre)
1959; Moses in the Green Pastures (Hallmark Hall of Fame)
1959; The Killers 1959; Simply Heavenly (Play of the Week)
1959; My Theory About Girls (CBS TV Workshop) 1960; Patrol-
man Wallace in Car 54 Where Are You? 1961-62; narrated
New York Illustrated 1962; The Patriots (Hallmark Hall of
Fame) 1963; Breaking Point 1964; In Darkness Waiting (Kraft
Suspense Theatre) 1965; Profiles in Courage 1965; Tarzan
1967.

Theater: As You Like It and Black Majesty (St. Louis) 1927; On
Striver's Row (ANT) 1940; Natural Man (ANT) 1941; Three's
a Family (ANT) 1943; Frank in Anna Lucasta (Bway debut)
1944; (Chicago) 1945-46; (London) 1947; title role in Henri
Christophe (ANT) 1945; A Lady Passing Fair (pre Bway tour)
1947; Head of the Family (Westport, Conn.) 1950; Lem in

Take a Giant Step 1953; House of Flowers 1954; The Winner
1954; The Man with a Golden Arm (O.B.) 1956; Lost in the
Stars (City Center) 1958; Antonio in Twelfth Night (Cambridge
Arts Festival) 1959; Shakespeare in Harlem 1960; Ballad for
Bimshire 1963; The Afro Philadelphian; Ballad of the Winter
Soldiers; Tell Pharaoh (O.B.) 1972, 75; Montage for Freedom
(Carnegie Hall) 1975; The World of a Harlem Playwright.

O'NEAL, RON
　　(Actor)
b.　September 1, 1937, Utica, N.Y.
Education: Ohio State University.
Special Interests: Teaching.
Address: Phil Gersh Agency, 222 N. Canon Drive, Beverly Hills,
　　Calif.
Honors: Obie, Clarence Derwent, Theatre World, Drama Desk
　　awards (for No Place to Be Somebody) 1969; Theatre World
　　award (for Dream on Monkey Mountain).
Career Data: Performed at Karamu Playhouse (Cleveland) in ap-
　　proximately 40 plays (including Walter Lee Younger in Raisin
　　in the Sun, Stanley in Streetcar Named Desire) 1957-66; worked
　　with N.Y. Shakespeare Festival; taught acting for HARYOU-
　　ACT 1964-66 and Kilpatrick-Cambridge School of Acting (L.A.)
　　1975.
Films: Move 1970; The Organization 1971; title role in Super Fly
　　1972; title role in Super Fly TNT 1973; The Master Gunfighter
　　1975; Brothers 1977.
Memberships: SAG.
Television: The Interns; Black Journal 1974; Today Show; Black
　　News 1975; Hot L Baltimore 1975.
Theater: Brother Julian in Tiny Alice; Basic Training of Pavlo
　　Hummel (O.B.); The Mummer's Play (O.B.); Dream on Mon-
　　key Mountain (NEC) 1971; American Pastorale (O.B.) 1968;
　　The Best of Broadway 1968; Gabe in No Place to Be Somebody
　　1969-70; Ceremonies in Dark Old Men (NEC) 1969; Taming
　　of the Shrew (tour) 1974; Poison Tree (pre-Bway) 1974; title
　　role in Macbeth (tour) 1974; All Over Town 1975; Agamemnon
　　(NYSF) 1977.

ORMAN, ROSCOE
　　(Actor)
b.　c.1944.
Education: High School of Art and Design.
Films: Title role in Willie Dynamite 1974.
Television: Sesame Street (series); Sanford and Son 1975.
Theater: If We Grow Up; Unfinished Business: Youth Sings Out
　　(O.B.) 1964; The Electronic Nigger (O.B.) 1968; The Sirens
　　(O.B.) 1974; The Secret Place (La Mama production) 1975;
　　When the Sun Goes Down (O.B.) 1976; Last Street Play (O.B.)
　　1977.

ORY, KID (Edward Ory)
    (Jazz Musician)
b. December 25, 1886, La Place, La.
d. January 23, 1973, Honolulu, Hawaii.
Special Interests: Trombone, conducting, cornet, alto saxophone,
    composing.
Honors: Record Changer all-time, all-star poll winner 1951.
Career Data: Led his own band (New Orleans) 1911-19 (L.A.)
    1919-25; played with bands of King Oliver 1925-27, Jelly Roll
    Morton, Buddy Bolden; reformed his own band in 1940's; Ber-
    lin Festival 1959, New Orleans Jazz Festival 1971.
Clubs: Sunset Café (Chicago) 1929; Club Araby 1931; Trouville
    Club (L.A.) 1942; Tiptoe Inn 1943; Jade Palace (L.A.);
    Beverly Cavern (L.A.); Child's 1955; On the Level (San
    Francisco) 1961.
Films: New Orleans, Crossfire 1947; Mahogany Magic 1950; The
    Benny Goodman Story 1956.
Memberships: ASCAP 1952.
Musical Compositions: Muskrat Ramble; Savoy Blues.
Radio: Orson Welles (series) 1944.
Records: Favorites (Good Time Jazz); Creole Jazz Band (Good
    Time Jazz); This Kid's the Greatest (Good Time Jazz); Tail-
    gate! (Good Time Jazz); Creole Jazz Band-Airchecks (Folk-
    lyric).
Theater: Appeared in Pantages Theatre circuit (L.A.) 1930.

OVERTON, BILL
    (Actor)
b. c.1947.
Address: William Morris Agency, 151 El Camino Drive, Beverly
    Hills, Calif. 90212.
Career Data: Former football player (with Dallas Cowboys and
    Kansas City Chiefs); former model.
Memberships: SAG.
Television: Firehouse 1972; Footsteps 1972; Night Train to Terror
    (Wide World Mystery); Harry O 1975; John Prentiss in Guess
    Who's Coming to Dinner (pilot) 1975.
Theater: Lord Shango 1975.

PACE, JUDY
    (Actress)
b. 1946, Los Angeles, Calif.
Education: Los Angeles City College; Studied with Lillian Randolph,
    Harvey Lembeck.
Address: Paul Kohner, 9169 Sunset Blvd., Los Angeles, Calif.
    90069.
Honors: NAACP Image Award as outstanding TV actress 1970.
Films: The Candy Web; 13 Frightened Girls 1963; The Fortune
    Cookie 1966; Three in the Attic; The Thomas Crown Affair
    1968; Cotton Comes to Harlem; Up in the Cellar; Getting
    Straight 1970; Cool Breeze; Frogs 1972; Slams 1973.

Memberships: SAG.
Television: The Danny Thomas Hour; I Dream of Jeannie; The
     Flying Nun; My Friend Tony; Bewitched; Insight; I Spy; Pro-
     files in Courage; Run for Your Life; Peyton Place (series);
     Medical Center; Kung Fu; That's My Mama; Tarzan 1968;
     Mod Squad 1968; N.Y.P.D. 1968; New People 1969; The Young
     Lawyers (series) 1970-71; Brian's Song 1971; Oh, Nurse 1972;
     Tilmon Tempo Show 1974; Ironside 1974; Caribe 1975; Fashion
     Fair commercial 1975; Good Times 1975.
Theater: Cindy (L.A.); My Fairfax Lady (L.A.); What This Coun-
     try Needs (L.A.); Goldfinkle (L.A.); The Zulu and the Zeda
     (L.A.); Guys and Dolls (Las Vegas) 1977.
Relationships: Sister of Jean Pace, singer; wife of Don Mitchell,
     actor.

PAGE, HARRISON
     (Actor)
Address: Rifkin-David, 9615 Brighton Way, Beverly Hills, Calif.
Films: Russ Meyer's Vixen 1969; Beyond the Valley of the Dolls
     1970.
Memberships: SAG.
Television: Sandcastles 1972; Love Thy Neighbor (series) 1973;
     Kojak 1974; Kung Fu 1974; Sepia Shock 1976; Adventurizing
     with the Chopper (pilot) 1976; CPO Sharkey (series) 1976.

PAGE, "HOT LIPS" (Oran Thaddeus Alfred Page)
     (Jazz Musician)
b. January 27, 1908, Dallas, Texas.
d. November 5, 1954, New York, N.Y.
Special Interests: Trumpet, conducting, mellophone.
Career Data: Worked with Ma Rainey, Bessie Smith; joined bands
     of Bennie Moten 1931-35; Count Basie 1935-36; his own band
     1936-41; Artie Shaw 1941; accompanist to Ethel Waters 1946;
     Paris Jazz Festival 1949; toured Europe 1950, 1951.
Clubs: Reno Club (Kansas City) 1936; Onyx Club 1937; Small's
     Paradise 1937; Plantation Club 1938; Brick Club 1938; Kelly's
     Stables; Famous Door; Savoy (Boston); Spotlite; Hotel Sherman
     (Chicago); West End Theatre Club; Café Society 1953.
Records: After Hours (Onyx); Trumpet at Minton's (Xanadu); The
     Hucklebuck/Baby It's Cold Outside 1949.
Theater: Appeared at Golden Gate Ballroom 1939, Apollo Theatre
     1943-45, Town Hall 1944.

PAGE, LAWANDA
     (Actress)
b. c.1920 St. Louis, Mo.
Special Interests: Fire-eating carnival act.
Address: Talent Inc. 1421 N. McCadden Place, Los Angeles, Calif.
Memberships: SAG.

Television: Aunt Esther on Sanford and Son (series) 1973-; Merv
Griffin Show 1975, 77; Mike Douglas Show 1975; Dinah! 1975;
Grady 1975; Clifton Davis Special 1976; Dean Martin Celebrity
Roast 1976, 77; Starsky and Hutch 1977; Richard Pryor Spe-
cial? 1977; Love Boat 1977.
Theater: Appeared at Howard Theatre (Washington, D.C.) 1975;
Apollo Theatre 1975.

PARKER, CHARLIE "Yardbird"; "Bird" (Charles Christopher Parker)
(Jazz Musician)
b. August 29, 1920, Kansas City, Mo.
d. March 12, 1955, New York, N.Y.
Special Interests: Alto saxophone, composing.
Honors: Esquire New Star award 1946; Metronome Poll winner
1948-53, Down Beat Poll 1950-54; Critic's Poll 1953-54;
Grammy best jazz soloist (posthumously) 1974; Ebony Music
award (posthumously) 1975.
Career Data: Co-founder, (with Dizzy Gillespie) of "The Bop"
movement; played with Cootie Williams, Andy Kirk, Noble
Sissle 1942, Earl Hines 1942-43, Billy Eckstine 1944; partici-
pated in Newport Jazz Festival, Paris Jazz Festival 1949.
Clubs: Birdland (named in his honor); Monroe's Uptown House;
Minton's.
Musical Compositions: Yardbird Suite; Ornithology; Confirmation;
Now's the Time; Relaxin' at Camarillo.
Records: Salt Peanuts; Be-Bop; New York 1208 Miles (Decca);
Groovin' High (Savoy); The Genius of Charlie Parker (Savoy);
Echoes of an Era (Roulette); Jazz at Massey Hall (Fantasy);
Charlie Parker (Prestige); Night and Day (Verve); The Char-
lie Parker Story (Verve); Charlie Parker's First Recordings
(Onyx); Bird: The Savoy Recordings (Savoy); The Greatest
Jazz Concert Ever (Prestige); April in Paris (Verve); Bird
and Diz (Verve); Birdology (Trip); Broadcast Performances
(ESP); Charlie Parker (Archive of Folk & Jazz Music); Es-
sential (Verve); Jazz Perennial (Verve); Live Performances
(ESP); Lullaby in Rhythm (Zim); The Master (Trip); New
Bird: Hi Hat Broadcasts (Phoenix); Now's the Time (Verve);
On Dial (Spotlite); ... Plays Porter (Verve); Return Engage-
ment (Verve); Swedish Schnapps (Verve); Verve Years 1948-
50 (Verve).
Theater: Appeared at Apollo Theatre.

PARKER, LEONARD (R.)
(Actor)
b. July 22, 1932, Cleveland, Ohio.
Education: Cleveland Institute of Music.
Special Interests: Directing, producing.
Address: 2311 Fifth Avenue, New York, N.Y. 10037.
Career Data: Worked with Karamu Playhouse (Cleveland); director
HARYOU Act's Arts and Cultural Delegate Agency 1975.
Films: Frankie in Nothing But a Man 1964; Brendo in Sweet Love
Bitter (a.k.a. It Won't Rub Off Baby) 1967; Johnson in

Stiletto 1969.
Memberships: AEA; SAG.
Records: Fly Black Bird (Mercury) 1962.
Television: Armstrong Circle Theatre; Espionage; N. Y. P. D.; The
    Doctors; As the World Turns; The Defenders; Naked City;
    The Doctors and the Nurses.
Theater: Dark of the Moon (O.B.) 1958; Carmen Jones (Theatre in
    the Park) 1959; The Long Dream 1960; Porgy and Bess (City
    Center) 1961; The Apple (O.B.) 1961; Fly Blackbird (O.B.)
    1962; The Connection (O.B.) 1963; One Flew Over the Cuckoo's
    Nest 1963; In White America (O.B.) 1963; The Physicist;
    Black Girl 1971; directed The Connection (O.B.) 1974; produced
    The Blacks (O.B.) 1975; produced The Yellow Pillow (Harlem
    Performance Center) 1976.

PARKS, GORDON (Alexander)
    (Director)
b. November 30, 1912, Fort Scott, Kan.
Special Interests: Composing music, photography, writing, produc-
    ing.
Address: 860 United Nations Plaza, New York, N. Y. 10017.
Honors: Rosenwald Fellowship 1942-43; ASMP Photographer of the
    Year 1960; Carr Van Anda award 1970; NAACP Spingarn Medal
    1972; Black Filmmakers Hall of Fame 1973.
Career Data: Photo-journalist, Life magazine 1949-70; editorial
    director, Essence magazine 1970-73; film director, Paramount
    Pictures.
Films: The World of Piri Thomas (doc.); The Diary of a Harlem
    Family (doc); wrote, produced, composed music and directed
    The Learning Tree 1969; directed Shaft 1971; directed Shaft's
    Big Score 1972; directed The Super Cops 1974; directed Lead-
    belly 1976.
Memberships: Authors Guild (past director); Directors Guild of
    America (National Board); ASMP (past director); NAACP;
    Urban League.
Musical Compositions: 5 piano sonatas; The Learning Tree Sym-
    phony; Symphonic Set: A Place for Piano and Wind Instru-
    ments.
Publications: The Learning Tree, Harper & Row, 1963; A Choice
    of Weapons, Harper & Row, 1966; Born Black, Lippincott,
    1971.
Television: Free Time 1971; Like It Is 1975; Black Pride 1975;
    Straight Talk 1975; Joe Franklin Show 1975; Positively Black
    1975.
Relationships: Father of Gordon Parks Jr., director.

PARKS, GORDON JR.
    (Director)
b. December 1934, Minneapolis, Minn.
Films: Africa and I (doc.); Super Fly 1972; Thomasine and Bush-
    rod, Three the Hard Way 1974; Aaron Loves Angela 1975.
Television: Kup's Show.

Television: Kup's Show.
Relationship: Son of Gordon Parks, director.

PATTERSON, LINDSAY
    (Critic)
b. July 20, 1937, Bastrop, La.
Education: Virginia State College B.A. (English).
Special Interests: Radio, films, theatre and television.
Address: 42 Perry Street, New York, N.Y. 10014.
Honors: National Foundation on the Arts & Humanities award;
    MacDowall Colony fellowships; Edward Albee Foundation fellow-
    ships.
Career Data: Feature writer and columnist, Associated Negro Press,
    editorial asst. to Langston Hughes; adjunct or guest lecturer
    at Columbia University, Kent State University, University of
    Iowa, New York University, Hunter College, Atlanta University,
    Harvard University, University of Connecticut.
Films: Publicity writer for Uptight 1968; wrote a screenplay Roper.
Publications: Anthology of the American Negro in the Theatre, The
    Negro in Music and Art (International Library of Negro Life
    and History volumes) 1967; Black Theatre: A 20th Century
    Collection of the Work of Its Best Playwrights, Dodd, Mead,
    1971; Black Films and Film-Makers: A Comprehensive An-
    thology from Stereotype to Superhero, Dodd, Mead, 1975; A
    Critical Study of the Best Black Playwrights, Dodd, Mead,
    1975; numerous articles and reviews on black theatre and
    black performers for Dictionary of Negro Biographies, The
    New York Times, Essence magazine, and In Black America.
Radio: Orde Coombs/LP Show (WRVR); co-hosted Celebrity Hour
    series (WRVR).
Television: Patterson & Coombs: Black Conversations (WPIX)
    1976-date.

PAUL, BILLY (Paul Williams)
    (Singer)
Honors: Ebony Music Awards 1975; Grammy.
Career Data: Organized Gamble Records (later called Philadelphia
    International); toured South America; Newport Jazz Festival
    1973.
Clubs: Red Rooster 1977.
Records: Me and Mrs. Jones; Got My Head on Straight (Philadelphia
    International); War of the Gods (Philadelphia International);
    When Love Is New (Philadelphia International); Let's Make a
    Baby; Ebony Woman (Philadelphia International); Live In Europe
    (Philadelphia International); Feeling Good (Philadelphia Interna-
    tional); Going East (Philadelphia International); 360 Degrees
    (Philadelphia International); Let 'Em In (Philadelphia Internation-
    al).
Television: Midnight Special; Soul Train 1976.
Theater: Appeared at Carnegie Hall 1976, 1977.

PAYNE, BENNIE (Benjamin E. Payne)
(Pianist)
b.   June 18, 1907, Philadelphia, Pa.
Education: Studied piano with Fats Waller.
Special Interests: Vocal directing.
Career Data: Worked with Wilbur Sweatman band 1928, Cab Callo-
way band 1931-43, 1946; accompanist for Elizabeth Welch,
Gladys Bentley, Pearl Bailey, Billy Daniels (since 1950);
toured Europe 1934, 1956.
Clubs: Cotton Club (Philadelphia) 1926.
Theater: Blackbirds of 1928; Hot Chocolates 1929.

PAYNE, FREDA
(Singer/Actress)
b.   c. 1944, Detroit, Mich.
Address: c/o Creative Attractions, 3125 Cadillac Tower, Detroit,
Mich. 48226.
Honors: Dame of Malta, 1974.
Career Data: Worked with Quincy Jones, Redd Foxx, Duke Elling-
ton, Billy Eckstine, Bob Crosby.
Clubs: Persian Room-Plaza Hotel; Mrs. Kelly's (Chicago); The
Coconut Grove (L. A.); Elegante (Brooklyn) 1962; Maisonette-
St. Regis Hotel 1974; Fairmont Hotel (Atlanta) 1974; Playboy
(McAfee, N. J.) 1975; Rainbow Grill 1976.
Films: Book of Numbers 1973.
Musical Compositions: Bring Back the Joy; You've Got What It
Takes.
Records: Payne and Pleasure (ABC-Dunhill); Out of Payne Comes
Love (ABC); Band of Gold; Bring the Boys Home 1973; You
Brought the Joy; Deeper and Deeper; After the Lights Go
Down (Impulse); Reaching Out (Invictus).
Television: Tonight Show; The Wayne Newton Special 1974; Positive-
ly Black 1974, 1975; Merv Griffin Show 1975; Mike Douglas
Show 1975; Dinah! 1975; Kup's Show 1975; Soul Train 1975;
Party 1975; Police Story 1976; American Bandstand 1976;
Celebrity Revue 1976; Sammy and Company 1977; Bobby Vinton
Show 1977.
Theater: Understudy for lead in Hallelujah Baby 1967; Lost in the
Stars (E. L. T.) 1968; appearance at Apollo Theatre; Sammy
Davis on Broadway 1974; Mill Run Theatre (Chicago) 1976;
Beacon Theatre 1976.

PEACHENA (Rebecca Lena Eure)
(Singer)
b.   May 15, 1948, Salisbury, Md.
Education: Morgan State College (Baltimore) B.A. 1970.
Special Interests: Acting, composing, teaching.
Address: 150-21 119 Road, Jamaica, N. Y. 11434.
Career Data: Sang with gospel group The Eure Trio.
Clubs: Rust Brown's; The Fallen Angel; The Grand Finale; Village
Gate 1976.
Membership: AEA.

Records: Let My People Come (Libra) 1974.
Television: Black Is 1972; Showcase 13 1972.
Theater: Let My People Come (O.B.) 1974-75.

PENDLETON, DAVID
     (Actor)
b. November 5, 1937, Pittsburgh, Pa.
Education: Lincoln University; City College of New York; studied
     acting with Stella Adler.
Special Interests: Teaching, music (cello, singing, tuba).
Career Data: Taught at Ophelia De Vore's Charm School.
Films: Dory in Abduction 1975; Mickey and Nickey 1976.
Television: The Guiding Light (series); The Doctors (series); The
     Edge of Night (series); Lieut. Ed Hall in One Life to Live
     (series); First National City Bank commercial; Prudential
     Life Insurance commercial; Luke Was There 1976.
Theater: Gilbert & Sullivan's The Gondoliers; Blueberry Mountain
     (O.B.); Screens (O.B.) 1971; No Place to Be Somebody 1971;
     Don't Bother Me, I Can't Cope 1972.

PENNIMAN, RICHARD see LITTLE RICHARD

PERKINSON, COLERIDGE TAYLOR
     (Composer)
b. 1932, New York, N.Y.
Education: Manhattan School of Music, B. Mus. 1953, M. Mus.
     1954, studied at The Berkshire Music Center, The Mozarteum,
     The Netherland Radio Union Hilversum.
Career Data: First associate director, Symphony of the New World
     1965.
Films: Music for Crossroads Africa (doc.).
Musical Compositions: Concerto for Viola and Orchestra 1954; At-
     titudes 1964, Freedom Freedom.
Theater: Music for NEC productions: Man Better Man, Song of the
     Lusitanian Bogey, God Is a (Guess What?) 1968-69; The Great
     MacDaddy 1974.

PERRY, FELTON
     (Actor)
Education: Roosevelt University B.A.
Special Interests: Playwriting, classic guitar.
Address: Michael Karg Agency, 470 S. Vicente Blvd., Beverly
     Hills, Calif. 90048.
Career Data: Acting workshops, Hull House (Chicago); Equity
     Library Theater program (Chicago); Second City Workshop
     (Chicago); Synergy Trust (L.A.); Actors Studio West; Rich-
     mond Shepherd's Pantomime Show.
Films: Medium Cool 1969; Trouble Man 1972; Magnum Force,
     Walking Tall 1973; The Towering Inferno 1974.

Memberships: SAG.
Television: Dragnet; Bracken's World; Julia; Here Come the Brides;
    Nanny and the Professor; Black Journal; Room 222; Ironside;
    Adam-12; The Name of the Game 1970; Matt Lincoln 1970-71;
    McMillan and Wife 1974; Police Story 1975; Mannix 1975;
    Kate McShane 1975; The Greatest Story Never Told (Bicenten-
    nial special) 1976.
Theater: Macbird (Chicago); What Did We Do Wrong (Chicago);
    Chemin de Fer (L. A.); Salvation (L. A.).

PERRY, ROD (Roderick Maurice)
    (Actor)
b. c.1941, Coatesville, Pa.
Education: Pennsylvania State University.
Address: International Creative Management, 8899 Beverly Blvd.,
    Los Angeles, Calif. 90048.
Films: The Black Godfather 1974; Black Gestapo 1975.
Memberships: SAG.
Television: Irving Mansfield's Talent Scouts; Merv Griffin Show;
    Joe Pittman in The Autobiography of Miss Jane Pittman 1974;
    Barney Miller 1975; Sgt. Deacon Kay in S. W. A. T. (series)
    1975.
Theater: Kicks and Company 1961; New Faces of 1968.

PERRY, SHAUNEILLE
    (Director)
Education: Howard University B.A. (drama); Goodman Theater,
    Art Institute (Chicago) M.A. directing; Royal Academy of
    Dramatic Art (London).
Special Interests: Acting, teaching.
Address: 444 Central Park West, New York, N.Y. 10025.
Honors: AUDELCO black theatre recognition award 1974 (best
    director).
Career Data: Member, Howard University Players; worked with
    AMAS Repertory Theatre, taught speech and theatre at
    Borough of Manhattan Community College; taught at Dillard
    University.
Films: The Long Night 1976.
Radio: The Kimball Hour.
Television: Catholic Hour (series).
Theater: Acted in: Dark of the Moon (ELT) 1960; Talent '60
    1960; The Goose (O.B.) 1960; Ondine (ELT) 1961; Clandestine
    on the Morning Line (O.B.) 1961; Octoroon (O.B.) 1961;
    wrote Mio 1971; wrote and directed The Music Magic of Neal
    Tate; directed The Sty of the Blind Pig (O.B.) 1971; Black
    Girl (O.B.) 1971; The Mau Mau Room (NEC workshop produc-
    tion); Rosalee Pritchett (NEC) 1972; The Prodigal Sister (O.
    B.) 1974; Bayou Legend (AMAS Repertory Theatre) 1974-75;
    Gilbeau (New Federal Theatre) 1976; Showdown (New Federal
    Theatre) 1976; Music Magic (Billie Holiday Theatre, Brooklyn)
    1976; wrote Clinton 1976; Relationship (O.B.) 1977.

PETERS, BROCK (Brock Fisher)
(Actor/Singer)
b.   July 2, 1927, New York, N.Y.
Education: Music and Art H.S.; University of Chicago 1944-45;
     City College of N.Y. 1945-47.
Special Interests: Directing.
Address: 131 Riverside Drive, New York, N.Y. 10024.
Honors: All American Press Assn. award for best supporting actor;
     Box Office Blue Ribbon award; American Society of African
     Culture Emancipation award (for To Kill a Mockingbird) 1962;
     Black Filmmakers Hall of Fame 1976.
Career Data: Bass soloist, De Paur Infantry Chorus 1947-50;
     chairman, board of directors, Dance Theatre of Harlem.
Clubs: Village Gate; Gate of Horn (Chicago); Purple Onion (Toronto);
     The Copa (Pittsburgh); The Troubadour (L.A.).
Films: Carmen Jones (debut) 1954; Crown in Porgy and Bess 1959;
     Tom Robinson in To Kill a Mockingbird, The L-Shaped Room,
     Heavens Above (Brit.) 1963; Major Dundee, The Pawnbroker
     1965; The Incident 1967; PJ 1968; Daring Game, Ace High
     1969; The McMasters 1970; Black Girl 1972; Soylent Green,
     Slaughter's Big Rip-Off, produced and acted in Five on the
     Black Hand Side 1973; narrated From These Roots (doc.) 1974;
     Rev. Kumalo in Lost in the Stars 1974; Framed 1975; Two
     Minute Warning 1976.
Memberships: AEA; AFTRA; AGVA; SAG.
Records: African Village Folktales; Ballad for Americans (United
     Artists).
Television: Arthur Godfrey's Talent Scouts 1953; The Hit Parade
     1953; The Garry Moore Morning Show 1953; Adventures in
     Paradise 1959; Music for a Summer Night 1959; Music for a
     Spring Night 1960; Snows of Kilimanjaro (special) 1960; Tonight
     Show 1961; Show Time (BBC London) 1961; Hootenanny 1963;
     Garry Moore Show 1963; Bloomer Girl (special); Sam Bene-
     dict (series) 1963; Great Adventure 1963; Eleventh Hour
     (series) 1964; Doctors/Nurses 1964; Rawhide 1965; Loner
     1965; Trials of O'Brian 1966; Run for Your Life 1966; The
     Girl from U.N.C.L.E. 1966; Mission: Impossible 1967;
     Tarzan 1967; It Takes a Thief 1968; Judd for the Defense
     1969; Felony Squad 1969; Outcasts 1969; Gunsmoke 1969; Man-
     nix 1970; Longstreet 1971; Mod Squad 1971; Welcome Home
     Johnny Bristol 1972; Streets of San Francisco 1974; McCloud
     1974; narrated The Black Cop (New York Illustrated) 1974;
     As the World Turns; NAACP commercial; Medical Center;
     Police Story 1976; Jigsaw John 1976; Tight As a Drum (Mys-
     tery of the Week); SST. Death Flight 1977; This Far by
     Faith 1977.
Theater: Jim in Porgy and Bess (debut) 1943; South Pacific 1943;
     Anna Lucasta 1944 (Chicago 1945); Head of the Family (West-
     port) 1950; My Darlin' Aida 1952; The Year Round; Mister
     Johnson 1956; The King in King of the Dark Chamber (O.B.)
     1961; Obitsebi in Kwamina 1961; title role in Othello (Arena
     Stage, Wash. D.C.) 1963; The Caucasian Chalk Circle (LRC);
     The Great White Hope (tour) 1969; produced Come Back to

Harlem at Apollo Theatre 1972; Rev. Kumalo in Lost in the
Stars 1972; directed Hallelujah: A Tribute to Black Gospel
Music (Forum, L.A.) 1975.

PETERSON, CALEB (J.)
    (Actor/Singer)
b. November 21, 1917, Peekskill, N.Y.
Education: Peekskill H.S. 1936; West Virginia State College 1941-
    42; Studied voice with Lawrence Brown.
Address: 4 Logwynn Lane, Peekskill, N.Y. 10566.
Honors: National Forensic League drama and speech contest winner
    1936.
Career Data: Presented recitals and concerts as bass baritone all
    over U.S.
Films: Stage Door Canteen 1943; Till the Clouds Roll By, Till the
    End of Time 1946; Scene of the Crime, Any Number Can
    Play 1949.
Memberships: AEA; AGVA; SAG.
Records: Sang Ole Man River on sound track album of Till the
    Clouds Roll By (M.G.M.) 1947.
Television: Papa Benjamin in The Thriller (series) 1958.
Theater: Minister in Run Little Chillun 1944; concert debut at
    Town Hall 1952; recital at Mahopec Farm Playhouse 1975.

PETERSON, LOUIS (Stamford)
    (Playwright)
b. June 17, 1922, Hartford, Conn.
Education: Morehouse College B.A. 1944; Yale University Drama
    School 1944-45; New York University M.A. 1947; studied with
    Lee Strasberg, Clifford Odets, Sanford Meisner.
Special Interests: Acting, piano.
Address: 440 West 22nd St., New York, N.Y. 10011
Honors: Benjamin Brawley Award for Excellence in English 1944;
    Emmy Nomination 1956; Black Filmmakers Hall of Fame
    Award 1975.
Films: Wrote screenplay for The Tempest (Italian) 1957; Take a
    Giant Step 1961.
Memberships: Writers Guild of America; Actors Equity Assn.;
    Dramatists Guild.
Television: Wrote following teleplays: Padlocks (Danger) 1954,
    Class of '58 (Goodyear) 1954, Joey (Goodyear) 1956, Emily Ros-
    siter Story (Wagon Train) 1957, Hit and Run (Dr. Kildare) 1961.
Theater: Acted in the following productions: A Young American
    (Blackfriars Guild) 1946; Our Lan' 1947; Member of the Wed-
    ding (tour) 1951-52; wrote: Take a Giant Step 1953; Entertain
    a Ghost 1962; Crazy Horse Have Jenny Now; Count Me for a
    Stranger.

PETERSON, MONICA (Dorothy A. Peterson)
    (Actress)
b. August 3, 1938, Va.

Education: University of Stockholm (Sweden) 1962; University of
     Southern California (Cinema) 1969-70; London School of Ballet
     and Music; studied acting with Jeff Corey, Paul Mann at Actors
     Studio, Sanford Meisner at Neighborhood Playhouse; Garfein
     Directors Lab (L.A.).
Special Interests: Directing, dancing, singing, writing.
Address: 7250 Franklin Avenue, Los Angeles, Calif. 90046 or
     c/o Edwards 607 North La Peer Drive, Los Angeles, Calif.
     90069.
Honors: Star of Tomorrow (ABC-TV) 1968; presented with Vietnam
     award by General Abrams 1969.
Career Data: Theatre in Park, U.C.L.A. Festival, Eagle Rock
     Park, L.A. 1975.
Films: Cleopatra 1963; Changes 1969; Kings Executive Style
     1974.
Memberships: SAG (its Minorities Committee); Women in Films
     (WIF).
Radio: Her own show, Barcelona, Spain, 1964.
Television: The Pigeon 1969.
Theater: Sarah in Funny House of a Negro (L.A.) 1973; assistant
     director, Ceremonies in Dark Old Men (L.A.).

PETERSON, OSCAR (Emmanuel)
     (Pianist)
b. August 15, 1925, Montreal, Quebec, Canada.
Special Interests: Composing, jazz, singing.
Address: 640 Roselawn Avenue, Toronto 5 Ontario, Canada.
Honors: Down Beat award 1950-54; Critics Poll 1953; Metronome
     award 1953-54; Grammy; Jazz & Pop 3rd annual readers poll
     winner 1968.
Career Data: Jazz at the Philharmonic tours 1952, 1953, 1954;
     toured Europe; led his own trio; faculty, School of Jazz, Len-
     ox, Massachusetts; appeared at Newport Jazz Festival, Strat-
     ford (Ontario) Shakespeare Festival.
Musical Compositions: Crunch.
Records: Oscar Peterson in Russia (Pablo); Walking the Line; Os-
     car Peterson and Dizzy Gillespie; The Jimmy McHugh Song
     Book (Verve); The Trio (Pablo); The History of an Artist
     (Pablo); Affinity (Verve); Another Day (BASF); Big 6 Mon-
     treux '75 (Pablo); Collection (Verve); Eloquence (Trip); Ex-
     clusively for My Friends (BASF); Featuring Stephane Grap-
     pelli (Prestige); Great Connection (BASF); Hello Herbie (BASF);
     In a Mellow Mood (BASF); In Tune (BASF); Motions and Emo-
     tions (BASF); Night Train (Verve); Plus One Clark Terry
     (Mercury); Rare Wood (BASF); Return Engagement (Verve);
     Reunion Blues (BASF); Something Warm (Verve); Tracks
     (BASF); Tristeza on Piano (BASF); Very Tall (Verve); Walk-
     ing the Line (BASF); We Get Requests (Verve); West Side
     Story (Verve); A Salle Pleyel (Pablo).
Television: Mike Douglas Show 1974; Like It Is 1976; Merv Griffin
     Show 1976; At the Top 1977.
Theater: Appeared at Carnegie Hall 1949; Salle Pleyel (Paris) 1974;

Westbury Music Fair 1975; Jazz at the Philharmonic Concert 1975; Confederation Centre of the Arts (Charlottetown, Prince Edward Island, Canada) 1976.

PHILLIPS, ESTHER
    (Singer)
b. December 23, 1935, Houston, Texas.
Honors: Ebony Music Award 1975; NAACP Image Award 1976.
Career Data: Sang with Johnny Otis Revue; known earlier as "Little Esther."
Clubs: Jupiter's (L.I.) 1975; Buddy's Place 1975; The Bottom Line 1976; Village Gate 1976.
Records: For All We Know (Kudu); What a Difference a Day Makes; Confessin' the Blues (Atlantic); Release Me (Lenox) 1962; Set Me Free (Atlantic) 1970; Burnin' (Atlantic); Alone Again (Kudu); And I Love Him (Atlantic); Black-Eyed Blues (Kudu); From a Whisper to a Scream (Kudu); Performance (Kudu); Capricorn Princess (Kudu).
Television: A.M. America 1975; Saturday Night 1975; Sunday 1975; Boarding House 1975; Soul Train 1975; Don Kirshner's Rock Concert 1976; Dinah! 1976.
Theater: Appeared at Felt Forum 1975; Apollo Theatre 1975; Avery Fisher Hall 1976; Salle Wilfrid-Pelletier (Montreal) 1976.

PICKETT, WILSON
    (Singer)
b. March 18, 1941, Prattsville, Ala.
Special Interests: Songwriting.
Address: c/o Atlantic Recording Corp., 75 Rockefeller Plaza, New York, N.Y. 10020.
Career Data: Sang with The Falcons, 1962-63.
Films: Soul to Soul 1971.
Musical Compositions: For Better or Worse; I'm Gonna Cry; The Midnight Hour.
Records: Greatest Hits (Atlantic); Join Me and Let's Be Free (RCA); If You Need Me (Double-L) 1963; In the Midnight Hour (Atlantic) 1965; Hey Jude (Atlantic) 1969; Call My Name, I'll Be There (Atlantic) 1971; In Philadelphia (Atlantic); Miss Lisa's Boy; Pickett in the Pocket (RCA); Best (Atlantic); Wickedness (Trip).
Television: Soul Train 1976.

PIERCE, PONCHITTA (Anne)
    (Broadcaster)
b. August 5, 1942, Chicago, Ill.
Education: University of Southern California B.A. (Journalism) 1964; Cambridge University (England) 1962.
Special Interests: Status of women.
Address: 780 Madison Avenue, New York, N.Y. 10021.

<u>Honors</u>: John Russwurm award (N.Y. Urban League) 1968; Woman
     Behind the News award (L.A. Chapter of Theta Sigma Phi)
     1969; Headliner award for outstanding work in the field of
     broadcasting (National Theta Sigma Phi) 1970.
<u>Career Data</u>: Ebony magazine (Johnson Publications) asst. editor
     1964-65, assoc. editor 1965-67, New York editor 1967-68.
<u>Memberships</u>: AFTRA; NATAS; American Women in Radio and Tele-
     vision (AWRT); Women in Communication (formerly Theta
     Sigma Phi).
<u>Television</u>: Girl Talk; special news correspondent (CBS) 1968-71;
     Sunday (NBC) co-host 1973-75, reporter 1975; narrated pro-
     gram on suicide (New York Illustrated) 1975.

PIGMEAT <u>see</u> MARKHAM, DEWEY

POITIER, SIDNEY
     (Actor)
b.   February 20, 1927, Miami, Fla.
<u>Education</u>: Studied Acting with Paul Mann and Lloyd Richards.
<u>Honors</u>: George Cini Cultural Foundation Award at Venice Film
     Festival for Something of Value; N.Y. Film Critics Award
     (Defiant Ones) 1958; Berlin Film Festival Best Acting (Defiant
     Ones) 1958; Academy Award Nominee (Defiant Ones) 1958;
     Winner (Lilies of the Field) 1964; Knight Commander of the
     British Empire (K.B.E.); Black Filmmakers Hall of Fame
     1975; NAACP Image Award (Let's Do It Again) 1976.
<u>Career Data</u>: Co-Founder, First Artists Prod. Co. 1968.
<u>Films</u>: From Whom Cometh My Help (U.S. Army documentary)
     1949; No Way Out, Cry the Beloved Country, Red Ball Ex-
     press 1952; Go, Man Go! 1954; The Blackboard Jungle 1955;
     Goodbye My Lady 1956; A Band of Angels, Edge of the City,
     Something of Value 1957; The Defiant Ones, The Mark of the
     Hawk 1958; Porgy in Porgy and Bess 1959; All the Young Men,
     Virgin Island 1960; A Raisin in the Sun, Paris Blues 1961;
     Pressure Point 1962; Lilies of the Field 1963; The Long Ships
     1964; The Greatest Story Ever Told, The Bedford Incident,
     Patch of Blue, The Slender Thread 1965; Duel at Diablo 1966;
     In the Heat of the Night, To Sir, with Love, Guess Who's
     Coming to Dinner 1967; For Love of Ivy 1968; The Lost Man
     1969; They Call Me Mr. Tibbs 1970; The Organization, Brother
     John 1971; directed and acted in Buck and the Preacher 1972;
     directed and acted in A Warm December 1973; produced, di-
     rected and acted in Uptown Saturday Night 1974; The Wilby
     Conspiracy 1975; directed and acted in Let's Do It Again 1975;
     directed and acted in A Piece of the Action 1977.
<u>Memberships</u>: AEA; AFTRA; ANT; SAG.
<u>Records</u>: Sidney Poitier Reads Poetry of the Black Man.
<u>Television</u>: Kup's Show; The Parole Officer (Philco Playhouse);
     Fascinating Stranger (Pond's Theatre) 1955; A Man Is Ten
     Feet Tall (Philco Playhouse) 1955; Strolling Twenties (special)
     1966; Dick Cavett Show 1972; Merv Griffin Show 1975; Wide
     World Special (Stanley Kramer Films) 1975; Black News 1975;

Columbia Pictures 50th Anniversary Salute 1975.
Theater: The Fisherman (ANT); Freight (ANT); Striver's Row
(ANT); You Can't Take It with You (ANT); Rain (ANT);
Riders of the Sea (ANT); Hidden Horizon (ANT); Sepia Cin-
derella (ANT); Days of Our Youth (ANT) 1945; Lysistrata
1946; Anna Lucasta 1948; Detective Story (Apollo Theatre)
1953; Walter Lee Younger in Raisin in the Sun 1959; directed
Carry Me Back to Morningside Heights 1968.

POLK, OSCAR
(Actor)
b. Marianna, Ar.
Education: Studied dance at Jack Blue's Dance Studio.
Special Interests: Tap dancing instruction, harmonica playing.
Films: Gabriel in The Green Pastures, Underworld 1936; Big Town
Czar, Gone with the Wind 1939; White Cargo, Reap the Wild
Wind 1942; Cabin in the Sky 1943.
Radio: Bright Horizon; Our Gal Sunday; Big Sister.
Theater: The Trial of Mary Dugan; A Roman Gentleman; Nona;
Bring on the Girls; The Brigand; Cross Roads; Once in a Life-
time 1930; Face the Music; Both Your Houses 1933; The Pur-
suit of Happiness 1933; It's a Great Life 1935; The Green Pas-
tures 1935; You Can't Take It with You 1937; Swingin' the
Dream 1939; Mr. Big 1941; Sunny River 1941; The Walking
Gentleman 1942; Dark Eyes 1943.

POMARE, ELEO
(Dancer/Choreographer)
b. October 20, 1937, Cartagena, Colombia.
Education: High School of Performing Arts; studied dance with
José Limon, Geoffrey Holder, Kurt Joos (in Germany).
Special Interests: Repertory, teaching.
Address: 325 West 16 Street, New York, N.Y. 10011.
Honors: John Hay Whitney Fellowship 1962; Guggenheim Fellowship
grant 1974; National Endowment for the Arts choreographer's
grant 1975.
Career Data: Founder, Eleo Pomare Dance Company 1958; founder,
Second Company in Amsterdam 1963 (toured Holland, Germany,
Sweden, Norway); performed and taught at National Ballet of
Holland, Scapino Ballet, Stockholm University and First Inter-
national Dancer Seminar of the Royal Danish Ballet; created
first Dance Mobile (N.Y.C.) 1967; founded Dance Workshop
in affiliation with Clark Center for the Performing Arts 1968;
participated in Adelaide Festival of the Arts (Australia);
toured U.S., Caribbean and Canada.
Television: National Educational Television (NET special) 1966.
Theater: Appeared with his company at major theatres including
Brooklyn Academy of Music; City Center Theatre; ANTA
Theatre; Delacorte Theatre; Hunter College Playhouse; John
F. Kennedy Center for the Performing Arts (Wash. D.C.);
Lyric Theatre (Baltimore); Theatre Maisonneuve (Montreal);

Warner Theatre (Adelaide); Conservatorium (Sydney). Dances choreographed include: Blues for the Jungle 1962 (rev. 1966); Missa Luba 1965; Serendipity 1966; Uptight 1967; Las Desena-moradas 1967; Climb 1967; Hex 1967; Over Here 1968; Faces of Noon 1968; Narcissus Rising 1968; Passage 1968; Radiance of the Dark 1969; Movements 1970-71; 'Nother Shade of Blue 1971; Roots 1972; De La Tierra 1975; Black on Black; Burnt Ash; Beginnsville; Junkie; Ode for Prophet Jones; Hushed Voices.

POPWELL, ALBERT
   (Actor)
b. New York, N.Y.
Education: Studied dance with Katherine Dunham and Pearl Primus; studied acting with Lee Strasberg.
Special Interests: Dancing, singing.
Address: 1300 N. Sanborn, Los Angeles, Calif. 90027.
Career Data: Danced in Paris with Chicago Ballet Co.
Films: The Joe Louis Story 1953; The Harder They Fall 1956; Coogan's Bluff, Journey to Shiloh 1968; Fuzz, Dirty Harry, Glass House 1972; Cleopatra Jones, Magnum Force 1973; Cleopatra Jones and the Casino of Gold 1975; The Enforcer 1976.
Memberships: AEA; SAG.
Television: Lamp unto My Feet; Drum Is a Woman; Danger; Captain Video; Medallion Theatre; Mannix; Ironside; Kojak; Name of the Game 1968; The Lost Flight 1970; Search (series) 1972-73; Shaft; Police Woman 1974; Emergency! 1975; Police Story 1975; Sanford and Son 1976.
Theater: The Pirate 1942; Beggars Holiday 1946; Lysistrata 1946; Finian's Rainbow 1947; Inside U.S.A. 1948; South Pacific 1949; House of Flowers 1954; Mr. Wonderful 1956; Shinbone Alley 1957; Saratoga 1959; Black Nativity (O.B.) 1961; Cabin in the Sky (O.B.) 1964; Golden Boy 1964-65.

POWELL, EARL "Bud"
   (Jazz Musician/Composer)
b. September 27, 1924, New York, N.Y.
Special Interests: Piano, bop.
Career Data: Played with Cootie Williams band 1943-44.
Clubs: Minton's; Birdland; Canada Lee's Chicken Coop; Chat Qui Pêche (Paris) 1959.
Musical Compositions: Hallucinations (a.k.a. Budo); Oblivion; Glass; Glass Enclosure.

PREER, EVELYN
   (Actress)
b. July 26, 1896 Vicksburg, Miss.
d. November 18, 1932 Los Angeles, Calif.
Career Data: Toured with Charley Johnson's vaudeville troupe; performed with Lafayette Players.

Films: The Homesteader 1918; The Brute, Within Our Gates 1920;
        Deceit, The Gunsaulus Mystery 1921; The Hypocrite 1922;
        Birthright 1924; The Conjur Woman, The Devil's Disciple, The
        Spider's Web 1926; Melancholy Dame 1929; Georgia Rose
        1930; Blonde Venus 1932.
Theater: Appeared in Lulu Belle; Rang Tang; Rain; Porgy; Scandals;
        Why Wives Go Wrong; The Good Little Bad Girl; The Chip
        Woman's Fortune (Negro Folk Theatre) 1923; title role in
        Salome (Negro Folk Theatre) 1923; The Warning 1924.

PREMICE, JOSEPHINE
        (Singer/Dancer)
b.   July 21, 1926, Brooklyn, N.Y.
Education: Columbia University; New School for Social Research;
        Cornell University; studied dance with Martha Graham and
        Katherine Dunham.
Special Interests: Acting, languages.
Address: 755 West End Avenue, New York, N.Y. 10025.
Clubs: Chez Florence (Paris); Blue Angel; Village Vanguard; Mo-
        cambo (Hollywood).
Memberships: AEA; AGMA; AGVA.
Television: Merv Griffin Show; The Autobiography of Miss Jane
        Pittman 1974; Positively Black 1976; Black Conversations
        1976; Not for Women Only 1977.
Theater: A Dance Festival (Carnegie Hall) 1943; Blue Holiday
        (Bway debut) 1945; Caribbean Carnival 1947; House of Flow-
        ers 1954; Bamm in Mister Johnson 1956; Ginger in Jamaica
        1957; The Blacks (O.B.) 1963; A Hand Is on the Gate 1966;
        Cherry Orchard (O.B.); Electra (O.B.); Mme. Fleur in House
        of Flowers (O.B.) 1968; appeared at Teatro Nuovo (Milan);
        American Night Cry (O.B.) 1973; Bubbling Brown Sugar 1976-
        77.

PRESTON, BILLY
        (Singer/Composer)
b.   c. 1947.
Special Interests: Film scoring.
Honors: Four gold records.
Career Data: Concert tour with George Harrison, former Beatle
        1975.
Films: W. C. Handy as a boy in St. Louis Blues 1958; The Con-
        cert for Bangladesh 1972.
Records: Sixteen Year Old Soul; Out of Space; Space Race; That's
        the Way God Planned It; Encouraging Words; Everybody Likes
        Some Kind of Music (A&M); Will It Go Round in Circles; The
        Kids and Me (A&M); Music Is My Life (A&M); I Wrote a
        Simple Song (A&M); It's My Pleasure (A&M); Nothing from
        Nothing (A&M); Gospel in My Soul (Peacock); Wildest Organ
        in Town (Capitol); Live European Tour (A&M); Soul'd Out
        (GNP Crescendo).
Television: The Tonight Show; Shindig; Sonny Bono Show 1974;

Mike Douglas Show 1975; The American Music Awards 1975;
Don Kirshner's Rock Concert 1975; Midnight Special 1975;
Superstars of Rock 1975; Saturday Night 1975; Dinah! 1975;
Soul Train 1976; Donny and Marie 1976; Merv Griffin Show
1977.
Theater: Appearances at Nassau Coliseum 1975; Madison Square
Garden (with Mick Jagger) 1975.

PRESTON, J. A.
(Actor)
Education: Louise Bramwell's Stage Studio (Wash. D.C.); studied
with Jerome Robbin's American Theatre Laboratory 1967-68.
Address: Natural Artists Enterprises, 8380 Melrose Avenue, Los
Angeles, Calif. 90069.
Films: Mississippi Summer 1971; The Spook Who Sat by the Door
1973; Two Minute Warning 1976.
Television: Another World (series); Hard Traveling; Good Times
1975; All in the Family 1975; All's Fair (series) 1976-77.
Theater: The Death of Bessie Smith (O.B.) 1961; King John (NYSF);
Comedy of Errors (NYSF); Henry IV pt. 1 & 2 (NYSF); title
role in Christophe (Bklyn Academy of Music) 1968; The Per-
sians (O.B.) 1970; The Gladiator (O.B.) 1970.

PRICE, GILBERT
(Singer)
b. September 10, 1942, Brooklyn, N.Y.
Education: Erasmus H.S. (Bklyn.); American Theatre Wing; studied
voice with Clare Gelda.
Special Interests: Acting, dancing.
Address: c/o International Creative Management, 41 West 57 Street,
New York, N.Y. 10019, and Variety Sound Corp., 130 West
42 Street, New York, N.Y. 10036.
Honors: Fanny Kemble award 1965; Theatre World award (for
Jerico-Jim Crow) 1964; Tony nomination (for Lost in the Stars)
1972; Tony nomination (for Night That Made America Famous)
1975.
Memberships: AEA; AGMA; AGVA; SAG.
Television: One More Time (Canada); guested on Merv Griffin
Show; Ed Sullivan Show, David Frost Show; Joey Bishop Show;
Red Skelton Show; Mike Douglas Show 1975.
Theater: Jacques Brel (Boston); Kicks and Company (O.B.) 1961;
Fly Blackbird (O.B.) 1962; A Midsummer Night's Dream
(NYSF) 1964; Jerico-Jim Crow (O.B.) 1964; Roar of the
Greasepaint, Smell of the Crowd (Bway debut) 1965; Slow
Dance on a Killing Ground (O.B.); Promenade (O.B.) 1969;
Dumas and Son (L.A.) 1970; Six (O.B.) 1971; Mahagonny
(Yale Repertory Theatre) 1971; Cavalcade of American Music
(L.A.) 1972; Lost in the Stars 1972; Two Gentlemen of Verona
(Australia) 1973; Leonard Bernstein's Mass (L.A.) 1973,
1974; I Got a Song (pre Bway tour) 1974; The Night That
Made America Famous 1975; 1600 Pennsylvania Avenue 1976.

PRICE, LEONTYNE (Mary Leontyne Price)
       (Opera Singer)
b. February 10, 1927, Laurel, Miss.
Education: Central State College (Wilberforce University) B.A.
       1948; Juilliard School of Music 1949-52.
Address: 1133 Broadway, New York, N.Y. 10010.
Honors: Ten Grammy awards; Mademoiselle merit award 1955;
       Presidential Medal of Freedom 1964; Order of Merit of
       Italian Republic 1965; sang Star Spangled Banner at Inaugura-
       tion of President Lyndon B. Johnson 1965; NAACP Spingarn
       Medal 1965; Mississippi Entertainment Hall of Fame 1976.
Career Data: Honorary chairman, Symphony of the New World;
       performed with San Francisco Opera Co. 1957-59, 1960-61;
       Vienna State Opera 1958, 1959-61; Salzburg Festival 1959-61;
       Bermuda Festival 1960; Metropolitan Opera debut 1961; opened
       new Metropolitan Opera at Lincoln Center 1966; Ravenna Festi-
       val (Highland Park, Ill.) 1975; opera repertoire includes
       Leonora in Il Trovatore, Cleopatra in Antony and Cleopatra,
       Donna Anna in Don Giovanni, Minnie in Girl of the Golden
       West, Aïda, Amelia in Un Ballo in Maschera, Liu in Turandot,
       Tosca, Mistress Ford in Falstaff, Fiordiligi in Cosi Fan Tutte,
       Cio-Cio San in Madama Butterfly, Carmen.
Memberships: AEA; AFTRA; AGMA.
Records: Christmas Offering (London); For RCA: I Wish I Knew
       How It Would Feel to Be Free; Leontyne Price Sings Richard
       Strauss; Verdi Heroines; Ernani; La Forza del Destino; Re-
       quiem; Il Tabarro; Favorite Hymns 1966; Prima Donna 3v
       1966-70; 5 Great Operatic Scenes 1972.
Television: Bell Telephone Hour; Television Opera Theatre (NBC)
       1955-58.
Theater: Four Saints in Three Acts 1952; Bess in Porgy and Bess
       1952-54; appeared at Constitution Hall (Washington, D.C.)
       1953; Town Hall (debut) 1954; Hollywood Bowl 1955-59; Dia-
       logues of the Carmelites at San Francisco Opera House 1957;
       Verona Opera Arena 1958-59; Covent Garden (London) 1958-59;
       Chicago Lyric Theatre 1959, 1960; La Scala Opera House
       (Milan) 1960; Metropolitan Opera House 1961-; Carnegie Hall
       1976; Westchester Premier Theatre 1976.
Relationships: Former wife of William Warfield, singer/actor.

PRIDE, CHARLEY (Frank)
       (Singer)
b. March 18, 1938, Sledge, Miss.
Education: Sledge Junior High School (Miss.).
Special Interests: Folk and country music, baseball.
Address: c/o Jack Johnson Enterprises, 306 Timberdale Ct.
       Nashville, Tenn. 37211.
Honors: Grammy awards 1971, 1972; 9 gold albums; Entertainer
       of the year (Music Operators of America); most promising
       male artist (Country Song Roundup) 1967; Entertainer of the
       year and Male Vocalist of the year (Country Music Assn.)
       1971; Cashbox's top male vocalist; Billboard's top male vocal-
       ist and top country artist; Mississippi Hall of Fame 1976.

Career Data: Played pro and semi-pro baseball: Birmingham
        Black Browns, Memphis Red Socks (Negro American League),
        Montana Timberjacks (Pioneer League) 1960; Los Angeles
        Angels 1961; first black to sing at Grand Ole Opry, Nashville
        1961; director, Guaranty Bank, Dallas.
Records: On RCA: Incomparable Charley Pride; Songs of Love;
        The Best of Charley Pride; A Sunshine Day with Charley
        Pride; Sweet Country; Country Feelin'; Hope You're Feelin'
        Me; The Happiness of Having You; Pride of America; Heart-
        aches by the Number; Kiss an Angel Good Morning; Let the
        Chips Fall; She Made Me Go; Let Me Help You Work It Out;
        Someday They Will; Day You Stopped Loving Me; Christmas
        in My Home Town; Sunday; In Person Panther Hall; Charley;
        Amazing; From Me to You; I'm Just Me; Make Country; Sen-
        sational; Songs of Pride; Tenth Album; Way; Just Play; Crawl
        at Night 1966; Just Between You and Me 1966; Does My Ring
        Hurt Your Finger 1967; I Know One 1967; Country Charley
        Pride 1967; Did You Think to Pray 1971; Let Me Live 1971;
        Charley Pride Sings Heart Songs 1972.
Television: Hee Haw; Tom Jones Show; Lawrence Welk Show;
        Joey Bishop Show; Encore; Flip Wilson Show; Vibrations;
        Johnny Cash Show; Eddy Arnold Christmas Show (Kraft Music
        Hall) 1970; Americans All 1974; Merv Griffin Show 1974, 75;
        Feeling Good 1974; Christmas with Oral Roberts (special)
        1974; Midnight Special 1974; Pop! Goes the Country 1975;
        Como Country ... Perry and His Nashville Friends 1975;
        The American Music awards 1975; Mike Douglas Show 1975;
        In Concert 1975; Dinah! 1975; Sammy and Company 1975;
        Mac Davis Show 1975; Phil Donahue Show 1975; Stars and
        Stripes Show 1975; Tonight Show 1975; Today 1975; Grand Ole
        Opry at 50 (A Nashville Celebration) 1975; Country Music
        Assn. Awards 1975; Saturday Night Live with Howard Cosell
        1976; Donny & Marie 1976.
Theater: Appearance at Felt Forum 1975.

PRIMUS, PEARL "Queen of Black Dance"
        (Choreographer/Dancer)
b.   November 29, 1919, Trinidad, West Indies.
Education: Hunter College B.A. 1940; Columbia University Ph.D.
        (anthropology).
Honors: Rosenwald Fellowship (for study of dances of Africa)
        1948; Star of Africa from Government of Liberia.
Career Data: Solo concerts N.Y. City, Chicago, Trenton, Newark
        1944-45; toured U.S. 1946-48; opened own School of Dance
        1947; dance repertoire includes The Wedding, Strange Fruit,
        Hard Times Blues, Slave Market, Rock Daniel, African Cere-
        monial Te Moana, Shouters of Sobo, Study in Nothing, The
        Negro Speaks of Rivers, Afro-Haitian Play Dance, Fanga,
        Yanvaloo, Eartha Theatre.
Clubs: Cafe-Society Downtown 1943-44.
Memberships: AEA; AGMA; AGVA; ANT; New Dance Group.
Theater: Appeared at YMHA 1943; A Dance Festival (Carnegie

Hall) 1943; Belasco Theatre (Bway debut) 1944; Roxy Theatre
1944; Show Boat 1946; Emperor Jones 1946; Caribbean Carnival 1947; asst. to director, Mister Johnson 1956.

PRINGLE, JOAN
    (Actress)
b. New York, N.Y.
Education: Columbia University.
Address: c/o Robert Baker Theatrical Associates, 119 West 57
    Street, New York, N.Y. 10019 and c/o Jerry B. Wheeler
    Artists' Management, 8721 Sunset Blvd., Los Angeles, Calif.
    90069.
Films: J.D.'s Revenge 1976.
Memberships: AEA; AFTRA; SAG.
Television: Bob Crane Show; Marcus Welby, M.D.; Ironside; Bana-
    cek; Toma, Lucas Tanner; Sanford and Son; Tracey (replacing
    Lynne Moody) on That's My Mama (series) 1975; Barnaby
    Jones 1977; Rafferty (series) 1977.
Theater: Operation Sidewinder (LCR) 1970.

PRYOR, RICHARD
    (Comedian/Actor)
b. December 1, 1940, Peoria, Ill.
Address: c/o Warner Brothers Reprise Records, 44 East 50th
    Street, New York, N.Y. 10022.
Honors: Grammy for Best Comedy Record 1974, 1976; Emmy 1974
    for Lily Tomlin Special; Gold Record for Album 1975.
Clubs: Harold's (Peoria); Collins' Corner (Peoria); Faust (East St.
    Louis); Shalimar (Buffalo); Poppa Hud's; Comedy Store; The
    Improvisation; Cafe Wha? 1960, 1963; El Alladin Hotel (Las
    Vegas) 1970.
Films: Busy Body 1967; Wild in the Streets, The Green Berets
    1968; The Phynx 1970; You've Got to Walk It Like You Talk
    It or You'll Lose That Beat 1971; Piano Man in Lady Sings
    the Blues, Dynamite Chicken 1972; Wattstax, The Mack, Hit,
    Some Call It Loving 1973; (writer) Blazing Saddles, Uptown
    Saturday Night 1974; Adios Amigo, Car Wash, Silver Streak
    1976; Greased Lightening 1977.
Records: Is It Something I Said? (Reprise); Pryor Goes Foxx
    Hunting (with Redd Foxx); Craps After Hours; Richard Pryor
    (Reprise) 1969; That Nigger's Crazy (Partee) 1974; Bicenten-
    nial Nigger (Reprise) 1976.
Television: Partridge Family; Kraft Summer Music Hall; On Broad-
    way Tonight; The Ed Sullivan Show; Midnight Special; Sanford
    and Son (writer); The Flip Wilson Show (writer); Mod Squad;
    Tonight Show; Merv Griffin Show 1965-75; Carter's Army 1970;
    Lily: A Special (writer) 1973; Salute to Redd Foxx 1974; Mike
    Douglas Show (co-host) 1974; Flip Wilson ... of Course
    (special) 1974; Salute to Dr. Martin Luther King 1974; Soul
    Train 1975; Sammy and Company 1975; Flip Wilson Special
    1975; hosted Saturday Night 1975; Sesame Street 1976; Dinah!

1976; Flip's [Wilson] Sun Valley Olympiad (special) 1976;
Dinah and Her New Best Friends 1976; Midnight Special 1977.
Theater: Apollo; Circle Star (San Carlos); Avery Fisher Hall (The
    Comedy of Richard Pryor) 1974; Felt Forum 1975; Kennedy
    Center (Washington, D.C.); Shubert Theatre (L.A.), Roxy
    Theatre (L.A.) 1976.

PRYSOCK, ARTHUR
    (Singer)
Address: 211 West 53 Street, New York, N.Y. 10019
Honors: Five gold records.
Career Data: Vocalist with Buddy Johnson orchestra.
Clubs: Flame Show Bar; Ebony Club; Black Hawk Restaurant;
    Across 110th St.; Copacabana; New Barrister (Bronx); Half
    Note 1974; Airport (Brooklyn) 1974; Seafood Playhouse 1975;
    San Su San (Mineola) 1975; Buddy's Place 1975; Club Daiquiri
    (St. Thomas) 1975.
Films: The Young Runaways (sang theme) 1968.
Records: I Worry About You; Blue Velvet; Ebb Tide; Stella by
    Starlight; In the Rain; This Is My Beloved (Verve); You Won't
    Find Another Fool Like Me; Best (Verve); All My Life.
Television: Black News: Caught in the Act 1944; Midday Live 1974;
    Positively Black 1974; This Is My Beloved 1974; Mark of Jazz
    1976.
Theater: Appeared at Howard Theatre (Wash. D.C.); Apollo Theatre
    1975; Felt Forum 1977.

QUARLES, NORMA (R.)
    (Broadcaster)
b. November 11, 1936, New York, N.Y.
Education: Hunter College; City College of New York.
Address: WNBC-TV, Merchandise Mart Plaza, Chicago, Ill. 60654.
Honors: Front Page award for TV journalism, Newswomen's Club
    1973; Sigma Delta Chi Deadline award.
Career Data: Instructor, New School for Social Research 1977.
Memberships: NATAS.
Publications: Women in Television News; Presstime.
Radio: News reporter, public service director, WSDM-FM (Chicago)
    1965-66.
Television: NBC news training program 1966-67; news reporter and
    anchorwoman, WKYC, Cleveland 1967-70; TV news reporter,
    NBC 1970-76; Positively Black 1975; News Center Five (Chi-
    cago) 1977.

RAGLAND, LARRY (Lawrence Cary Ragland)
    (Entertainer/Comedian)
b. February 21, 1948, Richmond, Va.
Education: Amherst College (Mass.) B.A. 1970.
Special Interests: Acting, flute, impressions, singing.
Address: 129 W. 85 Street, New York, N.Y. 10024.

Clubs: Across 110th Street; Reno Sweeney; Improvisation; Catch a
    Rising Star; Playboy (Baltimore); Fairmont Hotel (S.F.); Dan-
    gerfield's 1975, 1976.
Memberships: AFTRA; AGVA; ASCAP.
Television: Positively Black 1975; Keep on Truckin' 1975; Sammy
    and Company 1975; Tonight Show 1975; A.M. New York 1975;
    Tommy Banks Show (Canada) 1975; The Clifton Davis Special
    1976.

RAHN, MURIEL
    (Singer/actress)
b. 1911, Boston, Mass.
d. August 8, 1961, New York, N.Y.
Education: National Orchestral Assn., Atlanta University; Music
    Conservatory of University of Nebraska.
Career Data: Appeared with San Carlo Opera Co.; National Negro
    Opera Co.; performed in Mozart's The Abduction from Serag-
    lio (Carnegie Hall), Suor Angelica and Gianni Schicchi 1942;
    sang title role in Aïda for Salmaggi Opera Co. (Triboro Sta-
    dium) 1944; The Martyr (Carnegie Hall) 1947.
Films: King for a Day (short) 1934.
Memberships: AGMA.
Theater: Finian's Rainbow; title role in Carmen Jones (alternating
    with Muriel Smith) 1943-44; The Barrier 1951; Come of Age
    (City Center) 1952; The Ivory Branch (O.B.) 1956; musical
    director State Theatre of Frankfurt production of The Bells
    Are Ringing 1960.
Relationships: Wife of Dick Campbell, producer.

RAINEY, MA "Mother of the Blues" (Gertrude Malissa Nix Pridgett)
    (Singer)
b. April 26, 1886, Columbus, Ga.
d. December 22, 1939, Rome, Ga.
Career Data: Debut in A Bunch of Blackberries at Springer Opera
    House (Columbus Ga.) 1898; toured with Rabbit Foot Minstrels
    and Tolliver's Circus 1904; formed Georgia Jazz Band 1920's;
    performed in Fort Worth Stock Show 1930's; influenced Bessie
    Smith, her protégée; retired in 1933; made over 100 record-
    ings for Paramount starting 1923.
Records: Immortal (Milestone); Blame It on the Blues (Milestone);
    Blues the World Forgot (Biograph); Down in the Basement
    (Milestone); Ma Rainey (Milestone); Oh My Babe Blues (Bio-
    graph); Queen of the Blues (Biograph).
Theater: Appearance at Temple Theater (Cleveland); Smart Set
    1911.

RANDOLPH, AMANDA
    (Actress)
b. 1902 Louisville, Ky.
d. August 24, 1967, Duarte, Calif.

Special Interests: Singing.
Career Data: Teamed with Catherine Handy (daughter of W. C.
        Handy) as Dixie Nightingales 1932.
Films: Swing 1938; Lying Lips, At the Circus 1939; Comes Mid-
        night, The Notorious Elinor Lee 1940; No Way Out 1950; She's
        Working Her Way Through College 1952; Mr. Scoutmaster 1953;
        A Man Called Peter 1955.
Radio: Amos 'n' Andy (series); Aunt Jemima; Beulah (series).
Television: Mother-in-law of Kingfish on Amos 'n' Andy (series);
        Maid on Danny Thomas Show 1957-64.
Theater: In the Alley; Joy Cruise; Chili Peppers; Dusty Lane;
        Fall Frolics; Radiowaves.
Relationships: Sister of Lillian Randolph, actress.

RANDOLPH, JAMES (James Randolph Cheatham)
        (Singer/Actor)
b. February 21, 1934, Brewton, Ala.
Education: Long Island University B.A., (music) 1951.
Honors: Knighted by Republic of Liberia 1971.
Clubs: Riviera (Las Vegas); Star Dust Hotel (Las Vegas); Latin
        Quarter; Elegante (Brooklyn); Rat Fink Room.
Memberships: AEA; NAG.
Television: Arthur Godfrey's Talent Scouts; Tonight Show; Merv
        Griffin Show; Jackie Gleason Show; Mary Tyler Moore Show;
        Mike Douglas Show 1976.
Theater: Huskie Miller in Carmen Jones (debut at City Center)
        1954; Crown in Porgy and Bess (tour); Ballad for Bimshire
        (O.B.) 1963; To Broadway with Love; Free and Easy; Jump
        for Joy; Sky Masterson in Guys and Dolls 1976.

RANDOLPH, LILLIAN
        (Actress)
Special Interests: Singing.
Address: 4190 Sutro Avenue, Los Angeles, Calif. 90008.
Films: Life Goes On 1938; Mr. Smith Goes Ghost, Am I Guilty?,
        Little Men 1940; West Point Widow, Gentleman from Dixie,
        All American Coed 1941; The Glass Key 1942; The Mexican
        Spitfire Sees a Ghost, Hi Neighbor!, The Great Gildersleeve
        1943; Gildersleeve's Bad Day, Hoosier Holiday, Gildersleeve
        on Broadway 1943; Adventures of Mark Twain, Gildersleeve's
        Ghost, Three Little Sisters 1944; A Song for Miss Julie 1945;
        Child of Divorce, It's a Wonderful Life 1946; The Bachelor
        and the Bobby-Soxer 1947; Sleep My Love 1948; Once More,
        My Darling 1949; Dear Brat, That's My Boy 1951; Hush, Hush
        Sweet Charlotte! 1964; The Great White Hope 1970; How to
        Seduce a Woman 1974; Once Is Not Enough, Rafferty and the
        Gold Dust Twins 1975.
Memberships: SAG.
Radio: Lulu and Leander (WXYZ Detroit); Al Jolson Show; The Big
        Town; title role (replacing Hattie McDaniel) in Beulah Show
        (series); Madam Queen on Amos 'n' Andy (series); The Billie

Burke Show 1944-46; Birdie on The Great Gildersleeve (series)
1952-55.
Television: Mannix; title role in Beulah (series) 1952-53; Birdie
in The Great Gildersleeve (series) 1955-56; Mrs. Kincaid in
Bill Cosby Show (series) 1969; That's My Mama 1974; Sanford
and Son 1975; The Jeffersons 1976; Wesson Oil commercial
1976; Roots 1977; Nashville 99 1977.
Relationships: Sister of Amanda Randolph, actress.

RASULALA, THALMUS (Jack Crowder)
    (Actor)
b. November 15, 1939, Miami, Fla.
Education: University of Redlands; University of California.
Address: 1925 Weepah Way, Los Angeles, Calif. 90023.
Honors: Theatre World Award (for Hello, Dolly!) 1967.
Films: The Out of Towners 1970; Cool Breeze, Blacula 1972; The
Slams (asst. director) 1973; Willie Dynamite 1974; Mr. Ricco,
Cornbread, Earl and Me, Bucktown 1975; Friday Foster 1975;
The Last Hard Men, Adios Amigo 1976; Fun with Dick and
Jane 1977.
Television: Cannon; All in the Family; Sanford and Son; Perry
Mason Show; Run for Your Life; Kraft Suspense Theatre; One
Life to Live (series) 1969; The Bait 1973; The Autobiography
of Miss Jane Pittman 1974; Medical Center 1974; Khan! 1975;
Good Times 1975; Mannix 1975; Caribe 1975; Last Hours Be-
fore Morning 1975; Saturday Night 1975; Cop and the Kid 1976;
What's Happening (series) 1976; Most Wanted 1976; Monkey in
the Middle 1976; Roots 1977; Killer on Board 1977.
Theater: The Fantasticks (O.B.); Damn Yankees (stock); The Roar
of the Greasepaint (Calif.); The Zulu and the Zayda (Calif.);
No Time for Sergeants (stock); Irma La Douce (stock); One Is
a Crowd; Fly Blackbird (O.B.) 1962; Vandergelder in Hello,
Dolly! 1969.

RAWLS, LOU (Louis Allen Rawls)
    (Singer)
b. December 1, 1935, Chicago, Ill.
Address: c/o Creative Management Associates 8899 Beverly Blvd.,
Los Angeles, Calif. 90048 and 1120 S. Gramercy Place, Los
Angeles, Calif.
Honors: Two Grammys.
Career Data: Organized Dead End Productions (L.A.) to help
youths who seek show business careers; played with King
Curtis Band; member, Pilgrim Travelers (gospel group).
Clubs: Westside Room (L.A.); Pandora's Box (L.A.); Jimmy's
1974; Lion's Den of MGM Grand Hotel (Las Vegas) 1975;
Buddy's Place 1975; Great Gorge Resort Hotel (McAfee, N.J.)
1975.
Films: Angel, Angel Down We Go (a.k.a. Cult of the Damned)
1970.
Memberships: AFTRA.

Records: Natural Man; Lou Rawls Live! (Capitol); Unmistakably
          Love; She's Gone (Arista); Stormy Monday (Capitol); Tobacco
          Road; All Things in Time (Capitol); You'll Never Find Another
          Love Like Mine; Best (Capitol); Soulin' (Capitol); Come On in
          Mr. Blues (Pickwick); Nobody But You; Black and Blues.
Television: Big Valley; Jeanne Wolf with ...; The Wacky World of
          Jonathan Winters; Dick Clark Show; Steve Allen Show; Bourbon
          Street; 77 Sunset Strip; Trouble Comes to Town 1973; Mike
          Douglas Show 1974, 1975; The Tonight Show 1975; Dinah!;
          Merv Griffin Show 1975, 1976; Kup's Show; Positively Black
          1975; The Golddiggers (series) 1975; Musical Chairs 1975;
          Sammy and Company 1975; Midnight Special 1976; American
          Music awards show 1977; Disco '77 1977; The Captain and
          Tennille 1977; Budweiser commercial 1977.
Theater: Apollo Theatre; Felt Forum 1976; Satchmo '76 Show at
          Beacon Theatre 1976; Westbury Music Fair 1977.

RAZAF, ANDY (Andreamenentaia Paul Razafinkeriefo)
          (Lyricist)
b.   December 16, 1895, Washington, D.C.
d.   February 3, 1973, Los Angeles, Calif.
Special Interests: Composing.
Honors: U.S. Treasury Dept. Silver Medal 1946; Songwriters Hall
          of Fame 1972.
Career Data: Collaborated with composers including Fats Waller,
          Flournoy Miller and Eubie Blake.
Memberships: ASCAP 1929.
Musical Compositions: Stompin' at the Savoy; 12th Street Rag; Black
          and Blue; S'posin; Honeysuckle Rose; Memories of You; Ain't
          Misbehavin'; My Fate Is in Your Hands; Massachusetts; In the
          Mood; Keeping Out of Mischief Now; Gee, Baby Ain't I Good
          to You?; You're Lucky to Me; How Can You Face Me?; I'm
          Gonna Move to the Outskirts of Town; Make Believe Ballroom;
          Christopher Columbus; Milkman's Matinee; Concentratin' on
          You; That's What I Like 'Bout the South; Knock Me a Kiss;
          My Special Friend; Blue Turning Gray Over You; The Joint Is
          Jumpin'; If It Ain't Love; Shoutin' in the Amen Corner.
Theater: Connie's Hot Chocolates 1928; Keep Shufflin' 1928; Black-
          birds of 1930; Bubbling Brown Sugar (posthumously produced)
          1976.

REDDING, OTIS
          (Singer)
b.   September 9, 1941, Dawson, Ga.
d.   December 10, 1967, Madison, Wisc.
Special Interests: Composing.
Honors: Won English poll for World's Best Male Singer.
Career Data: Participated, Monterey Festival 1967.
Films: Monterey Pop 1969.
Records: The Best of Otis Redding (Atlantic); History of Otis Red-
          ding (Atlantic); The Legendary Otis Redding; Otis Redding in

Person at the Whiskey A-Go-Go; Immortal (ATCO); Live in
Europe (ATCO), On Volt: These Arms of Mine 1963; That's
What My Heart Needs 1963; Pain in My Heart 1963; Come to
Me 1964; Chained and Bound 1964; Mr. Pitiful 1965; I've Been
Loving You Too Long 1965; Respect 1965; Just One More Day
1965; Satisfaction 1966; My Lover's Prayer 1966; FA-FA-FA-
FA-FA- 1966; Try a Little Tenderness 1966; I Love You More
Than Words Can Say 1967; Shake 1967; Glory of Love 1967.

REED, ALAINA
    (Singer)
b. November 10, 1946, Springfield, Ohio.
Education: Kent State University.
Address: 225 West 106 Street, New York, N.Y. 10025.
Clubs: Downstairs; Improvisation; Brothers & Sisters; Reno Sween-
    eys; Mr. Kelly's (Chicago); The Continental Baths; Jimmy's;
    Rainbow Grill; Grand Finale 1974, 1975; Manhattan Theater
    Club 1975.
Television: Black News 1975; Sesame Street (series) 1976.
Theater: Hair (Chicago) 1969, (New York) 1971; Sgt. Pepper's Lone-
    ly Hearts Club Band on the Road (O.B.) 1974; A Matter of
    Time 1975; Alaina in Concert 1976.

REED, ALBERT
    (Actor)
Address: Granite Agency, 1920 La Cienega Blvd., Los Angeles,
    Calif. 90034.
Career Data: Co-producer, Miss Black Teenager Pageant.
Films: Where Does It Hurt 1972; Isis 1975.
Memberships: SAG.
Television: Sanford and Son; Emergency; Chase; Uncle Tom episode
    of The Jeffersons; Good Times 1975.

REED, TRACY
    (Actress)
b. c.1949, Fort Benning, Ga.
Education: U.C.L.A., B.A. 1970.
Address: Goldstein-Shapira, 9171 Wilshire Blvd., Beverly Hills,
    Calif.
Honors: Miss Teenage Los Angeles.
Films: A Shot in the Dark, Dr. Strangelove 1964; Casino Royale
    1967; Hammerhead 1968; Percy 1971; Trouble Man 1972; The
    Take 1974; Car Wash 1976; A Piece of the Action 1977.
Memberships: SAG.
Television: The Odd Couple; Cannon; Love, American Style; Journey
    into Midnight 1969; Barefoot in the Park (series) 1970; Incident
    in San Francisco 1971; I Want to Report a Dream (Kojak) 1975;
    McCloud 1975; Barnaby Jones 1975; The Great American Beauty
    Contest 1975; Policy Story 1975.

REED, VIVIAN
      (Singer)
b.   June 6, Pittsburgh, Pa.
Education: Juilliard School of Music; studied dance with George
      Faison.
Special Interests: Dancing, acting, composing.
Address: 60 West 142nd Street, New York, N.Y. 10037.
Honors: Tony nomination best musical actress (for Bubbling Brown
      Sugar) 1976.
Clubs: Snooky's; Copacabana; Pauline's Interlude; Kings Castle
      (Lake Tahoe); Shoreham Hotel (Washington, D.C.); Clay House
      Inn (Bermuda); Sahara (Las Vegas).
Records: Vivian Reed, Yours Until Tomorrow (Epic) 1969; Vivian
      Reed, Brown Sugar 1976.
Television: David Frost Show; Merv Griffin Show; Mike Douglas
      Show; Tonight Show; Tony Awards Show 1976; Apollo (special)
      1976; Sammy and Company 1976, 1977; Merv Griffin Show
      1977.
Theater: That's Entertainment at Apollo Theatre; Don't Bother Me
      I Can't Cope (Chicago) 1972; Bubbling Brown Sugar 1975-76;
      Carnegie Hall 1976.

REESE, DELLA (Deloreese Patricia Early)
      (Singer)
b.   July 6, 1932, Detroit, Mich.
Education: Wayne State University.
Special Interests: Acting, composing.
Honors: Gold Records; Most Promising Girl Singer 1957.
Career Data: Sang with Mahalia Jackson, Clara Ward; co-owner
      (with Carmen McRae) of boutique; vocalist with Erskine Haw-
      kins band.
Clubs: Flame Showbar (Detroit); The Cloisters (L.A.); Sheraton
      (Puerto Rico); Sahara (Tahoe); Caesar's Palace (Las Vegas);
      Coconut Grove (Las Vegas); Mr. Kelly's (Chicago); Caribe
      Hilton: Flamingo (Las Vegas); Birdland 1956; St. Regis-
      Maisonette 1975; Stevensville Country Club (Swan Lake, N.Y.)
      1976.
Films: Psychic Killer 1976.
Memberships: SAG.
Records: And That Reminds Me (Jubilee) 1957; Don't You Know
      (RCA) 1959; Bill Bailey (RCA) 1961; C'Mon and Hear (ABC);
      I Gotta Be Me (ABC); I Like It Like Dat (ABC); Live (ABC);
      On Strings of Blue (ABC); One More Time (ABC).
Television: Hollywood Squares; Merv Griffin Show; Mike Douglas
      Show; Tonight Show; Ed Sullivan Show; Flo in Twice in a
      Lifetime (Baselli's World); Celebrity Sweepstakes; Mod Squad;
      McCloud; Della Reese Show (series); Wide World Special;
      Flip Wilson Show; Name That Tune 1974; Police Woman 1974;
      Soundstage 1975; Petrocelli 1975; Rhyme and Reason 1975;
      Rookies 1975; Sanford and Son 1975; Sammy and Company
      1975; Kup's Show 1975; Chico and the Man 1975; The Return
      of Joe Forrester (Police Story) 1975; Magnificent Marble

Machine 1976; Medical Center 1976; Take My Advice 1976;
Break the Bank 1976; Nightmare in Badham County 1976.

RENARD, KEN
(Actor)
b. Trinidad.
Films: Murder with Music 1941; Killer Diller 1947; Lydia Bailey
    1952; Something of Value 1957; These Thousand Hills 1959;
    Home from the Hill 1960; Papa's Delicate Condition 1963; The
    Chase 1966; The Farmer 1977.
Memberships: AEA; AFTRA; SAG.
Radio: Gangbusters; Cavalcade of America; Ford Theatre; Camel
    Caravan; David Harum; Death Valley Days.
Television: Philco Playhouse; Schlitz Playhouse of Stars; Pulitzer
    Prize Playhouse; Studio One; Lights Out; Bonanza; Gunsmoke;
    Sanford and Son.
Theater: Macbeth (Lafayette Theatre) 1936; Androcles and the
    Lion (Federal Theatre) 1938; The Patriots (Washington, D.C.)
    1943; Janie (subway circuit) 1944; Native Son (subway circuit)
    1944; Strange Fruit 1945; Mr. Peebles and Mr. Hooker 1946;
    Another Part of the Forest (tour) 1947; The Skull Beneath
    (stock) 1947; A Long Way from Home (ANTA) 1948; Hope Is
    the Thing with Feathers 1948; The Respectful Prostitute 1949;
    The Shrike (tour) 1952.

RHODES, GEORGE A.
(Musician/Conductor)
b. October 20, 1918, Indianapolis, Ind.
Education: Crane College (Chicago); Chicago Music College;
    Juilliard School of Music.
Special Interests: Piano.
Address: 9000 Sunset Blvd., Suite 1212, Hollywood, Calif. 90069.
Honors: Royal Command Performance (Queen of England) 1960,
    1961, 1966; Emmy Awards 1964-65; Citation U.S.O. Perform-
    ances, Vietnam 1972.
Career Data: Music director, Sammy Davis Enterprises since 1955;
    president, Garshir Music Publishing Company.
Clubs: Coconut Grove (L.A.) 1971.
Films: Acted in A Man Called Adam 1966; Man Without Mercy
    (score) 1968.
Records: Music arranger for Apollo Records 1950-52; RCA Victor
    1954-55; King Records 1955-56; AMCO Records 1958-59.
Television: I Dream of Jeannie 1968; Sammy and Company (series)
    1975-76; Most Wanted 1976.
Theater: Golden Boy 1964-65.

RHODES, HARI
(Actor)
b. April 10, 1932, Cincinnati, Ohio.
Education: University of Cincinnati; Conservatory of Music.
Special Interests: Martial Arts (Judo, Karate)

Address: Diamond Artists Ltd., 8400 Sunset Blvd., Los Angeles,
          Calif. 90069.
Films: Let No Man Write My Epitaph 1959; Return to Peyton
          Place, The Sins of Rachel Cade, The Fiercest Heart 1961;
          Drums of Africa, Shock Corridor 1963; The Satan Bug, Mirage
          1965; Blindfold 1966; Conquest of the Planet of the Apes 1972;
          Detroit 9000 1973.
Memberships: SAG.
Television: Mannix; Name of the Game; Police Surgeon; Mike in
          Daktari (series) 1966-69; The FBI; To Sir, With Love; Dead-
          lock 1969; Earth II 1971; A Dream for Christmas 1973; Trou-
          ble Comes to Town 1973; Conquest of the Planet of the Apes
          (series) 1974; For Good or Evil on Streets of San Francisco
          1974; Six Million Dollar Man 1974; Police Story 1974, 1975;
          Cannon 1975; Matt Helm 1975; The Return of Joe Forrester
          (Police Story) 1975; Quincy 1976; May Day at 40,000 Feet
          1976; Most Wanted 1976; Roots 1977.

RICH, RON
     (Actor)
b. October 29, 1938, Pittsburgh, Pa.
Address: Beverly Hecht, 8949 Sunset Blvd., Los Angeles, Calif.
          90069.
Films: The Fortune Cookie 1966; Chubasco 1969.
Memberships: AEA; SAG.
Theater: Big Time Buck White (Bway debut) 1969.

RICHARDS, BEAH
     (Actress)
b. Vicksburg, Miss.
Education: Dillard University (New Orleans); San Diego Community
          Theatre.
Honors: Theatre World Award (The Amen Corner) 1965; Academy
          Award Nominee Best Supporting Actress (Guess Who's Coming
          to Dinner?) 1967; All American Press Assn. award 1968;
          Black Filmmakers Hall of Fame 1974.
Career Data: Teacher, Inner City Institute for Performing Arts;
          teacher, Ophelia DeVore Charm School.
Films: Take a Giant Step 1961; The Miracle Worker 1962; Gone
          Are the Days 1963; In the Heat of the Night, Guess Who's
          Coming to Dinner?, Hurry Sundown 1967; The Great White
          Hope 1970; The Biscuit Eater 1972; Mahogany 1975.
Memberships: AEA; SAG.
Television: Mrs. Kincaid in The Bill Cosby Show 1970; Dr. Kildare
          1966; Big Valley 1966; I Spy 1967; Hawaii Five O 1969; Iron-
          side 1969; Room 222 1969; It Takes a Thief 1970; On Stage
          1970; Sanford and Son 1972; Footsteps 1972; A Dream for
          Christmas 1973; Outrage 1975; Say Brother 1975; The Magi-
          cian; Just an Old Sweet Song (General Electric Theater) 1976.
Theater: Arturo Ui; Take a Giant Step (O.B.) 1956; A Raisin in
          the Sun 1959; The Miracle Worker 1959; Purlie Victorious

1961; Sister Margaret in The Amen Corner 1965; The Little
Foxes (Lincoln Repertory Theatre) 1967; authored and acted
in One Is a Crowd 1971; A Black Woman Speaks (tour) 1975;
This Far by Faith 1977.

RICHARDS, LLOYD (George)
      (Director)
b.   Toronto, Ontario, Canada.
Education: Wayne State University B.A. 1944; studied acting at
      Paul Mann Actors Workshop 1949-52.
Special Interests: Acting, teaching.
Address: 18 West 95 Street, New York, N.Y. 10025.
Honors: Wayne State University Alumni award for theatre achieve-
      ment 1962.
Career Data: Asst. Dir. and Teacher, Paul Mann Actors Workshop
      1952-62; resident dir., Great Lakes Drama Festival 1954;
      resident dir.; Northland Playhouse (Detroit) 1955-58; founder
      and teacher, Lloyd Richards Studio 1962-72; teacher, Negro
      Ensemble Co. 1967-68; teacher, National Theatre Institute
      1970-date; professor of cinema and theatre, Hunter College;
      artistic dir., O'Neill Center National Playwrights Conference
      1969-date; head actor training, N.Y.U. School of the Arts
      1966-72; founder, These Twenty People Co. (later called The
      Actor's Company Repertory) Detroit; founder. Greenwich
      Mews Theatre; conducted theatre survey and lectured in Ghana,
      Kenya, Uganda and Zambia.
Films: U.S. Army Signal Corps Films 1944-45.
Memberships: AEA; SAG; SSDC; Black Academy of Arts and Let-
      ters; Bd. of Advisors, The Street Theatre Inc.; National
      Advisory Council on Theatre and the Humanities; U.S. Bicen-
      tennial World Theatre Festival; First American Congress of
      Theatre; Theatre Hall of Fame Advisory Council; Bd. of Dir.,
      Theatre Development Fund.
Radio: Disc jockey WJLB (Detroit); narrated Little Church on the
      Air (WWJ) Detroit; Sam in Hotel for Pets; Front Page Drama;
      Helen Trent; Murder by Experts; Mysterious Traveller; Inheri-
      tance; Theatre Guild of the Air; Greatest Story Ever Told; Up
      for Parole; Jungle Jim; My True Story.
Records: Directed Jason Robards Jr. Reading Excerpts from Eugene
      O'Neill (Columbia); directed A Raisin in the Sun (Caedmon).
Television: Acted in: The Web; Studio One; Hallmark Hall of Fame;
      Pulitzer Television Playhouse; Famous Jury Trials; The Guiding
      Light; Search for Tomorrow; Lux Video Theatre; We the Peo-
      ple; Somerset Maugham Playhouse; Silver Theatre; Philco
      Playhouse. Directed: The Last Chapter (Wide World of En-
      tertainment); G.E. Theatre; The Committee; Kung Fu; Cable
      Car Murder; Miss Black America 1969, 1970; Sold on Soul
      (NAACP Tribute to Duke Ellington) 1970; You Are There 1971-
      72.
Theater: Acted in: Plant in the Sun (ELT) 1948; Freight 1950;
      The Egghead 1957; Winterset (ELT); Iago in Othello (O.B.);
      Oedipus (O.B.); Respectful Prostitute (O.B.); Home of the

Brave (O. B.); The Little Foxes (O. B.); Stevedore (O. B.);
Hedda Gabler (O. B.). Directed: A Raisin in the Sun 1959;
The Long Dream 1960; The Moon Besieged 1962; The Crucible
(Boston University) 1962; The Desperate Hours (stock); I Had
a Ball 1964; Lower Than the Angels (O. B.) 1965; The Year-
ling 1966; The Ox Cart (O. B.) 1966; Who's Got His Own (O.
B.) 1966; Summertree (O'Neill Memorial Theatre Center) 1967;
That's the Game Jack (Tanglewood Writer's Conference) 1967;
The Great I Am (American Place Theatre) 1972; Freeman
(American Place Theatre) 1974; The Past Is the Past and
Goin' Thru Changes (Billie Holiday Theatre, Brooklyn) 1974.

RICHARDSON, WILLIS
     (Playwright)
b. November 5, 1889, Wilmington, N. C.
Education: Dunbar High School (Washington, D. C.) 1906-10.
Honors: NAACP Spingarn medal for drama; Crisis Magazine con-
     test winner 1925, 1926; Opportunity Magazine contest winner
     1925.
Publications: Plays and Pageants from the Life of the Negro,
     Associated Publishers, 1930; co-editor, Negro History in Thir-
     teen Plays, Associated Publishers, 1935.
Theater: Wrote Alimony Rastus; The Amateur Prostitute; Bold
     Love (one act); The Brown Boy, Chase; The Curse of the
     Shell Road Witch; The Danse Calinda; The Dark Haven (one
     act); Hope of the Lonely; Imp of the Devil; The Jail Bird;
     Joy Rider; The New Generation; The Nude Siren; A Pillar of
     the Church; Protest; The Rider of the Dream; Rooms for
     Rent; The Victims; The Visiting Lady; The Man Who Married
     a Young Wife (one act); A Ghost of the Past 1920; The Dea-
     con's Awakening (one act) 1921; The Brownies Book 1921;
     The Chip Woman's Fortune 1923; Mortgaged 1923; The Broken
     Banjo 1925; Fall of the Conjurer 1925; Bootblack Lover 1926;
     Compromise 1926; The Flight of the Natives 1927; The Idle
     Head 1927; The House of Sham 1928; The Peacock's Feathers
     1928; The Black Horseman 1929; The King's Dilemma 1929;
     Sacrifice 1930; Antonio Maceo (one act) 1935; Attucks, the
     Martyr 1935; The Elder Dumas 1935; In Menelik's Court
     1935; Near Calvary, Easter Play for Children 1935; Place:
     America 1939; Miss or Mrs. 1941; Dragon's Tooth (one act)
     1956; The Gypsy's Finger Ring 1956; Man of Magic 1956; The
     New Santa Claus 1956.

RILEY, CLAYTON
     (Critic)
b. May 23, 1935, Brooklyn, N. Y.
Special Interests: Directing, playwriting, teaching.
Address: 523 West 112 Street, New York, N. Y. 10025.
Career Data: Entertainment editor, Amsterdam News (N. Y.); con-
     tributor, New York Times, Ebony magazine, CHAMBA Notes,
     The Liberator, Chicago Sun-Times and others; teacher (black

drama, music etc.) at Sarah Lawrence College, Fordham University, Howard University; lecture series on Blacks in American Films at American Film Institute 1975.

Films: Production asst., Nothing But a Man 1964.

Memberships: Drama Desk; Harlem Writers Guild.

Television: Is Sweetback Really Sweet? (Black Journal) 1971; Vince Amaker Show (Cable TV) 1974; Midday Live 1975; Black News 1977.

Theater: Directed On the Goddam Lock In (O.B.) 1975; wrote and directed Gilbeau (New Federal Theatre) 1976.

RIPERTON, MINNIE
    (Singer)
b. c.1947 Chicago, Ill.

Education: Hyde Park H.S. (Chicago); studied with Marian Jeffrey.

Special Interests: Composing.

Honors: Gold record; Female vocalist of the year; NAACP Image award 1975; Ebony Music Award 1976.

Career Data: Former member, The Rotary Connection.

Clubs: Riviera (Las Vegas) 1976.

Records: Come to My Garden (Janus); Loving You, Perfect Angel (Epic); Adventures in Paradise (Epic) 1975; Stay in Love 1976.

Television: American Bandstand 1975; American Music Awards 1975, 1976; Tonight Show 1975, 1976; Soul Train 1975; Dinah! 1975; Merv Griffin Show 1975; Midnight Special 1976; Sammy and Company 1976; Flip's [Wilson] Sun Valley Olympiad (special) 1976; Monty Hall's Variety Hour 1976; Mike Douglas Show 1977.

Theater: Appearance at Avery Fisher Hall 1975; Opera House-Kennedy Center for Performing Arts (Wash. D.C.) 1976.

RIPPY, RODNEY ALLEN
    (Actor)
b. c.1968.

Address: Dorothy Day Otis Agency, 6430 Sunset Blvd., Los Angeles, Calif. 90028.

Films: Blazing Saddles 1974.

Memberships: SAG.

Records: Take Life a Little Easier (Bell).

Television: Jack in the Box commercial; Fantasies Fulfilled (special); Mike Douglas Show; Mac Davis Show; Tonight Show 1974; Socko 1974; Harlem Globetrotter's Popcorn Machine (series) 1974; Merv Griffin and The Christmas Kids (special) 1974; Medical Center 1974; Dinah! 1974, 1975; Odd Couple (Cameo) 1975; Merv Griffin and The Easter Kids 1975; emcee, Ebony Music Awards 1975; Six Million Dollar Man 1975; Spring Event '75 with Oral Roberts; Police Story 1976; Tomorrow 1977.

RIVERS, LOUIS
    (Playwright)

b. September 18, 1922, Savannah, Ga.
Education: Savannah State College B.S. 1946; New York University
    M.A. 1949; Yale University 1958-59; Fordham University
    1970-1976; studied acting at Brette-Warren Studio with Howard
    da Silva 1952-53.
Special Interests: Acting, directing, teaching.
Address: 333 Lafayette Avenue, Brooklyn, N.Y. 11238.
Career Data: Stage manager, director and drama coach at institu-
    tions including Savannah State College, Waycross Georgia In-
    stitute, West Virginia State College, Southern University,
    Tougaloo College 1946-48; assoc. professor, N.Y.C. Communi-
    ty College, Brooklyn 1970-.
Memberships: The Dramatist Guild; The Authors League of Ameri-
    ca Inc.
Theater: Wrote Mr. Randolph Brown; Purple Passages; A Rose for
    Lorraine; Seeking; Scabs (one act) 1962; Madam Odum 1973;
    This Piece of Land (one act) 1975; Soldiers of Freedom 1976.
    Acted in: Danny in Night Must Fall; Joseph in Wuthering
    Heights; Gramps in On Borrowed Time; title role in Silas
    Marner.

ROACH, MAX (Maxwell)
    (Jazz Musician)
b. January 10, 1925, Brooklyn, N.Y.
Special Interests: Drums, composing, teaching.
Honors: Metronome Poll winner 1951, 1954; Down Beat Poll winner
    1955, 1957-59; Grand Prix Du Disque, France.
Career Data: Played with bands of Benny Carter 1944, Coleman
    Hawkins 1944; participated in Paris Jazz Festival 1949, Jazz
    at the Philharmonic Europe Tour 1952, Newport Jazz Festival
    1974; professor of music, Amherst College 1972-; faculty mem-
    ber, School of Jazz (Lenox, Mass.)
Clubs: Clarke Monroe's Uptown House; The Lighthouse (L.A.) 1954;
    Basin Street 1956; East (Brooklyn) 1976.
Musical Compositions: Freedom Now Suite.
Records: At Basin Street; Brown and Roach Inc.; Clifford Brown
    and Max Roach; The Best of Max Roach and Clifford Brown in
    Concert; Max Roach Plus Four; Max Roach 4 Plays Charlie
    Parker; Rich Versus Roach; Max Roach with The Boston Per-
    cussion Ensemble; Drummin' the Blues; Drums Unlimited (At-
    lantic); It's Time (Impulse); Percussion Bitter Sweet (Impulse);
    Speak Brother Speak (Fantasy); Plus Four (Trip).
Television: Like It Is 1975; Black News 1977.
Theater: Appeared at Carnegie Hall; Black Picture Show (music)
    1974; Avery Fisher Hall (Tribute to Dizzy Gillespie) 1975.
Relationships: Former husband of Abbey Lincoln, singer/actress.

ROBERTS, DAVIS
    (Actor)
b. March 7, 1917, Mobile, Ala.
Education: University of Chicago; UCLA; Actors Lab.

Address: Noah Sanders, 12108 Ventura Blvd., Studio City, Calif.
Films: Hotel 1967; Glass Houses, The Trial of the Catonsville
   Nine 1972; Detroit 9000 1973; Willie Dynamite 1974.
Memberships: AEA; SAG.
Television: Mission: Impossible; Name of the Game; Medical Center;
   Great Gettin' Up Mornin' (Repertoire Workshop) 1964; The
   Untouchables; Get Christie Love 1974; The Streets of San
   Francisco 1974; Ironside 1974; That's My Mama 1975; Police
   Story 1974, 1975; McMillan and Wife 1975; The Jeffersons
   1976; Roots 1977; Good Times 1977.
Theater: Trial of the Catonsville Nine 1971.

ROBERTSON, HUGH A.
   (Director)
b. Brooklyn, N.Y.
Honors: British Oscar Winner; Academy of Motion Picture Arts &
   Sciences Oscar Nominee.
Films: Hang Tough; edited Midnight Cowboy 1969; edited Shaft 1971;
   Melinda 1972; Georgia Georgia (consultant) 1972; Bim 1976.
Television: Dream a Monkey.

ROBESON, PAUL (Leroy)
   (Singer/Actor)
b. April 9, 1898, Princeton, N.J.
d. January 23, 1976, Phila., Pa.
Education: Rutgers University 1915-19 B.A.; Columbia University
   Law School 1919-22 LL.B.
Special Interests: Civil rights, football, labor movement.
Honors: Phi Beta Kappa, All-American 1918; Spingarn Medal 1945;
   Donaldson award (for Othello) 1944; The Gold Medal Award
   for best diction in American theatre; Stalin Peace Prize 1952;
   First Actors Equity Paul Robeson Citation 1974; Black Film-
   makers Hall of Fame 1974.
Career Data: Concert debut at Greenwich Village Theatre 1925;
   made many other concert appearances in U.S., Europe,
   U.S.S.R. from 1929-61; Sang for Loyalist Cause in Spain
   1938; Peekskill, N.Y. concert interrupted by mob violence
   1949.
Films: Body and Soul 1924; Borderline 1930; title role in Emperor
   Jones 1933; Sanders of the River 1935; Joe in Show Boat 1936;
   King Solomon's Mines, The Song of Freedom, Jericho (a.k.a.
   Dark Sands) 1937; Big Fella 1938; The Proud Valley 1941;
   narrated and sang songs in Native Land 1942; Tales of Man-
   hattan 1942.
Memberships: NAG.
Publications: Here I Stand, Othello Associates, 1958 (reprinted by
   Beacon Press, 1971).
Radio: Sang Ballad for Americans 1939.
Records: Paul Robeson (Vanguard); Essential (Vanguard); In Live
   Performance (Columbia) 1958; At Carnegie (Vanguard) 1958.
Television: Interface.

Theater: Simon the Cyrenian (debut) 1921; Taboo 1922 (a.k.a. The
Voodoo) London 1922; Brutus Jones in The Emperor Jones
1924 (London, 1925); Jim Harris in All God's Chillun Got
Wings 1924-25; Black Boy 1926; Crown in Porgy and Bess
1927; Joe in Show Boat (London) 1928; title role in Othello
(London) 1930; Yank in The Hairy Ape 1931; Joe in Show
Boat 1932; folk song concert at London Palladium 1932; Basilik
1935; Stevedore 1935; title role in Toussaint L'Ouverture 1936;
Emperor Jones (White Plains) 1939; title role in John Henry
1940; title role in Othello 1943 (London 1959); recital Royal
Albert Hall (London) 1958.

ROBINSON, BILL "Bojangles" (Luther Robinson)
(Dancer/Actor)
b. May 25, 1878, Richmond, Va.
d. November 25, 1949, New York, N.Y.
Honors: Winner 1st Prize, National Dancing Contests 1928-31;
Honorary Mayor of Harlem.
Career Data: Created "stair tap dance"; coined word "copacetic"
meaning O.K., fine; considered "King of the Tap Dancers,"
teamed in act of Butler & Robinson 1908.
Clubs: Zanzibar 1946.
Films: Dixiana 1930; Harlem Is Heaven 1932; King for a Day 1934;
The Little Colonel, In Old Kentucky, Hooray for Love, The
Big Broadcast of 1936, The Littlest Rebel, Curly Top 1935;
Dimples 1936; One Mile from Heaven 1937; Rebecca of Sunny-
brook Farm, Road Demon, Just Around the Corner, Up the
River, Hot Mikado, Cotton Club Revue 1938; Stormy Weather
1943.
Memberships: NAG.
Television: Milton Berle Texaco Show.
Theater: The South Before the War (tour) 1887; Blackbirds of 1928;
H.M.S. Pinafore; Brown Buddies 1930; Hot Rhythm 1930; N.Y.
World's Fair 1939; The Hot Mikado 1939; Memphis Bound 1945;
appearances at Roxy Theatre, Palace Theatre.

ROBINSON, MATT
(Producer)
b. January 1, 1937, Philadelphia, Pa.
Education: Pennsylvania State University B.A. 1958.
Special Interests: Writing songs and lyrics.
Address: c/o Hollymatt Inc., 445 Park Avenue (Suite 303), New
York, N.Y. 10022.
Honors: Gold record (for Sesame Street) 1970.
Career Data: Staff writer, WCAU Philadelphia, 1963-68.
Films: Wrote Possession of Joel Delaney 1972; Save the Children
1973; wrote and produced Amazing Grace 1974.
Radio: Hosted Black Book; The Discophonic Scene; Opportunity
Line.
Records: Year of Roosevelt Franklin (Columbia) 1970.
Television: Solomon Grundy; G. I. Johnson; Sesame Street 1968-
71; wrote Sanford and Son 1975.

ROBINSON, ROGER
    (Actor)
b. May 2, 1941, Seattle, Wash.
Education: University of Southern California.
Career Data: Participant, 12th National Playwrights Conference,
    Eugene O'Neill Memorial Theatre, Waterford, Conn.
Films: Willie Dynamite, Newman's Law 1974.
Memberships: SAG.
Television: Marcus Nelson Murders; Mallory; Ironside; The FBI;
    Get Christie Love 1974; Kojak 1974, 1975; Family Holvak
    1975; Baretta 1976.
Theater: Interrogation of Havana (O.B.); The Miser (London);
    Walk in Darkness (O.B.) 1963; Jerico-Jim Crow (O.B.) 1964;
    Who's Got His Own (O.B.) 1966; Trials of Brother Jero (O.
    B.) 1968; The Strong Breed (O.B.) 1968; Does a Tiger Wear
    a Necklace (Bway debut) 1969; Ain't Supposed to Die a Natural
    Death 1971; Flim Flam in Lady Day: A Musical Tragedy
    (Bklyn.) 1972.

ROBINSON, SMOKEY (William Robinson Jr.)
    (Singer/Producer)
b. February 9, 1940, Detroit, Mich.
Special Interests: Composing, recording.
Address: 6464 Sunset Blvd., Los Angeles, Calif. 90028.
Career Data: Has written more than 300 songs; former singer
    with The Miracles 1957-72; vice-president, Motown Industries
    Inc.
Clubs: Bachelor's III (Florida).
Musical Compositions: Ooh Baby, Baby; Don't Mess with Bill; Ain't
    That Peculiar; My Guy; My Girl; Got a Job (co-wrote) 1958;
    Bad Girl (co-wrote) 1959; Shop Around (co-wrote) 1960.
Records: Smokey Robinson and the Miracles (Tamla); A Quiet
    Storm (Tamla); Anthology (Motown); Smokey Robinson 1957-
    1972; Greatest Hits 2v (Tamla); Smokey's Family Robinson
    (Tamla); Deep in My Soul (Motown); Pure (Tamla); Tears of
    a Clown (Pickwick); Big Time (Motown).
Television: Sonny Comedy Revue 1974; Police Woman 1974; Police
    Story 1974; The American Music Awards 1975; Mike Douglas
    Show 1975; Dinah! 1975; Soul Train 1975; Mac Davis Show
    1975; Gettin' Over 1975; American Bandstand 1976; The Captain
    and Tennille 1977.
Theater: Appearances at Apollo Theatre 1958, 1975; Carnegie Hall
    1975; Los Angeles Forum 1975; Westchester Premier Theatre
    1975; Roxy (L.A.) 1975; Soul at Shea Stadium 1976.

ROBINSON, SUGAR CHILE (Frank Isaac Robinson)
    (Pianist)
b. 1940, Detroit, Mich.
Education: Olivet College, (Olivet, Michigan); Detroit Institute of
    Technology.
Special Interests: Singing.

Films: No Leave, No Love 1946.
Radio: Kate Smith Hour; Bob Hope Show.
Records: Hey, Bop A Re Bop; Numbers Boogie; Cal.
Theater: Appeared at Palladium (London); Apollo Theatre.

ROBINSON, "SUGAR" RAY (Walker Smith)
     (Entertainer)
b. May 3, 1920, Detroit, Mich.
Special Interests: Singing.
Address: Sugar Ray's Youth Center, 1905 Tenth Avenue, Los
     Angeles, Calif. 90018.
Career Data: Professional boxer; held middleweight championship
     of the world 1949; title lost and regained 3 times.
Films: Candy, The Detective, Paper Lion 1968.
Publications: Sugar Ray (autobiography), Viking, 1976.
Television: Mod Squad; What's My Line?; Dean Martin Comedy
     Hour (Roasting of Bob Hope) 1974; Tattletales 1975; The Way
     It Was 1976.

ROBY, LAVELLE
     (Actress)
Address: Kingsley Cotton & Associates, 321 S. Beverly Drive,
     Beverly Hills, Calif.
Films: Finders Keepers, Lovers Weepers 1968; Beyond the Valley
     of the Dolls 1970; Sweet Sweetback's Baadasssss Song 1971.
Memberships: SAG.

ROCCO, MAURICE (John)
     (Pianist)
b. June 26, 1915, Oxford, Ohio
d. March 25, 1976, Bankok, Thailand.
Education: Miami University (Oxford, Ohio).
Special Interests: Boogie Woogie, singing, dancing.
Career Data: Performed in Thailand 1961-76.
Clubs: Capitol Lounge (Chicago); Blackhawk Cafe' (Chicago); Kit
     Kat Club 1936; Copacabana; Cafe Zanzibar; Ruban Bleu; Chao
     Phya Hotel (Bangkok).
Films: 52nd Street, Vogues of 1938, 1937; The Incendiary Blonde
     1945.
Theater: Appearance at Roxy Theatre.

ROCHESTER see ANDERSON, EDDIE

RODGERS, ROD (Audrian Windsor Rodgers)
     (Dancer/Choreographer)
Education: Cass Technical H.S. (Detroit); Detroit Society of Arts
     & Crafts; Dance Repertoire Theatre, N.Y.C.; studied with
     Alvin Ailey (Clark Center) and with Eric Hawkins Dance Co.

Special Interests: Acting, directing, photography, teaching, com-
    mercial art.
Address: 8 East 12 Street, New York, N.Y. 10003.
Honors: Commissions from N.Y. Council on the Arts and the
    National Endowment for the Arts; John Hay Whitney fellowship;
    AUDELCO Black Theatre Recognition award 1975.
Career Data: Founder Rod Rodgers Dance Co.; toured colleges and
    universities throughout U.S.; directed and choreographed pro-
    ductions for Voices Inc.
Memberships: American Dance Guild; Assn. of American Dance
    Companies; National Entertainment Conference.
Television: Choreographed one program of Like It Is (ABC); chore-
    ographed productions for Journey into Blackness (CBS special);
    Black News 1976.
Theater: Choreographed The Prodigal Sister 1974; staged and di-
    rected Black Cowboys at City Center; choreographed The Box;
    Inventions; Shout; To Say Goodbye; Rhythm Ritual (with Dance-
    mobile at Harlem Performance Center) 1976; Tangents;
    Visions (at Barbizon Plaza Theater) 1976.

RODRIGUES, PERCY
    (Actor)
b. 1924, Montreal, Canada.
Address: c/o Lawrence Kuhlic Associates, 9000 Sunset Blvd.,
    Hollywood, Calif. 90069.
Career Data: Dominion Drama Festival Canada; professional boxer
    and winner of light-heavyweight championship, Canada; Negro
    Theatre Guild (Montreal).
Films: The Plainsman 1966; The Heart Is a Lonely Hunter, The
    Sweet Ride 1968; Come Back Charleston Blue 1972; Rhinoceros
    1974.
Television: Trio; Midsummer Theatre (Montreal); The Man from
    U.N.C.L.E.; Route 66; Naked City; Star Trek; Nurses 1963;
    Look Up and Live 1964; Carol for Another Christmas 1964;
    Slattery's People 1965; Ben Casey 1965; Daktari 1966; Wild
    Wild West 1966; Mission: Impossible 1966, 1967, 1970; Fugi-
    tive 1967; Tarzan 1967; Mannix 1967, 1968; Deadlock (Bob
    Hope Chrysler Theatre) 1967; Dr. Harry Miles in Peyton
    Place (series) 1968; Name of the Game 1969, 1970; Then Came
    Bronson 1969; Marcus Welby, M.D. 1969; Medical Center
    1970; 1971; The Silent Force 1970; The Old Man Who Cried
    Wolf 1970; World of Disney 1971; The Forgotten Man 1971;
    Ironside 1972; Banacek 1972; Owen Marshall 1972; Streets of
    San Francisco 1972; Sixth Sense 1972; Police Surgeon 1972;
    Toma 1973; Genesis II 1973; Faraday and Company 1974;
    Apple's Way 1974; Planet of the Apes 1974; The Last Survivors
    1975; Good Times 1975; The Lives of Jenny Dolan 1975; San-
    ford and Son 1975; Most Wanted 1976; The Rookies 1976; Doc
    1976; The Money Changers 1976.
Theater: Title role in The Emperor Jones (Canada), Irma La
    Douce (Montreal), Androcles and the Lion (Niagara), Toys
    in the Attic 1960, Blues for Mr. Charlie 1964.

ROGERS, TIMMIE
    (Comedian)
b. c.1915, Detroit, Mich.
Special Interests: Composing, dancing, singing.
Address: 555 Edgecombe Avenue, New York, N.Y. 10032 and
    William Morris Agency, 1350 Avenue of the Americas, New
    York, N.Y. 10019.
Career Data: Associated with phrase "Oh Yeaaah!"; composed
    songs for Tommy Dorsey, Sarah Vaughn and Nat Cole; led
    his own band 1954; appearances in Canada, London, Vietnam;
    participated in Newport Jazz Festival 1974.
Clubs: Basin Street East; New Frontier (Las Vegas); Mapes Hotel
    (Reno); Fontainebleu and Diplomat Hotels (Miami); Cafe Society
    1950; Elegante (Brooklyn) 1962.
Films: Sparkle 1976.
Memberships: AFM.
Records: Back to School Again 1957; If I Were President 1963;
    Alias Clark Dark (Partee).
Television: Sugar Hill Times (series) 1948; Jackie Gleason Show;
    Ed Sullivan Show; Mike Douglas Show; Melba Moore-Clifton
    Davis Show (summer series) 1972; Dinah! 1975; Sanford and
    Son 1975; Merv Griffin Show 1975.
Theater: Blue Holiday 1945; appeared at Apollo Theatre 1950, 1952,
    1958; Too Poor to Die (Ebony Showcase) 1956; No Time for
    Squares (revue) 1957; Town Hall 1974.

ROKER, RENNY
    (Actor)
Address: Moss Agency Ltd., 113 N. San Vicente Blvd., Beverly
    Hills, Calif. 90211.
Films: Skidoo 1968; Tick...Tick...Tick... 1970; Melinda 1972;
    Tough 1974; Deliver Us from Evil 1975; Brothers 1977.
Memberships: SAG.
Television: Harry O 1974; Sanford and Son 1976; What's Happening
    1976; Rafferty 1977; Good Times 1977.

ROKER, ROXIE
b. August 28, Miami, Fla.
Education: Howard University.
Address: 2901 4th Street, Santa Monica, Calif. 90405
Honors: Obie award and Tony nomination (for River Niger) 1973.
Career Data: Member, Howard University Players; production work
    for NBC-TV; Member, Negro Ensemble Company 1969-73;
    toured Scandinavia.
Clubs: Sang in Caribbean Fantasy at El Morocco (Montreal).
Films: Claudine 1974; Deliver Us from Evil 1975.
Television: Associate producer, Family Living (NBC); co-hostess,
    Inside Bedford Stuyvesant (WNEW series) 1967-68; Change at
    125th Street (special); Hollywood Squares; Helen Willis in The
    Jeffersons (series) 1975; Kojak 1976; Roots 1977.
Theater: Wild Duck; Mamba's Daughters; Ododo (NEC); Jamimma

(O.B.); The Blacks (O.B.) 1964; Behold Cometh the Vanderkellans (NEC) 1971; Rosalee Pritchett (NEC) 1972; River Niger
1973.

ROLLE, ESTHER
    (Actress)
b. November 18, 1922, Pompano Beach, Fla.
Education: Spelman College (Atlanta, Ga.); New School for Social
    Research; Hunter College.
Address: c/o Charter Management, 9000 Sunset Blvd., Los Angeles,
    Calif. 90069.
Honors: NAACP Image award, best actress in television series
    1975.
Career Data: Member of Negro Ensemble Company.
Films: Cleopatra Jones 1973.
Memberships: AEA; AFTRA; SAG.
Television: N.Y.P.D.; Sadie Gray in One Life to Live; Florida
    Evans in Maude (series) 1972-74; Good Time (series) 1974-77;
    Dinah's Place; Hollywood Squares 1974; Tony Orlando and Dawn
    1974; Harlem Globetrotter's Popcorn Machine 1974; Celebrity
    Sweepstakes 1975; Medix 1975; Sammy and Company 1975;
    Mike Douglas Show 1975; Match Game 1975; Golden Globe
    Awards Show 1976; Donny and Marie 1976.
Theater: Ballet Behind the Bridge (O.B.); Ride a Black Horse
    (O.B.); The Skin of Our Teeth (tour); The Crucible (tour);
    The Blacks (O.B.) 1961; Purlie Victorious (tour) 1962; Blues
    for Mr. Charlie (Bway debut) 1964; The Amen Corner 1965;
    Happy Ending (1966); Summer of the Seventeenth Doll (NEC)
    1968; God Is a (Guess What?) 1968; Evening of One Acts
    (NEC) 1969; Man Better Man (NEC) 1969; Okakawe (NEC)
    1970; Day of Absence (NEC) 1970; Brotherhood (NEC) 1970;
    The Dream on Monkey Mountain (NEC) 1971; Rosalee Pritchett
    (O.B.) 1972; Don't Play Us Cheap 1972; The Nearly Weds
    (stock) 1976; Lady Macbeth in Macbeth (O.B.) 1977.
Relationships: Sister of Estelle Evans, actress; aunt of Marti Evans-
    Charles, playwright.

ROLLINS, SONNY (Walter Theodore Rollins)
    (Musician)
b. September 7, 1930, New York, N.Y.
Education: N.Y. School of Music.
Special Interests: Saxophone, composing.
Address: Germantown, N.Y. 12526.
Honors: Guggenheim Fellowship 1972; Down Beat magazine Hall of
    Fame.
Career Data: Performed with Thelonius Monk, Art Blakey 1949,
    Bud Powell 1950, Miles Davis 1951; Max Roach-Clifford
    Brown Quartet 1956-57; toured England in 1967; performed at
    Smithsonian Institution Jazz Heritage series 1973 and his own
    group Nucleus 1976.
Clubs: 845 Club (Bronx); Basin Street 1956; Strode Lounge (Chicago);
    Jazz Gallery 1961; The Half Note 1974; Village Vanguard 1975.

Musical Compositions: Sonnymoon.
Records: Saxophone Colossus and More (Prestige); Sonny Rollins
    and the Big Brass (Metro Jazz); Sonny Rollins on Impulse
    (Impulse); Nucleus (Milestone); The Bridge (RCA); Sonny
    Rollins Saxophone; What's New and Our Man in Jazz (RCA);
    The Freedom Suite Plus (Milestone); Alfie (Impulse); Con-
    temporary Leaders (Contemporary); Cutting Edge (Milestone);
    E. Broadway Run Down (Impulse); First Recordings (Prestige);
    Horn Culture (Milestone); Jazz Classics (Prestige); Newk's
    Time (Blue Note); Next Album (Milestone); ...Plays for Bird
    (Prestige); Reevaluation: Impulse Years (Impulse); Sonny
    Rollins (Prestige); Sonny Rollins (Blue Note); Tenor Madness
    (Prestige); 3 Grants (Prestige); Way Out West (Contemporary);
    Worktime (Prestige); More from Vanguard (Blue Note); Night
    at Village Vanguard (Blue Note); Sonny Rollins (Archive of
    Folk & Jazz Music).
Television: Soundstage 1976.
Theater: Appearances at Avery Fisher Hall (Newport Jazz Festival)
    1975; Ira Aldridge Theatre, Howard University (Washington,
    D.C.) 1975; Carnegie Hall 1975, 1976.

ROSEMOND, CLINTON (C.)
    (Actor)
b. 1883.
d. March 10, 1966, Los Angeles, Calif.
Films: Black Network; Green Pastures 1936; Hollywood Hotel, They
    Won't Forget, Dark Manhattan 1937; The Toy Wife, Young Dr.
    Kildare 1938; Midnight Shadow, Stand Up and Fight, Golden
    Boy 1939; Safari, Jungle Queen (serial), Dr. George Washing-
    ton Carver (doc.), Maryland 1940; Blossoms in the Dust 1941;
    Syncopation, Yankee Doodle Dandy 1942; Flesh and Fantasy,
    Cabin in the Sky 1943.

ROSS, DIANA
    (Singer/Actress)
b. March 26, 1944, Detroit, Mich.
Education: Cass Technical High School (Detroit).
Special Interests: Fashion designing.
Address: 6464 Sunset Blvd., Los Angeles, Calif. 90028.
Honors: SCLS citation; Billboard, Cash Box and Record World
    awards; NAACP Image award 1970; Cue award as entertainer
    of the year 1972; Oscar nomination for best performance by
    an actress in a leading role 1973; Golden gardenia award (New-
    port Jazz Festival) 1974; American Music award 1974; gold
    records.
Career Data: Lead singer with The Supremes, vocal group, 1962-
    69.
Clubs: Sahara (Lake Tahoe); Caesar's Palace (Las Vegas) 1975.
Films: Billie Holiday in Lady Sings the Blues 1972; Mahogany 1975.
Records: On Motown: Baby Love 1964; Where Did Our Love Go?
    1964; My World Is Empty Without You 1966; The Happening

1967; Love Child 1968; Someday We'll Be Together 1969;
Diana Ross and The Supremes Greatest Hits; Anthology Diana
Ross and The Supremes; Last Time I Saw Him; Touch Me in
the Morning; Live at Caesar's Palace; Do You Know Where
You're Going?; Love Hangover; An Evening with....
Television: Bing Crosby (special); Ed Sullivan Show; Bob Hope Show
(special); Diana (special); Tarzan 1968; Like Hep (special)
1969; American Music Awards 1975; Fashion Awards 1975;
co-host, Rock Music Awards 1975; Tonight Show 1975; Dinah!
1975; An Evening with Diana Ross 1977.
Theater: Appearances at Apollo Theatre; Philharmonic Hall (with
Supremes) 1965; Tribute to Duke Ellington at Avery Fisher
Hall 1974; Westchester Premier Theatre 1975; Palais de Congress (Paris) 1976; An Evening with Diana Ross at the Palace
Theatre 1976.

ROSS, TED (Theodore Ross)
(Actor)
b. Ohio.
Honors: Tony award (for The Wiz) best supporting actor in a musi-
cal 1975; Television Critics Circle award (for Minstrel Man)
1977.
Films: The Bingo Long Traveling All-Stars and Motor Kings (debut)
1976.
Memberships: AEA; NAG.
Television: Ed Sullivan Show; An Evening with Ted Ross (Seattle);
Black Journal; Tonight Show 1975, 1976; Dinah! 1975; Mike
Douglas Show 1976; Sirota's Court 1976; Minstrel Man (special)
1977.
Theater: Sam in The Connection (Los Angeles); Weasel in Big Time
Buck White (title role in San Francisco) 1969; Purlie 1970;
Raisin 1973; Cowardly Lion in The Wiz 1975.

ROUNDTREE, RICHARD "Tree"
(Actor)
b. July 9, 1942, New Rochelle, N.Y.
Education: New Rochelle H.S.; Southern Illinois University.
Special Interests: Fashion modeling, football.
Address: Agency for Performing Arts, Sunset Blvd., Los Angeles,
Calif. 90069.
Honors: NAACP Image award.
Career Data: Teaches drama to Black Challengers Boys Club, Los
Angeles.
Films: What Do You Say to a Naked Lady 1970; Shaft 1971; Shaft's
Big Score 1972; Shaft in Africa, Embassy, Charley One-Eye
1973; Earthquake 1974; Man Friday, Diamonds 1975.
Memberships: SAG.
Television: Title role in Shaft (series) 1973-74; Tilmon Tempo
Show; Firehouse 1972; Hollywood Squares 1974; Dean Martin
Comedy Hour (Roasting of Telly Savalas) 1974; Dinah! 1974,
76; Celebrity Tennis 1976; Freedom Is (cartoon) 1976; Mike
Douglas Show 1977.

Theater: Mau Mau Room, Kongi's Harvest (NEC) 1968; Man Better
     Man 1969; The Great White Hope (Philadelphia) 1970; title
     role in Purlie Victorious (tour) 1977; Guys and Dolls (tour)
     1977.

RUSSELL, CHARLIE L.
     (Playwright)
b.   March 10, 1932, Monroe, La.
Education: University of San Francisco B.A. (English) 1959; New
     York University M.S.W. 1966.
Honors: NAACP Image award best screenwriter 1975.
Films: Five on the Black Hand Side 1973.
Television: A Man Is Not Made of Steel (WGBH, Boston); The
     Black Church (ABC); appeared on Like It Is 1973.
Theater: Five on the Black Hand Side 1969; Revival! (co-authored
     with Barbara Ann Teer).

RUSSELL, NIPSEY
     (Comedian)
b.   c.1924, Atlanta, Ga.
Education: University of Cincinnati B.A. 1946.
Special Interests: Dancing, poetry, rhymes.
Address: c/o Joseph Rapp, 1650 Broadway, New York, N.Y. 10019
     and 353 West 57 Street, New York, N.Y. 10019.
Career Data: Toured with Billy Eckstine.
Clubs: Carousel (L.I.); Elegante (Brooklyn); Paradise Island Hotel
     (Nassau, Bahamas); Palmer House (Chicago); Hilton Plaza
     (Miami Beach); Basin Street East; Eden Roc (Miami Beach);
     Casino (Toronto); Copacabana; The Baby Grand; Tamiment;
     Small's Paradise; Playboy Hotel Club (N.J.); Blue Angel 1962;
     Desert Inn (Las Vegas) 1975; Frontier Hotel (Las Vegas) 1975;
     Buddy's Place 1975; Sands (Las Vegas) 1975; Stevensville
     Country Club 1976.
Films: Rock and Roll Revue 1955; Rhythm and Blues Revue 1959.
Television: Arthur Godfrey Show; Jack Paar Show; Ed Sullivan Show;
     Tonight Show; I've Got a Secret; The Show Goes On 1949;
     Showtime at the Apollo 1954; Missing Links 1964; Car 54 Where
     Are You (series), 1961-63; co-host of Night Life (series with
     Les Crane); NBC Follies of 1965; Comedyworld; Strollin-
     Twenties (special) 1966; Colgate Comedy Hour (special) 1967;
     Barefoot in the Park (series) 1970; Masquerade Party 1974;
     Match Game 1974; Dean Martin Comedy Hour (Roastings of
     Lucille Ball, Bob Hope, Telly Savalas, Joe Garagiola, Jackie
     Gleason, Dennis Weaver, Sammy Davis Jr., Muhammad Ali)
     1974-76; Password 1975; $25,000 Pyramid 1975; Merv Griffin
     Show 1975, 1976; Blankety Blanks 1975; Dinah! 1975; Rhyme
     and Reason 1975; Celebrity Bowling 1975; Sammy and Company
     1976; Black Journal 1976; Donny and Marie 1976; Celebrity
     Revue 1976.
Theater: Little Joe in Cabin in the Sky (stock); appeared at Apollo
     Theatre 1950, 1951; Tambourines to Glory (O.B.) 1963;

appeared at Carnegie Hall; Nanuet Theatre-Go-Round 1975;
Colonial Music Fair (Latham, N.Y.) 1975.

ST. JACQUES, RAYMOND (James Arthur Johnson)
    (Actor)
b. 1930, Hartford, Conn.
Education: Hillhouse H.S. (New Haven); Yale University; Herbert
    Berghof Studio; Actors Studio.
Address: c/o William Morris Agency, 151 El Camino Drive,
    Beverly Hills, Calif. 90212.
Honors: Oscar Nominee for best performance in a supporting role
    (The Comedians) 1967.
Career Data: Founded St. Jacques Enterprises; teacher/director
    at American Shakespeare Festival, Stratford, Conn.
Films: Black Like Me (debut) 1964; The Pawnbroker, Mister
    Moses 1965; Mr. Buddwing 1966; The Comedians 1967; If He
    Hollers, Let Him Go, Uptight, Madigan, The Green Berets,
    Betrayal 1968; Change of Mind 1969; Cotton Comes to Harlem
    1970; Come Back Charleston Blue, Cool Breeze, The Final
    Comedown 1972; produced, directed and acted as Blueboy Har-
    ris in Book of Numbers 1973, Lost in the Stars 1974; Baron
    Wolfgang Von Tripps 1976.
Memberships: AEA; AFTRA; SAG.
Television: Dan August; Slattery's Hurricane 1965; Rawhide (series);
    Wackiest Ship in the Army 1966; I Spy 1966; Daniel Boone
    1966; The Girl from U.N.C.L.E. 1966; Tarzan 1967; Invaders
    1968; Name of the Game 1968; The Monk 1969; Police Story
    1974, 1975; Search for the Gods 1975; Bicentennial Minutes
    1975; McCloud 1975; The Rookies 1975; Police Woman 1976;
    The Greatest Story Never Told (Bicentennial Special) 1976;
    Roots 1977.
Theater: High Name Today (O.B. debut); Seventh Heaven; Romeo
    and Juliet (American Shakespeare Festival) 1959; Henry V.
    (New York Shakespeare Festival) 1960; The Cool World 1960;
    The Blacks (O.B.) 1961; Night Life 1962; Johnny Midnight
    (tour) 1976; Othello (Los Angeles) 1976.

ST. JOHN, CHRISTOPHER
    (Producer/Director/Actor)
Education: University of Bridgeport (Conn.); Actors Studio.
Address: Lew Sherrell Agency, 7060 Hollywood Blvd., Los Angeles,
    Calif. 90028.
Career Data: Former member, Yale Repertory Co.; founder, The
    Troupe Theatre.
Films: Acted in For Love of Ivy 1968; Shaft 1971; directed, pro-
    duced, wrote and acted in Top of the Heap 1972.
Memberships: SAG.
Television: That's My Mama 1975.
Theater: Directed Antigone (O.B.); directed Tennis Anyone? (O.B.)
    1968; directed End of a Summer's Drought (O.B.); acted in No
    Place to Be Somebody 1969.

SAMPSON, EDGAR (Melvin)
    (Musician/Composer)
b. August 31, 1907, New York, N.Y.
d. January 16, 1973, Englewood, N.J.
Education: Schillinger School of Music.
Special Interests: Arranging, piano, violin, saxophone (alto and
    tenor).
Career Data: Played with bands of Duke Ellington 1927, Charlie
    Johnson 1928-30, Fletcher Henderson 1931-33, Chick Webb
    1933-37, Benny Goodman and his own band 1949-51.
Clubs: Savoy Ballroom; Club 845 (Bronx).
Memberships: American Guild of Authors & Composers; ASCAP
    1940.
Musical Compositions: Stompin' at the Savoy; Blue Lou; If Dreams
    Come True; Don't Be That Way; Lullaby in Rhythm; I'm Not
    Complaining; Blue Minor; Serenade to Sleeping Beauty.

SANCHEZ, SONIA
    (Playwright)
b. September 9, 1934, Birmingham, Ala.
Honors: P.E.N. grant.
Theater: Wrote Dirty Hearts; The Bronx Is Next (one act) 1968;
    Sister Son/Ji (one act) 1969; Malcolm/Man Don't Live Here
    No Mo 1972; Un Huh, But How Do It Free Us 1973.

SANDERS, PHAROAH (Farrell Sanders)
    (Jazz Musician)
b. 1940.
Special Interests: Tenor saxophone.
Clubs: Top of the Gate; Village Vanguard 1975; The East (Brooklyn)
    1976.
Records: On Impulse: Karma; Jewels of Thought; Thembi; Summum,
    Bukmun, Umyun (Deaf, Dumb and Blind); Best; Black Unity;
    Elevation; Live at the East; Love in Us All; Tauhid; Village
    of the Pharoahs; Wisdom Through Music; Izipho Zam (Strata-
    East); Pharoah Sanders (ESP Disk).
Theater: Appeared at Carnegie Hall 1975.

SANDS, DIANA (Patricia)
    (Actress)
b. August 22, 1934, New York, N.Y.
d. September 21, 1973, New York, N.Y.
Education: H.S. of Performing Arts 1952; studied acting with Lloyd
    Richards and at Herbert Berghof Studio; studied dance with
    Louis Johnson and at International Dance Studio.
Special Interests: Dancing, singing, pantomime, poetry writing.
Honors: Off Broadway Magazine (Obie) award (for The Egg and I)
    1958; Outer Circle Critics award (for Raisin in the Sun) 1959;
    International Artist award (for film version of Raisin in the
    Sun) 1961; Theatre World award (for Tiger, Tiger, Burning
    Bright 1962-63.

Films: Caribbean Gold (debut) 1952; Four Boys and a Gun 1957;
    A Raisin in the Sun 1961; An Affair of the Skin 1963; Ensign
    Pulver 1964; The Landlord 1970; Doctors' Wives 1971; title
    role in Georgia Georgia 1972; Willie Dynamite, Honeybaby
    Honeybaby 1974.
Memberships: AEA; SAG.
Television: Bracken's World; Look Up and Live; Salute to Ameri-
    can Theatre 1960; Who Do You Kill? (East Side/West Side)
    1963; The Mice (The Outer Limits) 1964; The Nurses 1964;
    Beyond the Blues (Stage 2) 1964; Doctors/Nurses 1964; Dr.
    Kildare 1966; I Spy 1966; The Fugitive 1967; Julia 1970, 71;
    Medical Center 1971.
Theater: An Evening with Will Shakespeare (O.B.) 1953; The
    World of Sholom Aleichem (O.B.) 1953; Major Barbara (O.B.)
    1954; Pantomime Art Theatre Repertory Group 1955; The
    Man with the Golden Arm (O.B.) 1956; A Land Beyond the
    River (O.B.) 1957; The Egg and I (O.B.) 1958; Beneatha
    Younger in A Raisin in the Sun 1959; Another Evening with
    Harry Stoones (O.B.) 1961; Black Monday (O.B.) 1962; Brecht
    on Brecht (O.B.) 1962; Tiger, Tiger Burning Bright 1962;
    The Living Premise 1963; Blues for Mr. Charlie 1964; The
    Owl and the Pussycat 1964; Cleopatra in Caesar and Cleopatra
    (Atlanta) 1967; We Bombed in New Haven (pre-Bway) 1968;
    Cassandra in Tiger at the Gates (LCR) 1968; title role in St.
    Joan (LCR) 1968; Cleopatra in Antony and Cleopatra 1968;
    Phaedra.

SANFORD, ISABELL (Christine Virginia)
    (Actress)
Address: M.E.W. Company; 151 N. San Vicente, Beverly Hills,
    Calif.
Honors: NAACP Image award comedy actress (The Jeffersons)
    1976.
Career Data: Worked with American Negro Theatre.
Films: Guess Who's Coming to Dinner? 1967; The Young Runaways
    1968; The Comic 1969; Pendulum 1970; Hickey and Boggs,
    The New Centurions, Soul Soldier, Stand Up and Be Counted,
    Lady Sings the Blues 1972.
Memberships: SAG.
Television: Aunt Jenny in Bewitched (series); Mod Squad; Bill
    Cosby Show; Carol Burnett Show; Love, American Style 1971;
    The Great Man's Whiskers 1971; Louise Jefferson in All in
    the Family (series) 1972-75; Louise Jefferson in The Jeffer-
    sons (series) 1975-; Dean's [Martin] Place 1975; Tony Orlando
    and Dawn 1975; Kojak 1975; Dean Martin (Roasting of Evil
    Knievel) 1975; Thanksgiving Day Parade 1975; Match Game
    1976; Dean Martin (Roasting of Muhammad Ali) 1976; Holly-
    wood Squares 1976; Dinah 1977.
Theater: On Strivers Row (ANT) 1946; Purlie Victorious 1959;
    Dark of the Moon (ELT) 1960; The Blacks (O.B.) 1961; No-
    body Loves an Albatross 1963; The Amen Corner 1965; Funny
    Girl (tour) 1966.

SATCHMO see ARMSTRONG, LOUIS

SATTIN, LONNIE (Alonzo Louis Lee Staton)
        (Actor/Singer)
b. Jacksonville, Fla.
Education: Temple University 1949; Temple University Law School
        1949-50; Neighborhood Playhouse School of Theatre 1959;
        studied voice with Marian Brown and Edward Boatner; studied
        acting with Lloyd Richards.
Address: 200 Millington Street, Mt. Vernon, N.Y. 10553.
Career Data: Toured with Cab Calloway and George Kirby in The
        Cotton Club Revue.
Clubs: Jim Dolan's Cafe Gala (Hollywood) 1952; Oasis (Hollywood);
        Club De Lisa 1952-54; Jimmy Kelly's Dimension X Club 1954-
        56.
Films: For Love of Ivy 1968; Hello-Goodbye, The Invincible Six
        1970; Live and Let Die 1973.
Memberships: AEA; AFTRA; AGVA; Friars.
Television: Dave Garroway Show; Patti Page Show; Art Linkletter's
        House Party 1952; Ed Sullivan Show 1957; Jack Paar Show
        1958; hosted Schaefer Circle (musical series) 1960-61; Il Sig-
        nore Ventiuno (Ital.) 1962; Space 1999 1975.
Theater: The Body Beautiful (debut) 1958; The Ballad of Jazz Street
        (O.B.) 1959; Kicks and Company 1961; Explosion of the Beat
        (Town Hall) 1961; Kismet (E.L.T. production (O.B.) 1963;
        Golden Boy (tour) 1968; Bubbling Brown Sugar (London) 1977.
Relationships: Former husband of Tina Sattin, actress/singer.

SATTIN, TINA
        (Actress/Singer)
b. Philadelphia, Pa.
Education: Howard University.
Special Interests: Teaching (acting).
Address: 20 Millington Rd., Mount Vernon, N.Y. 10553.
Career Data: Tyrone Guthrie Theatre Repertory Co., Minneapolis.
Television: Just an Old Sweet Song (General Electric Theater) 1976;
        Kojak 1977.
Theater: Ballad of Jazz Street (O.B.) 1959; The Blacks (O.B.)
        1961; Tambourines to Glory (O.B.) 1963; The Sign in Sidney
        Brustein's Window 1964; The Amen Corner (European tour)
        1966; To Be Young, Gifted and Black (O.B.) 1969.
Relationships: Former wife of Lonnie Sattin, singer/actor.

SAVAGE, ARCHIE
        (Dancer/Choreographer)
Special Interests: Acting.
Career Data: Toured with his own group (appearing in Los Angeles
        for Dance Alliance Inc.) 1957.
Films: Carnival in Rhythm (Warner Bros. short) 1941; choreogra-
        phy for His Majesty O'Keefe 1954.
Memberships: AEA.

Theater: Macbeth 1935; Haiti 1938; Bal Negre 1946; Lysistrata 1946;
    Beggars Holiday 1946-47; South Pacific 1949; Kiss Me Kate
    (London) 1951; danced at Folk Studio (Rome) 1965.

SCHULTZ, MICHAEL A.
    (Director)
b. Milwaukee, Wisc.
Honors: Obie (for Song of the Lusitanian Bogey) 1968.
Films: Together for Days 1973; Cooley High 1975; Car Wash,
    Greased Lightning 1976.
Memberships: DGA; NEC; 1967-68.
Television: To Be Young, Gifted, and Black (PBS).
Theater: Waiting for Godot (Repertory) 1967; Song of the Lusitanian
    Bogey (NEC) 1968; Kongi's Harvest (NEC) 1968; Does a Tiger
    Wear a Necktie? 1969.
Relationships: Husband of Lauren Jones, actress.

SCHUYLER, PHILIPPA (Duke)
    (Pianist/Composer)
b. August 1931, New York, N.Y.
d. May 9, 1967, Danang, South Vietnam.
Education: Manhattanville College of The Sacred Heart.
Honors: Wayne University award; 1st Prize Detroit Symphony award;
    National Guild of Piano Teachers gold star (won 8 times);
    League of Nations Plaque; Decoration of Honor and Merit from
    Haiti 1950; command performances for Emperor Haile Selassie
    of Ethiopia, Queen Elizabeth of Belgium, King and Queen of
    Malaya.
Career Data: Soloist with major symphony orchestras including
    Detroit Symphony, N.Y. Philharmonic 1946, Boston Symphony
    1946 and New Haven Symphony 1948; concert tours of more
    than 50 countries including Viet Nam.
Memberships: ASCAP; National Assn. of Composers and Conductors.
Musical Compositions: Manhattan Nocturne; White Nile Suite; Rum-
    pelstiltskin; Sleepy Hollow Sketches; Six Little Pieces; Sanga;
    Chisamharu the Nogomo; Eight Little Pieces.
Publications: Adventures in Black and White (autobiography), R.
    Speller, 1960.
Theater: Performed at World's Fair 1940; Lewisohn Stadium 1946;
    Town Hall (debut) 1953.

SCOTT, HAROLD (Harold Russell Scott Jr.)
    (Actor)
b. September 6, 1935, Morristown, N.J.
Education: Phillips Exeter Academy (New Hampshire) 1953; Har-
    vard University B.A. 1957; studied dance with Anna Sokolow,
    voice with Kristin Linklater, acting with Paul Mann.
Special Interests: Directing, writing (plays and poetry).
Address: 466 Grand Street, New York, N.Y. 10002.

Honors: Obie (for Deathwatch) 1959; Variety Drama Critics Poll as
   most promising actor (for The Cool World) 1960.
Career Data: Lincoln Center Repertory Theatre Training Co. 1963-
   65; Pittsburgh Playhouse 1967-68; artistic dir., Cincinnati
   Playhouse in the Park; theater consultant, N.Y. State Dept.
   of Education; performed in stock and in university theaters
   throughout the U.S.
Memberships: AEA; AFTRA.
Television: Reading of God's Trombones on Lamp Unto My Feet
   1959; Open End 1961: Smash-Up (Armstrong Circle Theatre)
   1962; At Random 1963; Soul.
Theater: A Land Beyond the River (O.B.) 1957; I, Too, Have
   Lived in Arcadia (O.B.) 1957; The Egg and I (O.B.) 1958;
   Maurice in Deathwatch 1958; adapted and read God's Trom-
   bones at Town Hall 1959; Chester in The Cool World 1960;
   The Jackass (O.B.) 1960; The Witch Boy in Dark of the
   Moon (ELT) 1960; Program One (triple included Escurial,
   Calvary and Santa Claus) (O.B.) 1960; To Follow the Phoenix
   (Chicago) 1960; orderly in The Death of Bessie Smith (O.B.)
   1961; The Blacks (O.B.) 1961; After the Fall (LRC) 1964;
   Marco Millions (LRC) 1964; Incident at Vichy (LRC); Change-
   ling (LRC) 1964; But for Whom Charlie (LRC); The Cuban
   Thing; The Trials of Brother Jero (O.B.) 1968; The Strong
   Breed (O.B.) 1968; The Boys in the Band (O.B.) 1968; Eric
   in Les Blancs 1970; directed The Past Is the Past and Break-
   out for The Manhattan Theater Club 1975; wrote A Dream
   Deferred.

SCOTT, HAZEL (Dorothy)
   (Pianist/Singer)
b. June 11, 1920, Port of Spain, Trinidad.
Education: Juilliard School of Music.
Honors: Page One Award, Newspaper Guild of New York 1943.
Career Data: Made debut with American Creolians (her mother's
   all-girl band); saxophonist with Louise Armstrong's all-girl
   band; performed with N.Y. Philharmonic, Los Angeles Phil-
   harmonic and Philadelphia orchestra.
Clubs: Café-Society Downtown 1939; Café-Society Uptown; Roseland;
   Ritz Carlton Hotel Roof (Boston); Jimmy Weston's 1975; Down-
   beat 1975; Seafood Playhouse 1975; XII Birches (Jericho, L.I.)
   1975; The Cattleman 1976; Cleo's 1976; Ali Baba 1977; Hotel
   Carlyle 1977.
Films: Something to Shout About, I Dood It, The Heat's On 1943;
   Broadway Rhythm 1944; Rhapsody in Blue 1945; The Night
   Affair 1961.
Memberships: ASCAP 1952.
Musical Compositions: Love Comes Softly; Nightmare Blues.
Radio: Her own series 1936.
Records: Swinging the Classics; Mighty Like the Blues; Calling
   All Bars; Boogie Woogie.
Television: The Bold Ones; One Life to Live (series); Positively
   Black; The Hazel Scott Show 1950; Not for Women Only 1974;

Sunday 1974; Pat Collins Show 1974; Like It Is 1974; Right
Now 1974; Black Pride 1975; Midday Live 1975; Straight Talk
1975.
Theater: Debut at Town Hall 1925; Sing Out the News 1938; ap-
     pearances at Carnegie Hall; Paramount Theatre; San Francisco
     Opera House 1947; Brooklyn Academy of Music 1974.
Relationships: Former wife of Adam Clayton Powell, U.S. Congress-
     man (deceased).

SCOTT, LESLIE (Zakariya Abullah)
     (Actor/Singer)
b. January 26, 1921, New York, N.Y.
d. August 20, 1969, New York, N.Y.
Education: Harnett School of Music.
Special Interests: Guitar.
Career Data: Soloist, Sheloh Khall Electric Choir (Boston); vocal-
     ist, Louis Armstrong orchestra; toured Canada with Xavier
     Cugat band.
Films: The Spanish Gardener 1957; Island Women 1958; Porgy and
     Bess 1959.
Records: On RCA: Stars Fell on Alabama/Baby Get Lost 1947;
     Blue and Sentimental/So Long; You Go to My Head/Gaslight.
Television: Eddie Cantor Show.
Theater: Jazz Train 1950; appeared at Roxy Theatre 1951; Apollo
     Theatre 1951; Shuffle Along 1952; Porgy and Bess (Bway and
     tours) 1953; 1958-62; Cotton Club Revue 1959.

SCOTT-HERON, GIL
     (Musician)
b. 1949.
Education: Lincoln University 1967; Johns Hopkins University M.A.
Special Interests: Composing, creative writing, poetry, singing.
Career Data: Teaches creative writing at Federal City College,
     Washington, D.C.; formed his own musical group, Midnight
     Band.
Clubs: Village Gate 1976.
Films: Baron Wolfgang Von Tripps (score) 1976.
Records: From South Africa to South Carolina (Arista); Johannes-
     burg, The Revolution Will Not Be Televised (recorded by
     Labelle); The First Minute of a New Day (Arista); Winter in
     America (Strata-East).
Television: Saturday Night 1975; At the Top 1976.

SEBREE, CHARLES
     (Playwright/Designer)
b. August 1914, Madisonville, Ky.
Education: Art Institute of Chicago.
Special Interests: Art, painting.
Honors: Rosenwald fellowship 1944.
Career Data: Member, Katherine Dunham Dance Company; designed
     sets for the American Negro Theatre.

Theater: Costume and set designer for Garden of Time 1945;
    Henri Christophe 1945; Our Lan' 1947. Wrote My Mother
    Came Crying Most Pitifully; A Talent for Crumbs (one
    act); Mrs. Patterson (a.k.a. The Dry August) 1954;
    Fisher Boy.

SEJOUR, VICTOR (Juan Victor Sejour Marcon-Ferrand)
    (Playwright)
b. 1817, New Orleans, La.
d. September 21, 1874, Paris, France.
Education: Saint Barbe Academy (New Orleans).
Honors: Chevalier, Legion d' Honneur 1860.
Theater: Le Vampire; Diégarias 1844; La Chute de Séjan (The Fall
    of Sejanus) 1849; Richard III 1852; Les Noces Venitiennes
    (The Venetian Wedding) 1855; Le Marquis Caporal (The Cor-
    poral Is a Marquis) 1856; Les Fils de la Nuit (Sons of the
    Night) 1856; Les Enfants de La Louvre (The Kids of the
    Louvre) 1856; Les Massacres de La Syrie (Syrian Massacre)
    1856; André Gerard 1857; L'Argent du Diable (The Devil's
    Coin) 1857; Le Martyr du Coeur 1858; Les Grands Vassaux
    1859; Les Aventuriers (The Adventurers) 1860; Compère Guil-
    lery (Friend Guillery) 1860; Le Paletot Brun (the Brown Over-
    coat) 1860; La Tireuse de Cartes (The Fortune Teller) 1860;
    Les Mystères du Temple 1862; Les Volontaires de 1814 (The
    1814 Volunteers) 1862; Les Fils de Charles-Quint (The Sons
    of Charles the Fifth) 1864; La Madon des Roses (Our Lady of
    the Roses) 1869.

SEKKA, JOHNNY
    (Actor)
b. 1939, Dakar, Senegal.
Education: Royal Academy of Dramatic Art (London).
Films: Flame in the Streets 1962; East of Sudan, Young and Willing,
    Woman of Straw 1964; Khartoum 1966; The Last Safari 1967;
    The Southern Star 1969; Bullfrog in the Sun 1971; A Warm
    December, Charley One Eye 1973; A Visit to a Chief's Son,
    Uptown Saturday Night 1974; Mohammad Messenger of God
    1976.
Memberships: BAEA.
Television: Avengers, Rivals of Sherlock Holmes 1975; Black News
    1977; Good Times 1977; The African Queen (pilot) 1977.
Theater: Look Back in Anger (London); Flesh Is a Tiger (London);
    Moon on a Rainbow Shawl (London) 1958; Mr. Johnson (London)
    1960.

SELLERS, BROTHER JOHN (John B. Sellers)
    (Singer/Actor)
b. May 27, 1924, Clarksdale, Miss.

Special Interests: Composing, dancing.
Address: 236 West 64 Street, New York, N. Y. 10023.
Career Data: Toured with Mahalia Jackson; toured with U.S.
        Government Cultural Exchange Program 1962.
Musical Compositions: Lucy Mae Blues; Love Is a Story; You've
        Been Gone Too Long.
Theater: Danced in Ailey's Blues Suite, Tambourines to Glory
        (O.B.) 1963.

SEMBENE, OUSMANE "Father of African Cinema"
        (Producer/Director)
b.   January 8, 1923, Ziguinchor, Casamance, Senegal.
Education: Moscow Film School, U.S.S.R. , Gorki Film Studios
        (Moscow).
Special Interests: Writing.
Honors: Cannes Film Festival award 1967; Venice Film Festi-
        val award 1969; Atlanta (Georgia) Film Festival award
        1970.
Career Data: Films shown at World Festival of Negro Arts, Dakar
        1966; Venice Film Festival 1968; New York Film Festival
        1969.
Films: Barom-Saret (a.k.a. Borom Sarrett) 1963; Le Noire
        (a.k.a. Black Girl) 1967; Mandabi (a.k.a. The Money Order,
        Le Mandat); Vehi Ciosane 1968; Emitai (a.k.a. God of Thunder
        1973; Xala 1975.

SHANGE, NTOZAKE (Paulette Williams)
        (Playwright)
b.   October 18, 1948, Trenton, N.J.
Education: Barnard College B.A.; University of Southern California
        M.A.
Special Interests: Acting, poetry writing, teaching.
Honors: Obie award 1977.
Memberships: AEA.
Radio: Celebrity Hour (WRVR) 1976.
Television: Straight Talk 1976; Sunday 1976; Black Journal 1977;
        An Evening with Diana Ross 1977.
Theater: Wrote and acted in For Colored Girls Who Have Consid-
        ered Suicide/When the Rainbow Is Enuf (O.B.) 1976; writing
        A Photograph: A Still Life with Shadows/A Photograph: A
        Study of Cruelty.

SHARP, SAUNDRA
        (Actress)
b.   c.1943, Cleveland, Ohio.
Education: Bowling Green State University (Ohio).
Special Interests: Singing, writing.
Address: 884 West End Avenue, New York, N. Y. 10025 and

Victoria Lucas Associates, 1414 Avenue of the Americas,
New York, N.Y. 10019.
Career Data: Poetry reading tours of colleges throughout U.S.
   1974; worked with Theatre for the Forgotten (presentations in
   prisons).
Clubs: Playboy Club (Baltimore); Le Royalty Llave (Puebla, Mexi-
   co); Holiday Inn (Antigua); Holiday Inn (Paramus, N.J.); The
   East; The Grand Finale 1974.
Films: Prissy in The Learning Tree 1969.
Memberships: AEA; AFTRA; SAG.
Radio: Norma on Sounds of the City (WWRL series) 1974; The
   Story Hour (with Ossie Davis and Ruby Dee); Guest moderator,
   Black Dialog (WWRL).
Television: As the World Turns (series); Guiding Light (series);
   Soul; acted role of Kathy and wrote script The Way It's
   Done for Our Street (series); Black News; Like It Is; Posi-
   tively Black 1974; commercials: Campbells soup, Avon cos-
   metics, Quaker Oats, Pampers diapers; The Minstrel Man
   (special) 1977; The Jeffersons 1977.
Theater: Appeared at Town Hall; wrote The Sistuhs (two-act play
   with music); To Be Young, Gifted and Black (O.B.) 1969;
   Hello, Dolly! 1969; Five on the Black Hand Side (NEC) 1970;
   Netta in Black Girl (O.B.) 1971; The Great MacDaddy (NEC)
   1974.

SHAW, MARLENA
   (Singer)
b.   New Rochelle.
Special Interests: Piano.
Career Data: Vocalist with Count Basie band 1968-71.
Clubs: Playboy (Chicago) 1966.
Records: Wade in the Water (Cadet); Mercy, Mercy, Marlena
   (Blue Note); From the Depths of My Soul (Blue Note); Who Is
   This Bitch Anyway? (Blue Note); Just a Matter (Blue Note);
   Out of Different Bags (Cadet); Spice of Life (Cadet); Sweet
   Beginning (Columbia) 1977.
Television: Positively Black 1975; Sammy and Company 1975; Mike
   Douglas Show 1975.
Theater: Appeared at Apollo Theatre; Westbury Music Fair (with
   Sammy Davis Jr.) 1975; Mill Run Theatre (Chicago); Avery
   Fisher Hall 1977.

SHEPP, ARCHIE (Vernon)
   (Musician)
b.   May 24, 1937, Fort Lauderdale, Fla.
Education: Goddard College (Plainfield, Vermont) B.A. 1959.
Special Interests: Tenor saxophonist, jazz, teaching, composing.
Address: 27 Cooper Square, New York, N.Y. 10003.
Honors: Down Beat Magazine new star award 1965.
Career Data: European tour 1962; Scandinavian tour 1963; artist-in-
   residence, Mobilization for Youth Musical 1963; Newport Jazz

Festival and Chicago Jazz Festival 1965.
Clubs: Five Spot Cafe 1961; Village Gate 1965; St. James Infirmary
1975; Village Vanguard 1975.
Memberships: Jazz Composers Guild.
Records: Attica Blues (Impulse); Black Gypsy (Prestige); Coral
Rock (Prestige); Cry of the People (Impulse); Donaulschingen
Festival (BASF); Fire Music (Impulse); Four for Trane
(Impulse); In Europe (Delmark); In San Francisco (Impulse);
Kwanza (Impulse); Magic of Ju-Ju (Impulse); Mama Too Tight
(Impulse); Montreux (Arista/Freedom); On This Night (Impulse);
There's a Trumpet in My Soul (Arista/Freedom); 3 for a
Quarter (Impulse); Way Ahead (Impulse); Mariamar (Horo);
A Sea of Faces (Black Saint).
Theater: Appeared in concert at Goddard College 1960; played in
The Connection at Living Theatre 1960; Judson Hall Concert
1965; wrote music for Junebug Graduates Tonight 1967;
Revolution 1968; Slave Ship 1969.

SHERRIL, JOYA
(Actress/Singer)
Career Data: Vocalist with Duke Ellington orchestra.
Clubs: Le Reuben Bleu.
Memberships: AEA; NAG.
Television: Time for Joya (series) WPIX 1971.
Theater: The Cool World 1960.

SHINE, TED
(Playwright)
b.   April 26, 1936, Baton Rouge, La.
Education: Howard University B.A. 1953; State University of Iowa
M.A. 1958; University of California, Santa Barbara Ph.D.
1973.
Address: Prairie View A&M College, Prairie View, Texas 77445.
Theater: Herbert III; Cold Day in August (one act) 1950; Sho' Is
Hot in the Cotton Patch (one act) 1951; Dry August 1952; Bats
Out of Hell 1955; Epitaph for a Bluebird 1958; Entourage
Royale (musical) 1958; A Rat's Revolt 1959; Morning Noon
and Night 1964; Miss Victoria (one act) 1965; Pontiac (one
act) 1967; Flora's Kisses (one act) 1968; Revolution 1968;
Jeanne West (musical) 1968; The Coca-Cola Boys (one act)
1969; Hamburgers at Hamburger Heaven Are Impersonal (one
act) 1969; Idabel's Fortune (one act) 1969; Shoes (one act)
1969; Waiting Room (one act) 1969; Come Back after the Fire
1969; Contribution (one act) 1969; Plantation (one act) 1970.

SHIPP, JESSE A.
(Playwright/Actor)
b.   c.1859.
d.   May 1, 1934, Richmond Hill, Long Island.
Career Data: Toured with Sam P. Jacks Revue 1879-1881; with

Primrose and West Minstrel circuit 1885-89; The Porto Rican
Girls; The Tennessee Ten (vaudeville acts) 1911-1917.
Memberships: The Frogs (a theatrical association).
Theater: Co-wrote musicals including: Senegambian Carnival 1898;
The Policy Players 1900; In Dahomey 1902; Abyssinia 1906;
Bandanna Land 1908; Mr. Lode of Koal 1909. Performed in:
Simon the Cyrenian 1917; Abraham in The Green Pastures
1930.

SHIRLEY, DON (Donald Walbridge)
(Pianist)
b. January 29, 1926, Kingston, Jamaica.
Education: Harvard University M. A. (psychology) 1948, Ph. D.
1952; Oberlin College; Leningrad Conservatory; Catholic Uni-
versity.
Special Interests: Composing, jazz arranging.
Address: c/o Torrence-Perrotta Management, 1860 Broadway,
New York, N. Y. 10023.
Career Data: Faculty, New York University; founder, Free
Southern Theatre; toured in Europe; made debut with Boston
Pops; performed with La Scala Symphony, Cleveland Orches-
tra, Miami Philharmonic, St. Louis Symphony, Detroit Sym-
phony, Minneapolis Symphony and Cincinnati Symphony.
Clubs: Embers; The Bottom Line 1976.
Musical Compositions: Finegan's Wake; Legacy; Duke Ellington
Suite.
Records: Piano (Audio Fidelity); Don Shirley Point of View (At-
lantic); Gospel According ... (Columbia); In Concert (Colum-
bia).
Television: Like It Is 1976.
Theater: Town Hall (5:45 Interlude Series) 1976; Carnegie Hall
1977.

SHIRLEY, GEORGE (Irving)
(Opera Singer)
b. April 18, 1934, Indianapolis, Ind.
Education: Wayne State University B. S. 1955.
Address: c/o Show Concerts Inc., 233 East 49th Street, New
York, N. Y. 10019.
Honors: National Arts Club award 1960; winner, Il Concorso di
Musica e Danza, Italy 1960; American Opera Audition 1960;
Metropolitan Opera Audition 1961.
Career Data: Member, Turnau Opera Players, Woodstock, N. Y.
1959; participated in Festival of Two Worlds, Spoleto, Italy
1961 and Glyndebourne Festival, Sussex, England 1966.
Memberships: AGMA.
Radio: WQXR (series) 1974.
Theater: Performances include Teatro Nuovo, Milan and Teatro
Della Pergola, Florence 1960; New England Opera Theatre,
Soring Opera San Francisco, N. Y. C. Opera, Metropolitan
Opera Co., Santa Fe Opera 1961; Opera Society Washington

1962; Teatro Colon, Buenos Aires, Argentina 1964; La Scala, Milan 1965; Scottish Opera, Royal Opera, Covent Garden 1967; An Evening of Negro Spirituals, Alice Tully Hall 1975.

SHORT, BOBBY (Robert Waltrip Short)
        (Singer/Pianist)
b. September 15, 1924, Danville, Ill.
Address: 154 West 57 Street, New York, N.Y. 10019
Honors: Harold Jackman Memorial award 1977.
Clubs: The Beverly Club; The Red Carpet; Le Cupidon; The Arpeg-
        gio; The Haig (L.A.); Spivy's (Paris); Embassy (London);
        The Living Room; L'Intrigue; Frolics Café 1937; La Grande
        Pomme 1937; Capitol Lounge (Chicago) 1942; Radio Room
        (L.A.) 1943; Chase Hotel (St. Louis) 1944; Blue Angel 1944;
        Café-Gala (L.A.) 1948-51; Le Caprice 1964; Café Carlyle
        (Hotel Carlyle) 1968-date; The Bottom Line 1976; Venetian
        Room-Fairmont Hotel (San Francisco).
Films: Call Me Mister 1951.
Publications: Black and White Baby, Dodd Mead, 1971.
Records: For Atlantic: Bobby Short Is K-RA-ZY for Gershwin;
        Live at the Café Carlyle; The Very Best of Bobby Short;
        The Mad Twenties; Bobby Short Loves Cole Porter; My Per-
        sonal Property; Rodgers & Hart (Atlantic); Mad About Noel
        Coward (Atlantic).
Television: O.T.B. commercial; Evening at Pops (Cole Porter
        Show) 1973; Mabel Mercer, Bobby Short and Friends 1974;
        Sunday 1975; Dinah! 1975; Black Conversations 1976.
Theater: Alice Tully Hall; Apollo; Night Life 1962; The New Cole
        Porter Revue (O.B.) 1965; Town Hall (with Mabel Mercer)
        1968; Avery Fisher Hall 1975.

SHORTE, DINO
        (Actor)
b. March 28, 1947, Tifton, Ga.
Education: Studied with Sanford Meisner at Neighborhood Playhouse
        1971.
Address: P.O. Box 1322, FDR Station, New York, N.Y. 10022.
Films: The Hospital, Such Good Friends 1971; The Hot Rock 1972;
        Ganja and Hess (a.k.a. Blood Couple); Badge 373, Shamus,
        Gordon's War, Serpico 1973; Death Wish, Noa Noa, Crazy
        Joe, Super Cops 1974.
Memberships: AEA; AFTRA; SAG.
Radio: Joey Adams Show 1974.
Television: All My Children; Search for Tomorrow; Love Is a
        Many Splendored Thing; Guiding Light (series) 1973-75; Love
        of Life (series) 1973-75; Joe Franklin Show 1974; McCloud
        1974; Monkey Monkey 1974.
Theater: Member of the Wedding (O.B.) 1959-60; Shoes (O.B.);
        The Mummer's Play (O.B.); In White America (O.B.); Cream
        of the Crop (O.B.) 1973; Who's Who in Hell 1974; We Inter-
        rupt This Program... 1975.

SIDNEY, P. J. (Jay)
    (Actor)
b. Virginia.
Education: City College of New York.
Special Interests: Civil rights, announcing.
Address: 19 Maple Street, Brooklyn, N.Y. 11225.
Career Data: Appeared in Federal Theatre productions in 1930s;
    campaigned for congressional hearings which altered image
    of blacks in advertising and television 1963-63; picketed Batten
    Barton Durstine and Osborn and Lever Brothers in protest
    of depiction of blacks in commercials 1967.
Films: The Joe Louis Story 1953; A Face in the Crowd 1957; Black
    Like Me 1964; Brother John 1971.
Memberships: AEA; AFTRA; SAG.
Television: The Doctors and The Nurses; Camera Three; Philco
    Playhouse; Hallmark Hall of Fame; East Side West Side;
    Kraft Theatre 1955; Ed Sullivan Show 1955; Sgt. Bilko Show
    1955; Brenner 1959; Look Up and Live 1960.
Theater: Dance with Your Gods (debut) 1934; The Green Pastures
    1935; The Conjur Man; The Last Mile; Black Panther; La Belle
    Helene; In Abraham's Bosom; The Cradle Will Rock; Noah
    1935; Processional 1937; Androcles and the Lion (Federal
    Theatre) 1938; stage mgr., Head of the Family; Run Little
    Chillun' 1943; Carmen Jones; Arsenic and Old Lace (black
    cast); title role in Othello (ELT) 1946; Lysistrata 1946; Jeb
    1946; Twentieth Century 1950; Captain Brassbound's Conver-
    sion 1950; The Emperor's Clothes 1953; The Winner 1954;
    The Cool World 1960; The Octoroon (O.B.) 1961; King Lear
    (NYSF) 1962; The Playroom 1965.

SILVERA, FRANK (Alvin)
    (Actor/Director)
b. July 24, 1914, Kingston, Jamaica.
d. June 11, 1970, Pasadena, Calif.
Education: Northeastern University Law School 1934-36; Boston
    University; Old Vic School 1948; Actors Studio 1950.
Special Interests: Playwriting, producing.
Honors: Tony nomination (for The Lady of the Camellias) 1963.
Career Data: Boston Federal Theatre 1935-39; New England Reper-
    tory Theatre 1939-40; bd. of dirs., New Playwrights Company;
    co-founder, The Theatre of Being (L.A.)
Films: The Cimarron Kid, The Fighter, The Miracle of Our Lady
    of Fatima, Viva Zapata! 1952; Fear and Desire 1953; Killer's
    Kiss 1955; Crowded Paradise, The Mountain, The Lonely
    Night 1956; Hatful of Rain 1957; The Bravados 1958; Crime
    and Punishment, U.S.A. 1959; The Mountain Road, Key Wit-
    ness 1960; Mutiny on the Bounty 1962; Toys in the Attic 1963;
    The Greatest Story Ever Told 1965; The Appaloosa 1966; Hom-
    bre, The St. Valentine's Day Massacre 1967; Betrayal, Up-
    tight 1968; The Stalking Moon, Che!, Guns of the Magnificent
    Seven 1969; Valdez Is Coming 1971.
Memberships: AEA; AFTRA; SAG.

Radio: Two Billion Strong; UN Story; Up for Parole; Perry Mason;
    Counterspy, Someone You Know.
Records: Hearing Poetry; Everyman: A Morality Play; The Life
    and Death of Dr. Faustus; Othello.
Television: Captain Video; Big Story; The Skin of Our Teeth (spe-
    cial) 1955; Guitar (Studio One) 1957; Wanted Dead or Alive
    1958; Ellery Queen 1958; Alfred Hitchcock Presents 1964,
    1969; Seven Against the Wall (Playhouse 90) 1959; Lineup 1959;
    Law and Mr. Jones 1960; Thriller 1960; Hong Kong 1960; Mr.
    Garland 1960; Rebel 1960; Bonanza 1961, 1964; Twilight Zone
    1962; Defenders 1963; The Travels of Jaimie McPheeters 1963;
    Channing 1964; Great Adventures 1964; Mr. Novak 1964; That
    Time in Havana (Kraft Suspense Theatre) 1965; Profiles in
    Courage 1965; Rawhide 1965; Gunsmoke 1966; I Spy 1966; Rat
    Patrol; High Chaparral (series) 1967-70; Dundee and the Cul-
    hane 1967; Wild Wild West 1967; World of Disney 1968, 1971;
    Marcus Welby, M.D. 1969; Hawaii Five-O 1969, 1970; Flying
    Nun.
Theater: Potters Field (Boston) 1934; wrote Unto the Least (play)
    1938; Big White Fog (Lincoln Theatre, Harlem) 1944; Anna
    Lucasta (Bway debut) 1945, (London) 1947; John Loves Mary
    1947; Longitude '49 1950; title role in Nat Turner (O.B.) 1950;
    Gutman in Camino Real 1953; Mademoiselle Colombe 1954;
    Saint Joan (pre-Bway tour) 1954; directed Juno and the Pay-
    cock (O.B.) 1955; John Pope Sr. in A Hatful of Rain 1955,
    (tour) 1956-57; The Skin of Our Teeth (ANTA Salute to France)
    Paris and on Bway, 1955; Richard Mason in Jane Eyre 1958;
    Dr. Stockman in An Enemy of the People (Hollywood) 1958;
    A Tribute to Carl Sandburg (U.C.L.A.) 1958; directed and
    played Eddie Carbone in A View from the Bridge (Hollywood)
    1958; Semi-Detached 1960; Vershinin in The Three Sisters
    (UCLA) 1960; directed A Hatful of Rain (L.A.) 1962; title
    role in King Lear (NYSF) 1962; M. Duval in The Lady of the
    Camellias 1963; produced and directed The Amen Corner (L.A.
    and N.Y.) 1964; directed Anouilh's Medea (Hollywood) 1966.

SIMMS, HILDA (Hilda Theresa Moses)
    (Actress)
b. April 15, 1920, Minneapolis, Minn.
Education: University of Minnesota; Hampton Institute B.S. 1943;
    University of Paris (de la Sorbonne) 1950-52; American Aca-
    demy of Dramatic Arts 1958-59; Carnegie Hall Drama School
    1959-60; studied acting with Abbie Mitchell, Ezra Stone.
Special Interests: Modeling, singing.
Address: 272 East 10 Street, New York, N.Y. 10009.
Honors: Chicago Defender's Race Relations Honor Roll 1944; Allied
    Forces (Central Europe) award 1951; Minneapolis Urban
    League award 1953; N.Y.C. Y.M.C.A. award 1954; National
    Council of Negro Women award 1956.
Career Data: Worked with American Negro Theatre 1943-44; made
    U.S.O. tours; hostess, Exposition of Progress 1956; head,
    Arts Communication Dept., Addiction Research and Treatment
    Corp.

Films: Narrated Day After Day 1943; Marva in The Joe Louis
       Story 1953; Black Widow 1954.
Memberhips: AEA (Council Member 1962); AFTRA; SAG (Council
       Member 1963).
Radio: Scriptwriter for O.W.I. broadcasts; Joe Bostic's The Negro
       Sings (WLIB); Ladies Day with Hilda Simms 1954-57.
Television: A Man Is Ten Feet Tall (Philco Television Playhouse)
       1955; Profiles in Courage (Kraft Television Theatre) 1956;
       Black Monday (Play of the Week) 1960; The Nurses (series)
       1962-65.
Theater: Three's a Family (ANT) 1943; title role in Anna Lucasta
       (Bway debut) 1944, Chicago 1945, London 1947; Desire Caught
       by the Tail (London) 1950; Stella Goodman in the Gentle Peo-
       ple 1950; Pervaneh in Hassan (Cambridge) 1951; The Cool
       World 1960; The Captain's Paradise and Black Monday (summer
       stock) 1961; Love Letters of Famous Courtesans; One Woman
       Show (tour) 1961; Laura Wright Reed in Tambourines to Glory
       (O.B.) 1963; Madwoman of Chaillot (O.B.) 1970; Tell Pharaoh
       1972; Montage for Freedom at Carnegie Hall 1975.

SIMON, JOE
       (Singer)
b. c.1941, Simmesport, La.
Honors: Three Grammys.
Clubs: Barney Google's 1975.
Films: Cleopatra Jones (theme) 1973.
Records: Come Get to This; Power of Love; Drowning in the Sea
       of Love; My Adorable; Let's Spend the Night Together; Get
       Down (Polydor); Today (Spring); Simon Sings (Monument);
       Mood, Heart & Soul (Spring); Chokin' Kind/Better Than Ever
       (Monument); Hits (Monument); World of... (Monument); Easy
       To Love (Spring).
Television: Soul Train 1975; American Bandstand 1975.

SIMONE, NINA (Eunice Kathleen Waymon)
       (Singer/Pianist/Composer)
b. February 21, 1933, Tryon, N.C.
Education: Curtis Institute of Music 1950-53, Juilliard School of
       Music 1954; studied acting with Vladimir Sokoloff.
Special Interests: Teaching, jazz.
Address: 1 Lincoln Plaza, New York, N.Y. 10023.
Honors: Most Promising Singer of the Year 1960; Woman of the
       Year, Jazz at Home Club (Philadelphia, 1966); Female Jazz
       Singer of the Year 1967.
Career Data: Newport Jazz Festival 1974.
Clubs: Village Gate.
Memberships: AFM; AFTRA; ASCAP 1959; National Assn. of Com-
       posers and Conductors.
Musical Compositions: Central Park Blues; Return Home; African
       Mailman; If You Knew; Sugar in My Bowl; To Be Young, Gifted
       and Black; Blackbird; Children Go Where I Send You; Flo Me

La; Nina's Blues; Go Limp; Mississippi Goddam 1963; Four
Women 1964; Backlash Blues 1966.

Publications: Still Out in the Wind (autobiography), 1973.

Records: Emergency Ward; Black Gold; Nina Simone Sings Billie
Holiday; High Priestess of Soul; Nuff Said (RCA); At the Vil-
lage Gate (Colpix); Wild Is the Wind (Philips); The Original
and Best of Nina Simone (Bethlehem); Little Girl Blue (Beth-
lehem); Broadway Blues Ballads (Philips); I Loves You Porgy
(Bethlehem, 1959); Do What You Gotta Do (RCA 1968); To Be
Young, Gifted and Black (RCA 1969); It Is Finished (RCA,
1974); Best (Philips); Best (RCA); Black Is the Color (Trip);
Here Comes Sun (RCA); Live in Europe (Trip); Poets (RCA);
Portrait (Trip).

Relationships: Sisters of Sam Waymon, singer/composer.

SIMPSON, O. J. "Juice" (Orenthal James Simpson)
     (Actor)
b.   July 9, 1947, San Francisco, Calif.
Education: City College of San Francisco; University of Southern
     California.
Address: International Creative Management, 8899 Beverly Blvd.,
     Los Angeles, Calif 90048.
Honors: Heisman Trophy 1968.
Career Data: Pro-football star, Buffalo Bills (running back).
Films: Garth in the Klansman, The Towering Inferno 1974; Killer
     Force, The Cassandra Crossing 1976.
Memberships: SAG.
Publications: O.J.: The Education of a Rich Rookie (autobiography),
     Macmillan, 1970.
Television: Tonight Show; Wide World of Sports; Hertz commercial;
     Medical Center 1969; Funny World of Sports 1974; O. J.
     Simpson Is Alive and Well and Getting Roasted Tonight on Wide
     World of Entertainment 1974; Juice on the Loose 1974; The
     Superstars 1975; Celebrity Superstars 1975; Mac Davis Show
     1975; NFL Action 1975; Bobby Vinton Show 1975; Easter Seal
     Telethon 1976; Emmy Awards Show 1976; Good Morning Ameri-
     ca 1976; Roots 1977; Tree-Sweet commercial 1977; A Killing
     Affair 1977.

SINCLAIR, MADGE
     (Actress)
b.   April 28, 1940, Kingston, Jamaica.
Education: Shortwood College for Women, (Kingston, Jamaica).
Address: 1999 N. Sycamore Avenue, Hollywood, Calif. 90068.
Honors: NAACP Image Award (for Conrack).
Films: Conrack 1974; Cornbread, Earl and Me 1975; Leadbelly, I
     Will I Will for Now, Not Fade Away 1976.
Memberships: AEA; AFTRA; SAG.
Television: Mama Prentiss in Guess Who's Coming to Dinner?
     (pilot) 1975; Joe Forrester 1975; Doctors Hospital 1975; The
     Waltons 1975; Belle in Roots 1977; Almos' a Man 1977.

Theater: Mod Donna (NYSF); Iphigenia (NYSF); T-Jean and His
          Brothers (NYSF); Blood (NYSF); Kumaliza (NYSF); Lady Day
          (Bklyn. Academy of Music).

SIR LANCELOT
          (Singer)
Special Interests: Calypso.
Films: I Walked with a Zombie 1943; Curse of the Cat People, To
          Have and Have Not 1944; Brute Force 1947; Romance on the
          High Seas 1948; The Buccaneer 1958.
Memberships: SAG.

SISSLE, NOBLE
          (Musician/Conductor)
b. July 10, 1889, Indianapolis, In.
d. December 17, 1975, Tampa, Fla.
Education: De Pauw University, (Greencastle, Indiana), Butler
          University (Indianapolis).
Special Interests: Banjo, mandolin, writing lyrics, singing.
Honors: (Unofficial) Mayor of Harlem; Ellington Medal (Yale Uni-
          versity) 1972.
Career Data: Toured as singer with Thomas male quartet, Hann's
          Jubilee Singers 1911-13; formed band at Severin Hotel, Indi-
          anapolis 1914; teamed with Eubie Blake as partner in perform-
          ing and composing 1915-; toured as drum major with James
          Reese Europe's band 1916-1919; led own orchestra 1935-36;
          toured with U.S.O. shows 1943-45; managed own publishing
          company 1960s.
Clubs: Coconut Grove (Palm Beach, Fla.) 1915, Ritz Carlton
          Roof, Kit Kat Club (London) 1926, Les Ambassadeurs (Paris)
          1928, Park Central Hotel 1931, Billy Rose's Diamond Horse-
          shoe 1938-42, 1945.
Films: Snappy Tunes 1923; Pie Pie Blackbird (short) 1931; Murder
          with Music 1941; Junction 88 1947.
Memberships: ASCAP; NAG (founder and first president).
Musical Compositions: Wrote lyrics for It's All Your Fault; In
          Honeysuckle Time; When Emaline Said She'd Be Mine; I'm
          Just Wild about Harry; Love Will Find a Way; You Were
          Meant for Me; Gypsy Blues; Hello Sweetheart Hello; Yeah
          Man; Okey Doke; Characteristic Blues; Slave of Love; Lowdown
          Blues; Goodnight Angeline; Boogie Woogie Beguine; The Red
          Bull Line; Bandana Days.
Radio: Emcee, Swingtime at the Savoy.
Theater: Appeared at Palace Theatre; wrote lyrics and appeared
          in Shuffle Along 1921; produced The Chocolate Dandies (a.k.a.
          In Bamville) 1924; wrote Shuffle Along of 1933; wrote and
          produced O'Sing a New Song (Chicago) 1934; appeared at
          Loew's State Theatre 1939; wrote Shuffle Along 1952; wrote
          The Rhythms of America (Brooklyn) 1967.

SMITH, BESSIE "Empress of the Blues"
    (Singer)
b. April 15, 1894, Chattanooga, Tenn.
d. September 26, 1937, Clarksdale, Miss.
Special Interests: Composing.
Honors: Record Changer All Time; All Star Poll winner 1951.
Career Data: Sang for United Hot Clubs of America; hits include
    Gimme a Pigfoot and T'Ain't Nobody's Bizness If I Do.
Films: St. Louis Blues 1929.
Musical Compositions: Backwater Blues.
Records: Down Hearted Blues 1923; Blues to Barrelhouse; Any-
    Woman's Blues; The World's Greatest Blues Singer (Columbia);
    Empty Bed Blues (Columbia); Nobody's Blues But Mine (Colum-
    bia); The Empress (Columbia); Nobody Knows You When You're
    Down and Out 1929; The Bessie Smith Story (Columbia) 1933.
Theater: Appeared at Lafayette Theatre (Harlem); Apollo Theatre;
    Midnight Steppers 1929; toured her own show Harlem Frolics;
    sang in F. C. Woolcott's Rabbit Foot Minstrel Show; Charles
    P. Bailey's "81" Theatre; toured TOBA (Negro vaudeville) cir-
    cuit; toured Silas Green Show 1937.

SMITH, HALE
    (Musician/Composer)
b. 1925, Cleveland, Ohio.
Education: Cleveland Institute of Music B.M. 1950, M.M. 1952.
Special Interests: Arranging.
Address: 222 Independence Avenue, Freeport, L.I. 11520.
Honors: Broadcast Music Student Composers award 1953.
Career Data: Associate professor, University of Connecticut; ad-
    junct associate professor (Music), C. W. Post College, Long
    Island University 1968; Karamu House, Cleveland; arranger
    for Chico Hamilton, Oliver Nelson, Quincy Jones, Ahmad
    Jamal.
Films: Bold New Approach (doc.) 1966.
Memberships: ACA (bd. of govs.); Composers Recordings Inc.
    (bd. of dir.).
Musical Compositions: In Memoriam--Beryl Rubinstein 1953; Yerma
    (score); Blood Wedding (score); Epicedial Variations 1956;
    Sonata for Cello and Piano; Two Love Songs of John Donne;
    Three Brevities for Flute; Contours for Orchestra 1962; Bold
    New Approach (score); Somersault; Take a Chance; Evocation;
    Orchestral Set 1962; Music for Harp and Orchestra 1967;
    Three Songs for Voice; Trinial Dance; By Yearning and by
    Beautiful; Faces of Jazz; Comes Tomorrow.

SMITH, LONNIE LISTON
    (Singer)
b. December 28, 1940, Richmond, Va.
Education: Morgan State College B.S. (music).
Special Interests: Arranging, composing, teaching.
Address: Suite 17D 207 West 106 Street, New York, N.Y. 10025.

Honors: International Jazz Critics Poll 1972; 37th annual Down Beat
     Poll citation; National Endowment for the Arts Grant 1973;
     Judge at Notre Dame Collegiate Jazz Festival 1974; Best new
     jazz artist of 1975 (Record World Magazine) 1975.
Career Data: Worked with The Royal Stage Band; worked with
     Pharoah Sanders, Miles Davis, Joe Williams, Art Blakey,
     Ethel Ennis, Rahsaan Roland Kirk, Gato Barbieri and others;
     leads his own group The Cosmic Echoes; participated in
     Montreux Jazz Festival 1969-71; Nice Jazz Festival 1969,
     1971; Hammerveld Jazz Festival 1972; Newport Jazz Festival
     (at New York) 1972; Berliner Jazz Tage 1972; Schaefer Music
     Festival 1975.
Clubs: Slugs; Village Vanguard; Jazzboat; Jazz Workshop (Boston);
     Gilly's (Dayton); Baker's Keyboard Lounge (Detroit); Top of
     the Gate 1975; East (Brooklyn) 1976.
Musical Compositions: Jewels of Thought; Let Us Go into the House
     of the Lord; Astral Traveling; Morning Prayer; Imani (Faith);
     Aspirations; Rejuvenation; In Search of Truth; Cosmic Funk;
     Beautiful Woman; Peaceful Ones; Summer Days; Expansions;
     Shadows; Desert Nights; Voodoo Woman.
Records: For Flying Dutchman: Astral Traveling; Cosmic Funk;
     Expansions; Reflections of a Golden Dream; Visions of a New
     World; Renaissance.
Television: Montreux Jazz Festival 1971; The Jazz Set 1972; Posi-
     tively Black 1975.
Theater: Appearances at Apollo Theatre 1975; Carnegie Hall 1975;
     Avery Fisher Hall 1975.
Relationships: Son of Lonnie Liston Smith Sr., singer; brother of
     Donald Smith, singer (with the Cosmic Echoes).

SMITH, MILDRED JOANNE
     (Actress)
b. Mary 16, 1923, Struthers, Ohio.
Education: Western Reserve University B.A.; Columbia University
     M.A.; Manhattanville College M.A.; Actors' Studio.
Address: 14 Madison Place, White Plains, N.Y. 10603.
Career Data: Worked with Karamu Theatre (Cleveland); owner and
     president of Black Beauty Inc. Talent Agency.
Films: (Sidney Poitier's wife) in No Way Out 1950.
Memberships: AFTRA; AGVA; NAACP; SAG.
Television: Jack Benny Show.
Theater: Beggar's Holiday; Men to the Sea (debut); S.S. Glencairn
     (City Center Revival); The Insect Comedy; Forward the Heart;
     Cockles and Champagne (London); Mamba's Daughters 1939;
     Blue Holiday 1945; Lysistrata 1946; St. Louis Woman 1946;
     Set My People Free 1948.
Relationships: Wife of David Hepburn, producer.

SMITH, MURIEL
     (Actress/Singer)
b. February 23, 1923, New York, N.Y.

Education: Curtis Institute (Philadelphia, Pa.); Columbia University;
     studied with Gian Carlo Menotti.
Special Interests: Poetry.
Address: 17 Spencer Mans, Queens Club Gardens, London, England
     W 14.
Films: Narrated Strange Victory 1948; Moulin Rouge 1953; The
     Crowning Experience 1960; Voice of the Hurricane 1964.
Memberships: AEA; British AEA; SAG.
Radio: Major Bowes Amateur Hour.
Theater: Title role (alternating with Muriel Rahn) in Carmen Jones
     (debut) 1943; Our Lan' 1947; The Cradle Will Rock 1947;
     Phaedra in Hippolytus (O.B.) 1948; Bella in Sojourner Truth
     (YMHA) 1948; title role in Carmen (Triborough Stadium) 1948;
     Sauce Tarter (London) 1949; Sauce Piquante (Cambridge) 1950;
     Bloody Mary in South Pacific (London) 1950; Lady Thiang in
     The King and I (London) 1953; title role in Carmen Jones
     (City Center) 1956; title role in Carmen (Covent Garden) 1956;
     Moral Rearmament Production 1958.

SMITH, O. C. (Ocie Smith)
     (Singer)
b. June 21, 1932, Mansfield, La.
Address: c/o Prince and Bash, Suite 302, 8150 Beverly Road,
     Los Angeles, Calif. 90048.
Career Data: Performed with bands of Count Basie, Sy Oliver,
     Horace Heidt.
Records: On Columbia: La La Peace Song; Greatest Hits; Help
     Me Make It; The Son of Hickory Hollers Tramp 1968; Little
     Green Apples 1968; Friend, Lover, Woman, Wife 1969;
     Daddy's Little Man 1969.
Television: Arthur Godfrey's Talent Scouts; Sammy and Company
     1976.

SNOW, VALAIDA
     (Singer)
b. June 2, c.1900, Chattanooga, Tenn.
d. May 30, 1956, Brooklyn, N.Y.
Special Interests: Trumpet.
Career Data: Toured with Will Masten's Revue 1920s, worked with
     Ananias Berry (former husband) in act (L.A.) 1935; performed
     in concerts, shows and clubs in Middle East, Russia 1929,
     Far East 1936, Europe 1936-41, U.S. 1946-56.
Clubs: Barron Wilkins (Phila.) 1922; Grand Terrace 1936.
Films: Take It from Me 1926; Irresistible You; Alibi (French)
     1939.
Theater: Rhapsody in Black; The Chocolate Dandies 1924; Black-
     birds of 1929; Apollo Theatre 1936, 1943; Palace Theatre (last
     appearance) 1956.

SOUTH, EDDIE "Dark Angel of the Violin" (Edward South)
     (Jazz Musician)

b. November 27, 1904, Louisiana, Mo.
d. April 25, 1962, Chicago, Ill.
Education: Chicago College of Music; studied with Charles Elgar.
Special Interests: Violin.
Career Data: Performed with Jimmy Wade 1924-27; Erskine Tate
1927-28; led his own combo The Alabamians; toured Europe in
1930, 1937 and 1938; led his own groups in 1940s and 1950s.
Clubs: Moulin Rouge Cafe (Chicago); Club des Oiseaux (Paris);
Cafe-Society; Jigs; The Garrick (Chicago); Trocadero (Holly-
wood); Du Sable Hotel (Chicago).
Records: The Distinguished Violin of Eddie South (Mercury); South
Side Jazz (Chess); Dark Angel of Fiddle (Trip).

SOYINKA, WOLE (Akinwande Oluwole Soyinka)
(Playwright)
b. July 13, 1934, Abeokuta, Nigeria.
Education: University College of Ibadan; University of Leeds (Eng-
land) 1954-57.
Special Interests: Acting, teaching.
Address: c/o School of The Arts, University of Ibadan, Ibadan,
Nigeria, West Africa.
Honors: Rockefeller Fellowship 1960-61; Encounter Magazine
Literary Prize 1960, African Arts Festival Award 1966.
Career Data: Play reader, Royal Court Theatre (London); faculty,
University of Ife (Ibadan) 1962; founded Orisun Repertory Co.
1964; faculty, University of Lagos 1965; founder, Calpenny-
Nigeria Ltd. (film company).
Films: Kongi's Harvest (screenplay) 1973.
Theater: Wrote: The Invention; Dance of the Forests 1965; The
Swamp Dwellers 1965; The Road 1965; The Lion and the
Jewel 1965; Kongi's Harvest 1967; The Trials of Brother
Jero 1967; The Strong Breed 1967; Madmen and Specialists;
Jero's Metamorphosis.

SPEARMAN, RAWN W.
(Concert Singer)
b. February 4, 1923, Bexar, Ala.
Education: Florida A & M College B.S., Columbia University
M.A., Ed.D. American Theatre Wing.
Address: 103 Splitbrook Road, Nashua, N.H. 01854
Honors: Marian Anderson award; John Hay Whitney Fellowship;
Ville de Fontainebleau award.
Career Data: Concert tour with Fisk Jubilee Singers 1947-48;
Hunter College (faculty member) 1969-73; Coordinator, Per-
forming Arts, Borough of Manhattan Community College 1973-
76; Lowell State College (Mass).
Publications: Theatre Music for Young People: A Handbook for
Teachers. Far Rockaway, N.Y., Peripole Publishing Corp.,
1969.
Records: Christmas Sounds of Peripole (Peri-Scope).
Television: Fred Waring Show.

Theater: Four Saints in Three Acts 1952; House of Flowers 1955;
     Sportin' Life in Porgy and Bess (City Center) 1961.

SPEED, CAROL
     (Actress)
Special Interests: Singing, songwriting.
Address: Jules Katz, 9201 Wilshire Blvd., Suite 104-A, Beverly
     Hills, Calif.
Films: The New Centurions 1972; The Mack, Savage 1973; Black
     Samson, title role in Abby 1974.
Memberships: SAG.
Television: Sanford and Son 1975.

SPELL, GEORGE
     (Actor)
Films: They Call Me Mr. Tibbs 1970; The Organization 1971; Man
     and Boy, The Biscuit Eater 1972.
Memberships: SAG.
Television: Bracken's World; Flying Nun; Bill Cosby Show; Kung
     Fu; A Dream for Christmas 1973; Harry O 1974; That Girl
     1976.

SPENCE, EULALIE
     (Playwright)
b. June 11, 1894, Nevis, British West Indies.
Education: New York University B.S. 1937; Columbia University
     M.A. (Speech) 1939.
Special Interests: Coaching, directing, producing, teaching.
Address: 475 F.D.R. Drive, New York, N.Y. 10002.
Honors: Second Prize Krigwa Contest sponsored by The Crisis
     1926.
Career Data: Teacher and Dramatic Society Coach, Eastern Dis-
     trict H.S. (Brooklyn).
Films: Wrote screenplay The Whipping for Paramount 1933.
Theater: Wrote one act plays including Fool's Errand 1927; Foreign
     Mail 1927; Her 1927; The Hunch 1927; The Starter 1927; Epi-
     sode 1928; Help Wanted 1929; Undertow 1929; directed Before
     Breakfast and Joint Owners of Spain (Dunbar Garden Players)
     1929.

SPENCER, CHRISTINE
     (Actress/Singer)
Memberships: AEA; NAG.
Television: American Musical Theatre.
Theater: Carmen Jones (Theatre in the Park) 1959; Ballad for
     Bimshire 1963; The Zulu and the Zayda 1965.

SPENCER, KENNETH (L.)
     (Actor/Singer)

b.   1913, Los Angeles, Calif.
d.   February 25, 1964 near New Orleans, La.
Education: Eastman School (Rochester).
Career Data: Performed as soloist with Los Angeles Philharmonic,
     N.Y. Philharmonic and symphony orchestras of Detroit, Austin,
     Houston, Rochester, Ottawa, Vancouver and London; sang with
     St. Louis Opera Co.
Films: Cabin in the Sky, Bataan 1943.
Theater: Sang in Gettysburg (an opera) at Hollywood Bowl; Joe in
     Showboat 1946.

STANIS, BERNNADETTE (Bernadette Stanislaus)
     (Actress)
b.   December 22, 1953, Brooklyn, N.Y.
Education: Juilliard School of Music.
Special Interests: Dancing, modeling.
Address: P.O. Box 1838 Studio City Station, 305 N. Hollywood,
     Calif. 91604.
Honors: Pepperdine Outstanding Service award 1974-75; Miss
     Brooklyn, 1st runner-up for Miss N.Y. State in Miss Black
     America Pageant 1974; Certificate of Merit, United Negro Col-
     lege Fund 1975; American Heart Fund Award 1975.
Career Data: Participant American Heart Fund Bike-A-Thon 1974;
     Mistress of Ceremonies, United Negro College Fund Kick-Off
     Campaign 1975.
Memberships: AFTRA.
Television: Thelma on Good Times (series) 1974-; Tattletales 1975;
     Saturday Preview Special 1975.
Theater: Appeared on amateur night at Apollo Theatre.

STATON, DAKOTA (Aliyah Rabia)
     (Singer)
b.   June 3, 1932, Pittsburgh, Pa.
Education: Filion School of Music (Pittsburgh).
Honors: Down Beat award for most promising newcomer 1955.
Clubs: Thwaites Inn (City Island); Baby Grand 1975; Seafood Play-
     house 1975.
Records: Confessin' (Groove Merchant); Late Late Show (Capitol).
Theater: Appeared at Apollo Theatre 1950.

STEWART, ELLEN
     (Producer)
b.   Alexandria, La.
Education: Arkansas State University.
Address: c/o La Mama Experimental Theater Club, 74 A East 4
     St., New York, N.Y. 10003.
Special Interests: Designing clothes.
Honors: Margo Jones Award for developing new playwrights under
     workshop conditions 1969; N.Y. State Council on the Arts
     Award for the La Mama Experimental Theater 1973; Harold
     Jackman Memorial award.

Career Data: Founded La Mama July 22, 1962; formed branches
of La Mama in Japan, Colombia, England, Canada, Soviet
Union, Lebanon, Israel, Australia.
Theater: Productions include Tennessee Williams' One Arm 1962;
Megan Terry's Viet Rock; Jean-Claude van Itallie's America;
Hurrah!; Rochelle Owens' Futz!; Michael Locasio's In a Cor-
ner of the Morning 1962; Harold Pinter's The Room 1962; Paul
Foster's Balls 1963; Tom Paine, Jerzy Grotoroski and his
Polish Laboratory Theater 1969; Tom Eyen's Caution: A Love
Story 1969; Euripides' Medea 1972; Sam Shepard's Chicago;
Adrienne Kennedy's Black Mass; Lanford Wilson's This Is the
Pill Speaking; Electra (Bordeaux, France) 1973; Adrienne
Kennedy's A Beast Story 1974; House of Leather; Short Bullins;
Horse Opera; Serban/Swados Trilogy; Good Woman of Setzuan
1975.

STEWART, MEL (Melvin)
(Actor)
Address: Sackheim Agency, 9301 Wilshire Blvd., Los Angeles,
Calif.
Career Data: Worked at Karamu Playhouse, Cleveland.
Films: Odds Against Tomorrow 1959; Shadows, The Hustler 1961;
Nothing But a Man 1964; Petulia 1968; A Session with the Com-
mittee 1969; Halls of Anger, The Landlord 1970; Hammer 1972;
Trick Baby, Scorpio, Kid Blue, Steelyard Blues 1973; The
Conversation, Newman's Law 1974; Let's Do It Again 1975.
Memberships: AEA; NAG; SAG.
Television: Simply Heavenly (Play of the Week) 1959; Deadlock 1969;
All in the Family (series) 1972-74; Roll Out (series) 1973;
Marcus Welby, M.D. 1974; Good Times 1975; Harry O 1975;
Lucas Tanner 1975; Rockford Files 1975; The Last Survivors
1975; Salt and Pepe 1975; That's My Mama 1975; Police
Story 1975; Gibson in On the Rocks (series) 1975; Parkay
Margarine commercial 1977; The Double Con 1977.
Theater: Simply Heavenly 1957; The Cool World 1960; Brouhaha
(O.B.) 1960; The Hostage 1961; Moon on a Rainbow Shawl
(O.B.) 1962; In the Counting House 1962; My Mother, My
Father and Me 1963; The Last Minstrel (O.B.) 1963; No Place
to Be Somebody 1970.

STILL, WILLIAM GRANT
(Composer)
b. May 11, 1895, Woodville, Miss.
Education: Wilberforce University; Oberlin College; New England
Conservatory of Music; studied with Edgar Varese.
Special Interests: Conducting, oboe, violin.
Address: 1262 Victoria Avenue, Los Angeles, Calif. 90019.
Honors: Harmon award 1927; Rosenwald and Guggenheim (1st 1934)
fellowships; Cincinnati Symphony Orchestra's composition con-
test 1st prize 1944; Phi Beta Sigma's George Washington Carver
achievement award 1953; National Assn. for American Com-

posers and Conductors Citation for Outstanding Service to
American Music 1961; League of Allied Arts in L.A. trophy
1965; APPA (Washington, D.C.) trophy 1968; West Point
Sesquicentennial Freedom Foundation award; NFMC & Aeolian
Music Foundation award for best composition honoring the U.N.

Career Data: Works commissioned by World's Fair New York 1939-
40; arranger for W. C. Handy, Sophie Tucker, Paul Whiteman,
Artie Shaw and others.

Clubs: Plantation Club.

Memberships: ASCAP 1936.

Musical Compositions: Sahdji (ballet); La Guiablesse (ballet); Seven
Traceries; Blue Steel (opera); From the Black Belt; Afro-
American Symphony; Symphony in G-Minor; To You America;
Blues; Old California; Danzas de Panama; From the Heart of
the Believer; Dismal Swamps; From the Delta; Lenox Avenue;
Poems for Orchestra; Africa: A Symphonic Poem; The Ameri-
can Scene; Incantation and Dance; A Deserted Plantation; Three
Visions; Death of a Rose; Summerland; A Southern Interlude;
Winter's Approach; Festive Overture, Poem for Orchestra;
Violin and Piano Suite; Darker America 1924; Troubled Island
(opera) 1937; A Bayou Legend (opera) 1940; Costaso 1949;
Highway U.S.A. 1963; From the Land of Dreams; Log Cabin
Ballads; If You Should Go.

Radio: Deep River Hour (WOR).

Theater: Played oboe in Shuffle Along 1921; Eastman School (Rochester) 1929; Carnegie Hall 1935; Symphony Under the Stars,
Hollywood Bowl 1936.

STITT, SONNY (Edward Stitt)
    (Jazz Musician)
b. February 2, 1924, Boston, Mass.

Special Interests: Tenor, alto and baritone saxophone, conducting.

Honors: Esquire new star award 1947.

Career Data: Played with bands of Tiny Bradshaw, Dizzy Gillespie
1945-46, 1958; led his own band and later his own combo;
participated in Jazz at the Philharmonic 1958, 1959; Newport
Jazz Festival.

Clubs: The Bottom Line 1975; Starlight Roof-Waldorf Astoria 1975;
Top of the Gate 1976.

Films: Jazz on a Summer's Day (doc.) 1960.

Records: New Sounds in Modern Music (Savoy); Jazz at the High
Hat (Roost); Best (Prestige); Best for Lovers (Prestige); Bits
(Prestige); Black Vibrations (Prestige); Bud's Blues (Prestige);
The Champ (MUSE); Dumpy Mama (Flying Dutchman); Genesis
(Prestige); Goin' Down Slow (Prestige); I Cover the Waterfront
(Cadet); Inter-Action (Cadet); Jug & Sonny (Cadet); Made for
Each Other (Delmark); Make Someone Happy (Roulette); Mellow
(MUSE); Move on Over (Cadet); Mr. Bojangles (Cadet); My
Main Man (Cadet); Never Can Say Goodbye (Cadet); Night Let-
ter (Prestige); Night Work (Black Lion); 'Nuther Fu'ther (Pres-
tige); Now (Atlantic); ...Plays Bird (Atlantic); Pow (Prestige);
Primitivo (Prestige); Salt and Pepper (Impulse); Satan (Cadet);

Shangri-La (Prestige); So Doggone Good (Prestige); Soul Electricity (Prestige); Soul Girl (Paula); Soul in the Night (Cadet); Soul People (Prestige); Soul Shack (Prestige); Stardust (Roulette); Stomp Off Let's Go (Flying Dutchman); Turn It On (Prestige); 12! (MUSE); Two Sides of... (Trip); We'll Be Together Again (Prestige).

Theater: Appeared at Avery Fisher Hall (tribute to Dizzy) 1975; Radio City Music Hall 1976.

STOKER, AUSTIN
    (Actor)
b. October 7, Trinidad.
Education: College of Our Lady of Fatima (Trinidad); studied acting with Paul Mann and Herbert Berghof.
Special Interests: Singing, dancing, drums.
Address: Barr/Gilly Agency, 8721 Sunset Blvd., Los Angeles, Calif. 90069.
Career Data: Geoffrey Holder dance troupe; musical comedy club act (with Vivian Bonnell).
Films: Parrish 1961; Battle for the Planet of the Apes 1973; The Zebra Killer, Abby, Airport 1975, 1974; Sheba Baby 1975.
Memberships: SAG.
Television: Monte Nash; Mod Squad; Trouble Comes to Town 197?; Police Story 1974; S.W.A.T. 1975; Bronk 1975; Jigsaw John 1976; Victory at Entebbe 1976; Roots 1977.
Theater: House of Flowers 1955; Boys in the Band (tour).

STONE, SLY (Sylvester Stewart)
    (Singer)
b. March c.1944, Calif.
Education: Vallejo Junior College (Calif.).
Special Interests: Arranging, composing, drums, guitar, organ.
Career Data: Former disc jockey (San Francisco).
Clubs: Sahara (Las Vegas).
Records: On Epic: A Whole New Thing 1967; Dance to the Music 1968; Life 1968; Stand 1969; Fresh 1973; Small Talk; High on You; Sly and the Family Stone Greatest Hits.
Television: Geraldo Rivera's Good Night America 1974; Mike Douglas Show 1974; Midnight Special 1974; Hollywood Palladium 1974; Wide World in Concert 1974; American Music Awards 1975.
Theater: Appearances at Fillmore East 1968; Madison Square Garden 1974; Radio City Music Hall 1975.

STRAYHORN, BILLY "Swee' Pea" (William Thomas Strayhorn)
    (Jazz Musician/Composer)
b. November 29, 1915, Dayton, Ohio.
d. May 31, 1967, New York, N.Y.
Special Interests: Arranging, piano, writing lyrics.
Honors: Esquire (silver) award 1945.
Career Data: Composed and arranged for Duke Ellington orchestra 1939-67; toured Europe 1950.

Memberships: ASCAP 1946.
Musical Compositions: Take the "A" Train; After All; Something
    to Live For; Lush Life; Chelsea Bridge; Day Dream; Rain-
    check; Johnny Come Lately; Clementine; Passion Flower; Mid-
    riff; Satin Doll; Grievin'; Perfume Suite; Far East Suite;
    Blood Count.
Records: Cue for Sax (Master Jazz).

STRODE, WOODY (Woodrow Strode)
    (Actor)
b. 1914, Los Angeles, Calif.
Education: U.C.L.A.
Address: c/o Jack Fields & Associates, 9255 Sunset Blvd., Los
    Angeles, Calif. 90069.
Career Data: Wrestler; football player (all-pro end, Canadian
    League 1948), Hollywood Bears, Los Angeles Rams, Calgary
    Stampeders.
Films: Sundown 1941; The Lion Hunters 1951; Caribbean 1952;
    Androcles and the Lion, The City Beneath the Sea 1953; De-
    metrius and the Gladiators, The Gambler from Natchez 1954;
    The Ten Commandments 1956; Tarzan's Fight for Life, The
    Buccaneer 1958; Pork Chop Hill 1959; Sergeant Rutledge, The
    Last Voyage, Spartacus 1960; The Sins of Rachel Cade, Two
    Rode Together 1961; The Man Who Shot Liberty Valance 1962;
    Tarzan's Three Challenges 1963; Genghis Khan 1965; Seven
    Women, The Professionals 1966; Shalako 1968; Che, Once
    Upon the Time in the West 1969; Black Jesus, The Last Rebel,
    The Gatling Gun, The Deserters 1971; narrated Black Rodeo,
    The Revengers 1972; Boot Hill, The Italian Connection 1973;
    Winterhawk 1976.
Television: Lothar in Mandrake The Magician (series) 1954; Soldiers
    of Fortune 1955; The Savage 1960; Thriller 1960; Rawhide 1961;
    Lieutenant 1964; Farmer's Daughter 1964; Daniel Boone 1966;
    Batman 1966; Tarzan 1966-68; Key West 1973; Manhunter 1975;
    Quest 1976; Martinelli; Outside Man (pilot) 1977.

STUBBS, LOUISE
    (Actress)
Education: Barnard College 1952; Goodman School of Drama (Chi-
    cago).
Career Data: Richard B. Harrison Players (Chicago).
Films: The Cool World 1964; The Pawnbroker 1965; A Fine Mad-
    ness 1966; Sweet Love Bitter 1967; Black Girl 1972.
Memberships: NEC.
Television: Naked City; The Guiding Light; The Defenders; Harlem
    Detective; Directions '66; The Crucible; East Side/West Side.
Theater: Tryout (O.B.); Light in the Cellar (O.B.); The Jackal
    (O.B.); The Other Foot (O.B.); Take a Giant Step 1953; The
    Blacks (O.B.) 1961-62; Day of Absence (NEC) 1966; Happy
    Ending (NEC) 1966; The Trial of Lee Harvey Oswald 1967;
    American Pastoral (O.B.) 1968; The Reckoning (O.B.) 1969;

Open 24 Hours (O.B.) 1969; Contribution (O.B.) 1970; Black
Girl (O.B.) 1971-72; title role in Sister Sadie (O.B.) 1972;
The Anniversary (O.B.) 1973; The Prodigal Sister (O.B.)
1974; What the Winesellers Buy (Chicago) 1975; Secret Service
(O.B.) 1976; Tribute to Duke Ellington at Avery Fisher Hall
1976; Macbeth (O.B.) 1977.

SULLIVAN, MAXINE "The Loch Lomond Lark" (Marietta Williams)
    (Singer)
b. May 13, 1911, Homestead, Pa.
Address: c/o House That Jazz Built, 1312 Stebbins Avenue, Bronx,
    N.Y. 10459.
Career Data: Vocalist with World's Greatest Jazz Band and bands
    of Count Basie and Benny Goodman; toured Great Britain 1948,
    1954; popularized songs Loch Lomond and Molly Malone.
Clubs: Reuben Bleu; Blue Angel; Village Vanguard; Penthouse; Blues
    Alley; Benjamin Harrison Literary Club (Pittsburgh); Onyx
    1938; Thwaites Inn 1975; Dutch Inn 1975; Seafood Playhouse
    1975; The Cookery 1975; Rainbow Room 1976; Riverboat 1977.
Films: Going Places, St. Louis Blues 1939.
Radio: Flow Gently, Sweet Rhythm (CBS) 1940.
Records: Looking for a Boy (King); Flow Gently Sweet Rhythm
    (Period); Shakespeare and Hyman (Monmouth-Evergreen).
Theater: Swinging the Dream 1939; Take a Giant Step 1953; ap-
    peared at Carnegie Hall (Newport Jazz Festival 1974); South
    Street Seaport Pier 15 (with Marshall Brown Septet 1975).
Relationships: Former wife of John Kirby, bandleader; widow of
    Cliff Jackson, jazz pianist.

SUN RA (Sonny Blondt, a.k.a. Le Sony'Ra)
    (Jazz Musician)
Special Interests: Piano.
Address: Variety Sound Corp. 130 W. 42 Street, New York, N.Y.
    10036.
Career Data: Performed with Fletcher Henderson; formed his own
    orchestra.
Clubs: Five Spot 1975; The East (Brooklyn) 1976; The Bottom Line
    1976.
Records: Nothing Is (ESP); Bad and Beautiful (Impulse); Continua-
    tion (Saturn); Heliocentric Worlds (ESP); It's After the End of
    the World (BASF); Jazz in Silhouette (Impulse); Pathways to
    Unknown Worlds (Impulse); Pictures of Infinity (Black Lion);
    Universe in Blue (Saturn); Sound of Joy (Delmark); Sun Song
    (Delmark).
Theater: Appeared at Beacon Theatre.

SYKES, BRENDA
    (Actress)
b. June 25, c.1949, Shreveport, La.
Education: U.C.L.A.

Address: Sackheim Agency, 9301 Wilshire Blvd., Los Angeles,
    Calif.
Films: The Liberation of L. B. Jones, Getting Straight 1970; The
    Baby Maker 1970; Pretty Maids All in a Row, Honky, Skin
    Game 1971; Black Gunn 1972; Cleopatra Jones 1973; Mandingo
    1975; Drum 1976.
Memberships: SAG.
Television: The Dating Game; Mayberry R.F.D.; Room 222; My
    Friend Tony; Streets of San Francisco; Ozzie's Girls (series);
    The New People 1969; The Sheriff 1971; Young Love (Doris
    Day comedy series) 1971; Police Woman 1974; Harry O 1975;
    Mobile One 1975; Executive Suite (series) 1976; Love Boat
    1977.

SYREETA (Syreeta Wright)
    (Singer)
b. August 13, Pennsylvania.
Clubs: The Bottom Line; Troubadour (L.A.) 1974
Records: Stevie Wonder Presents (Motown); Syreeta; Signed Sealed
    and Delivered (with Stevie Wonder); I Wanna Be by Your Side.
Television: Soul Train 1974; Black News 1974; Mike Douglas Show
    1974.
Relationships: Former wife of Stevie Wonder, singer.

TAMU
    (Actress)
b. Brooklyn, N.Y.
Address: Rifkin-David, 9615 Brighton Way, Beverly Hills, Calif.
Career Data: Member, Al Fann Theatrical Ensemble; given her
    stage name by Amiri Baraka.
Films: Up the Sandbox, Come Back Charleston Blue 1972; Gordon's
    War 1973; Super Cops, Charlene in Claudine 1974.
Memberships: SAG.
Television: Maude (series); Police Story 1974; That's My Mama
    1975; Good Times 1976.
Theater: Slaveship 1969; King Heroin (O.B.) 1971; Ain't Supposed
    to Die a Natural Death 1971; Masks in Black (O.B.) 1974.

TANISHA, TA
    (Actress)
Address: Lil Cumber, 6515 Sunset Blvd., Los Angeles, Calif.
    90028.
Films: Halls of Anger 1970.
Memberships: SAG.
Television: Mission: Impossible; Bill Cosby Show; Mod Squad;
    Room 222; Barnaby Jones 1974; Lucas Tanner 1975; Sanford
    and Son 1975; Good Times 1976.

TARKINGTON, ROCKNE
    (Actor)

Films: South Pacific, The Buccaneer 1958; Porgy and Bess 1959;
        Soldier in the Rain 1963; The Great White Hope 1970; Melinda,
        Beware! The Blob 1972; title role in Black Samson 1974;
        Black Starlet 1976.
Memberships: SAG.
Television: Danger Island; The Shirley Temple Show; Meet McGraw;
        Day in Court; Man with a Camera; Tarzan; Have Gun Will
        Travel; The Red Skelton Show; The Texan; Andy Griffith Show;
        Police Story 1975; City of Angels 1976.
Theater: Picnic (Hollywood); The Grass Harp (Hollywood); A Raisin
        in the Sun (L.A.) 1960; Mandingo 1961.

TATUM, ART (Arthur Tatum)
        (Jazz Pianist)
b. October 13, 1910, Toledo, Ohio.
d. November 5, 1956, Los Angeles, Calif.
Special Interests: Violin.
Honors: Esquire (gold) award 1944; (silver) award 1945; (tied for
        silver) award 1947; Metronome Poll 1945; Down Beat Critics
        Poll 1954.
Career Data: Almost blind from birth; appeared in London 1938;
        formed his own band, then a trio (Slam Stewart, Tiny Grimes)
        1943.
Clubs: Onyx 1933; Three Deuces (Chicago).
Radio: Programs on WSPD (Toledo) and WUJ (Toledo).
Records: Solo Masterpieces (Pablo); Art Tatum: Solo Piano (Capi-
        tol); Dvorak's Humoresque; 9:20 Special; Massenet's Elegy;
        Tea for Two; Get Happy; Wee Baby Blues; Solos and Trio
        (Stinson); At the Crescendo (GNP); Footnotes to Jazz (Folk-
        ways); Genius (Black Lion); God Is in the House (Onyx); Group
        Masterpieces (Pablo); Masterpieces (MCA); Piano Starts Here
        (Columbia); Rarest Solos (CMS/SAGA).

TAYLOR, BILLY (William Edward Taylor)
        (Musician/Conductor)
b. July 21, 1921, Greenville, N.C.
Education: Virginia State College B. Mus. 1942, University of
        Massachusetts (Amherst) Ph.D. in Music Education 1975.
Special Interests: Piano, arranging, teaching.
Honors: Down Beat Critics' Poll New Star 1953.
Career Data: Member, Ben Webster quartet; Cozy Cole quintet
        1945; worked with Slam Stewart 1946; formed his own quartet
        1949-50; own trio 1952; worked with Dizzy Gillespie, Tito
        Puente, Ethel Smith, Gerry Mulligan, Slim Gaillard and
        others; vice president, Musicians Clinic; president, Jazzmobile
        1965-74; director, New York Jazz Repertory Co.; advisory
        board, on Jazz, Lincoln Center; taught at Columbia University,
        Yale University, C.W. Post College, Manhattan School of
        Music and other institutions; guest conductor, Oakland Sym-
        phony, Utah Symphony 1974, Minneapolis Symphony 1975.
Clubs: Three Deuces; Birdland 1951; Half Note 1974; Drake Hotel

1975; The Café in Hoppers 1976; New Barrister 1976.
Memberships: ASCAP; National Council on the Arts; N.Y. City
    Cultural Council.
Musical Compositions: More than 300 including Suite for Jazz
    Piano and Orchestra; Just the Thought of You; Midnight Piano;
    Feeling Frisky; Ever So Easy; A Bientot; Capricious; It's a
    Grand Night for Swinging; Theodora; I Wish I Knew How It
    Would Feel.
Radio: Own programs on WNEW and WLIB.
Records: Taylor Made Piano (Roost); Billy Taylor Introduces Ira
    Sullivan (ABC); My Fair Lady Loves Jazz (Impulse); A Bientot-
    Touch (Prestige).
Television: The Electric Company (music); Sesame Street (music);
    conductor, The Subject Is Jazz; conductor, David Frost Show
    (series) 1969-72; musical director, Black Journal 1975-76;
    Sunday 1976.
Theater: Seven Lively Arts 1945; Wesley in The Time of Your Life
    1955; appeared at Billie Holiday Theatre (Brooklyn); Carnegie
    Hall 1974; Delacorte Theatre 1975.

TAYLOR, CECIL (Percival)
    (Jazz Musician/Composer)
b. March 15, 1933, New York, N.Y.
Education: New York College of Music; New England Conservatory.
Special Interests: Piano.
Career Data: Formed his own quartet; helped organize Jazz Com-
    posers Guild 1965; participated in Newport Jazz Festival 1957.
Clubs: Five Spot 1975; Village Vanguard 1976; Village Gate 1977.
Musical Compositions: Ila Ila Todo 1973.
Records: Silent Tongues (Arista); Cecil Taylor in Transition (Blue
    Note); Conquistador (Blue Note); Spring of Two Blue-J's (Unit
    Core); Looking Ahead (Contemporary); Cafe Montmartre (Fan-
    tasy); Nefertiti, the Beautiful One (Arista/Freedom); Unit
    Structures (Blue Note).

TAYLOR, CLARICE
    (Actress)
b. September 20, Buckingham County, Va.
Education: New Theater School.
Special Interests: Directing.
Honors: Show Business award for best actress of 1969.
Films: Change of Mind 1969; Tell Me That You Love Me Junie Moon
    1970; Play Misty for Me, Such Good Friends 1971; Mrs.
    Brooks in Five on the Black Hand Side 1973; Willie Dynamite
    1974.
Memberships: ANT; The Committee for the Negro in the Arts;
    NEC.
Television: Ironside; Sanford and Son; Owen Marshall; Like It Is
    1973; Fanny in Wedding Band 1974; Salt and Pepe 1975;
    Sesame Street (series) 1977.
Theater: On Striver's Row (O.B. debut) 1943; Home Is the Hunter
    (ANT) 1945; Major Barbara (O.B.); A Medal for Willie (O.B.)

1951-1952; Gold Through the Trees (O.B.) 1952; In Splendid
Error (O.B.) 1954-1955; directed Trouble in Mind (O.B.)
1956; The Egg and I (O.B.) 1958; Simple Speaks His Mind
(O.B.); Nat Turner (O.B.) 1960; Wedding Band (O.B.) 1966;
God Is a (Guess What?) (NEC) 1968; Song of the Lusitanian
Bogey (NEC) 1968; Summer of the Seventeenth Doll (NEC)
1968; Kongi's Harvest (NEC) 1968; Daddy Goodness (NEC)
1968; An Evening of One Acts (NEC) 1969; Man Better Man
(NEC) 1969; Duplex (O.B.) 1969; Brotherhood (NEC) 1970;
Akokawe (NEC) 1970; Day of Absence (NEC) 1970; Sty of the
Blind Pig (O.B.) 1970; Five on the Black Hand Side (O.B.)
1970; Rosalee Pritchett (NEC) 1972; Addaperle in The Wiz
1975.

TAYLOR, LIBBY
       (Actress)
Career Data: Noted for servant roles in films of the 1930s and
       1940s.
Films: Jasmine in Belle of the Nineties 1934; Mississippi,
       Shanghai 1935; Fury and the Woman 1937; The Toy Wife 1938;
       The Great McGinty 1940; The Howards of Virginia 1940; Flight
       from Destiny 1941; My Gal Sal 1942; The Foxes of Harrow
       1947; Another Part of the Forest 1948; You're My Everything
       1949.
Memberships: SAG.

TEAGUE, BOB (Robert Teague)
       (Newscaster)
b. 1929, Milwaukee, Wisc.
Education: University of Wisconsin B.A.
Address: WNBC, 30 Rockefeller Plaza, New York, N.Y. 10020.
Honors: Harold Jackman Memorial award.
Career Data: Former "Big Ten" ranking half back; news reporter
       for National Broadcasting Company 1963.
Publications: Letters to a Black Boy, Walker, 1968.
Television: 11th Hour News (WNBC); News Center Four (WNBC).
Theater: Wrote Soul Yesterday and Today (based on Langston
       Hughes' work) 1969.

TEER, BARBARA ANN
       (Actress/Director)
b. June 18, 1937, East St. Louis, Ill.
Education: University of Illinois B.A. (Dance Education); studied
       drama with Sanford Meisner, Paul Mann, Phillip Burton and
       Lloyd Richards.
Special Interests: Dance, teaching, producing, writing.
Address: 213 West 137 Street, New York, N.Y. 10030.
Honors: Vernon Rice Drama Desk award (for Home Movies) 1965;
       AUDELCO Black Theatre Recognition award 1973; International
       Benin award 1974; National Assn. of Media Women's Black

Film Festival award (for Rise) 1975.

Career Data: Taught dance and drama in N. Y. C. public schools;
co-founder of the Group Theatre Workshop which later became
the Negro Ensemble Co.; danced with Alvin Ailey and Louis
Johnson Dance Companies; cultural director, teenage workshop, Harlem School of the Arts; founder, producing director
and playwright, The National Black Theatre 1968-date; created
Sunday Afternoon Blackenings and Ritualistic Revivals for tours
in theatres, colleges and universities throughout the East
Coast, the Caribbean and Nigeria; Theatre Committee for 2nd
International Black and African Festival of Arts and Culture
1975.

Films: Acted in Slaves 1969; acted in Angel Levine 1970; wrote,
produced and directed Rise/A Love Song for a Love People
1974.

Memberships: Black Theatre Alliance; bd. of dir., Theatre Communications Group; Harlem Philharmonic Society.

Publications: Contributing editor, Black Theatre Magazine; articles
for New York Times Sunday Drama Section.

Television: Black Heritage (CBS series); Lenox Avenue Sunday
(CBS Repertory Workshop); Soul; Positively Black 1976.

Theater: Acted in: Kwamina 1961; Living Premise (O.B.) 1963;
Home Movies (O.B.) 1965; Prodigal Son (O.B.) 1965; Who's
Got His Own (O.B.) 1966; The Experiment (O.B.) 1967;
Where's Daddy?; Day of Absence (O.B.) 1970. Directed:
The Believers (O.B.) 1969; Five on the Black Hand Side (O.
B.) 1970. Adapted and produced We Sing a New Song (O.B.).
Co-wrote: A Revival: Change/Love Together/Organize (NBT)
1972; Soul Journey into Truth (NBT) 1975.

Relationships: Former wife of Godfrey Cambridge, comedian.

THARPE, (SISTER) ROSETTA (Rosetta Nubin)
(Gospel Singer)
b. March 20, 1921, Cotton Plant, Ark.
Special Interests: Guitar.
Address: 759 South 19 Street, Philadelphia, Pa. 19146.
Career Data: Sang with Cab Calloway band and Lucky Millinder
band.
Clubs: Café Society; Cotton Club 1938.
Records: Precious Memories (Savoy); Singing in My Soul (Savoy).
Theater: Appeared at Apollo Theatre; Town Hall 1959.

THOMAS, PHILIP (Michael)
(Actor)
b. May 26, 1949, Columbus, Ohio.
Education: Oakwood College; University of California.
Address: Agency for Performing Arts, 9000 Sunset Blvd., Los
Angeles, Calif. 90067.
Films: Come Back Charleston Blue, Stigma 1972; Book of Numbers
1973; Coonskin, Mr. Ricco 1975; Sparkle 1976.
Memberships: SAG.

Television: Police Woman 1974; Caribe 1975; Movin' On 1976;
     Medical Center 1976; Roosevelt and Truman (pilot) 1977.
Theater: No Place to Be Somebody 1971; The Selling of the Presi-
     dent.

THOMPSON, ARTHUR CHARLES
     (Singer)
b. December 27, 1942, New York, N.Y.
Education: Hartt College of Music (Hartford, Conn.) B. Mus. 1965;
     Juilliard School of Music 1965-68; studied with Adele Addison
     at Aspen School of Music (Colorado) and with Hans Heinz
     (Dartmouth).
Address: 33 Riverside Drive, New York, N.Y. 10023.
Honors: Young concert artists auditions 1968; Ezio Pinza award
     1969; Marian Anderson award 1970.
Memberships: AEA; AGMA.
Radio: Listening Room (WQXR) 1974; Afro-Americans in Arts
     1975.
Records: Jake in Porgy and Bess (London) 1976.
Television: Young Artists (series) 1973.
Theater: Sang at Aspen Music Festival, Dartmouth Festival and
     with Metropolitan Opera, St. Louis Symphony, Milwaukee
     Symphony, Miami Symphony; Symphony of the New World at
     Avery Fisher Hall 1977.

THOMPSON, CLIVE
     (Dancer/Choreographer)
b. October 20, Kingston, Jamaica.
Education: University College of West Indies; Soohih School of Clas-
     sical Dance; Ivy Baxter's Dance Co.
Career Data: Represented Jamaica at Federal Festival of Arts
     1958; joined Martha Graham Company 1961; danced Legend of
     Judith, Circe for Martha Graham Troup; danced The Lark
     Descending for Alvin Ailey Dance Company 1975; danced in
     Blood Memories 1976.

THOMPSON, GARLAND LEE
     (Playwright)
b. February 14, 1938, Muskegee, Okla.
Address: 252 West 76 Street, New York, N.Y. 10023.
Honors: Winner 42nd annual One Act Tournament, Washington, D.C.
Career Data: Founder and director, Frank Silvera Writers Work-
     shop; Directors and Playwrights Unit, Actors Studio; founder,
     Black Theatre Alliance.
Theater: Stage manager, No Place to Be Somebody 1970; wrote
     Sisyphus and the Blue-Eyed Cyclops 1972; production stage
     manager, The River Niger 1973; wrote Papa Bee on the "D"
     Train 1975.

THURMAN, WALLACE
      (Playwright)
b. 1902, Salt Lake City, Utah.
d. December, 1934, New York, N.Y.
Education: University of Utah; University of Southern California.
Honors: Noted as being second black playwright to have work
      produced on Broadway.
Films: High School Girl (screenplay) 1935.
Theater: Wrote Harlem: A Melodrama of Negro Life in Harlem
      (a.k.a. Black Belt) 1929; Jeremiah the Magnificent 1930;
      Singing the Blues 1931; Savage Rhythm 1932.

TILLIS, FREDERICK (Charles)
      (Composer)
b. 1930, Galveston, Texas.
Education: Wiley College (Marshall, Texas); University of Iowa
      M.A., Ph.D.
Special Interests: Arranging, conducting, teaching.
Career Data: Director, 3560th Air Force Band 1954; guest com-
      poser, Symposium of Contemporary Music at Illinois Wesleyan
      University 1967; Festival of Contemporary Music, Spelman
      College 1968; head, music department, Kentucky State College
      1967-.
Musical Compositions: Design for Orchestra No. 2; Quartet for
      Flute; Passacaglia for Brass Quintet; Clarinet, Bassoon and
      Cello; The End of All Flesh, Baritone and Piano; A Prayer
      in Faith; Psalms; Capriccio for Viola and Piano; Concert Piece
      for Clarinet and Piano; Overture to a Dance Band; Militant
      Mood for Brass Sextet; String Trio; Phantasy for Viola and
      Piano; Passacaglia for Organ in Baroque Style; Brass Quintet;
      Quintet for Four Woodwinds and Percussion; Three Movements
      for Piano; Motions for Trombone and Piano; Music for Alto
      Flute, Cello and Piano; Sequences and Burlesque for Strings;
      Two Songs for Soprano and Piano; Music for an Experimental
      Lab Ensemble no. 1; Gloria: Music for an Experimental Lab
      Ensemble no. 2; Freedom-Memorial for Dr. Martin Luther
      King Jr. for Chorus; Music for Tape Recorder no. 1; Alleuia
      for Chorus; Three Plus One for Guitar, Clarinet and Tape
      Recorder 1969.

TODD, BEVERLY
      (Actress)
b. July 11, 1946, Ohio.
Special Interests: Singing.
Address: 870 Riverside Drive, New York, N.Y. 10032 and 3651
      Olympiad Drive, Los Angeles, Calif. 90043.
Clubs: Playboy; Paul's Mall (Boston); Key Club (Cleveland).
Films: Dolly Map 1967; Some Kind of a Nut, Lost Man 1969; They
      Call Me Mister Tibbs 1970; Brother John 1971.
Memberships: AEA; AFTRA; SAG.
Publications: Origins (a play written with Hazel Bryant and Hank
      Johnson) 1969.

Television: Today Show; Sunday Night at the Palladium (London);
     Night of the Diva; Wild Wild West; Summerkill; N.Y.P.D.;
     Which Side Are You On?; Love of Life (series); Tonight
     Show; Girl Talk; Deadlock 1969; J.T. 1970; Barnaby Jones
     1976; Six Characters in Search of an Author (PBS) 1976;
     Roots 1977.
Theater: The Owl and the Pussy Cat (London); Deep Are the Roots
     (O.B.) 1960; The Octoroon (O.B.) 1961; No Strings (London
     and on tour) 1963; Blues for Mister Charlie (London) 1964;
     Carry Me Back to Morningside Heights 1968; Gettin' It To-
     gether (O.B.) 1970.
Relationships: Wife of Kris Keiser, producer.

TOLBERT, BERLINDA
     (Actress)
b. November 4, 1949, Charlotte, N.C.
Education: North Carolina School for the Arts (Winston Salem)
     B.F.A.; Rose Bruford's School of Acting; Stockwell College
     (London).
Address: Twentieth Century Artists, 13273 Ventura Blvd., Studio
     City, Calif. 91604.
Films: Airport '75.
Memberships: SAG.
Television: Streets of San Francisco; Mannix; Sanford and Son;
     That's My Mama; Shoot Anything That Moves (PBS); Jennie
     in The Jeffersons (series) 1974-; Police Woman 1975.
Theater: What the Winesellers Buy 1973; Godspell (Washington,
     D.C.).
Relationships: Wife of Ray Vitte, actor.

TOLLIVER, MELBA
     (Broadcaster)
b. December 1939, Akron, Ohio.
Education: Columbia University (journalism); New York University;
     University of Michigan 1976-77.
Address: c/o WNBC-TV, 30 Rockefeller Plaza, New York, N.Y.
     10020 and William Morris Agency, 1350 Avenue of the Ameri-
     cas, New York, N.Y. 10019.
Honors: Outstanding Woman in Media (National Assn. of Media
     Women) 1975; National Endowment for the Humanities Fellow-
     ship 1976.
Television: (ABC) 1968-76: reporter, Eyewitness News; anchor
     person and associate producer, Sunday Hours News; co-host
     Like It Is; Melba Tolliver's New York; Americans All; People,
     Places and Things; One Life to Live 1974; Who's News? (Wide
     World of Entertainment) 1975; N.Y. Emmy Award Show 1976;
     News Center 4 (NBC) 1977-.
Theater: Co-host of Truckin (Black Theatre Alliance production at
     Harlem Cultural Council) 1974.

TREADWELL, GEORGE (McKinley)
    (Composer/Musician)
b. December 21, 1919, New Rochelle, N. Y.
Special Interests: Trumpet, arranging, theatrical booking.
Career Data: Played with bands of Benny Carter 1942-43, Tiny
    Bradshaw, Cootie Williams 1943-46; as theatrical representa-
    tive his clients included Ruth Brown, The Drifters, Sarah
    Vaughan.
Clubs: Monroe's Uptown House 1941-42; Café Society 1946.
Relationships: Former husband of Sarah Vaughan, singer.

TUBBS, VINCENT (Trenton)
    (Publicist)
b. September 25, 1915, Dallas, Texas.
Education: Morehouse College A. B. 1938; Atlanta University 1939;
    Blackstone College of Law LL. B. 1949.
Special Interests: Journalism.
Address: 4000 Warner Blvd., Burbank, Calif. 91522.
Honors: War Dept. citation 1947; Newsman's Newsman award;
    Windy City Press Club award 1957; Male Decision Maker in
    Communications, National Assn. of Media Women 1974; Black
    Filmmakers Hall of Fame 1974.
Career Data: Correspondent and Editor, Baltimore Afro-American
    1943-54; associate editor, Ebony 1954-55; managing editor,
    Jet Magazine 1955-59; founder and president, Windy City Press
    Club 1956; senior publicist, Warner Bros., American Interna-
    tional Pictures, Columbia, Paramount, CBS Cinema Center
    1959-71; director of community relations, Warner Bros. 1971-
    date.
Memberships: Academy of Motion Picture Arts and Sciences; Pub-
    licists Guild of America (Past President and Treasurer);
    Overseas Press Club; Hollywood Press Club.

TUCKER, LEM(UEL)
    (Broadcaster)
b. May 26, 1938, Saginaw, Mich.
Education: Central Michigan University B. A.; University of Michi-
    gan.
Address: 175 West 13 Street, New York, N. Y. 10011.
Memberships: AFTRA.
Television: News reporter, ABC-TV.

TUCKER, LORENZO "The Black Valentino"
    (Actor)
b. June 27, 1907, Philadelphia, Pa.
Education: Temple University; Cambridge School of Radio Broad-
    casting; The School of Radio Technique and Television Studios
    New York; N. Y. Institute of Photography.
Special Interests: Photography.
Address: 2109 Broadway, New York, N. Y. 10023.

Honors: Oscar Micheaux Film Makers award and Black Filmmakers
 Hall of Fame 1973.
Career Data: Starred in all-black cast silent films; worked the
 Borscht circuit as actor and manager; organized Negro Drama
 Players; organizer and president of Universal Theatre Co.
 (a repertory group); wrote, produced, directed and hosted
 shows for U.S. Army Air Force, World War II; managed shows
 for international artists.
Films: Wages of Sin, Fool's Errand 1926; Bewitching Eyes 1927;
 Easy Street, When Men Betray 1928; Daughter of the Congo
 1930; The Black King 1931; Veiled Aristocrats 1932; Harlem
 After Midnight 1934; Temptation 1936; The Underworld, Mira-
 cle in Harlem 1937; Straight to Heaven 1939; Boy, What a
 Girl!, One Round Jones 1946; Sepia Cinderella, Reat, Petite
 and Gone 1947.
Memberships: AEA; SAG.
Radio: The Vaudeville Theatre of the Air; The Unexplained; Heart
 of Gold; Triumph Over Yellow Jack.
Television: Free Time 1971.
Theater: Queen of Sheba; Ole Man Satan; Make Me Know It 1929;
 The Constant Sinner 1931; Humming Sam 1933; Harvey (tour);
 Bell Book and Candle (tour); Born Yesterday (tour); Spring
 Time for Henry (tour); Sheriff in Porgy and Bess (tour);
 Father in Anna Lucasta (England) 1952-54.

TURMAN, GLYNN (Russell)
 (Actor)
b. c.1946, New York, N.Y.
Education: High School of Performing Arts.
Special Interests: Singing, dancing.
Address: International Creative Management, 8899 Beverly Blvd.,
 Los Angeles, Calif. 90048.
Career Data: Tyrone Guthrie Theatre (Minneapolis); teacher, Inner
 City Cultural Center, Los Angeles.
Films: Five on the Black Hand Side 1973; Thomasine and Bushrod,
 Together Brothers 1974; Cooley High 1975; The River Niger,
 J.D.'s Revenge 1976.
Memberships: SAG.
Television: Sing a Song (debut); Hawaii Five-O; Room 222; Rookies;
 Lew Miles in Peyton Place (series) 1968; Carter's Army 1970;
 Mod Squad 1972; Ceremonies in Dark Old Men 1975; The Blue
 Knight 1975; Minstrel Man (special) 1976; This Far by Faith
 1977.
Theater: Member of Chorus in Puccini's Tosca (Amato Opera);
 Slow Dance on the Killing Ground (Los Angeles); One in a
 Crowd; Raisin in the Sun 1959; Who's Got His Own (O.B.)
 1966; Junebug Graduates Tonight (O.B.) 1967; What the Wine-
 sellers Buy 1974.

TURNER, TINA (Annie Mae Bullock)
 (Singer)

b. November 25, 1939, Brownsville, Tenn.
Address: Associated Booking, 445 Park Avenue, New York, N.Y. 10022.
Honors: Golden European Record award.
Career Data: Teamed at various times with Ike Turner, The Iketts, The King of Rhythm orchestra.
Clubs: Basin Street West (San Francisco); Barney Google's 1975; Empire Room-Waldorf Astoria 1976; Caesar's Palace 1977.
Films: The Big T.N.T. Show 1966; Taking Off, Soul to Soul 1971; The Acid Queen in Tommy 1975.
Records: Sexy Ida (United Artists); River Deep, Mountain High; Proud Mary; Honky Tonk Woman; Acid Queen (United Artists); Her Man, His Woman; Workin' Together; A Fool in Love (Sue) 1960; It's Gonna Work Out Fine (Sue) 1961; Country On (United Artists); Let Me Touch Your Mind (United Artists).
Television: Ike and Tina Turner Show; Ed Sullivan Show; Andy Williams Show; Name of the Game 1968; Soul Train 1975; Ann-Margaret Olsson (special) 1975; Don Kirshner's Rock Concert 1975; Mike Douglas Show 1975; Dinah! 1975; Mac Davis Show 1975; Cher 1975; Midnight Special 1975; Dick Van Dyke (special) 1975; Dancin' Time 1975; Gimme Shelter 1976; Hollywood Squares 1976; Donny and Marie 1976; The Brady Bunch Hour 1977; Merv Griffin Show 1977.
Theater: Appeared at Madison Square Garden (with Rolling Stones) 1969.
Relationships: Wife of Ike Turner, musician.

TYLER, WILLIE
    (Ventriloquist)
b. Detroit, Mich.
Career Data: Teams for act with puppet, Lester.
Clubs: Copacabana 1969, 1971; Blue Max Room-Regency Hyatt Hotel (Chicago).
Television: Ann Margaret Special 1969; Tonight Show 1969; Peggie Lee Variety Program 1970; Flip Wilson Show 1973; Sammy and Company 1975; Vegetable Soup 1975; Vaudeville 1975; American Bandstand 1976; Merv Griffin Show 1976; Apollo (special) 1976; Hagger Clothes commercial 1976; Music Hall America 1977.
Theater: Tour with Diana Ross 1964; appeared at Apollo Theatre 1974; Westbury Music Fair 1975.

TYNES, MARGARET
    (Opera Singer)
b. Virginia.
Career Data: Sang with New York City Opera Co.; repertoire includes Jenny in Weill's Mahagonny, Idamante in Idomeneo, title role in Salome, title role in Norma, title role in Tosca, title role in Aida, The Kaiserin in Die Frau Ohne Schatten, Lady Macbeth in Verdi's Macbeth, title role in Jenufa; Festival of Two Worlds, Spoleto 1961; The Music Festival of Coruña,

Spain 1968; debut with New York Metropolitan Opera Co. 1974.
Records: Porgy and Bess (DCF).
Television: Positively Black 1974.
Theater: Sang at Town Hall 1960.

TYSON, CICELY
     (Actress)
b. December 19, 1939, New York, N.Y.
Education: Charles Evans Hughes H.S.; New York University;
     Actors Studio; Lee Strasberg; Paul Mann Workshop; Barbara
     Watson Modeling School.
Address: William Morris Agency, 151 El Camino Drive, Beverly
     Hills, Calif. and 315 West 70 Street, New York, N.Y. 10023.
Honors: Vernon Rice Award 1962 (for Virtue in The Blacks); Vernon
     Rice Award 1962 (for Mavis in Moon on a Rainbow Shawl);
     NAACP Image Award (Best Actress) 1970; Nomination Academy
     of Motion Picture Arts & Sciences, Best Performance by
     Leading Actress in 1972; Emmy for best actress in a television
     comedy or drama special 1974; Best Actress Jamaica's First
     Black Film Festival 1974 (for Autobiography of Miss Jane
     Pittman); Black Filmmakers Hall of Fame 1977.
Career Data: Board of Governors, Urban Gateways (organization
     that exposes children to the arts); first vice-pres., board of
     directors, Dance Theatre of Harlem; trustee, American Film
     Institute.
Films: Odds Against Tomorrow, The Last Angry Man 1959; A Man
     Called Adam 1966; The Comedians 1967; The Heart Is a Lone-
     ly Hunter 1968; Rebecca Morgan in Sounder 1972; River Niger,
     Bluebird 1976.
Memberships: SAG.
Television: Between Yesterday and Today (Camera Three); Bill
     Cosby Show; Kup's Show; Soul; Dating Game; Americans: A
     Portrait in Verse (special); The Nurses; To Tell the Truth;
     Naked City; Frontiers of Faith; Brown Girl, Brown Stones
     1960; East Side/West Side (series) 1963; Slattery's People
     1965; I Spy 1965, 1966; The Guiding Light (series) 1967; Cow-
     boy in Africa 1967; The F.B.I. 1968, 1969; Medical Center
     1969; On Being Black 1969; Courtship of Eddie's Father 1969;
     Here Come the Brides 1969, 1970; Mission: Impossible 1970;
     Gunsmoke 1970; Marriage: Year One 1971; Emergency 1972;
     Wednesday Night Pout (pilot) 1972; The Autobiography of Miss
     Jane Pittman 1974; Mike Douglas Show 1974, 1976; Dream
     Girls of Hollywood (special) 1974; Marlo Thomas and Friends--
     Free to Be You and Me (special) 1975; Today 1975; Good
     Morning, America 1976; Merv Griffin Show 1976; Positively
     Black 1976; Dinah! 1976; Black Conversations 1976; Just an
     Old Sweet Song (General Electric Theater) 1976; Everybody
     Rides the Carousel 1976; Roots 1977.
Theater: Talent '59 1959; Jolly's Progress 1959; The Dark of the
     Moon (E.L.T.) 1960; The Cool World 1960; The Blacks (O.B.)
     1961; Moon on a Rainbow Shawl (O.B.) 1962; Tiger, Tiger,
     Burning Bright 1962; The Blue Boy in Black (O.B.) 1963; A
     Hand Is on the Gate 1966; Carry Me Back to Morningside

Heights 1968; Trumpets of the Lord 1968 (O.B. 1963); To Be
Young, Gifted and Black (O.B.) 1969; Desire Under the Elms
(Lake Forest, Illinois) 1974.

UGGAMS, LESLIE (Eloise C. Uggams)
    (Singer/Actress)
b. May 25, 1943, New York, N.Y.
Education: Professional Children's School; Juilliard School of Music.
Address: Kurt Frings Agency, 9440 Santa Monica Blvd., Beverly
    Hills, Calif.
Honors: Best Singer on TV 1962, 1963; Tony, Drama Critics and
    Theatre World awards (for Hallelujah Baby) 1969; Television
    Critics Circle Award (for Roots) 1977.
Clubs: Thunderbird (Las Vegas) 1975; Sahara (Las Vegas) 1976;
    Turn of the Century (Denver) 1976.
Films: Two Weeks in Another Town 1962; Black Girl, Skyjacked
    1972; Poor Pretty Eddie 1975.
Memberships: AEA; SAG.
Radio: Peter Lind Hayes/Mary Healy Show.
Records: What's an Uggams?; Leslie Uggams (Motown); I Want to
    Make It Easy for You.
Television: Ed Sullivan Show; Johnny Olsen's TV Kids (debut);
    Beulah 1945-50; Arthur Godfrey Show; Jack Paar Show; Milton
    Berle Star Time; Garry Moore Show; Name That Tune 1958;
    Sing Along with Mitch 1962; The Girl from U.N.C.L.E. 1966;
    The Leslie Uggams Show (series) 1969; Mod Squad 1972; Mar-
    cus Welby, M.D. 1974; Johnny Carson Tonight Show; Words
    and Music (special) 1974; Soul Train 1975; Ice Palace 1971;
    Magnificent Marble Machine 1975; Easter Is (cartoon) 1975;
    In Concert 1975; Hollywood Squares 1975; Dinah! 1975; Swing
    Out, Sweet Land 1976; Merv Griffin Show 1976; Your Choice
    for the Oscars (special) 1976; Perry Como's Spring in New
    Orleans (special) 1976; Tony Awards Show 1976; Celebrity
    Concert 1976; Kup's Show 1976; Roots 1977; Tony Awards
    Show 1977.
Theater: The Boy Friend (San Francisco); Hallelujah Baby 1967;
    Her First Roman 1968; Nanuet Theatre Go Round; Mill Run
    Playhouse (Chicago) 1974; Maria in West Side Story (tour)
    1976; Guys and Dolls (Aladdin Hotel, Las Vegas) 1977.

VAN PEEBLES, MELVIN
    (Actor/Director/Playwright)
b. August 21, 1932, Chicago, Illinois.
Education: Ohio Wesleyan University B.A. 1953.
Special Interests: Composing, singing.
Address: Suite 1203, 850 Seventh Avenue, New York, N.Y. 10019
    and 132 Rue d'Assas, Paris 6, France.
Honors: San Francisco Film Festival award 1967; Belgian Festival
    1st Prize; NAACP Image award best film director; Black Film-
    makers Hall of Fame 1976.
Clubs: The Bottom Line.

Films: Sunlight (short), Three Pickup Men for Herrick (short)
1957; directed The Story of a Three Day Pass (a.k.a. La
Permission) 1968; directed Watermelon Man 1970; wrote,
directed, produced and acted in Sweet Sweetback's Baadasssss
Song 1971; wrote and directed Don't Play Us Cheap.
Memberships: French Directors Guild; Directors Guild of America.
Publications: A Bear for the FBI (autobiography), Trident Press,
1968.
Records: What the ... You Mean I Can't Sing (Atlantic); Don't
Play Us Cheap (Yeah!).
Television: A.M. New York; Free Time 1971; Black Journal 1971,
1975, 1976; Today Show 1971; Midnight Special 1974; One to
One Telethon 1974; The Bachelor of the Year (Wide World
Special) 1974; Kup's Show 1975; wrote Just an Old Sweet Song
(General Electric Theater) 1976.
Theater: The Hostage (Dutch National Theatre tour); wrote Ain't
Supposed to Die a Natural Death 1971; wrote Don't Play Us
Cheap 1972.

VAN SCOTT, GLORY
(Actress/Dancer)
Education: Goddard College; Union Graduate School (Ohio) Ph.D.
(Educational Theatre).
Special Interests: Playwriting.
Career Data: Member, Katharine Dunham Company; member, The
American Ballet Theatre.
Memberships: AEA; NAG.
Television: Girl Talk; Look Up and Live; Mitch Miller Show; Sing
America Sing 1976.
Theater: Carmen Jones (City Center); Show Boat (City Center);
Kwamina 1961; Porgy and Bess (City Center) 1961; Fly Black-
bird (O.B.) 1962; Prodigal Son (O.B.) 1965; Who's Who Baby?
(O.B.) 1968; House of Flowers (O.B.) 1968; The Great White
Hope 1968; Billy No Name (O.B.) 1970; Don't Bother Me I
Can't Cope 1971-72; Step Lively Boys (O.B.) 1973; A Matter
of Time 1975; wrote Miss Truth: A Poetic Suite on Sojourner
Truth; acted in Love! Love! Love! (O.B.) 1977.

VAUGHAN, SARAH (Lou) "Miss Sassy"; "The Divine One"
(Singer)
b. March 27, 1924, Newark, N.J.
Address: Hidden Hills, San Fernando Valley, Calif. and c/o James
Harper, 13063 Ventura Blvd., Studio City, Calif. 91604.
Honors: Winner Apollo amateur contest 1942; Down Beat annual
vocalist award 1946-52; Esquire new star award 1947; Metro-
nome poll winner 1948-53.
Career Data: Sang with bands of Earl "Fatha" Hines 1943-44,
Billy Eckstine 1944-45; participated in Monterey Jazz Festival
1974 and Newport Jazz Festival 1974, 75.
Clubs: Fairmount (San Francisco); Broadmoor Hotel (Colorado
Springs); Copacabana 1945-46; Café Society 1946; Tropicana

(Las Vegas) 1970; St. Regis-Maisonette 1975.

Films: Rhythm and Blues Revue 1959.

Records: Echos of An Era (Roulette); Feelin' Good (Mainstream);
Life in Japan (Mainstream); More From Japan Live (Main-
stream); No Count Sarah (Trip); Send In The Clowns (Main-
stream); Time In My Life (Mainstream); You're Mine, You
(Roulette); Swingin' Easy (Trip); In The Land of Hi-Fi (Trip);
After Hours (Columbia Special Products); I Cover The Water-
front; Misty; Lullaby of Birdland; Don't Blame Me; Sassy
(Trip); Sarah Vaughan's Golden Hits (Mercury); It's Magic
(Musicraft) 1948; Make Yourself Comfortable (Mercury) 1954;
Mr. Wonderful (Mercury) 1956; Passing Strangers (Mercury)
1957; Broken Hearted Melody (Mercury) 1959.

Television: Ed Sullivan Show; This Is Music; Day at Night; Showtime at the Apollo 1954; In Performance at Wolf Trap (special) 1974; Mike Douglas Show 1975; Dinah! 1975; Smoganza
(special) 1975; Positively Black 1975; Sammy and Company
1975; Al Hirt Show 1975; Entertainment '76 Hall of Fame
awards 1976; Midnight Special 1976; Evening at Pops 1976;
Soundstage 1977.

Theater: Appeared at Paramount Theatre; Carnegie Hall; Apollo
Theatre; Symphony Hall (Boston); Music Center (L.A.);
Kennedy Center for the Performing Arts (Wash. D.C.); Nas-
sau Coliseum 1975; Avery Fisher Hall 1975, 1977; Symphony
Hall (Newark) 1975; Radio City Music Hall 1976; Hollywood
Bowl 1974, 1976.

Relationships: Former wife of George Treadwell, composer/musi-
cian.

VEREEN, BEN (Benjamin Augustus Vereen)
        (Singer/Dancer)
b. October 10, 1946, Miami, Fla.
Education: High School of Performing Arts; studied at Dance
Theatre of Harlem School; Manhattan's Pentecostal Theological
Seminary.
Address: Wm. Morris Agency, 1350 Avenue of the Americas, New
York, N.Y. 10019.
Honors: Tony nomination and Theatre World award for Jesus Christ
Superstar 1972; Tony and Drama Desk award for Pippin; Clio
for Pippin commercial; AGVA's Entertainer of the Year, Song
and Dance Star and Rising Star 1975; Television Critics Circle
Award (for Roots) 1977.
Clubs: Kutsher's Country Club (Monticello); Odysseus; Caesar's
Palace (Las Vegas) 1975; Empire Room-Waldorf Astoria 1975;
Diplomat (Hollywood by the Sea, Fla.) 1975; Persian Room-
Plaza 1976; Blue Max Room-Hyatt Regency Hotel (Chicago).
Films: Gas 1971; A Piece of the Action (doc.) 1974; Bert Robbins
in Funny Lady 1975.
Records: Off Stage (Buddah).
Television: Good Night America; Tonight Show; Clio Awards 1974;
Comin' at Ya (Summer series) 1975; Gladys Knight and the
Pips 1975; Merv Griffin Show 1975, 1976; Kup's Show 1975;

A.M. New York 1975; A.M. America 1975; Dinah! 1975; Black
News 1975; Mike Douglas Show 1975, 76; Positively Black
1975; Entertainment Hall of Fame Awards 1975; Midday Live
1975; Saturday Night Live with Howard Cosell 1975; Louis
Armstrong-Chicago Style 1976; Entertainer of the Year Awards
1976; Mary's Incredible Dream (special) 1976; American Music
Awards 1976; Today Show 1976; Jubilee (Bell Telephone Spe-
cial) 1976; Second Annual Comedy Awards 1976; Entertainment
Hall of Fame Awards '76 1976; Kup's Show 1976; Sammy and
Company 1976; Chicken George in Roots 1977; Evening at Pops
1977.
Theater: Jesus Christ Superstar; Hair; Prodigal Son (O.B. debut)
    1965; Sweet Charity (tour) 1967; Golden Boy (London) 1968;
    No Place to Be Somebody 1970; Pippin 1972-74; Westbury
    Music Fair 1975; Westchester Premier Theatre 1976; Mill
    Run Theatre (Chicago) 1976.

VERRETT, SHIRLEY
    (Opera Singer)
b.   May 31, 1931, New Orleans, La.
Education: Ventura College (California) A.A. 1951; Juilliard
    School of Music 1961; studied voice with Anna Fitziu and
    Marian Szekeley-Freschl.
Address: c/o Basil Horsfield Artists International Management,
    5 Regents Park Road, London NW 1, England.
Honors: Marian Anderson award 1955; Walter Naumberg award
    1958; Grantee, William Matteus Sullivan Fund 1959; Martha
    Baird Rockefeller Aid to Music Fund Fellowship 1959-61;
    Blanche Thebom award 1960; National Federation of Music
    Clubs award 1961; Ford Foundation Fellowship 1962-63.
Career Data: Appeared as soloist with Philadelphia Orchestra
    1960, N.Y. Philharmonic 1961-63, Washington Opera Society
    1962, Chicago Symphony 1963, Minneapolis Symphony 1963,
    Pittsburgh Symphony 1964; performed at Spoleto 1961, 62,
    Stratford (Ontario) Festival 1963; Lausanne (Switzerland)
    Festival 1964; operatic roles include Second prioress in Dia-
    logues of the Carmelites; Judith in Bluebeard's Castle; Norma;
    Dalila in Samson et Dalila; Carmen; Azucena in Il Trovatore;
    Clytemnestra in Oedipus Rex; Dido in The Trojans; Princess
    Selika in L'Africaine; Amneris in Aida; Neocle in Siege of
    Corinth; Leonora in La Favorita; Lady Macbeth in Macbeth;
    Amelia in Un Ballo in Maschera; Queen Elizabeth in Maria
    Stuarda; Queen of Judea; Metropolitan Opera debut in 1968.
Records: Norma; How Great Thou Art, Precious Lord 1964; Car-
    negie Hall Recital 1965; Seven Popular Spanish Songs 1965;
    Singing in the Storm 1966.
Television: Arthur Godfrey's Talent Scouts 1955; Ed Sullivan Show
    1963; Mike Douglas Show 1963; A.M. New York 1976.
Theater: Appeared at Town Hall (recital debut) 1958; Lost in the
    Stars 1958; Bolshoi Theatre (Moscow) 1963; La Scala (Milan);
    Carnegie Hall 1965; Covent Garden (London) 1967; Metropolitan
    Opera House (debut) 1968; San Francisco Opera House 1972.

VITTE, RAY
       (Actor)
b. New York, N. Y.
Address: Twentieth Century Artists, 13273 Ventura Blvd., Studio
       City, Calif. 91604.
Films: Airport '75 1975; Car Wash 1976.
Memberships: SAG.
Television: Sanford and Son; Police Story; Starsky and Hutch 1975;
       That's My Mama 1975; What's Happening 1977; Martinelli:
       Outside Man (pilot) 1977.
Theater: What the Winesellers Buy 1973.
Relationships: Husband of Berlinda Tolbert, actress.

WADE, ADAM (Patrick Henry Wade)
       (Singer/Actor)
b. March 17, 1935, Pittsburgh, Pa.
Education: Virginia State College 1952-55; University of Pittsburgh;
       studied acting with Al Fann.
Special Interests: Emceeing, modeling, announcing, teaching.
Address: 45 West 132 Street, New York, N. Y. 10037.
Honors: Billboard award 1960; Cash Box award 1960; Play Boy Jazz
       Poll nomination 1962; Clio award 1972 (for Virgin Islands 50
       Dollar Days); Clio award 1973 (for Baby Sitter Campbell Soup).
Career Data: Member, Al Fann Theatrical Ensemble 1970-75;
       teacher, Don Ramsey's Modeling School.
Clubs: Fontainebleau (Miami); Latin Casino (N. J.); Freemont Hotel
       (Las Vegas); Playboy (Ocho Rios, Jamaica).
Films: Shaft, The Anderson Tapes 1971; Across 110th Street, Come
       Back Charleston Blue, The Hot Rock, Shaft's Big Score,
       (trailer for) The Legend of Nigger Charley 1972; Brother on
       the Run (sang title song), Gordon's War 1973; Crazy Joe,
       Claudine, The Taking of Pelham 1-2-3, Serpico, Super Cops,
       Education of Sonny Carson 1974; Phantom of the Paradise 1974.
Memberships: AEA; AFTRA; SAG.
Radio: Reflections (WWRL); Sounds of the City (series) 1974-75;
       Barry Gray Show.
Records: And Then Came Adam 1960; Ruby 1960; Tell Her for Me
       1960; Take Good Care of Her 1961; The Writing on the Wall
       1961; As If I Didn't Know 1961; Tonight I Won't Be There 1961;
       Adam and Evening 1962; Very Good Year for Girls 1964; One
       Is a Lonely Number 1964.
Television: Adam Wade Presented by The Playboy Hotel of Jamaica
       (special); The FBI; Positively Black; Madigan; Adam-12; Nicky's
       World; The Edge of Night; Somerset; Where the Heart Is;
       Children's TV Workshop; Miss Teenage Black America; Like It
       Is; Eyewitness News; As the World Turns; Love of Life; Feelin'
       Good; commercials for Geritol, Mott's Tomato Juice, Final
       Touch fabric softener, Dream Whip, Campbell Soup; Della
       Reese Show; Merv Griffin Show; Virgin Island tourism com-
       mercial; Black News; Tonight Show; That Was the Year That
       Was; This Is the Year That Will Be; John Burroughs in Search
       for Tomorrow (series) 1971; Midday Live 1975; Mike Douglas

Show 1975; emceed Miss Black America Pageant 1974, 1975; hosted Musical Chairs (series) 1975; Flic My Bic commercial 1975; Sammy and Company 1976; Tattletales 1976; Street Killing 1976; Police Woman 1976.

Theater: Lost in the Stars (Pittsburgh Playhouse); Falling Apart (O.B.); Too Late (O.B.); My Sister, My Sister (O.B.); Hallelujah Baby (tour) 1968-69; Masks in Black '70 (tour) 1970; King Heroin (O.B.) 1971; Westbury Music Fair 1975; Guys and Dolls (Aladdin Hotel, Las Vegas) 1977.

WADE, ERNESTINE (JONES)
      (Actress)
b. Jackson, Miss.
Special Interests: Singing, organ.
Address: Warren Wever, 1104 S. Robertson Blvd., Los Angeles, Calif. 90035.
Career Data: Member, Hall Johnson choir 1939-45.
Films: Eddies Laugh Jamboree; The Song of the South 1946; The Girl He Left Behind 1956; Bernadine, Three Violent People, The Guns of Fort Petticoat 1957; Critic's Choice 1963.
Memberships: SAG.
Television: Jackson Five cartoon series (voice); Sapphire on Amos 'n' Andy (series) 1951-54; That's My Mama 1974; Tomorrow 1976.

WALCOTT, DEREK
      (Playwright)
b. 1930, Castries, St. Lucia.
Education: University of the West Indies (Jamaica) B.A. 1959.
Honors: Rockefeller Foundation Grant; Jamaica Drama Festival Prize 1958; Jamaica Government Award for contribution to the West Indian Theatre 1961; Obie (for Dream on Monkey Mountain) 1972.
Career Data: Founder and artistic director, Trinidad Theater Workshop, 1959-.
Films: In a Fine Castle (unproduced script).
Television: Black Journal 1972.
Theater: Wrote Henri Christophe; The Sea at Dauphin; The Charlatan; Franklin, A Tale of the Island; Malcochon 1969; Dream on Monkey Mountain 1971; wrote and directed Ti Jean and His Brothers 1972; appeared reading his works at Hunter College Playhouse 1972; Remembrance.

WALKER, ADA OVERTON
      (Entertainer)
b. 1880, New York, N.Y.
d. October 10, 1914.
Special Interests: Dancing, singing, comedy.
Career Data: Performed for Black Patti Co., Williams and Walker Co. and The Frogs.
Theater: Sons of Ham 1900-01; In Dahomey 1902-05; Abyssinia 1906;

The Red Moon 1907; Bandana Land 1908-09; The Smart Set 1911.
Relationships: Wife of George W. Walker, entertainer.

WALKER, BILL
(Actor)
Films: The Killers 1946; Free for All, Sand, Bad Boy 1949; Bright Leaf, No Way Out 1950; The Harlem Globetrotters, Francis Goes to the Races, The Well, The Family Secret 1951; Night Without Sleep, Bloodhounds of Broadway, Lydia Bailey 1952, Killer Leopard, The Outcast 1954; Good Morning, Miss Dove, The Big Knife, Queen Bee, A Man Called Peter, Prince of Players, The View from Pompey's Head 1955; A Kiss Before Dying 1956; Hot Spell, Ride a Crooked Mile 1958; Porgy and Bess 1959; The Mask 1961; To Kill a Mockingbird 1962; Wall of Noise 1963; Kisses for My President 1964; The Third Day 1965; A Dream of Kings, Riot 1969; The Great White Hope, Tick... Tick... Tick... 1970; Big Jake 1971; Maurie 1973.
Memberships: SAG.
Television: Perry Mason; Run, Joe, Run; Alfred Hitchcock Presents; Good Times; Another Part of the Forest (Hollywood Television Theatre) 1972; Rockford Files 1976.

WALKER, GEORGE THEOPHILUS
(Composer/Pianist)
b. June 27, 1922, Washington, D.C.
Education: Oberlin College B. Mus. 1941; Curtis Institute of Music (Philadelphia) 1945; Conservatoire Americaine (Fontainebleau, France) 1947; Eastman School of Music (Rochester) 1957.
Special Interests: Teaching.
Honors: Philadelphia youth auditions winner 1945; John Hay Whitney Fellowship; Fulbright Fellowship 1957; Bok award 1963; Harvey Gaul Prize 1964; MacDowell Colony Fellowship 1966-69; Rhea Sosland Chamber Music Contest award 1967; Guggenheim Fellowship 1969; Rockefeller Foundation Grant 1970.
Career Data: Taught at Dillard University, Smith College, New School for Social Research, Rutgers University; participated in the Bennington Composers Conference; soloist, World Youth Festival Prague, Czeckoslovakia 1947; Cherry Blossom Festival, National Gallery of Art (Washington, D.C.) 1948; concert tours of U.S., Canada, Europe and the West Indies.
Musical Compositions: So We'll Go-A-Roving; The Bereaved Maid; Lament; I Went to Heaven; Two Poems; Piano Sonatas nos. 1 & 2; Sonata for Violin and Piano; Stars for Mixed Chorus; Sonata for Cello and Piano; Spatials; Fifteen Songs; Concerto for Trombone and Orchestra; String Quartet; Ten Works for Chorus; Perimeters for Clarinet and Piano; Three Lyrics for Chorus; Caprice; Lyric for MK 1946; Gloria in Memoriam 1963.
Theater: Town Hall (debut) 1945, 1958; Carnegie Hall 1948.

WALKER, GEORGE W.
    (Entertainer)
b. 1873, Lawrence, Kan.
d. January 6, 1911, Central Islip, L.I.
Special Interests: Composing, singing, comedy.
Career Data: Teamed with Bert Williams as vaudeville act Williams
    and Walker (a.k.a. Two Real Coons) 1895.
Memberships: The Frogs (a theatrical association).
Theater: Co-wrote Sons of Ham 1899; appeared in In Dahomey 1902;
    Abyssinia 1906; Bandana Land 1908.
Relationships: Husband of Ada Overton Walker, actress.

WALKER, JIMMIE "The Black Prince" (James C. Walker)
    (Comedian)
b. June 25, 1949, Bronx, N.Y.
Education: De Witt Clinton High School; City College of New York.
Special Interests: Acting, writing.
Address: International Creative Management, 8899 Beverly Blvd.,
    Los Angeles, Calif. 90048.
Honors: Most Popular TV Performer, Family Circle Magazine
    1975; NAACP Image Award best actor in television series
    1975.
Career Data: Member, The Last Poets.
Clubs: East Wind; Folk City; Champagne Gallery; Bitter End; Catch
    a Rising Star; At the Metro; The African Room; Upstairs at
    the Downstairs; The Improvisation; Comedy Store (L.A.); Play-
    boy (Boston); Grossingers 1975; Riviera (Las Vegas) 1975;
    Buddy's Place 1975; Diplomat (Hollywood by the Sea, Fla.)
    1975; Cellar Door (Washington, D.C.) 1975; Tamiment (Pa.)
    1976; Latin Casino (Cherry Hill, N.J.) 1976.
Films: The Last Detail, Badge 373 1974; Let's Do It Again 1975.
Memberships: SAG.
Records: Dyn-O-Mite (Buddah) 1975.
Television: Jack Paar Show (debut); Calucci's Department (audience
    warmup); The Nancy Wilson Show (L.A.); J.J. in Good Times
    (series) 1974-date; Comedy World; $10,000 Pyramid; Tony
    Orlando and Dawn Show; Perry Como's Summer of '74; Match
    Game 1974, 1975; Dinah! 1974, 1975; Cotton Club '75 1974;
    Mike Douglas Show 1974, 1975; Tattletales 1974; Merv Griffin
    Show 1975, 1976; Celebrity Sweepstakes 1975, 1976; American
    Bandstand 1975; Wide World Special 1975; The First Annual
    Comedy Awards 1975; Hollywood Squares 1975; Smoganza (spe-
    cial) 1975; American Music Awards 1975; People's Choice
    Awards 1975; Cher 1975; Panasonic commercial 1975; Gladys
    Knight and the Pips (special) 1975; Magnificent Marble Machine
    1975; Rhyme and Reason 1975; The Dyn-O-Mite Saturday Pre-
    view (special) 1975; Donny and Marie 1975; Phil Donahue Show
    1975; Midnight Special 1975; Supernight at the Superbowl (spe-
    cial); Joys (Bob Hope Special); Kup's Show 1976; Tonight Show
    1976; Second Annual Comedy Awards 1976; Black News 1976;
    Sammy and Company 1976; The John Davidson Show (special)
    1976; Good Morning, America 1976; Bob Hope Bicentennial

Special (cameo) 1976; Dean Martin Roasts Angie Dickinson
1977; Love Boat 1977.
Theater: Appearances at Apollo Theatre; Westbury Music Fair
1975; Paramount Theatre (Oakland, Ca.) 1975.

WALKER, JOSEPH A.
(Playwright)
b. February 23, 1935.
Education: Howard University B.A.; Catholic University M.F.A.
1970.
Special Interests: Acting, directing, choreography.
Honors: Obie award 1973; Tony award 1973; AUDELCO Black
Theatre Recognition award 1973.
Career Data: Howard University Players; Negro Ensemble Company;
co-founder and artistic director, The Demi-Gods (repertory
company); playwright in residence, Yale University; professor,
Speech and Theatre Department, City College of New York.
Films: Acted in: April Fools 1969; Bananas 1971.
Television: Narrated In Black America; acted in Deadly Circle of
Violence (N.Y.P.D.); appeared on Postively Black 1976.
Theater: Wrote: The Believers 1968; Ododo 1968; The Harangues
1969; Themes of the Black Struggle 1970; The River Niger
1972; Yin-Yang 1973; The Lion Is a Soul Brother 1976; The
Hiss; Old Judge Mose Is Dead; Out of the Ashes; Tribal
Harangue Two.

WALLACE, ROYCE
(Actress)
b. c.1923.
Special Interests: Singing.
Address: 156-20 Riverside Drive, New York, N.Y. 10024.
Career Data: Member, Karamu Playhouse, Cleveland, Ohio.
Clubs: Village Vanguard 1951; Chez Nous (Paris); The Mars Club
(Germany).
Films: Take a Giant Step 1961; Goodbye, Columbus 1969; Willie
Dynamite 1974; Funny Lady 1975.
Television: East Side/West Side; The Storefront Lawyers 1970;
Shaft; The Waltons 1973; Barnaby Jones 1975; Good Times
1976; The Last of Mrs. Lincoln 1976.
Theater: Carmen Jones (debut); St. Louis Woman 1946; Beggars
Holiday 1946; Lysistrata 1946; Inside U.S.A. 1948; Arms and
the Girl 1950; Happy as Larry 1950; Dark of the Moon (ELT)
1950; Take a Giant Step (O.B.) 1956; Jamaica 1957; Talent
58 1958; On the Town (O.B.) 1959; The Pretender (O.B.)
1960; My Mother, My Father and Me 1963; Funny Girl 1964.

WALLER, "FATS" (Thomas Wright Waller)
(Musician)
b. May 21, 1904, New York, N.Y.
d. December 15, 1943, Kansas City, Mo.

Special Interests: Composing, piano, organ, singing.
Career Data: Played with bands of Fletcher Henderson, Erskine
        Tate 1925 and his own orchestra 1941-42; accompanist to Bes-
        sie Smith (tour) 1926; collaborated with Andy Razaf, lyricist.
Clubs: Panther Room-Sherman Hotel (Chicago); Cabaine Cuban;
        Boudon's Cafe; Gavarnie's Melody Bar (Paris); Connie's Inn
        1929; Sebastian's Cotton Club (L.A.) 1935; Famous Door;
        Yacht Club 1938; Tic Toc Club (Boston) 1943; Zanzibar Club
        (L.A.) 1943.
Films: Hooray for Love 1935; King of Burlesque 1936; Stormy
        Weather 1943.
Memberships: ASCAP 1931.
Musical Compositions: Boston Blues (a.k.a. Squeeze Me); Honey-
        suckle Rose; Ain't Misbehavin'; The Spider and the Fly; Willow
        Tree; My Fate Is in Your Hands; I've Got a Feeling I'm Fall-
        ing; I'm Crazy 'Bout My Baby; Take It from Me; Harlem Fuss;
        Viper's Drag; Numb Fumblin'; St. Louis Shuffle; Handful of
        Keys; Rollin' Down the River; Black and Blue; Georgia Bo Bo;
        I'm Gonna Sit Right Down and Write Myself a Letter; Jitterbug
        Waltz; Blue Turning Grey Over You; Keeping Out of Mischief
        Now.
Radio: CBS (with his Beale Street Boys); WABC (series) 1930; WLW
        (Cincinnati) 1932.
Records: The Fats Waller Legacy; African Ripples; The Complete
        Fats Waller vol. 1 (Smithsonian); Ain't Misbehavin' (RCA);
        The Complete Fats Waller (Bluebird); A Legend in His Life-
        time (Trip); On the Air (Trip); Rare Piano Rolls (Biograph);
        Undiscovered (Stanyan).
Television: Back to U.S.A. (B.B.C.) 1938.
Theater: Appeared at Empire Theater (Glasgow); organist at Laf-
        ayette and Lincoln Theatres (Harlem) 1923; appeared at Para-
        mount Theatre; Vendome, Regal, Metropolitan Theatres (Chi-
        cago) 1927; performed and wrote score for Keep Shufflin' 1928;
        Carnegie Hall 1928, 1942; wrote score for Hot Chocolates 1929;
        appeared in Blackbirds of 1930; Apollo Theatre 1935; wrote
        score for Early to Bed 1943.

WAN, MADAME SUL TE (Nellie Conley)
        (Actress)
b. September 12, 1873, Louisville, Ky.
d. February 1, 1959, Hollywood, Calif.
Films: The Birth of a Nation 1915; Narrow Street 1925; Uncle
        Tom's Cabin 1927; Thunderbolt 1929; Heaven on Earth 1931;
        Ladies They Talk About 1933; Black Moon 1934; Tituba in Maid
        of Salem 1937; Kentucky, In Old Chicago 1938; Maryland 1940;
        Rhapsody in Blue 1945; Carmen Jones 1954; The Buccaneer 1958.

WARD, CLARA
        (Gospel Singer)
b. April 21, 1924, Philadelphia, Pa.
d. January 16, 1973, Los Angeles, Calif.

Special Interests: Arranging, conducting, composing.
Honors: Gold record; Grammy nominee.
Career Data: Leader, The Ward Singers; performed at Newport
    Jazz Festival 1957.
Clubs: Village Vanguard 1961; Caesar's Palace (Las Vegas); The
    Bitter End; New Frontier (Las Vegas) 1962-64.
Films: It's Your Thing.
Records: Surely God Is Able; Clara Ward Memorial Album (Savoy);
    Receive Me Lord (Nashboro); We Remember Clara Ward
    (HOB).
Theater: Appeared at Apollo Theatre; Olympia Theatre (Paris);
    Ziegfeld Theatre; Carnegie Hall; Tambourines to Glory (O.B.)
    1963; God Is Back Black 1969; Singing Gospel 1969.

WARD, DOUGLAS TURNER
    (Actor/Playwright)
b. May 5, 1930, Burnside, La.
Education: Wilberforce University; University of Michigan; Paul
    Mann Actors Workshop.
Special Interests: Directing.
Address: 222 East 11 Street, New York, N.Y. 10003.
Honors: Margo Jones award; Vernon Rice Drama Desk award and
    Obie (for playwright of Happy Ending) 1966; Tony nomination
    as best supporting actor (The River Niger) 1974; AUDELCO
    theatre recognition award 1974.
Career Data: Co-founder (with Robert Hooks) of Negro Ensemble
    Company 1967.
Films: Acted in Man and Boy 1972.
Memberships: AEA.
Television: Acted in: Dupont Show of the Month; Studio One; East
    Side West Side; The Edge of Night; Look Up and Live; Bicen-
    tennial: A Black Perspective 1975; Sunday 1975; Ceremonies
    in Dark Old Men 1975; Like It Is 1975. Directed The First
    Breeze of Summer 1976; Black Pride 1976.
Theater: Wrote: Happy Ending 1965; The Reckoning 1969; Brother-
    hood 1970. Acted in: The Iceman Cometh (O.B.); Frederick
    Douglass Through His Own Words (O.B.); Land Beyond the
    River (O.B.) 1957; Lost in the Stars (City Center) 1957; A
    Raisin in the Sun (Bway debut) 1959; The Blacks (O.B.) 1961-
    62; Pullman Car Hiawatha (O.B.) 1962; One Flew Over the
    Cuckoo's Nest 1963; Bloodknot (O.B.) 1964; Rich Little Rich
    Girl (Pre-Bway) 1964; Happy Ending (O.B.) 1965; Coriolanus
    (NYSF) 1965; Day of Absence (O.B.) 1965; Kongi's Harvest
    (NEC) 1968; Daddy Goodness (NEC) 1968; The Reckoning (O.
    B.) 1969; Ceremonies in Dark Old Men (NEC) 1969; The
    Harangues (NEC) 1970; The River Niger (NEC) 1972; The
    Brownsville Raid (NEC) 1976. Directed: Daddy Goodness
    (NEC) 1968; Contribution (NEC) 1969; The River Niger (O.B.
    and Bway) 1972-73; The Great MacDaddy (NEC) 1974; Waiting
    for Mongo (O.B.) 1975; The First Breeze of Summer 1975;
    Livin' Fat (NEC) 1976.

WARD, RICHARD (Richard Waugh)
    (Actor)
b. March 15, 1915, Glenside, Pa.
Education: Tuskegee Institute.
Special Interests: Writing, teaching, directing, producing.
Address: 411 East 10 Street, New York, N.Y. 10009.
Honors: Award for best short story in Saturday Evening Post
    1947.
Career Data: Vaudeville tour with Florida Blossoms as Dot, Flo
    and Dick 1928-32; later toured as emcee throughout U.S. and
    Canada; member of American Negro Theatre; founder and di-
    rector (drama dept.) of the International School of Performing
    Arts 1960; directed at Hartford Stage Co. (Hartford, Conn.)
    and Center Stage (Baltimore, Md.).
Films: Tarzan (M.G.M. series) 1937-39; Public Enemy #1 (a.k.a.
    The Most Wanted Man in the World) (French) 1962; Black Like
    Me, The Cool World, Nothing But a Man 1964; The Learning
    Tree 1969; Brother John 1971; Across 110th Street 1972;
    Cops and Robbers 1973; For Pete's Sake 1974; Mandingo 1975.
Memberships: AEA; AFTRA; NAG; SAG; SSD; Author's Guild;
    Dramatist's Guild.
Publications: Penance (3 act drama); Rock & Roll Has Gotta Go
    (2 act musical); The Long Chase (TV script).
Television: Wrote When the World Has Found a Man (Camera
    Three); acted in Studio One; Playhouse 90; Kraft Theatre;
    Danger; Naked City; The Immortal; Barefoot in Athens; The
    Little People; Snap Finger Creek; Our American Heritage; Sty
    of the Blind Pig; Savings Bank Assn. of N.Y. commercial;
    Harlem Detective (series) 1953-54; The Green Pastures (Hall-
    mark Hall of Fame) 1957; Black Monday (Play of the Week)
    1961; Petrocelli; N.Y.P.D.; Sanford and Son; Starsky and
    Hutch; Baretta; William Piper in Beacon Hill (series) 1975;
    Good Times 1975; The Jeffersons 1976; Mary Hartman, Mary
    Hartman 1977.
Theater: South Sea Island Holiday (European tour) 1933; St. Louis
    Woman 1946; Jeb 1946; Ride the Right Bus (People's Showcase
    Theatre) 1951; Shuffle Along 1952; Anna Lucasta (European
    tour) 1954; Member of the Wedding (tour) 1956; Portrait of a
    Madonna and A Happy Journey (Berlin) 1957; A Land Beyond
    the River (O.B.) 1957; Christopher Columbus Brown (O.B.);
    The Cellar (O.B.); My Heart's in the Highlands (O.B.); The
    Midnite Caller (O.B.) 1958; The Man Who Never Died (O.B.)
    1958; The Ballad of Jazz Street (O.B.) 1959; title role in Nat
    Turner (O.B.) 1960; produced Giovanni's Room (International
    School of Performing Arts) 1960; Walk in Darkness (O.B.)
    1963; The Firebugs (O.B.) 1963; Blues for Mr. Charlie 1964;
    The Amen Corner (European tour) 1965; The Sweet Enemy
    (O.B.); Banners of Steel (O.B.); Bedford Forrest (O.B.);
    Willie Loman in Death of a Salesman (Center Stage, Balti-
    more); Ceremonies in Dark Old Men (Center Stage, Baltimore);
    directed An American Night Cry (O.B.) 1974; Every Night
    When the Sun Goes Down 1976.

WARD, THEODORE
        (Playwright)
b. September 15, 1902, Thibodeaux, La.
Education: University of Utah.
Honors: Zona Gale fellowship for creative writing; AUDELCO
        Black Theatre Outstanding Pioneer 1975.
Career Data: Co-founder/member, Negro Playwrights Co.
Theater: Wrote Big White Fog: A Negro Tragedy 1937, The Life
        of Harriet Tubman; The Daubers; Falcoln of Adowa; Our Lan'
        1946; John Brown 1949; Sick and Tired; Skin Deep; Whole Hog
        or Nothing.

WARFIELD, MARLENE
        (Actress)
b. June 19, 1941, New York, N.Y.
Education: Brooklyn Conservatory of Music; N.Y. Actors Repertory
        Theatre; José Quintero's Circle in the Square workshop; Lee
        Strasberg's workshop.
Career Data: Former member, Bill Frank Dance Co.; former
        member, Lincoln Center Repertory Co.
Films: Joe, The Great White Hope 1970; Across 110th Street 1972;
        Network 1976.
Memberships: AEA; SAG.
Television: The Nurses; The Defenders; For the People; Wide
        Wide World; Fab commercial (voice); The Time Is Now
        (Name of the Game) 1970; Cutter 1972; Madigan--The Midtown
        Beat 1973; Hortense in Beacon Hill (series) 1975; That's My
        Mama 1975; Maude (series) 1977.
Theater: Androcles and the Lion (LRC); The Bald Soprano (LRC);
        Thurber Carnival (LRC); Taming of the Shrew (LCR); Electra
        (O.B.); Antigone (O.B.); Cradle Song (O.B.); The Owl and
        the Pussycat (Canada); The Blacks (O.B.) 1962; A Matter of
        Life and Death (O.B.) 1963; Who's Got His Own (N.Y. State
        Council of the Arts) 1966; Helena in Alls Well That Ends
        Well (NYSF) 1967; Celia in Volpone (NYSF) 1967; The Great
        White Hope 1968; title role in Janie Jackson (London) 1968;
        A Midsummer Night's Dream (NYSF) 1975; So Nice They
        Named It Twice (O.B.) 1975.

WARFIELD, WILLIAM (C.)
        (Singer/Actor)
b. January 22, 1920, West Helena, Ark.
Education: Eastern School of Music (Rochester) B. Mus. 1942;
        American Theatre Wing 1948-50; studied with Rosa Ponselle
        1958-65.
Special Interests: Teaching.
Address: c/o Larney Goodkind, 30 East 60 Street, New York,
        N.Y. 10022.
Honors: National Music Educators Competition 1st Prize; Gold
        Medal from Emperor Haile Selassie, Ethiopia.
Career Data: Since 1950, toured U.S., Africa, Europe, Near

East; Berkshire Music Festival, Tanglewood; toured Australia 1950, 1958, Europe with Philadelphia Orchestra 1956; Africa and Middle East 1956; Asia 1958; Brussels World's Fair, Belgium 1958; Cuba 1959; Casals Festival in Puerto Rico 1962, 1963; Arts Festival in Brazil 1963; Western Europe 1964; repertoire includes Handel's Messiah, Bach's St. Matthew Passion, Mendelssohn's Elijah, Mozart's Requiem, Verdi's Requiem, Casal's El Peselbre, Bloch's Hebrew Service, Berlioz' Romeo and Juliet, Menotti's Death of the Archbishop of Brindisi, Schoenberg's Gurre Lieder; professor of music, University of Illinois, Champaign-Urbana.

Films: Joe in Show Boat 1951; narrated Masters of the Congo Jungle 1960; That's Entertainment 1974.

Memberships: AEA; AFTRA; AGMA; SAG.

Records: Show Boat (M.G.M.); Porgy in Porgy and Bess (RCA).

Television: DeLawd in The Green Pastures (Hallmark Hall of Fame) 1957.

Theater: Hollywood Bowl; Lewisohn Stadium; Symphony Hall (Atlanta); Garden State Arts Center (New Jersey); Call Me Mister 1947-48; Aneas in Set My People Free (debut) 1948; Cal, the butler in Regina 1949; Town Hall (debut) 1950; Porgy in Porgy and Bess (Bway and Europe tour) 1952-53, (City Center) 1961, 1964; Joe in Show Boat (City Center) 1966; Alice Tully Hall 1970; Central Park Mall 1975; Carnegie Hall 1975.

Relationships: Former husband of Leontyne Price, opera singer.

WARREN, MARK (Edward)
    (Director)
b. September 24, 1938, Harrodsburg, Ky.

Education: Lincoln Institute 1955; Pennsylvania State University B.A. (theatre).

Special Interests: Producing.

Honors: Emmy as best director of a musical variety series 1971; Sickle Cell Research Special award 1972; NAACP Image award 1973.

Films: Come Back Charleston Blue 1972.

Memberships: Directors Guild of America; Los Angeles Film Development Council; NATAS; American Academy of Humor.

Television: Rowan & Martin's Laugh-In (series); Bill Cosby Show (series); Burns and Schreiber Comedy Hour; Sanford and Son (series); Funny Side of Sports (special); Diahann Carroll (special); Get Christie Love 1974; Cotton Club 75 (special) 1974; Salute to Redd Foxx 1974; Joey [Heatherton] and Dad 1975; Second Annual Unofficial Bachelor of the Year Awards 1975; Cher 1975; Diahann Carroll Show 1976; What's Happening 1976.

Theater: Selma (L.A.) 1975.

WARWICK, DIONNE (Dionne Warrick)
    (Singer)
b. December 12, 1940, East Orange, N.J.

Education: Hartt School of Music; University of Hartford (Conn.).
Special Interests: Acting, piano.
Address: c/o Wand Management, 254 West 54 Street, New York,
N.Y. 10019.
Honors: National Assn. of Record Merchandisers most popular
female vocalist 1964, 1970; Cash Box Poll as number one
R & B singer and number two pop singer 1966; Gold record
1968; Grammy 1969, 1971; NAACP Image Award 1971, 1974
Howard University Hasty Pudding Award Woman of the Year
1970; B'nai B'rith Creative Achievement Award 1971.
Career Data: Vocalist with Bill Elliott band; participated in Cannes
Television and Film Festival 1964, San Remo Festival and
Newport Jazz Festival 1968; night club and concert tours in-
clude Europe, South America, Mexico and Japan; owns boutique
in Beverly Hills.
Clubs: Harrahs (Tahoe); Savoy Hotel (London) 1965; Diplomat Hotel
(Hollywood by the Sea, Florida) 1971, 1975; Riviera (Las Ve-
gas) 1972, 1975; Shady Grove (Wash. D.C.) 1975; Cunard
International Hotel (London) 1975.
Films: Acted in Slaves 1969; The April Fools (theme song) 1969;
Valley of the Dolls (theme song) 1967; The Love Machine
(theme song) 1971.
Records: On Scepter: From Within; Greatest Motion Picture Hits;
Here I Am; Here Is Love; Magic of Believing; Make Way;
Soulful; The Golden Hits; Don't Make Me Over 1962; Anyone
Who Had a Heart 1963; Walk on By 1964; A House Is Not a
Home 1964; Message to Michael 1966; Alfie 1967; I Say a
Little Prayer 1967; Do You Know the Way to San Jose 1968;
Promises, Promises 1968; This Girl's in Love with You 1969;
I'll Never Fall in Love Again 1970; A Decade of Gold 1972.
On Warner Bros.: Track of the Cat; Dionne 1972; Just Being
Myself 1973; Then Came You 1975. On Springboard Interna-
tional: One Hit After Another; ...Sings Her Very Best;
Greatest Hits; A Man and a Woman (ABC); Very Dionne
Dionne (Pickwick); Make It Easy on Yourself (Pickwick) 1970.
Television: Music Country USA; Merv Griffin Show; Hollywood
Squares; Bob Hope (special); Hullabaloo 1965, 66; The Dupont
Show 1966; Garry Moore Show 1966; Tonight Show 1966, 1976;
Grand Gale Du Disque (Amsterdam) 1966; Ed Sullivan Show
1967, 68; Song Makers (special) 1967; Carol Burnett Show
1967, 68; Red Skelton Show 1967, 68; Kraft Music Hall 1967;
Operation Entertainment 1968; Jerry Lewis Show 1968; Name
of the Game 1968; Jose Feliciano (special) 1969; Glen Camp-
bell Show 1969; Dionne Warwick (special) 1969; Marlo Thomas
and Friends (special) 1975; Dinah! 1975; Dionne Warwick (special) 1975; Dean Martin Comedy Hour (Roasting of Sammy
Davis Jr.) 1975; Soul Train 1975; Tattletales 1975; In Performance at Wolf Trap 1975; Dean Martin's California Christmas
(special) 1975; Celebrity Sweepstakes 1976; Celebration: The
American Spirit 1976; Switch 1976; Festival of Lively Arts for
Young People 1976.
Theater: Appearances at Uris Theatre; Olympia Theatre (Paris)
1963, 1964; Mill Run Theatre (Chicago) 1974, 1976; West-

chester Premier Theatre 1975; Westbury Music Fair 1976;
Garden State Arts Center 1976.
Relationships: Former wife of Bill Elliott, actor; sister of Dee
Dee Warwick, singer.

WASHINGTON, DINAH "The Queen" (Ruth Jones)
(Singer)
b. August 29, 1924, Tuscaloosa, Ala.
d. December 14, 1963, Detroit, Mich.
Honors: Grammy 1959.
Career Data: Vocalist with Lionel Hampton 1943-46.
Clubs: Garrick Bar 1942.
Films: Rock and Roll Revue 1955; Jazz on a Summer's Day (doc.)
1960.
Records: Best (Roulette); Dinah Washington (Pickwick); Discovered
(Mercury); Echoes of an Era (Roulette); For Lonely Lovers
(Mercury); I Don't Hurt Anymore (Pickwick); Immortal (Rou-
lette); Queen of the Blues (Roulette); Tears and Laughter
(Trip); This Is My Story (Mercury); Unforgettable (Mercury);
... Sings Bessie Smith (Trip); The Swingin' Miss D (Trip);
Greatest Hits (Pickwick); Love for Sale. On Mercury: It
Isn't Fair 1950; I Won't Cry Anymore 1951; Cold Cold Heart
1951; Wheel of Fortune 1952; Teach Me Tonight 1954; I Con-
centrate on You 1955; What a Diff'rence a Day Makes 1959;
A Rockin' Good Way (with Brook Benton) 1960; Baby You've
Got What It Takes (with Brook Benton) 1960; Love Walked
In 1960; Our Love Is Here to Stay 1961; Where Are You 1962;
You're Nobody Til' Somebody Loves You 1962; For All We
Know; After Hours with Miss D; Dinah Jams.
Television: Showtime at the Apollo 1954.
Theater: Appeared at Regal Theatre (Chicago) 1940; Apollo Theatre
1953, 1955.

WASHINGTON, FORD LEE "Buck"
(Comedian/Musician)
b. October 16, 1903, Louisville, Ky.
d. February, 1955, New York, N.Y.
Special Interests: Dancing, piano, singing, trumpet.
Career Data: Teamed with John Sublett as Buck and Bubbles 1919-
53; Timmie Rogers Combo 1954.
Films: Cabin in the Sky 1943; Buck and Bubbles Laugh Jubilee
1945; A Song Is Born 1948.
Theater: Appeared at Apollo Theatre; Palace Theatre; Ziegfeld
Follies of 1921; Palladium (London) 1931; Capitol Theatre 1943.

WASHINGTON, FREDI (Fredricka Carolyn Washington)
(Actress)
b. December 23, 1903, Savannah, Ga.
Education: St. Elizabeth's Convent (Cornwell Heights, Pa.); Egri
School of Dramatic Writing; Christophe School of Languages;

Julia Richmond H. S.
Special Interests: Civil rights, casting, writing, dancing, singing.
Address: Mrs. Bell, 54 W. North Street, Stamford, Conn. 06902.
Honors: Black Filmmakers Hall of Fame 1975.
Career Data: Organized dance team, Moiret & Fredi 1927-28;
    danced with Duke Ellington orchestra; danced on tour of South
    (with Eubie Blake and Noble Sissle orchestras) 1932; founded
    Negro Actors Guild, served as its first executive secretary
    1937-38; theatre editor and columnist, The People's Voice;
    administrative secretary, Joint Actors Equity-Theatre League
    Committee on Hotel Accommodations for Negro Actors through-
    out the U.S.; registrar for Howard da Silva School of Acting.
Clubs: Reisenweber's Cafe; Alabam; St. Regis Hotel; Gaumont
    Palace (Paris); Chateau Madrid (Paris); Green Park Hotel
    (London); Cafe de Paris (Monte Carlo); Casino (Nice); New
    Casino (Dieppe); Casino (Ostend); Trocadero (Berlin); Barber-
    ina Cafe (Dresden); Alkazar (Hamburg); Gloria Palast (Ber-
    lin); Lincoln Tavern (Chicago).
Films: Black and Tan Fantasy 1929; The Old Man of the Mountain
    1933; Emperor Jones 1933; Peola in Imitation of Life 1934;
    Drums of the Jungle 1935; One Mile from Heaven 1937; casting
    consultant for Cry, the Beloved Country 1952.
Memberships: AEA; AFRA; NAG; Newspaper Guild.
Radio: The Goldbergs; Specials for National Urban League (CBS).
Records: Worked with Black Swan Record Co. 1921.
Television: The Goldbergs.
Theater: Shuffle Along (tour) 1922-26; Black Boy 1926; Great Day
    1929; Hot Chocolates 1929; Sweet Chariot 1930; Singin' the
    Blues 1931; Run Little Chillun 1933; Mamba's Daughters 1939;
    casting consultant for Carmen Jones and Porgy and Bess 1943;
    Lysistrata 1946; A Long Way from Home 1948; How Long Till
    Summer 1949.
Relationships: Sister of Isabel Washington, former actress; first
    wife of U.S. Congressman Adam Clayton Powell (deceased).

WASHINGTON, GROVER JR.
    (Jazz Musician)
Special Interests: Saxophone.
Honors: NAACP Image Award (Jazz Artist) 1976.
Clubs: Bottom Line 1975.
Records: A Secret Place; On Kudu: Mister Magic; Feels So Good;
    Inner City Blues; All the King's Horses; Soul Box.
Television: Don Kirshner's Rock Concert 1976.
Theater: Appeared at Convention Hall (Asbury Park, N.J.); Felt
    Forum 1975; Avery Fisher Hall 1976; The Paladium 1977.

WASHINGTON, KENNY (Kenneth)
    (Actor)
b. 1918.
d. June 24, 1971.
Career Data: Played pro football with Los Angeles Rams 1946.

Films: While Thousands Cheer; The Foxes of Harrow 1947; Rogues
    Regiment 1948; Easy Living, Rope of Sand, Pinky 1949; The
    Jackie Robinson Story 1950; Weekend of Fear 1966; Changes
    1969.
Television: Hogan's Heroes 1970.

WASHINGTON, LAMONT
    (Singer)
b. c.1944, New York, N.Y.
d. August 25, 1968, New York, N.Y.
Education: High School of Performing Arts.
Career Data: Vocalist with Count Basie band.
Television: Call Back; The New Yorkers.
Theater: One upon an Island (O.B.); The Cool World 1960; Golden
    Boy (understudy and substitute for Sammy Davis Jr.) 1965;
    Hair 1968.

WATERS, ETHEL
    (Actress/Singer)
b. October 31, 1896, Chester, Pa.
d. September 1, 1977, Los Angeles, Calif.
Special Interests: Dancing, religion.
Honors: Academy award nomination (for Pinky) 1949 and (for Mem-
    ber of the Wedding) 1952; Plaque from Negro Actors Guild
    (for Pinky) 1949; St. Genesius Medal from ANTA 1951; Black
    Filmmakers Hall of Fame 1976.
Career Data: Vocalist with Fletcher Henderson band; Seventh Wom-
    an's Ambulance Corps and honorary captain of California State
    Militia during World War II; during career introduced many
    songs including Dinah, Am I Blue, Stormy Weather, Heat Wave,
    Suppertime, Happiness Is Just a Thing Called Joe, Takin' a
    Chance on Love, and St. Louis Blues; participated in Billy
    Graham Evangelism crusades.
Clubs: Edmond's Cellar (debut); Plantation Club; Lenox Avenue
    Club; Cotton Club 1932; Zanzibar, Blue Mirror (Wash., D.C.)
    1950.
Films: Sunny Side Up; On with the Show (debut) 1929; The Cotton
    Club New York, New York Nights 1930; Rufus Jones for Presi-
    dent 1931; International House 1933; Gift of Gab, Bubbling Over,
    Hot n' Bothered 1934; Cairo, Tales of Manhattan 1942; Stage Door
    Canteen, Cabin in the Sky 1943; Pinky 1949; Carib Gold, Mem-
    ber of the Wedding 1952; The Heart Is a Rebel 1956; Dilsey
    in The Sound and the Fury 1959.
Memberships: AEA (executive council 1942-43); AFTRA; AGMA;
    AGVA; NAG (Exec. Vice Pres. 1942-43); SAG.
Publications: His Eye Is on the Sparrow (autobiography), Doubleday,
    1951; To Me It's Wonderful (autobiography), Harper & Row,
    1972.
Radio: U.S.O. Camp Shows 1942.
Records: Performing in Person: Highlights from Her Illustrious
    Career on Stage and Screen 1925-1940 (Columbia); His Eye Is

on the Sparrow (Word); Jazzin' Babies Blues (Biograph);
Greatest Years (Columbia); Miss Ethel Waters (Monmouth-
Evergreen); 1921/4 (Biograph).
Television: Tex and Jinx Show (series); Daniel Boone; title role
    in Beulah (series) 1950; Speaking to Hannah (Favorite Play-
    house) 1955; Climax 1955; Winner by Decision (G.E. Theatre)
    1955; The Sound and the Fury (Playwrights '56) 1955; Sing for
    Me (Matinee Theatre) 1957; Good Night Sweet Blues (Route 66)
    1961; Go Down Moses (Great Adventures) 1963; Something
    Special 1966; Run, Carol, Run (Owen Marshall) 1972; Soul Free
    1974; Billy Graham Crusade.
Theater: Vaudeville at Lincoln Theatre, Baltimore (debut) 1917;
    Sweet Mama Stringbean and act with Hill Sisters trio 1917-27;
    Howard Theatre (Washington, D.C.) 1926; Africana 1927; Lew
    Leslie's Blackbirds 1930; Rhapsody in Black 1931; As Thousands
    Cheer 1933; At Home Abroad 1935; appearances at Carnegie
    Hall 1938, Roxy Theatre, Lafayette Theatre, Palace Theatre,
    Monogram (Chicago); Hagar in Mamba's Daughters 1938;
    Petunia Jackson in Cabin in the Sky 1940; Laugh Time 1943;
    Blue Holiday 1945; The Voice of Strangers (stock); Berenice
    in The Member of the Wedding 1950; At Home with Ethel
    Waters 1953; Happy Journey (Berlin) 1957.

WATERS, MUDDY (McKinley Morganfield)
    (Singer)
b. April 4, 1915, Rolling Fork, Miss.
Special Interests: Guitar, harmonica, blues, songwriting.
Honors: Grammy award (best ethnic or traditional recording) 1976.
Career Data: Joined Silas Green tent show as accompanist 1941;
    formed his own band in early 1950s; toured England in 1958;
    appeared at jazz and folk festivals including Monterey and New-
    port (1960, 1967, 1976); his tune "Rollin' Stone" became name
    of British rock music group.
Clubs: The Bottom Line 1975.
Musical Compositions: Rollin' Stone (a.k.a. Catfish Blues) 1954.
Records: On Archive of American Folk Song: I Be's Troubled
    1940; Country Blues 1940. On Aristocrat: Gypsy Woman
    1946; Little Anna Mae 1946; I Feel Like Going Home; I Can't
    Be Satisfied. On Chess: Louisiana Blues 1951; Long Distance
    Call 1951; Mad Love 1953; I'm Your Hootchie Coochie Man
    1954; Just Make Love to Me 1954; I'm Ready 1954; Manish
    Boy 1955; Forty Days and Forty Nights 1956; Close to You
    1958; The Best of Muddy Waters 1958; Muddy Waters at New-
    port 1960, 1961; Folk Singer 1964; Live; The Muddy Waters
    Woodstock Album; Hard Again; Brass and Blues; AKA McKinley
    Morganfield; Can't Get No Grindin'; London; Sail On; "Unk" in
    Funk. On Cadet: After the Rain; Electric Mud. On Testa-
    ment: Stovall's Plantation.
Theater: Paladium 1977.

WATKINS, LOVELACE
    (Singer)

b. March 6, 1938, New Brunswick, N.J.
Special Interests: Organ
Career Data: Former Golden Gloves Champion; toured South Africa
    1974.
Clubs: Birdland; Latin Quarter; Flamingo (Las Vegas) 1974; El
    San Juan Hotel (Puerto Rico) 1974; Empire Room-Waldorf
    Astoria 1975; Rainbow Grill 1976.
Television: Merv Griffin Show 1974, 1975; Black News 1975; Kup's
    Show 1975; Midday Live 1975, 1976.

WATSON, IRWIN C.
    (Comedian)
b. January 12, 1934, Brooklyn, N.Y.
Special Interests: Singing, composing, acting, saxophone.
Address: 887 Sterling Place, Brooklyn, N.Y. 11216.
Clubs: Royal Box; Frontier (Las Vegas); Landmark (Las Vegas);
    Sands (Las Vegas); Caesar's Palace (Las Vegas); New Grove
    (Las Vegas); Diplomat Hotel (Miami); Latin Casino (Phila.);
    Harrah's (Tahoe); Sahara (Tahoe); Waldorf's Starlight Roof
    1975.
Films: Cotton Comes to Harlem 1970.
Memberships: AFTRA; AGVA; SAG.
Musical Compositions: Many Many Facts; Sacrifice for You; Try to
    Fall in Love with Me.
Radio: Disc jockey on Gene Klavin Show (WNEW) 1970.
Television: Tonight Show; Mike Douglas Show; Jackie Gleason Show;
    Ed Sullivan Show; Hollywood Palace; Steve Allen Show; Virginia
    Graham Show; Spring Thing (special); Rhythm and Blues (spe-
    cial); TW 3 (London) 1963; Good Times 1976.
Theater: Performed at the following: Mill Run Playhouse (Chicago)
    1975; Royal Theatre (Chicago); Howard Theatre (Wash., D.C.);
    Royal Theatre (Baltimore); Uptown Theatre (Phila.); Apollo
    Theatre 1961; Madison Square Garden.

WATSON, JAMES A. JR.
    (Actor)
Films: Halls of Anger 1970; The Organization 1971; Lady Coco
    1976.
Memberships: SAG.
Television: Love, American Style; Mod Squad; Kung Fu; Killdozer;
    Name of the Game; The Old Man Who Cried Wolf 1970; The
    Strangers in 7A 1972; Mannix 1975; Karen 1975; Joe Forrester
    1975; Kojak 1975; Rockford Files 1976; Blue Knight 1976;
    Police Woman 1976; What's Happening! 1976; Sanford and Son
    1977.

WATTS, ANDRE
    (Pianist)
b. June 20, 1946, Nuremburg, Germany.
Education: Lincoln Prep School; Peabody Conservatory of Music
    (Baltimore).

Address: c/o William Judd, Columbia Artists Management Inc.,
     165 West 57 Street, New York, N.Y. 10019.
Career Data: Debut at age 9 with Philadelphia orchestra youth
     concerts 1955; adult debut with Leonard Bernstein and N.Y.
     Philharmonic orchestra 1963; performed with numerous sym-
     phony orchestras including: San Francisco, Montreal, Nation-
     al 1966, London 1966, Berlin 1967, Los Angeles 1967.
Records: An André Watts Recital; Beethoven's Piano Sonata no. 7.
Television: Camera Three; Evening at Symphony 1975; Live at
     Lincoln Center 1976.
Theater: Appearances at Carnegie Hall; Gershwin Theatre-Brooklyn
     College; Ford Theatre (Wash., D.C.) 1975; Avery Fisher
     Hall 1976.

WAYMON, SAM(UEL)
     (Singer/Composer)
Clubs: Marco Polo (Vancouver); Marty's on The Hill (L.A.);
     Hungry I (San Francisco); Village Gate.
Films: Ganja and Hess (a.k.a. Blood Couple) 1973.
Records: It's Finished (with Nina Simone).
Television: Tonight Show; David Frost Show.
Theater: Appeared at Carnegie Hall; Philharmonic Hall; Apollo
     Theatre; Black Picture Show 1974.
Relationships: Brother of Nina Simone, singer/pianist/composer.

WEBB, ALYCE ELIZABETH
     (Actress)
b. June 1, 1935, Greensboro, N.C.
Education: Juilliard School of Music B.A.; New York University
     M.A.; Union Theological Seminary M.A.; studied dance with
     Katherine Dunham, Pearl Primus, Syvilla Fort; studied acting
     with José Quintero.
Special Interests: Singing, dancing, stagemanaging.
Address: 875 Columbus Avenue, New York, N.Y. 10025.
Career Data: First black woman stage manager on Broadway (for
     N.Y. City Opera and N.Y. City Light Opera Companies);
     member, Lincoln Center Repertory Company 1973; member,
     American Shakespeare Festival, Stratford, Connecticut 1974.
Films: Cotton Comes to Harlem 1970; Claudine 1974.
Memberships: AEA; AFTRA; AGMA; NAFM; SAG.
Radio: Community News (WLIB).
Television: Ed Sullivan Show; Harry Belafonte special.
Theater: Street Scene (Bway debut) 1946; Lost in the Stars 1949;
     Finian's Rainbow (City Center) 1955; Guys and Dolls (City
     Center) 1955; Kiss Me, Kate (City Center) 1956; Carousel;
     Simply Heavenly 1957; Ballad for Bimshire 1963; Trumpets of
     the Lord 1963; Wonderful Town (City Center) 1963; Bloody
     Mary in South Pacific (tour) 1969; Hello, Dolly! 1969; Purlie
     1970; The Grass Harp 1971; Don't Play Us Cheap 1972; A
     Streetcar Named Desire 1973; The Women 1974; Raisin (stand-
     by) 1975; Show Boat (Jones Beach) 1976.

WEBB, CHICK (William Webb)
    (Jazz Musician)
b. February 10, 1907, Baltimore, Md.
d. June 16, 1939, Baltimore, Md.
Special Interests: Drums, cymbals.
Career Data: Led his first band 1926; introduced Ella Fitzgerald
      as vocalist 1935; popularized A Tisket A Tasket, Stomping at
      the Savoy, Don't Be That Way and other songs.
Clubs: Black Bottom 1926; Paddocks Club; Savoy Ballroom; Strand
      Roof; Roseland; Cotton Club; Casino de Paris 1934.
Records: Stompin' at the Savoy (Columbia Special Products).
Theater: Hot Chocolates Revue (tour) 1930; appeared at Apollo
      Theatre.

WEBSTER, BEN (Benjamin Franklin Webster)
    (Jazz Musician)
b. February 27, 1909, Kansas City, Mo.
Special Interests: Tenor saxophone, piano.
Career Data: Played with Andy Kirk, Bennie Moten 1932, Benny
      Carter and Fletcher Henderson 1933-34, Duke Ellington 1939-
      43, 1948; toured with Jazz at the Philharmonic.
Records: Cotton Tail; Conga Brava; Just a Settin' and a Rockin';
      All Too Soon; Jam Blues. On Verve: The Kid and the Brute;
      Sophisticated Lady; Soulville; King of the Tenors; Coleman
      Hawkins Encounters Ben Webster; Ben Webster and Associates;
      Ballads (Verve Select); See You at the Fair (Impulse); At
      Work in Europe (Prestige); Atmosphere for Lovers and Thieves
      (Black Lion); Duke's in Bed (Black Lion); Live at Pio's (Enja);
      Ben Webster Meets Don Byas (BASF); Giants of the Tenor
      Saxophone (Columbia).

WESLEY, RICHARD (Errol)
    (Playwright)
b. July 11, 1945, Newark, N.J.
Education: Howard University B.F.A. 1963-67.
Honors: National Collegiate Playwrighting contest (Honorable Men-
      tion) 1965; N.Y. Drama Desk Prize 1972; AUDELCO Black
      Theatre Recognition Award 1974.
Career Data: Co-editor, Black Theatre Magazine; Playwriting Work-
      shop, New Lafayette Theatre 1968; playwright-in-residence,
      New Lafayette Theatre 1973.
Films: Uptown Saturday Night 1974.
Theater: Wrote: Ace Boon Coon, Another Way 1969; The Black
      Terror 1971; Gettin' It Together 1970; Goin' Through Changes
      (one act); Headline News 1970; Knock, Knock, Who Dat 1970;
      The Past Is the Past 1973; The Sirens; Springtime High (one
      act) 1968; The Street Corner 1970; Strike Heaven on the Face
      1973; Steady Rap 1972; Put My Dignity on 307; The Mighty
      Gents.

WESTON, KIM
    (Singer)
b. December 20, 1939, Detroit, Mich.
Education: Studied acting with Herbert Berghof.
Special Interests: Acting, gospel.
Address: Stax Records, 98 N. Avalon Avenue, Memphis, Tenn.
    38104.
Career Data: Sang with Wright Specials, gospel group.
Films: Changes 1969; Wattstax 1973.
Memberships: National Council of Negro Women.
Records: Lift Every Voice and Sing (a. k. a. Black National Anthem);
    It's Got to Be a Miracle; Love Me All the Way (Tamla, 1963);
    What Good Am I Without You (Tamla, 1964); Take Me in Your
    Arms (Gordy, 1965); Helpless (Gordy, 1966); It Takes Two
    (Tamla, 1967).
Television: Gloria in The Bill Cosby Show.
Theater: Hallelujah Baby (tour) 1968.

WESTON, RANDY (Randolph E. Weston)
    (Pianist/Composer)
b. April 6, 1926, Brooklyn, N. Y.
Special Interests: Writing, lyrics, lecturing.
Honors: Pianist Most Deserving of Wider Recognition 1972.
Career Data: Newport Jazz Festival 1958; toured Europe, Africa.
Clubs: Bohemia; Vanguard; Five Spot; Composer.
Musical Compositions: Little Niles; Pam's Waltz; Machine Blues;
    Hi Fly; Bantu Suite; Tangiers Bay; Niger Mambo.
Records: Berkshire Blues (Arista); Blues (Trip); Blue Moses
    (CTI); Blues to Africa (Arista); Carnival (Arista).
Theater: Appeared at Town Hall 1976.

WHEELER, HAROLD
    (Conductor/Musician)
Special Interests: Arranging.
Address: 200 East End Avenue, New York, N. Y. 10028.
Career Data: Arranged and conducted record albums for Lena
    Horne, Nina Simone, Billy Taylor and others.
Films: The Bride; Don't Play Us Cheap; musical supervisor for
    Cotton Comes to Harlem 1970; Fortune and Men's Eyes 1971.
Television: George M; The Real American Music; Wedding Band
    1974.
Theater: Promises, Promises 1968; Coco 1969; Ain't Supposed to
    Die a Natural Death 1971; Don't Play Us Cheap 1972; Two
    Gentlemen of Verona 1972; The Wiz 1975.

WHIPPER, LEIGH
    (Actor)
b. 1877, Charleston, S. C.
d. July 26, 1975, New York, N. Y.

Education: Howard University Law School L. L. B. 1895.
Special Interests: Playwriting, producing.
Honors: Howard University alumni award; Screen Actors Guild
         award, Black Filmmakers Hall of Fame 1974; Harold Jackman
         Memorial award.
Career Data: Began theatrical career 1899 with Philadelphia Stand-
         ard Theatre stock company; first black member of Actors
         Equity Association 1920; formed Renaissance Company to pro-
         duce all-black newsreels 1922.
Films: The Symbol of the Unconquered 1920; Crooks in Of Mice
         and Men 1940; King of the Zombies, Virginia 1941; White
         Cargo, Bahama Passage, The Vanishing Virginian 1942; Sparks
         in The Ox-Bow Incident, Haile Selassie in Mission to Moscow
         1943; The Negro Sailor (doc) 1945; Undercurrent 1946; narrated
         Untamed Fury 1947; Lost Boundaries 1949; The Harder They
         Fall 1956; The Young Don't Cry 1957; Marjorie Morningstar
         1958.
Memberships: AEA; NAG (co-founder 1920); SAG.
Theater: Uncle Tom's Cabin 1898; wrote De Board Meetin' (with
         Porter Grainger) 1925; Georgia Minstrels (debut); In Abra-
         ham's Bosom 1926; Crabman in Porgy 1927; wrote We's Risin':
         A Story of the Simple Life in the Souls of Black Folk (with
         Porter Grainger) 1927; wrote Runnin' de Town (with J. C.
         Johnson) 1930; wrote Yeah Man (with Billy Mills) 1932; Jim
         Veal in Stevedore 1934; Three Men on a Horse; Of Mice and
         Men; Volpone; Lysistrata 1946; Set My People Free 1948; The
         Shrike 1955.

WHITE, BARRY
     (Singer/Composer)
b. September 12, 1944, Galveston, Texas.
Education: Reese High School, (L.A.).
Special Interests: Piano, producing.
Honors: NAACP Image award 1975; 9 gold records.
Career Data: Member, Love Unlimited, singing group and orches-
         tra.
Films: Together Brothers (music) 1974; Coon Skin 1975.
Musical Compositions: I'm Going to Love You Just a Little Bit
         More, Baby; Honey, Please.
Records: Walking in the Rain; Together Brothers; Got So Much to
         Give; Can't Get Enough (20th Century); White Gold; Rhapsody
         in White; Stone Gon'; Just Another Way to Say I Love You
         (20th Century); Barry White's Greatest Hits (20th Century);
         Let the Music Play (20th Century).
Television: Speakeasy; Midnight Special 1974; Soul Train 1975.
Theater: Appeared at Felt Forum 1974, Radio City Music Hall
         1976; Westchester Premier Theatre 1976.

WHITE, EDGAR B.
     (Playwright)
b. April 4, 1947, Montserrat, West Indies.
Education: New York University B.A. 1968; Yale University.

Special Interests: Music (flute, clarinet).
Address: 230 East 4th Street, New York, N.Y. 10009.
Honors: Rockefeller Foundation Grant 1974; New York State Council
on the Arts Grant 1975.
Career Data: Worked with Cincinnati Playhouse; Shakespeare Festi-
val Public Theatre.
Memberships: The Authors Guild of New York.
Radio: Survey of the Arts (WNYC) 1973.
Theater: Les Femmes Noires; Ode to Charlie Parker; La Gente;
Seigismundo's Tricycle; The Cathedral at Chartres (one act)
1969; The Mummer's Play (one act) 1969; The Wonderful Year
1969; The Life and Times of J. Walter Smintheus 1970; Fun
in Lethe 1970; The Burghers of Calais 1971; Underground:
Four Plays 1971; The Crucificado (Two Plays) 1973; Sati:
The Rastofarian 1973; Omar at Christmas 1973; The Children
of Night 1974.

WHITE, JANE
(Actress)
b. October 30, 1922, New York, N.Y.
Education: The Ethical Culture School; Smith College, B.A. 1944;
studied Modern Dance with Hanya Holm 1945, acting with
Herbert Berghof 1945 and Uta Hagen 1950-52.
Address: 35 West 9 Street, New York, N.Y. 10011.
Honors: Obie 1965 as best actress for performance in Coriolanus.
Career Data: Board member, The American Negro Theatre; co-
founder and vice president, Torchlight Productions Inc. 1947-
49 (promoted interracial casting).
Clubs: Piccolo Cabaret 1975; Alfredo's Settebello 1976.
Films: Non Sommettere Con il Diavolo (Fellini); Pinky (technical
adviser), Lost Boundaries (script consultant) 1949; Klute 1971.
Memberships: AEA; AFTRA; SAG.
Radio: Arlene Francis Show 1974.
Television: Lydia Holiday in Edge of Night (series); Stage 13 1950;
Casey, Crime Photographer 1951; Alcoa Presents 1956; Lamp
Unto My Feet 1956; Kraft Television Theatre 1957; Studio One
1957; Car 54 Where Are You? 1961; The Shari Lewis Show
1962, 1963; Queen in Once Upon a Mattress 1964.
Theater: Trumpets of the Lord (Paris, France); The Cuban Thing;
French Princess in Love's Labours Lost (NYSF); Volumnia in
Coriolanus (NYSF); Clytemnestra in Iphigenia in Aulis; Nonnie
in Strange Fruit (debut) 1945; Curley's wife in Of Mice and
Men (O.B.) 1946; Peer Gynt (E.L.T.), 1947; Almost Faithful
(Allentown, Pa.) 1947; The Washington Years (A.N.T.) 1948;
The Insect Comedy (City Center) 1948; Blithe Spirit (O.B.)
1948; City of Kings (Blackfriars Guild) 1949; Dark of the
Moon (O.B.) 1949; Come What May (O.B.) 1950; Razzle Daz-
zle (O.B.) 1951; The Climate of Eden 1952; Take a Giant
Step 1953; Time of Storm (O.B.) 1954; title role in Hedda
Gabler (Y.M.H.A.) 1956; The Real Me (Connecticut) 1956;
title role in Lysistrata (O.B.) 1956; Liliom (New Hampshire)
1957; mad wife in Jane Eyre 1958; The Power and the Glory

(O. B.) 1958; The Queen in Once Upon a Mattress 1959; Katherine in The Taming of the Shrew (NYSF) 1960; Hop, Signor! (O. B.) 1962; Helen of Troy in The Trojan Women (O. B.) 1963; Helen of Troy in Troilus and Cressida 1965; The Burnt Flower (O. B.) 1974; Goneril in King Lear (ASF Stratford, Conn.) 1975.

Relationships: Daughter of Walter White, NAACP leader (deceased).

WHITE, JOSH (Joshua Daniel White)
    (Singer)
b.   February 11, 1908, Greenville, S. C.
d.   September 5, 1969, Manhasset, L. I.
Special Interests: Folk music, guitar, tambourine.
Career Data: Became known early in his career as the Singing Christian and "Pinewood Tom"; made U. S. goodwill tour of Mexico 1941; popularized songs including John Henry, Hard Time Blues, Strange Fruit, Evil Hearted Man, The Girl with the Delicate Air, The House I Live In, I Am Goin' to Move on the Outskirts of Town.
Clubs: Blue Angel; Cafe-Society Downtown.
Films: The Crimson Canary; The Walking Hills 1949.
Records: Josh White; The Best of Josh White; Spirituals (Columbia) 1933; Chain Gang (Columbia) 1940; Southern Exposure (Keynote) 1941; Chain Gang Songs (Elektra); Empty Bed Blues (Elektra); The House I Live In (Elektra); In Memoriam (Tradition); Josh White (Archive of Folk & Jazz Music); ... Sings the Blues (Stinson); Spirituals and Blues (Elektra).
Theater: Appeared at Apollo Theatre; Blind Lemon in John Henry 1940; appeared with Pearl Primus Company 1944; Blue Holiday 1945; A Long Way from Home 1948; How Long Till Summer 1949.
Relationships: Father of Josh White Jr., actor/singer.

WHITE, SLAPPY
    (Comedian)
Career Data: Teamed in comedy act with Redd Foxx in 1950s.
Clubs: Club Alabam; Great Gorge Resort Hotel (McAfee, N. J.); Playboy Club (New Orleans).
Films: The Man from O. R. G. Y. 1970; Amazing Grace 1974.
Records: First Negro Vice President (Brunswick); The First Slappy White Astronaut (Brunswick).
Television: Comedy World; Sanford and Son (series); O. J. Simpson Is Alive and Well and Getting Roasted Tonight (Wide World of Entertainment) 1974; Salute to Redd Foxx (Wide World Special) 1974; That's My Mama 1974; Merv Griffin Show 1975; Celebrity Revue 1976.
Theater: Appearances at Apollo Theatre.
Relationships: Former husband of Pearl Bailey, singer.

WHITMAN, ERNEST
    (Actor)

b. 1893.
d. August 6, 1954, Hollywood, Calif.
Films: The Prisoner of Shark Island, White Hunter, The Green
        Pastures 1936; Daughter of Shanghai 1937; Jesse James 1939;
        Congo Maisie, Buck Benny Rides Again, Maryland, The Return
        of Frank James, Third Finger, Left Hand 1940; Among the
        Living, The Get-Away, The Pittsburgh Kid 1941; Drums of the
        Congo, The Bugle Sounds 1942; Cabin in the Sky, Stormy
        Weather 1943; My Brother Talks to Horses, Blonde Savage
        1947.
Radio: The Gibson Family; Circus Days 1933; Bill Jackson on
        Beulah (series).
Television: Bill Jackson on Beulah (series).
Theater: Savage Rhythm; Bloodstream 1932.

WILLIAMS, BERT (Egbert Austin Williams)
        (Entertainer)
b. November 12, 1874, Antigua, West Indies.
d. March 4, 1922, New York, N.Y.
Education: Riverside High School (Calif.)
Special Interests: Acting, comedy, composing.
Career Data: Teamed with George Walker 1895-1909 in vaudeville
        act as Two Real Coons; introduced The Cakewalk dance 1896;
        recorded for The Victory Talking Machine Co.
Clubs: Tony Pastor's; Koster and Bial's.
Films: Darktown Jubilee 1914; A Natural Born Gambler 1916.
Memberships: AEA; The Frogs; (a theatrical assn.).
Musical Compositions: Nobody; I'm a Jonah Man; I May Be Crazy
        but I Ain't No Fool; Woodman Spare That Tree; I Don't Like
        No Cheap Man; The Medicine Man; Good Morning Carrie;
        The Fortune Telling Man; When It's All Goin' Out and Nothin'
        Comin' In; He's a Cousin of Mine; I'd Rather Have Nothin' All
        of the Time, Than Somethin' for a Little While; When the
        Moon Shines on the Moonshine.
Records: It's Nobody's Business But My Own (Columbia); Oh Death
        Where Is Thy Sting? (Columbia); It's Getting So You Can't
        Trust Nobody (Columbia).
Theater: The Gold Bug 1896; Clorindy, or The Origin of the Cake
        Walk 1898; A Lucky Coon 1899; The Policy Players 1899; The
        Sons of Ham 1900; In Dahomey 1902 (London) 1903-05); In
        Abyssinia 1908; Bandana Land 1909; Mr. Lode of Koal 1910;
        Ziegfeld Follies 1910-19; Broadway Brevities 1920; Under the
        Bamboo Tree 1922.

WILLIAMS, BILLY
        (Singer)
b. December 28, 1916, Waco, Texas.
d. October 17, 1972, Chicago, Ill.
Career Data: Member, Charioteers until 1949; Billy Williams
        Quartet from 1950.
Clubs: DeVille (South Fallsburg).

Radio: WLW (Cincinnati); WOR; Bing Crosby Show.
Records: On Coral: I'm Gonna Sit Right Down and Write Myself
    a Letter 1957; Got a Date with an Angel 1957; Baby Baby 1958.
Television: Sid Caesar's Your Show of Shows (series) 1950-54.

WILLIAMS, BILLY DEE (William December Williams)
    (Actor)
b. April 6, 1937, New York, N.Y.
Education: Music and Art H.S.; National Academy of Fine Arts
    and Design; Actors Workshop in Harlem.
Address: International Creative Management, 8899 Beverly Blvd.,
    Los Angeles, Calif. 90048.
Honors: Emmy Nomination (for Brian's Song) 1971.
Films: The Last Angry Man 1959; The Out of Towners 1970; Louis
    McKay in Lady Sings the Blues, The Final Comedown 1972;
    The Hit 1973; The Take 1974; Mahogany 1975; The Bingo Long
    Traveling All-Stars and Motor Kings 1976.
Memberships: AEA; SAG.
Television: Hallmark Hall of Fame; Another World; Look Up and
    Live; Hawk; Eye on New York; The Medicine Men (Mod Squad);
    The Interns; The FBI; Mission: Impossible; Lost Flight 1970;
    Carter's Army 1970; Gayle Sayers in Brian's Song 1971; The
    Glass House 1972; Dinah! 1974, 1976; Kup's Show 1975, 1976;
    Positively Black 1975; Lola Falana (special) 1976; Mike Doug-
    las Show 1976; Black News 1976; Black Conversations 1976;
    Like It Is 1976.
Theater: The Firebrand of Florence (debut) 1947; Take a Giant
    Step (O.B.) 1956; A Taste of Honey 1960; The Cool World
    1960; The Blacks (O.B.) 1962; The Blue Boy in Black (O.B.)
    1963; The Firebugs (O.B.) 1963; Hallelujah Baby! 1967; Slow
    Dance on the Killing Ground (O.B.) 1970; Ceremonies in Dark
    Old Men (O.B.) 1970; Trial of Abraham Lincoln 1972; Martin
    Luther King Jr. in I Have a Dream 1976.

WILLIAMS, CAMILLA
    (Opera Singer)
b. Danville, Va.
Education: Virginia State College B.A. 1941; University of Penn-
    sylvania 1942; studied voice with Mme. Marian Szekely-Freschi
    1943 and Sergius Kagen 1958-62.
Special Interests: Teaching.
Address: 309 West 104 Street, New York, N.Y. 10025.
Honors: Marian Anderson award 1943, 1944; Philadelphia orchestra
    youth award 1944; N.Y. Newspaper Guild Page One award 1947;
    Chicago Defender's Honor Role 1951; White House Command
    Performance 1960; Gold medal from Emperor of Ethiopia 1962;
    Art, Culture and Civic Guild award 1962; Negro Musicians'
    Assn. plaque 1963; Harlem Opera and World Fellowship Society
    award 1963; WLIB Radio award 1963; honored by Governor of
    Virginia 1972; Hall of Fame, Danville, Va. Museum of Fine
    Arts and History 1974; Cooper Union's Great Hall 1975.

Career Data: Music Instructor, Danville, Va. public schools 1941-
    42; first black to sing Cio Cio San in Madame Butterfly at
    N.Y.C. Center 1946; sang Mozart's Idomeneo with Little Or-
    chestra Society; Menotti's Saint of Bleecker Street at Vienna
    State Opera; operatic roles include Aida, Mimi in La Boheme,
    Nedda in Pagliacci, Marguerite in Faust; tours include New
    Zealand and Australia 1955, Africa (U.S. State Dept.) 1958,
    Europe (12th tour) 1960, Japan, Korea, Laos, Philippines,
    Viet Nam (U.S. State Dept.) 1961; appearances with orches-
    tras: Royal Philharmonic, Vienna Symphony, BBC, Stuttgart,
    Zurich, Geneva, Berlin Philharmonic, Belgium, N.Y. Phil-
    harmonic, Chicago Symphony and Philadelphia; adjunct profes-
    sor, Brooklyn College 1970-73; first N.Y. performance of
    Handel's Orlando 1971.
Memberships: NAACP.
Radio: Library of Congress Founder's Day Concert WETA-FM
    (Washington, D.C.) 1973.
Records: Porgy and Bess (Columbia).

WILLIAMS, CLARENCE III
b. August 21, 1939, New York, N.Y.
Honors: Theatre World award 1965.
Films: The Last Angry Man 1959; The Cool World 1964.
Television: Daktari 1967; Danny Thomas Show 1968; Linc on Mod
    Squad (series) 1968-70.
Theater: Dark of the Moon (ELT) 1960; The Long Dream (Bway
    debut) 1960; The Egg and I (O.B.); Double Talk (O.B.); Walk
    in Darkness (O.B.) 1963; Slow Dance on the Killing Ground
    1964; Sarah and the Sax (O.B.) 1964; The Great Indoors (O.B.);
    King John (Central Park); Party on Greenwich Avenue (O.B.)
    1967.
Relationships: Husband of Gloria Foster, actress.

WILLIAMS, COOTIE (Charles Melvin Williams)
    (Musician/Conductor)
b. July 24, 1908, Mobile, Ala.
Special Interests: Trumpet, composing.
Honors: Esquire magazine (silver) award 1944, (gold) award 1945-
    46.
Career Data: Played with bands of Fletcher Henderson, Duke Elling-
    ton 1929-40, Benny Goodman (sextet) 1941; formed his own
    band 1942; noted for virtuoso use of "plunger mute"; Newport
    Jazz Festival 1976.
Musical Compositions: Concerto for Cootie (a.k.a. Do Nothing Till
    You Hear from Me).
Theater: Appeared at Apollo Theatre; New School 1975; Carnegie
    Hall 1976.

WILLIAMS, DICK ANTHONY
    (Actor)
b. August 9, 1938, Chicago, Ill.

Special Interests: Directing, playwriting.
Address: 100 Riverside Drive #11E, New York, N.Y. 10024.
Honors: Drama Desk award, Tony nomination and AUDELCO Theatre
    award (for What the Winesellers Buy) 1974; Tor award, Tony
    nomination (for Black Picture Show) 1975, AUDELCO Black
    Theatre Recognition award 1975.
Career Data: Co-founder, The New Federal Theatre.
Films: Uptight 1968; The Lost Man 1969; Who Killed Mary What's
    'Er Name, The Anderson Tapes 1971; The Mack, Five on the
    Black Hand Side, Slaughter's Big Rip-Off 1973; Dog Day After-
    noon 1975; The Long Night, Deadly Hero 1976; The Deep 1977.
Television: Ironside; Positively Black 1975; Starsky and Hutch 1975;
    Black News 1976.
Theater: Wrote and directed One (O.B.); directed Pig Pen (A.P.T.);
    directed In New England Winter (O.B.); directed Don't Let It
    Go to Your Head (O.B.); wrote Black and Beautiful (produced
    in L.A.); wrote A Big of Black (produced in Chicago and
    L.A.); co-wrote, directed and acted in Big Time, Buck White
    1968; Jamimma (O.B.); co-produced Black Girl; Ain't Supposed
    to Die a Natural Death 1971; Rico in What the Winesellers Buy
    1973; Black Picture Show 1974; We Interrupt This Program...
    1975; The Poison Tree 1976.
Relationships: Husband of Gloria Edwards, actress.

WILLIAMS, HAL
    (Actor)
Address: Sackheim Agency, 9301 Wilshire Blvd., Suite 606, Los
    Angeles, Calif.
Memberships: SAG.
Television: Smitty on Sanford and Son (series) 1972-; Kung Fu;
    Police Woman 1974; Sgt. Earl Danning in Harry O 1974, 1975;
    Caribe 1975; S.W.A.T. 1975; DeMott in On the Rocks (series)
    1975; The Jeffersons 1977.

WILLIAMS, JOE (Joseph Goreed)
    (Singer)
b. 1918, Cordele, Ga.
Special Interests: Jazz, blues, soul.
Honors: Down Beat Male vocalist 1955; International Critics Best
    Male Vocalist of the Year 1974.
Career Data: Vocalist with bands of Lionel Hampton, Coleman
    Hawkins, Andy Kirk and Count Basie; popularized song Every-
    day All Right O.K. You Win; participated in Newport Jazz Fes-
    tival 1973, 1976.
Clubs: Buddy's Place 1975; The New Barrister 1976; Hoppers 1976,
    1977.
Records: Count Basie Swings and Joe Williams Sings; A Man Ain't
    Supposed to Die; Live (Fantasy); Man Ain't Supposed to Cry
    (Roulette); Something Old, New and Blue (Solid State); Worth
    Waiting For (Blue Note).
Television: Merv Griffin Show; The Strollin' Twenties (special)

1966; Mike Douglas Show 1974; Sammy and Company 1975;
Festival of Lively Arts for Young People 1976; At the Top
1976.
Theater: Black Music 1975 at Apollo Theatre 1975; appeared at
    Radio City Music Hall 1976; sang role of John Henry in Big
    Man (Carnegie Hall) 1976.

WILLIAMS, MARION
(Gospel Singer)
b. 1927, Miami, Fla.
Career Data: Member Ward Singers 1947-58; formed Stars of
    Faith 1959-65; toured Africa 1966; Bryant Park Noon Concert
    1974; Newport Jazz Festival 1975; among her hits are Surely
    God Is Able, Prayer Changes Things, How Far Am I from
    Canaan, Packin' Up 1957.
Records: O Holy Night (Savoy).
Television: Soundstage 1975.
Theater: Black Nativity (Bway, Europe, Australia) 1961; Town
    Hall 1975; Carnegie Hall 1975.

WILLIAMS, MARY LOU (Mary Louise Burley-Winn)
(Musician/Composer)
b. May 8, 1910, Atlanta, Ga.
Special Interests: Arranging, jazz, lecturing, piano, secular music.
Address: P.O. Box 32, Hamilton Grange Station, New York, N.Y.
    10031.
Honors: Four honorary doctorates; Guggenheim fellowship; N.Y.
    State Council on the Arts grant; her mass performed and cele-
    brated at St. Patrick's Cathedral 1975.
Career Data: Performed, arranged and composed for Andy Kirk
    band 1931, Count Basie; Duke Ellington 1943, Jimmy Lunce-
    ford, Cab Calloway, Earl Hines, Benny Goodman 1948, Louis
    Armstrong, The Dorsey Brothers and many others; founder,
    Pittsburgh Jazz Festival and participant in Newport, Monterey
    and Bay Area Jazz Festivals; President, Mary Records; toured
    England and France 1952-54; made lecture tours of colleges
    and universities throughout U.S.
Clubs: Cafe Carlyle; Copley Plaza (Boston); The Cookery; Bourbon
    Street (Toronto); Encore II (Pittsburgh); The Embers; Village
    Vanguard; Chez Mary Lou (her own club in Paris); Café Society
    Uptown and Downtown; Storyville (Boston); Three Deuces; Down-
    beat; Le Beouf sur Le Toit (Paris); Grand Terrace (Chicago);
    The Composer Room; Bop City; Kelly's Stables; Skybar (Cleve-
    land); Sheraton Palace (San Francisco); Timme's Club (Copen-
    hagen); Rhythm Club.
Memberships: AFM (Local 802); ASCAP 1943; NARAS.
Musical Compositions: Mary Lou's Mass (Mass #3); The Zodiac
    Suite 1945; Black Christ of the Andes; Hymn to St. Martin de
    Porres 1962; What's Your Story Morning Glory; In the Land of
    Oo Bla Dee; Little Joe from Chicago; Zoning Fungus II; A
    Fungus Amungus; Praise the Lord; Rosa Mae; Play It Momma;

Froggy Bottom; Elijah Under the Juniper Tree; Mass for the
Lenten Season (Mass #2); The Beggar Man (a.k.a. Lazarus);
Trumpet No End; Whistle Blues; Nite Life; The Scarlet Creep-
er; Drag Em; Lotta Sax Appeal; Steppin' Pretty; Pretty Eyed
Baby; You Know Baby; Timme's Blues; Blues for Peter; Dirge
Blues; Easy Blues; I Love Him (a.k.a. Amy); Fan Dangle;
Miss D.D.; Joycie; The Devil; Tisherome; Mary's Idea; Just
an Idea; My Mama Pinned a Rose on Me; Nursery Ryme 2-
Mary's Lamb; Cloudy; Lonely Moments; Walking and Swinging;
Roll Em; Overhand; Camel Hop; Fifth Dimension; The Juniper
Tree; Lamb of God.

Radio: Jack O'Brian Show; Arlene Francis Show; Sherrye Henry
Show; Women In; In Conversation; Mike Wallace Show; The
Mary Lou Williams Piano Playhouse (WNEW); Voice of Amer-
ica.

Records: On Mary: Zoning; Mary Lou's Mass; Mary Lou Williams
Presents St. Martin De Porres; Black Christ of the Andes.
On Chiaroscuro: From the Heart; Live at the Cookery; The
Zodiac Suite (Folkways); The Mary Lou Williams Trio 1975
(Steeplechase); Mary Lou Williams in London (GNP Crescendo);
Mary Lou Williams (Folkways).

Television: Today Show; Tonight Show; Dick Cavett Show; Sesame
Street; A.M. New York; Sunday; Joe Franklin Show; The First
Estate; Black Pride; Like It Is; To Tell the Truth; What's My
Line?; Steve Allen Show; Eyewitness News; Positively Black
1974; A.M. America 1975; Look Up and Live 1975; Bicentennial: A Black Perspective 1975; Christopher Closeup 1976,
1977.

Theater: Appearances at Apollo Theatre; Chicago Civic Auditorium;
Toledo Auditorium; Atlanta Auditorium; Crown Center (Kansas
City); Radio City Music Hall; Avery Fisher Hall; Hollywood
Bowl; John Drew Theatre (East Hampton); Walnut Street The-
atre (Philadelphia); Carnegie Music Hall (Pittsburgh); Palais
de Chaillot (Paris); Salle Pleyel (Paris); Olympia Theatre
(Paris); New York City Center (with Alvin Ailey Dance The-
atre); Blue Holiday 1945; Town Hall 1945; Carnegie Hall 1946;
Philharmonic Hall 1946; Guggenheim Bandshell, Damrosch
Park 1976.

WILLIAMS, OSCAR
    (Director/Producer)
b. 1939, Virgin Islands.
Education: Lagos Egri, School of Writing; New York City Community College; C.C.N.Y.; San Francisco State College B.A., M.
A. (Radio, Television and Film); U.S. Army Signal Corps
(cinematography) 1963.
Special Interests: Writing.
Films: Wrote Sudden Death; The Great White Hope (intern) 1970;
wrote, directed and produced The Final Comedown 1972;
directed Five on the Black Hand Side 1973; wrote Truck Turner; wrote and associate producer of Black Belt Jones 1974;
wrote and directed Hot Potato 1976.

WILLIAMS, SPENCER
    (Actor/Director)
b. July 14, 1893, Vidalia, La.
d. December 13, 1969, Los Angeles, Calif.
Special Interests: Writing
Films: Oft in the Silly Night (short); The Lady Fare (short);
    Music Hath Charms (short); The Framing of the Shrew (short);
    The Girl in Room 20; wrote, acted in and directed Tender-
    feet 1928; Melancholy Dame 1929; Georgia Rose 1930; The
    Virginia Judge, wrote and acted in Son of Ingagi 1937; Bronze
    Buckaroo 1938; Harlem Rides the Range, Two Gun Man from
    Harlem, Bad Boy, Harlem on the Prairie 1939; Toppers Take
    a Bow 1941; directed The Blood of Jesus 1942; wrote, acted
    in and directed Go Down Death, Of One Blood 1944; Bad Street
    Mama, Dirty Gerty from Harlem USA 1946; Jivin in Be Bop,
    Juke Joint 1947.
Records: It Feels So Good (Okeh) 1929.
Television: Andy on Amos 'n' Andy (series) 1951-54.

WILLIAMS, SPENCER
    (Jazz Musician/Composer)
b. October 14, 1889, New Orleans, La.
d. July 14, 1965, Flushing, N.Y.
Education: St. Charles University 1901-03.
Special Interests: Piano.
Career Data: Wrote Josephine Baker's songs for Folies Bergere
    and Casino de Paris 1925-35; partner with Fats Waller in
    vaudeville act, London 1932.
Memberships: ASCAP 1921.
Musical Compositions: Basin Street Blues; Everybody Loves My
    Baby; I Found a New Baby; Royal Garden Blues; I Ain't Got
    Nobody 1915; Squeeze Me (with Fats Waller) 1918; Careless
    Love 1921; She'll Be Comin' Round the Mountain 1923; I'm
    Sending a Letter to Santa Claus 1939.
Theater: Wrote score for Put and Take 1921.

WILLIAMSON, FRED "The Hammer"
    (Actor)
b. March 5, 1938, Gary, Ind.
Education: Northwestern University B.A. 1959.
Special Interests: Architecture, football, karate, directing, pro-
    ducing, singing.
Address: c/o Po Boy Productions, 1040 North Las Palmas Avenue,
    Los Angeles, Calif. 90038.
Career Data: Pro-football player (San Francisco Forty Niners,
    Pittsburgh Steelers, Oakland Raiders, Kansas City Chiefs)
    1959-68; karate demonstration in The Oriental World of Self
    Defense at Madison Square Garden 1974.
Films: Spearchucker in M*A*S*H*, Tell Me That You Love Me
    Junie Moon 1970; title role in Hammer, The Legend of Nigger
    Charley 1972; Black Caesar, The Soul of Nigger Charley, That

Man Bolt, Hell Up in Harlem 1973; Black Eye, Three Tough
Guys, Crazy Joe, Three the Hard Way 1974; Hero's Welcome,
Buck Town, Take a Hard Ride, wrote, co-produced and acted
in Boss Nigger; produced, directed and acted in Mean Johnny
Barrows 1975; Adios Amigo, No Way Back, directed and acted
in Death Journey 1976; Joshua 1977.
Radio: Movie Talk.
Records: Goodnight Sweetheart.
Television: Dating Game; Police Story; Laugh-In; Merv Griffin
    Show; Julia (series) 1969-70; Rookies 1974; Mike Douglas
    Show 1974; NFL Monday Night Football 1974; Bachelor of the
    Year (Wide World Special) 1974; O. J. Simpson Is Alive and
    Well and Getting Roasted Tonight (Wide World of Entertainment)
    1974; Ebony Music awards 1975; Dinah! 1976; Miss Universe
    Beauty Pageant 1976.

WILSON, BILLY
    (Choreographer /Dancer)
b. c.1936, Philadelphia, Pa.
Honors: Tony nominee (Bubbling Brown Sugar) 1976.
Career Data: Soloist, National Ballet of Holland 1961-65; visiting
    professor (drama), Brandeis University.
Theater: Carmen Jones (City Center) 1956: danced in chorus of
    Bells Are Ringing 1956; Jamaica 1957; West Side Story 1960;
    Two, If by Sea (O. B.); choreographed Bubbling Brown Sugar
    1976; directed and choreographed Guys and Dolls 1976.

WILSON, DEMOND
    (Actor)
b. October 13, 1946, Valdosta, Ga.
Education: High School of Performing Arts; Hunter College.
Clubs: Hilton (Las Vegas) 1975.
Films: The Organization 1971; Dealing 1972.
Records: America Is 200 Years and There Is Still Hope (Capitol).
Television: Mission: Impossible; Mannix; All in the Family 1971;
    Lamont in Sanford and Son (series) 1972-; Tonight Show;
    Hollywood Squares; Go (A Day at the San Diego Zoo) 1974;
    Salute to Redd Foxx (Wide World Special) 1974; Bluffers 1974;
    Merv Griffin Show 1975; Tony Orlando and Dawn 1975; Dinah!
    1975.
Theater: Green Pastures (debut) 1951; Jazznite (O. B.); Obsidian
    (O. B.); Touchstone in As You Like It 1960; Bernard in Boys
    in the Band (tour) 1969; Ceremonies in Dark Old Men (O. B.)
    1970; Five on the Black Hand Side (O. B.) 1970.

WILSON, DOOLEY
    (Actor /Musician)
b. April 3, 1894, Tyler, Texas.
d. May 30, 1953, Los Angeles, Calif.
Special Interests: Piano, singing.

Career Data: Drummer with Clarence Tisdale band; toured Europe
      with his own band 1919-30; performed with Federal Theatre
      Productions 1934.
Films: Sam in Casablanca, Night in New Orleans, Cairo, Take a
      Letter, Darling, My Favorite Blonde 1942; Two Tickets to
      London, Stormy Weather 1943; Higher and Higher, Seven Days
      Ashore 1944; Racing Luck 1948; Come to the Stable 1949;
      Free for All 1949; Passage West 1951.
Memberships: NAG.
Television: Bill Jackson in Beulah (series) 1952-53.
Theater: "Little Joe" Jackson in Cabin in the Sky 1940; Bloomer
      Girl 1944-45; Harvey (tour with all-black cast); Booker T.
      Washington (O. B.); Crooks in Of Mice and Men.

WILSON, FLIP (Clerow Wilson)
      (Comedian)
b.   December 8, 1933, Jersey City, N. J.
Address: International Famous Agency, 9255 Sunset Blvd., Los
      Angeles, Calif. 90069.
Honors: Grammy award for best comedy record 1971.
Clubs: Manor Plaza Hotel (San Francisco) 1954.
Films: Uptown Saturday Night 1974.
Records: Cowboys and Colored People (Atlantic); Funny and Live
      (Springboard International); Pot Luck (Scepter).
Television: Ed Sullivan Show; guest and substitute host, Tonight
      Show 1965-; Love, American Style 1969; The Flip Wilson Show
      (series) 1970-73; Here's Lucy 1971, 1972; Today Show; Merv
      Griffin Show; Glen Campbell Show; New Ballgame for Willie
      Mays; Flip Wilson... of Course (special) 1974; Dean Martin
      Comedy Hour (Roasting of Bob Hope) 1974; Clerow Wilson's
      Great Escape (special) 1974; Dinah! 1975; Muhammad Ali
      Variety Special 1975; Co-host Mike Douglas Show 1975; Milton
      Berle's More Mad World of Comedy 1975; Cher (special) 1975;
      Entertainment Hall of Fame Awards 1975; Mac Davis Show
      1975; Bob Hope Special 1975; Sammy and Company 1975; Em-
      my Awards Show 1975; Midnight Special 1975, 1976; Travels
      with Flip (special) 1976; Joys (Bob Hope Special) 1976; Six
      Million Dollar Man 1976; Good Morning America 1977; Tomor-
      row 1977.

WILSON, FRANK H.
      (Actor/Playwright)
b.   May 4, 1886, New York, N. Y.
d.   February 16, 1956, Jamaica, N. Y.
Education: American Academy of Dramatic Arts.
Honors: Command Performance for King George V of England;
      Opportunity Magazine Prize 1926.
Career Data: Organized singing quartet for vaudeville tour.
Films: Acted in Melody Makers 1932; The Emperor Jones 1933;
      The Green Pastures 1936; The Devil Is Driving, All American
      Sweetheart, A Dangerous Adventure, Life Begins with Love
      1937; Extortion 1938; Paradise in Harlem (acted and wrote)

1939; Murder on Lenox Avenue (wrote), Sunday Sinners (wrote)
1941; Watch on the Rhine 1943; Beware 1946.
Memberships: AEA; AFTRA; SAG.
Radio: Circus Days 1933.
Television: Studio One; Ethel and Albert.
Theater: Wrote: Brother Mose (a.k.a. Meek Mose) 1928; Back
Home Again, Confidence (one act) 1922; The Frisco Kid, The
Good Sister Jones, Sugar Cane (one act) 1926; Walk Together,
Chillun 1936; Race Pride, Colored Americans; acted: All
God's Chillun Got Wings 1924; Lem in Emperor Jones 1925;
The Dreamy Kid 1925; In Abraham's Bosom 1926; title role
in Porgy 1927, 1929; Sweet Chariot 1930; We the People 1931;
Singin' the Blues 1931; Bloodstream 1932; They Shall Not Die
1934; The Green Pastures 1935; All the Living 1938; Journey-
man 1938; Kiss the Boys Goodbye 1938; Emperor Jones (White
Plains) 1939; Watch on the Rhine 1941; South Pacific 1943;
Memphis Bound (tour) 1945; Anna Lucasta 1946-47; Set My
People Free 1948; The Big Knife 1949; How Long till Summer
1949; Take a Giant Step 1953.

WILSON, JACKIE "Mr. Excitement"
    (Singer)
b. June 9, 1934, Detroit, Mich.
Address: 400 Market Street, Camden, N.J. 08102.
Career Data: Former Golden Gloves boxing winner; member, The
    Dominoes, quartet, 1954-57.
Clubs: Black Knight (New Orleans); Latin Casino (Cherry Hill,
    N.J.)
Films: Go, Johnny, Go 1959.
Records: On Brunswick: Nowstalgia; At the Copa; Body and Soul;
    Greatest Hits; It's All a Part of Love; Jackie Sings the Blues;
    Manufacturers of Soul; My Golden Favorites; ... Sings the
    World's Greatest Melodies; This Love Is Real; Whispers; Reet
    Petite 1957; Lonely Teardrops 1958; To Be Loved 1958; That's
    Why (I Love You So) 1959; I'll Be Satisfied 1959; Night 1960;
    Doggin' Around 1960; Baby Workout 1963.
Television: Ed Sullivan Show; American Bandstand; Soundstage 1975;
    Merv Griffin Show 1975.
Theater: Appeared at Apollo Theatre.

WILSON, MARY
    (Singer)
b. March 4, 1944, Detroit, Mich.
Education: Northwestern High School (Detroit).
Career Data: Member, The Supremes vocal group 1962-73.
Clubs: Magic Mountain (L.A.); Flamboyant Hotel (Puerto Rico).

WILSON, NANCY
    (Singer)
b. February 20, 1937, Chillicothe, Ohio.

Education: Central State University (a.k.a. Wilberforce University).
Special Interests: Acting.
Address: 9465 Wilshire Blvd., Beverly Hills, Calif. 90212.
Honors: Grammy 1964.
Career Data: Sang with Rusty Bryant band 1956; toured U.S. and
    Canada until 1958; solo since 1959.
Clubs: Tropicoro; Fairmount Hotel (San Francisco); Coconut Grove
    Ambassador Hotel 1964; Riviera (Las Vegas) 1974; El San
    Juan Hotel (Puerto Rico) 1975.
Films: Save the Children 1973.
Records: On Capitol: Tell Me the Truth 1963; (You Don't Know)
    How Glad I Am 1964; I Wanna Be with You 1964; Don't Come
    Running Back to Me 1965; Face It Girl, It's Over 1968; Peace
    of Mind 1968; Can't Take My Eyes Off You 1969; All in Love
    Is Fair; Come Get to This; This Mother's Daughter 1976; Hurt
    So Bad; Now I'm a Woman; Son of a Preacher Man; Right to
    Love; But Beautiful; Close-Up; How Glad I Am; For Once in
    My Life; Who Can I Turn To; Best (Capitol); Good Life (Pick-
    wick); Free Again (Pickwick); Goin' Out of My Head (Pick-
    wick); I Know I Love (Capitol); Kaleidoscope (Capitol); I've
    Never Been to Me (Capitol).
Television: The FBI; Hawaii Five-O; Tonight Show; Phil Donahue
    Show; Bob Hope Show; Danny Kaye Show; Carol Burnett Show;
    Hollywood Palace; I Spy 1966; Room 222 1970; The Nancy Wil-
    son Show (L.A.) 1974; Police Story 1974; Soul Train 1974;
    Jerry Visits 1975; presenter, Ebony Music Awards 1975; Sam-
    my and Company 1975; Merv Griffin Show 1976; Kup's Show
    1976.
Theater: Appeared at Apollo Theatre 1960-62, 1969, 1970; West-
    bury Music Fair 1962, 1976; Carnegie Hall 1962, 1975, 1976;
    National Theatre-Kennedy Center for the Performing Arts
    (Washington D.C.) 1975; Avery Fisher Hall 1975; Soul at Shea
    Stadium 1976; Mill Run Theatre (Chicago) 1976.

WILSON, TEDDY (Theodore Wilson)
    (Pianist/Jazz Musician)
b. November 24, 1912, Austin, Texas.
Education: Tuskegee Institute; Talladega College.
Special Interests: Composing, teaching.
Address: 213 Knickerbocker Avenue, Hillside, N.J. 07205.
Honors: Down Beat Poll winner 1936-38; Metronome Poll winner
    1937, 1939, 1946; Esquire magazine award (gold) 1945, 1947,
    (silver) 1946; Newport Jazz Hall of Fame 1975.
Career Data: Played with bands of Benny Carter 1933, Willie
    Bryant 1934-35, Benny Goodman 1935-39, own band 1939-45,
    leader of sextets and trios 1945-59; appeared at Jazz Festival
    Aspen, Colorado; Brussels World's Fair 1958; taught at
    Juilliard School of Music 1945-52; toured Australia 1960,
    U.S.S.R. 1962, Europe 1965.
Clubs: Cafe-Society Uptown and Downtown; Michael's Pub 1974;
    Eddie Condon's 1975; Sweet Basil 1976.

Films: Hollywood Hotel 1938; Something to Shout About 1943;
        Boogie Woogie Dream 1944; The Benny Goodman Story 1955.
Memberships: ASCAP 1960.
Musical Compositions: Something to Shout About; Dizzy Spells;
        Warming Up; Sunny Morning; Early Session Hop; I'm Really
        Through.
Radio: WNEW (series) 1949-52; Peter Lind Hayes Show (WCBS)
        1954-55; Crime Photographer.
Records: And Then They Wrote (Columbia Special Products); Billie
        in Mind (Chiaroscuro); Moonglow (Black Lion); Runnin' Wild
        Montreux (Black Lion); Striding After Fats (Black Lion); Teddy
        Wilson and His All-Stars (Columbia).
Television: Bell Telephone Hour; Tonight Show; Today Show; Mike
        Douglas Show; What's My Line? 1975; Soundstage 1975.
Theater: Seven Lively Arts (musical) at Carnegie Hall; The Es-
        tablishment (O.B.) 1963; Town Hall (5:45 Interlude series)
        1975; N.Y. Jazz Museum 1975; Avery Fisher Hall (Newport
        Jazz Festival).

WILSON, THEODORE (R.)
        (Actor)
b. December 10, 1943, New York, N.Y.
Education: Florida A & M University.
Films: Cotton Comes to Harlem 1970; Come Back Charleston
        Blue 1972; Newman's Law 1974; River Niger 1976; The Great-
        est 1977.
Memberships: AFTRA; NEC 1968-69.
Television: The Waltons; Rev. Dooley in The Partridge Family
        (series) 1972; Roll Out (series) 1973; Earl the postman in
        That's My Mama (series) 1974; Police Woman; AAMCO Trans-
        mission commercial; Good Time 1976; Tonight Show 1976;
        Risko 1976; What's Happening! 1976; Sanford and Son 1976;
        The Love Boat 1976; Phil Wheeler in Sanford Arms (series)
        1977.
Theater: Daddy Goodness (NEC) 1968; Song of the Lusitanian Bogey
        (NEC) 1968; God Is a (Guess What?) (NEC) 1968; An Evening
        of One Acts (NEC) 1969.

WINFIELD, PAUL
        (Actor)
b. May 22, 1941, Los Angeles, Calif.
Education: Los Angeles City College; U.C.L.A. B.A. (drama);
Special Interests: Cello.
Honors: CORE plaque (Sounder) 1973; Oscar nomination for best
        performance by an actor in a leading role (Sounder) 1973.
Career Data: Inner City Repertory Theatre (L.A.); Actors Studio
        West; artist-in-residence, University of Hawaii.
Films: Who's Minding the Mint?, Perils of Pauline 1967; The Lost
        Man 1969; R.P.M. 1970; Brother John 1971; Trouble Man,
        Father in Sounder 1972; Gordon's War 1973; Huckleberry Finn,
        Conrack 1974; Hustle 1975; High Velocity 1976; Twilight's Last

Gleaming, The Greatest (cameo) 1977.
Memberships: Board member, ANTA (West Coast).
Television: Perry Mason; The Young Rebels; Nichols; Mannix;
    Ironside; Mission: Impossible; Room 222; The Suntan Mob
    episode of The Name of the Game; High Chaparral; Julia;
    Stones (Movie of the Week) 1973; The Horror at 37,000 Feet
    1973; Mike Douglas Show 1974; Roy Campanella in It's Good
    to Be Alive 1974; With All Deliberate Speed 1976; Green Eyes
    1977.
Theater: Sisyphus and the Blue-Eyed Cyclops (Studio-West, Calif.);
    A Raisin in the Sun (Inner City Repertory Co., Los Angeles);
    Duke of Buckingham in Richard III (NYSF) 1974.

WINSTON, HATTIE
    (Actor/Singer)
b. March 3, 1945, Greenville, Miss.
Education: Howard University.
Address: 200 East End Avenue, New York, N.Y. 10028.
Clubs: Reno Sweeney's 1976; Barbarann 1976.
Memberships: AEA; NAG; NEC 1968-69; SAG.
Television: Callback; The Electric Company; Musical Chairs 1975;
    Midday Live 1975; Positively Black 1976; Midnight Special 1977.
Theater: Sambo (O.B.); Weary Blues (O.B.); Prodigal Son (O.B.)
    1965; Day of Absence (NEC) 1966; Pins and Needles (O.B.)
    1967; God Is a (Guess What?) (NEC) 1968; Song of the Lusi-
    tanian Bogey (NEC) 1968; Man Better Man (NEC) 1969; The
    Me Nobody Knows 1970; Billy No Name (O.B.) 1970; Silvia
    in Two Gentlemen of Verona (replaced Jonelle Allen) 1972;
    Scapino 1974; The Great MacDaddy (NEC) 1974.

WINTERS, LAWRENCE (Lawrence Wisonant)
    (Opera Singer)
b. November 12, 1915, Kings Creek, S.C.
d. September 24, 1965, Hamburg, Germany.
Education: Howard University.
Career Data: Howard University Players and Choir; first black
    male to sing leading role, New York City Opera Company
    1951-61; lead baritone, Hamburg State Opera Company 1961-
    65; operatic roles include Tonio in Pagliacci, messenger in
    The Dybbuk, Amonasro in Aida, Rigoletto.
Records: Porgy in Porgy and Bess.
Television: All About Music 1957.
Theater: Porgy and Bess (debut) 1942; Call Me Mister 1946; My
    Darlin' Aida 1952; The Long Dream 1960; Show Boat.

WITHERS, BILL
    (Singer)
b. c.1940, Slab Fork, W. Va.
Special Interests: Composing, guitar.
Address: William Morris Agency, 151 El Camino Drive, Beverly
    Hills, Calif. 90212.

Clubs: Riviera (Las Vegas); The Bottom Line 1976.
Films: Save the Children 1973.
Records: Use Me; Bill Withers Live; Still Bill (Sus); It's All Over
     Now (with Bobby Womack); Just As I Am (Sus); Ain't No Sun-
     shine; Lean on Me; Live at Carnegie Hall (Sus); Making Music
     (Columbia); Naked and Warm (Columbia); And Justments (Sus);
     Live.
Television: Flip Wilson Show; guest/co-host Mike Douglas Show;
     Tonight Show 1974; Action 1974; Feeling Good 1975; American
     Bandstand 1976; Merv Griffin Show 1976; Dinah! 1976; Soul
     Train 1976.
Theater: Appeared at Avery Fisher Hall; Carnegie Hall 1972, 1976;
     Felt Forum 1976.
Relationships: Former husband of Denise Nicholas, actress.

WOMACK, BOBBY
     (Musician)
b.   1944.
Films: Across 110th Street (score) 1972.
Records: On United Artists: I Don't Know What the World Is
     Coming To; Safety Zone; B. W. Goes C & W; Hits; Home Is
     Where the Heart Is; Communication; Facts; Lookin' For...;
     Understanding; Live (Liberty); My Prescription (Minit); It's
     All Over Now.
Television: American Bandstand 1976; Soul Train 1976.
Theater: Appeared at Radio City Music Hall 1976; Nassau Coliseum
     1976.

WONDER, STEVIE (Steveland Judkins Morris Hardaway)
     (Singer)
b.   May 13, 1950, Saginaw, Mich.
Education: Michigan School for the Blind (Lansing); University of
     Southern California.
Special Interests: Harmonica, organ, drums, piano, composing.
Address: 325 East 18 Street, New York, N. Y. 10003.
Honors: Winner of 12 Grammies, 14 Gold singles; 2 platinum al-
     bums; 4 gold albums; Amsterdam News (N. Y.) Entertainer of
     the Year   1973; Best male vocalist of 1974 (National Assn.
     of Television and Radio Artists); Show Business Inspiration
     award; National Assn. of Record Merchandisers' Presidential
     award; winner of 5 Ebony Poll music awards 1975; NAACP
     Image award, male recording artist, songwriter 1976; Playboy
     Music Hall of Fame 1976.
Career Data: First performed as Little Stevie Wonder; formed his
     own company, Black Bull Productions; performed in England,
     France, Japan, Okinawa.
Clubs: Cellar Door (Washington, D. C.); Village Gate; Copacabana
     1970.
Films: Bikini Beach, Muscle Beach Party 1964.
Memberships: ASCAP.
Records: For Tamla: You Haven't Done Nothin'; Fingertips-Pt. 2

1963; For Once in My Life 1968; Super Woman 1972; Super-
stition 1972; Living for the City 1973; You Are the Sunshine
of My Life 1973; Signed Sealed and Delivered 1970; Where I'm
Coming From 1970; Talking Book; Music of My Mind 1972;
Innervisions 1973; Fulfillingness First Finale; My Cherie
Amour; I Call It Pretty Music; Songs in the Key of Life (Motown); Hits (Tamla).

Television: Ed Sullivan Show; Mike Douglas Show; Tom Jones Show;
American Bandstand; Touch of Gold (special) 1974; The American Music Awards 1975, Dinah! 1975; Grammy Awards 1976,
1976; Burt Bacharach...Opus No. 3 1976.

Theater: Appearances at Philharmonic Hall 1969; Carnegie Hall
1973; Nassau Coliseum 1974; Madison Square Garden 1974.

Relationships: Former husband of Syreeta, singer.

WOODS, ALLIE
    (Actor)
b.   September 28, 1940, Houston, Texas.
Education: Texas Southern University B.A. 1962; Tennessee A & I
State University M.S. 1964; New York University 1973; New
School for Social Research 1973.

Special Interests: Directing, producing, teaching, music.
Address: 255 West 108 Street, New York, N.Y. 10025.
Honors: Ford Foundation Fellowship 1973.
Career Data: Teacher, public schools, Houston 1964-66; taught or
lectured at John Jay College, Rutgers University, University
of Missouri, University of Ibadan, University of Washington,
Brooklyn College 1970-date; theatrical tours of Italy with La
Mama E.T.C. 1972; theatrical tours of U.S., England and
Italy with N.E.C. 1967-70; chorus, N.Y.C. Opera Co.

Films: Paper Lion 1968.
Memberships: AEA; SAG; SSDC.
Television: Day of Absence (PBS) 1967; Gateway (CBS) 1968;
Intern in Love Is a Many Splendored Thing (series) 1969; Free
Time 1972.

Theater: Acted in: Day of Absence (NEC) 1966; Big City Break-
down (O.B.) 1968; Kongi's Harvest (NEC) 1968; Song of the
Lusitanian Bogey (NEC) 1968; Daddy Goodness (NEC) 1968;
God Is a (Guess What)? (NEC) 1968; Man Better Man (NEC)
1969; Contribution (NEC) 1969; Akokawe (NEC) 1970; Brother-
hood (NEC) 1970; For Sale (O.B.) 1970; Noah's Trip (Mobile
Unit) 1970; How Do You Do? (La Mama) 1972; Dialect Tele-
vision (La Mama) 1972. Directed: Miss Weaver/Two in a
Trap (NEC) 1968; A Black Quartet (O.B.) 1969; Short Stuff
(New Dramatists Committee) 1970; Clara's Ole Man/Sister
Sadie (La Mama) 1972; Cotillion (New Federal Theatre) 1975.

WORK, JOHN WESLEY
    (Composer)
b.   June 15, 1901, Tullahoma, Tenn.
d.   May 18, 1967, Nashville, Tenn.

Education: Fisk University B. A. 1923; Columbia University M. A.
    1931; Yale University B. Mus. 1933; Juilliard School of
    Music.
Special Interests: Conducting.
Honors: Rosenwald Foundation Fellowship; 1st Prize, Fellowship
    of American Composers (for The Singers) 1946.
Career Data: Fisk University; conductor, Men's Glee Club 1927-31,
    assistant professor (music) 1933-40, professor and head,
    Music Dept. 1940-65, director Fisk Jubilee Singers 1948-57.
Memberships: ASCAP 1941; Composers-Authors Guild; National
    Assn. of American Composers and Conductors; National Assn.
    of Negro Musicians.
Musical Compositions: Go Tell It on the Mountain; My Lord, What
    a Morning; Sing O Heavens; Soliloquy; Three Glimpses of Night;
    Dusk at Sea; To a Mona Lisa; Every Mail Day; There's a
    Meetin' Here Tonight; For the Beauty of the Earth; Into the
    Woods My Master Went; Do Not I Love Thee, O Lord?; The
    Singers (cantata); Yenvalou; Isaac Watts Contemplates the
    Cross (choral cycle); Appalachia and Sassafras; For All the
    Saints Who from Their Labors Rest; Scuppernong.

WRIGHT, RICHARD
    (Playwright)
b. September 4, 1908, Natchez, Miss.
d. November 28, 1960, Paris, France.
Honors: NAACP Spingarn Medal 1941.
Career Data: Publicity agent, Federal Negro Theatre; member,
    Federal Writers' Project 1935.
Films: Wrote and starred as Bigger Thomas in Native Son 1950.
Publications: Black Boy (autobiography), Harper, 1945.
Theater: Wrote Native Son 1941; The Long Dream 1960; Daddy
    Goodness (produced posthumously) 1968.

YANCY, EMILY
    (Actress)
b. April 28, 1939, New York, N. Y.
Education: New York City Community College A. A. S. 1960; studied
    at Ophelia De Vore School of Charm and acting with Lloyd
    Richards.
Special Interests: Modeling, singing.
Address: Henderson Hogan Agency, 247 S. Beverly Drive, Beverly
    Hills, Calif.
Honors: National Negro Beauty Contest Winner 1962; 2nd Place,
    Miss Cannes Film Festival Contest.
Clubs: Bricktop's (Rome); Living Room; Blue Angel 1963.
Films: Sodom and Gomorrah 1963; What's So Bad About Feeling
    Good? 1968; Tell Me That You Love Me, Junie Moon, Cotton
    Comes to Harlem 1970; Blacula 1972.
Memberships: AEA; NAG; SAG.
Records: Yancy (Mainstream).

Television: Tonight Show; Merv Griffin Show; Mod Squad; Sanford
        and Son; The Rookies 1974; That's My Mama 1975; Starsky and
        Hutch 1947.
Theater: Your Own Thing (NYSF); Tuptim in The King and I (L.A.);
        Shakespeare in Harlem (O.B.) 1960; No Strings (stock) 1964;
        Hallelujah Baby (standby for Leslie Uggams) 1967; Mrs. Mol-
        loy in Hello, Dolly! 1967-69; Don't Bother Me, I Can't Cope
        1972; 1600 Pennsylvania Avenue 1976; Aldonza in Man of La
        Mancha 1977.

YARBOROUGH, SARA
        (Dancer)
b. 1951, Brooklyn, N.Y.
Education: George Balanchine's School of American Ballet 1963-66;
        Professional Children's School; Harkness School for Ballet
        Arts.
Career Data: Member of Harkness Ballet 1968-70 (danced Firebird,
        John Butler's Sebastian, Jerome Robbins' New York Export:
        Opus Jazz, Alvin Ailey's Feast of Ashes); member of Alvin
        Ailey Dance Theatre 1970-date (danced Cry, Carmina Burana,
        After Eden, Portrait of Billie, Time Out of Mind 1971, Rev-
        elations 1971, Mary Lou's Mass 1971, Icarus 1972, Lark As-
        cending 1972, Metallics 1972, Rainbow 'Round My Shoulder
        1972, Leonard Bernstein's Mass 1973).

YOUNG, A. S. "Doc" (Andrew Sturgeon)
        (Publicist)
b. October 29, 1924, Va.
Education: Hampton Institute B.S.; Pepperdine College; California
        State University.
Special Interests: Writing.
Address: c/o The Sentinel, 112 East 43 Street, Los Angeles,
        Calif. 90011.
Career Data: Writer, radio commercials 1950; Hollywood Studio
        Publicist 1957.
Films: Publicity for: The Defiant Ones 1958; The Bus Is Coming
        1971.
Memberships: Publicists Guild of Hollywood; Greater Los Angeles
        Press Club.

YOUNG, LESTER "Pres" (Willis)
        (Jazz Musician/Composer)
b. August 27, 1909, Woodville, Miss.
d. March 15, 1959, New York, N.Y.
Special Interests: Tenor saxophone, clarinet.
Honors: Down Beat poll winner 1944; Esquire Silver award 1945,
        1947; Down Beat Hall of Fame 1959; Ebony Music award
        (posthumously) 1975.
Career Data: Played with King Oliver, Bennie Moten, Fletcher
        Henderson 1934, Andy Kirk 1936, Count Basie 1936-40, led
        own combo 1941-42.

Clubs: Reno (Kansas City); Kelly's Stable 1941; Cafe Society 1942.
Films: Jammin' the Blues 1945.
Memberships: ASCAP 1959.
Musical Compositions: Tickle Toe; Jumpin' with Symphony Sid;
     Taxi War Dance; Lester Leaps In; Nobody Knows.
Records: Pres: The Complete Savoy Recordings (Savoy); Lester
     Young the Aladdin Sessions (Blue Note); Tenor Saxes (Verve);
     Pres and Sweets (Verve); Lester's Here (Verve); Lester
     Swings Again (Verve); Lester Leaps In (Epic); Also Blue
     Lester (Savoy); The Lester Young Story (Verve); Newly Dis-
     covered Performances (ESP); Pres (Archive of Folk & Jazz
     Music); Pres and Teddy and Oscar (Verve); Pres at His Very
     Best (Trip); Pres in Europe (Onyx); Prez Leaps Again (Soul).

YOUNG, OTIS (Edwin)
     (Actor)
b. 1932, Providence, R.I.
Education: New York University B.S. (Education); University of
     Dayton; Neighborhood Playhouse 1957; studied theatre with
     Frank Silvera.
Address: Herman Zimmerman, 12077 Ventura Place, Studio City,
     Calif.
Films: Don't Just Stand There 1968; Right on Brother 1969; The
     Last Detail 1974.
Memberships: SAG.
Television: A Bride for Oona (U.S. Steel Hour); The Green Pas-
     tures (Hallmark Hall of Fame) 1957; East Side West Side
     1963; Jemal David in The Outcasts (series) 1968; The Clones
     1973; Get Christie Love 1975; Colombo 1975; Cannon 1976;
     Ellery Queen 1976; Twin Detectives 1976.
Theater: Second City Troupe; stage mgr., Call Me by My Rightful
     Name (O.B.) 1961; stage mgr., In the Counting House 1962;
     production asst., Days and Nights of Beebee Fenstermaker
     (O.B.) 1962; Tambourines to Glory 1963; Blues for Mister
     Charlie 1964.

ZULEMA
     (Singer)
b. c.1947.
Special Interests: Songwriting.
Career Data: Started vocal group, Faith Hope and Charity; partici-
     pated in Save the Children Festival, Watts.
Clubs: Half Note; Brody's Supper Club 1975; New Barrister (Bronx)
     1976.
Films: Save the Children 1973.
Records: On RCA: Zulema; RSVP; Suddenly There Was You; Ms Z
     (Sus).
Television: Positively Black 1975.
Theater: Appeared at Avery Fisher Hall; Town Hall 1975.

DIRECTORY OF ORGANIZATIONS

Academy of Motion Picture
Arts and Sciences (AMPAS)
8949 Wilshire Blvd.
Beverly Hills, Calif. 90211

Actors Equity Association (AEA)
165 West 46 Street
New York, N.Y. 10036

Afro-American Studio Theatre
415 West 127 Street
New York, N.Y. 10027

Afro-American Total Theatre
c/o Empire Hotel
44 West 63 Street
New York, N.Y. 10023

Afro-Asian Artistes
34 Grafton Terrace
London, England NW 5

Alonzo Players
395 Clinton Avenue
Brooklyn, N.Y. 11238

AMAS Repertory Theatre
Church of Sts. Paul and Andrew
263 West 86 Street
New York, N.Y. 10024

American Academy of Arts and
Sciences (AAAS)
280 Newton Street
Boston, Mass. 02146

American Federation of Musicians (AFM) of the United
States & Canada
641 Lexington Avenue
New York, N.Y. 10022

American Federation of Television and Radio Artists
(AFTRA)
1350 Avenue of the Americas
New York, N.Y. 10019

American Film Institute (AFI)
c/o John F. Kennedy Center
for the Performing Arts
Washington, D.C. 20566

American Guild of Musical
Artists (AGMA)
1841 Broadway
New York, N.Y. 10023

American Guild of Variety
Artists (AGVA)
1540 Broadway
New York, N.Y. 10036

American National Theatre &
Academy
245 West 52 Street
New York, N.Y. 10019

American Society of Music Ar-
rangers (ASMA)
c/o Local 47, A.F. of M.
816 Vine Street
Los Angeles, Calif. 90038

Arena Players Inc.
406 Orchard Street
Baltimore, Md. 21201

Armstead-Johnson Foundation
for Theater Research
222 West 23 Street
New York, N.Y. 10011

Associated Actors and Artistes
  of America (AAAA)
165 West 46 Street
New York, N.Y. 10036

Association of Theatrical Press
  Agents and Managers (ATPAM)
268 West 47 Street
New York, N.Y. 10036

Audience Development Co.
  (AUDELCO)
155 West 126 Street
New York, N.Y. 10027

Black Experience Ensemble
5 Homestead Avenue
Albany, N.Y. 12203

The Black Theatre Alliance
  (BTA)
162 West 56 Street, Suite 303
New York, N.Y. 10019

British Actors Equity Association (BAEA)
8 Harley Street
London WIN 2AB, England

British Film Institute
81 Dean Street
London W.1, England

Composers and Lyricists Guild
  of America (CLGA)
6565 Sunset Blvd.
Hollywood, Calif. 90028

Concept East
60 Harper Street
Detroit, Mich. 48202

The Cornbread Players
29 Hamilton Terrace
New York, N.Y. 10021

Dance Theatre of Harlem
466 West 152 Street
New York, N.Y. 10031

D.C. Black Repertory Company
4935 Georgia Avenue N.W.
Washington, D.C. 20011

The Demi-Gods
415 West 127 Street
New York, N.Y. 10027

Directors Guild of America
  (DGA)
7950 Sunset Blvd.
Hollywood, Calif. 90046

Ebony Showcase Theatre
4718 West Washington Blvd.
Los Angeles, Calif. 90007

Equity Library Theatre (ELT)
165 West 46 Street
New York, N.Y. 10036

Al Fann Theatrical Ensemble
207 West 133 Street
New York, N.Y. 10027

Free Southern Theatre
1240 Dryades Street
New Orleans, La. 70113

Harlem Performance Center
2394 Adam Clayton Powell Blvd.
New York, N.Y. 10030

Harlem Philharmonic Society
  Inc.
P.O. Box 445, Cathedral Sta-
  tion
New York, N.Y. 10025

Billie Holiday Theatre
1368 Fulton Street
Brooklyn, N.Y. 11216

Inner City Repertory Co.
1308 South New Hampshire
  Avenue
Los Angeles, Calif. 90006

Karamu House Theatre
2355 East 89 Street
Cleveland, Ohio 44160

Mafundi Institute
Drama Workshop
103rd and Wilmington
Los Angeles, Calif. 90002

William Morris Agency
151 El Camino Drive
Beverly Hills, Calif. 90212

National Academy of Recording
    Arts and Sciences (NARAS)
6430 Sunset Blvd.
Hollywood, Calif. 90028

National Academy of Television
    Arts and Sciences (NATAS)
291 South La Cienega Blvd.
Beverly Hills, Calif. 90211

National Black Theatre (NBT)
9 East 125 Street
New York, N.Y. 10035

National Society of Film Critics
562 West End Avenue
New York, N.Y. 10024

Negro Actors Guild (NAG)
1674 Broadway
New York, N.Y. 10019

Negro Ensemble Company (NEC)
133 Second Avenue
New York, N.Y. 10003

New Federal Theatre
Henry Street Playhouse
466 Grand Street
New York, N.Y. 10002

New Heritage Theatre
43 East 125 Street
New York, N.Y. 10035

New Lafayette Theatre
2349 Seventh Avenue
New York, N.Y. 10030

New York Shakespeare Festival
    (NYSF)
150 West 65 Street
New York, N.Y. 10023

100 Black Men
60 East 86 Street
New York, N.Y. 10028

Performing Arts Society of
    Los Angeles (PASLA)
3701 West 54 Street
Los Angeles, Calif. 90043

Poet-Tential Unlimited Theater
303 West 125 Street
New York, N.Y. 10027

Public Theatre
425 Lafayette Street
New York, N.Y. 10023

Screen Actors Guild (SAG)
7750 Sunset Blvd.
Hollywood, Calif. 90046

Society of Stage Directors and
    Choreographers (SSDC)
1619 Broadway
New York, N.Y. 10019

Spirit House Movers and
    Players
13 Belmont Avenue
Newark, N.J. 07102

Spotlight Casting Directing &
    Contacts
42 Cranbourn Street
London, England WC2

Symphony of the New World
250 West 57 Street
New York, N.Y. 10019

Theatre Guild
226 West 47 Street
New York, N.Y. 10036

Theatre Owners Booking Assn.
    (TOBA)
c/o The First Congregational
    Church
464 East Walnut Street
Pasadena, Calif. 91101

Urban Arts Corps.
26 West 20 Street
New York, N.Y. 10011

Writers Guild of America,
  East (WGAE)
1212 Avenue of the Americas
New York, N. Y. 10036

Writers Guild of America,
  West (WGAW)
8955 Beverly Blvd.
Los Angeles, Calif. 90048

BIBLIOGRAPHY

The Afro-American Encyclopedia. 10 volumes. North Miami, Fla.:
Educational Book Pub., Inc., 1974.

The American Society of Composers, Authors and Publishers. The
ASCAP Biographical Dictionary of Composers, Authors and
Publishers. 1966 ed.

Amory, Cleveland, ed. Celebrity Registry: An Irreverent Compendium of American Quotable Notables. New York: Simon
and Schuster, 1973.

Arata, Esther and Rotoli, Nicholas. Black American Playwrights,
1800 to the Present: A Bibliography. Metuchen, N.J.:
Scarecrow Press, 1976.

Archer, Leonard C. Black Images in the American Theatre.
Brooklyn: Pageant-Poseidon Ltd., 1973.

Baskin, Wade and Runes, Richard N. Dictionary of Black Culture.
New York: Philosophical Library, 1973.

Bogle, Donald. Toms, Coons, Mulattoes, Mammies and Bucks:
An Interpretive History of Blacks in American Films. New
York: Viking, 1973.

Chambers, Lucille Arcola, ed. America's Tenth Man. New York:
Twayne, 1957.

Chilton, John. Who's Who of Jazz: Storyville to Swing Street.
Radnor, Pa.: Chilton, 1972.

Chujoy, Anatole and Manchester, P. W. The Dance Encyclopedia.
Rev. and enl. ed. New York: Simon and Schuster, 1967.

Ebony Editors. The Ebony Handbook. Chicago: Johnson Pub. Co.,
1974.

Ebony Editors. Ebony Pictorial History of America. v.4. Chicago:
Johnson Pub. Co., 1973.

Ebony Editors. The Negro Handbook. Chicago: Johnson Pub. Co.,
1966.

412

Emery, Lynne F. Black Dance in the United States from 1619 to
     1970. Palo Alto, Calif.: National Press Books, 1972.

Feather, Leonard. The Encyclopedia of Jazz. New York: Horizon
     Press, 1955.

Gertner, Richard, ed. International Television Almanac. New
     York: Quigley Pub. Co., 1975.

Halliwell, Leslie. The Filmgoer's Companion. 4th ed. New York:
     Hill and Wang, 1974.

Hughes, Langston and Meltzer, Milton. Black Magic: A Pictorial
     History of the Negro in American Entertainment. Englewood
     Cliffs, N.J.: Prentice-Hall, 1967.

Hughes, Langston. Famous Negro Music Makers. New York:
     Dodd, Mead, 1955.

Landay, Eileen. Black Film Stars. New York: Drake, 1974.

Leab, Daniel J. The Black Experience in Motion Pictures. New
     York: Houghton Mifflin, 1975.

Leab, Daniel J. From Sambo to Superspade: The Black Experience
     in Motion Pictures. New York: Houghton Mifflin, 1975.

Mapp, Edward. Blacks in American Films: Today and Yesterday.
     Metuchen, N.J.: Scarecrow Press, 1972.

Matney, William C., ed. Who's Who Among Black Americans.
     v.1 1975-1976. Northbrook, Ill.: W.W.A.B.A., Inc., 1976.

Mitchell, Loften. Black Drama: The Story of the American Negro
     in the Theatre. New York: Hawthorn, 1967.

Mitchell, Loften. Voices of the Black Theatre. Clifton, N.J.:
     James T. White & Co., 1975.

Munden, Kenneth. The American Film Institute Catalog. New
     York: Bowker, 1971.

Murray, James P. To Find an Image, Black Films from Uncle
     Tom to Super Fly. New York: Bobbs-Merrill, 1973.

The New York Times Obituaries Index 1858-1968. (New York Times)
     1970.

The New York Times Film Reviews. 3 v. (New York Times)
     Arno Press, 1970.

Nite, Norm N. Rock On: The Illustrated Encyclopedia of Rock n'
     Roll The Solid Gold Years. New York: Crowell, 1974.

Noble, Peter. The Negro in Films. (Reprint of 1949 ed.) New
York: Arno, 1970.

Null, Gary. Black Hollywood: The Negro in Motion Pictures.
Secaucus, N.J.: Citadel, 1975.

Parish, James R. Actors' Television Credits 1950-1972. Metuchen,
N.J.: Scarecrow Press, 1973.

Patterson, Lindsay. Anthology of the American Negro in the
Theatre: A Critical Approach. The Assn. for the Study of
Negro Life and History (International Library of Negro Life
and History). Cornwell Hghts., Pa.: Publishers Agency,
Inc., 1967.

Patterson, Lindsay. Black Films and Film-Makers: A Compre-
hensive Anthology from Stereotype to Superhero. New York:
Dodd, Mead, 1975.

Performing Arts Libraries and Museums of the World. 2d ed.
New York: Theatre Arts Books, 1967.

Pines, Jim. Blacks in Films; A Survey of Racial Themes and
Images in American Films. London: Studio Vista Publishers, 1975.

Players' Guide. New York: Paul L. Ross, 1943-.

Ploski, Harry A. and Brown, Roscoe C. The Negro Almanac.
New York: Bellwether Pub. Co., 1966.

Powell, C. B. ed. Amsterdam News (weekly). New York. Various issues, 1974-1976.

Primus, Marc. Black Theater: A Resource Directory. Washington, D.C.: American Theatre Assoc., 1973.

Ragan, David. Who's Who in Hollywood 1900-1976. New Rochelle,
N.Y.: Arlington House, 1977.

Rigdon, Walter, ed. The Biographical Encyclopaedia & Who's Who
of the American Theatre. New York: James H. Heineman,
1966.

Roach, Hildred. Black American Music: Past and Present. Boston: Crescendo Publishing Co., 1973.

Rollins, Charlemae. Famous Negro Entertainers of Stage, Screen
and TV. New York: Dodd, 1967.

Rush, Theressa Gunnels, Carol F. Myers and Esther Spring Arata.
Black American Writers Past and Present: A Biographical
and Bibliographical Dictionary. 2 v. Metuchen, N.J.:
Scarecrow Press, 1975.

Sampson, Henry T. Blacks in Black and White: A Source Book
    on Black Films. Metuchen, N.J.: Scarecrow Press, 1977.

Schiffman, Jack. Uptown: The Story of Harlem's Apollo Theatre.
    New York: Cowles, 1971.

Schwann Record and Tape Guide (monthly). Boston: W. Schwann,
    Inc.

Shockley, Ann Allen and Chandler, Sue P. Living Black American
    Authors: A Biographical Directory. New York: Bowker,
    1973.

Smythe, Mabel M. ed. The Black American Reference Book.
    Englewood Cliffs, N.J.: Prentice-Hall, 1976.

Southern, Eileen. The Music of Black Americans: A History.
    New York: W. W. Norton, 1971.

Stambler, Irwin and Landon, Grelun. Encyclopedia of Folk, Coun-
    try and Western Music. New York: St. Martin's Press,
    1969.

Terrace, Vincent. The Complete Encyclopedia of Television Pro-
    grams 1947-1976. 2 v. Cranbury, N.J.: A. S. Barnes,
    1976.

Truitt, Evelyn Mack. Who Was Who on Screen. New York:
    Bowker, 1974.

TV Guide (weekly). Radnor, Pa.: Triangle Pub. Co.

Weaver, John T. Forty Years of Screen Credits 1929-1969. 2 v.
    Metuchen, N.J.: Scarecrow Press, 1970.

Who's Who in Colored America: A Biographical Dictionary of Nota-
    ble Living Persons of Negro Descent in America. 7th ed.
    Yonkers, N.Y.: Christian E. Burckel & Assocs., 1950.

Who's Who in Music and Musicians' International Directory. 6th
    ed. London: Burke's Peerage Ltd., 1972.

Who's Who in Show Business: The International Directory of the
    Entertainment World. New York: WWSB, Inc., 1971.

Willis, John, ed. Dance World [annual]. New York: Crown.

Willis, John, ed. Screen World [annual]. New York: Crown.

Willis, John, ed. Theatre World [annual]. New York: Crown.

CLASSIFIED INDEX

Persons listed in this Directory have been indexed under one or more of the following categories:

Actors	Dancers	Opera Singers
Actresses	Designers	Pianists
Broadcasters	Directors	Playwrights
Choreographers	Disc Jockeys	Producers
Comedians	Entertainers	Publicists
Composers	Folk Singers	Singers
Concert Singers	Gospel Singers	Theatrical
Conductors	Jazz Musicians	Agents
Critics	Musicians	Ventriloquist

ACTORS

Adams, Joe
Adams, Robert
Aldridge, Ira
Amos, John
Anderson, Carl
Anderson, Eddie
Anderson, Ernest
Anderson, Thomas
Atkins, Pervis
Attles, Joseph
Baskett, James
Beard, Matthew
Belafonte, Harry
Bernard, Ed
Best, Willie
Bibb, Leon
Blakely, Donald
Bledsoe, Jules
Bosan, Alonzo
Brooks, Clarence
Brown, Everett
Brown, George Stanford
Brown, Graham
Brown, Jim
Browne, Roscoe Lee
Burghardt, Arthur
Bush, Norman

Calloway, Kirk
Calloway, Northern
Cambridge, Ed
Cambridge, Godfrey
Cameron, Earl
Carter, Ben
Carter, Ralph
Carter, Terry
Casey, Bernie
Challenger, Rudy
Chenault, Lawrence
Chester, Slick
Childress, Alvin
Christian, Robert
Clanton, Rony
Colley, Don Pedro
Cook, Lawrence
Cooper, Ralph
Copage, Marc
Corbin, Clayton
Cosby, Bill
Crosse, Rupert
Crothers, Scatman
Crudup, Carl
Cumbuka, Ji-Tu
Davis, Clifton
Davis, Ossie

Mitchell, Don
Mitchill, Scoey
Moore, Archie
Moore, Tim
Moreland, Manton
Morris, Garrett
Morris, Greg
Morton, Joe
Mosley, Roger
Muse, Clarence
O'Neal, Frederick
O'Neal, Ron
Orman, Roscoe
Overton, Bill
Page, Harrison
Parker, Leonard
Perry, Felton
Perry, Rod
Peters, Brock
Peterson, Caleb
Poitier, Sidney
Polk, Oscar
Popwell, Albert
Preston, J. A.
Randolph, James
Rasulala, Thalmus
Reed, Albert
Renard, Ken
Rhodes, Hari
Rich, Ron
Rippy, Rodney Allen
Roberts, Davis
Robeson, Paul
Robinson, Bill
Robinson, Roger
Rodrigues, Percy
Roker, Renny
Rosemond, Clinton
Ross, Ted
Roundtree, Richard
St. Jacques, Raymond
St. John, Christopher
Sattin, Lonnie
Scott, Harold
Sekka, Johnny
Sellers, Brother John
Shorte, Dino
Sidney, P. J.
Silvera, Frank
Simpson, O. J.
Spell, George
Spencer, Kenneth
Stewart, Mel

Stoker, Austin
Strode, Woody
Tarkington, Rockne
Thomas, Philip M.
Tucker, Lorenzo
Turman, Glynn
Van Peebles, Melvin
Vitte, Ray
Wade, Adam
Walker, Bill
Ward, Douglas Turner
Ward, Richard
Washington, Kenny
Watson, James A.
Whipper, Leigh
Whitman, Ernest
Williams, Billy Dee
Williams, Clarence III
Williams, Dick Anthony
Williams, Hal
Williams, Spencer
Williamson, Fred
Wilson, Demond
Wilson, Dooley
Wilson, Frank H.
Wilson, Theodore
Winfield, Paul
Woods, Allie
Young, Otis

ACTRESSES

Allen, Deborah
Allen, Jonelle
Alice, Mary
Anderson, Esther
Anderson, Myrtle
Angelou, Maya
Archer, Osceola
Attaway, Ruth
Avery, Margaret
Ayler, Ethel
Bailey, Pearl
Batson, Susan
Beavers, Louise
Belgrave, Cynthia
Bell, Jeanne
Bennett, Fran
Bey, Marki
Bowman, Laura
Brown, Chelsea

Randolph, Amanda
Randolph, Lillian
Reed, Tracy
Richards, Beah
Roby, Lavelle
Roker, Roxie
Rolle, Esther
Ross, Diana
Sands, Diana
Sanford, Isabell
Sattin, Tina
Sharp, Saundra
Sherril, Joya
Simms, Hilda
Sinclair, Madge
Smith, Mildred Joanne
Smith, Muriel
Speed, Carol
Spencer, Christine
Stanis, BernNadette
Stubbs, Louise
Sykes, Brenda
Tamu
Tanisha, Ta
Taylor, Clarice
Taylor, Libby
Teer, Barbara Ann
Todd, Beverly
Tolbert, Berlinda
Tyson, Cicely
Uggams, Leslie
Van Scott, Glory
Wade, Ernestine
Walker, Ada Overton
Wallace, Royce
Wan, Madame Sul Te
Warfield, Marlene
Washington, Fredi
Waters, Ethel
Webb, Alyce
White, Jane
Winston, Hattie
Yancy, Emily

BROADCASTERS

Brown, Tony
Jackson, Hal
Jenkins, Carol
Johnson, John
Lamont, Barbara

McCreary, Bill
Murray, Joan
Noble, Gil
Pierce Ponchitta
Quarles, Norma
Teague, Bob
Tolliver, Melba
Tucker, Lem

CHOREOGRAPHERS

Ailey, Alvin
Ashley, Frank
Beatty, Talley
Bey, La Rocque
Borde, Percival
Collins, Janet
Dafora, Asadata
Destiné, Jean-León
Dunham, Katherine
Faison, George
Fort, Syvilla
Holder, Geoffrey
Johnson, Louis
McKayle, Donald
Mitchell, Arthur
Pomare, Eleo
Primus, Pearl
Rodgers, Rod
Savage, Archie
Thompson, Clive
Wilson, Billy

COMEDIANS

Ajaye, Franklin
Anderson, Eddie
Best, Willie
Brown, Johnny
Cambridge, Godfrey
Cosby, Bill
Fetchit, Stepin
Foxx, Redd
Green, Eddie
Gregory, Dick
Kirby, George
Mabley, Jackie
Markham, Dewey
Mitchill, Scoey

Moreland, Manton
Pryor, Richard
Ragland, Larry
Rogers, Timmie
Russell, Nipsey
Walker, Jimmie
Washington, Ford Lee
Watson, Irwin C.
White, Slappy
Wilson, Flip

COMPOSERS

Benjamin, Bennie
Bland, James
Boatner, Edward
Bonds, Margaret
Brown, Oscar
Burgie, Irving
Burleigh, Harry
Clevalier de Saint Georges,
 J. B.
Coleridge-Taylor, Samuel
Cook, Will Marion
Cordero, Roque
Cunningham, Arthur
Da Costa, Noel
Dawson, William Levi
Dett, Robert Nathaniel
Diton, Carl
Dorsey, Thomas A.
Ellington, Duke
Grant, Micki
Handy, W. C.
Johnson, James Weldon
Johnson, J. Rosamond
Jones, Quincy
Joplin, Scott
Kay, Ulysses
Lucas, Sam
Lyles, Aubrey
Mayfield, Curtis
Miller, Flournoy
Moore, Carman Leroy
Moore, Undine Smith
Perkinson, Coleridge Taylor
Razaf, Andy
Sampson, Edgar
Simone, Nina
Sissle, Noble
Smith, Hale

Still, William Grant
Strayhorn, Billy
Tillis, Frederick C.
Waller, Fats
Walker, George Theophilus
Williams, Mary Lou
Work, John W.

CONCERT SINGERS

Addison, Adele
Allen, Betty
Anderson, Marian
Boatwright, McHenry
Brice, Carol
Brown, Anne
Davis, Elabelle
Duncan, Todd
Hayes, Roland
Maynor, Dorothy
Norman, Jessye
Robeson, Paul
Thompson, Arthur
Warfield, William

CONDUCTORS

Armstrong, Louis
Basie, Count
Calloway, Cab
Dawson, William Levi
De Paur, Leonard
De Priest, James
Dixon, Dean
Ellington, Duke
Ellington, Mercer
Europe, James Reese
Frazier, James Jr.
Hampton, Lionel
Hawkins, Erskine
Hines, Earl
Jacquet, Illinois
Jessye, Eva
Johnson, Hall
Jordan, Louis
Lee, Everett
Lewis, Henry
Millinder, Lucky
Rhodes, George

Taylor, Billy
Wheeler, Harold
Williams, Cootie

CRITICS

Abdul, Raoul
Burrell, Walter
Holt, Nora
Mason, Clifford
Murray, James
Patterson, Lindsay
Riley, Clayton

DANCERS

Adams, Carolyn
Ailey, Alvin
Ashley, Frank
Bates, Peg Leg
Beatty, Talley
Bey, La Rocque
Borde, Percival
Bubbles, John
Collins, Janet
Defora, Asadata
De Lavallade, Carmen
Destiné, Jean-León
Dunham, Katherine
Faison, George
Fort, Syvilla
Hillman, George
Holder, Geoffrey
Jamison, Judith
Johnson, Louis
Kelly, Paula
McKayle, Donald
Mitchell, Arthur
Moore, Charles
Pomare, Eleo
Premice, Josephine
Primus, Pearl
Robinson, Bill
Rodgers, Rod
Savage, Archie
Thompson, Clive
Van Scott, Glory
Vereen, Ben
Wilson, Billy

Yarborough, Sara

DESIGNERS

Burbridge, Edward
Chanticleer, Raven

DIRECTORS

Alonzo, Cecil
Atkins, Pervis
Belgrave, Cynthia
Bourne, St. Clair
Campbell, Dick
Carroll, Vinnette
Crain, William
Davis, Ossie
Dixon, Ivan
Fann, Al
Franklin, Wendell
Frazier, Cliff
Furman, Roger
Glanville, Maxwell
Lathan, Stan
McClintock, Ernie
Moses, Gilbert
Parks, Gordon
Parks, Gordon Jr.
Perry, Shauneille
Poitier, Sidney
Richards, Lloyd
Robertson, Hugh A.
St. John, Christopher
Schultz, Michael A.
Sembene, Ousmane
Teer, Barbara Ann
Van Peebles, Melvin
Warren, Mark
Williams, Oscar
Williams, Spencer

DISC JOCKEYS

Crocker, Frankie
Higginsen, Vy
Jackson, Hal

Henderson, Fletcher
Henderson, Luther
Hinderas, Natalie
Joplin, Scott
Larkins, Ellis
Lewis, Ramsey
Moore, Phil
Payne, Bennie
Robinson, Sugar Chile
Rocco, Maurice
Schuyler, Philippa
Scott, Hazel
Shirley, Don
Short, Bobby
Walker, George Theophilus
Waller, Fats
Watts, André
Weston, Randy
Wilson, Teddy

PLAYWRIGHTS

Alonzo, Cecil
Anderson, Garland
Angelou, Maya
Aranha, Ray
Baraka, Imamu
Branch, William
Bryant, Hazel
Bullins, Ed.
Caldwell, Ben
Childress, Alice
Cullen, Countee
Davis, Ossie
Dean, Phillip Hayes
Dodson, Owen
Dumas, Alexandre (fils)
Edmonds, Randolph
Elder, Lonne
Evans-Charles, Marti
Franklin, J. E.
Fuller, Charles H. Jr.
Gaines, James
Gordone, Charles
Goss, Clay
Grainger, Porter
Gunn, Bill
Hairston, William
Hansberry, Lorraine
Harrison, Paul Carter
Hill, Abram

Hill, Errol
Hughes, Langston
Hunter, Eddie
Hurston, Zora Neale
John, Errol
Kennedy, Adrienne
Killens, John O.
Lee, Leslie
McIver, Ray
Mackey, William W.
Mason, Clifford
Mayfield, Julian
Milner, Ronald
Mitchell, Loften
Norford, George
Okpaku, Joseph
Peterson, Louis
Richardson, Willis
Rivers, Louis
Russell, Charlie L.
Sanchez, Sonia
Sebree, Charles
Sejour, Victor
Shange, Ntozake
Shine, Ted
Shipp, Jesse
Soyinka, Wole
Spence, Eulalie
Thompson, Garland Lee
Thurman, Wallace
Van Peebles, Melvin
Walcott, Derek
Walker, Joseph A.
Ward, Douglas Turner
Ward, Theodore
Wesley, Richard
White, Edgar B.
Wilson, Frank H.
Wright, Richard

PRODUCERS

Bourne, St. Clair
Brown, Tony
Bryant, Hazel
Campbell, Dick
Cole, Bob
Frazier, Cliff
Goodwin, Robert L.
Gordy, Berry Jr.
Greaves, William

Haizlip, Ellis
Harper, Ken
Hepburn, David
Johnson, George P.
Johnson, Noble P.
Jordan, Jack
Kennedy, Scott
King, Woodie Jr.
Mapp, Jim
Micheaux, Oscar
Norford, George
Sembene, Ousmane
Stewart, Ellen
Williams, Oscar

PUBLICISTS

Jones, Robert G.
Leaks, Sylvester
Tubbs, Vincent
Young, A. S.

SINGERS

Allen, Deborah
Allen, Jonelle
Anderson, Carl
Attles, Joseph
Bailey, Pearl
Baker, Josephine
Balthrop, Carmen
Barnes, Mae
Bassey, Shirley
Belafonte, Harry
Benton, Brook
Berry, Chuck
Bland, Bobby
Bledsoe, Jules
Blind Tom
Bradford, Alex
Bridgewater, Dee Dee
Brown, James
Brown, Maxine
Brown, Ray
Brown, Ruth
Brown, Timothy
Bryant, Joyce
Bryant, Willie
Butler, Jerry

Caesar, Shirley
Calloway, Cab
Carpenter, Thelma
Carroll, Diahann
Carter, Betty
Carter, Ralph
Charles, Ray
Checker, Chubby
Cliff, Jimmy
Cole, Nat "King"
Cole, Natalie
Cooke, Sam
Daniels, Billy
Davis, Clifton
Domino, Fats
Donaldson, Norma
Dowdy, Helen
Dyson, Ronnie
Eckstine, Billy
Edwards, Tommy
Falana, Lola
Fitzgerald, Ella
Flack, Roberta
Foxx, Inez
Franklin, Aretha
Frierson, Andrew
Gaye, Marvin
Gaynor, Gloria
Grant, Earl
Grant, Micki
Green, Al
Guyse, Sheila
Hall, Adelaide
Hall, Juanita
Hamilton, Roy
Hartman, Johnny
Hayes, Isaac
Hendrix, Jimi
Hibbler, Al
Hill, Ruby
Holiday, Billie
Hopkins, Linda
Horne, Lena
Houston, Thelma
Jackson, Millie
Jeffries, Herb
Jones, Sisseretta
Kendricks, Eddie
Kenny, Bill
King, B. B.
King, Ben E.
Kitt, Eartha
Knight, Gladys

Laine, Cleo
Leonardos, Urlyee
Lester, Ketty
Lincoln, Abbey
Little Anthony
Little Richard
Lord Observer
Lucien, Jon
Lutcher, Nellie
Lymon, Frankie
McNair, Barbara
McPhatter, Clyde
McRae, Carmen
Makeba, Miriam
Marrs, Stella
Mathis, Johnny
Melvin, Harold
Mercer, Mabel
Mills, Florence
Mills, Stephanie
Moore, Melba
Moten, Etta
Murphy, Rose
Nash, Johnny
Nelson, Gail
Nelson, Novella
Oliver, Thelma
Paul, Billy
Payne, Freda
Peachena
Peters, Brock
Peterson, Caleb
Phillips, Esther
Pickett, Wilson
Premice, Josephine
Preston, Billy
Price, Gilbert
Prysock, Arthur
Rahn, Muriel
Rainey, Ma.
Randolph, James
Rawls, Lou
Redding, Otis
Reed, Alaina
Reed, Vivian
Reese, Della
Riperton, Minnie
Robinson, Smokey
Ross, Diana
Sattin, Lonnie
Sattin, Tina
Scott, Hazel
Scott, Leslie

Shaw, Marlena
Sherril, Joya
Short, Bobby
Simon, Joe
Simone, Nina
Sir Lancelot
Smith, Bessie
Smith, O. C.
Smith, Muriel
Snow, Valaida
Spearman, Rawn
Spencer, Christine
Spencer, Kenneth
Staton, Dakota
Stone, Sly
Sullivan, Maxine
Syreeta
Turner, Tina
Uggams, Leslie
Vaughan, Sarah
Vereen, Ben
Wade, Adam
Warwick, Dionne
Washington, Dinah
Washington, Lamont
Waters, Ethel
Watkins, Lovelace
Waymon, Sam
Weston, Kim
White, Barry
Williams, Billy
Williams, Joe
Wilson, Jackie
Wilson, Mary
Wilson, Nancy
Winston, Hattie
Withers, Bill
Wonder, Stevie
Zulema

THEATRICAL AGENTS

Bowen, Ruth
McClendon, Ernestine
Treadwell, George

VENTRILOQUIST

Tyler, Willie